Echoes 12

Fiction, Media, and Non-Fiction

Francine Artichuk

Susanne Barclay

Wouter Broersma

Janeen Werner-King

Diana Knight

Liz Orme

Kevin Reed

Peter Weeks

OXFORD

UNIVERSITY PRESS

OXFORD
UNIVERSITY PRESS

70 Wynford Drive, Don Mills, Ontario M3C 1J9
www.oup.com/ca

Oxford University Press is a department of the University of Oxford.

It furthers the University's objective of excellence in research, scholarship, and
education by publishing worldwide in

Oxford   New York
Auckland   Bangkok   Buenos Aires   Cape Town
Chennai   Dar es Salaam   Delhi   Hong Kong   Istanbul
Karachi   Kolkata   Kuala Lumpur   Madrid   Melbourne   Mexico City
Mumbai   Nairobi   São Paulo   Shanghai   Singapore   Taipei   Tokyo   Toronto

National Library of Canada Cataloguing in Publication Data

Main entry under title:
Echoes 12: fiction, media, and non-fiction / Francine Artichuk . . . [et al.].

ISBN 0–19–541631–7 (bound).—ISBN 0–19–541781–X (pbk.)

1. Readers (Secondary). 2. English language—Rhetoric—Problems, exercises, etc.
I. Artichuk, Francine. II. Title: Echoes: fiction, media and non-fiction.

PE1121.E293 2002   808'.0427   C2002–900045–9

Printed and bound in Canada
This book is printed on permanent (acid-free) paper ∞

2 3 4 — 05 04 03 02

Acquisitions editors: Patti Henderson, Marian Marsh
Developmental and managing editor: Monica Schwalbe
Anthologists / Researchers: Chelsea Donaldson, Todd Mercer,
Nancy Mackenzie, Evelyn Maksimovich,
Monika Croydon, Carolyn Black
Cover art and unit opening illustrations: Derek Lea
Cover and text design: Brett Miller

Contents (by genre)

Narrative and Dramatic Poems

Unit 2 Drama   121

Stage Plays

Contents (by theme)

Identity and "Otherness"

Short Fiction Echo:
The Allure of "the Other"

Mysteries and Paradoxes of the Human Spirit

Longings and Ideals

Poetry Echo: The Quest for the Ideal

Wonders of Nature

Epiphanies (moments of revelation)

Life's Passages

Humour and Satire

Introduction

ઝ

Echoes is a multi-genre anthology featuring a wide range of quality selections designed to engage student interest. The *Echoes 12* anthology is organized into six key genres. The genres represented are diverse, reflecting a broad definition of "text." The texts included range from poems, short stories, dramas, and essays to film scripts, fine art, photo essays, informational texts, pamphlets, and advertisements. While the anthology is organized by genre, a detailed table of contents by theme also allows students and teachers the flexibility to approach their study by the themes of their choice.

Each selection in the anthology begins with a clear set of Learning Goals presented in student-accessible language, so that students are immediately aware of some key focus points for their study. Following each selection is a short author biography and a set of Responding activities categorized into Meaning, Form and Style, Exploring Context, and Creative Extension. These activities offer a variety of reading, writing, listening, speaking, viewing, and representing opportunities. Students both analyze texts closely and develop their own creative responses.

Echo Sections

One of the most unique features of the anthology is the "Echo" sections. Each unit includes at least one, if not two, "Echoes." These sections include a core selection from the genre (a poem in the Poetry unit; an essay in the Essays unit), along with a number of related texts from different genres, media, and often time periods. Students have the opportunity to make connections among texts, to compare different forms and styles, and to examine a theme or universal question from a number of different perspectives. In some cases, the Echo allows students to study closely the work and interpretations of the work of a particular author (e.g., Margaret Atwood).

Each Echo section includes the following elements:
- a title that identifies the key theme of the section
- a provocative question to stimulate and focus student thinking
- a paragraph summarizing the overall issues raised by the different selections
- learning goals related to the whole section
- a core selection from the genre followed by a full set of Responding activities
- related selections from different genres, media, and often time periods including such varied texts as fine art, photographs, film scripts, poems, informational texts, songs, interviews, and essays
- Connecting questions after each Echo piece that allow students to analyze it and relate it to the central theme of the Echo
- Reflecting on the Echo activities that allow students to reflect on the Echo theme after studying the selections, and to develop their own creative responses. These activities are designed to appeal to different learning styles and multiple intelligences.

Poetry

Michael Ondaatje on poetry:

The stories within the poems don't matter, the grand themes don't matter. The movement of the mind and language is what is important.... We can come back to these fragile drawings again and again, taking another look, discovering something new, not hearing what we heard the first time we read it. Somehow the poems move when you are not watching, so that new objects and tones come into relief.

Constantly risking absurdity and death

ℑ Lawrence Ferlinghetti

Constantly risking absurdity
                          and death
       whenever he performs
                     above the heads
                                of his audience
     the poet like an acrobat
                     climbs on rime
                          to a high wire of his own making
and balancing on eyebeams
                     above a sea of faces
          paces his way
                     to the other side of day
       performing entrechats
                     and sleight-of-foot tricks
and other high theatrics
                     and all without mistaking
          any thing
                     for what it may not be

     For he's the super realist
                          who must perforce perceive
          taut truth
                     before the taking of each stance or step
     in his supposed advance
                     toward that still higher perch

where Beauty stands and waits
with gravity
to start her death-defying leap

And he
a little charleychaplin man
who may or may not catch
her fair eternal form
spreadeagled in the empty air
of existence

Lawrence Ferlinghetti was a leading figure in the Beat movement of the 1950s. The Beats were a group of writers in San Francisco and New York who shared an antagonism for middle-class values, commercialism, and conformity. Ferlinghetti's poems can be light and satirical in tone, but they often focus on major social and political issues. His first book of poetry was *Pictures from the Gone World* (1955). "Constantly risking absurdity and death" appeared in *A Coney Island of the Mind* (1958). (*Born New York 1919*)

(*Responding Activities p. 12*)

betting on the muse

ᔐ Charles Bukowski

Jimmy Foxx died an alcoholic
in a skidrow hotel
room.
Beau Jack ended up shining
shoes,
just where he
began.
there are dozens, hundreds
more, maybe
thousands more.
being an athlete grown old
is one of the cruelest of
fates,
to be replaced by others,
to no longer hear the
cheers and the
plaudits,
to no longer be
recognized,
just to be an old man
like other old
men.

to almost not believe it
yourself,
to check the scrapbook
with the yellowing
pages.
there you are,
smiling;
there you are,
victorious;
there you are,
young.

the crowd has other
heroes.
the crowd never
dies,
never grows
old
but the crowd often
forgets.

now the telephone
doesn't ring,
the young girls are
gone,
the party is
over.

this is why I chose
to be a
writer.
if you're worth just
half-a-damn
you can keep your
hustle going
until the last minute
of the last
day.
you can keep
getting better instead
of worse,
you can still keep
hitting them over the
wall.

(Responding Activities p. 12)

Like Lawrence Ferlinghetti, Charles Bukowski was originally a Beat poet and novelist in the 1950s. Raised in Los Angeles, Bukowski wrote often about the anger felt by outsiders. Because of its provocative subject matter, much of Bukowski's work was originally published in limited editions and underground magazines. His poetry collections include *Drowning in Flame: Selected Poems 1955–1973* (1974) and a collection of work published after his death called *Betting on the Muse: Poems & Stories* (1996), in which this poem appeared. (*Born Andernach, Germany 1920; died 1994*)

The Story

ᡦ Karen Connelly

Eventually each of us
will tell a story
of scars and ocean,
the way you never
know what's in deeper water
while the seaweed shadows
twist below you
and the slow fear
fills your thin arms.

You know you are a fool
for having come this far.
You know you could never
swim fast enough.
In your mouth your heart
dissolves like a holy tablet
of salt.

In the end, it is
only a drifting body
of wood. Or a dolphin.

But what we own
beyond a shadow
of a doubt
is our fear
of being eaten
alive, torn apart
in depths we have entered
willingly.

❧ Canadian writer Karen Connelly has published four books of poetry: *The Small Words in My Body* (1990), which received the Pat Lowther Award, *This Brighter Prison: A Book of Journeys* (1993), *The Disorder of Love* (1997), and *The Border Surrounds Us* (2000), the collection that includes "The Story." She has also written two works of non-fiction, including the best-seller *Touch the Dragon: A Thai Journal* (1992), which won a Governor General's Award. At the time, she was the youngest writer to win the English non-fiction prize. (*Born Calgary, Alberta 1969*)

(Responding Activities pp. 12–13)

Naming myself

ᘒ Barbara Kingsolver

Learning Goals

- interpret theme
- analyze form and imagery
- examine how context is used to create irony
- create a dramatic monologue
- write a feature article

I have guarded my name as people
in other times kept their own clipped hair,
believing the soul could be scattered
if they were careless.

I knew my first ancestor.
His legend. I have touched
his boots and moustache, the grandfather
whose people owned slaves and cotton.
He was restless in Virginia
among the gentleman brothers, until
one peppered, flaming autumn he stole a horse,
rode over the mountains to marry
a leaf-eyed Cherokee.
The theft was forgiven but never
the Indian blood. He lost his family's name
and invented mine, gave it fruit and seeds.
I never knew the grandmother.
Her photograph has ink-thin braids
and buttoned clothes, and nothing that she was called.

I could shed my name in the middle of life,
the ordinary thing, and it would flee
along with childhood and dead grandmothers
to that Limbo for discontinued maiden names.

But it would grow restless there.
I know this. It would ride over leaf smoke mountains
and steal horses.

(Responding Activities pp. 13–14)

ᘒ Barbara Kingsolver's fiction and poetry are rich with the language and imagery of her native Kentucky and often focus on the experiences of mixed race families. Best-selling works of fiction include *The Bean Trees* (1988) and *The Poisonwood Bible* (1998). Kingsolver published "Naming myself" in a collection of poetry entitled *Another America: Otra America* (1992). *(Born Kentucky 1955)*

All-Star Action

ↄ Richard Harrison

*—January 19, 1991: Desert Storm begins the war on
Iraq 3 days before the Annual All-Star Game*

Even the greatest player in the world asks *What
are we here for?* and votes to cancel play. But
they don't just as I am writing this, when the war
has begun, and bombs become the Thousand
Points of Light once the bad joke of an American
election. The men shift listlessly on their skates as
a woman whose brother is a pilot in the Gulf sings
the National Anthem. The puck is dropped. Later I
will scan the papers for the numbers that mean the
acts of men. And as they score the surface, we
hear again the scour of metal on ice; the crowd
stares past them, dizzy with fear for the boys they
are so proud of. Below the ice, distant at first, and
moving under the sliding men, they appear: blade-
shaped, graphic the way insects are, the airplanes.
They rise towards the ice from the sky below,
larger now, faster, their steel tails scraping the ice;
they move under the men, imitating them perfectly
—passing, shooting . . . passing, shooting.

ↄ Richard Harrison lives in Calgary. His poems appear in a number of anthologies and journals, and he has received several poetry awards, including a silver medal for the Milton
Acorn People's Poet of Canada Award. His collection *Big Breath of a Wish* was nominated
for the Governor General's Award in 1999. Other collections include *Fathers Never Leave
You* (1987) and *Hero of the Play* (1994), which contains "All-Star Action." (*Born Ontario 1957*)

(Responding Activities pp. 14–15)

Guilt

ও Leona Gom

Learning Goals

- compare theme and purpose in two poems
- analyze use of key metaphors
- transform the poem into a short story
- write a comparative essay

your mother giving you a set of dishes
and all you said was *but I move around
so much* and you can never forget
her hurt face turning away.
the best friend you accused of
flirting with your boyfriend when
all the time you knew it was him
you just couldn't face it.
the argument with your father about
not having seen his damned magazine
then finding it in your room
and never admitting it.
telling your office mate you
agreed with her motion then
voting with the others after all.

thousands of them, little knots
you can't shake loose from your memory.
it's too late now to say you're sorry.
they contract along your nerves
to consciousness, whenever you think
you are not a bad person, there
they come, little lumps of guilt
making their daily rounds,
like doctors, keeping you sick.

ও   Leona Gom is a teacher, an editor, and a writer of both poetry and prose. She spent her university career at the University of Alberta, where she studied for her B.Ed. and M.A. She won the CAA Award for Best Book of Poetry for *Land of Peace* in 1980 and the Ethel Wilson Fiction Prize for *Housebroken* in 1986. "Guilt" is from *Private Properties* (1986). (*Born Alberta 1946*)

(Responding Activities p. 15)

This Day in History

෨ Bert Almon

The radio tells me
that back in 1950
the sun rose blue
over Great Britain,
from forest fires
in Western Canada.
I know the dust of
exploding Krakatoa
gave the whole world
a year of fine sunsets.

I try to imagine
whose labour I lift
on my fork, what
ashes sift in my tea,
and get about as far
as the corner market.
We can say "brother"
to everyone, but
only a blue sunrise
might make us feel it.

෨ Bert Almon was born in Texas, but he has lived in Canada since 1968, where he teaches modern poetry and creative writing at the University of Alberta. He has published several books of poetry, along with many academic articles. "This Day in History" appears in *Blue Sunrise* (1980). The collection *Earth Prime* won the Writers' Guild of Alberta poetry award in 1995, and Almon went on to publish *Mind the Gap* in 1996. (*Born Texas 1943*)

(*Responding Activities p. 15*)

RESPONDING ACTIVITIES

Contemporary Lyric Poems (pages 2 – 11)

Constantly risking absurdity and death – Lawrence Ferlinghetti
betting on the muse – Charles Bukowski
(A comparison)

Meaning

1. Describe each author's beliefs about the role of the poet in society. Support your interpretations with specific evidence from the poems.

2. a) Imagine that you are an editor recommending some revisions to these authors. You recommend to Bukowski that he title his poem "Constantly risking absurdity and death," and to Ferlinghetti that he title his poem "betting on the muse." Find evidence in each poem to support the suggestion for this change.
   b) Which title change could work? Which is least effective? Why?

Form and Style

3. Analyze the effects of line breaks in each poem. Refer to specific examples in your answer.

4. *Tone* refers to a writer's attitude to his or her subject. Describe the tone of each poem and identify two examples of diction or imagery that contribute to the tone.

Exploring Context

5. Ferlinghetti and Bukowski were both originally Beat poets. Find out more about these poets and their views. To what extent do these two poems reflect those views? Present your findings in a short oral or written report.

Creative Extension

6. Working with a partner, assume the persona of Ferlinghetti or Bukowski. A magazine has contracted the two of you to co-author an article about the role of the poet in society. Use the ideas that these authors develop in "Constantly risking absurdity and death" and "betting on the muse." You may add to their ideas, but anything you add should be consistent with their beliefs about poetry as expressed in these poems.

7. Choose a line or two that you see as essential to understanding one of the poems. Create a visual representation of the line(s) for a page in an illustrated book or magazine. Use colour, layout, style, and medium to enhance the tone and emphasize the ideas in the line(s).

The Story – Karen Connelly

Meaning

1. Examine the speaker's *analogy* of swimming in the ocean. Describe the swimmer's actions, thoughts, and feelings. Make inferences about deeper layers of meaning in the swimming imagery to suggest a theme for the poem.

2. Analyze the contrast between the imagery in stanzas three and four. Connect this contrast to the theme of the poem.

Form and Style

3. With a small group, read the poem aloud several times. Note that both stanzas one and four are one sentence, but that stanzas two and three contain several short sentences. Assess the effect of this punctuation on your oral reading of the poem. How does this use of punctuation relate to the poem's central idea?

4. Trace the speaker's use of first- and second-person pronouns. What effect does the use of these pronouns have on your response to the poem?

Exploring Context

5. The last three lines of stanza two allude to the sacrament of Holy Eucharist in some forms of Christian worship. How does this *allusion* to a symbol of bodily sacrifice extend your understanding of the poem?

Creative Extension

6. Research Abraham Maslow's theory of the Hierarchy of Needs. Prepare an oral or multimedia presentation that links this poem to the highest need, the need to reach beyond oneself. Alternatively, or as part of your presentation, design a graphic organizer that assesses the psychological truth of the poem based on Maslow's theory.

7. Write a dialogue or a short narrative to "tell a story / of scars and ocean." Focus on a particular experience and free-write around this experience to generate ideas. Then organize your ideas and revise your writing until you have a coherent piece.

Naming myself – Barbara Kingsolver

Meaning

1. Trace the events that led to the creation of the narrator's name.

2. a) How does the narrator describe her name in the poem? Refer to specific words (verbs, adjectives) and images she uses.
   b) How do these words and images reveal the significance the narrator gives to her name? How does her name define her identity?

Form and Style

3. What is Kingsolver's purpose in specifically repeating the images of stealing horses and riding over mountains? Support your interpretation.

4. Explain the symbolic significance of "fruit and seeds" in the lines "He lost his family's name / and invented mine, gave it fruit and seeds."

Exploring Context

5. *Irony* is created when there is a contrast between what is expected and what actually occurs. What irony results from the historical context in which the grandfather lived? What lines in the poem foreshadow this irony? Explain how they set the stage for the ironic revelation.

6. This poem could be interpreted as presenting a feminist point of view. What lines reveal this point of view? How could this poem be interpreted as presenting a more universal theme?

Creative Extension

7. Transform the poem into a *dramatic monologue* written from the grandfather's point of view. Consider the time period, the implied audience, and what you will reveal about the grandfather's character. Perform your monologue for an audience, or record it on audio or videotape. Use pitch, pace, volume, and gestures to convey the character.

8. Write a feature article for a local paper, published at the time in which the poem is set, about the grandfather's scandalous behaviour. You may add specific details to flesh out the story, but the details you add should be consistent with the story and the historical context in "Naming myself." Build upon as many details in the poem as you can.

All-Star Action – Richard Harrison

Meaning

1. Examine the sentence "And as <u>they</u> score the surface, <u>we</u> / hear again the scour of metal on ice; the crowd / stares past <u>them</u>, dizzy with fear for the boys <u>they</u> / are so proud of." To whom does each underlined pronoun refer?

2. It is physically impossible that airplanes are flying below the ice, yet Harrison draws the reader's attention to this image twice. First he writes, "Below the ice, distant at first, and / moving under the sliding men they appear: blade- / shaped, graphic the way insects are, the airplanes." Then, in the next sentence, he states, "They rise towards the ice from the sky below." What is the significance of the airplanes below the ice or rising towards the ice?

Form and Style

3. Harrison uses *puns* and *ambiguity* liberally. Explain the double meanings of the following words and phrases:
    a) "the greatest player in the world"
    b) "the puck is dropped"
    c) "scan the papers for the numbers that mean the / acts of men"
    d) "score the surface" and "scour of metal"
    e) "passing, shooting"
    f) "all-star action"

4. Harrison *juxtaposes* watching an all-star hockey game with the Gulf War. What are the effects of this juxtaposition? (HINT: Refer to specific lines such as "The men shift listlessly on their skates as / a woman whose brother is a pilot in the Gulf sings / the National Anthem.")

Exploring Context

5. Research the Gulf War and the beginning of operation "Desert Storm." Who was involved? What was the cause of the war? How was the war fought? How does the historical context enhance your understanding of the following lines in the poem?
    *   "and bombs become the Thousand / Points of Light once the bad joke of an American / election"
    *   "votes to cancel play. But / they don't"
    *   "a woman whose brother is a pilot in the Gulf sings / the National Anthem"

6. Transform Harrison's poem into a personal editorial column for a newspaper. Carefully consider the *tone* and point of view your column will present.

7. Create a *storyboard* for one sentence of Harrison's poem. Use at least five frames. Consider a variety of camera shots and angles. Your storyboard should represent not only the events expressed in the lines, but also their tone, mood, and point of view.

Guilt – Leona Gom
This Day in History – Bert Almon
(A comparison)

Meaning

1. What are the sources of the narrator's guilt in Gom's poem? What makes the narrator in Almon's poem feel a sense of guilt? How do the sources of guilt differ in these poems?

2. Explain and compare the significance of each poem's title. Support your interpretations.

Form and Style

3. What *metaphors* does Gom use to describe guilt in stanza two of her poem? Why do you think the author chose these metaphors?

4. a)   Examine the images in Almon's poem. How do they create a sense of *irony?*
   b)   Explain the reason for Almon's sardonic tone as he refers to a "blue sunrise" in the last stanza.

Exploring Context

5. Research Almon's historical *allusion* to Krakatoa and how the dust from it gave the world a year of fine sunsets. Explain how your understanding of the history and science enhances your understanding of the poem.

Creative Extension

6. Transform Gom's poem into a short story. You may wish to select one event from the first stanza as the focus of your story and work some other events in as flashbacks. Or, adapt Almon's poem into a radio or television news commentary. Use one of the events mentioned in the first stanza to begin the commentary. Stay true to Almon's message and intent.

7. Both Gom and Almon reflect on the sources and effects of guilt in their poems. Write an essay comparing the two poems. Consider the titles, themes, points of view, stylistic devices, and tone of both poems. Conclude with your assessment of each poem's effectiveness.

The Woman I Am in My Dreams

ॐ Maxine Tynes

The woman I am in my dreams
is taller than I am
and sees the world as she walks
unlike me with eyes on every step
      with eyes ever and always on the ground
that woman walks only when
she feels like not running
not jogging
the woman I am in my dreams
lifts one leg effortlessly over the other
crosses them
high up on the knee
    the hip
    the thigh
not just at the ankle like I do.

The woman I am in my dreams
breaks all the rules about shoes
wears them high and red
with killer spike heels
    moves from Nikes to spikes
    and the kind of pumps
    that go with a dress
    and having your hair done
the woman I am in my dreams
her legs are straight and sure
they don't fly out from under her
they don't hide under long skirts
her legs and feet are well
they speak for her in footsteps on the road
they laugh at hills and

at rolling, unforgiving gravel
they dialogue with ice and snow
and they always win that argument

the woman I am in my dreams
I wake up and carry part of her
with me everywhere.

ᜰ Maxine Tynes, a poet of Africadian descent, writes dramatic poetry about social and
   personal issues. Her first book, *Borrowed Beauty* (1987), won the Milton Acorn People's
   Poet of Canada Award. Two later volumes, *Woman Talking Woman* (1990) and *The Door of
   My Heart* (1993), include both poems and stories. (*Born Dartmouth, Nova Scotia 1950*)

(Responding Activities p. 26)

Today's Learning Child

ℰ Rita Joe

I see the bronze hue of skin
The dark eyes flashing.
The arrogant hold of that stare
Into the dream of that softness of life
Just out of reach.

The angry hold onto the reality
Into determination.
To see the life of improvement
Someday soon.

The head is bent, the shoulders round
That force upon learning, commanding,
Until dignity nods.

We are different to this age
We rely so much.

Please understand;
The chisel must continue to carve an image
Because all our life has already been labelled.

ℰ Many of Rita Joe's poems focus on her Mi'kmaq culture and heritage. She is especially concerned with the revival of that culture and with promoting understanding among peoples, particularly because of her experience at the Indian Residential School in Shubenacadie, Nova Scotia, where her culture was suppressed. Joe's first book of poems, *Poems of Rita Joe*, was published in 1978. She received the Order of Canada in 1990. (*Born Whycocomogh, Nova Scotia 1932*)

(Responding Activities pp. 26–27)

Field of Vision

ॐ Seamus Heaney

Learning Goals

- examine the thematic connection between two poems
- analyze use of imagery
- script and perform a dialogue
- create a visual representation

I remember this woman who sat for years
In a wheelchair, looking straight ahead
Out the window at sycamore trees unleafing
And leafing at the far end of the lane.

Straight out past the TV in the corner,
The stunted, agitated hawthorn bush,
The same small calves with their backs to wind and
      rain,
The same acre of ragwort, the same mountain.

She was steadfast as the big window itself.
Her brow was clear as the chrome bits of the chair.
She never lamented once and she never
Carried a spare ounce of emotional weight.

Face to face with her was an education
Of the sort you got across a well-braced gate—
One of those lean, clean, iron, roadside ones
Between two whitewashed pillars, where you could see

Deeper into the country than you expected
And discovered that the field behind the hedge
Grew more distinctly strange as you kept standing
Focused and drawn in by what barred the way.

ॐ Irish poet Seamus Heaney worked as an English teacher and lecturer before being
appointed Professor of Poetry at Oxford in 1989. Economic in his use of language, his first
collection, *Death of a Naturalist* (1966), revealed his preoccupation with environmental
themes and Irish history. "Field of Vision" appears in *Seeing Things* (1991), a collection of
poems that explores the simultaneous seeing of experience in the present and the past.
Heaney won the Nobel Prize for Literature in 1995. (*Born Northern Ireland 1939*)

(*Responding Activities pp. 27–28*)

Where There's A Wall

ᘒ Joy Kogawa

Learning Goals

- examine the thematic connection between two poems
- analyze use of parallel structure, repetition, and imagery
- research contextual elements to enhance understanding
- script and perform a dialogue
- create a visual representation

Where there's a wall
there's a way through a
gate or door. There's even
a ladder perhaps and a
sentinel who sometimes sleeps.
There are secret passwords you
can overhear. There are methods
of torture for extracting clues
to maps of underground passages.
There are zeppelins, helicopters,
rockets, bombs, battering rams,
armies with trumpets whose
all at once blast shatters
the foundations.

Where there's a wall there are
words to whisper by loose bricks,
wailing prayers to utter, birds
to carry messages taped to their feet.
There are letters to be written—
poems even.

Faint as in a dream
is the voice that calls
from the belly
of the wall.

(Responding Activities pp. 27–28)

ᘒ Joy Kogawa has published several collections of poetry, including *A Choice of Dreams* (1974) and *Woman in the Woods* (1985), where "Where There's A Wall" appears. Many of her poems are characterized by a direct but understated voice and tight, short lines. She is perhaps best known for her novel *Obasan* (1981), which drew on her family's experience during the evacuation and internment of Canadians of Japanese descent in World War II. She currently lives in Toronto. *(Born Vancouver, British Columbia 1935)*

gravity

ॐ Marilyn Dumont

earning Goals

- describe character as presented in a poem
- consider use of condensed time
- examine point of view
- create a storyboard
- write a story based on a poem

my brother wasn't born
he fell from the sky
while I was drying dishes
friction, the only natural law
suspended him for me
through the sound of limbs cracking
their dry rhythm announcing
his delivery to earth
and mom's gasp to see him walk
and flop on the couch
where it seemed he lay
for his adolescence
but through his example
she wouldn't have to repeat herself
her warning of danger
to this family of falling things.

ॐ Marilyn Dumont is of Métis descent and is currently working as a teacher and writer. Before writing and teaching full-time, she worked in video production. Her poetry and prose have appeared in several literary journals and anthologies. She received the Gerald Lampert Memorial Award in 1997 for *A Really Good Brown Girl* (1996). "gravity" is from the collection *green girl dreams Mountains* (2000). (Born Alberta 1955)

(Responding Activities pp. 28–29)

Ghosts

§ Tom Dawe

I remember: cow-bells waking me
and mid-wives walking
in yellow flowers after June rain
and stone doorsteps
brought somewhere up from spindrift
and crying babies with eyes closed
like drowned kittens
and old women tying silver coins
around the necks of the newborn
and waving nettles over driftwood
and our short-cut to a swimming hole
and granite under crystal tide
and going with buckets to a well
under green-gage trees
where a big trout waited to be fed
and every leaf-killing fall of the year
a loon coming to the salt pond
to be shot again
and people leaving houses for cellars
on nights when the wind blew hard
and lead jiggers hanging in haylofts
where boys and girls went hide-and-seek
and men with faith that the fish would stay
and pirates leaving graves and gold
and guardian spirits
and thin boys stumbling behind horse ploughs
in silver fog low over turnip clay
and fat men dressed for Sunday
walking ahead of their women
and young men flinging their hats
from trains to Canada

and Americans building their bases
and sick young girls leaving home for good
and flower-gardens
and kitchen-gardens
and lilacs in the lane dust
and pendulum clocks always swinging
at weddings and wakes
and sun and moon and tide and wind
and wallpaper leaves
and lamplight
and window-blinds
all up and down . . .
all ghosts.

ℰ Tom Dawe's poems often reflect upon the changing lives of people in his native Newfoundland. His work has been published in journals, anthologies, and magazines around the world. Collections include *In Hardy Country*, *Hemlock Cove*, and *After*. The poem "Ghosts" is from *Island Spell: Poems by Tom Dawe* (1981). (*Born Conception Bay, Newfoundland*)

(*Responding Activities p. 29*)

Students

♋ Tom Wayman

The freshman class-list printouts
showed birthdates so recent
Wayman was sure the computer was in error.
One young man, however, was curious
about Wayman's mention near the start of term
of his old college newspaper:
"You were an editor *when*? Wow,
that's the year I was born."
The wisdom of the students
hadn't altered, though.
Wayman observed many clung to
The Vaccination Theory of Education
he remembered: once you have had a subject
you are immune
and never have to consider it again.
Other students continue to endorse
The Dipstick Theory of Education:
as with a car engine, where as long as the oil level
is above the add line
there is no need to put in more oil,
so if you receive a pass or higher
why put any more into learning?

At the front of the room, Wayman sweated
to reveal his alternative.
"Adopt The Kung Fu Theory of Education,"
he begged.
"Learning as self-defence. The more you understand
about what's occurring around you
the better prepared you are to deal with difficulties."

The students remained skeptical.
A young woman was a pioneer
of The Easy Listening Theory of Learning:
spending her hours in class
with her tape recorder earphones on,
silently enjoying a pleasanter world.
"Don't worry, I can hear you,"
she reassured Wayman
when after some days he was moved to inquire.

Finally, at term's end
Wayman inscribed after each now-familiar name on the list
the traditional single letter.
And whatever pedagogical approach
he or the students espoused,
Wayman knew his notation would be pored over
with more intensity
than anything else Wayman taught.

Tom Wayman is a poet, editor, and teacher. He has worked at a wide variety of jobs in Canada and the United States, and his poetry often focuses on what he describes as "the central experience of everyday life—which is what people do for a living, their work." His poems are often humorous and ironic. He won the A. J. M Smith Prize for distinguished achievement in Canadian poetry in 1976. *Waiting for Wayman* (1973) was his first collection of poetry. *Did I Miss Anything?: Selected Poems* appeared in 1993. Born in Ontario, Wayman now lives in Vancouver. *(Born Hawkesbury, Ontario 1945)*

(Responding Activities p. 30)

RESPONDING ACTIVITIES

Contemporary Lyric Poems (pages 16 – 25)

The Woman I Am in My Dreams – Maxine Tynes

Meaning

1. The narrator implies that she is different from the woman in her dreams. What can the reader infer about the narrator based on the contrasts she reveals?
2. Create a brief character sketch of the woman in the narrator's dreams. Refer to specific words (verbs and adjectives) in the poem.

Form and Style

3. Identify the turning point in the poem and explain the shift that occurs in the reader's understanding.
4. a) Why does Tynes repeat her title at the beginning of each stanza?
   b) What is the effect of the indentations in the poem?

Exploring Context

5. Speculate on why Maxine Tynes wrote this poem. Who is her audience? What social and cultural factors might have influenced her writing? Do further research into the life, work, and career of Maxine Tynes. Read other poems by this writer. How does your research extend your understanding of this author's goals and the common themes in her work?

Creative Extension

6. Working with a partner, script or improvise a dialogue between the woman in the narrator's dreams and the narrator. Decide on the approach you wish to take—humorous, serious, satirical, etc.—and keep your purpose in mind. Tape or perform your dialogue for an audience. Ask for responses to tone, intent, and authenticity of your performance.
7. Using Maxine Tynes's poem as a model, write a poem using a different voice. Start your poem with a line such as "The man I am in my dreams...," "The actor I am in my dreams...," "The politician I am in my dreams...," etc. You may change the tone of the poem (satirical, ironic, inspirational, etc.), but you must sustain the voice throughout and incorporate the key turning point in the last stanza. Present a dramatic reading of your poem.

Today's Learning Child – Rita Joe

Meaning

1. Rita Joe's choice of words in this poem is vital to the message she wishes to convey. Identify the *concrete nouns* (name something physical) and *abstract nouns* (name what cannot be seen, touched, etc.) in the first four stanzas. Which are dominant? What do the concrete nouns portray? What are the implications of the abstract nouns?

2. The speaker is addressing an unidentified listener, someone who is separate from "I" and "we." Read the following lines aloud several times. Then in a small group, discuss to whom the words "dignity," "different," and "rely" are connected and what they convey.

   > Until dignity nods.

   > We are different to this age
   > We rely so much.

Form and Style

3. Describe the *tone* and *diction* of the speaker's voice. Are they effective? Support your response with direct quotations from the poem.

4. Analyze the *connotations* of the imagery in the last two lines. Explain how the imagery makes the speaker's purpose clear.

Exploring Context

5. Many of Rita Joe's poems deal with her experience in the Indian Residential School in Shubenacadie, Nova Scotia. In the past, the Canadian government placed many Aboriginal children in residential schools. Research the purpose of these schools. How does this background knowledge deepen your appreciation of the tone and purpose of Rita Joe's poem? How does it enhance your understanding of the following lines in the poem?
   a) "Into the dream of that softness of life"
   b) "That force upon learning, commanding"
   c) "We are different to this age"
   d) "all our life has already been labelled"

Creative Extension

6. Rita Joe's poetry often focuses on the positive, even in the most difficult circumstances. Imagine a situation that would seem to carry only negative feelings and images. Using that situation, create a written, visual, or oral representation that depicts a gentle portrait of a person, that advocates understanding, or that corrects misinformation by focusing on positive images.

7. Research another poem, song, short narrative, or essay in which the author is reacting against some form of oppression. Carefully analyze the *tone* and *diction* of this selection, and write a short critical analysis in which you draw comparisons with Rita Joe's poem.

Field of Vision – Seamus Heaney
Where There's A Wall – Joy Kogawa
(A comparison)

Meaning

1. After a close reading of both poems, explain the thematic connection between "Field of Vision" and "Where There's A Wall." Refer to specific evidence from the poems to support your interpretation.

2. Analyze the significance of each poem's title. Support your analysis with reference to the poems.

Form and Style

3. Kogawa employs parallel structure and repetition of "Where there's a wall" and "there's" or "there are" in her poem. What might her purpose be in repeating "Where there's a wall" only twice, while following these lines with seven phrases beginning with "there is" or "there are"?

4. a) What techniques does Heaney use in his poem to create the sense of time passing slowly?

   b) What kind of diction and imagery does Heaney use to describe the woman who is the protagonist of his poem? What can you infer about the woman from the diction and imagery?

Exploring Context

5. Research print and electronic sources to find pictures and stories about the walls of Jericho, the Wailing Wall in Jerusalem, the Berlin Wall, and the wall in the story of Pyramus and Thisbe. Share the pictures and stories and explain how they enhance your understanding and appreciation of Kogawa's poem.

Creative Extension

6. Script a dialogue between the woman in Heaney's poem and Kogawa's narrator. Present a dramatic reading of your dialogue or record it on audio or videotape. Use the techniques of effective oral performance including pitch, pace, volume, gestures, and facial expressions to convey the characters' thoughts and emotions.

7. Choose a line or two that you see as essential to understanding one of the poems. Create a visual representation (drawing, poster, painting, collage, etc.) illustrating your interpretation of the lines. Use colour, layout, style, and medium to enhance the tone and emphasize the ideas. Present your representation to a group and explain the choices you made to create particular effects.

gravity – Marilyn Dumont

Meaning

1. a) Describe the brother's character based on the description of him and his actions in the poem.

   b) Describe the mother's character based on the description of her and her actions in the poem.

2. Link the various meanings of the word "gravity" to specific lines in the poem. Analyze and explain the connections between the lines and the different meanings of the title.

Form and Style

3. How much time passes in this poem? Quote the lines in which Dumont condenses time. Why do you think she uses condensed time?

4. How would this poem change if it were written from the mother's point of view? From the brother's point of view? Why do you think Dumont chose to write from a sibling's point of view?

Exploring Context

5. Readers create context by bringing their own prior knowledge to a text. What experiences, either personal or literary, influence your understanding of the family snapshot presented in this poem?

Creative Extension

6. Create a *storyboard* of at least five frames based on what you understand to be several key lines from Dumont's poem. Use a variety of camera shots and angles purposefully and choose appropriate sound effects and music to create a specific mood. Explain why you think the lines you selected were key lines.

7. Write the story that is suggested between the lines (i.e., in the *subtext*) of the poem. What would the dialogue be like between the mother and the brother in this household?

Ghosts – Tom Dawe

Meaning

1. Identify images that help you to locate the speaker's memories in time and place. What emotions and values are implied by the images?

2. Explain how, through concrete images in the poem, the speaker conveys thoughts about time. Which images are connected to time? What mood do they create and what is their significance?

Form and Style

3. Describe the *form* of this poem. Refer specifically to the punctuation and use of repetition. How does the form of the poem reflect the speaker's mood and purpose?

4. Examine the sequence of images carefully. What pattern can you see that gives coherence to this seemingly random list of memories?

Exploring Context

5. Describe, from your imagination, the scene or the circumstance in which the speaker is talking of these memories. What might have prompted the recollections? To whom might they be directed? Support your interpretations.

Creative Extension

6. Write a free-verse poem using Dawe's poem as a model. Begin the poem with the line, "I remember: . . ." Use the poet's technique of having concrete images suggest themes, values, and emotions.

7. Many places in Canada have ghost towns: places people have abandoned for a variety of reasons. Research the history of your own area and compose a photo essay depicting a settlement that exists now only as a memory. Include two to three lines of verse or commentary with each photo, capturing its mood or message.

Students – Tom Wayman

Meaning

1. Identify what separates Wayman from the students in his class.
2. Wayman describes two old theories of education and two new theories. What *connotations* might these labels have beyond those in his own description?

Form and Style

3. The poet refers to himself in the third person throughout the poem. What effect does this point of view create?
4. Analyze the *irony* of the last stanza. How does the irony include both Wayman and the students?

Exploring Context

5. Wayman frequently writes about the workplace, using ordinary language and work-related diction. Describe your own response as a student to Wayman's perspective on his job and on his students.

Creative Extension

6. Take Wayman's idea of poetry on the job as a model for a poem of your own conveying a point of view on a job you have held.
7. Write a review of a feature-length film that depicts some form of school. In your review, assess the credibility of the central character's point of view on school and on learning.

The Six Strings

ᕓ Federico Garcia Lorca

.earning Goals

- compare metaphors and their connections to theme
- analyze diction, syntax, and spacing
- compare personal perspectives to those in a poem
- compose a free-verse poem
- research or create a visual to express the dynamic in a poem

The guitar
makes dreams cry.
The crying of lost
souls
escapes from its round
mouth.
And like the tarantula
it weaves a huge star
to catch sighs
that float on its black
wooden tank.

Translated by Donald Hall

ᕓ Federico Garcia Lorca is one of Spain's most respected poets and playwrights, and his works have been translated into many languages. He was a friend of the Surrealist painter Salvador Dali. Dark, surreal images fill the poems in *Romancero Gitano (The Gypsy Ballads)*, published in 1928, and *Poeta en Nueva York (Poet in New York)*, published in 1940. "The Six Strings" appeared in *The Rattle Bag* (1982), a collection of Lorca's works translated into English. Because of Lorca's political opinions, he was executed by a firing squad during the Spanish Civil War. *(Born Granada, Spain 1898; died 1936)*

eagle's work

ᕓ Wayne Keon

eagle strikes her prey
out of the air
with

one screaming blow
of blood nd
talon

swift nd clean nd proud
i torture this page
for hours
til

finally my soul stumbles
out sick of being the
official witness

starts walkin nd talkin nd dancin right out loud

ℰ Wayne Keon is an Ojibwe writer of poetry and fiction. His poetry collections include *My Sweet Maize* (1997) and *Storm Dancer* (1993). He also published a work of fiction entitled *Thunderbirds of Ottawa* in 1977. (*Born Pembroke, Ontario 1946*)

Dog

ℰ Kojo Laing

I bark
      into the orchestra
with my four paws
      going in different
            directions,
and all my bones finished
Agyeeei! I am the
      ouch of the year,
            I am the percussion of the jaws.

(Responding Activities p. 42)

ℰ Novelist and poet Kojo Laing worked as a civil servant and a chief executive of a private school in Ghana. His novels include *Search Sweet Country* (1986) and *Woman of the Aeroplanes* (1988). "Dog" appears in his collection of poems *Godhorse* (1989). (*Born Kumasi, Ghana 1946*)

The Uninvited

ଏ Dorothy Livesay

earning Goals

examine how a poet
creates mystery

analyze point of
view

relate a poem to
quotations from
other authors

adapt the poem into
a short story

create a photo or
art essay

Always a third one's there
where any two are walking out
along a river-bank   so mirror-still
sheathed in sheets   of sky
pillows of cloud—
their footprints crunch the hardening earth
their eyes delight in trees   stripped clean
winter-prepared
with only the rose-hips red
and the plump fingers of sumach

And always between the two
(scuffing the leaves, laughing
and fingers locked)
goes a third lover   his or hers
who walked this way with one or other   once
flung back the head   snapped branches of dark pine
in armfuls   before snowfall

    I walk beside you
    trace
    a shadow's shade
    skating on silver
    hear
    another voice
    singing under ice

(Responding Activities pp. 42–43)

ଏ Dorothy Livesay is particularly admired for her love poems and her poems on political
issues. Born in Winnipeg, she moved in 1920 to Toronto where she became involved in
socialism and women's rights. When she was eighteen, she published *Green Pitcher* (1928),
her first poetry collection. Her political concerns were expressed in collections such as *Day
and Night* (1944), winner of a Governor General's Award. "The Uninvited" appeared in
Livesay's *Collected Poems* (1972). (*Born Winnipeg, Manitoba 1909; died 1996*)

Myth

ᔤ Anne Simpson

There were other people moving in that room,
but she was watching the illuminated lenses

of his glasses as he talked about a Russian love story:
a man in love with a woman,

a distant woman, who was, of course, beautiful
and who only fell in love with the man

after a long time, although that wasn't the end of it
(she didn't trust anything so simple

but listened, curious about his glasses,
like mirrors, in which she saw things)

because neither the man nor the woman knew
the depth of the other's love

except that it was a door
opening to another door, until she couldn't think about it

anymore and looked away in the direction
of Orion and the Pleiades through the dark

glass of the window where the stars were obscured
by reflections of people dancing

so that it was impossible
to find what she was looking for. Anyway, it was clear

that constellations weren't really connected
like dot-to-dot figures

except in myths.

Anne Simpson lives in Nova Scotia, where she writes poetry, fiction, and non-fiction. Her work has appeared in many literary journals and anthologies. She published "Myth" in her first book of poetry, *Light Falls Through You* (2000). Her novel, *Canterbury Beach*, was published in 2001. *(Born 1956)*

(Responding Activities pp. 43–44)

puce fairy book

⁓ Alice Major

you wanted Rapunzel waiting in a tower
braids of hair like ropes
stairs that only you could climb

my hair would never grow long enough

you wanted a lady sleeping in a garden
no rings on her fingers
never been kissed

other princes had made it through my forest

so you tried revisionist tale-telling
and turned them into dwarves—
you wanted happy ever after

I forgot to water the roses round the door

I piled up mattresses to cushion you
but you tossed and turned
bruised by that one small nub—

the part of me that is no fairy tale

you brought me a crystal slipper
on a heart-shaped pillow
pretty   but slightly passé

my foot was too big to fit into it

you might have been the one true prince
but on mature consideration
I declined, with thanks, the honour

of cutting off my toe

Alice Major moved to Toronto from Scotland at the age of eight. She attended the University of Toronto, and after receiving her degree, went on to work for a newspaper association. This took her to Edmonton in 1981, where she lives today. Her first novel for young adults, *The Chinese Mirror* (1988), won the Alberta Writing for Youth Competition. She also writes short stories and award-winning poetry books, including *Tales for an Urban Sky* (1999) and *Some Bones and a Story* (2001). (*Born Scotland*)

(*Responding Activities pp. 44–45*)

The Diverse Causes

ଈ Michael Ondaatje

Learning Goals

- describe setting
- analyze use of imagery and juxta-position
- create an illustrated adaptation of a poem
- write a comparative essay

for than all erbys and treys reneweth a man and a woman, and in lyke wyse calleth to their mynde olde jantylnes and olde servyse, and many kynde dedes that was forgotyn by neylgence

Three clouds and a tree
reflect themselves on a toaster.
The kitchen window hangs scarred,
shattered by winter hunters.

We are in a cell of civilized magic.
Stravinsky roars at breakfast,
our milk is powdered.

Outside, a May god
moves his paws to alter wind
to scatter shadows of tree and cloud.
The minute birds walk confident
jostling the cold grass
the world not yet of men.

We clean buckets of their sand
to fetch water in the morning,
reach for winter cobwebs,
sweep up moths who have forgotten to waken.
When the children sleep, angled
behind their bottles, you can hear mice prowl.

I turn a page
careful not to break the rhythms
of your sleeping head on my hip,
watch the moving under your eyelid
that turns like fire,
and we have love and the god outside
while ice starts to limp
in brown hidden waterfalls,
or my daughter burns the lake
by reflecting her red shoes in it.

꿁 Internationally acclaimed writer Michael Ondaatje was born in Sri Lanka, but moved to
England in 1954, and then to Canada in 1962. He received Governor General's Awards for
the poetry collection *There's a Trick with a Knife I'm Learning to Do* (1979), *The Collected
Works of Billy the Kid* (1970), a combination of prose and poetry, and the novel *The English
Patient* (1992), co-winner of the Booker Prize and the basis for a Hollywood movie.
Ondaatje's novel *Anil's Ghost* won the Giller Prize and Governor General's Award in 2000.
"The Diverse Causes" is from *The Cinnamon Peeler* (1992). (*Born Sri Lanka 1943*)

(*Responding Activities p. 45*)

And If You Should Leave Me

ও Ben Okri

And if you should leave me
I would say that the ghost
Of Cassandra
Has passed through
My eyes
I would say that the stars
In their malice
Merely light up the sky
To stretch my torment
And that the waves crash
On the shores
To bring salt-stings on
My face:
For you re-connect me with
All the lights of the sky
And the salt of the waves
And the myths in the air.
And with your passing
The evening would become too dark
        To dream in
And the morning
        Too bright.

ও Ben Okri is known as a poet, novelist, short fiction writer, and essayist. He received his education in his native Nigeria and in England. His partly autobiographical novels, *Flowers and Shadows* (1980) and *The Landscapes Within* (1981), and two collections of short stories, *Incidents at the Shrine* (1986) and *Stars of the New Curfew* (1988), established his international reputation. His novel, *The Famished Road*, won the prestigious Booker Prize in 1991. "If You Should Leave Me" is from the collection *An African Elegy* (1992). (*Born Lagos Nigeria, 1959*)

(*Responding Activities pp. 45–46*)

Refugee Mother and Child

ᕦ Chinua Achebe

earning Goals

examine tension

make inferences
about a speaker's
values and emotions

adapt the poem to
film

prepare a research
report or Web page

No Madonna and Child could touch
that picture of a mother's tenderness
for a son she soon would have to forget.

The air was heavy with odours
of diarrhoea of unwashed children
with washed-out ribs and dried-up
bottoms struggling in laboured
steps behind blown empty bellies. Most
mothers there had long ceased
to care but not this one; she held
a ghost smile between her teeth
and in her eyes the ghost of a mother's
pride as she combed the rust-coloured
hair left on his skull and then—
singing in her eyes—began carefully
to part it . . . In another life this
would have been a little daily
act of no consequence before his
breakfast and school; now she
did it like putting flowers
on a tiny grave.

ᕦ Chinua Achebe is a Nigerian novelist, short-story writer, essayist, editor, and writer of children's literature. He explores the effects of British colonization on Nigeria in novels such as *Things Fall Apart* (1958) and *Anthills of the Savannah* (1987), which was shortlisted for the Booker Prize. Achebe won the Commonwealth Poetry Prize in 1972. The poem "Refugee Mother and Child" comes from the collection *Christmas in Biafra and Other Poems* (1973). (*Born Eastern Nigeria 1930*)

(*Responding Activities p. 46*)

RESPONDING ACTIVITIES

Contemporary Lyric Poems (pages 31 – 41)

The Six Strings – Federico Garcia Lorca
eagle's work – Wayne Keon
Dog – Kojo Laing

Meaning

1. Each of these poems uses striking and unusual *metaphors*. Analyze how the metaphors convey meaning in each poem. Then create a graphic organizer to show similarities and differences among the three poems. Write a short paragraph to explain which metaphors seem most effective and why.

2. Examine how each poem implies the presence of music. Analyze thematic connections in each poem between the presence of music and the metaphors.

Form and Style

3. In groups of three or four, read the poems aloud. Take turns reading until each person in the group has read all the poems. Pay particular attention to the *diction* in each poem. What effects does the diction have on you as readers and listeners?

4. *Syntax* refers to the way words and clauses are ordered and connected to form sentences. Examine the syntax and the spacing in the poems. Analyze the effectiveness of one of these elements in all three poems.

Exploring Context

5. Choose the poem with which you most closely identify. Compare the perspective presented in the poem to your own. What views do you have in common with the speaker in the poem you have chosen?

Creative Extension

6. Write a free-verse poem centring on your own ideas of creativity. Use some of the devices you have examined in these three poems, such as metaphor, imagery, unusual diction, syntax, and spacing to express your ideas and emotions.

7. Research or create a piece of art or a photograph that you feel best captures the dynamic between the speaker and the theme in one of these poems. Consider how colour, images, focus, and perspective in the visual can reflect mood and ideas. Imagine the poem and visual are paired in an exhibition and write the brochure copy that would accompany this piece.

The Uninvited – Dorothy Livesay

Meaning

1. a) Who are "the uninvited"? What other nouns and adjectives are used in the poem to describe "the uninvited"? What impression do these words create?
    b) Why are the uninvited "always" there?

2. To whom does the pronoun "their" in "their footprints" (line 6) and in "their eyes" (line 7) refer?

Form and Style

3. a) The narrator uses third-person pronouns in stanzas one and two, but in stanza three, she switches to the first-person pronoun and point of view. The reader then realizes that all along, she was describing a personal situation. Identify the third-person pronouns in stanzas one and two. What is the effect of having a narrator describe her own situation from the third-person point of view?

    b) What does the switch to the first-person pronouns in the last stanza reveal about the narrator?

4. a) How does Livesay create a sense of mystery at the beginning of the poem?

    b) The dash at the end of the fifth line in the poem can be seen as a kind of turning point. How do the words and images before this point compare with those following it? Explain how this change foreshadows the ending of the poem.

Exploring Context

5. Choose one of the following quotations and, in a well-developed paragraph, explain how it illuminates the theme expressed in Livesay's poem.

    a) "Nothing changes more constantly than the past; for the past that influences our lives does not consist of what actually happened, but of what men believe happened." (Gerald W. Johnson, American writer, from *American Heroes and Hero-Worship*, 1943)

    b) "I want to do away with everything behind man, so that there is nothing to see when he looks back. I want to take him by the scruff of his neck and turn his face toward the future!" (Leonid Andreyev, Russian writer, from *Savva*)

    c) "The present contains nothing more than the past, and what is found in the effect was already in the cause." (Henri Bergson, French philosopher, from *Creative Evolution*)

Creative Extension

6. Rewrite the poem as a short story told from the viewpoint of one of "the uninvited." Be sure to

    •   incorporate seasonal symbolism into your story.

    •   consider the most effective order of events. What will hook your reader at the beginning? What will be the initial incident that leads to various obstacles?

    •   add details that will flesh out the characters and develop them more fully; however, the details you add should be consistent with the portraits given in the poem.

7. Create a photo or art essay based on the theme of "the uninvited." Research appropriate pieces or develop your own. Carefully consider various camera angles and perspectives, use of colour or black and white, the sequencing of your images, and the use of words, if any.

Myth – Anne Simpson

Meaning

1. What might the relationship be between the narrator and the man telling the story? What details in the poem support your interpretation?

2. Based on the *context* provided by the poem, what do you think the title means?

Form and Style

3. Explain the *symbolism* of reflections in this poem.

4. What point of view is used in this poem? How does it affect the tone of the poem? Consider both the poet's attitude toward what occurs and what remains unsaid.

Exploring Context

5. Research the connection between constellations and myths. Explain how this connection illuminates your understanding of the narrator's experiences in the poem.

Creative Extension

6. Create a short *shooting script* for a scene in a film based on this poem. Carefully select different camera angles and include music and sound effects. Keep the words in your script to a minimum. Rely on the images to tell the story. Aim to capture the mystery and elusiveness of the poem.

7. Rewrite this poem as a short story. Incorporate the symbolism of reflections, the images of the story within the story, the contrast between science and myth, and build upon the details provided about the setting and characters. You may add details to flesh out both the major and minor characters in the poem.

puce fairy book – Alice Major

Meaning

1. What is a fairy tale? Name a favourite fairy tale and explain why it appeals to you. Why do fairy tales have such universal appeal?

2. a) What unrealistic or fairy-tale expectations does the woman feel her partner has of her in this poem? Identify the five fairy tales the speaker mentions as the source of these expectations. Discuss folk tales from other cultures that reflect a similar theme.

   b) In what ways does the woman fail to live up to these expectations? How does she try to protect the relationship when she knows she has failed the expectations?

Form and Style

3. How does Major use the form of the poem to emphasize her ideas?

4. Identify what technique makes the ending of this poem, the last four stanzas, so powerful. Explain how the technique emphasizes Major's point.

Exploring Context

5. Why have feminists criticized fairy tales? Is the criticism justified? Why or why not? How are men portrayed in the five fairy tales to which Major alludes? Is a revisionist retelling, from a male perspective, necessary?

6. Revisionism makes us think about the way our culture represents individuals, but revisionism taken to extremes has disadvantages. Read "There Was Once..." by Margaret Atwood on pages 57–59 of this anthology.

   a) What aspects of the revisionist movement does Atwood satirize?

   b) Is revisionism ever justified? In what contexts? Why? If you argue it cannot be justified, explain why.

Creative Extension

7. Work with a partner to create a picture book of Major's poem. Include as many of Major's images as you can in your illustrations. Use the style, layout, and colour in your

art to convey the poem's tone and ideas. Prepare a one- to two-page written analysis of your picture book explaining your choices and the effects you aimed to create.

8. Write a revisionist version of a fairy tale or folk tale of your choice. You may choose a tale from any culture or time period. Decide what your purpose is in revising the details, and keep your audience in mind. Prepare your tale on computer, if possible, and choose type styles, layout, and graphics to best represent your purpose.

The Diverse Causes – Michael Ondaatje

Meaning

1. Describe the physical environment in which the narrator lives. Refer to the poem for details, but summarize the description with several well-chosen adjectives.

2. What image in the poem best reveals the narrator's tenderness? Support your answer.

Form and Style

3. Why does Ondaatje *juxtapose* the line "Stravinsky roars at breakfast" with the next line "our milk is powdered"?

4. How does Ondaatje prepare the reader for the unusual image at the end of the poem: "or my daughter burns the lake / by reflecting her red shoes in it"? What is the significance of this *metaphor*?

Exploring Context

5. The poem twice refers to the May god. What is the significance of the May god?

Creative Extension

6. Create a limited edition illustrated version of "The Diverse Causes." Carefully plan the scenes or images you will illustrate and the number of pages you will use. Decide on a style that you feel best reflects the mood of the poem. Present your book in electronic form or as a hardbound copy.

7. In a short essay, compare and contrast the *tone* of "The Diverse Causes" with that in Alice Major's "puce fairy book."

And If You Should Leave Me – Ben Okri

Meaning

1. This lyric poem uses *apostrophe*, in which a poet addresses directly another absent person or an abstract quality. Explain the dramatic situation in the poem. What is the relationship between the speaker and the person being addressed? In what situation are they at the moment of the poem? What does the word "passing" in line 18 suggest about their situation?

2. Argue that the "you" addressed in the poem may be something other than an individual person. In preparing your argument, examine how the speaker views the elements of the natural world throughout the poem—specifically "stars," "waves," and "night and day."

Form and Style

3. In the first thirteen lines of the poem, Okri uses several specific words that suggest violence or death. Identify three of these words and explain how each is appropriate to the speaker's mood and meaning in this first part of the poem.

4.   The poem ends with a *double paradox:* "The evening would become too dark / To dream in / And the morning / Too bright." A *paradox* is a statement that appears to be absurd or contradictory, but that may in fact be true. Explain why the speaker concludes his or her lyric in this way.

Exploring Context

5.   In the third line of the poem, Okri uses a *classical allusion*, a reference to a character or work of classical mythology or art. Research and summarize briefly the story of Cassandra in ancient Greek mythology. Explain why Okri's choice of this mythological character is appropriate for this poem.

Creative Extension

6.   Assume that the poem is addressed to a lover who is breaking off a romantic relationship. Write a poem from his or her point of view, using some of the same words and images from the original poem.

7.   Two other poems in this unit also deal with the theme of separation from a loved one: "A Valediction: Forbidding Mourning" by John Donne and "The River-Merchant's Wife: A Letter" by Li Po. Write a 500-word essay in which you compare and contrast Ben Okri's poem with one of these other poems. Focus on such aspects as dramatic situation, form, imagery, mood, and characterization. Quote directly from the poems to support your points.

Refugee Mother and Child – Chinua Achebe

Meaning

1.   What images in this poem suggest death? How does the poet create images of life to imply a sense of life-in-death?

2.   Explore the *connotations* of the reference to the Madonna and Child. What emotions might the two images of motherhood share?

Form and Style

3.   What is the effect of the absence of sound in the poem? Given this absence, what might the image "singing in her eyes" mean?

4.   The speaker uses verbs in both the *indicative* and the *subjunctive mood*. Identify where in the poem the verbs shift mood and describe any connections between the mood of the verbs and the speaker's feelings. Speculate why all the indicative verbs are in the past tense.

Exploring Context

5.   In the first and last sentences of the poem, the speaker implies a commentary on the scene he or she is describing. What values and attitudes lie behind the speaker's responses to seeing this mother and her child? What responses do the speaker's comments evoke from the reader?

Creative Extension

6.   Imagine you were filming this poem. Take each sentence in turn and describe effective camera angles. How would you represent the images in the final sentence?

7.   Research the career and accomplishments of Chinua Achebe. Prepare a report or create a Web page introducing others to this writer. Include a short profile, a bibliography of his major works, and a close analysis of one or two examples of his writings. Conclude with an assessment of this writer's importance.

Illusions and Reality

Can we trust appearances?

Many artists focus on the discrepancy between reality and illusion. How do we know what is real? Can we trust appearances? What influences our perceptions? Margaret Atwood frequently explores this tension between fiction and reality in her work. In this Echo, two poems and a dialogue by Margaret Atwood, an excerpt from Eleanor Wachtel's interview with Atwood, and Canadian art that influenced Atwood offer the opportunity to explore this key theme in an influential author's work.

Learning Goals

- explore the development of a key theme in an author's work
- examine and analyze contextual influences on an author
- analyze how differences in genre, form, and style affect the development of a key theme

This is a Photograph of Me

ᔆ *Margaret Atwood*

This poem appeared in Margaret Atwood's first collection of poetry, The Circle Game, *published in 1966. It immediately established her fascination with appearances and illusions. In her characteristically wry style, she challenges her readers to carefully examine their perceptions.*

It was taken some time ago.
At first it seems to be
a smeared
print: blurred lines and grey flecks
blended with the paper;

then, as you scan
it, you see in the left-hand corner
a thing that is like a branch: part of a tree
(balsam or spruce) emerging
and, to the right, halfway up
what ought to be a gentle
slope, a small frame house.

In the background there is a lake,
and beyond that, some low hills.

(The photograph was taken
the day after I drowned.

I am in the lake, in the centre
of the picture, just under the surface.

It is difficult to say where
precisely, or to say
how large or small I am:
the effect of water
on light is a distortion

but if you look long enough,
eventually
you will be able to see me.)

Morning in the Burned House

ᔕ Margaret Atwood

"Morning in the Burned House" was written much later in Margaret Atwood's career than "This is a Photograph of Me". "Morning in the Burned House" appeared in a collection of the same name published in 1995, yet the theme of reality and illusion is still very prevalent.

In the burned house I am eating breakfast.
You understand: there is no house, there is no breakfast,
yet here I am.

The spoon which was melted scrapes against
the bowl which was melted also.
No one else is around.

Where have they gone to, brother and sister,
mother and father? Off along the shore,
perhaps. Their clothes are still on the hangers,

their dishes piled beside the sink,
which is beside the woodstove·
with its grate and sooty kettle,

every detail clear,
tin cup and rippled mirror.
The day is bright and songless,

the lake is blue, the forest watchful.
In the east a bank of cloud
rises up silently like dark bread.

I can see the swirls in the oilcloth,
I can see the flaws in the glass,
those flares where the sun hits them.

I can't see my own arms and legs
or know if this is a trap or blessing,
finding myself back here, where everything

in this house has long been over,
kettle and mirror, spoon and bowl,
including my own body,

including the body I had then,
including the body I have now
as I sit at this morning table, alone and happy,

bare child's feet on the scorched floorboards
(I can almost see)
in my burning clothes, the thin green shorts

and grubby yellow T-shirt
holding my cindery, non-existent,
radiant flesh. Incandescent.

ᔥ Margaret Atwood is one of Canada's most prominent contemporary writers. A poet, novelist, short-story writer, and literary critic, she first attracted attention with her poetry in collections such as *The Circle Game* (1966) and *The Journals of Susanna Moodie* (1970). Both volumes won Governor General's Awards. *Morning in the Burned House* received the Trillium Award in 1995. Atwood's many novels include *The Handmaid's Tale* (1986) and *The Blind Assassin* (2000). *Good Bones* (1992) is a collection of short stories, monologues, prose poems, and non-fiction, and it includes the dialogue "There Was Once." Atwood's work has been translated into over thirty languages, and she has been awarded several Canadian and international awards including the Giller Prize and the Booker Prize. (*Born Ottawa, Ontario 1939*)

RESPONDING

Meaning

1.   As a class or in small groups, paraphrase the literal details (what the *text* actually says) in each poem. That is, answer the 4Ws: Who are the characters? Where does the poem take place? When does it take place? What events occur?

2.   Next, consider what is not said in the poems (*the subtext*). What does Atwood leave out? What key questions are unanswered in your (the reader's) mind?

Form and Style

3.   a)   Identify key elements and techniques (e.g., setting, mood, tone, punctuation, irony, etc.) Atwood uses in "This is a Photograph of Me" and analyze their effects.
     b)   Write a theme statement for "This is a Photograph of Me" that answers the question, "Why did Atwood write this poem?"

4.   a)   Reread the two poems focusing specifically on similarities and differences in content and style. Develop a graphic organizer to present your findings.
     b)   Discuss the significance of fire in "Morning in the Burned House" and water in "This is a Photograph of Me." Support your interpretations.

Exploring Context

5.   In her essay, "Atwood and a Canadian Tradition," Sandra Djwa states: "The poem is often a journey . . . down into the water. Many of these journeys are seen as a descent, ultimately a journey down into the psychological self. As such the mythic descent is related to questions of identity . . . . In the Canadian critical tradition, landscape has always been closely associated with identity" (22). Apply Djwa's analysis to specific excerpts from "This is a Photograph of Me."

ECHO

Creative Extension

6. Write a front-page article for a newspaper based on the tragedy that occurs in one of these poems. Remember to follow the conventions of good newspaper writing and investigative journalism. What are the facts? What are the unanswered questions? What is appearance and what is reality?

7. Write an essay comparing and contrasting "Morning in the Burned House" and "This is a Photograph of Me." Consider specifically ideas Atwood develops about illusion versus reality. Present your essay in a seminar.

An Interview with Margaret Atwood

ᕦ Eleanor Wachtel

In this interview, Eleanor Wachtel prompts Margaret Atwood to look back over her career and to explore some of the key themes and influences in her work. The results are interesting and revealing.

WACHTEL You produced your first book of poems when you were seven—which, you said, didn't indicate promise. Why did you start writing poetry?

ATWOOD Because I was writing everything else at the time. I started a novel about then. It featured as its central character an ant. Don't ask me why. I did not finish that book, but it started off quite well. And I was writing other things as well—I think our main form was comic books. We probably did more of those than anything, but I also did a play around that time. I think children—this is the pre-television generation—imitate the art forms they see around them. . . .

WACHTEL When did you really start reading poetry seriously?

ATWOOD I didn't really start reading poetry seriously, apart from the stuff we had to do in school—you know, *Poems Chiefly Narrative* and things like that—until I started writing it. The poetry I was exposed to was not written in the twentieth century. I didn't even really know that there was such a thing as modern poetry until I was at university.

WACHTEL Which is when you really started to write poetry.

ATWOOD No, I started when I was sixteen, in high school. It all sounds like Edgar Allan Poe on a very bad day; you know, Byron with a hangover.

It all rhymes and scans. Actually, it's rather startlingly bad poetry. It's written by a sixteen-year-old; what can we expect?

WACHTEL   Is it full of angst?

ATWOOD   Lots of angst. I looked back through some of it, which I still have, and noticed I had written a poem about the Hungarian uprising of 1956 which I had quite forgotten. But there is a reasonable amount of angst, more so as I hit the coffee shop. Let's face it, once you hit the coffee shop—once I hit T. S. Eliot—then lots of empty vessels appeared in my poems, you know, empty cups.

WACHTEL   I remember measuring out my life in coffee spoons around that time.

ATWOOD   They had a big impact. Also, the fact that you could put garbage in a poem very much impressed me because, if all you had was nineteenth-century poetry, that had no garbage in it. It was much more noble. But once you hit the twentieth century—

WACHTEL   What kind of garbage?

ATWOOD   Garbage, you know, garbage blowing around on the street, the kind you have in garbage cans. So I put some of that in my early poems, and leaves, decaying leaves, not spring leaves.

WACHTEL   What draws you to poetry both as a writer and a reader?

ATWOOD   I go through long phases of neither writing it nor reading it. Then I'll go through a phase in which I really can't get enough of it. I go to the bookstore and I catch up on all the books of poetry I haven't read over the past three or four years. It's like another life, or let me put it this way: It's like another language. I always have the sense of opening up a box and finding amazing things in there which are suddenly very attractive—you know, coming across something you had hidden away, finding it again. I think for me it has a lot to do with the rediscovery of language or concentration on the word.

If you're writing a novel, you're concentrating on much larger units—not that you don't pay attention to your sentences et cetera, but the potency of the individual word tends to be more spread out. You're really concentrating on starting something on page 30 that you finish on page 250. The wavelengths are a lot longer, the pattern much larger. Poetry is a very concentrated form, and therefore the explosiveness of each word becomes much greater.

. . .

WACHTEL   The first poem in your selected poems, "This is a Photograph of Me," is from *The Circle Game*, which came out back in 1966. I've always liked that poem a lot, even before I realized that it touches on a number of themes that you've returned to or developed. One is in the line, "I am in the lake in the centre of the picture just under the surface." It's a very evocative image, being in the photograph but invisible, drowned, and I wonder, what is it about photographs that you find so fascinating?

ATWOOD   Photographs are stopped time. All that they can portray is appearances. You see the moment, you see the instant when that photograph was taken. But the camera cannot take a picture of your thought, it cannot take a picture of what was really going on. It's a completely odd phenomenon when you come to think of it. Photographs are frozen light. There is always either much less in them than meets the eye or much more.

I adore looking at photographs. They're mysterious. They purport to be very flat and visible, and they have no depth on the page; they're just a flat surface. But if you look into them rather than at them you can go underneath the surface of the photograph. That sounds creepy. I find them a very Gothic form. . . .

WACHTEL   There's another tantalizing line in the poem, at the end where your write, "If you look long enough, eventually you will be able to see me." I know the "me" isn't necessarily you, but you are very elusive in your poetry. George Woodcock described your poetry as "inclined to an almost Buddhist objectivity."

ATWOOD   I don't know exactly what is meant by those things. I suppose some people when they write poems create *dramatis personae* for themselves. They write roles for themselves, which they then play in the poems: me, person who drinks a lot; me, who wears loud, plaid shirts; you know, whatever their thing happens to be, whatever the costume happens to be. And there is another kind of poem in which the narrator really is the reader, the "I." Because the "I" is not described and is not specific it becomes the reader, so that the reader, instead of viewing the poet, as if the poet were cavorting about on the stage, is able to enter the poem as a co-creator.

WACHTEL   Is that a deliberate strategy? It sounds suspiciously post-modern.

ATWOOD   No, I think it's just the way it works, and it's not postmodern. I was already old by the time postmodern came along.

WACHTEL   A lot of readers think they recognize you in your novels.

ATWOOD   You know what they really recognize? They really recognize themselves. When they write letters, it tends to be not, "Gosh, that was an interesting description of your childhood," but "Gosh, that was *my* childhood."

   That's what we do when we read books. We enter in. They know, from wiring up people's brains, that when you watch television there is less activity than when you are asleep. But when you read a book there is a great deal of brain activity, because you, the reader, are creating all the sound effects, all the visuals; you are making that world. That's why people are deeply influenced by books in a way that they are not by TV. You can have a momentary interest in TV, but try to remember all the TV shows you've seen, and now tell me the plots. I double-dare.

   But you could tell me the plots of quite a few books because you have lived those plots. They also know that reading a book is, in terms of brain activity, the nearest equivalent to actually doing it, whatever *it* is.

WACHTEL   The poem "This is a Photograph of Me" also picks up the idea of a human figure in relation to nature—in this case, quite literally submerged in nature, underwater. You spend a lot of your early childhood close to nature. Your father was an entomologist and your family spent a lot of time in the bush. How do you think that affected you?

ATWOOD   I also spent a lot of time in the early sixties looking at Canadian paintings, among them the paintings of Jack Chambers, and one of the things that Jack Chambers was very interested in showing was the human figure disappearing into a landscape. In fact, the whole tradition of Canadian painting and how and where figures enter landscapes was very interesting to me at that time. It connected with my own experience of growing up in the North, and the fact that if you are watching a figure in that landscape, one minute you see it and the next minute you don't. It disappears among the trees, it goes around the corner, people dive. There is a constant metamorphosis going on between human figures, foliage, and water surfaces in that sort of landscape.

WACHTEL   Was your childhood a kind of bush idyll?

ATWOOD   I don't think it's quite like that in the Canadian North. It's a large place, it's easy to get lost and there is always the possibility that something may come out of the woods. It's a landscape with a lot of spiritual resonance. How can I say that without sounding pretentious? Well, I can't, so we'll just keep that, that phrase.

WACHTEL   Did you feel that even as a child?

ATWOOD   Who can remember what they felt as a child, precisely? It was my home, so all those home feelings you have—this is familiar, that's familiar—all those kinds of feelings I associate with that landscape. I also knew that one false step and . . . You had to watch where you were going and what you were doing. It was not a feeling of complete safety, but on the other hand, it wasn't the kind of paranoia you get living in the city. . .

Connecting

1. On the third page of the interview (page 53), Atwood explains her fascination with photographs. How does this discussion relate to her poem, "This is a Photograph of Me"? Choose two sentences or phrases from the interview and relate them directly to themes and images in the poem.
2. a)   In this interview, Atwood contrasts the process of reading books with the process of viewing television. Summarize her argument. Do you agree or disagree? Why?
    b)   How might Atwood's ideas influence the worlds she creates in her poems?
3. Wachtel and Atwood also discuss the importance of the Canadian landscape during Atwood's childhood. Select a key sentence or two about this topic from the interview and explain how it enhances your understanding of "This is a Photograph of Me" or "Morning in the Burned House."

✍ Eleanor Wachtel is a well-known writer and broadcaster in Canada. Since 1990, she has been the host of the popular radio show *Writers & Company*, where she conducts interviews with respected authors. Selections of her interviews have been published in two volumes, *Writers & Company* (1993), which contains her interview with Margaret Atwood, and *More Writers & Company* (1996). *(Born Montreal, Quebec 1947)*

All Things Fall

ᴐ Jack Chambers

In the interview with Eleanor Wachtel, Margaret Atwood mentions that she was influenced early in her career by the paintings of Jack Chambers. This painting represents Chambers's fascination with figures disappearing into the landscape.

Connecting

1. Describe your impressions of this painting. What thoughts and emotions does it evoke?

2. a) Describe the human figures in this painting. How do they relate to the background landscape?
    b) How does the title connect with images in the painting?

3. Choose a line or sequence of lines from "This is a Photograph of Me" and Eleanor Wachtel's interview that you feel best relate to this painting. Analyze your choices. How do they relate to the theme of illusions versus reality?

֍ Canadian artist Jack Chambers painted his family, his home, the city of London, where he lived, and the surrounding landscape. His work in the 1960s often contained dreamlike images, combining his immediate personal experience and memories. He also worked as a filmmaker, producing eight films during his lifetime. (*Born London, Ontario 1931; died 1978*)

There Was Once

֍ *Margaret Atwood*

In this satirical dialogue, Margaret Atwood explores another aspect of the blurred line between fiction and reality.

—There was once a poor girl, as beautiful as she was good, who lived with her wicked stepmother in a house in the forest.

—Forest? *Forest* is passé, I mean, I've had it with all this wilderness stuff. It's not a right image of our society, today. Let's have some *urban* for a change.

—There was once a poor girl, as beautiful as she was good, who lived with her wicked stepmother in a house in the suburbs.

—That's better. But I have to seriously query this word *poor*.

—But she *was* poor!

—Poor is relative. She lived in a house, didn't she?

—Yes.

—Then socio-economically speaking, she was not poor.

—But none of the money was *hers!* The whole point of the story is that the wicked stepmother makes her wear old clothes and sleep in the fireplace—

—Aha! They had a *fireplace!* With *poor*, let me tell you, there's no fireplace. Come down to the park, come to the subway stations after dark, come down to where they sleep in cardboard boxes, and I'll show you *poor!*

—There was once a middle-class girl, as beautiful as she was good—

—Stop right there. I think we can cut the *beautiful*, don't you? Women these days have to deal with too many intimidating physical role models as it is, what with those bimbos in the ads. Can't you make her, well, more average?

—There was once a girl who was a little overweight and whose front teeth stuck out, who—

—I don't think it's nice to make fun of people's appearances. Plus, you're encouraging anorexia.

—I wasn't making fun! I was just describing—

—Skip the description. Description oppresses. But you can say what colour she was.

—What colour?

—You know. Black, white, red, brown, yellow. Those are the choices. And I'm telling you right now, I've had enough of white. Dominant culture this, dominant culture that—

—I don't know what colour.

—Well, it would probably be *your* colour, wouldn't it?

—But this isn't *about* me! It's about this girl—

—Everything is about you.

—Sounds to me like you don't want to hear this story at all.

—Oh well, go on. You could make her ethnic. That might help.

—There was once a girl of indeterminate descent, as average-looking as she was good, who lived with her wicked—

—Another thing. *Good* and *wicked*. Don't you think you should transcend those puritanical judgmental moralistic epithets? I mean, so much of that is conditioning, isn't it?

—There was once a girl, as average-looking as she was well-adjusted, who lived with her stepmother, who was not a very open and loving person because she herself had been abused in childhood.

—Better. But I am so *tired* of negative female images! And stepmothers— they always get it in the neck! Change it to step*father,* why don't you? That would make more sense anyway, considering the bad behaviour you're about to describe. We all know what those twisted . . . middle-aged men are like.

—*Hey, just a minute!* I'm *a middle-aged*—

—Stuff it, Mister Nosy Parker. Nobody asked you to stick in your oar, or whatever you want to call that thing. This is between the two of us. Go on.

—There was once a girl—

—How old was she?

—I don't know. She was young.

—This ends with marriage, right?

—Well, not to blow the plot, but—yes.

—Then you can scratch the condescending paternalistic terminology. It's woman, pal. Woman.

—There was once—

—What's this *was, once?* Enough of the dead past. Tell me about *now.*

—There—

—So?

—So, what?

—So, why not *here?*

Connecting

1. *Satire* is a mode of writing that exposes the failings of individuals, institutions, or societies to ridicule and scorn. What is Atwood satirizing in "There Was Once"? How do the devices and techniques she uses make her satire effective?

2. Atwood uses dialogue to demonstrate an argument rather than simply tell it. On what support does Atwood base her argument? What are her conclusions?

3. What ideas does Atwood develop in "There Was Once" about fiction and reality? How do Atwood's attitudes and ideas about appearance and reality in this selection compare with the tone and theme in "This is a Photograph of Me" and "Morning in the Burned House"?

☐ REFLECTING ON THE ECHO

1. Create a photo essay or multimedia presentation on the theme of illusion and reality. Use images of people and landscapes in your presentation. Carefully consider the use of words, lighting, colour, music, and sound effects. Include a memo in which you explain your choices. Note two challenges you faced and the strategies you used to meet them.

2. Choose another selection from this anthology in which the author or artist explores the theme of illusion and reality. Write an analytical essay in which you examine how the theme is developed in the work. Consider aspects such as form, style, point of view, diction or colour, and imagery in your essay. Conclude with your interpretation of the author's views on the theme.

3. Create a *shooting script* for a short film based on Atwood's poem "Morning in the Burned House." Your film could be a documentary in which you include voice-overs with readings or interpretations of the poem. Focus on the theme of illusion and reality.

Sonnet 147

My love is as a fever, longing still
For that which longer nurseth the disease,
Feeding on that which doth preserve the ill,
Th' uncertain sickly appetite to please.
My reason, the physician to my love,
Angry that his prescriptions are not kept,
Hath left me, and I desperate now approve[1]
Desire is death, which physic did except.[2]
Past cure I am, now reason is past care,[3]
And frantic mad with evermore unrest;
My thoughts and my discourse as madmen's are,
At randon[4] from the truth vainly express'd;
    For I have sworn thee fair, and thought thee bright,
    Who art as black as hell, as dark as night.

An unrivalled dramatist and poet in his time, William Shakespeare is still considered England's greatest playwright. In addition to comedies such as *Much Ado About Nothing* and tragedies such as *Romeo and Juliet*, he wrote 154 sonnets. Many dealt with themes of love, fate, and the ravages of time. A number were addressed to a woman commonly referred to as "the Dark Lady". The sonnets were first printed in 1609. (*Born Stratford-upon-Avon, England 1564; died 1616*)

---

1 approve = learn by experience
2 that desire, which refused medical treatment (from reason), is fatal
3 care = medical care
4 randon = random

(*Responding Activities p. 73*)

A Valediction: Forbidding Mourning[1]

ᓃ John Donne

As virtuous men pass mildly away,
    And whisper to their souls to go,
Whilst some of their sad friends do say,
    "The breath goes now," and some say,
    "No."

So let us melt, and make no noise,
No tear-floods, nor sigh-tempests move;
'Twere profanation of our joys
    To tell the laity our love.

Moving of th' earth[2] brings harms and
      fears;
Men reckon what it did, and meant;
But trepidation of the spheres,
    Though greater far, is innocent.[3]

Dull sublunary[4] lovers' love
(Whose soul is sense) cannot admit
Absence, because it doth remove
Those things which elemented it.[5]

But we by a love so much refined,
    That ourselves know not what it is,
Inter-assured of the mind,
    Care less, eyes, lips, and hands to miss.

Our two souls therefore, which are one,
    Though I must go, endure not yet
A breach, but an expansion,
    Like gold to airy thinness beat.[6]

If they be two, they are two so
      As stiff twin compasses are two;
Thy soul, the fix'd foot, makes no show
      To move, but doth, if th' other do.   30

And though it in the centre sit,
      Yet, when the other far doth roam,
It leans, and hearkens after it,
      And grows erect, as that comes home.

Such wilt thou be to me, who must   35
      like th'other foot, obliquely run;
Thy firmness makes my circle just,
      And makes me end where I begun.

⇢ John Donne's poetry shaped the style of many important twentieth-century writers, including T. S. Eliot and Ezra Pound. Donne was one of the Metaphysical poets of the seventeenth century. These poets blended ingenuity and wit to create unconventional imagery, such as the "twin compasses" in "A Valediction: Forbidding Mourning." Donne's passionate, colloquial, and sometimes abrupt tone distinguished his poems from those of the Elizabethan poets before him. His work consists of love poems, religious poems, verse satires, and sermons. (*Born London, England c. 1572; died 1631*)

---

1 Izaack Walton says that John Donne wrote this poem for his wife before he left for France in 1611.

2 Moving of th' earth = earthquakes

3 trepidation of the spheres, / Though greater far, is innocent—In Ptolemaic astronomy, the motion of the eighth or ninth sphere was believed to cause the "innocent or harmless variation in the date of the equinox." The movement of the celestial spheres though greater than earthquakes causes less harm.

4 sublunary = under the moon; therefore earthly and characterized by change

5 elemented = compose or constitute

6 Like gold to airy thinness beat = refers to the making of gold filigree

(*Responding Activities pp. 73–74*)

Ode on a Grecian Urn

୭ John Keats

Thou still unravish'd bride of quietness,
    Thou foster-child of silence and slow time,
Sylvan historian, who canst thus express
    A flowery tale more sweetly than our rhyme:
What leaf-fring'd legend haunts about thy shape
    Of deities or mortals, or of both,
        In Tempe or the dales of Arcady?
What men or gods are these? What maidens loth?
    What mad pursuit? What struggle to escape?
        What pipes and timbrels? What wild ecstasy?   10

Heard melodies are sweet, but those unheard
    Are sweeter; therefore, ye soft pipes, play on;
Not to the sensual ear, but, more endear'd,
    Pipe to the spirit ditties of no tone:
Fair youth, beneath the trees, thou canst not leave   15
    Thy song, nor ever can those trees be bare;
        Bold Lover, never, never canst thou kiss,
Though winning near the goal—yet, do not grieve;
    She cannot fade, though thou hast not thy bliss,
        For ever wilt thou love, and she be fair!   20

Ah, happy, happy boughs! that cannot shed
    Your leaves, nor ever bid the Spring adieu;
And, happy melodist, unwearied,
    For ever piping songs for ever new;
More happy love! more happy, happy love!   25

For ever warm and still to be enjoy'd,
    For ever panting, and for ever young;
All breathing human passion far above,
    That leaves a heart high-sorrowful and cloy'd,
      A burning forehead, and a parching tongue.   30

Who are these coming to the sacrifice?
    To what green altar, O mysterious priest,
Lead'st thou that heifer lowing at the skies,
    And all her silken flanks with garlands drest?
What little town by river or sea shore,   35
    Or mountain-built with peaceful citadel,
    Is emptied of this folk, this pious morn?
And, little town, thy streets for evermore
    Will silent be; and not a soul to tell
      Why thou art desolate, can e'er return.   40

O Attic shape! Fair attitude! with brede
    Of marble men and maidens overwrought,
With forest branches and the trodden weed;
    Though, silent form, dost tease us out of thought
As doth eternity: Cold Pastoral!   45
    When old age shall this generation waste,
    Thou shalt remain, in midst of other woe
Than ours, a friend to man, to whom thou say'st,
    'Beauty is truth, truth beauty,'—that is all
      Ye know on earth, and all ye need to know.   50

ও John Keats is considered a part of a group of writers known as the Romantics. Influenced by William Wordsworth, the Romantics believed in the power of the imagination and the prophetic power of the poet. Keats's early poems received harsh criticism, but he continued to write. Many of his best-known poems including "Ode on a Grecian Urn," "Ode to a Nightingale," and "Ode to Melancholy" were written in one year, 1818, and published in 1820. Keats died at the age of 26 of tuberculosis. (*Born London, England 1795; died 1821*)

(*Responding Activities pp. 74–75*)

After Great Pain a Formal Feeling Comes

ℰ Emily Dickinson

After great pain, a formal feeling comes—
The nerves sit ceremonious, like Tombs—
The stiff Heart questions was it He, that bore,
And Yesterday, or Centuries before?

The Feet, mechanical, go round—
Of Ground, or Air, or Ought—
A Wooden way
Regardless grown,
A Quartz contentment, like a stone—

This is the Hour of Lead—
Remembered, if outlived,
As Freezing Persons, recollect the Snow—
First—Chill—then Stupor—then the letting go—

ℰ Only seven of Emily Dickinson's poems were published during her lifetime. She lived in seclusion and her work became well known only in the twentieth century. Much of the dramatic tension in her short lyrics stems from religious doubt and her own inner struggles. Her innovative techniques, however, influenced many twentieth century poets. *The Poems of Emily Dickinson* (1955) contains all 1775 known poems. (*Born Massachusetts 1830; died 1886*)

(Responding Activities p. 75)

The Goblet

ᖇ Gabriela Mistral

arning Goals

define words from
context

examine a speaker's
state of mind

speculate about the
meaning of symbols

present a dramatic
reading

discuss archetypes in
literature

I have carried a goblet from one island
to another and never waked its gift of water.
If I had spilled it, I would have betrayed a thirst;
one drop lost, its boon destroyed;
all lost, its owner would have wept.

I did not pause to greet cities
or stay to praise their flight of towers.
I did not fling my arms wide before the great pyramid.
I did not establish a home and a circle of sons.

Delivering the goblet, the new sun
on my throat, I said:
"My arms are now free as vagrant clouds,
and I loll on crests of the hills,
rocked with allure of the valleys below."

It was a lie, my alleluia. Look at me.
My eyes are lowered to empty hands.
I walk slowly, without my diamond of water.
I go in silence. I carry no treasure.
And in my breast and through my veins
falls my blood, struck with anguish and fear.

Translated by Doris Dana   *(Responding Activities p. 76)*

ᖇ Gabriela Mistral was the pseudonym of Lucila Godoy y Alcayaga, a Chilean schoolteacher.
Her love poems in memory of the dead, *Sonetos de la muerte* (1914), brought her fame in
Latin America, but the collection *Desolación (Despair)*, published in 1922, cemented her
international success. English translations of "The Goblet" and "The Other" were published in 1971 in the *Selected Poems of Gabriela Mistral*. After her poetry became popular,
she taught Spanish literature at universities around the world. She won the Nobel Prize for
Literature in 1945. *(Born Vicuna, Chile 1889; died 1957)*

Sailing to Byzantium[1]

ᔆ W. B. Yeats

1

That is no country for old men. The young
In one another's arms, birds in the trees
—Those dying generations—at their song,
The salmon-falls, the mackerel-crowded seas,
Fish, flesh, or fowl, commend all summer long
Whatever is begotten, born, and dies.
Caught in that sensual music all neglect
Monuments of unaging intellect.

2

An aged man is but a paltry thing,
A tattered coat upon a stick, unless
Soul clap its hands and sing, and louder sing
For every tatter in its mortal dress,
Nor is there singing school but studying
Monuments of its own magnificence;
And therefore I have sailed the seas and come
To the holy city of Byzantium.

3

O sages standing in God's holy fire
As in the gold mosaic of a wall,
Come from the holy fire, perne in a gyre,[2]
And be the singing-masters of my soul.
Consume my heart away; sick with desire
And fastened to a dying animal
It knows not what it is; and gather me
Into the artifice of eternity.

4

Once out of nature I shall never take   25
My bodily form from any natural thing,
But such a form as Grecian goldsmiths make
Of hammered gold and gold enamelling
To keep a drowsy Emperor awake;
Or set upon a golden bough to sing   30
To lords and ladies of Byzantium
Of what is past, or passing, or to come.

Byzantine mosaic panel of the Empress Theodora and her court, 540s

Irish poet William Butler Yeats revived Irish literature by writing about Ireland's politics, history, and folklore. His poem "Sailing to Byzantium" in *The Tower* (1928) employed an almost romantic lyricism, while his later collections of poetry were harsher, criticizing modern civilization. They include *The Wild Swans at Coole* (1917) and *The Winding Stair* (1929). Yeats received a Nobel Prize for Literature in 1923. (*Born Dublin, Ireland 1865; died 1939*)

---

1 Yeats refers to the ancient city of Byzantium, on the site of modern Istanbul, capital of the Eastern Roman Empire and the centre, especially in the fifth and sixth centuries, of highly developed forms of art and architecture. Byzantine paintings and mosaics were stylized and formal, making no attempt at full naturalistic renderings of human forms. For Yeats, the city and its art symbolized a way of life in which art is accepted as artifice, as a work of intellect, and so is not subject to the decay and death that overtake the life of "natural things." Yeats also felt the civilization had achieved a rare "Unity of Being," in which religious, aesthetic, and practical life were one.

2 perne in a gyre = move in a spiral pattern; the speaker calls the sages to descend to him in this way, to come down into the gyres of history, the cycles of created life, out of their eternity in "the simplicity of fire" where is "all music and all rest."

(*Responding Activities pp. 76–77*)

Do Not Go Gentle Into That Good Night

ꙮ Dylan Thomas

Learning Goals

- make inferences about a narrator and his message
- analyze use of oxymorons
- examine the villanelle form
- develop a story-board
- script a dramatic scene

Do not go gentle into that good night,
Old age should burn and rave at close of day;
Rage, rage against the dying of the light.

Though wise men at their end know dark is right,
Because their words had forked no lightning they
Do not go gentle into that good night.

Good men, the last wave by, crying how bright
Their frail deeds might have danced in a green bay,
Rage, rage against the dying of the light.

Wild men who caught and sang the sun in flight,
And learn, too late, they grieved it on its way,
Do not go gentle into that good night.

Grave men, near death, who see with blinding sight
Blind eyes could blaze like meteors and be gay,
Rage, rage against the dying of the light.

And you, my father, there on the sad height,
Curse, bless, me now with your fierce tears, I pray.
Do not go gentle into that good night.
Rage, rage against the dying of the light.

(Responding Activities pp. 77–78)

ꙮ Dylan Thomas began writing poetry as a child, and by the age of twenty, his first book of poetry, *18 Poems*, appeared in London. He worked as a broadcaster, journalist, and film-maker in addition to writing poetry, stories, and a popular radio drama *Under Milk Wood* (1952). His Romantic, rhetorical style was influential and was imitated by many other writers. Thomas's *Collected Poems* appeared in 1953. *(Born Swansea, South Wales 1914; died 1953)*

From Stone to Steel

♪ E. J. Pratt

From stone to bronze, from bronze to steel
Along the road-dust of the sun,
Two revolutions of the wheel
From Java[1] to Geneva[2] run.

The snarl Neanderthal[3] is worn
Close to the smiling Aryan[4] lips,
The civil polish of the horn
Gleams from our praying finger tips.

The evolution of desire
Has but matured a toxic wine,
Drunk long before its heady fire
Reddened Euphrates or the Rhine.[5]

Between the temple and the cave
The boundary lies tissue-thin:
The yearlings still the altars crave
As satisfaction for a sin.

The road goes up, the road goes down—
Let Java or Geneva be—
But whether to the cross or crown
The path lies through Gethsemane.[6]

♪ E. J. Pratt is regarded as one of Canada's leading poets of the twentieth century. Narrative
poems such as *Towards the Last Spike* (1952) mythologized the Canadian experience. Other
poems, such as *The Titanic* (1935), echoed Victorian themes, including the conflict between
humans and nature. Pratt also wrote shorter lyrics, such as "From Stone to Steel." (*Born
Western Bay, Newfoundland 1882; died 1964*)

1 indicating an early period and place of violence before civilization; 2 indicating civilization
and the search for international peace (Geneva was the headquarters of the League of Nations
between World Wars I and II); 3 a form of primitive human; 4 a sarcastic allusion to Hitler's
theory of the superiority of the Aryan race; 5 references to ancient and modern battles;
6 where Christ suffered the agony in the Garden of Gethsemane. The suggestion is that human
beings must undergo deep suffering.

(*Responding Activities pp. 78–79*)

Night

ॐ Anne Hébert

Learning Goals

- analyze imagery and tone
- examine use of synaesthesia
- create a multimedia presentation
- write an original poem based on a model

Night
The silence of the night
Engulfs me
Like vast underwater currents.

I rest at the bottom of mute and sea-green water.
I hear my heart
Flashing on and off
Like a lighthouse.

Pulsing rhythm
Secret code
I can't decipher any mystery.

With each flash of light
I close my eyes
To continue this night
Perpetuate this silence
Where I'm shipwrecked.

Translated by A. Poulin, Jr.

ॐ Anne Hébert is considered one of the major French poets of the twentieth century. Born in Quebec, she moved to France in 1967 after receiving a scholarship and lived there most of her life. In addition to poems, she also wrote major novels, short stories, dramas, and screenplays. She received several international and Canadian awards for her work including three Governor General's Awards, the Prix France-Quebec, the Prix David, and the Prix du Roman de l'Académie française. Her novels include *Kamouraska, Children of the Black Sabbath, Héloise,* and *In the Shadow of the Wind.* Her *Selected Poems,* including both English and French texts, was published in 1988. Many of her works explore the theme of escaping personal and social restrictions and behaviours. (*Born Sainte-Catherine-de-Fossambault, Quebec 1916; died 2000*)

(*Responding Activities p. 79*)

RESPONDING ACTIVITIES

Pre- and Early Twentieth Century Lyric Poems (pages 61 – 72)

Sonnet 147 – William Shakespeare

Meaning

1. In a Shakespearean *sonnet*, each quatrain functions as a paragraph. In groups, read the poem aloud. Stop after each quatrain and paraphrase the meaning.
2. The final couplet contains the key theme of the sonnet. What message is contained in the last two lines?

Form and Style

3. Shakespeare compares passion for his lady to a fever and a disease.
   a) Identify the disease and medical imagery. How does each image reflect the speaker's emotional state? What *tone* do they create in the poem?
   b) How does the modern proverb "feed a cold and starve a fever" relate to the images and ideas in this sonnet?
4. Shakespeare is a master of the *pun* and this sonnet is no exception. Find an example of his use of double meanings and explain its significance.

Exploring Context

5. Research the Renaissance idea that each individual is a microcosm or little world and that each individual's reason, emotions, and physical needs are linked to "The Chain of Being." Based on this understanding of the Elizabethan context, explain the significance of the fact that reason leaves the speaker in this poem.

Creative Extension

6. In an essay, present your interpretation of the ideas about the power of love that are developed in Shakespeare's "Sonnet 147," Ondaatje's "The Diverse Causes," or Donne's "A Valediction: Forbidding Mourning."
7. Imagine you are the dark lady. Write a sonnet in modern English that replies to Shakespeare's sonnet. Or, write a *parody* (a humorous, exaggerated imitation) of Shakespeare's sonnet. Keep the sonnet form and "disease" imagery, or change the dominant images and present a different view of love. Present a dramatic reading of your sonnet.

A Valediction: Forbidding Mourning – John Donne

Meaning

1. a) To whom is the narrator speaking? Describe the situation that leads to this monologue.
   b) What is the *tone* or attitude of the speaker towards the listener? What is his tone or attitude about their situation? Refer to specifics from the poem to support your interpretation.
2. With a partner or small group, reread the poem several times. Summarize the speaker's message. Choose one stanza of the poem that you believe best expresses this message, and support your choice.

Form and Style

3. How does Donne make the opening of his poem very dramatic?

4. A *conceit* is an unusually far-fetched or elaborate metaphor or simile presenting a surprisingly fitting parallel between two apparently dissimilar things or feelings. The Metaphysical poets of the seventeenth century were noted for their ingenious use of conceits. What unusual comparison does Donne make from line 27 to the end of the poem? Analyze and explain the parallels involved in this extended metaphor.

Exploring Context

5. Re-read stanza three and the footnote for lines 10-13. This is the beginning of an astronomical conceit and an argument that Donne extends in stanzas four and five. What is being compared to the oscillation of the spheres? Why does Donne contrast the oscillation of the spheres with an earthquake? Analyze the argument that Donne builds based on the contrast between heaven and earth in stanza four.

Creative Extension

6. Both "A Valediction: Forbidding Mourning" and "The River-Merchant's Wife: A Letter" by Li Po on page 100 of the anthology describe relationships in which one partner has left or is about to leave. What ideas about absence within an intimate relationship do Donne and Li Po develop? What is your response to these views? Present your ideas in a short informal speech.

7. Imagine you are the woman who has listened to "A Valediction: Forbidding Mourning." Write a response to your partner's monologue. Build on the representation of the relationship conveyed in the poem, but take the woman's point of view. Write in modern English, but imagine you are part of Renaissance culture. Try to develop a metaphysical conceit to express your feelings.

Ode on a Grecian Urn – John Keats

Meaning

1. Imagine the speaker in this poem turning the Grecian urn and examining each of the pictures. Describe in sequence the scenes depicted in stanza one, stanzas two and three, and stanza four.

2. The real stories painted on the urn have been lost in time, but in his imagination, the speaker composes a story for each image. Provide evidence that the speaker is more than an observer of these stories.

Form and Style

3. The tension in the poem is based on several *paradoxes*: the frozen images on the urn versus the energy of the life they portray; change versus permanence; life versus art. Choose one of these paradoxes and explain its significance in the poem.

4. Locate images of both the spiritual passion and the earthly passion of love. Which does the speaker prefer? What *irony* is there in his choice? To what extent does this irony include the speaker's vision of an ideal life?

Exploring Context

5. This poem is a Romantic *ode*, a lyrical form that has a characteristic structure of thought.
   a) The ode begins with the description of a scene or an object that stimulates the speaker's imagination.

b)   The speaker contemplates life in response to the scene or object.

c)   The speaker achieves an understanding and returns to the starting point, the original scene or object, with new insight or perspective.

Assess the extent to which this ode follows this structure.

Creative Extension

6.   The closing couplet has troubled readers ever since the poem was first published. There are at least four versions of the punctuation.

Experiment with the punctuation and the quotation marks to arrive at answers to the questions of who is actually speaking the last lines, and to whom they are addressed. In a small group, read your different versions aloud. Which best fits your interpretation of the poem?

7.   Write an argumentative essay or an opinion piece in which you consider the question of whether art can be a substitute for real life. Refer to the contemporary media (television shows, films, the Internet, etc.) in your argument. If appropriate, organize a formal debate on the question.

After Great Pain a Formal Feeling Comes – Emily Dickinson

Meaning

1.   Specific detail is often what makes writing immediate and real, yet Dickinson does not state what caused the "great pain." Why does she leave out this detail?

2.   Who does "He" refer to in line three? (NOTE: Use the context of line 4 to assist with this question.) Why is "He" referred to here?

Form and Style

3.   a)   In stanzas one and two, Dickinson uses two *similes*. What is compared in each simile?

b)   What qualities do the items compared share? Explain how the two similes are connected.

4.   a)   In stanza three, Dickinson uses a *metaphor:* "This is the Hour of Lead." What feelings are suggested by the metaphor? Explain your answers.

b)   Dickinson also uses a *simile,* that if one outlives this, it is remembered "As Freezing Persons, recollect the Snow— / First—Chill—then Stupor—then the letting go." Explain why this comparison is so appropriate for describing the aftermath of surviving "great pain."

Exploring Context

5.   How does using religious *allusions* add to Dickinson's description of the numbness of pain?

Creative Extension

6.   Write three diary entries from the point of view of the speaker in this poem. Have one entry describe the experience. In another, take one line from the poem that describes the aftermath of great pain and describe what the person does on that day to demonstrate his or her feelings. The third entry can be written before or after the event.

7.   Create a *storyboard* for an animated version of one stanza of Dickinson's poem. Use a variety of camera shots and angles purposefully and select music to enhance the mood. Use at least ten frames. One of these stanzas requires combining dialogue and narration.

The Goblet – Gabriela Mistral

Meaning

1. Define the following words in context: *goblet, waked, boon, vagrant, allure, alleluia.* Comment on any unusual or unexpected use of words in the poem.

2. Prepare a three-column chart to compare the speaker's thoughts and actions in stanzas one and two, stanza three, and stanza four. For each of these three stages of the experience with the goblet, compose one sentence to summarize the speaker's state of mind.

Form and Style

3. Use a dictionary of symbols to analyze words and images that have symbolic meaning in the poem. Determine the importance of the goblet. Speculate about who gave the goblet to the speaker. To whom did the speaker deliver it?

4. Discuss *irony* in the poem. What do you think the speaker's sudden statement "It was a lie, my alleluia" means?

Exploring Context

5. The goblet may be connected to the myth of the Grail, the vessel that holds together the opposites of life and preserves life. Discuss similar connections to myths or legends in other cultures. What indications are there in the poem that the goblet has been both a blessing and a burden? How does the connection to this symbol of the Grail extend your understanding of the speaker's state of mind in the final stanza?

Creative Extension

6. With a small group, prepare a readers' theatre presentation of this poem. Use pace, pitch, volume, and gestures to create particular effects.

7. Using a dictionary of literary terms, define an *archetype.* What aspects of Mistral's poem could be considered archetypal or related to universal experience? Discuss other works of literature you have studied in which symbols are used to represent human experience.

Sailing to Byzantium – William Butler Yeats

Meaning

1. a) On what do "the young" focus in the first stanza? What do they ignore? Why? On what do "the young" focus in stanza two?
    b) What phrases in stanzas one and two reveal the poet's bitterness about aging in a world geared towards youth?
    c) According to Yeats, in the first half of this poem, how can an elderly man become more than "a tattered coat upon a stick"? What does the narrator do to achieve this goal?

2. Stanza three is the poet's prayer. For what does he pray? Quote the lines and paraphrase them.

Form and Style

3. Throughout the poem the natural world is contrasted with the world of art.
    a) How is each described throughout the poem? Provide examples from the poem to support your answer.

b) How does the contrast between the natural world and the world of art relate to the contrast between youth and age?

c) Quote the lines in the poem where the two worlds come together, and explain how they are reconciled.

4. Yeats's repetition of images helps create a rich symbolic meaning in the poem. Locate references to each of the following images in the poem and interpret the symbolic meaning.
   a) singing
   b) birds
   c) monuments
   d) fire
   e) Byzantium

Use an organizer such as a T-chart to organize your ideas.

References to an Image	Symbolic Meaning(s)
Singing / Music • "Caught in that sensual music" (line 7) • "Soul clap its hands and sing, and louder sing / For every tatter in its mortal dress" (lines 11–12)	• sensual music refers to nature captured by art, writing, or poetry—this art is attractive and beguiling, but not lasting • • •

Exploring Context

5. Research Byzantine paintings or mosaics. Describe how human forms are presented in the examples you find. How do these works of art relate to Yeats's poem? Why do you think Yeats was attracted to this form of art?

Creative Extension

6. Improvise the dialogue between a character representing "the young" in stanza one and the old poet as the young person tries to convince the old poet that he has misinterpreted the focus young people have on the physical world.

7. a) Select a line or phrase that you see as being important to Yeats's argument in this poem. Design one page of a coffee table book illustrating this line or phrase.

   b) Write a short paragraph explaining why you see this line or phrase as important and how you have used colour, layout, and style to emphasize the ideas in the line or phrase or the mood associated with it.

Do Not Go Gentle Into That Good Night – Dylan Thomas

Meaning

1. a) Who is the speaker in this poem? To whom is he speaking?
   b) What is the speaker's message?

2. Thomas presents four kinds of men who resist death. Identify these four kinds of men. Explain in your own words why they resist death.

Form and Style

3. An *oxymoron* is a contradiction created by two opposing words set side by side. Though seemingly contradictory, the words contain a truth. Find five examples of oxymorons in Thomas's poem and explain how the contradictions are true given the context.

4. This poem is a *villanelle*, a form that is even more restrictive than the sonnet. A villanelle has five tercets (three-line stanzas) and a final quatrain of four lines. Two of the lines must be repeated at set points. In addition, Thomas uses only two rhymes within nineteen lines.
    a) What two lines does Thomas repeat? Write out each of the lines once and provide the line numbers to show when and where they are repeated.
    b) What are the effects of the repetition?
    c) How does this very restrictive form enhance the depth of the speaker's emotion?

Exploring Context

5. Dylan Thomas wrote this poem when his father was dying. What emotions are behind the speaker's voice in this poem?

Creative Extension

6. Develop a *storyboard* for stanza two, three, four, *or* five. Use a variety of camera shots and angles purposefully and choose music to enhance the mood. Although the stanzas are only three lines long, use at least six frames—if a word is important, it may have a frame to itself. Also consider adding dialogue.

7. Script the scene where Thomas's father replies to the request, "Do not go gentle into that good night." Think about how you could dramatize some of the symbols in the poem. Be sure to provide the setting for the scene by
    • describing and drawing the setting
    • describing the character's costumes.

From Stone to Steel – E. J. Pratt

Meaning

1. Pair-share the reading of this poem. Together with your partner, decide on and record the main visual image in each stanza. Discuss the meaning and effect of each image.

2. Speculate on the possible meaning of the following phrases. Keep in mind the context of the whole poem.
    a) the horn
    b) reddened Euphrates
    c) as satisfaction for a sin

Form and Style

3. Describe the rhythm and rhyme scheme in this poem. What effects do they create?

4. Literary critics of Pratt's "From Stone to Steel" agree for the most part that the last two lines of the fourth stanza and the whole fifth stanza could be omitted from the poem. Do you agree? Explain your answer.

Exploring Context

5. a) The publication date of this poem is not stated. Make an educated guess as to when this poem was written. What word(s) in the poem gives you a clue to the answer?

    b) List other *allusions* in this poem and explain their significance.

Creative Extension

6. Using history and its lessons as a theme, create a poem that balances the bitterness of Pratt's. Find remarkable people/events that celebrate the good in humankind. You may wish to scan this text or *Echoes 11* to begin your search.

7. Picasso, a modern painter, is another artist who often depicts the brutal side of human nature. Research his work on the Internet or in the library. Create a poster or Web page that pairs these two artists' works and themes.

Night – Anne Hébert

Meaning

1. Describe a time when you woke up at night, but wanted to stay in bed and go back to sleep. What images or comparisons would you use to describe those transitory moments between sleeping and waking?

2. What is the narrator's *tone* or attitude towards being shipwrecked? Explain, with reference to the poem, the words or phrases that indicate this attitude.

Form and Style

3. Explain the *simile* in stanza one. What two things are being compared? What qualities do they have in common?

4. *Synaesthesia*, according to the *Concise Oxford Dictionary of Literary Terms*, is "a blending or confusion of different kinds of sense-impression, in which one type of sensation is referred to in terms more appropriate to another. Common synaesthetic expressions include the descriptions of colours as 'loud' or 'warm,' and of sounds as 'smooth.'

    Find an example of synaesthesia in the poem and explain how the ambiguity created by the blending and confusion of the senses enhances the meaning.

Exploring Context

5. What is Morse code? How does your knowledge of what Morse code is enhance your understanding of the poem?

Creative Extension

6. Create a multimedia presentation of images to enhance a dramatic reading of the poem. Be sure to document the sources of the images you select.

7. Use Anne Hébert's poem as a model for your own poem about night. Your goal is to create a sustained tone or attitude of the narrator's feeling towards night. Begin your poem in the following way:

    The _____ (insert your own noun) of the night
    _____ (insert an appropriate verb) me
    Like _____ (finish the simile).

    Do not use images related to the sea; find your own comparison. Your second stanza should introduce a related simile that uses synaesthesia. Identify the techniques used in the third and fourth stanzas and adapt them to finish your poem.

The Quest for the Ideal

How can striving for an ideal affect the human spirit?

The quest for a goal we desire to achieve can encourage us to grow and evolve. But if that goal is for perfection (something that by definition is impossible to attain), the results can be devastating. What happens when we close ourselves off from the world around us to pursue an ideal? How does that pursuit affect our place in the world around us? In this Echo, poems, paintings, a song, and a novel excerpt provide various perspectives on this theme.

Learning Goals
- examine different perspectives on a key theme
- analyze how different genres, forms, and styles contribute to meaning and affect audience
- create original works in a modern context using elements found in a focus text

The Lady of Shalott

Alfred Tennyson

In this poem, Tennyson recreates the artist's dilemma using the Authurian legend as a base. This lyrical narrative eventually became a parable adopted by many artists who wished to explain their situation in the world.

Part I

On either side of the river lie
Long fields of barley and of rye,
That clothe the wold and meet the sky;

And through the field the road runs by
      To many-towered Camelot;   5
And up and down the people go,
Gazing where the lilies blow
Round an island there below,
      The island of Shalott.

Willows whiten, aspens quiver,   10
Little breezes dusk and shiver
Thro' the wave that runs for ever
By the island in the river
      Flowing down to Camelot.
Four gray walls, and four gray towers,   15
Overlook a space of flowers,
And the silent isle imbowers
      The Lady of Shalott.

By the margin, willow veil'd
Slide the heavy barges trail'd   20
By slow horses; and unhail'd
The shallop flitteth silken-sail'd
      Skimming down to Camelot:
But who hath seen her wave her hand?
Or at the casement seen her stand?   25
Or is she known in all the land,
      The Lady of Shalott?

Only reapers, reaping early
In among the bearded barley,
Hear a song that echoes cheerly   30
From the river winding clearly,
      Down to tower'd Camelot;
And by the moon the reaper weary,
Piling sheaves in uplands airy,
Listening, whispers "Tis the fairy   35
      Lady of Shalott."

Waterhouse, John William. British, 1849–1917. "I am half sick of shadows, said the Lady of Shalott" (The Lady of Shalott, Part II) 1915. Oil on canvas 100.3 x 73.7 cm. ART GALLERY OF ONTARIO, Toronto. Gift of Mrs. Philip B. Jackson, 1971.

Part II

There she weaves by night and day
A magic web with colours gay.
She has heard a whisper say,
A curse is on her if she stay   40
        To look down to Camelot.
She knows not what the curse may be,
And so she weaveth steadily,
And little other care hath she,
        The Lady of Shalott.   45

And moving thro' a mirror clear
That hangs before her all the year,
Shadows of the world appear.
There she sees the highway near
        Winding down to Camelot: 50
There the river eddy whirls,
And there the curly village-churls,
And the red cloaks of market girls,
        Pass onward from Shalott.

Sometimes a troop of damsels glad,   55
An abbot on an ambling pad,
Sometimes a curly shepherd lad,
Or long-hair'd page in crimson clad,
        Goes by to towered Camelot;
And sometimes thro' the mirror blue   60
The knights come riding two and two:
She hath no loyal knight and true,
        The Lady of Shalott.

But in her web she still delights
To weave the mirror's magic sights,   65
For often thro' the silent nights
A funeral, with plumes and lights,
        And music, went to Camelot:

Or when the moon was overhead,
Came two young lovers lately wed;   70
"I am half sick of shadows" said
    The Lady of Shalott.

Sidney Harold Meteyard, "I am half-sick of shadows," said *The Lady of Shalott,* 1913.

Part III

A bow-shot from her bower-eaves,
He rode between the barley-sheaves,
The sun came dazzling thro' the leaves,   75
And flamed upon the brazen greaves
    Of bold Sir Lancelot.

A red-cross knight for ever kneel'd
To a lady in his shield,
That sparkled on the yellow field,   80
    Beside remote Shalott.

The gemmy bridle glitter'd free,
Like to some branch of stars we see
Hung in the golden Galaxy.
The bridle bells rang merrily   85
       As he rode down to Camelot:
And from his blazon'd baldric slung
A mighty silver bugle hung,
And as he rode his armour rung,
       Beside remote Shalott.   90

All in the blue unclouded weather
Thick-jewell'd shone the saddle-leather,
The helmet and the helmet-feather
Burn'd like one burning flame together,
       As he rode down to Camelot.   95
As often thro' the purple night,
Below the starry clusters bright,
Some bearded meteor, trailing light,
       Moves over still Shalott.

His broad clear brow in sunlight glow'd;   100
On burnish'd hooves his war-horse trode;
From underneath his helmet flow'd
His coal-black curls as on he rode,
       As he rode down to Camelot.
From the bank and from the river   105
He flash'd into the crystal mirror,
"Tirra lirra" by the river
       Sang Sir Lancelot.

She left the web, she left the loom,
She made three paces thro' the room,   110
She saw the water-lily bloom,
She saw the helmet and the plume,
       She looked down to Camelot.
Out flew the web and floated wide;

The mirror crack'd from side to side;   115
"The curse is come upon me," cried
    The Lady of Shalott.

William Holman Hunt, *The Lady of Shalott,* 1886–1905.

Part IV

In the stormy east-wind straining,
The pale yellow woods were waning,
The broad stream in his banks complaining,   120
Heavily the low sky raining
        Over tower'd Camelot;
Down she came and found a boat
Beneath a willow left afloat,
And round about the prow she wrote   125
        The Lady of Shalott.

And down the river's dim expanse
Like some bold sëer in a trance,
Seeing all his own mischance—
With a glassy countenance   130
        Did she look to Camelot.
And at the closing of the day
She loosed the chain, and down she lay;
The broad stream bore her far away,
        The Lady of Shalott.   135

Lying, robed in snowy white
That loosely flew to left and right—
The leaves upon her falling light—
Through the noises of the night
        She floated down to Camelot: 140
And as the boat-head wound along
The willowy hills and fields among,
They heard her singing her last song,
        The Lady of Shalott.

Heard a carol, mournful, holy   145
Chanted loudly, chanted lowly,
Till her blood was frozen slowly,
And her eyes were darkened wholly,
        Turned to tower'd Camelot.

John William Waterhouse, *The Lady of Shalott,* 1888.

For ere she reach'd upon the tide   150
The first house by the water-side,
Singing in her song she died,
    The Lady of Shalott.

Under tower and balcony,
By garden-wall and gallery,   155
A gleaming shape she floated by,
Dead-pale between the houses high,
    Silent into Camelot.
Out upon the wharfs they came,
Knight and burgher, lord and dame,   160
And round the prow they read her name,
    The Lady of Shalott.

Who is this? and what is here?
And in the lighted palace near
Died the sound of royal cheer;   165
And they cross'd themselves for fear,
    All the knights at Camelot:
But Lancelot mused a little space;
He said, "She has a lovely face;
God in his mercy lend her grace,   170
    The Lady of Shalott."

ᴇᵴ Alfred Lord Tennyson is one of the best-known English poets of the Victorian age. He is famous for the majestic and musical quality of his verse and for such narrative and dramatic poems as "The Charge of the Light Brigade," "The Idylls of the King," and "The Lady of Shalott." Tennyson was Poet Laureate of Great Britain from 1850 to 1892. *(Born Lincolnshire, England 1809; died 1892)*

RESPONDING

Meaning

1. In groups, discuss the significance of the following lines:
   a) She has heard a whisper say,
      A curse is on her if she stay
          To look down to Camelot.
   b) And moving thro' a mirror clear
      That hangs before her all the year,
      Shadows of the world appear.
   c) "I am half sick of shadows," said
          The Lady of Shalott.
2. Write a clear and concise *theme statement* for this poem. Discuss your statement with other members of your class.

Form and Style

3. This poem is an *allegory*, a narrative with a second distinct meaning partially hidden behind its literal or visible meaning. There is a continuous parallel between two (or more) levels of meaning in the story. If the Lady of Shalott is the artist, and Shalott is the artist's shadow world, decide what the following could represent:
   a) Camelot
   b) Lancelot
   c) the web (the tapestry on which the Lady of Shalott works)
   d) the mirror
   e) the Lady's death

4. In Part III of the poem, the *mood* and *tone* change dramatically. Identify specific lines, rhythms, and images that illustrate the shift. Then write a paragraph explaining the effectiveness of this section. Focus on word choice, subject focus, colour references, and changes in lyrical rhythm.

Exploring Context

5. This poem is based on one of the incidents in Malory's *Morte d'Arthur*. The incident centres on Lancelot, one of the knights of the Round Table, and his connections to Elaine, the lady of the tower. Research the Arthurian legend of Lancelot and Elaine. How does Tennyson reinterpret the myth to suit his theme?

Creative Extension

6. Assume, instead of the role of an artist, a different life role such as a renowned doctor, famous athlete, popular musician, superior teacher, or successful businessperson. Create your own allegory in poetry or prose. Carefully plan your main storyline, the symbols you will use, and the parallel storyline they will represent.

7. Research the life of a famous person who has always interested you. Investigate the sacrifices this individual has made to attain his or her "perfection." Share your research with the class in a three to five minute informal presentation.

Paintings of the Lady of Shalott

Many artists through the centuries have been captivated by the powerful theme and narrative of Tennyson's poem and have created their own interpretations. The Pre-Raphaelite artists in particular produced several representations of the Lady of Shalott.

2

3

4

1

Connecting

1. Choose the painting you find most striking and reread the section of the poem it represents. What four words or phrases from the poem best match this painting?
2. Of the four paintings, which has the most energy? How is this energy projected? Consider the perspective, use of colour, body language, facial expression, etc.
3. a) Which of the four visuals best suits the mood of the entire poem? Justify your choice.
    b) Which visual best reflects the main theme of the poem—the pursuit of an ideal and its consequences. Write a short paragraph explaining your view.

Lancelot with Bicycle

ᔓ *Phyllis McGinley*

This poem by Phyllis McGinley is a playful parody of Tennyson's "Lady of Shalott." Though light and quaint, it makes an important comment on the main theme of Tennyson's text.

> Her window looks upon the lane.
> From it, anonymous and shy,
> Twice daily she can see him plain,
> Wheeling heroic by.
> She droops her cheek against the pane
> And gives a little sigh.
>
> Above him maples at their bloom
> Shake April pollen down like stars
> While he goes whistling past her room
> Toward unimagined wars,
> A tennis visor for his plume,
> Scornful of handlebars.
>
> And, counting over in her mind
> His favours, gleaned like windfall fruit
> (A morning when he spoke her kind,
> An afternoon salute,
> A number that she helped him find,
> Once, for his paper route).
>
> Sadly she twists a stubby braid
> And closer to the casement leans—
> A wistful and a lily maid

ECHO

In moccasins and jeans,
Despairing from the seventh grade
To match his lordly teens.

And so she grieves in Astolat
(Where other girls have grieved the same)
For being young and therefore not
Sufficient to his fame—
Who will by summer have forgot
Grief, April, and his name.

೨ Even as a teenager, Phyllis McGinley's poetry was published in such distinguished magazines as *The New Yorker*. McGinley used humour to praise the virtues of ordinary life and
she celebrated but also satirized life's absurdities. She defended femininity, morality, and
domestic and suburban living in *Times Three: Selected Verse from Three Decades*, which won
the 1961 Pulitzer Prize for poetry. She also wrote a series of humorous, autobiographical
essays about being a suburban housewife, which were published in *The Province of the
Heart* (1959) and *Sixpence in Her Shoe* (1964). *(Born Oregon 1905; died 1978)*

Connecting
1. According to the narrator, what seems to be the major impediment to the relationship
    between the young girl and her Lancelot?
2. What key idea is McGinley satirizing in Tennyson's poem? Explain.
3. Parallel four lines from "The Lady of Shalott" with four lines from this poem. What tech-
    niques does Phyllis McGinley use to *parody* Tennyson's imagery and style? Comment on
    the effectiveness of her techniques.
4. Which of the visuals matched with the Tennyson poem comes closest to the main focus
    of this poem? Explain. How does this poem relate to the theme of striving for an ideal?

Candle in the Wind

೨ *Elton John and Bernie Taupin*

*This eulogy, written for actress Marilyn Monroe, poignantly expresses the loneliness and despair of
the modern artist in a world that doesn't seem to care for the individual.*

Goodbye Norma Jean
Though I never knew you at all
You had the grace to hold yourself
While those around you crawled

They crawled out of the woodwork
And they whispered into your brain
They set you on the treadmill
And they made you change your name

And it seems to me you lived your life
Like a candle in the wind
Never knowing who to cling to
When the rain set in
And I would have liked to have known you
But I was just a kid
Your candle burned out long before
Your legend ever did

Loneliness was tough
The toughest role you ever played
Hollywood created a superstar
And pain was the price you paid
Even when you died
Oh the press still hounded you
All the papers had to say
Was that Marilyn was found in the nude

And it seems to me you lived your life
Like a candle in the wind
Never knowing who to cling to
When the rain set in
And I would have liked to have known you
But I was just a kid
Your candle burned out long before
Your legend ever did

Goodbye Norma Jean
From the young man in the 22nd row
Who sees you as something more than sexual

More than just our Marilyn Monroe

And it seems to me you lived your life
Like a candle in the wind
Never knowing who to cling to
When the rain set in
And I would have liked to have known you
But I was just a kid
Your candle burned out long before
Your legend ever did

ও   Born Reginald Kenneth Dwight, rock singer Elton John has entertained fans across the world, often dressed in flamboyant, colourful costumes. The singer accompanies himself on the piano for many of his songs, which he co-writes with Bernie Taupin. Although some critical favour followed the release of John's first album, *Empty Sky* (1969), and the later *Tumbleweed Connection* (1970), *Goodbye Yellow Brick Road* (1973) was his first huge success. It featured the song "Candle in the Wind," a eulogy for Marilyn Monroe. (*Born Pinner, England 1947*)

Connecting

1.   Read the lyrics of the song thoughtfully. Explain three of the following phrases and connect them to the core text and, if possible, to one other selection in this Echo:
     a)   those around you crawled
     b)   they set you on the treadmill
     c)   when the rain set in
     d)   the toughest role
     e)   pain was the price
     f)   like a candle in the wind

2.   Which painting from page 90 would you associate with this song? Why?

3.   Who are "they" in Elton John's song? How does Elton John portray them in his song? In one sentence, describe the attitude of the outside world to the individual artist, and of the individual artist to the outside world, as it is revealed in each selection in this Echo.

4.   In 1998, Elton John revised this song to perform at the funeral of Princess Diana. What parallels can be drawn between the Lady of Shalott, Marilyn Monroe, and Princess Diana?

The Mountain and the Valley

ও   *Ernest Buckler*

In these excerpts from Ernest Buckler's novel, the protagonist David Canaan is an aspiring writer who feels a strong sense of isolation from the world around him. His situation has interesting parallels with Tennyson's poem.

David Canaan had lived in Entremont all his thirty years. As far back as childhood, whenever anger had dishevelled him, or confusion, or the tick, tick, tick, of emptiness like he felt today, he had sought the log road that went to the top of the mountain. As he moved along this road, somewhere the twist of anger would loosen; a shaft of clarity would strike through the scud of confusion; blood would creep back into the pulse and pallor of the emptiness. He would take happiness there, to be alone with it; as another child might keep hidden for a day a toy that wasn't his.

He stood at the kitchen window now, watching the highway.

The highway was irregularly noduled with whitewashed wooden houses. It cut through the Annapolis Valley; and on either side of it lay the flat frozen fields.

On the north side, the fields and orchards ran down to the big bend of the river, cut wide by the Fundy tides. Blocks of grimy, sun-eaten ice were piled up in Druidic formations on the river's banks, where the tides had tumbled them. The North Mountain rose sharply beyond the river. It was solid blue in the afternoon light of December that was pale and sharp as starlight, except for the milky ways of choppings where traces of the first snow never quite disappeared.

On the south side of the highway, beyond the barn and the pastures, the South Mountain rose. Solid blue too at the bottom where the dark spruces huddled close, but snow-grey higher up where the sudden steepness and the leafless hardwood began. At the peak the gaunt limbs of the maples could be seen like the bones of hands all along the lemon-coloured horizon.

The mountain slopes were less than a mile high at their topmost point but they shut the valley in completely.

• • •

Detail came clearly enough to David's sight; but it was as if another glass, beyond the glass of the window pane, covered everything, made touch between any two things impossible. He saw the children skating on the flooded marshes, but the sound of their voices fell in the thin air before it reached the house. Their movements were like line drawings of movements. His eyes followed the peopled cars as they passed down the long straight stretch of road; yet when they disappeared around the corner there was no impression of severance.

He stood absolutely still. He was not quiet with thought or interest. It was simply that any impulse to movement receded before the compulsion of the emptiness: to suspend the moment and prolong it, exactly as it was, in a kind of spell.

At a first glance his face looked young. The tentative, blue-eyed look of a boy's face still shadowed it. A touch of sun still lingered in the quick blond hair. The eyes and mouth were sober, but a trigger-readiness to grin lurked in them. At a second glance his face seemed old. The flesh was firm over the broad bones (so much broader than the tall slender body seemed to call for); but it had the cast of a bad night's sleep. The longer you looked, the less you could be sure whether the face was young or old.

"What are you doing, David?" Ellen turned from the rug as she spoke. The patience in his face was his father's; the quickness that disputed the patience his mother's. Its fine graining was hers.

He didn't reply. She scarcely noticed now, whether you answered or not.

"What are you looking at, child?" she asked again.

"Nothing," he said.

She turned back to the rug.

• • •

Most mornings there was pain. It wasn't exclamatory, but a bleaching ache that whitened his senses like thumb pressure whitens flesh. For the first time he knew steady pain, not as something that grazed him in passing, but as a thing resident inside. Yet he didn't wrestle with it. When they asked him if his head hurt, he said no. He let the pattern of the pain imprint itself on him; as if by grudging a thing, whose nature it was to be fought against, and such reaction, he could deny it.

He personalized it: as if it were blows struck first in pardonable anger but continued, through momentum, to unjust excess; and then, achieving no effect other than intensification of his privacy, became the weapon of their own defeat. He lay there, listening to it, hating it, but subtly possessing it.

But sometimes, in the afternoons, he would doze and awake and the pain would be gone. The thumb would be relaxed. The blood would course colourful through the vein again.

Then it would seem as if the pain had been something made real only by his attitude toward it, that it had tired itself out, vanished so completely there could be no seed of it left. If someone asked him then if his head hurt, he'd say, "No. But it hurt like hell this morning." They would seem to glow, for asking him about his head—now that the ache was gone.

There would be a quality quite wonderful in these afternoons then. Lying there, exempt from any possible task, listening to the others below go about *their* tasks (tasks with so much brighter faces on them, now that someone in the house had been grazed by death but miraculously not struck down), there would be a strange heightening of perception in him. There would be instants when the simplest things—a chance undulation of the curtain frill in the breeze, the sound of his mother's mixing spoon against the bowl— would be suddenly, sweepingly, shot with universality. As if he had happened on some shockingly bright phrase in the very language of meaning.

That afternoon there was the instant with the book.

It was a book Dr. Engles had sent him. It was different from any book he'd ever read. It was supposed to be a good book; but at first it seemed dusty, like something old.

And then his eyes fell on one sentence: "He turned back to the empty house and his heart bent forward against a wind." He caught his breath. That's exactly the way *he'd* felt when anyone had gone away.

Then there was: "A shaft of memory stabbed him like the slash of a branch against a window pane in the night . . . ," "the sound of crickets winding their watches . . . ," "Lint made a knitting pattern in the interstices of the screen," "It was that shocking cry of a child in extreme pain, which you mistake at first for laughing. . . ." He had the flooding shock of hearing things stated exactly for the first time.

Suddenly he knew how to surmount everything. That loneliness he'd always had . . . it got forgotten, maybe, weeded over . . . but none of it had ever been conquered. (And all that time the key to freedom had been lying in these lines, this book.) There was only one way to possess anything: to say it exactly. Then it would be outside you, captured and conquered.

There was a scribbler by the bed. He reached for it and a pencil.

He wrote quickly, "Roger was angry with his brother." He hesitated. When he did, a listening seemed to spring up in everything around. It stiffened him. But he forced himself to go on. "He didn't want to climb the ladder, but something made him. His brother's face looked . . ." He thought: sad? . . . sober? . . . hurt? . . . *struck.* Yes, sure: His brother's face looked struck."

He couldn't go any farther. The cleansing cathartic of the first accurate line (*there* was the thing itself, outside him, on the page) made him close his eyes. He felt as if he were going to cry.

His mother's voice brought him up short.

"Is that Rachel coming?" he heard her say to Chris. They were alone in the kitchen.

"Yeahhhhh," Chris said disgustedly, "that's *her*."

"Is she past Ora's gate?"

"Yeahhh. She's comin here. What does *that* old bitch want?"

"Christopher!"

David slipped the scribbler under his pillow. Rachel might be coming to see *him*. He could just hear her. She'd whisper to his mother outside the door, "Well, that's fine . . . if Doctor Engles knows. He's made so many mistakes . . ." He could see her looking at him and saying, "Well, *Daaaaaavid* . . ." She'd draw out the syllables of his name as if she were comforting someone at a funeral.

And if the scribbler were in sight, she'd be sure to pick it up. She'd open it to that very page. She'd never come into the house that she hadn't brought up something that someone wanted to keep hidden. The thought of Rachel being the first one to look at these words he'd just written was awful.

ᔌ During the 1940s and 1950s, Ernest Buckler wrote and published stories that dramatized rural family relationships. He worked this theme into his first and best-known novel, *The Mountain and the Valley* (1952), where the main character, David Canaan, does not reach his full potential as a writer because of his rural surroundings. Other novels by Buckler include *The Cruelest Month* (1963) and *Ox Bells and Fireflies* (1968). (*Born Dalhousie West, Nova Scotia 1908; died 1984*)

Connecting

1. Translate into English the name of David's village. What could the name *connotatively* suggest?
2. If you were to create a visual of this artist, what paragraph or paragraphs from the text would you focus on? Why? What mood would you project? What objects would you include in the visual? Would the style of your visual be realistic, romantic, or abstract? Might you use photography as your medium? Explain your choices.
3. Reread the excerpt twice. Note the paragraph(s), words, and images that parallel images and events in "The Lady of Shalott." How does this novel excerpt reflect the theme in Tennyson's poem?

☐ REFLECTING ON THE ECHO

1. Society seems to teach that sacrifice and commitment are the price of excellence but also warns that perfectionism and striving for it often lead to stress and stress-related illness. Contact a local Human Resource manager or your local guidance counsellor. Ask him/her to speak to your class on Perfectionism or "Doing things well without 'doing in' your Wellness."

2. The Pre-Raphaelites of the nineteenth century often used literature as a base for their art. Research this period of art in your library or on the Internet. Locate another painting which is an interpretation of literature. In a PowerPoint presentation or other multimedia presentation, "teach" the class about the painting and the literary work it represents.

3. Northrop Frye, the famous Canadian literary critic, said "... we may come to realize that two essential facts about a work of art—that it is contemporary with its own time and that it is contemporary with ours—are not opposed but complementary facts." Tennyson's "Lady of Shalott," and Elton John's "Candle in the Wind" reinforce this statement. Write a persuasive essay convincing the reader that the plight of the artist in society has not changed over the centuries—that to be a master in a field is to be alone, isolated, and alienated.

4. "Lancelot with Bicycle" is a parody of sorts on "The Lady of Shalott." Create your own modern parody on the theme of longing for the unattainable.

ECHO

The River-Merchant's Wife: A Letter

☙ Li Po

While my hair was still cut straight across my forehead
I played about the front gate, pulling flowers.
You came by on bamboo stilts, playing horse,
You walked about my seat, playing with blue plums.
And we went on living in the village of Chokan:
Two small people, without dislike or suspicion.

At fourteen I married My Lord you.
I never laughed, being bashful.
Lowering my head, I looked at the wall.
Called to, a thousand times, I never looked back.

At fifteen I stopped scowling,
I desired my dust to be mingled with yours
Forever and forever and forever.
Why should I climb the look out?

At sixteen you departed
And went into far Ku-to-yen, by the river of swirling
        eddies,
And you have been gone five months.
The monkeys make sorrowful noise overhead.
You dragged your feet when you went out.

By the gate now, the moss is grown, the different mosses,
Too deep to clear them away!
The leaves fall early this autumn, in wind.
The paired butterflies are already yellow with August
Over the grass in the West garden;

They hurt me. I grow older.
If you are coming down through the narrows of the river
      Kiang
Please let me know beforehand,
And I will come out to meet you
      As far as Cho-fu-sa.

A version by Ezra Pound

Li Po is one of the most respected, pre-modern Chinese poets. Around 1100 of his poems, mainly ballads and songs, are still read today and have been translated into several languages. Li Po is best known for his poems that describe voyages through imaginary landscapes. "The River-Merchant's Wife: A Letter" was rendered in English by American poet Ezra Pound in 1926. (*Born Sichuan, China 701; died 762*)

(Responding Activities p. 117)

The Canterbury Tales

❧ Geoffrey Chaucer

Pilgrims leaving Canterbury from the "Troy Book and Siege of Thebes", 1412–22.

PROLOGUE

When in April the sweet showers fall
And pierce the drought of March to the root, and all
The veins are bathed in liquor of such power
As will bring on the engendering of the flower,
When also Zephyrus[1] with his sweet breath

---

1 Zephyrus = the warm west wind

Exhales an air in every grove and heath
Upon the tender shoots, and the young sun
His half-course in the sight of the Ram has run.
And the small fowl are making melody,
That sleep away the night with open eye   10
(So nature pricks them and their heart engages),
Then people long to go on pilgrimages,
And palmers² long to seek the stranger strands
Of far-off saints, hallowed in sundry lands,
And specially, from every shire's end   15
In England, down to Canterbury they wend
To seek the holy blissful martyr,³ quick
In giving help to them when they were sick.
      It happened in that season that one day
In Southwark, at the Tabard, as I lay   20
Ready to go on pilgrimage and start
For Canterbury, most devout at heart.
At night there came into that hostelry
Some nine and twenty in a company
Of sundry folk happening then to fall   25
In fellowship, and they were pilgrims all
That towards Canterbury meant to ride.
The rooms and stables of the inn were wide;
They made us easy, all was of the best.
And shortly, when the sun had gone to rest,   30
By speaking to them all upon the trip
I soon was one of them in fellowship,
And promised to rise early and take the way
To Canterbury, as you heard me say.
      But none the less, while I have time and space,   35
Before my story takes a further pace,
It seems a reasonable thing to say
What their condition was, the full array
Of each of them, as it appeared to me,

---

2 palmers = pilgrims
3 Saint Thomas Becket, the archbishop of Canterbury who was murdered in 1170.

According to profession and degree,   4
And what apparel they were riding in;
And at a knight I therefore will begin.

There was a KNIGHT, a most distinguished man,
Who from the day on which he first began
To ride abroad had followed chivalry,   4
Truth, honour, generousness and courtesy.
He had done nobly in his sovereign's war
And ridden into battle, no man more,
As well in Christian as in heathen places,
And ever honoured for his noble graces. . . .   5
And though so much distinguished, he was wise
And in his bearing modest as a maid.
He never yet a boorish thing had said
In all his life to any, come what might;
He was a true, perfect gentle-knight.   5
               Speaking of his equipment, he possessed
Fine horses, but he was not gaily dressed.
He wore a fustian tunic stained and dark
With smudges where his armour had left mark;
Just home from service, he had joined our ranks   6
To do his pilgrimage and render thanks.

               He had his son with him, a fine young SQUIRE,
A lover and cadet, a lad of fire
With locks as curly as if they had been pressed.
He was some twenty years of age, I guessed.   6
In stature he was of a moderate length,
With wonderful agility and strength.
He'd seen some service with the cavalry
In Flanders and Artois and Picardy
And had done valiantly in little space   7
Of time, in hope to win his lady's grace.
He was embroidered like a meadow bright
And full of freshest flowers, red and white.
Singing he was, or fluting all the day;

He was as fresh as is the month of May.   75
Short was his gown, the sleeves were long and wide;
He knew the way to sit a horse and ride.
He could make songs and poems and recite,
Knew how to joust and dance, to draw and write.
He loved so hotly that till dawn grew pale   80
He slept as little as a nightingale.
Courteous he was, lowly and serviceable,
And carved to serve his father at the table.

    There also was a NUN, a Prioress,
Her way of smiling very simple and coy;   85
Her greatest oath was only "By Saint Loy!"
And she was known as Madame Eglantyne.
And well she sang a service, with a fine
Intoning through her nose, as was most seemly,
And she spoke daintily in French, extremely,   90
After the school of Stratford-atte-Bowe;
French in the Paris style she did not know.
At meat her manners were well taught withal;
No morsel from her lips did she let fall,
Nor dipped her fingers in the sauce too deep;   95
But she could carry a morsel up and keep
The smallest drop from falling on her breast.
For courtliness she had a special zest.
And she would wipe her upper lip so clean
That not a trace of grease was to be seen   100
Upon the cup where she had drunk; to eat,
She reached a hand sedately for the meat.
She certainly was very entertaining,
Pleasant and friendly in her ways, and straining
To counterfeit a courtly kind of grace,   105
A stately bearing fitting to her place,
And to seem dignified in all her dealings,
As for her sympathies and tender feelings,
She was so charitably solicitous
She used to weep if she saw but a mouse   110

Caught in a trap, if it were dead or bleeding.
And she had little dogs she would be feeding
With roasted flesh, or milk, or fine white bread.
Sorely she wept if one of them were dead
Or someone took a stick and made it smart;   11
She was all sentiment and tender heart.
Her veil was gathered in a seemly way,
Her nose was elegant, her eyes glass-grey;
Her mouth was very small, but soft and red,
Her forehead, certainly, was fair of spread,   12·
Almost a span across the brows, I own;
She was indeed by no means undergrown.
Her cloak, I noticed, had a graceful charm.
She wore a coral trinket on her arm,
A set of beads, the gaudies tricked in green.   12·
Whence hung a golden brooch of brightest sheen
On which there first was graven a crowned *A*,
And lower, *Amor vincit omnia*.[4]
　　Another NUN, the chaplain at her cell,
Was riding with her, and three PRIESTS as well.   13·

　　A MONK there was, one of the finest sort
Who rode the country; hunting was his sport.
A manly man, to be an Abbot able;
Many a dainty horse he had in stable.
His bridle, when he rode, a man might hear   13·
Jingling in a whistling wind as clear,
Aye, and as loud as does the chapel bell
Where my lord Monk was Prior of the cell.
The Rule of good Saint Benet or Maur
As old and strict he tended to ignore;   14·
He let go by the things of yesterday
And took the modern world's more spacious way.
He did not rate that text at a plucked hen
Which says that hunters are not holy men

---

4 Latin phrase meaning "love conquers all."

And that a monk uncloistered is a mere 145
Fish out of water, flapping on the pier,
That is to say a monk out of his cloister.
That was a text he held not worth an oyster;
And I agreed and said his views were sound;
Was he to study till his head went round 150
Poring over books in cloisters? Must he toil
As Austin[5] bade and till the very soil?
Was he to leave the world upon the shelf?
Let Austin have his labour to himself.
   This Monk was therefore a good man to horse; 155
Greyhounds he had, as swift as birds, to course.
Hunting a hare or riding at a fence
Was all his fun, he spared no expense.
I saw his sleeves were garnished at the hand
With fine grey fur, the finest in the land, 160
And on his hood, to fasten it at his chin
He had a wrought-gold cunningly fashioned pin;
Into a lover's knot it seemed to pass.
His head was bald and shone like looking glass;
So did his face, as if it had been greased. 165
He was a fat and personable priest;
His prominent eyeballs never seemed to settle
And glittered like the flame beneath a kettle;
Supple his boots, his horse in fine condition.
He was a prelate[6] fit for exhibition, 170
He was not pale like a tormented soul.
He liked a fat swan best, and roasted whole.
His palfrey was as brown as is a berry. . . .

A worthy WOMAN from beside BATH city
Was with us, somewhat deaf, which was a pity. 175
In making cloth she showed so great a bent
She bettered those of Ypres and of Ghent.

---

5 Austin = Saint Augustine, who wrote much on the subject of self-discipline.
6 prelate = one who ranks high in the Church.

In all the parish not a dame dared stir
Towards the altar steps in front of her,
And if indeed they did, so wrath was she   180
As to be quite put out of charity.
Her kerchiefs were of finely woven ground;
I dared have sworn they weighed a good ten pound,
The one she wore on Sunday, on her head.
Her hose were of the finest scarlet red   185
And gartered tight; her shoes were soft and new.
Bold was her face, handsome, and red in hue.
A worthy woman all her life, what's more
She'd had five husbands, all at the church door,
Apart from other company in youth;   190
No need just now to speak of that, forsooth.
And she had thrice been to Jerusalem,
Seen many strange rivers and passed over them;
She'd been to Rome and also to Boulogne,
St. James of Compostella and Cologne,   195
And she was skilled in wandering by the way,
She had gap-teeth, set widely, truth to say.
Easily on an ambling horse she sat
Well wimpled up, and on her head a hat
As broad as is a buckler or a shield;   200
She had a flowing mantle that concealed
Large hips, her heels spurred sharply under that.
In company she liked to laugh and chat
And knew the remedies for love's mischances,
An art in which she knew the oldest dances.   205

Medieval poet Geoffrey Chaucer made a crucial contribution to English literature—he wrote in English at a time when English was not considered a suitable language for poetry. Most of the other poets in England were writing in French or Latin, but the merit of Chaucer's poetry encouraged them to write in English. His humour and attention to detail can be found in the long poem called *The Book of the Duchess*. His most famous work, a long poem written sometime after 1387, is *The Canterbury Tales*. (*Born London, England c. 1346; died 1400*)

(*Responding Activities pp. 117–118*)

The Love Song of J. Alfred Prufrock

ᔐ T. S. Eliot

Learning Goals

- make inferences about the narrator
- recognize elements of mock-heroic poems
- analyze patterns of imagery
- develop a dramatic dialogue
- write an analytical essay

S'io credesse che mia riposta fosse
A persona che mai tornasse al mondo,
Questa fiamma staria senza piu scosse.
Ma perciocche giammai di questo fondo
Non torno vivo alcun, s'i'odo il vero,
Senza tema d'infamia ti rispondo.[1]

Let us go then, you and I,
When the evening is spread out against the sky
Like a patient etherized upon a table;
Let us go, through certain half-deserted streets,
The muttering retreats   5
Of restless nights in one-night cheap hotels
And sawdust restaurants with oyster-shells:
Streets that follow like a tedious argument
Of insidious intent
To lead you to an overwhelming question . . .   10
Oh, do not ask, 'What is it?'
Let us go and make our visit.

In the room the women come and go
Talking of Michelangelo.

The yellow fog that rubs its back upon the window-panes,   15
The yellow smoke that rubs its muzzle on the window-panes

---

1 If I thought my answer were being made to one
who could ever return to the world,
this flame could shake no more [i.e., I would not speak to you];
but since if what I hear is true,
no one ever returned alive from this depth,
I answer you without fear or shame.
—from Dante Alighieri's *Divine Comedy, The Inferno*, Canto 27, lines 61–66
written during 1306–1321

Licked its tongue into the corners of the evening,
Lingered upon the pools that stand in drains,
Let fall upon its back the soot that falls from chimneys,   20
Slipped by the terrace, made a sudden leap,
And seeing that it was a soft October night,
Curled once about the house, and fell asleep.

And indeed there will be time
For the yellow smoke that slides along the street   25
Rubbing its back upon the window-panes;
There will be time to murder and create,
And time for all the works and days of hands
That lift and drop a question on your plate;
Time for you and time for me,   30
And time yet for a hundred indecisions,
And for a hundred visions and revisions,
Before the taking of toast and tea.

In the room the women come and go
Talking of Michelangelo.   35

And indeed there will be time
To wonder, 'Do I dare?" and, 'Do I dare?'
Time to turn back and descend the stair,
With a bald spot in the middle of my hair—
[They will say: 'How his hair is growing thin!']   40
My morning coat, my collar mounting firmly to the chin,
My necktie rich and modest, but asserted by a simple pin—
[They will say: 'But how his arms and legs are thin!']
Do I dare
Disturb the universe?   45
In a minute there is time
For decisions and revisions which a minute will reverse.

For I have known them already, known them all—
Have known the evenings, mornings, afternoons,
I have measured out my life with coffee spoons;   50
I know the voices dying with a dying fall
Beneath the music from a farther room.
        So how should I presume?

And I have known the eyes already, known them all—
The eyes that fix you in a formulated phrase,   55
And when I am formulated, sprawling on a pin,
When I am pinned and wriggling on the wall,
Then how should I begin
To spit out all the butt-ends of my days and ways?
        And how should I presume?   60

And I have known the arms already, known them all—
Arms that are braceleted and white and bare
[But in the lamplight, downed with light brown hair!]
Is it perfume from a dress
That makes me so digress?   65
Arms that lie along a table, or wrap about a shawl.
        And should I then presume?
        And how should I begin?

                • • •

Shall I say, I have gone at dusk through narrow streets
And watched the smoke that rises from the pipes   70
Of lonely men in shirt-sleeves, leaning out of windows?...

I should have been a pair of ragged claws
Scuttling across the floors of silent seas.

                • • •

And the afternoon, the evening, sleeps so peacefully!
Smoothed by long fingers,   75
Asleep...tired...or it malingers,

Stretched on the floor, here beside you and me.
Should I, after tea and cakes and ices,
Have the strength to force the moment to its crisis?
But though I have wept and fasted, wept and prayed,   8(
Though I have seen my head [grown slightly bald] brought
     in upon a platter,
I am no prophet—and here's no great matter;
I have seen the moment of my greatness flicker,
And I have seen the eternal Footman hold my coat, and   85
     snicker,
And in short, I was afraid.

And would it have been worth it, after all,
After the cups, the marmalade, the tea,
Among the porcelain, among some talk of you and me,   9(
Would it have been worth while,
To have bitten off the matter with a smile,
To have squeezed the universe into a ball
To roll it toward some overwhelming question,
To say: 'I am Lazarus, come from the dead,   95
Come back to tell you all, I shall tell you all'—
If one, settling a pillow by her head,
     Should say: 'That is not what I meant at all.
     That is not it, at all.'

And would it have been worth it, after all,   10(
Would it have been worth while,
After the sunsets and the dooryards and the sprinkled
     streets,
After the novels, after the teacups, after the skirts that trail
along the floor—   105
And this, and so much more?—
It is impossible to say just what I mean!
But as if a magic lantern threw the nerves in patterns on a
     screen:

Would it have been worth while   110
If one, settling a pillow or throwing off a shawl,
And turning toward the window should say:
       'That is not it at all,
       That is not what I meant, at all.'

          .   .   .   .

No! I am not Prince Hamlet, nor was meant to be;   115
Am an attendant lord, one that will do
To swell a progress, start a scene or two,
Advise the prince; no doubt, an easy tool,
Deferential, glad to be of use,
Politic, cautious, and meticulous;   120
Full of high sentence, but a bit obtuse;
At times, indeed, almost ridiculous—
Almost, at times, the Fool.

I grow old . . . I grow old . . .
I shall wear the bottoms of my trousers rolled.   125

Shall I part my hair behind? Do I dare to eat a peach?
I shall wear white flannel trousers, and walk upon the
       beach.
I have heard the mermaids singing, each to each.

I do not think that they will sing to me.   130

I have seen them riding seaward on the waves
Combing the white hair of the waves blown back
When the wind blows the water white and black.

We have lingered in the chambers of the sea
By sea-girls wreathed with seaweed red and brown   135
Till human voices wake us, and we drown.

ᴄ Considered one of the fathers of modern poetry, T. S. Eliot favoured intellect and wit over the emotional unrestraint of the Romantic poets. He left America in 1914 and settled in London a year later, where he worked as a banker and editor. "The Love Song of J. Alfred Prufrock" appeared in an American magazine in 1915, as well as the *Collected Poems 1909–1962*. Eliot's major work is a long poem entitled *The Wasteland*, published in 1922. This pessimistic poem, innovative in its use of a fragmented narrative, is now accepted as a central work of Modernism. In 1948, Eliot received the Nobel Prize for Literature. (*Born Missouri 1888; died 1965*)

(*Responding Activities pp. 118–119*)

The City of Yes and the City of No

ဒ Y. Yevtushenko

Learning Goals

▸ paraphrase meaning
▸ analyze irony and
foreshadowing
▸ create a tourist
brochure
▸ rewrite the poem in
a different form

I am like a train
                    rushing for many years now
between the city of Yes
                    and the city of No.
My nerves are strained
                    like wires
between the city of No
                    and the city of Yes.
Everything is deadly,
                    everyone frightened,
                              in the city of No.
It's like a study furnished with dejection.
Every morning its parquet floors are polished with bile.
It's sofas are made of falsehood, its walls of misfortune.
Every portrait looks out suspiciously.
Every object is frowning, withholding something.
You'll get lots of good advice in it—like hell you will!—
neither a bunch of flowers nor even a greeting.
Typewriters chatter a carbon-copy answer:
"No-no-no . . .
              No-no-no . . .
                        No-no-no . . ."
And when the lights go out altogether,
the ghosts in it begin their gloomy ballet.
You'll get a ticket to leave—
                        like hell you will!—
to leave
        the black town of No.

But in the town of Yes—life's like the song of a thrush.
This town's without walls—just like a nest.
The sky is asking you to take any star you like in your hand.
Lips ask for yours, without any shame,
softly murmuring: "Ah—all that nonsense..."—
and daisies, teasing, are asking to be picked,
and lowing herds are offering their milk,
and in no one is there even a trace of suspicion,
and wherever you want to be, you are instantly there,
taking any train, or plane, or ship that you like.
And water, faintly murmuring, whispers through the years:
"Yes-yes-yes...
                Yes-yes-yes...
                            Yes-yes-yes..."
Only to tell the truth, it's a bit boring, at times,
to be given so much, almost without any effort,
in that shining multicoloured city of Yes...

                    •   •   •

Better let me be tossed around
                            to the end of my days,
between the city of Yes
                    and the city of No!
Let my nerves be strained
                    like wires
between the city of No
                    and the city of Yes!

Yevgeny Yevtushenko's ancestors were among many Ukrainians exiled to Siberia. Yevtushenko moved to Moscow in 1944, and published his first important narrative poem "Zima Junction" in 1956. He gained international fame in 1961 with the poem "Babii Yar," in which he denounced Nazi and Russian anti-Semitism. Since the 1970s, he has been writing, acting, and directing films. He was appointed an honorary member of the American Academy of Arts and Sciences in 1987. The English translation of "The City of Yes and the City of No" appears in *The Poetry of Yevgeny Yevtushenko: 1953–1965* (1965). (*Born Siberia 1933*)

(*Responding Activities pp. 119–120*)

RESPONDING ACTIVITIES

Narrative and Dramatic Poems (pages 100 – 116)

The River-Merchant's Wife: A Letter – Li Po

Meaning

1. Trace the stages in the speaker's feelings for her husband, from their childhood to the point at which she writes this letter.
2. a) The wife is very conscious of time and change. Compare her thoughts about time in childhood, at fifteen, and at sixteen-and-a-half.
   b) What might her use of "still" in her recollections of herself as a child imply? What might lie behind her use of "already" in describing the paired butterflies, and her despairing statement, "I grow older"?

Form and Style

3. Consider what the phrases "without dislike or suspicion" and "If you are coming" imply about her feelings as she waits for him to return.
4. Explain how the poet creates reticence (not saying all one knows or feels) and dignity in the wife's voice.

Exploring Context

5. Research Ezra Pound and Imagist poetry. Write a short summary of the Imagists' ideas and views. How does "The River-Merchant's Wife: A Letter" exemplify their approaches to writing poetry?

Creative Extension

6. Write, in prose or poetry, a letter from the river-merchant in reply to his wife. Echo the formal dignity and the subtle restraint of the wife's letter. What would be the effect on your interpretation of both letters if you were to resolve the husband's absence in some way?
7. Present a readers' theatre interpretation of this poem. Focus on capturing both the restraint and emotion in the speaker's voice.

The Canterbury Tales – Geoffrey Chaucer

Meaning

1. In a small group, read the text several times. Then answer the 5W+H questions—who, what, when, where, why, and how. Share your responses with other groups.
2. Scan each of the descriptions of the pilgrims. Record their names and list two adjectives and three items of clothing or three possessions that you feel best describe each traveller.

Form and Style

3. a) Chaucer seems to set a *leitmotif* for each pilgrim in the first two lines of description. A *leitmotif* is an image, symbol, phrase, event, or other element of special significance that is repeated throughout a work. Read the first two lines of each pilgrim's description. What word or idea is set as the focus of the character study to follow?

b) Choose one of the pilgrims and review each line of the description. Support your choice of leitmotif with a list of supporting words.

4. Literary scholars suggest that there are actually two narrators of the *Tales*. One is Chaucer the pilgrim and the other is the *ironic* Chaucer, the poet. The first Chaucer sees the pilgrims through the eyes of a "camera." The other Chaucer looks more deeply into the travellers' situations.

Create a two-column organizer like the one below for each of the pilgrims. Choose a line from your pilgrim's description. In the first column state the *literal* or *denotative* meaning of the words. In the second column state the *figurative* or *connotative* meaning of the phrase.

Chaucer/Pilgrim	Chaucer/Poet
Squire: "short was his gown, the sleeves were long and wide"	"the squire is well dressed in the stylish clothing of the time"

Exploring Context

5. The society of Chaucer's day was built on the foundation of two powerful institutions —Feudalism and the Church. The two clashed repeatedly, but were closely intertwined. To acquire a better understanding of the system of Church and State, research the law of inheritance in the noble class. What effect did it have on the second and third son or daughter of a nobleman? How did it affect the Church?

Creative Extension

6. Assume the persona of one of the pilgrims. In the setting of a hostelry at mealtime, tell a story about one of your possessions or journeys, or recount your reason for coming on this pilgrimage. Consider which of the character's traits you will subtly infer, what item best epitomizes the character you will assume, and to whom you relate your story.

7. Surf the Internet for medieval music that would set the mood for the introduction to two or three of the pilgrims. The choice of music should be based on the character's personality as Chaucer reveals it. Record your selection along with a short reading from the introductions you have chosen.

The Love Song of J. Alfred Prufrock – T. S. Eliot

Meaning

1. To whom would you expect a love song to be addressed? To whom is Prufrock speaking? Might there be more than one answer? How do you know?

2. In stanza one, Prufrock says, "Streets that follow like a tedious argument / Of insidious intent / To lead you to an overwhelming question . . ."
    a) List all the questions Prufrock asks in the poem. Who does Prufrock often refer to before he asks his questions?
    b) What is the overwhelming question that Prufrock cannot bring himself to ask?

Form and Style

3. A *mock-heroic poem* is shorter than a *mock-epic*, but like the mock-epic, it is written in an ironically grand style that is in comic contrast with the low or trivial subject matter. These satirical poems may also make fun of the conventions of epic poetry such as battles, supernatural machinery, epic similes, and formulaic descriptions (such as funeral rites or warriors arming for combat).

    a) Reread the translation of the epigraph from Dante's epic, *The Inferno*, at the beginning of the poem. Why do you think Eliot opens his poem with this *allusion* to Dante's epic? Explain the parallels and the contrasts.

    b) Eliot refers to a number of well-known historical figures in the poem. List at least three heroic figures to whom Eliot contrasts Prufrock. What serious tragedies or mental conflicts did these men face? What is Prufrock's mental conflict? Is his tragedy as serious as those faced by heroic figures? Why or why not?

    c) List at least three examples where an elevated or grand style of language is *juxtaposed* with common, ordinary speech. What point is Eliot making about his modern-day hero, Prufrock?

4. Consider each of the following patterns of imagery in the poem:

    i.   fog / smoke
    ii. domestic or daily life
    iii. sleep / somnolence
    iv. women

    a) Choose one and trace each reference to the image in the poem (note the line numbers).

    b) Explain what each group of images could represent.

Exploring Context

5. Many twentieth-century artists have explored humankind's shared feelings of alienation and helplessness. Identify a modern song that you think helps to illuminate Prufrock's character or some of the ideas in "The Love Song of J. Alfred Prufrock." Copy the lyrics of the song and write an explanation of how the song reflects the character of Prufrock or the poem's themes.

Creative Extension

6. Many people have internal dialogues as they strive for reassurance or try to convince themselves to take some action. Write a script between the two sides of Prufrock's character. Add dialogue and create some action or dramatic tension. Build on clues Eliot provides about the setting and costumes.

7. Write an essay on one of the following topics:

    •   What is Prufrock's attitude toward taking risks? What is Eliot's attitude toward risk taking? Provide specific evidence from the poem to support your opinions. (Hint: When examining Prufrock's attitude, consider what he says and what he does; when examining Eliot's attitude toward Prufrock, consider his tone, diction, and imagery).

    •   Modern literature often comments on human alienation. Alienation may be the result of external circumstances, or of personal attitudes and perceptions. What ideas does Eliot develop about the average person's ability to come to terms with personal alienation?

The City of Yes and the City of No – Y. Yevtushenko

Meaning

1. Describe the city of No in your own words. Paraphrase Yevtushenko's description of the city of Yes.

2. What lines in the description of each city do you find to be most effective? Why?

Form and Style

3. What is *ironic* about the ending of the poem? Explain how the title and the names of the cities contribute to the situational irony found in the conclusion.

4. What techniques does Yevtushenko use to foreshadow the turning point of the poem?

Exploring Context

5. Yevtushenko's poems, like T. S. Eliot's, often reflect the inner struggles and conflicts associated with modern life. Research the life and accomplishments of this poet and find at least two other poems he has written. Compare the themes in the poems with those in "The City of Yes and the City of No." How do you think Yevtushenko's life may have influenced the theme he chose for his poems?

Creative Extension

6. Create a tourist brochure for the city of Yes or the city of No. Locate appropriate images or create your own representations. Your brochure may be light or serious.

7. Yevtushenko expresses a desire to "be tossed around / to the end of [his] days / between the city of Yes / and the city of No!" Rewrite the poem by breaking apart the long stanzas that describe the city of No and the city of Yes and juxtaposing lines from each to enhance the contrast and tension that Yevtushenko wants to convey.

Drama

David Mamet on drama:

The theatre is an expression of our dream life—of our unconscious aspirations.
It responds to that which is best, most troubled, most visionary in our society.
As the society changes, the theatre changes.

What we act out, design, write, springs not from meaningless individual
fancy, but from the soul of the times—

A Marriage Proposal

୭ Anton Chekhov
translated from the Russian

Learning Goals

- examine satire
- analyze how struc-
  ture and punctuation
  contribute to tone
- examine use of
  melodramatic
  techniques
- transpose a dramatic
  scene into a
  narrative form
- prepare a readers'
  theatre presentation

CHARACTERS

Stepan Stepanovitch Tschubukov, a country farmer

Natalia Stepanovna, his daughter (aged twenty-five)

Ivan Vassiliyitch Lomov, Tschubukov's neighbour

Time. The present [1890s]

Scene. The reception room in TSCHUBUKOV's country home in Russia. TSCHUBUKOV discovered as the curtain rises. Enter LOMOV, wearing a dress suit.

TSHUBUKOV (*going towards him and greeting him*): Who is this I see? My dear fellow! Ivan Vassiliyitch! I'm so glad to see you! (*shakes hands*) But this is a surprise! How are you?

LOMOV: Thank you! And how are you?

TSCHUBUKOV: Oh, so-so, my friend. Please sit down. It isn't right to forget one's neighbour. But tell me, why all this ceremony? Dress clothes, white gloves, and all? Are you on your way to some engagement, my good fellow?

LOMOV: No, I have no engagement except with you, Stepan Stepanovitch.

TSCHUBUKOV: But why in evening clothes, my friend? This isn't New Years!

LOMOV: You see, it's simply this, that—(*composing himself*) I have come to you, Stepan Stepanovitch, to trouble you with a request. It is not the first time I have had the honour of turning to you for assistance, and you have always, that is—I beg your pardon, I am a bit excited! I'll take a drink of water first, dear Stepanovitch. (*He drinks.*)

TSCHUBUKOV (*aside*): He's come to borrow money! I won't give him any. (*To LOMOV*) What is it, then, dear Lomov?

LOMOV: You see-dear-Stepanovitch, pardon me, Stepan-Stepan-dearvitch-I mean-I am terribly nervous, as you will be so good as to see! What I mean to say—you are the only one who can help me, though I don't deserve it, and—I have no right whatever to make this request of you.

TSCHUBUKOV: Oh, don't beat about the bush, my dear fellow. Tell me!

LOMOV: Immediately—in a moment. Here it is then, I have come to ask for the hand of your daughter, Natalia Stepanovna.

TSCHUBUKOV (*joyfully*): Angel! Ivan Vassiliyitch! Say that once again! I didn't quite hear it!

LOMOV: I have the honour to beg—

TSCHUBUKOV (*interrupting*): My dear, dear man! I am so happy that everything is so—everything! (*embraces and kisses him*) I have wanted this to happen for so long. It has been my dearest wish! (*He represses a tear.*) And I have always loved you, my dear fellow, as my own son! May God give you His blessings and His grace and—I always wanted it to happen. But why am I standing here like a blockhead? I am completely dumbfounded with pleasure, completely dumbfounded. My whole being—! I'll call Natalia—

LOMOV: Dear Stepan Stepanovitch, what do you think? May I hope for Natalia Stepanovna's acceptance?

TSCHUBUKOV: Really! A fine boy like you—and you think she won't accept on the minute? Lovesick as a cat and all that—! (*He goes out, right.*)

LOMOV: I'm cold. My whole body is trembling as though I was going to take my examination! But the chief thing is to settle matters! If a person meditates too much, or hesitates, or talks about it, waits for an ideal or true love, he never gets it. Brrr! It's cold! Natalia is an excellent housekeeper, not at all bad-looking, well educated—what more could I ask? I'm so excited my ears are roaring!

(*He drinks water.*) And not marry, that won't do! In the first place, I'm thirty-five—a critical age, you might say. In the second place, I must live a well-regulated life. I have a weak heart, continual palpitation, and I am very sensitive and always getting excited. My lips begin to tremble and the pulse in my right temple throbs terribly. But the worst of it all is sleep! I hardly lie down and begin to doze before something in my left side begins to pull and tug, and something begins to hammer in my left shoulder—and in my head, too! I jump up like a madman, walk about a little, lie down again, but the moment I fall asleep I have a terrible cramp in the side. And so it is all night long!

(*Enter* NATALIA STEPANOVNA.)

NATALIA: Ah! It's you. Papa said to go in: there was a dealer in there who'd come to buy something. Good afternoon, Ivan Vassiliyitch.

LOMOV: Good day, my dear Natalia Stepanovna.

NATALIA: You must pardon me for wearing my apron and this old dress: we are working today. Why haven't you come to see us oftener? You've not been here for so long! Sit down. (*They sit down.*) Won't you have something to eat?

LOMOV: Thank you, I have just had lunch.

NATALIA: Smoke, do, there are the matches. Today it is beautiful and only yesterday it rained so hard that the workmen couldn't do a stroke of work. How many bricks have you cut? Think of it! I was so anxious that I had the whole field mowed, and now I'm sorry I did it, because I'm afraid the hay will rot. It would have been better if I had waited. But what on earth is this? You are in evening clothes! The latest cut! Are you on your way to a ball? And you seem to be looking better, too—really. Why are you dressed up so gorgeously?

LOMOV (*excited*): You see, my dear Natalia Stepanovna—it's simply this: I have decided to ask you to listen to me—of course it will be a surprise, and indeed you'll be angry, but I—(*aside*) How fearfully cold it is!

NATALIA: What is it? (*A pause.*) Well?

LOMOV: I'll try to be brief. My dear Natalia Stepanovna, as you know, for many years, since my childhood, I have had the honour to know your family. My poor aunt and her husband, from whom, as you know, I inherited the estate, always had the greatest respect for your father and your poor mother. The Lomovs and the Tschubukovs have been for decades on the friendliest, indeed the closest, terms with each other, and furthermore my property, as you know, adjoins your own. If you will be so good as to remember, my meadows touch your birch woods.

NATALIA: Pardon the interruption. You said "my meadows"—but are they yours?

LOMOV: Yes, they belong to me.

NATALIA: What nonsense! The meadows belong to us—not to you!

LOMOV: No, to me! Now, my dear Natalia Stepanovna!

NATALIA: Well, that is certainly news to me. How do they belong to you?

LOMOV: How? I am speaking of the meadows lying between your birch woods and my brick-earth.

NATALIA: Yes, exactly. They belong to us.

LOMOV: No, you are mistaken, my dear Natalia Stepanovna, they belong to me.

NATALIA: Try to remember exactly, Ivan Vasiliyitch. Is it so long ago that you inherited them?

LOMOV: Long ago! As far back as I can remember they have always belonged to us.

NATALIA: But that isn't true! You'll pardon my saying so.

LOMOV: It is all a matter of record, my dear Natalia Stepanovna. It is true that at one time the title to the meadows was disputed, but now everyone knows they belong to me. There is no room for discussion. Be so good as to listen: my aunt's grandmother put these meadows, free from all costs, into the hands of your father's grandfather's peasants for a certain time while they were making bricks for my grandmother.

These people used the meadows free of cost for about forty years, living there as they would on their own property. Later, however, when—

NATALIA: There's not a word of truth in that! My grandfather, and my great-grandfather, too, knew that their estate reached back to the swamp, so that the meadows belong to us. What further discussion can there be? I can't understand it. It is really most annoying.

LOMOV: I'll show you the papers, Natalia Stepanovna.

NATALIA: No, either you are joking, or trying to lead me into a discussion. That's not at all nice! We have owned this property for nearly three hundred years, and now all at once we hear that it doesn't belong to us. Ivan Vassiliyitch, you will pardon me, but I really can't believe my ears. So far as I am concerned, the meadows are worth very little. In all they don't contain more than five acres and they are worth only a few hundred rubles, say three hundred, but the injustice of the thing is what affects me. Say what you will, I can't bear injustice.

LOMOV: Only listen until I have finished, please! The peasants of your respected father's grandfather, as I have already had the honour to tell you, baked bricks for my grandmother. My aunt's grandmother wished to do them a favour—

NATALIA: Grandfather! Grandmother! Aunt! I know nothing about them.

All I know is that the meadows belong to us, and that ends the matter.

LOMOV: Natalia Stepanovna, I don't need the meadows, I am only concerned with the principle. If you are agreeable, I beg of you, accept them as a gift from me!

NATALIA: But I can give them to you, because they belong to me! That is very peculiar, Ivan Vassiliyitch! Until now we have considered you as a good neighbour and a good friend; only last year we lent you our threshing machine so that we couldn't thresh until November, and now you treat us like thieves! You offer to give me my own land. Excuse me, but neighbours don't treat each other that way. In my opinion, it's a very low trick—to speak frankly—

LOMOV: According to you I'm a usurper, then, am I? My dear lady, I have never appropriated other people's property, and I shall permit no one to accuse me of such a thing! (*He goes quickly to the bottle and drinks water.*) The meadows are mine!

NATALIA: That's not the truth! They are mine!

LOMOV: Mine!

NATALIA: Eh? I'll prove it to you! This afternoon I'll send my reapers into the meadows.

LOMOV: W—h—a—t?

NATALIA: My reapers will be there today!

LOMOV: And I'll chase them off!

NATALIA: If you dare!

LOMOV: The meadows are mine, you understand? Mine!

NATALIA: Really, you needn't scream so! If you want to scream and snort and rage you may do it at home, but here please keep yourself within the limits of common decency.

LOMOV: My dear lady, if it weren't that I were suffering from palpitation of the heart and hammering of the arteries in my temples, I would deal with you very differently! (*in a loud voice*) The meadows belong to me!

NATALIA: Us!

LOMOV: Me!

(*Enter* TSCHUBUKOV, *right.*)

TSCHUBUKOV: What's going on here? What is he yelling about?

NATALIA: Papa, please tell this gentle-man to whom the meadows belong, to us or to him?

TSCHUBUKOV (*to* LOMOV): My dear fellow, the meadows are ours.

LOMOV: But, merciful heavens, Stepan Stepanovitch, how do you make that out? You at least might be reasonable. My aunt's grandmother gave the use of the meadows free of cost to your grandfather's peasants; the peasants lived on the land for forty years and used it as their own, but later when—

TSCHUBUKOV: Permit me, my dear friend. You forget that your grand-mother's peasants never paid, because there had been a lawsuit over the meadows, and everyone knows that the meadows belong to us. You haven't looked at the map.

LOMOV: I'll prove to you that they belong to me!

TSCHUBUKOV: Don't try to prove it, my dear fellow.

LOMOV: I will!

TSCHUBUKOV: My good fellow, what are you shrieking about? You can't prove anything by yelling, you know. I don't ask for anything that belongs to you, nor do I intend to give up anything of my own. Why should I? If it has gone so far, my dear man, that you really intend to claim the meadows, I'd rather give them to the peasants than you, and I certainly shall!

LOMOV: I can't believe it! By what right can you give away property that doesn't belong to you?

TSCHUBUKOV: Really, you must allow me to decide what I am to do with my own land! I'm not accus-tomed, young man, to have people address me in that tone of voice. I, young man, am twice your age, and I beg you to address me respectfully.

LOMOV: No! No! You think I'm a fool! You're making fun of me! You call my property yours and then expect me to stand quietly by and talk to you like a human being. That isn't the way a good neighbour behaves, Stepan Stepanovitch! You are no neighbour, you're no better than a land-grabber. That's what you are!

TSCHUBUKOV: Wh—at? What did he say?

NATALIA: Papa, send the reapers into the meadows this minute!

TSCHUBUKOV (to LOMOV): What was that you said, sir?

NATALIA: The meadows belong to us and I won't give them up! I won't give them up! I won't give them up!

LOMOV: We'll see about that! I'll prove in court that they belong to me.

TSCHUBUKOV: In court! You may sue in court, sir, if you like! Oh, I know you, you are only waiting to find an excuse to go to law! You're an intriguer, that's what you are! Your whole family were always looking for quarrels. The whole lot!

LOMOV: Kindly refrain from insulting my family. The entire race of Lomov has always been honourable! And never has one been brought to trial for embezzlement, as your dear uncle was!

TSCHUBUKOV: And the whole Lomov family were insane!

NATALIA: Every one of them!

TSCHUBUKOV: Your grandmother was a dipsomaniac, and the younger aunt, Nastasia Michailovna, ran off with an architect.

LOMOV: And your mother limped. (He puts his hand over his heart.) Oh, my side pains! My temples are bursting! Lord in Heaven! Water!

TSCHUBUKOV: And your dear father was a gambler—and a glutton!

NATALIA: And your aunt was a gossip like few others!

LOMOV: And you are an intriguer. Oh, my heart! And it's an open secret that you cheated at the elections—my eyes are blurred! Where is my hat?

NATALIA: Oh, how low! Liar! Disgusting thing!

LOMOV: Where's the hat? My heart! Where shall I go? Where is the door? Oh—it seems—as though I were dying! I can't—my legs won't hold me—(goes to the door)

TSCHUBUKOV (following him): May you never darken my door again!

NATALIA: Bring your suit to court! We'll see!

(LOMOV staggers out, centre.)

TSCHUBUKOV (angrily): The devil!

NATALIA: Such a good-for-nothing! And then they talk about being good neighbours!

TSCHUBUKOV: Loafer! Scarecrow! Monster!

NATALIA: A swindler like that takes over a piece of property that doesn't belong to him and then dares to argue about it!

TSCHUBUKOV: And to think that this fool dares to make a proposal of marriage!

NATALIA: What? A proposal of marriage?

TSCHUBUKOV: Why, yes! He came here to make you a proposal of marriage.

NATALIA: Why didn't you tell me that before?

TSCHUBUKOV: That's why he had on his evening clothes! The poor fool!

NATALIA: Proposal for me? Oh! (*falls into an armchair and groans*) Bring him back! Bring him back!

TSCHUBUKOV: Bring whom back?

NATALIA: Faster, faster, I'm sinking! Bring him back! (*She becomes hysterical.*)

TSCHUBUKOV: What is it? What's wrong with you? (*his hands to his head*) I'm cursed with bad luck! I'll shoot myself! I'll hang myself!

NATALIA: I'm dying! Bring him back!

TSCHUBUKOV: Bah! In a minute! Don't bawl! (*He rushes out, centre.*)

NATALIA (*groaning*): What have they done to me? Bring him back! Bring him back!

TSCHUBUKOV: (*comes running in*) He's coming at once! The devil take him! Ugh! Talk to him yourself, I can't.

NATALIA (*groaning*): Bring him back!

TSCHUBUKOV: He's coming I tell you! "Oh, Lord! What a task it is to be the father of a grown daughter!" I'll cut my throat! I really will cut my throat! We've argued with the fellow, insulted him, and now we've thrown him out!—and you did it all, you!

NATALIA: No you! You haven't any manners, you are brutal! If it weren't for you, he wouldn't have gone!

TSCHUBUKOV: Oh, yes, I'm to blame! If I shoot or hang myself, remember *you'll* be to blame! You forced me to it! You! (LOMOV appears in the doorway.) There, talk to him yourself! (*He goes out.*)

LOMOV: Terrible palpitation! My leg is lamed! My side hurts me—

NATALIA: Pardon us, we were angry, Ivan Vassiliyitch. I remember now—the meadows really belong to you.

LOMOV: My heart is beating terribly! My meadows—my eyelids tremble —(*They sit down.*) We were wrong. It was only the principle of the thing—the property isn't worth much to me, but the principle is worth a great deal.

NATALIA: Exactly, the principle! Let us talk about something else.

LOMOV: Because I have proofs that my aunt's grandmother had, with the peasants of your good father—

NATALIA: Enough, enough. (*aside*) I don't know how to begin. (*to LOMOV*) Are you going hunting soon?

LOMOV: Yes, heath-cock shooting, respected Natalia Stepanovna. I expect to begin after harvest. Oh, did you hear? My dog, Ugadi, you know him—limps!

NATALIA: What a shame! How did that happen?

LOMOV: I don't know. Perhaps it's a dislocation, or maybe he was bitten by some other dog. (*He sighs.*) The best dog I ever had—to say nothing of his price! I paid Mironov a hundred and twenty-five rubles for him.

NATALIA: That was too much to pay, Ivan Vassiliyitch.

LOMOV: In my opinion it was very cheap. A wonderful dog!

NATALIA: Papa paid eighty-five rubles for his Otkatai, and Otkatai is much better than Ugadi!

LOMOV: Really? Otkatai is better than Ugadi? What an idea! (*He laughs.*) Otkatai better than Ugadi!

NATALIA: Of course he is better. It is true Otkatai is still young; he isn't full-grown yet, but in the pack or on the leash with two or three, there is no better than he, even—

LOMOV: I really beg your pardon, Natalia Stepanovna, but you quite overlooked the fact that he has a short lower jaw, and a dog with a short lower jaw can't snap.

NATALIA: Short lower jaw? That's the first time I ever heard that!

LOMOV: I assure you, his lower jaw is shorter than the upper.

NATALIA: Have you measured it?

LOMOV: I have measured it. He is good at running, though.

NATALIA: In the first place, our Otkatai is purebred, a full-blooded son of Sapragavas and Stameskis, and as for your mongrel, nobody could ever figure out his pedigree; he's old and ugly, and as skinny as an old hag.

LOMOV: Old, certainly! I wouldn't take five of your Otkatais for him! Ugadi is a dog, and Otkatai is—it is laughable to argue about it! Dogs like your Otkatai can be found by the dozens at any dog dealer's, a whole pound full!

NATALIA: Ivan Vassiliyitch, you are very contrary today. First our meadows belong to you, and then Ugadi is better than Otkatai. I don't like it when a person doesn't say what he really thinks. You know perfectly well that Otkatai is a hundred times better than your silly Ugadi. What makes you keep on saying he isn't?

LOMOV: I can see, Natalia Stepanovna, that you consider me either a blind man or a fool. But at least you may as well admit that Otkatai has a short lower jaw!

NATALIA: It isn't so!

LOMOV: Yes, a short lower jaw!

NATALIA (*loudly*): It's not so!

LOMOV: What makes you scream, my dear lady?

NATALIA: What makes you talk such nonsense? It's disgusting! It is high time that Ugadi was shot, and yet you compare him with Otkatai!

LOMOV: Pardon me, but I can't carry on this argument any longer. I have palpitation of the heart!

NATALIA: I have always noticed that the hunters who do the most talking know the least about hunting.

LOMOV: My dear lady, I beg of you to be still. My heart is bursting! (*He shouts.*) Be still!

NATALIA: I won't be still until you admit that Otkatai is better! (*Enter* TSCHUBUKOV)

TSCHUBUKOV: Well, has it begun again?

NATALIA: Papa, say frankly, on your

honour, which dog is better: Otkatai or Ugadi?

LOMOV: Stepan Stepanovitch, I beg of you, just answer this: has your dog a short lower jaw or not? Yes or no?

TSCHUBUKOV: And what if he has? Is it of such importance? There is no better dog in the whole country.

LOMOV: My Ugadi is better. Tell the truth, now!

TSCHUBUKOV: Don't get so excited, my dear fellow! Permit me. Your Ugadi certainly has his good points. He is from a good breed, has a good stride, strong haunches, and so forth. But the dog, if you really want to know it, has two faults: he is old and has a short lower jaw.

LOMOV: Pardon me, I have palpitation of the heart!—Let us keep to facts—just remember in Maruskins's meadows, my Ugadi kept ear to ear with the Count Rasvachai and your dog.

TSCHUBUKOV: He was behind, because the Count struck him with his whip.

LOMOV: Quite right. All the other dogs were on the fox's scent, but Otkatai found it necessary to bite a sheep.

TSCHUBUKOV: That isn't so!—I am sensitive about that and beg you to stop this argument. He struck him because everybody looks on a strange dog of good blood with envy. Even you, sir, aren't free from the sin. No sooner do you find a dog better than Ugadi than you begin to—this, that—his, mine—and so forth! I remember distinctly.

LOMOV: I remember something, too!

TSCHUBUKOV (mimicking him): I remember something, too! What do you remember?

LOMOV: Palpitation! My leg is lame—I can't—

NATALIA: Palpitation! What kind of hunter are you? You ought to stay in the kitchen by the stove and wrestle with the potato peelings, and not go fox-hunting! Palpitation!

TSCHUBUKOV: And what kind of hunter are you? A man with your diseases ought to stay at home and not jolt around in the saddle. If you were a hunter! But you only ride around in order to find out about other people's dogs, and make trouble for everyone. I am sensitive! Let's drop the subject. Besides, you're no hunter.

LOMOV: You only ride around to flatter the Count! My heart! You intriguer! Swindler!

TSCHUBUKOV: And what of it? (shouting) Be still!

LOMOV: Intriguer!

TSCHUBUKOV: Baby! Puppy! Walking drugstore!

LOMOV: Old rat! Jesuit! Oh, I know you!

TSCHUBUKOV: Be still! Or I'll shoot you—with my worst gun, like a partridge! Fool! Loafer!

LOMOV: Everyone knows that—oh, my heart!—that your poor late wife beat you. My leg—my temples—Heavens—I'm dying—I—

TSCHUBUKOV: And your housekeeper wears the trousers in your house!

LOMOV: Here-here-there-there-my heart has burst! My shoulder is torn apart. Where is my shoulder? I'm dying! (*He falls into a chair.*) The doctor! (*faints*)

TSCHUBUKOV: Baby! Half-baked clam! Fool!

NATALIA: Nice sort of hunter you are! You can't even sit on a horse. (*to* TSCHUBUKOV) Papa, what's the matter with him? (*She screams.*) Ivan Vassiliyitch! He is dead!

LOMOV: I'm ill! I can't breathe! Air!

NATALIA: He is dead! (*She shakes* LOMOV *in the chair.*) Ivan Vassiliyitch! What have we done! He is dead! (*She sinks into a chair.*) The doctor—doctor! (*She goes into hysterics.*)

TSCHUBUKOV: Ahh! What is it? What's the matter with you?

NATALIA (*groaning*): He's dead! Dead!

TSCHUBUKOV: Who is dead? Who? (*looking at* LOMOV) Yes, he is dead! Good God! Water! The doctor! (*holding the glass to* LOMOV's *lips*) Drink! No, he won't drink! He's dead! What a terrible situation! Why didn't I shoot myself? Why have I never cut my throat? What am I waiting for now? Only give me a knife! Give me a pistol! (LOMOV *moves.*) He's coming to! Drink some water—there!

LOMOV: Sparks! Mists! Where am I?

TSCHUBUKOV: Get married! Quick, and then go to the devil! She's willing! (*He joins the hands of* LOMOV *and* NATALIA.) She's agreed! Only leave me in peace!

LOMOV: Wh—what? (*getting up*) Whom?

TSCHUBUKOV: She's willing! Well? Kiss each other and—the devil take you both!

NATALIA (*groans*): He lives! Yes, yes, I'm willing!

TSCHUBUKOV: Kiss each other!

LOMOV: Eh? Whom? (NATALIA *and* LOMOV *kiss*). Very nice! Pardon me, but what is this for? Oh, yes, I understand! My heart—sparks—I am happy. Natalia Stepanovna. (*He kisses her hand.*) My leg is lame!

NATALIA: I'm happy, too!

TSCHUBUKOV: Ahh! A load off my shoulders! Ahh!

NATALIA: And now at least you'll admit that Ugadi is worse than Otkatai!

LOMOV: Better!

NATALIA: Worse!

TSCHUBUKOV: Now the domestic joys have begun. Champagne!

LOMOV: Better!

NATALIA: Worse, worse, worse!

TSCHUBUKOV (*trying to drown them out*): Champagne, champagne!

ᔆ Anton Chekhov began writing plays, short stories, and comic sketches as a medical student in Russia. He started writing primarily for personal pleasure, but was encouraged by a friend to pursue his talent. Today he is considered a master of the short story and of modern drama. His major plays include *Uncle Vanya* (1899) and *The Three Sisters* (1901). *(Born Taganrog, Russia 1860; died 1904)*

RESPONDING

Meaning

1. Identify the object of Chekhov's *satire* in this play. Support your interpretation with specific reference to the text.

2. Why do you think Chekhov included the character of Tschubukov in the play? What function does he serve?

Form and Style

3. The play has a strong emotional *tone*. Explain how both the structure of the play and the punctuation of the text contribute to the emotional tone. Cite specific examples to support your answer.

4. *Melodrama* is defined in the *Canadian Oxford Dictionary* as "a sensational dramatic piece with crude appeals to the emotions and usually a happy ending." Comment on how Chekhov uses melodramatic techniques to create humour in this piece.

Exploring Context

5. What information about life in Czarist Russia do we learn from this script? Explain how this information creates the context for the drama in the play.

Creative Extension

6. Choose a segment of the play and rewrite it in a narrative (short story) form. Be prepared to discuss changes you needed to make to transpose one form to another.

7. Prepare a readers' theatre presentation of a portion of the script. Focus on capturing the emotional tension created through the dialogue. If possible, record your presentation on audio or videotape and share it with other groups.

Glory in the Flower

᭧ William Inge

The play is set inside a small roadhouse called the Paradise, close to a Midwestern town. It is a totally unpretentious sort of place, yet there has been a serious attempt, in the decor, to create, successfully or not, an atmosphere of gaiety. A kewpie doll, wearing a Hawaiian grass skirt, stands on the shelf behind the bar, and the walls have been painted with amateur murals depicting some fantasized seashore, edged by swaying palm trees, topped by a crescent moon and a starry sky. The total effect, whether intended or not, is primitive. The bar is extreme R., and the entrance extreme L. One can see the gaudy neon sign outside, PARADISE. At the back are an enormous jukebox and a row of about six booths for customers. A gang of teenagers fills the Paradise now, jiving and jitterbugging, making a background of noisy zestful activity. There is one customer at the bar, a SALESMAN, a stout, weary man in his fifties who already has had a few too many drinks. His conversation to HOWIE, the bartender, is in a melancholy, nostalgic vein.

SALESMAN (*to HOWIE, showing his drinks*): Nothing ever stays the same. Why is that?

HOWIE (*detached but human*): I couldn't say.

SALESMAN: It used t' be, when I came into this town, I'd leave it with . . . sometimes ten thousand dollars' worth of orders. Ten thousand!

HOWIE: I wouldn't doubt it.

SALESMAN: 'Course I did. Know what I do in this town now? I'm doin' good if I make my expenses. That's right. I'm doin' good if I make my expenses.

HOWIE: Is that a fact?

SALESMAN (*conscious of his repetitions*): I'm doin' good if I make my expenses. It don't hardly pay me anymore to make this town. I might as well cut it outa my territory, cause I hardly make enough commission here to keep goin'.

HOWIE: Things is pretty bad all over, ain't they?

SALESMAN: Sure. Things is bad all over. I don't know why I stay on the road, Howie. The road's gone. (*Now JACKIE comes in from the outside. She is a woman nearing forty, but pretty, with a clear, fair skin and a pleasing fullness about the body, and a sweet, girlish smile that makes her attractive. JACKIE has tried to keep her youthful looks and succeeded. At this particular time, perhaps she has tried too hard, for her dress is quite frilly and fussy, there are flowers in her hair, and a little too much makeup. Only her sweetness and her seeming naïveté prevent her from seeming cheap. She hurries to the bar, radiating the excitement she feels, seeking* HOWIE.)

JACKIE: Howie, has Bus Riley been in here?

HOWIE: No, he hasn't, Jackie. You expectin' to meet Bus here?

JACKIE: Yes, I'm so excited. *(One of the teenagers calls to* JACKIE. *He is* JOKER, *a husky, handsome kid of eighteen, a dynamo of youthful energy.)*

JOKER *(calling)*: Hi, Miss Bowen!

JACKIE *(calling back)*: Hi, Joker! *(To the others)*: Hi kids! *(And she sounds like a kid herself.)*

TEENAGERS: Hi! Hi, Miss Bowen!

JACKIE *(back to* HOWIE): I guess I'm a little early. I was so excited when Bus called, and I didn't wanta be late, so I hurried so much gettin' ready that here I am, ahead of time.

A GIRL *(to* JOKER, *teasing)*: Jackie Bowen's in love with Joker. Jackie Bowen's in love with Joker.

JOKER: So what? Maybe I'm in love with her, too. *(The others all laugh.)*

BOY 1: No fool, Joker. I think she's got her eye on you.

JOKER *(embarrassed)*: Cut it out, will you? She's a swell dame. Gives me a can of beer when I deliver the groceries, and we stand and talk sometimes. She always asks me about my schoolwork . . . things like that . . . like she was really interested.

GIRL *(sarcastically)*: I bet!

GIRL 2: My mother says she doesn't have a very good reputation, something that happened a long time ago.

JOKER: I don't care about her reputation. I *like* her.

JACKIE *(who has turned to the bartender —breathlessly)*: Have you seen him, Howie?

HOWIE: Who? Bus?

JACKIE: Bus Riley was a *god.*

HOWIE: He never seemed like no god to me.

JACKIE: You just didn't like him.

HOWIE: No, I just didn't like him, and I know quite a few other people felt the same way I did.

JACKIE: They just didn't *know* Bus.

HOWIE: Anyway, I seen him. He was in here the other night, gettin' a load on.

JACKIE *(taken aback)*: He was in here?

HOWIE: Yep!

JACKIE *(almost to herself)*: Why he told me he hadn't been out of the house since he . . .

HOWIE: He came in here, wearin' a spiffy suit, full of big stories, just as ornery and bad natured as he ever was.

JACKIE: Bus really isn't like that, Howie. Not when you know him. Bus and I went steady, you know, for a long time. Of course, we were only kids then, but I think, lotsa times, a girl sees lots of very fine things about a boy. . . that other people . . . maybe just don't *wanta* see.

HOWIE: I think lotsa times a young girl, smitten by a boy, just sees lotsa "very fine things" in him that aren't there at all.

JACKIE (*giving thought*): Do you, Howie?

HOWIE: Kids! Kids get head-over-heels in love, and maybe even kill themselves for love, without even knowin' what they're in love with.

JACKIE (*trying to laugh it off*): Oh! You just wanta sound cynical Howie. (JOKER *suddenly grabs* JACKIE *by the arm and pulls her out on the dance floor with him.*)

JOKER: C'mon and dance, Miss Bowen.

JACKIE (*while he drags her onto the floor*): Oh, Joker! You don't mean it. You don't wanta dance with *me*.

JOKER: Sure I do. I got an Oedipus complex. C'mon!

JACKIE (*trying to follow his jiving, sounding a little uncertain*): Well . . . I'll try. . .

HOWIE (*to the* SALESMAN): If you ask me, she's still a kid herself.

SALESMAN: Kinda pretty. S'pose she wants a little company?

HOWIE: No. Not Jackie. Not when Bus Riley's in town.

SALESMAN: That her husband?

HOWIE (*evasively*): No . . . Bus wasn't ever her husband. (*Now* JACKIE *comes back to the bar with* JOKER.)

JOKER: Miss Bowen, don't be a square.

JACKIE: Goodness, Joker, I can't do all those wild, crazy steps you kids do.

JOKER: Just get the swing and it's easy.

JACKIE: When I was your age, we used to like to dance . . . *soft* and *romantic* and dreamy.

HOWIE (*to* JOKER): You sure all your gang's eighteen and over?

JOKER (*kidding*): On my Boy Scout oath, Howie. (*Returns to his gang.*)

HOWIE (*eyeing a young couple in one of the back booths, the boy kissing the girl with youthful ardour. Calls to* JOKER): Now watch your behaviour back there. (*A number of the young people are dancing with quick, spontaneous rhythm, very "hep."*)

JACKIE (*to* HOWIE, *a little self-consciously*): I've always been one of the best dancers in town, haven't I, Howie? Remember when I did the tango in the American Legion show?

HOWIE: Sure, Jackie.

JACKIE (*recalling a bit of a tango step, executing it just to make sure she remembers it*): I just loved the tango. Remember that black-haired fellow that did it with me? I heard he got run outta town, for passing bad cheques.

HOWIE: Don't remember. What're you gonna have, Jackie?

JACKIE: I'll have a Tom Collins, Howie. Very sweet. (*Starts off.*) If Bus comes, tell him I'll be out in a minute. (*She disappears behind a door marked* DOLLS, *at the back of the dance floor, opposite a door marked* GUYS.)

HOWIE: When them mines was operatin', this was the wealthiest town in the whole darn Midwest . . . *per capita*. That's what people said.

SALESMAN: Oh, this was a fine town in its day. No doubt about it.

HOWIE: The college professors had come here to look at them mines, and they told us they didn't run very deep. Folks didn't pay any attention.

SALESMAN: Well, who's gonna believe a college professor?

HOWIE: Seems like folks b'lieve pretty much what they *wanta* b'lieve.

SALESMAN: But this was sure a fine town while . . . while it *was* a fine town.

HOWIE: I got no objection to it *now*. It's no *utopia* . . . or anything, but the wife and I got friends here, I like my work. Shoot! You can't expect . . . well you can't expect *paradise* until you *die*.

SALESMAN (*has not been listening*): It used t' be, I'd drive my car into town . . . I had a Buick then . . . and park in front of the hotel and there'd be a porter right there, waiting to take my things inside. And then when I got inside, he'd have a couple bottles waitin' for me . . . they had Prohibition then . . . and I'd have my customers up and offer 'em a few drinks. Then I'd take 'em out to dinner.

HOWIE: Oh, those were the days, all right.

SALESMAN: Now I drive into town, pull up at the hotel and have to wake 'em up so they'll let me register. I carry my bags up to my room, myself, cause there ain't any porter, and I eat my dinner alone. (*Shakes his head sadly.*) You can't even get a good meal in this town any more. (BUS RILEY *enters. He is a handsome man of thirty-nine or forty, but still young-looking, with a boyish face that has become somewhat hard and bitter. His dress is sharp, rather dapper. His physique is powerful and finely proportioned, with broad shoulders and slim waist. His walk and his manner are a little arrogant, a little disdainful. He goes straight to the bar.*)

BUS (*to* HOWIE): Jackie Bowen been here?

HOWIE (*nods at the door marked* DOLLS): Be out in a minute, Bus. Sit down and make yourself at home.

BUS (*sitting*): Draw me a beer. Jigger of whiskey on the side.

HOWIE (*reaching for a glass*): One boiler-maker! This your first trip home in quite a while, ain't it, Bus?

BUS: It's gonna be my last one, too.

HOWIE: Don't the old home town look very good to you?

BUS: This *snob* town? Why should I come back here? I'd like to tell a few jerks in this town . . . I'd like to *show* 'em. People aren't like they are here *everywhere*. Out in Hollywood, I can go to places like *Ciro's*, and the *Mocambo*. . . places the hicks in this town never even heard of, places that've got *class*.

HOWIE (*unimpressed but interested*): That right, Bus? You have yourself a good time out there, do you?

BUS (*taking out his wallet, producing a snapshot*): See her? She's a starlet . . . one of the biggest studios out there. Drives around in a Jaguar. Every night we go off dancin' at *Ciro's* . . . or some place like that. I shouldn't waste my time comin' back to this jerk town!

HOWIE: You still in the ring, Bus?

BUS: Won a fight last November. I had the slob on the mat in three rounds.

HOWIE: You're gettin' a little old to fight, aren't you, Bus? You're gonna have to start lookin' for a new job soon, aren't you?

BUS: What're you talkin' about? (*Doubles a fist to display before* HOWIE.) See that? That's still hard as a rock, and it's gonna stay that way. I can still dish it out, and I'll always be able to. Know why? Cause I got fight in *here*. (*Pounds his fist over his chest.*)

HOWIE: All the same, Bus, when a man gets past thirty-five, he begins to slow up, and . . .

BUS: Not me. I got it in here. I got fight in here. (*He pounds his heart.*) And I'm never givin' up.

SALESMAN (*who has been studying the picture of the starlet*): They tell me these Hollywood girls are . . . pretty hot stuff.

BUS: They're all right. (*It's not in his self-image to show too much enthusiasm.*)

JACKIE (*suddenly appears at BUS's side. Her face is almost beatific with the joy of seeing him*): Bus! Bus Riley!

BUS (*turning quickly. He feels some true joy in seeing her*): Jackie! How ya, Doll? (*He throws his arms around her.*)

JACKIE: Bus Riley! I just can't believe it.

BUS: You're lookin' swell, Jackie. Not a day older.

JACKIE: You're still the best-lookin' guy I ever saw.

BUS (*more cautiously*): You're . . . you're not sore at me?

JACKIE (*thinks a moment*): No. Of course not, Bus.

BUS (*relieved*): Sit down, Doll, and have yourself a drink.

JACKIE (*picking up her Tom Collins*): I got one already. I was so surprised when you called. Someone told me you were in town, but I didn't believe it. I didn't believe Bus Riley would ever come back to town without calling me.

BUS: I wasn't too sure you'd *wanta* see me, Doll.

JACKIE (*still in a personal voice*): Oh, Bus! You *knew* I did. I never blamed you for anything, Bus. Of course I wanted to see you.

BUS: Well . . . the old man, Jackie . . .

JACKIE (*seriously*): I heard about it, Bus. How is he?

BUS: I guess he's all right now. But when they wired me, they thought he was done for. I had to come back and give him some blood. See, I got the same type he has. He's gonna pull through now.

JACKIE: I'm glad, Bus.

BUS: So tomorrow morning, I'm pullin' out.

JACKIE: Tomorrow?

BUS (*trying to relieve tension*): I can't get over how swell you look, Doll. Hey, tell you what, I'll take you back to California with me and put you in movies. How ya like that? (*They laugh together.*) Don't think I couldn't. I gotta lotta pull out there. Yah, I had dinner just the other night at *Ciro's* . . . with some very big people. *Very* big.

JACKIE (*thrilled. This is her dream man*): Oh, Bus! Thanks, just the same.

BUS: How 'bout a little dance, Doll?

JACKIE: That's what I've been waiting for all day. When you called, my heart began to swell out like a balloon and I was afraid I was gonna pop. And I told myself, "Tonight I'll be dancing with Bus again. After all these years."

BUS (*laughs*): You're a silly dame. (*They stand by the bar and talk before dancing.*) Hey, we had some great times together, didn't we?

JACKIE: Yes . . . we did.

BUS: It don't seem so long ago. Remember the Senior Picnic?

JACKIE: Of course I do.

BUS: Remember the Thanksgiving game at Midwest?

JACKIE: You made all the touchdowns, and I was so proud to be your girl. Sure I remember.

BUS: The Commencement dance?

JACKIE: I . . . I remember everything, Bus. Everything.

BUS: And remember the English class we had together!

JACKIE: Yes, Miss Carson was the teacher.

BUS: That her name? Remember when she accused me of cribbin' off your test paper?

JACKIE: I told you she'd suspect something if you quoted the same lines a poetry I did.

BUS: But I had to write *something*.

JACKIE: She asked us to quote some poetry by William Wordsworth, and I wrote . . . I even remember the lines.

BUS: Yah?

JACKIE:
"Though nothing can bring back the hour
Of splendour in the grass, glory in the flower,
We will grieve not, rather find
Strength in what remains behind."

BUS (*impressed*): Well, what'ya know about that?

JACKIE: Sometimes . . . lines a poetry just stay with me. I don't know why.

BUS (*feeling awkward*): I never knew much about poetry . . . stuff like that.

JACKIE: I never did either. . . except for certain lines that I'd remember . . . just like songs I'd hear. . . (*Brightly, snapping back to the present.*) Oh, I'm a longhair now. Honest!

BUS: You used to play the hottest piano in town.

JACKIE: Oh, I still like to play ragtime and popular stuff, but I got out some of my old music a few years ago, the things I studied when I was a kid. (*Laughs.*) Chopin and Schubert and Brahms, they didn't make sense to me then, but I started playing them again, and I couldn't believe it. They seemed. . . so beautiful and. . . and. . . Well, I wondered, where have I been all these years that I thought this stuff was dull.

BUS: Well, you're not too highbrow to dance to the jukebox now, are you?

JACKIE (*laughs*): Don't be silly.

BUS: . . . cause I never dance very well to. . . to Brahms. (*The jukebox has now turned sentimental. A recording of "Stardust" has turned up. It is a straight playing of the piece, simple, sweet, and tender.*)

JACKIE (*clutches BUS's arm*): Listen! It's "Stardust," Bus. You and I remember when that piece first came out, don't we?

BUS: Yah!

JACKIE: Kids have been dancing to that piece ever since, but we danced to it when it was *new*. I was dancing with you the first time I heard it played. Oh, Bus, let's. . . let's dance to this again.

BUS (*stretching out his arms to her*): Here's my arms, Doll. Just crawl into 'em again. (*He folds her into his arms and they dance softly together.*)

SALESMAN (*with the wonder of recall*): It used to be, I'd come into town, come in on the Northeast highway, over the new white bridge, and all the way down Elm Street, there was them fine big houses on both sides of the street. *Mansions!* Them high trees overhead, they was like a big green, leafy canopy, that let the sunlight through. And all the lawns was trimmed and smooth, and there was always a shiny big car sitting in the driveway. . .

HOWIE: Yah. When this town had it, we really *had* it.

SALESMAN: Them's all rooming houses now, ain't they?

HOWIE: The old Forester home's a business college.

SALESMAN: It. . . it just don't seem right. All them houses with the big trees, and the big cars sittin' out in front. . . they was so dern beautiful. Why couldn't they stay that way? Can you tell me that? Why couldn't they have stayed that way?

HOWIE: Don't ask *me*.

SALESMAN: There oughta be a law to keep things the way they are. Goll darn it, there oughta be a law. (*JACKIE and BUS are dancing.*)

JACKIE: Are you still fighting, Bus?

BUS: You said it, Doll. I'm still in there sluggin'. I've still got the hardest punch in . . .

JACKIE (*naïvely*): Maybe you'll be champion someday, huh.

BUS (*a little embarrassed*): Naw. I don't go in for championship bouts. I just fight once in a while now, when I feel like it. And I do a little movie work, too. Sure. When I feel like it. Yah, I been in quite a few pictures. Just small parts, of course. I never take parts where I have to speak lines. You have to study to do that, and I don't wanta be a star or anything. I just like to take a few parts once in a while . . . just for the fun of it. It's kind of a hobby with me, when I'm not fightin'. (*They stop dancing as the music stops. They are L. near the window and front door.*)

JACKIE: I always knew you'd get someplace, Bus.

BUS (*you can fool some of the people and still feel embarrassed about it*): Yah . . . Well . . . (*Hurrying to change the subject.*) Tell me about *you*, Doll. I thought I'd come back and find you an old married woman.

JACKIE (*now it is her turn to feel embarrassed*): No. I never got married, Bus.

BUS (*his face now turns serious. Something has been recalled*): Oh . . .

JACKIE (*quick to reassure him*): Oh, but I *could* have, Bus. Lotsa times. I dated Bunny Byram after you left . . .

BUS: Old Bunny?

JACKIE: He wanted to marry me, but he drank so much.

BUS: Yah. You stayed outa trouble there.

JACKIE: And I went with Dick Parsons a while, but I never really cared for him . . . much. And I got a boyfriend now. Yes. His name is Gerald Baker. He sells dental supplies. I met him once in Dr. Millard's office, and he called me for a date that night. He's an awful nice fellow and a peck of fun. He wants to marry me . . . and I've been thinking it over. He . . . he's . . . well, he's nothing like *you*, Bus. But I seem to like him *more* every time we go out together. He . . . he seems to . . . to really like me. (*She gives a little laugh of embarrassment.*)

BUS (*feeling a little morose*): Well . . . I used to wonder about you at times . . . *you* know.

JACKIE: People really were very nice about it, Bus. After a while. At first they weren't. I mean . . . when I first came back to town, lotsa people wouldn't speak to me, and I didn't go to church or anything because I knew how all the women would look at me, but I got busy right away. I teach piano lessons. That was the only thing I knew how to do very well, was play the piano, and I had to earn a living. I didn't have many pupils at first, but people soon forgot and now I got all the pupils I can take care of,

and no one ever tries to remind
me . . .

BUS (*this is very hard for him to ask*):
What . . . what ever happened to . . .

JACKIE: It was a little girl, Bus. I
never saw her. I figured the best
thing I could do for her was to give
her to that place in Chicago. They
see the babies are adopted by nice
families and . . . Well, they took her
from me the very first thing. The
nurse said it would be easier that
way, if I never saw her. So I never
did.

BUS (*completely inadequate to the situation*): Yah . . . well . . . you did the
right thing. Sure. You did the right
thing. (*Now the music has changed.
The rhythm is high and fast and exciting. Teenagers start dancing, their
young bodies full of quickness and zest,
their faces smiling and full of life.*)

BUS: Let's get back to the bar, Doll.
What d'ya say? (*They go to the bar
and BUS calls out to HOWIE*): Set
'em up for us again, Howie.

HOWIE: OK (*There is a long pause
between JACKIE and BUS. They sit
together at the bar now with their own
private thoughts. Finally JACKIE
speaks, in a very private voice.*)

JACKIE: Bus?

BUS: Yah, Doll?

JACKIE (*gives a little laugh*): I just can't
get used to having you call me
"Doll." I mean . . .

BUS: Out in L.A. that's all you ever
hear. *Doll.*

JACKIE: I know, but . . . Well, when
we were kids, you called me other
things . . . like "honey," or "sweetie-
pie," or "precious."

BUS: Well, what's wrong with *doll?*

JACKIE: Nothing's wrong with it.
I . . . I just can't get used to it,
that's all.

BUS: Every girl I see . . . I call "doll."

JACKIE: Oh.

BUS: . . . but you're a special doll,
Jackie, cause you're the first doll I
was ever really gone on. (*JACKIE
smiles wistfully.*) And how 'bout me,
Doll? You were pretty gone on me,
weren't you?

JACKIE: Yes . . . yes, Bus. I *was.*

BUS: . . . and I'm just sayin' this cause
it's true, Doll, but right now I don't
think you're so bad either.

JACKIE (*of course she is thrilled to hear
him say this*): Oh, Bus! When you
say that, I . . . I feel just as thrilled
and excited as I did . . . when you
said it before, all those times you
said it, you could say it to me a
hundred times a day, and each time,
I'd feel thrilled . . . quiver inside
like a bird.

BUS (*laughs and throws a bearlike arm
around her*): You're OK, Jackie.
You're OK.

JACKIE (*drawing from him for she has
serious things to say*): Bus . . . I was
in love with you.

BUS (*not knowing for sure how to
respond to her seriousness*):
Well . . . after all, Doll . . .

JACKIE: I was in love with you. There. I've said it. And I've wanted to say it all these years.

BUS (*unequal to the situation*): Yah? Well . . .

JACKIE: We were just kids then, and it's hard for kids to say. . . "I love you." So I never said it . . . in so many words, even though you musta known it.

BUS: I guess I did.

JACKIE: Then after you were gone . . .

BUS: Look, Jackie, the only thing for me to do was leave. You know that. This town was flat. I couldn't find a job.

JACKIE: I never blamed you for leaving, Bus.

BUS (*his guilt is within himself*): Well . . . I just wondered . . .

JACKIE: But after you'd gone, and I . . . I had to go away. . . you know. . . I missed you so, Bus, I wanted you so bad, I thought my heart was gonna pound its way out of my bosom . . .

BUS (*embarrassed*): Jackie!

JACKIE: Then after I'd had the baby taken care of and come back home . . . I felt so empty inside, I . . . I wanted to die. I almost . . .

BUS: Jackie! You didn't.

JACKIE: I . . . I did try. Finally Dr. Henry, that's Bernice's father, he knew I didn't have any money so he and Bernice took me up to Kansas City to see a psychiatrist.

BUS: Those guys don't know anything.

JACKIE: Anyway, I talked with him a few times and it helped. I came back home then and got to work.

BUS: Golly, Jackie, I wish you didn't have to bring all this up.

JACKIE: I've *got* to, Bus. You've got to know how I felt. 'Cause I was in love with you, and if you love someone and he's gone, and you can't say you love him, it all begins to hurt inside and it's gotta come out when it *can*.

BUS: OK, Doll. Shoot!

JACKIE: Well . . . I guess I've said it now. Anyway, when I came back, Bernice Henry was the only friend I could count on. She used to take me riding of an evening. She did for more'n a year. Every evening, I'd ask her to drive by your house. She said it was just making things worse, but I couldn't resist. I just wanted to see the places where I knew you'd been. I used to look up in your window and remember all the times I used to see your face in it. And I used to look at the old hot-rod in the backyard, and remember all the joy rides we had . . .

BUS (*here's a chance to lift the pressure*): Hey, it's still there. Was I ever surprised to find the old hot-rod in the backyard?

JACKIE: . . . and I . . . Now don't laugh, Bus . . . I used to pray for you. I did.

BUS: Pray for me?

JACKIE: You always seemed so discontent in lots of ways, and I used to pray that you'd pass American History and graduate, and then get a good job that'd keep you happy and . . .

BUS (*his belligerence returns*): Think anyone in this snob town'd give a job to a miner's son?

JACKIE: Bus, they *would* have. You imagined most of those things.

BUS: Oh yah! Oh sure! I *imagined* there wasn't any decent jobs around. I just imagined I had to dig ditches . . .

JACKIE: You'da got something better, if you'd been patient.

BUS (*going on, paying no attention*): I just *imagined* that the old lady had to take in washings. I just *imagined* that the old man used to come home drunk and beat up all his kids just to get his exercise . . .

JACKIE: I knew what it was like for you. I knew all the time.

BUS: And I suppose I'm to come back home now and *smile* at people and be *nice*.

JACKIE: Bus, there's *no* one can ever arrange things in his own life, when he's a kid anyway, to suit himself. You . . . you gotta make peace sometime with the life you were born with . . .

BUS: Not me, Doll!

JACKIE: But you got to, Bus, if you ever really make your life any better.

BUS: My life's a lot better.

JACKIE: I mean . . . to keep from going on . . . hating people . . . blaming other people . . . for things they couldn't help . . . or didn't mean . . .

BUS (*gritting his teeth*): It makes you feel strong . . . to *hate*.

JACKIE (*pained*): Oh, Bus!

BUS: Yah! It makes you feel strong.

JACKIE: . . . and I did know a time . . . when . . . sometimes . . . you *did* smile at people. I did know times you could be nice. There were even times when . . . Oh, you were sweet, Bus. You were very sweet.

BUS: A guy don't stay smiling . . . and nice . . . and sweet. A guy's gotta *fight*.

JACKIE: It hurts, Bus, to hear you talk like that. I can't tell you how it hurts.

BUS (*now he forces himself back into a party mood*): Hey, Doll! Fer cryin' out loud, let's stop it! Get that lost look off your face. We're out to celebrate tonight. Order another round of drinks. I wanta make a phone call. Be back in two seconds. (*He hurries off to the telephone booth. JACKIE sits at the bar, her face in her hands, a heavy sadness upon her. HOWIE and the SALESMAN resume their conversation, the latter has become a little more plastered than before.*)

SALESMAN: You know, sometimes I think about givin' up the road. The wife wants me to. She wants me to buy a little chicken farm, close to St. Louis. We'll never get rich that way, I tell her. She says we're not gettin' rich *this* way, and she's right. I know we could make a good living on the farm, but . . . but a man . . . always wants . . . somethin' *better*.

HOWIE: Take my brother Elmo. He's makin' big money up in Kansas City now, used-car business. He says to me, "Howie! ya gonna be a bartender all your life? Let me get you started in Kansas City and I'll have you drivin' around in a Cadillac." (*Chuckles.*) Yah! that's my brother Elmo. He's got his fourteenth Cadillac now and his third wife. 'Course . . . I'm not sayin' that tendin' bar is the greatest job in the world . . . but I kinda like it. I take a kind of pride in doin' my work well . . . (*Suddenly sniffs something in the air, then hollers back at the teenagers.*) Hey! Who's smokin that stuff back there? (*He rushes back to the gang.*) I don't allow that in here. You kids know I don't. I'm disgusted with you. Now who's got it? (*The kids are mum.*) I don't wanta have to run you *all* out. (*Finally one boy steps forward. His name is BRONCO.*)

BRONCO: Aw, fer cryin' out loud, Howie. Let a guy have a little fun, will you?

HOWIE (*worked up about it*): Was it you, Bronco? Anyone else?

JOKER: No one else, Howie.

HOWIE: You swear to that, Joker? The rest of you kids swear to it, you weren't smokin' that weed?

THE GANG: Honest, Howie! Give us the benefit of the doubt. Honest. No one else had any.

HOWIE (*taking BRONCO by the collar*): Now look, Bronco! I don't like to spoil anyone's fun, but there's just certain kinds of fun I can't allow you to have here. And if that's the only kinda fun you enjoy, well . . . I personally feel darn sorry for you, kid, but I gotta force you to have your fun someplace else. That's all.

BRONCO (*straightening up*): You can't order me around like that. I'm not gonna take orders from you.

HOWIE: Look, boy, someday you're gonna have to take orders from *someone.*

BRONCO (*belligerent*): No one's gonna tell me what to do.

HOWIE: Yes, they are kid. I can feel it in my bones. Someday you're gonna force 'em to. And if you force a man to tell you what to do, then you got a pretty unholy kinda man that's not gonna let you do *anything.* Now beat it.

BRONCO: I was goin' anyway. I don't enjoy this two-bit dump.

HOWIE: Just beat it, Bronco. Just beat it. (BRONCO *thrusts his hands into his hip-pockets and strides arrogantly out.* HOWIE *returns to behind bar.*)

I don't know what's got into kids today. If I don't watch 'em, they'd turn this place into an opium den.

SALESMAN: But I'll never give up the road. I know I'll never give it up, even if I don't make a dime.

HOWIE: Kids today *beat* me. Every one of them kids in there knows more'n I knew when I was thirty. They throw orgies that'd surprise a Roman emperor, but they go home to their folks and their folks still wanta read 'em bedtime stories. I don't know what's gonna happen to 'em. They're all ambitious but they all wanta be movie stars or band-leaders or disc-jockeys. They're too *good* for plain, ordinary, everyday work. And what's gonna happen to us if everyone becomes a bandleader, I'd like to know.

SALESMAN (*who has been immersed in his own liquid thoughts*): What's that, Howie?

HOWIE: Oh . . . nothin', I guess. Nothin'.

SALESMAN: You know, Howie, I'll never give up the road 'cause I keep tellin' myself *some*day it's gonna come back.

HOWIE: Maybe it will, for all *I* know.

SALESMAN: I don't think so. (*Now* BUS *comes hurrying back to* JACKIE's *side. He is worked up about something. He whispers to her privately.*)

BUS: Hey, Jackie! What ya say, Doll? I just called Fred Beamis. Remember old Fred? His wife's gone. Yah. He's got the whole house there to him-self. He says you and me can take it over and . . . Well, how 'bout it, Jackie?

JACKIE (*as though coming out of a dream*): Fred Beamis?

BUS: Yah! His wife's gone, Doll. Look, Doll, I'm lonesome. What ya say? It's your old boyfriend Bus talkin' to you, Doll. Yah!

JACKIE: Bus . . . you been in town a whole week now and you . . . you never even called me till today.

BUS (*squirming a little*): Yah. Well, I told you how it was at home, Doll, there with the family, first time I've seen 'em in all these years, and the old man sick and the old lady about to blow a gasket . . .

JACKIE: You . . . you coulda *called*, Bus. You coulda called up and said, "Hi, Jackie! How are you?"

BUS: OK, I didn't call. I tell you, I had a lotta things on my mind.

JACKIE (*without rancour*): It just didn't occur to you to call . . . until tonight . . . when you began to feel "lonesome" . . . and you knew Fred Beamis's wife was gone . . .

BUS: Aw, come off it, Jackie. Fer cryin' out loud!

JACKIE: No, Bus. I'm not goin' with you.

BUS (*all his plans wrecked*): Jackie!

JACKIE (*quietly but firmly*): No, Bus, I'm not goin' with you.

BUS (*this is a blow to his ego he can hardly counter*): Well, I'll be a . . .

JACKIE (*standing*): I guess I may as well go home now.

BUS (*bitterly mocking her previous claims of affection*): I was in *love* with you, Bus. I never loved anyone else, in quite the same way. Oh, you were the only one, Bus. I used to pray for you, Bus.

JACKIE (*this is too much for her. She covers her face with her hands*): Don't! Don't!

BUS: All I gotta say is, if you're so nuts about me, you gotta darn funny way of showin' it.

JACKIE: (*she sounds strong but not vengeful*): I'm not *nuts* about you, Bus. Not anymore. And I can say it now and feel like I'd just shed a heavy mantle that'd been weighing me down for years. (*Now BUS jumps off his stool and grabs JACKIE in his arms and kisses her fiercely, with a kiss he always had complete confidence in to get him what he wanted.*)

BUS: You can't go off and leave Bus. You *know* you can't. You know you're *nuts* about me. You still are. Yah. I seen it in your eyes when I first come into this joint. You're *nuts* about me.

JACKIE: No, Bus. I'm really not. You gotta believe me. I'm not nuts about you. I'm not anymore. I got no hard feelings... I'm just not nuts about you.

BUS (*now he has to get mad*): Who do you think you are to turn me down? You're a small town pick-up, that's

what, and you earn fifty dollars a week, maybe, givin' piano lessons. Out in Hollywood, I got girls that have got class. Yah! If I wanta doll, all I have to do is drop a dime in the telephone. Yah! I can have myself a different doll every night.

JACKIE: So long, Bus. (*She starts slowly out.*)

HOWIE (*from behind her, to BUS*): Now look here, Bus Riley, I ain't gonna let no one talk to Jackie Bowen that way in my bar.

BUS: And *who's* gonna stop me?

JACKIE (*turning back*): It's all right, Howie. It didn't mean anything at all. (*Out.*)

BUS (*over the bar*): Gimme another boiler-maker.

SALESMAN (*to himself*): Man, this was a pretty town in its day. That long street with all them high elm trees, the Country Club... that nice, big colonial house with the big columns... all the big, high-powered automobiles ridin' around in the street...

BUS: Hey, Howie! whatever happened to Zelma Buckley? Remember her?

HOWIE: Zelma, she got married a while back and moved to Oklahoma.

BUS: That right? (*Thinks again.*) How about Dorothy Pierson? She around?

HOWIE: No, Bus. Dorothy got herself a big radio job up in Kansas City. Makin' good money. Just comes home once in a while to show off her mink coats.

BUS: Oh, a big-time girl, huh?

SALESMAN (*reduced to childish murmuring*): No. I'll never give up the road. I don't wanta start life on any chicken farm. You can't ever tell. The road might come back someday. (JACKIE *reappears, coming slowly back to the bar. HOWIE is the first to see her.*)

HOWIE: Leave something behind, Jackie?

JACKIE (*going to BUS*): No, Howie, I . . . I . . . (BUS *lifts his head and looks at her.*) Bus, I . . .

BUS: I s'pose you had to come back to gimme hell.

JACKIE: No, Bus, I can't leave you feeling that way. You've *got* to understand, I . . . I want to remember you with no hard feelings. Please, Bus.

BUS (*finally*): OK, Jackie.

JACKIE: . . . and I hope we can always be friends.

BUS: Sure, Jackie. Shake. (*They shake hands on it. Then JACKIE hurries off. She gets to the door when JOKER catches up with her, his feet jiggling with rhythm, his arms extended to her.*)

JOKER: Hey, Miss Bowen, wanta try again?

JACKIE: No, Joker. You young people have your own dances. I'm not gonna try again. (*She takes the roses out of her hair as if suddenly she felt they didn't belong.*)

JOKER: Aw, come on. You're only as old as you feel.

JACKIE: Right now, I feel very old, and I'm kinda proud.

JOKER: Don't you like me? (*He winks at her, a little devilishly.*)

JACKIE (*maybe placing a fond hand on his cheek while she speaks*): Yes, Joker, I *do* like you. You're a vision of life itself, boy, with a face like a lamp and a lively spring in your step like you was attached to a current. How could I help but like you, Joker-boy?

JOKER (*putting an arm around her, trying to coax her to dance*): C'mon. Let's dance.

JACKIE (*holding him off*): But all that life you got, all that energy and pep, they're no good just in themselves . . . you gotta grow up, Joker-boy.

JOKER: Hey, I'm nineteen next month. I can lift a hundred pounds over my head.

JACKIE: I mean *really* grow up, not just in your body, but in the way you think and feel. Really grow up, Joker.

JOKER (*sober*): I know what you mean. It's hard.

JACKIE: Yes, boy. It's awful hard. It takes some people half their lives . . . (*She throws her roses on the floor, disgustedly*) and some people never do. Goodbye, boy. (*She hurries out. JOKER, rather mystified, returns to his gang and sits thoughtfully in the midst of their dancing.*)

BUS: Gimme another, Howie.

HOWIE: Look, Bus. I've served you four of those boiler-makers already, and I don't like to serve you another.

BUS (*in the most belligerent voice*): Who's askin' you what you like? (*The SALESMAN is asleep now. His head lies on his arm, curved on the bar. He snores loudly.*)

HOWIE: OK. If you wanta knock yourself out, I'm not stoppin' you. (*Sets the jigger of whiskey and the glass of beer before* BUS.) One boiler-maker!

CURTAIN

   William Inge started his career as a high-school teacher. He then moved to St. Louis, where he was the drama critic for the *St. Louis Star-Times* and his interest in playwriting was sparked. His first major success was *Come Back, Little Sheba*. In 1953, he won the Pulitzer Prize and the New York Drama Critics' Circle award for *Picnic*. *Glory in the Flower* was written in 1958 and was broadcast as a teleplay starring Hume Cronyn and Jessica Tandy. Inge's other plays include *Bus Stop* and *The Dark at the Top of the Stairs*. (*Born Independence, Kansas 1913*)

RESPONDING

Meaning

1. Jackie quotes the following lines from a Wordsworth poem. She tells Bud that some lines of poetry "just stay with me."
   Though nothing can bring back the hour
   Of splendour in the grass, glory in the flower,
   We will grieve not, rather find
   Strength in what remains behind.
   a) Explain why these lines are significant to Jackie.
   b) Why are the lines significant to the audience?
2. To play a role effectively, an actor must understand the relationship between characters. Imagine you are the director of a production of this play. What would you want your actors to communicate through their performances about the connection between Bus and Jackie? How would you suggest they communicate this connection in their performance?

Form and Style

3. a) Explain how the language of the play creates a feeling for the time period being portrayed.
   b) What other features of the play communicate the atmosphere of the time period?
4. Most of Inge's plays and screenplays are set in small-town America. Why do you think he chose a small-town setting for *Glory in the Flower*? Support your answer with reference to the play.

Exploring Context

5. Two years after writing this play, Inge wrote one of his most famous screenplays, *Splen-dour in the Grass,* for which he won an Academy Award in 1961. The script tells the story of the relationship between Bus and Jackie in high school. Using information gleaned from *Glory in the Flower,* write a plot outline presenting your ideas on what you think the script would be about.

Creative Extension

6. *We will grieve not, rather find*
    Strength in what remains behind.
    Write an essay in which you discuss the quality of "strength" as it relates to this play.

7. *Glory in the Flower* was written as a teleplay. Select a scene from the play and prepare a video shooting script for the scene.

The Black and White

୬ Harold Pinter

The FIRST OLD WOMAN is sitting at a milk bar table. Small. A SECOND OLD WOMAN approaches. Tall. She is carrying two bowls of soup, which are covered by two plates, on each of which is a slice of bread. She puts the bowls down on the table carefully.

SECOND: You see that one come up and speak to me at the counter? *[She takes the bread plates off the bowls, takes two spoons from her pocket, and places the bowls, plates, and spoons.]*

FIRST: You got the bread, then?

SECOND: I didn't know how I was going to carry it. In the end I put the plates on top of the soup.

FIRST: I like a bit of bread with my soup. *[They begin the soup. Pause.]*

SECOND: Did you see that one come up and speak to me at the counter?

FIRST: Who?

SECOND: Comes up to me, he says, hullo, he says, what's the time by your clock? Bloody liberty. I was just standing there getting your soup.

FIRST: It's tomato soup.

SECOND: What's the time by your clock? he says.

FIRST: I bet you answered him back.

SECOND: I told him all right. Go on, I said, why don't you get back into your scraghole, I said, clear off out of it before I call a copper. *[Pause.]*

FIRST: I not long got here.

SECOND: Did you get the all-night bus?

FIRST: I got the all-night bus straight here.

SECOND: Where from?

FIRST: Marble Arch.

SECOND: Which one?

FIRST: The two-nine-four, that takes me all the way to Fleet Street.

SECOND: So does the two-nine-one. *[Pause.]* I see you talking to two strangers as I come in. You want to stop talking to strangers, old piece of boot like you, you mind who you talk to.

FIRST: I wasn't talking to any strangers. *[Pause. The FIRST OLD WOMAN follows the progress of a bus through the window.]* That's another all-night bus gone down. *[Pause.]* Going up the other way. Fulham way. *[Pause.]* That was a two-nine-seven. *[Pause.]* I've never been up that way. *[Pause.]* I've been down to Liverpool Street.

SECOND: That's up the other way.

FIRST: I don't fancy going down there, down Fulham way, and all up there.

SECOND: Uh-uh.

FIRST: I've never fancied that direction much. *[Pause.]*

SECOND: How's your bread? *[Pause.]*

FIRST: Eh?

SECOND: Your bread.

FIRST: All right. How's yours? *[Pause.]*

SECOND: They don't charge for the bread if you have soup.

FIRST: They do if you have tea.

SECOND: If you have tea they do. *[Pause.]* You talk to strangers they'll take you in. Mind my word. Coppers'll take you in.

FIRST: I don't talk to strangers.

SECOND: They took me away in the wagon once.

FIRST: They didn't keep you though.

SECOND: They didn't keep me, but that was only because they took a fancy to me. They took a fancy to me when they got me in the wagon.

FIRST: Do you think they'd take a fancy to me?

SECOND: I wouldn't back on it.
    [The FIRST OLD WOMAN gazes out of the window.]

FIRST: You can see what goes on from this top table. *[Pause.]* It's better than going down to that place on the embankment, anyway.

SECOND: Yes, there's not too much noise.

FIRST: There's always a bit of noise.

SECOND: Yes, there's always a bit of life. *[Pause.]*

FIRST: They'll be closing down soon to give it a scrub-round.

SECOND: There's a wind out. *[Pause.]*

FIRST: I wouldn't mind staying.

SECOND: They won't let you.

FIRST: I know. *[Pause.]* Still, they only close hour and half, don't they? *[Pause.]* It's not long. *[Pause.]* You can go along, then come back.

SECOND: I'm going. I'm not coming back.

FIRST: When it's light I come back. Have my tea.

SECOND: I'm going. I'm going up to the Garden.

FIRST: I'm not going down there. *[Pause.]* I'm going up to Waterloo Bridge.

SECOND: You'll just about see the last two-nine-six come up over the river.

FIRST: I'll just catch a look of it. Time I get up there. *[Pause.]* It don't look like an all-night bus in daylight, do it?

❧ Harold Pinter is known for inventing a new kind of comedy, sometimes called the "comedy of menace." The majority of Pinter's plays are set in a single room, where characters are threatened by forces or people whose intentions are unclear to the characters and the audience. *The Dumb Waiter* (1960) and *The Caretaker* (1960) established Pinter as a major playwright. *(Born London, England 1930)*

RESPONDING

Meaning

1. Describe the life of the two characters presented in this sketch. Refer to specific elements of the text in your answer.

2. Why do you think Pinter entitled this sketch "The Black and White"? Support your interpretation.

Form and Style

3. Pinter once said, "There are two silences—one when no word is spoken; the other when perhaps a torrent of language is employed. This speech is speaking a language locked beneath it.... The speech we hear is an indication of the speech we don't hear. It is a necessary avoidance, a violent, sly, anguished or mocking smokescreen which keeps the other in its place. When true silence falls, we are still left with an echo but are nearer nakedness. One way of looking at speech is to say it is a contrast stratagem to cover nakedness."

   Look carefully at the frequent moments of silence in this sketch, indicated by the word *Pause*. Discuss whether the moments of silence and the nature of the dialogue between the two characters support Pinter's ideas in the above quote.

4. This short play is referred to as a *sketch*, which is defined as a brief, self-contained dramatic scene. Comment on how the scene is "self-contained."

Exploring Context

5. The term "Theatre of the Absurd" is used to describe many plays written in the twentieth century that have stressed the absurd nature of human existence by focusing on the drama found in everyday interaction. Why do you think Pinter is often included in a list of absurdist writers?

Creative Extension

6. Write a monologue delivered by one of the two characters when the other leaves the café. Consider what she might reveal about her life.

7. With a partner, practise a section of the dialogue of the play. In addition to the dialogue that is written, include in your interaction the dialogue that is unsaid.

The Transformative Power of Art

Is art, as Picasso claimed, a lie that makes us realize the truth?

Picasso also said, "Art washes away from the soul the dust of everyday life." By "cleaning the dust from our souls," art in its various forms may be a medium through which we can find our true selves, and potentially transform our lives for the better. In this Echo, a stage play, dramatic sketch, mural art, and two poems allow you to explore various perspectives on the transformative power of art.

Learning Goals
- examine a key theme from a variety of perspectives and in a variety of genres
- analyze how various aspects of form, style, and medium convey theme
- create original works based on a key theme

The Drawer Boy
ᔥ *Michael Healey*

In this contemporary stage play, Canadian playwright Michael Healey challenges us to consider the role of theatre in forcing us to face our hidden truths.

CHARACTERS
MORGAN, in his fifties
ANGUS, also in his fifties
MILES, in his twenties

The stage set from a Theatre New Brunswick production of *The Drawer Boy*. Visualize the action as you read the play.

ACT ONE

Act 1, Scene 1

The kitchen of a central Ontario farmhouse, in the summer of 1972. It is dominated by a large, old oak table; there is a wood stove for heat and a rather modern oven in some ghastly colour. The decorating touches are either from the forties, or are non-existent. There is a back door stage-left, with a small, unheated mud room. Downstage is a yard (with chickens? small vegetable garden?), and off stage-right is the barn.

Lights up. ANGUS is alone in the kitchen. There is a long moment where he sits, then eventually gets up and starts making sandwiches. Just as he finishes one, MORGAN comes into the kitchen.

ANGUS: Morgan! Hello!

MORGAN takes the sandwich, eats a couple of bites, and then leaves, taking the sandwich. ANGUS starts to make another sandwich. Meanwhile, MILES wanders into the yard. He looks at the farmhouse, leaves, then comes back and knocks on the door. ANGUS opens the door.

ANGUS: Hello!

MILES: Good morning, sir. My name's—

ANGUS: Hey! Who're you?

MILES: I'm . . . My name's Miles.

ANGUS: Miles! Hello!

MILES: Hi. I'm from Toronto.

ANGUS: Oh. That's too bad.

MILES: Yes. Uh, I'm here with a group of actors. We're making up a play about farmers.

ANGUS: Oh.

MILES: Yes. I was wondering—could I help out here in any way? We want to spend time with—

ANGUS: We're farmers.

MILES: I . . . Yes. Could you use some help around the farm for the next couple of weeks? Free of charge. I just need a place to stay and the chance to watch you.

ANGUS: Watch me.

MILES: Uh, yes.

ANGUS: Watch me what?

MILES: Well, whatever you do all day. As a farmer.

ANGUS: As a farmer.

MILES: Yes.

ANGUS: I better ask Morgan.

MILES: Okay.

ANGUS: Okay.

ANGUS goes inside. MILES waits. ANGUS heads across the room. He

notices the sandwiches and this stops him. He returns to the counter and continues making sandwiches. As he finishes one, MORGAN comes in and takes it.

ANGUS: Morgan! Hello!

MORGAN: Angus. Did I hear you talking?

ANGUS: Talking?

MORGAN: Forget it. Thanks.

MORGAN goes. ANGUS makes a sandwich and starts to eat. MILES waits patiently outside. Slow fade out of lights, as ANGUS eats and MILES waits.

Act 1, Scene 2

In the blackout, there is noise off right: a tractor engine being gunned. The following dialogue should be only partially audible over the tractor.

MORGAN: Alright, now. Alright. Give 'er. Little more . . . little more.

ANGUS: Give 'er. Give 'er. Give 'er.

MILES: Okay . . .

MORGAN: You got to line up those parts—

MILES: Right.

MORGAN: —so I can connect them.

ANGUS: Give 'er. Give 'er. Give 'er.

MORGAN: That's it, son. That's it. Now back it up into place. You want it to go left, so turn the wheel right, yeah? Back it up. Reverse! REVERSE!

MILES: Right on, okay. How do I— where's the—*(the gears grind terribly)* Oh, sh—.

ANGUS: Give 'er. GIVE 'ER! GIVE 'ER!

MILES: Alright. I got it. I got it. Okay! *(The motor dies; there's a pause.)* Wow. Sorry.

ANGUS: Uh oh.

MORGAN: Alright, son. Just—start 'er up again.

He starts the engine up again.

MORGAN: Now. Just back it up slow. Just a few feet's all. Just a few more . . .

ANGUS: Give 'er!

MILES: Oooookay. Oooooooookaaaaaay . . .

Suddenly the engine roars, then dies. After the briefest of pauses, the following occurs all at once.

MORGAN: Eeeezuz Rice! Sonnova . . . ! Arrrgh!

MILES: Oh, no. Oh, Jesus.

ANGUS: Oh boy. Oh boy, Morgan. OH BOY. Morgan?

MILES: Are you okay? Sir? Are you—?

MORGAN: Goddamn it.

ANGUS: Oh boy, oh boy, oh boy. Oh my.

Lights have come up by now. ANGUS runs on and into the kitchen; as soon as he gets there, he forgets why. MORGAN enters, sits on the stoop, examining his wounded arm. MILES comes in, writing in a small notebook.

MORGAN: Farm's a dangerous place. Put that in yer . . . play.

MILES: You okay?

MORGAN: Eyuh.

MILES *(writing)*: I'm really, really sorry.

MORGAN: Thought you said you knew how to drive a tractor.

MILES: Just a sec *(finishes writing)*. I really, really thought I did.

ANGUS wanders out to the stoop and sees MORGAN.

ANGUS: Christ! Morgan! What happened to you?

MORGAN: Angus. You were there! He backed the tractor over me.

ANGUS: Who did?

MORGAN: He did.

ANGUS *(noticing MILES)*: Hello!

MILES: Hi.

ANGUS: Morgan. Who's that?

MORGAN: Angus. Get me a wet towel, will yeh?

ANGUS: Sure.

ANGUS goes inside, to the sink. He pauses, and during the following gets a tablespoon out of a drawer, puts water in it from the tap, and carefully walks it out to the stoop.

MILES: There's no little "R" on your knob.

MORGAN: 'Scuse me?

MILES: And your clutch goes, I think, abnormally far in. I think I should probably not do anything but watch you guys from now on, and take notes. If I just do that, rather than actually help you guys around the farm, I think it'd be better for everyone.

MORGAN: If you want to stay here, you'll help out. Don't mind you being here and doing your playwriting, but I can't see having a pair of hands around here that don't do nothing.

MILES: Alright, I guess I could...
ANGUS comes out with the spoonful of water.

ANGUS: Morgan. Here.
ANGUS shoves the spoon in MORGAN's mouth.

MORGAN: Thanks. A towel?

ANGUS: You bet.
ANGUS goes back indoors.

MILES: I think I might be better off if I stick to the animals. Animals like me.

MORGAN: Uh huh.

MILES: Could you tell me about the milking operation?

MORGAN: Cows are milked twice a day, milk goes to the dairy, dairy gives us money.

MILES: Okay, but what's it like? Do the cows mind being milked continually?

MORGAN: Do they mind?

MILES: Yeah, well, you know—how does a cow feel about getting interfered with twice a day?
ANGUS returns with another spoonful of water.

MORGAN (*to* ANGUS): Thanks. A towel?

ANGUS: You bet.
ANGUS goes back inside, and gets another spoonful of water.

MORGAN: How does the cow feel. About getting milked.

MILES: Yeah. Do they find it traumatic at all?

MORGAN: Well, even though you're from the city, you must know that your cow is the laziest of God's creatures.

MILES: Right.

MORGAN: And I'm sure you realize that we slaughter some of the cows we got. For eatin'.

MILES: Right.

MORGAN: 'Bout one a week we slaughter. Keeps the deep freeze full. Maybe you can help us with the next one. Well, the way we choose which cow to kill for meat is related to their milk output. Lowest producer gets the axe. The cows know this, and they produce as much milk as they can, to keep from—you know—being chosen.

MILES: I see.

MORGAN: Otherwise, the dang things would stand around all day.

MILES: Really.

MORGAN: Here's what I suggest you do. Go into the barn, sit down with the cows. At first, they'll seem real casual. But just watch them for a while, and before long you'll see just how much pressure they're labouring under. They're all as tense as cats.

MILES: Right. Okay! Thanks. (*He starts to leave, then comes back.*) Morgan? I'm sorry I hit you with the tractor.

MORGAN: Think nothing of it. Hardly a day goes by on most farms when something or somebody doesn't get run over. I expect you'll find that out firsthand.

ECHO

MILES: Thanks.

MILES *exits.* ANGUS *returns with the water, and shoves the spoon in* MORGAN's *mouth.*

MORGAN: Thanks. A towel?

ANGUS: Morgan, I'm tired.

MORGAN: Okay.

ANGUS: Morgan? What happened. I smell bread. Oh boy.

MORGAN *goes to* ANGUS *and feels his head.*

MORGAN: Okay, Angus. Get upstairs and get to bed. I'll come up and close the curtains. Go now.

ANGUS: Okay. Oh my. The smell . . . I wonder, I wish . . . I . . .

MORGAN: Angus? Upstairs now.

Act 1, Scene 3

Later. MORGAN *is in the kitchen, making a sandwich.* MILES *wanders into the yard. He is staring at his notebook, talking softly.*

MILES: Mooo. Mooo—low. Loooow. Lowing. Loooow. Soooooo. Sooooo scared. Don't want to get eaaten. Muuuust maaaake miiiilk.

MILES *practises bovine look and movements. Satisfied, he makes a final notation and goes into the house.*

MORGAN: You were right. All those cows are absolutely terrified.

MORGAN: Sandwich?

MILES: Sure. What kind?

MORGAN: Spleen. Beef Spleen.

MILES: Sure. Great. A small one. How's your hand?

MORGAN: Numb. Some of the nerves are crushed, I expect.

MILES: Oh, my God. . . .

MORGAN: Well, at least the throbbing's stopped. If it's not right in a week or so, I'll get it removed.

MILES: You'll . . . ?

MORGAN: Government'll pay for a hook or something. How'er things in the barn?

MILES: Uhh, well, I sat there for a long time, watching your cows. One of them, a brown one—

MORGAN: Which brown one?

MILES: Uh . . .

MORGAN: Bow-legged brown one, or the brown one that smells like vanilla beans?

MILES: The bow-legged one. I guess.

MORGAN: Daisy.

MILES: She kept trying to turn around to look at me. I think she thought I was coming to choose the next one to get—you know. She looked me in the eye, she—Daisy has these eyes that are like brown tennis balls. She stared and stared right at me. For a long time. It felt like we . . . exchanged something. Daisy's not . . . next, is she?

MORGAN: 'Fraid so.

MILES: Jeez *(eating).* You said this was beef? Tastes like ham.

MORGAN: That's because we feed the pigs to the cows.

MILES: Really?

MORGAN: Well, not the whole pig.

MILES *(takes notebook out):* What's

it like, being around death and rebirth all the time? To grow things and kill things for a living, year in and year out? You've been here how long?

MORGAN: We bought the place in '42.

MILES: So, for thirty years you've been doing this. Planting, nurturing, building up; then harvesting, reaping, destroying, eviscerating.

MORGAN: Uh huh.

MILES: Must be . . . difficult. I mean, you grow wheat and corn out of the dirt, out of literally nothing, then you cut it down and sell it. You raise animals, feed them and house them for years, name them; and then you kill them and eat them.

MORGAN: Uh huh.

MILES: What is that like? How does that make you feel?

MORGAN: Miles, it's an emotional rollercoaster.

MILES: I bet. Is Angus going to have lunch?

MORGAN: Angus is upstairs asleep. He's got one of his headaches.

MILES: Is there something wrong with him? I mean, apart from his being . . .

MORGAN: Being what?

MILES: Well, uh, you know. . .

MORGAN: Simple?

MILES: Yeah, I guess.

MORGAN: 'The hell do you mean by that?

MILES: Uuuuhh . . .

MORGAN: He gets headaches. Says he sees lights flashing, sometimes he smells bread baking. Lasts for a day, then he's fine. Sometimes, just before a headache comes on, he'll get giddy. Excited. Then I know to put him to bed.

MILES: Was he always like this?

MORGAN: Angus got knocked down by the front door of a house, in London in '41, during the bombing. He's got a plate in his skull that keeps the two broken parts of it from rubbing together. Before that, he was just like you or me. We went over together, and came back together. We grew up.

MILES: And you've taken care of him since the war?

MORGAN: He doesn't need much taking care of. Angus's no invalid. I show him how to do things, remind him. He can run the tractor, he can use the stove. Knits. Does the accounts. You should see him with a bunch of figures. Only thing that makes Angus different is he can't remember from one minute to the next. He only knows right now. He won't remember you.

MILES: Ever?

MORGAN: Nope. You'll have to tell him who you are, what you're doing here, probably every morning.

MILES: What do the doctors say?

MORGAN: They say he's normal, for someone who's had done to him what he's had.

MILES: Will he ever—I mean, is he . . .

ECHO

MORGAN: Angus's fine. He stays here, does what I've taught him—we're just fine.

MILES: You've lived here alone since the war?

MORGAN: Yup. We bought this land right after. Finish up. Plenty to do this afternoon.

MILES (*wolfing sandwich and rising*): Right. Nothing dangerous, I hope.

MORGAN: Nah. Ever gutted anything?

MILES: You mean—what—like, cut the guts out of something?

MORGAN: Uh huh. Do you know how to use a chainsaw?

MILES: I, uhh (*remembers the tractor*). No. No sir, I don't.

MORGAN: Nothing to it. Just put on the welder's mask and the raincoat, and hold on tight when things get slippery.

MILES: Think it's a good idea? After the tractor?

MORGAN: Probably not. But there'll be no mollycoddling on this farm while there's work to do. Plus, I'll stand well back.

MILES: They're not going to believe this at rehearsal.

ANGUS *enters, disoriented and in pain. The light hurts him. He's looking for something.*

ANGUS: Morgan? Hello. The car got scratched. Right?

MORGAN: You need to be lying down. You know, Angus.

ANGUS: Right. (*Points to MILES.*)

Who'r . . . you?

MILES: My name's Miles. I'm staying here with you while I put on a play about farmers.

ANGUS: Tall. You look like . . . standing there, beside the . . . the girl.

MORGAN (*to MILES*): You go ahead, meet you in the barn.

MILES: Sure.

MILES *exits.*

MORGAN: Angus. Come now. Come up.

ANGUS (*softly, as MORGAN leads him out*): You bet.

Act 1, Scene 4

Lights up. ANGUS enters the kitchen. He's looking for something, and begins his search by examining a wall. Eventually he starts to look around, opening cupboard doors and looking under things. He's on his hands and knees when MILES limps into the farm house, his hands and thighs raw from moving hay bales. He has some trouble getting the door open.

MILES: Wow. Ow, Jeez.

ANGUS: Hullo. Hey. Get outta here.

MILES: Hello, Angus. My name is Miles and I'm staying with you and Morgan to learn about farming so I can write a play about it.

ANGUS (*throws a hand up in the air*): Hello, Miles. Okay.

MILES *limps to the sink, starts to tend to his wounds.*

ANGUS: Are yuh hurt? Yuh want some Freshie?

ECHO

MILES: I was just out helping Morgan with the hay bales. I musta hauled six hundred of the damn things off the wagon and on to the . . . escalator thing . . .

ANGUS: The what?

MILES: The—you know—the thing that takes the bales up to the top of the barn.

ANGUS: Oh, yeah, that thing's called the . . . uh.

ANGUS *goes to the sink during the following, gets* MILES *a spoonful of water.*

MILES: The only way to do that's to drag them off the wagon and sorta throw the bale onto the escalator using your leg. Look at my leg.

ANGUS: It's called the, uh . . .

MILES: Morgan looks at me and says: "Folks wear long pants around a farm." I bet this is infected. (ANGUS *shoves the water into* MILES's *mouth.*) Thanks.

ANGUS: Uh huh. Help yourself.

MILES: Then I go up into the barn to stack the bales, and that's even worse, 'cause there's no air up there—lots of dust, but no air—and I have to pick the damn things up, lift them over my head, and pile them up.

ANGUS: Hey. We got Freshie.

MILES: I wrestled in high school. I've done hard things, Angus. I was a hedgehog in a show last year about a group of dead animals. That show was three hours long. *I didn't move.* I've done hard things. And I wasn't about to quit, not with Morgan watching. I just picked them up, (*demonstrating*) one by one, hauled them over to the side of the barn, built a wall of hay. Look at my hands. Splinters inside of exploded blisters. "The twine, city boy, pick them up by the twine!" For God's sake. I'm not supposed to be doing this. I'm supposed to be writing a play.

ANGUS: Was it hay or straw you were loadin'?

MILES: I dunno. What's the difference?

ANGUS: Between hay and straw?

MILES: Yeah.

ANGUS: Hmmmmm. Nope. Don't know. Wouldn't eat no straw, though.

MILES: Do you think that Morgan's still upset with me over the thing with the tractor?

ANGUS: Thing with the . . . ?

MILES: Running him over with the tractor. I ran him down two mornings ago, remember?

ANGUS: Uuuhhhh. Nope. Tractor, eh?

MILES: Yes. Never mind.

ANGUS: Someone got hit by the tractor?

MILES: Yes, it's okay, Angus. Forget it.

ANGUS: You bet.

MILES (*points to fridge*): Angus, what's that called?

ANGUS: That's the uuuhhhh. Nope.

MILES: Is that the refrigerator?

ANGUS: Sure it is.

MILES: Or the stove?

ANGUS: Morgan. We better ask Morgan that.

MILES: It's okay. (*Points to the table.*) That's the chair, right?

ANGUS: Chair.

MILES: Angus. What's my name?

ANGUS: Don't you know?

MILES: Do you?

ANGUS: Ha ha.

MILES: Okay.

ANGUS: Okay then.

MILES: My name's Miles.

ANGUS: Hello, Miles, okay.

MILES: Angus? Twelve, fifty-six, one-oh-seven, twelve again, and six seventy-nine.

ANGUS: Uh huh.

MILES: What's my name?

ANGUS: Oh. Uuuuhhh. Ha ha.

MILES: Okay, Angus. What about those numbers I said. Can you add them up?

ANGUS: Eight hundred, sixty-six.

MILES: Right! I think that's right. . . .

ANGUS: Oh, yes.

MILES: How old are you?

ANGUS: 'Bout your age.

MILES: Oh yeah? Is Morgan our age, too?

ANGUS: Naw. He's an old feller.

MILES: Did you ever fight in the war?

ANGUS: Yes, I did. Sure. Prince's Pats. Went to France, went to England. With Morgan.

MILES: What did you have for breakfast this morning?

ANGUS: Ha ha. Sure.

MILES: And what's my name?

ANGUS *looks at* MILES. *This is starting to upset him.*

MILES: My name's Miles. Angus. Tell me about your head.

ANGUS: Hurts . . . sometimes . . . always . . .

MILES: How'd you hurt it? Do you know?

ANGUS: Morgan says . . . they were waiting for . . . hey. What's your name?

MILES: You tell me.

ANGUS: Don't know. Didn't tell me.

MILES: Angus—

ANGUS: Me too! My name's Angus too! Ha ha ha!

MILES: No, Angus. Listen. Your head. In London, did you get hit by a—

ANGUS: Noo, no. NO.

MILES: In the bombing—by a, a front door.

ANGUS: Front . . . ? No no no no. I did not.

MILES: Is that what happened, or do you just not remember. Morgan said.

ANGUS: Morgan knows. He knows. He tells me. I . . . the drawer boy. The tall girls. You see . . . Morgan . . . he knows. He knows. He . . . oh boy. (ANGUS *holds his head and starts to weep*) Ohhh boy. . . .

MILES: Angus. What is it? Are you— (*runs to the door*) Morgan! Morgan! Come quick! Angus, I'm sorry. . . . Morgan!

MORGAN *enters.*

MORGAN: Jesus. Alright now, Angus. Alright.

MORGAN *goes to the sink and gets a tablespoon of water.*

ANGUS: Morgan? Hello. How did I get hurt?

MORGAN *shoves the spoon into ANGUS's mouth. ANGUS calms down somewhat.*

Thanks. Okay. But.

MORGAN: Hush now.

ANGUS: Was it the front door? Was it?

MORGAN: Hush.

ANGUS: He says . . .

MORGAN *(suddenly)*: Angus! Make me a sandwich.

ANGUS: Eyuh.

ANGUS gets up, goes to the fridge, and gets out sandwich materials. He is almost instantaneously distracted by this task, and stops crying.

MORGAN: 'The hell have you been doing?

MILES: I didn't mean to upset him. I asked him a few questions about the war. His accident. . . .

MORGAN: I thought you were here to find out *about farming.*

MILES: Yes, I. . . .

MORGAN: You don't know what you're doing, asking him about that. I told you, his memory's faulty. You upset him, he spends the day in bed, and I have to do everything by myself. You got questions, ask me. I said I'd tell you everything you need to know about farming. Stick to the cows and the chickens. If you can't do that, you'd better leave. Can you do that?

MILES: Yes.

MORGAN: Miles? You better.

MILES: Yes, sir. I'm sorry. *(To ANGUS)* Angus? I'm sorry I . . . I'm sorry about what just happened.

ANGUS has no idea what MILES is talking about.

ANGUS: Oh. Well, uh . . . no, no. That's fine. Hey! Who wants Freshie?

Act 1, Scene 5

Night. MILES and MORGAN are seated at the table. Dinner is over. ANGUS has finished washing up and starts to make bread. He gets out the ingredients and makes dough through-out the scene. MILES makes notes furiously through the following.

MORGAN *(to MILES)*: You know what a steak costs? Per pound?

ANGUS: Dollar forty-seven.

MILES: Dollar forty-seven?

MORGAN: One dollar forty-seven cents. People scream over a price like that. Drop down dead in the meat aisle when they see that price, but let me tell you something: if the price of that steak had increased in the last ten years as much as the price of a postage stamp, that steak would be dollar fifty-seven per pound.

ANGUS: Eight point oh-two percent.

MORGAN: If that steak had gone up like the price of a newspaper, it'd cost a dollar seventy-five.

ANGUS: Ten point three percent.

MILES: Per pound.

MORGAN: Per pound. If that pound of steak had gone up like wages have in the last ten years, it'd cost two-oh-eight a pound.

ANGUS: Thirty-nine percent.

MORGAN: And if it'd gone up like the income tax has, that steak would be three-eighty a pound.

ANGUS: Fifty-eight point three three three three three. Percent.

MORGAN: And wouldn't that make people scream blue murder in the grocery store. We get nothing for what we do. An egg costs nine cents in the store, there's practically an armed uprising in the city over how expensive an egg is. Know how much it costs me to produce that egg? Nine point one three cents. Care to guess what my profit margin is on that egg?

ANGUS: Negative eighteen point seven-two cents per gross of eggs.

MORGAN: And if I drop one or two, it gets even worse.

MILES: How can you afford to run a losing business, year in, year out?

MORGAN: I make a little on the milk, and that almost evens things out with the eggs. The rest of the debt I put over to next year, until the year when my crops finally go for what they're actually worth. That year, of course, will never come. Government gets wind of that, they'll start doin' business that way. Then, God help us all.

Public complains about us, they believe all us farmers are making a killing. Politicians complain about us, tired of giving us subsidies that just get us to next year—maybe. Kids are leaving the farms, moving to Toronto; nobody wants to do this anymore. Soon nobody will.

ANGUS: Morgan? Why're you shouting?

MORGAN: Farms in a strip from Windsor to Montreal provide forty percent of the food for the country, and soon they'll all just stop. You'll get your food imported from God knows where, then see how much a pound of steak goes for. You go to university?

MILES: Yeah.

MORGAN: What'd you study?

MILES: English and drama. And political science, and geology, and law, and French. Phys Ed and a little Latin.

MORGAN: Uh huh. Graduate?

MILES: Well, I was living at this place called Rochdale College, and we really didn't believe that the point was to graduate; we thought that we should be able to—

MORGAN: How big a student loan didja run up?

MILES: That's a little personal, Morgan, I—

MORGAN: More than two thousand dollars?

MILES: Oh, yeah.

MORGAN: More than three?

MILES: Well, I sort of missed a term in there—a whole year, really, once the customs thing got cleared up—

never mind—so, actually I went for five years, on and off. So it wound up being around thirty-six hundred dollars. All together.

MORGAN: The government gave you more than I paid myself for the last four years.

ANGUS: 1968: eight sixty-one. 1969: nine hundred and five. 1970: seven hundred, seventy four. And 1971: seven hundred and ninety.

MORGAN: Don't you write that down. I make about the same as everyone else out here, but nobody needs to hear the exact figures from your stage.

MILES: Can I use the figures about the pound of steak?

MORGAN: Wish you would.

MILES: This is going to blow people's minds in rehearsal. You know, we all just go to the store, buy some fruit or a steak, and never think about where it comes from. Did you ever think of starting up a communal farm?

MORGAN: Eh?

MILES: Have you ever studied the Soviet model? They've been farming communally for decades in Russia, and the results are incredible.

ANGUS: Goddamn communists.

MILES: Productivity is up, the people all have enough to eat, money's not a—

ANGUS: *Goddamn communists.*

MILES: —worry. Anybody who looks at it sees it's the wave of the future.

Who are your neighbours to the north?

MORGAN: Lobbs. Don and Alison Lobb.

MILES: What if the fence came down between your two places. What if you and the Lobbs agreed—

ANGUS: *Goddamn communists.*

MILES: —agreed that from now on you'd both work the fields, take turns, maybe even sell one of the tractors—you'd only need the one, one barn for all the animals, an equal division of labour, materials, and profits—

ANGUS: GOD. DAMN. COMMUNISTS!

MORGAN: Angus! Why're *you* shouting?

ANGUS: Was I?

MORGAN: How's that bread coming?
    ANGUS *puts the bread in the oven.*

ANGUS: Done!
    During the following, ANGUS *goes outside and stands in the yard. He stares up at the stars and becomes transfixed.*

MORGAN: Good. Miles. Let me ask you a question. Now, your answer to this question may have a direct bearing on where you sleep tonight, on how comfortable a place it is you're sleeping in. A place where the humans normally sleep, or a place where furred and feathered animals generally lay their heads. A place that smells a bit. Miles? How would you describe yourself, politically?

MILES (*after a pause*): Oh. Well, I'm an actor. We don't have politics.

MORGAN: I think that's best. Angus. Don't you let that bread burn.

ANGUS: Bread?

MORGAN: He's ruined more bread... Where will you be putting on this play of yours?

MILES: Ray Bird is lending us his barn for the first show. Eventually, we hope to do it all over the county. Hope you'll come and see it, both of you. In fact, we're inviting some people to a rehearsal day after tomorrow, just so they can tell us if we're on the right track. Maybe you'd come to that?

MORGAN: Prob'ly will, seeing as how you're going to give your rendition of our cow Daisy.

MILES: Well, maybe not. I did the monologue for the others in the show—you know, "Have to make milk, don't want to get eaten"—and nobody believed it. I couldn't convince anybody that cows are petrified all the time. They want to do the stereotypical cow—you know, placid, dumb, cud-chewing. Bourgeois theatrical cow; that cow that we've seen onstage for years and years. And which of course I now know is a lie. I said, If you want to do a scene about a cow that's a lie, we could have stayed in Toronto and made it up out of our heads. I said I wasn't going to insult Daisy by portraying her without exploring her pain, her anxiety. Her reality. The director said okay, fair enough. And then he cut the scene.

MORGAN: Tough break.

MILES: Yeah. So far they aren't using anything I've brought to rehearsal. Remember the day we piled up all those hay bales? I made up a dance, the dance of the hay-bale stacker. It got cut too.

MORGAN (*to* MILES): Lemme ask you something. (*Goes to the door.*) Lie down, Angus.

ANGUS: Morgan. Hello.

MORGAN: Lie down if you want to look at them stars. You'll hurt your neck again.

ANGUS: Okay, sure.

ANGUS *lies down.*

MORGAN (*to* MILES): What happens if none of the...things you make up get put in the show?

MILES: Jeez. I don't know. I guess they'd probably have to kick me out of the collective.

MORGAN: So, if you don't produce, you die—is that it?

MILES: ...I guess so.

MORGAN: Well, there you go. You have something in common with me, too. I don't produce, I go as sure as you or the cows do.

MILES: Right on. That's good. Mind if I use that?

MORGAN: Guess not.

MILES: Thanks. Think I'll take this upstairs and try to put it into some kind of shape for rehearsal tomorrow.

MORGAN: Right. You'd better get some sleep. We're rotating the crops tomorrow.

MILES: Is that right? That a big job?

MORGAN: Uh-huh. We have to dig up all the hay growing on the east side of the field, the hay that gets all the morning sun, and move it to the west side, to get the afternoon sun. Big job. And we have to do it in the dark. Set your alarm for three.

MILES: Three? A.M.??

MORGAN: That's right. And I don't want to have to call you.

MILES: I'll be ready.

MORGAN: See that you are.

MILES: Yes, sir.

MILES *exits.* MORGAN *goes outside and sits on the back step. Silence, as he looks at the sky and at* ANGUS.

MORGAN: Angus? Bread in the oven.

ANGUS: Uh huh.

MORGAN: Don't forget.

ANGUS: Aww.

MORGAN: How many?

ANGUS: Nineteen thousand, four hundred and forty-four. Total.

MORGAN: That's a lot.

Silence.

ANGUS: Tell it.

MORGAN: Naw. . . . Not tonight, Angus.

ANGUS: Sure, tonight. You never tell it.

MORGAN: I tell it daily, you just don't. . . . Alright. Just . . . listen. A couple of boys played shinney and went to school and grew up. One drew pictures of a cabin—fine pictures of the inside and the out-side—until finally they built the cabin together. Stole nails, played hookey until it was done.

They finished school. One just barely. The other finished easily, but never got his diploma because he wouldn't give back the poetry book. That one almost went off to school, to keep drawing. The other one never would of. He was all set to work for his father, to start in on the farm. And then they both got called up, both went off to Europe. No school for the one, no farm for the other. They managed to stick together.

MILES *comes into the kitchen to retrieve his pen, and overhears the following.*

They fired their guns straight up in the air, and they yelled to each other the louder things got. When it got so loud they couldn't hear, they sang. They had three boots between them.

In England they met two girls, one tall and one taller. The taller one liked the drawer; the tall one, the farmer. They talked, they made plans. The girls talked together, the boys talked together.

The tall girl and the farmer would talk all night. The taller girl and the drawer would walk and talk all night. One girl would talk to the other boy about the boy she liked; so would the other girl to the other boy about the first boy.

Also, they talked in threes. Drawer boy, two tall girls; farmer boy, two tall girls; tall girl and two boys; taller girl and two boys. They talked to themselves, too.

The plans they made were like something the one boy would draw: Inside and out, all the details mixed, and when they were done talking, all four got ready to come home.

One night, in an air raid, the drawer boy was outside. The tall English girls and his friend were together and safe, in the butler's pantry of a large and empty house. They lit candles and made jokes about where the other one might be.

Well, he was down the street, looking at another large house. Probably staring at the wrought iron, or memorizing the slope of the roof. The front door of the house flew off when the shell hit, and the drawer boy watched it come for him.

A doctor took two inches of copper plate out of the boy's head, from the front-door door-knocker. The doctor put in twenty-six millimetres of stainless steel. Before the doctor could close up the wound, the boy's memory escaped.

His hair grew back and the boy's three friends slowly put his memory back, too. One day he woke up and remembered right and left, and up and down. One day he woke up and remembered he loved the taller English girl. They got ready to go

home again, talked about their plans again. They showed the drawer boy pictures he made of the house all four would live in, pictures he had made before the front door came. He could not remember making the pictures, but he agreed to the plan: They would come home. There would be a double wedding. There was money enough for one piece of land. The house would be built on a farm they would share, and it would be two houses joined. Two families would be started, life would begin for the four friends.

They came home. There was a double wedding. The drawer boy recited a poem from the stolen book. They bought one piece of land. They started to build the house. They bought a car. They bought an old black car.

ANGUS: Right.

MORGAN: The taller English girl loved to drive, and one day she and the tall English girl went in the old black car to a berry bush the farmer boy had shown them. Coming home, there were two pails of raspberries between them on the seats. They knew what side of the road to be on. They did. An old army transport came over the hill on their side, coming toward them; the transport was passing a horse. The taller English girl turned, turned her side of the old black car into the transport, because she knew they could not miss. Her side of the car was just ruined. Not a scratch on the tall girl's side. But the tall girl died too.

ANGUS: Right. My Sally. My . . . Sally. Your?

MORGAN: My Frances. Then the two tall English girls went to a hill, both in the same carriage, pulled by a horse. The hill is the highest point in the county. That's where they are now. And then, it was the two friends again. And the drawer makes bread and adds rows of numbers in his head, and the farmer farms and tends to the place on the hill and keeps their memories safe, like a pail of raspberries between them.

ANGUS: Right. Morgan. I smell bread.

MORGAN: You do? How do you feel? How's your head?

ANGUS: No. I smell bread.

MORGAN (*jumping up*): Jesus.
    MORGAN *runs into the kitchen to rescue the bread.* MILES *escapes without being seen.*

MORGAN (*pulling the burnt bread out of the oven*): Jesus! Angus! Goddamn it!

ANGUS: Nineteen thousand, four hundred and forty . . . five.

Act 1, Scene 6

Late that night. MILES *comes into the kitchen. He pulls out his notebook.*

MILES: Two friends built a cabin with nails they stole from . . . Two friends grew up together; one was a farmer, one drew pictures. They made plans, they went to school. They went off to war. They shot their guns in the air and sang war songs. They had three boots between them. They met two English girls, one tall and one taller.

ANGUS *enters in his pyjamas. He's searching for something. As* MILES *watches, he goes carefully through the kitchen, beginning again with the blank space on the wall. Eventually, he sees* MILES.

ANGUS: Hey! Who are you??

MILES: My name's Miles. I'm staying with you and Morgan to learn about farming so I can write a play about it.

ANGUS (*waves*): Okay. Hello, Miles.
    ANGUS *sits down at the table. He looks at* MILES.

MILES: Did you come down for something? It's a couple of hours until we have to rotate the crops.

ANGUS: Eh?

MILES: Were you looking for something?

ANGUS: Sure.

MILES: What?

ANGUS: No idea.

MILES: . . . Should you go to bed then?

ANGUS: You bet.
    ANGUS *gets up, hesitates, then heads outside.* MILES *follows, and watches as* ANGUS *stands, looking at the stars.*

MILES: Angus?

ANGUS: You bet.

MILES: Nice night.

ANGUS: That's right. (*Silence.*) You organize it into sections. The whole sky. It's just pieces. No bigger than you. Then you count it. (*Silence, then ANGUS turns to MILES.*) See?

MILES: Uh huh.

ANGUS goes inside. He repeats exactly the same moves from earlier, looking for something. MILES watches him for a while.

MILES: Can I help you find it?

ANGUS: Jeez. I couldn't tell ya. You hungry?

MILES: Not really.

ANGUS: Me neither.

ANGUS leaves. After a moment, MILES returns to his notebook.

Act 1, Scene 7

An afternoon, a couple of days later. MORGAN and ANGUS enter, ANGUS is excited.

ANGUS: That was exactly right, wasn't it? The tractor? Them two girls were the tires, and the one fella on the other's shoulders, and he was driving the fella and the two girls, because they were the tractor. And telling about the tractor breaking down when the harvest hasta come in, and how you gotta be awake when you go over hills and the like. The fella sitting on top of the fella's shoulders, talking away to us while he's driving the tractor. That was exactly right.

MORGAN: Uh huh.

ANGUS: And that girl who came out and said she was . . . was . . .

MORGAN: Alison Lobb.

ANGUS: That's right. D'you know for a long while there I thought she was Alison Lobb? I thought, good Lord, Alison Lobb's lost her senses and gone up there on the stage and was talking to us. It wasn't, you know. That was an actress. Acting.

MORGAN: I know.

ANGUS: *I laughed.* And then . . . Miles comes out and starts with that story about the two tall English girls and the war and all, in that funny voice, and all of a sudden I realized—it's you! He's pretending to be you and that's why I knew the story just before he said each word. He told it just the way you do! I remembered all of it as he said it. I could have said it along with him. . . . Hey! That other fella! The simple-looking fella he was telling the story to! That was me! The one fella was you and the other one was supposed to be me! Jesus, that was something. That was us.

MORGAN: That was us.

ANGUS: He got us, didn't he? Miles. He got us.

MORGAN: He did.

ANGUS: He did. I'll never forget that. I can't wait until everyone—

MORGAN: Angus? Want a sandwich?

ANGUS: Sure. (*Gets sandwich materials out of fridge, starts to make two.*) I'll tell yuh, Morgan, that was just . . . I never seen. . . .

MORGAN: Angus? How many stars you count last night?

ANGUS: Six-hundred and eighteen I never counted before. One thousand and seventy-nine I already did.

MORGAN: Got a new total?

ANGUS: Sure. Twenty-two thousand, seven-hundred and fifty-seven. New total.

MORGAN: Good. What did we do today?

ANGUS: Aaww. We just got back.

MORGAN: From where.

ANGUS: From . . . town?

MORGAN: What on earth were we doing in town?

ANGUS: Well, Morgan, I don't know. We were . . . I don't . . . I'm hungry, though. Sandwich?

MORGAN: Okay.

MORGAN *sees* MILES *coming into the yard, and goes out to intercept him.*

MILES: What'd you think of the rehearsal? A lot of it's pretty rough, but I thought some of it went—

MORGAN: You get out of here.

MILES: . . . I'm sorry?

MORGAN: You heard. Get out. You can't stay here.

MILES: Morgan, hold it. You're upset that I used that story and didn't tell you—I wanted that to be a surprise.

MORGAN: It was. You put that in your play and I'll see to it you never put it on.

MILES: Look, if I didn't get the story exactly right, it's because I only heard it once. You can give me the details, we can work on it together. It's important. We're here to get your history and give it back to you.

MORGAN: It ain't—you can't use that. It's private between Angus and me, and I don't want people to hear it.

MILES: Everyone around here must know the story already. I just want to tell it to them in the play, so they can see how important it is.

MORGAN: Just get out of here. You can't stay. You lied.

MILES: What does Angus say about it?

MORGAN: Angus's already forgotten it, thank God. You oughta be ashamed, coming here, stealing . . .

MILES: Morgan, listen to me. It's the only thing I've got in the show right now. If I cut this scene—which the director loves, by the way—I'm out of the show. Produce or die, remember?

ANGUS *comes outside, sees* MILES.

ANGUS: Hey!!!

MILES: Hello, Angus. My name's—

ANGUS: Miles! We saw you! You were Morgan and that other fella was me! You got us!

MILES: (*Pause.*) That's right. You remember the play?

MORGAN: You know who that is?

ANGUS: Sure. You're Miles, and you're staying with Morgan and me while you learn about farming and write that play! You were Morgan. You told about us. God! I'll never forget it. Come in and have a sandwich, Miles.

MILES (*to* MORGAN): Has he ever . . . ?

MORGAN: Never recognized anyone but me.

ANGUS: You were him. You sounded just like Morgan. Come in and have a sandwich.

MORGAN: He has to go now. He's gonna get his things and leave.

ANGUS: Why?

MILES: I don't know, exactly.

ANGUS: Well, that's just silly. You can't go. Just got here.

MORGAN: He's leaving.

ANGUS: Why?

MILES: Because of what I did on stage.

ANGUS: Whatareyuh...?

MILES: Your story. About the two tall English girls. Morgan says I can't use it.

ANGUS: Oh. Well. That's not a story. That's us. You have to use that.
ANGUS goes back inside. MILES and MORGAN stare at each other.
He has to use that. He's here because he's Miles! Get in here! 'Kinda sandwich you want?
MILES goes inside and sits with ANGUS.

ACT TWO

Act 2, Scene 1

The next day. MILES sits on the ground outdoors, talking to ANGUS. There are two piles of gravel beside him: a big pile and a little pile. He takes a stone from the big pile, dunks it in a bucket of soapy water, scrubs it

with a vegetable brush, and dries it carefully with a small towel. Then he puts it onto the small pile.
ANGUS sits on the back step, listening.

MILES: ...and I have these two friends. From university. They're funny. They talk alike, and they sort of dress alike, and they're always together. And because I'm sad, my stepfather calls them up and says, "He mopes around wearing black all day, come and visit and cheer him up"—and so they do. Except what my stepfather really wants them to do is spy on me. In case I get it into my head that I want to kill him.

ANGUS: Why would you...?

MILES: Because, like I said, he killed my father and married my mum, and my father told me to. Sort of. His ghost sort of told me to.

ANGUS: Right.

MILES: Their names are Rosencrantz and Guildenstern.

ANGUS: You're kidding.

MILES: I am not.

ANGUS: Hee hee.

MILES: So they show up, and I know right off that they're here to spy on me for my stepfather. So I put on an antic disposition. I pretend to go mad. I threaten them, and call them names, and kick them out. Except you start to wonder—am I acting mad, or am I really going mad? I'm all sad and angry, I keep hearing voices, and I can't decide what to do, so I do nothing, and that makes

Miles tells Angus a story on the front step during a National Arts Centre production of *The Drawer Boy*.

me even worse. I start treating my
girlfriend really badly. I yell at her
and call her bad names. I just treat
her terribly, until she goes mad for
sure and drowns herself in a pond.

ANGUS: Miles. You went mad.

MILES: And then I yell at my mother.
And—Angus, you aren't baking,
are you?

ANGUS: Who knows? You yelled at
your mum?

MILES: And then I kill this nice old guy
who talked all the time. I stabbed
him through the arras.

ANGUS: The arras. Ouch. Were you
mad then? Or just pretending?

MILES: Well, you still weren't sure.
You still couldn't tell.

ANGUS: But—could you?

MILES: I. . . . Yes. I think I was a little
mad then. I think stabbing a guy
makes you go even more mad.

ANGUS: Oh, I know.

MILES: Anyway, by the time I finish
talking to my mum and stabbing
the old guy, I decide I have to kill
my stepfather.

ANGUS: 'Cause of hearing your dad's
voice?

MILES: Yes.

ANGUS: But, Miles! What if the voice
in your head is just some voice?

You can't go killing people because of that.

MILES: That's right. . . .

ANGUS: I mean—Jesus!—what if everybody acted that way?

MILES: I know.

ANGUS: Killing people just 'cause of something they heard in their head once or twice.

MILES: I know.

ANGUS: Everybody did that, there'd be no one left. S'not right.

MILES: You're right. That's what I'm so worried about. That's why I went mad.

MORGAN *comes in from the barn, and speaks to* MILES *as he passes.*

MORGAN: Hurry up. I'll need that gravel by after lunch.

ANGUS: Morgan! Hello.

MORGAN *goes inside.*

ANGUS: That's a tough job you've got.

MILES: Yeah, the actor's life's a difficult one.

ANGUS: No. The . . . (*points at what* MILES *is doing*)

MILES: Have you ever done this?

ANGUS: Well, I guess I must of, some time. Tough job. So . . . what . . . where . . . Oh! Your stepfather. Didja kill him?

MILES: Well, not right away. My girl-friend's brother comes home. He's mad at me because she killed her-self, so we have a couple of sword fights, everybody takes some drugs sort of by accident, and then every-body dies.

ANGUS: Everybody dies by accident?

MILES: Sort of.

ANGUS: Helluvan accident.

MILES: And then I die too.

ANGUS: I should hope so. Did people clap?

MILES: Oh, yeah. People loved it. The people that saw it. The critics hated it.

ANGUS: Why?

MILES: I don't know. They said I was too Canadian.

ANGUS: Well, that makes sense.

MORGAN *comes back outside with a dessert fork.*

ANGUS: Morgan. Hello. He went mad.

MORGAN (*to* MILES): Here. Know what this is? This is a short-handled insilage fork. After the gravel's washed, I want you to muck out the cow stalls. Using this. Cows have been eating corn lately, and not all of it gets digested. You use this to retrieve the undigested corn and put it into a bucket. We feed the chickens that fortified corn. You understand me?

MILES: Yes. (MORGAN *exits.*) He must think I'm so stupid.

ANGUS: Oh, he does.

MILES: As if I'd go through all the cow crap with this. With a stupid little fork.

ANGUS: It's crazy.

MILES: It sure is.

ANGUS: I'll get you a spoon. Tell me another.

MILES: Let's see. Did one about a family from out around here, called the Donnellys. Bad bunch. They were so nasty to so many people, that one night a mob came and burned down their house.

ANGUS: Jeez. Who made that up? That Shakespeare?

MILES: No, a Canadian wrote it, but it's not made up. It's a true story. It really happened.

ANGUS: Whadda ya mean! It was on stage, wasn't it? It was a play.

MILES: It was a play from a true story. Like the one that we're making up now. It's a play about farmers, but the stories we tell in it are true ones. Like the story I heard Morgan tell you.

ANGUS: The two tall English girls.

MILES: Right.

ANGUS: Tell it.

MILES: I don't think so, Angus.

ANGUS: Go on.

MILES: No, I don't think Morgan would like it.

ANGUS: 'Course he would. Why wouldn't he?

MILES: Well, because it's his story. His and yours. And he should tell it to you, not me.

ANGUS: Okay.

MILES: Sorry.

ANGUS: No. (*Pause.*) What if you pretended you were him. You be Morgan, and I'll pretend I'm Angus, and you tell it that way.

MILES: I can't do that.

ANGUS: Can too.

MILES: No, I can't.

ANGUS: Sure, just pretend you're Morgan sitting there washing rocks, and you think to yourself, "Geez, I'd better tell Angus that there tall-girl story before I do another thing." And then say "Angus," and I'll say "What?" and you say the story of the two English tall-girls now hurry up.

MILES: No, look, I can't. It's Morgan's story to tell. It's not right that I start telling it to you.

ANGUS: Oh. Unless you're up on stage telling everybody, right?

MILES: Uhh. Right.

ANGUS: Oh.

MILES: Right, so . . .

ANGUS: It'd be okay for me, though? To tell it?

MILES: Of course. Yes. I'd love to hear it.

ANGUS: Okay. I'll pretend to be you pretending to be Morgan telling the story. (*He looks around.*) Now, would I be on a stage, or . . .

MILES: No. You're just sitting on the back step.

ANGUS: Oh. Right. Okay then. (*He contorts himself, raises his voice an octave.*) Now I'm you. (*He hunches over, drops his voice two octaves.*) And now I'm you being Morgan. Any good?

MILES: Perfect.

ANGUS: Perfect. (*Pause.*) How's it start?

MILES: (*Pulls out his notebook.*) Once there were two friends . . .

ANGUS: Once there were two friends...

As MILES leads ANGUS through the story, MILES falls into his "Morgan" persona, until there are two slightly grotesque "Morgans" telling the story back and forth.

MILES: Two boys. They played hockey together, they did everything together.

ANGUS: Boys who played hockey. And everything.

MILES: The one boy drew pictures.

ANGUS: The one boy drew pictures. The drawer boy.

MILES: Yes. He drew pictures of a cabin. Inside and out, lots of pictures. Then they built the cabin.

ANGUS: Drawer boy drew a cabin, inside and out. Then they stole nails, and played hookey, and built the cabin.

MILES: And then they went off to war together.

ANGUS: And then they went off to war together.

MILES: They fought together, and hid together, and sang when it was loudest. They had three boots between them.

ANGUS: They fired up in the air together, and hid, and sang together when it got too loud, and... three boots.

MILES: In England they met two girls....

ANGUS: One tall and one taller.

MILES: The taller one liked the drawer.

ANGUS: And the tall one liked Morgan. Liked me.

MILES: The tall girl and the farmer would talk all night; the taller girl and the drawer would walk all night and talk. One girl would talk to the other boy about the boy she liked, so would the other girl to the other boy....

ANGUS: They talked....

MILES: When they were done talking, their plans were as complete as something the boy would draw.

ANGUS: When they were done talking, they had a picture of the next thing they would make together, the four of them. They came home and had a double wedding....

MILES: No, Angus. Next is the air raid. The front door flying. Remember?

ANGUS: Uh huh. But. I don't want to.

MILES: Okay.

ANGUS: They went home. There was a double wedding, he said the stolen poem. They started the house, the two houses joined.

MILES: Right.

ANGUS: Where?

MILES: Where what?

ANGUS: Where's the houses joined and separate?

MILES: I don't know.

ANGUS: He said—you said, "They started to build the house."

MILES: You're right.

ANGUS: Where?

MILES: Let's ask him later.

ANGUS: Okay.

MILES: They bought a car.

ANGUS: They bought a black car. Now, Angus, you say "My Sally."

MILES: My Sally. Your...?

ANGUS: My Frances. Your Sally loved to drive the car, the black car. To where raspberries grew wild. A horse came the other way, and the army headed straight for my Frances, but my Sally—your Sally— Sally....

MILES: She turned her side into the truck, to save her friend, Angus. Your Sally tried to save Frances.

ANGUS: She...yes.

MILES: And now it's the two friends again.

ANGUS: And now it's the...No. They got taken in a cart to the highest point in the county. Buried there.

MILES: Yes. That's right. And now it's the two friends again.

ANGUS: And now it's...I've never been there. The highest point in the country. Hey.

He's being led by a memory so faint, he behaves as though he's smelling something. ANGUS walks inside, drops to his knees, and pulls up a floorboard. He pulls out a beat-up metal tube, khaki green, about three feet long. He opens the tube, pulls out several architectural drawings, and spreads them out on the table.

The houses joined. Together and separate.

MORGAN enters. ANGUS greets him without looking up.

Morgan! Hello! The houses joined. They never got started. Did they? You said they did. I want to go to them.

MORGAN (*to* MILES): How did you find these?

MILES: I didn't.

MORGAN: How did you find these?

ANGUS: You hid them. I saw you. You didn't see me.

MORGAN: You remember that?

ANGUS: I...I guess I do....

MILES: You made these?

ANGUS: The two houses joined up. I drew these. Separate and joined. I was the drawer boy.

MORGAN: You did. You were.

ANGUS: I am. I want to see her, Morgan. Take me to where they are. Up on that hill. The tallest point. (*To* MILES) You should come, too. You did this. Let's go right now. ANGUS *goes outside.*

MORGAN: No, Angus. You're baking.

ANGUS: Well, just—turn off the damn...whatever that is! I want to go now. My Sally.

MORGAN (*following* ANGUS *out*): Listen to me. We can't go, Angus. Now, just stop this.

ANGUS: Can too. I have to.

MORGAN: Angus! Make me a sandwich. I'm hungry.

ANGUS: Make you...? Make your own damn sandwich, old fella! I got to...Damn it! I WANT TO GO! MILES *comes outside.*

I been waiting so long. I never—

why'd you not ever take me? That's my Sally. That's my WIFE.

MILES: Angus. I'm sure he must of. You don't remember things, you know.

ANGUS: I want to go to them. I'll remember them now.

MORGAN: I'm hungry. I want to eat something.

ANGUS: I'll cook once we get back. Let's go. Why'd you never take me there before?

MORGAN: No.

ANGUS: Yes.

MORGAN: No.

ANGUS/MILES (*together*): Yes!

MORGAN (*to* MILES): I beg your pardon?

MILES: Well, I mean, he seems to want to go. I just thought—

MORGAN: Would you excuse us, please? Wait inside.

MILES: Sure.

ANGUS: He'll come too!

MILES: Yes, but, I'm going to go inside for a while.
MILES *goes inside.*

ANGUS: I'll get the truck—or, you should get the truck, you know where we're going. Plus, do I know how to drive?

MORGAN: Angus, I'm tired. I want my lunch. There's so much I need to do this afternoon.

ANGUS: Not more important than this! There's a picture of the place in my head—the tallest spot—I want to go and match it. Now.

MORGAN: Feed came this morning. Usual amount, and I wrote Wally a cheque. Can we cover it?

ANGUS: Leaves forty-four dollars and sixteen cents. Dairy gives us ninety-one twenty-one in the next three days, we can cover the loan and have sixteen-oh-eight to spare—now, let's go.

MORGAN: Angus. No. We aren't going.

ANGUS (*after a pause*): You eat lunch first. *Then.*

MORGAN: No. Not then.

ANGUS: Yes then. Go now and quick—there's some, there's some . . . something for a sandwich in the . . . thing. Quick. Go. I'll wait out here.

MORGAN: Listen to me.

ANGUS: You go! I'll wait patiently for you to come out, and we'll go see—

MORGAN: Listen.

ANGUS: —SEE MY SALLY.
ANGUS *holds his head, has to sit.*

MORGAN: Angus, are you—

ANGUS: GO IN! Go in and come out.
MORGAN *goes inside. He starts to make a sandwich.*

MILES: I believe he will remember this time, if you take him.

MORGAN: I'm not taking him.

ANGUS: Morgan. Done yet?

MILES: But why?

ANGUS: Morgan.

MORGAN: That's between him and me.

MILES: Fine, I don't want to interfere—

ANGUS: Morgan! Time's up!

MILES: —but he's better now, he seems better. Since rehearsal. He's remembering things. And he wants to go.

MORGAN: I told him no, and I'm telling you no.

ANGUS (*holding his head*): Aw, God. Moorgan!
Silence while MORGAN *finishes making the sandwich, sits, and begins to eat.* Morgan! Let's go! Morgan! Moorgan! You got to drive!
ANGUS *is in more and more pain.* Moooorgan!!

MILES: Morgan, Jesus. . . .

MORGAN: How's the gravel coming?

MILES: I'll take him myself. Just tell me where it is.

ANGUS: Mooorgan! Get the . . . truck!

MORGAN: You got too much to do. Gravel and then the muckin' out.

ANGUS: Aaaahhh. Morgan! Morgan.

MILES: This is, just, cruel.

ANGUS (*suddenly no longer in pain*): Morgan! Get the jeep!

MILES: Morgan, for God's sake.

ANGUS: Get a, we need a jeep! Don't tell anyone! Morgan!

MORGAN: (*Goes to the door.*) Angus! Come indoors.

ANGUS: Morgan! Hello! We need a ride. We can't tell anyone. WE got to go.

MORGAN: Come inside.
They go inside.

ANGUS: What did you do to get us passes? Sergeant says don't tell any-one, and be back by oh-six-hundred. Jesus, Morgan! Miles. You can't come.

MORGAN: Angus, listen—

ANGUS: Sally will just—let's go now. Surprise them.

MORGAN: Angus? You need to go upstairs. To bed, now.

ANGUS: To hell with that! They're waiting for us. Did you call? Did you?

MORGAN: I. . . . Yes. I did.

ANGUS: I knew it! Jesus, you did. Goddamn it! You set it all up.

MORGAN: That's right. I did.

ANGUS: Yuh clever bastard! Let's go. Miles. You can't go. The girls are waiting, but we got just the two passes. Morgan set it up.

MILES: Angus. I'm sorry. I don't understand you.

MORGAN: This happened.

MILES: What?

MORGAN: I got leave for the two of us overnight. It was his birthday. It was a surprise.

MILES: He remembers!

MORGAN: This is your fault.

ANGUS: You've got to lend me some shoes, mine are still wet from the ditch. Sergeant says we have to . . . we have to be back . . . (*his headache resumes*) Morgan? It's too bright.

MORGAN: Let's go, Angus. Upstairs.

ANGUS: No! She's waiting with . . . to give me . . . cufflinks.

MORGAN: You can't go like that. Can you.

ANGUS: No. Not like this.

MORGAN: Let's go up and get your uniform on.

ANGUS: Okay.

MORGAN: Get you that shoe.

ANGUS: Let's . . . hurry. (*Looks at MILES.*) Hey. Who're you?

MORGAN: That's the man who did this to you.

MORGAN leads ANGUS upstairs.

Act 2, Scene 2

Late that night. ANGUS walks into the kitchen. As in Act One, he's looking for something. He comes across the architectural drawings, and stares at them for a while.

ANGUS: "God with honour hang your head,

Groom, and grace you bride, your bed,

With lissome scions, sweet scions,

Out of hallowed bodies bred.

Each be other's comfort kind:

Deep, deeper than divined—"

He looks up.

Morgan?

He gets no response, and goes back to the blueprints.

I want to . . .

He looks out the door, then looks back toward the stairs.

I'll go. I'll go now.

He goes out the back door and off into the night. After a moment, MORGAN comes into the kitchen.

MORGAN: Angus? (*Sees the open back door and goes out.*) Angus? Angus!!

He walks off. MILES comes into the kitchen.

MILES: Morgan? What is it?

MORGAN comes back into the house. He pulls on his boots, puts on a jacket.

MORGAN: He's gone.

MILES: Oh, no. He went to the graveyard. I'll go. . . .

MORGAN: You stay here.

MILES: Look—I'm "the man who did this." I want to help.

MORGAN: You stay here.

MORGAN exits.

Act 2, Scene 3

Dawn. MILES is sitting in the kitchen, waiting impatiently. He gets up and goes outside. He sees the two piles of rocks left over from the day before; picks up a rock, dunks it in the pail of water, dries it with the cloth, and sets it on the small pile. He does this again, distractedly. Then he looks around, surreptitiously; picks up the bucket of water, dumps the water on the larger pile of rocks, pats the pile dry a couple of times, and then pushes the big pile and the little pile together.

MORGAN enters.

MORGAN: Anybody call?

MILES: No. Any luck?

MORGAN: No.

MORGAN goes inside. He doesn't know what to do with himself. He makes a sandwich. MILES goes in. ANGUS walks through the yard unseen, his arm bleeding, and then goes off again.

MILES: He'll turn up. (*Pause.*) Finished the gravel.

MORGAN: Huh? Oh. Goes in the culvert.

MILES: Sure. Is the culvert that shed thing out behind the barn?

MORGAN: No, it's . . . never mind. I'll do it. (*Goes to the phone and dials.*) Tom? Morgan. Any sign of him? Okay. Thanks. (*Hangs up.*)

MILES: What about the graveyard?

MORGAN: What about it?

MILES: Did you look there.

MORGAN: No.

MILES: But that's where he wanted to go.

MORGAN: I'm gonna say this once, as nice as I can under the circumstances: You are not being helpful.

MILES: Fine. I'm sorry. Tell me how I can help.

MORGAN: Go to the henhouse. Shuffle the eggs.

MILES: Morgan—

MORGAN: Take the eggs out from underneath each chicken, put them under a different chicken.

MILES: Look—

MORGAN: That way, they don't raise a fuss when we take their eggs away for good.

MILES: Stop it.

MORGAN: And no chicken has to suffer.

MILES: Tell me why you wouldn't take him to the graveyard. Why you won't look for him there now.

MORGAN: Why? Your play not long enough yet?

MILES: Because I did something to Angus, and I hurt you, and I don't know how I did that. And I want to fix it.

MORGAN: I'll fix it.

MILES: Tremendous. Fix it. Go to the graveyard and get him. Go now.

MORGAN: Cows need to be milked.

MILES: I'll milk the goddamn cows!

MORGAN: Oh, you will, will you? Think you could figure out the milking machine on your own?

MILES: Yes. I do.

ANGUS *walks into the yard again.*

MORGAN: You can't recognize the useful end of a shovel. You go out there, the barn'll fall over.

MILES: I'll do it. Go. Or I'll call the cops and send them up there for him.

MORGAN: You'll what?

MILES: And I'll tell them that you knew he was out there wandering around, and you wouldn't go to get him.

MORGAN: You're gonna call the police?

MILES: I. . . . No, of course not. I just —I don't understand it. We both know where he is, we both know why he went there, and I can't figure out why you won't—

MORGAN: Stop trying.

MILES: —why you won't go and get him. He could be hurt, he could be God knows what. Jesus, Morgan, don't you care?

MORGAN: You watch your step, young man.

MILES: Tell me why you won't go. Tell me why you're just standing there.

MORGAN: (*Tosses his truck keys to MILES.*) You go.

MILES: Okay. Thank you. I will.
MILES *turns to go. But before he gets outside, he stops suddenly and turns to MORGAN.*

MILES: It's not true. What you tell him isn't true. That's why you won't go. Isn't it?

MORGAN: You get out of here.
MILES *leaves the house, then sees ANGUS.*

MILES: Angus!
MORGAN *comes outdoors. Through the following, ANGUS will not look at MORGAN.*

MORGAN: Angus! Are you alright? What happened to you? Where did you get to? (*He pauses, then turns to MILES.*) You leave us alone?

MILES: Sure. (*He exits.*)

MORGAN: Angus? You alright? Come inside. (*They go in together.*) Sit down. Lemme look at that arm. How did this happen? (*Pause.*) You hungry? Want a sandwich?

You haven't walked off for some time. Once I found you up in the mow; looked all day, and your one leg had gone through a hole, and you were just stuck there. You didn't care. Looking off, like you were waiting for a train or something. Do you know, I pulled you out, carried you down, and it took you till the next day to come back to yourself. You scared me.

What were you thinking about? You'd do it when we were kids. I'd find you up a tree somewhere; you'd be staring off, I'd be yelling, "Angus, Angus," and you'd come back to yourself, climb back down, ask what day it was. It was funny when we were kids.

I'm gonna make you something to eat and I want you to eat it. MORGAN *goes to the fridge, and begins to make a sandwich. He stops, goes to the sink, gets a spoonful of water, and gives it to ANGUS. Then he finishes making the sandwich.*

ANGUS (*looking at the blueprints*): The houses joined. Together and separate.

MORGAN: Yes.

ANGUS: I drew these.

MORGAN: Yes.

ANGUS: Don't remember doing that. Remember him hiding them, though. I saw him hide them.

MORGAN: Saw who?

ANGUS: Him. He didn't see me.

MORGAN: Angus. Look at me. Who am I?

ANGUS: You're the man who did this to me.

MORGAN: What's my name.

ANGUS: Don't you know?

MORGAN: Look at me.

ANGUS: You played the farmer boy. You got us.

MORGAN: No, Angus.

ANGUS: Sure.

MORGAN: No, Angus. Please. Tell me who I am.

ANGUS: Why should I?

MORGAN: I want to know if you're okay.

ANGUS: I don't care. I was in the dark, walking, and I got stopped. I heard a voice. It was a ghost. It stopped me, warned me against you.

MORGAN: What?

ANGUS: It told me what you did. It told me I should be afraid of you. It said: "HE KILLED YOUR FATHER. HE MARRIED YOUR MUM."

MORGAN: Angus, you're scaring me.

ANGUS *pauses, then looks at* MORGAN.

ANGUS: Okay. I was just pretending I was mad. There was no voice. It was my antic disposition.

I'm scared. Listen, I was out there, and I heard. He said—Miles said, "It's not true. What you tell him isn't true." I heard.

MORGAN: You did.

ANGUS: Yes. Miles said, "It's not true. What you tell him isn't true." Did he mean me?

MORGAN: Yes.

ANGUS: Oh. What did he mean?

MORGAN: He means I lied. I lied to you.

ANGUS: Is that true?

MORGAN: Yes.

ANGUS: Oh. Okay. You lied. You're a bastard. God. Look. The houses joined. Where's Miles. I want him to tell it.

MORGAN: Not now.

ANGUS: Yes, now. I want—Miles to. He, what did he do? Oh God, Morgan.

MORGAN: What's wrong?

ANGUS: What'd he do to me? I have, in my head . . .

MORGAN: What. Tell me.

ANGUS: Just everything. Just . . . every-thing. It came all night. Listen: I'm a boy, and I have a cough and a nose-bleed on my shirt. On my short pants. I remembered that. Then, another time, I'm writing a test, and the smell of you sittin' beside me, smell of you failing it. I remember France, that boy running away. You would not shoot the boy running away. Sally, the first sight of her from behind in that church. Oh, God, oh no, I remember that. Her hair, my finger trapped in the pages of the hymn book. And then, I got hurt—God, the noise, I'm lying on the ground. . . . I remember when my head didn't hurt, I think. I remember Miles, who was you on that . . . stage. I remember the double wedding.

MORGAN: You remember the double wedding?

ANGUS: I do. I stood up, I said: "God with honour hang your head, groom—"

MORGAN: You remember getting hurt?

ANGUS: I do. I remember the door flying. At me. The three of you safe, and me on my way to you, and I got stopped by the architecture.

MORGAN: No, that's—oh, Jesus.

ANGUS: I remember everything.

MORGAN: No, you don't.

ANGUS: Yes. Yes, I do! It came all night. I walked. I was looking for them.

MORGAN: You remember the story. What he said on stage.

ANGUS: No. I remember *it*.

MORGAN: What was in your hand?

ANGUS: My hand?

MORGAN: What were you carrying?

ANGUS: Nothing. I don't think . . .

MORGAN: What you just told me is what I've told you all these years. That's our story. What you had in your hand was a bottle of cheap brandy, given to me in a card game. I sent you to fetch it. Remember? *We laughed,* and I made you get it. You were safe, and I sent you out— you understand? Angus? I did that. I did that to you. That's the first thing.

ANGUS: That's the first thing? See. You're a bastard. What do I remember?

MORGAN: You remember the story.

ANGUS: Aw, God.

MORGAN: Angus. What'd I get for that car?

ANGUS: Car?

MORGAN: The black car.

ANGUS: It got wrecked. The army truck.

MORGAN: Did it? If you can remember, then remember.

ANGUS: Don't.

MORGAN: What'd I get for that car.

ANGUS: It got wrecked, my Sally was driving, and she turned it into the truck—

MORGAN: No. It's a number.

ANGUS: I don't want to. I want him— I want the story.

MORGAN: How much'd I get for that car?

ANGUS: Hundred and ten dollars.

MORGAN: That's right.

ANGUS: Hundred and ten dollars. Oh. From Doug Hamm. It didn't crash.

MORGAN: That's right. We sold it. You do remember.

ANGUS: No, I don't.

MORGAN: Angus, listen—

ANGUS: No. It's not true. "What you tell him isn't true." I heard.

MORGAN: It is true.

ANGUS: Where's Miles? Hey Miles! Get in here!

MORGAN: No, Angus, wait.

ANGUS: I want him. Miles!
MILES *runs in.*
(*to* MILES) You said, "What you tell him isn't true." He said, "I lied." He lied. He's a bastard. Now he says something . . . else. You have to tell it.

MILES: Morgan'll tell you.

ANGUS: No, he won't. He's a bastard. You will. You know.

MILES: Angus. Do you know what I am? I'm an actor. I play at things. I was playing Morgan when you saw me. But he's here. He's right there, and he can tell you.

ANGUS: He lied. I remember you.

MILES: Listen to me. Do you know what I did? Just now? I was out in the barn, pretending to be a farmer. All those cows were in agony, they were all begging to be milked, and do you know what I did? I broke the milking machine. I hooked it up to Daisy and switched it on, and she groaned, and then the whole thing stopped. I broke it. I don't know what I'm doing, Angus. Let Morgan tell you.

ANGUS: You broke the milking machine?

MILES: Yes.

ANGUS: Oh boy.

MORGAN (*simultaneous with the above*): Aw, Jesus.

MILES: Sorry. You were right. But you don't need to rush out there. Daisy's okay. They're all okay. I milked them by hand.

MORGAN: You milked nine cows by hand?

MILES: Well, a little bit each. Just to take the pressure off. I was standing there amid all these weeping cows. I had to do something. I just sat down, grabbed hold, and got the hang of it pretty fast. I just went from cow to cow, one after another —grab, milk, grab, milk, grab, milk, grab, milk.... Suddenly, I looked up, and it was done.

MORGAN: What'd you do when the bucket got full?

MILES: You're supposed to use a bucket?

ANGUS: Oh boy.

MILES: I've got to go. I've got rehearsal....

ANGUS: No! Tell it.

MORGAN: I am. I will.

ANGUS: No. Him.

MILES: Angus, no.

ANGUS: Okay. Both of you. Tell it.

MORGAN: I will, but not with him here.

ANGUS: Yes, with him here. I'm scared. You're scaring me, yuh bastard. From the start. Both of you.

MORGAN: Angus, don't—

ANGUS: BOTH OF YOU. Please. So I can match them. Find me in them. I'm starved to know.

MORGAN: Alright.

ANGUS: Right. Go. You start.

MILES: Okay.

ANGUS: But, as him.

MILES: Right.

ANGUS: Like you did, on the... thing.

MILES: I got it. (*As MORGAN*) A couple of boys played shinney, and went to school, and grew up.

ANGUS: Now you.

MORGAN: They built—

ANGUS: But, as you.

MORGAN: —we built a cabin together. You dreamed it up, I did all the work.

MILES: Stole nails, and played hookey, and built a cabin. From the drawer boy's pictures.

MORGAN: You were about to go to university. I talked you out of it.

The war started, and I talked you into volunteering with me. It was going to be an adventure. We were so excited. No. I was excited, and you were—you were my friend. We joined up. As soon as we got over there, we were at an air field, and we saw something. A stupid accident during training. Do you remember?

ANGUS: I . . .

MORGAN: We watched three men burn to death. We couldn't help. It was awful. And then the only thing we did was survive. We never volunteered for anything, we hid when things got bad. We'd use up ammunition by shooting straight up.

MILES: Then, they met two girls. One tall, and one taller. The taller one liked the drawer, the tall one, the farmer.

MORGAN: They agreed to marry us. They agreed to come home with us. They were friends, like we were friends. The four of us were together as much as possible. We would spend whole nights talking the four of us. You and Sally would take long walks and count the stars. She taught you how. She knew the names of stars, and how to cut the sky up into manageable pieces for counting. It was the first thing she gave you.

MILES: They made plans. By the time they were done talking, they had a picture of what they would do, like something the one boy would draw.

MORGAN: All we had to do was wait out our tour. All we had to do was keep hiding. Then, one night in an air raid, I sent you out, to get a bottle of brandy I left in Sally's car. We decided we wanted a drink. We were all together, we felt indestructible, because of—because of each other. Like the war was just a dream or something. You took a long time to come back. We made jokes about where you might be. I said to Sally, "He's found someone else."

MILES: The drawer boy was standing down the street, looking at a large house.

MORGAN: You were running like hell down the street, trying to get back. Jesus. You were laughing.

MILES: The front door of the house flew off when the shell hit, and the drawer boy watched it come for him.

MORGAN: A piece of shrapnel caught you from behind. I watched you get carried through the air. You flew right at me. You nearly died. But you didn't. You woke up. But your memory was . . . gone. We came home. They came with us. There was no double wedding. Sally wanted to wait. Until you were better.

ANGUS: But—the stolen poem . . .

MORGAN: You never said it. You've been waiting to say it.

We bought this land. We lived here, in the house that came with the land, English girls in one room, us in the other. The house you designed was never started. We tacked the plans up over there (*indicates the spot where* ANGUS *looks first when he's searching*), so that we could see every day what we intended to do. Eventually, they became just a . . . reminder. So, one day when you were asleep, when I thought you were asleep, I took them down and I hid them. We did buy an old car, so they could go into town. They were lonely. The car didn't help much.

Sally looked after you. She stayed by you all the time, every minute. She watched you wander off, she'd follow behind, hiding behind trees so you wouldn't see. You'd get lost, she'd be there, and she'd bring you back home. She'd clean you. She'd feed you. She gave you medicine from a spoon.

You kept having headaches. They made you different, Angus. They made you mean. Because she was always there, you'd get mean at Sally.

ANGUS (*to himself*): At Sally.

MORGAN: One day, she was very tired. It was hot, hot like they'd never felt at home. You had another headache. Sally was cooking, baking bread, and you came up to her, and without saying a thing, you hit her. She cried and cried; she wasn't hurt much, but she was tired. You looked at her, and then you had to ask me who that crying girl was. And it was then that Sally decided to leave.

ANGUS: Your Frances . . . ?

MORGAN: They were friends. They were here alone.

The day they went, they called a taxi from town. You were asleep. I was here (*in the kitchen doorway*), I couldn't move. The taxi came, and I went to help Frances with her suitcase, and she said, "This is the worst thing I could do to you. Don't you dare help me do it." She dragged it outside and snarled at the taxi driver when he tried to help her. She was crying from the effort of it. The suitcase made a little trench across the driveway where she dragged it. They got in the taxi. They left. I've not heard a word from her in all this time. When you woke up—

ANGUS: No.

MORGAN: When you woke up, you knew something was wrong. You went into their room. Looked in the closet, looked under the bed. Tore the room apart. You didn't know what you were looking for. You went through all the rooms, looking, and when you had searched the whole house, you started again. You tore through the house, faster and faster— you wouldn't stop, Angus, and you couldn't say what you were looking for. Finally, when you were racing up the stairs to start over again, I tackled you. I hauled you down, and we sat on the stairs, and I told you the lie. I told you the story of the black car crashing for the first time. I told it again, and you stopped crying. I told it again, and you fell asleep. I kept telling it 'cause it made you feel better. Goddamn it, it made me feel better. *Pause.*

ANGUS: I hit my Sally, and you lost your...

MORGAN: Yes.

ANGUS: That's what I did to you. God, you must hate me.

MORGAN: I guess I did, Angus.

ANGUS: So. That's me. I'm scared I'll forget *that* now.

MORGAN: We'll tell it to each other. Daily.

ANGUS: Okay. Thank you.

MORGAN: We'll fill it all in. If you can remember, we'll do that.

ANGUS: Even if I don't. Let's do that.

MORGAN: Okay.

ANGUS (*to* MILES): He was right. You are the man who did this to me.

MILES: I'm late. I should go.

ANGUS: Go?

MILES: I have to go to work. To rehearse.

ANGUS: Yes. You're making a...

MILES: That's right.

ANGUS: Miles? That was just a story.

MILES: I know.

ANGUS: No, I mean—you can use it if you want.

MILES: Thanks. But—thanks.
MILES takes his notebook out of his pocket, hands it to MORGAN, then leaves.

ANGUS: That was Miles. He's here staying with you and me while he puts on a play about farming. You told him awful stories.

MORGAN: Yes.

ANGUS: And you're Morgan.

MORGAN: Yes. And you're Angus.

ANGUS: You carried me—and all that—around all this time? Since the taxi went?

MORGAN: Yes.

ANGUS: Must be tired. I'll make you a sandwich. Or—here—someone made this one already.

MORGAN: Thanks. I'd better go outside and see what he's done to the barn. *MORGAN exits.*

ANGUS: "God with honour hang your head,
Groom, and grace you bride, your bed
With lissome scions, sweet scions,
Out of hallowed bodies bred.
Each be other's comfort kind:
Deep, deeper than divined..."

MORGAN (*from off*): Angus! The bulk cooler's full of milk! He used the milking machine after all. He was—he was lying to us, the silly bugger!

ANGUS: "...Divine charity, dear charity,
Fast you ever, fast bind.
"Then let the march tread our ears:
I to him turn with tears
Who to wedlock, his wonder wedlock,
Deals triumph and immortal years."
As the lights fade, ANGUS *takes the drawings and holds them up where they used to live.*

The End.

❦ Michael Healey's works have been much lauded and widely received throughout Canada. His first play, *Kicked,* was nominated for a Chalmers Award and won a Dora for Best New Play (1998). He often works with Jason Sherman, another Toronto-based actor/writer, and was nominated for another Dora for his role as Nathan in Sherman's *League of Nathans. The Drawer Boy* (1999) has been played in eight provinces across Canada.

RESPONDING

Meaning

1. Speaking about the relationship of the two friends in the play, Healey said, "They need each other to do certain things. They also need each other not to do certain things." Explain what you think Healey meant by this.

2. A reviewer suggested that the central themes of the play were appropriation and theatre-as-self-discovery. In a short piece of writing, comment on how this play presents each of these themes.

Form and Style

3. Storytelling and role-play are essential elements in the play's structure.
    a) Identify the various points in the play where stories are told and analyze their importance to the development of the drama.
    b) Consider how the characters are affected by the performances they witness and explain the purpose of role-playing in this drama.
    c) What are some other plays in which role-playing is an important device? How does the use of role-play in other plays compare with its use in *The Drawer Boy?*

4. Healey uses the clash between rural and urban culture to create humour in his play. Identify specific examples from the text that illustrate this humour and comment on their effectiveness.

Exploring Context

5. Explain why this play has been so successful in crossing cultural barriers, appealing to urban as well as rural audiences.

Creative Extension

6. From within your community, interview someone who might have a unique and interesting story to tell. Retell the story you hear and consider the impact of your storytelling both on you as the storyteller and on your audience.

7. Script a scene from a parallel drama in which Sally and Francis respond to the episode of leaving the farm and the two friends. If possible, stage your scene or record it on videotape to share with other groups.

The Farm Show

ε∫   *A Theatre Passe Muraille Company Creation*

This excerpt, from a production called "The Farm Show," suggests one way in which artists can find truth and authenticity through role-playing.

Introduction

"This is a record of our version of 'grass roots' theatre. The idea was to take a group of actors out to a farming community and build a play out of what we could see and learn. There is no 'story' or 'plot' as such. The form of the play is more like a Canadian Sunday School or Christmas Concert where one person does a recitation, another sings a song, a third acts out a skit, etc. Nevertheless, we hope that you can see many stories woven into the themes of this play and that out if it will emerge a picture of a complex and living community.

"The play was not written down, but developed out of interviews, visits, and improvisations. Most of the words used were given to us by the community, along with their stories. We spent a great deal of our time trying to imitate these people both in the way they move and the way they speak. We wanted to capture the fibre of what they are and this seemed the best way to do it. In any case, it taught us to watch and listen. I'm not sure how much of this will come through the printed word."

—Paul Thompson, Artistic Director

Opening Scene and Speech

One of the more easy-going members of the cast is present on stage for about half an hour before the show begins, helping people find seats, talking to them, or, especially when the show is on tour through rural areas, listening to the fiddle music or country music frequently supplied by local musicians. During the last ten minutes or so the other members of the cast gradually move on stage and take up their positions sitting on the bales, waiting for the signal to start and the introduction by one of the cast, which takes various forms, but, when playing to city audiences, goes something like this:

Last summer we visited a farming community near Clinton, Ontario. Clinton is about a hundred and twenty miles due west of Toronto. You go down near Kitchener and then take the number eight highway to Stratford, Mitchell, Seaforth, *Clinton*. Which would be right about here *(just off front stage left)* if it were on this map.

It's a nice town of about three thousand, but people blast on through it along the number eight, past the village of Holmesville and on up to

Goderich (*just off the front of stage right*). Because Goderich is on Lake Huron, it's the county seat, and that's where the tourists want to get to.

Now, beside the number eight highway is the community we lived in. This map (*marked on raked stage*) shows the roads and the names of the different farmers in the area.

We lived there for about six weeks and put this show on for the people there. They seemed to enjoy it, so we brought it back to see if we could brighten up the dull lives of the people who live in Toronto.

Picture Frame

HUSBAND: This farm has been in our family for a long time now. I think it was my grandfather who came over from England and bought a lot of eighty acres along the Maitland in the 1860s. My cousin is making up a book . . .

WIFE: There's a picture in there of the log cabin they built.

HUSBAND: They had to pull the cedars out of the swamp and without machinery they had to . . .

FIRST GIRL: (*Moves out of frame. Others freeze.*) I just finished my Grade Thirteen and I decided I don't want to go to university. I've got a job in London working for an insurance company, London Life. I'm sharing an apartment with a couple of friends of mine. I'm really looking forward to it because I've never lived off the farm before. I don't know if I'll come back to the farm again or not.

HUSBAND: This stone house you're looking at our grandfather built. We put in the plumbing and the electricity.

WIFE: Oh you wouldn't know the dampness of it now, not with the way he's fixed it up with the wood panelling and all.

SECOND GIRL: (*Moves out of frame. Freeze.*) Several years ago, I met a boy and we decided we wanted to get married. Well, my parents didn't like him and we fought, and I left home. We're living in Toronto now and I haven't been back for almost two years.

HUSBAND: We've added a lot of land, we've gone more into livestock than my father did.

WIFE: I have my own source of income from the chickens . . .

HUSBAND: Oh yeah, of course with the machinery what it is now I don't think . . .

BOY: (*Moves out of frame. Freeze.*) I managed, gee I don't know how, to get a scholarship to study English at university and I'm going to get my degree and I'm going to be a teacher. I'd like to go out West to teach. Hope my father understands.

HUSBAND: The kids today don't want to work hard and it is hard work.

Then they've got the TV and everything telling them how they can live in the city and make a lot of money.

WIFE: Oh, they'll work. But even if they did want to buy the farm, we'd be dead by the time they got enough money. Oh yes, of course, you know, it's not easy, you can't just hand your farm down to your children. There's taxes to pay, and the government . . .

HUSBAND: Succession taxes and the forms that they make you fill out make it very difficult . . .

WIFE: I think farming is the best of both worlds though. You can go into town when you want and . . .

(Cut off by auctioneer. Freeze.)

AUCTIONEER: Now, let's see what we have here. Oh yes, we have a nice picture, with a nice handcrafted picture frame. And well, if you don't like the picture you can cut it out, put in your own, and it would look good against anybody's wall. Well, what do you give me to start it off? Anybody give me a five . . . ? I got two, two, two—give me a half, got a half, half, half. Give me three, three, three, got three, three, three, give me a half? A half? Give me three and a half, give me four, four, four, give me five!

The girls who left the picture frame have been bidding as women in the audience.

OK lady. You bought it! Take it away.

❧ "The Farm Show" was the most popular of Theatre Passe Muraille's "collective creations" and was a runner-up for the Chalmers Award in 1972. The production was described as "a tribute to rural life today." A television version was broadcast on the CBC and a documentary film by Michael Ondaatje entitled "The Clinton Special" showed the play being prepared and performed by rural people.

Connecting

1. Artistic director Paul Thompson says in his introduction to "The Farm Show," "we hope that you can see many stories woven into the themes of this play." Explain how "The Picture Frame" both tells a story and serves to illustrate a theme.

2. How do the dramatic structures of these two scenes differ from scenes in a traditional play?

3. The late Urjo Kareda, while drama critic for *The Toronto Star*, wrote, "A collective creation is a play made communally by a group of actors, a director and a designer, as well as perhaps—and only perhaps—a writer. On the baldest level, it's a play prepared without the benefit of a script written in advance, a play for which the actors write their own roles from material they have gathered themselves. . . . For Paul Thompson and those who work with him, the collective creation is more than a technique. It is both a means of approaching the theatre and a means of approaching the Canadian experience itself."

   Discuss with a small group whether or not the collective creation approach taken for "The Farm Show" produces an authentic representation of the Canadian experience. Support your opinions by referring to this script and the text of *The Drawer Boy*.

Two Paintings

The following two paintings illustrate how visual artists use their art to provoke new ways of thinking, to celebrate the culture and history of their people, and to empower their audiences.

Pow Wow Dream

ᕫ *Joane Cardinal-Schubert*

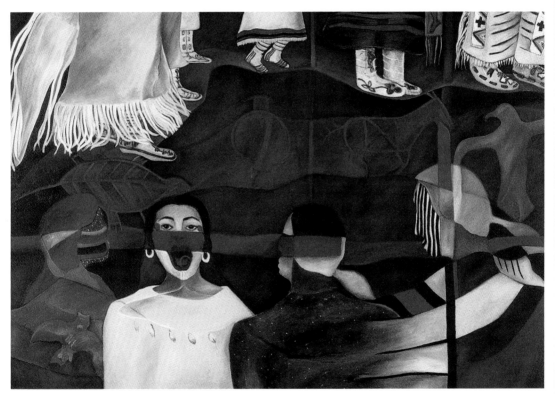

Joane Cardinal-Schubert, RCA, *Pow Wow Dream*, 1992, acrylic on canvas, 121.92 cm x 182.88 cm. Reproduced by permission of the artist.

Patio De Fiestas

Diego Rivera

ECHO

❧ Contemporary artist Joane Cardinal-Schubert uses images from her Aboriginal heritage to express both a personal and universal message. Many of her works are concerned with memory, Aboriginal history, and social injustice. Her art attempts to express connection in a chaotic world that has lost respect for nature and its past. *(Born Red Deer, Alberta 1942)* Diego Rivera received many public commissions during his career to paint murals on the theme of the Mexican revolution. He studied in both Mexico and Europe and established himself as a pupil of post-modernism and cubism. He painted both murals and canvases to display his brightly coloured visions and social commentary. *(Born Guanajuato, Mexico 1886; died 1957)*

Connecting

1. a) Look carefully at the paintings. What strikes you first about the paintings? What other key features do you notice? What do you think each artist wanted you to see?
    b) What story do the pictures tell?
    c) What feelings do the pictures evoke?
    d) Do these pictures remind you of anything? Explain.
    Compare your responses with those of a partner. Consider what factors influence the varying responses individuals might have to a work of art.

2. With your partner, discuss Rivera's choice of colour and use of line in the painting. What effects do they create? Comment on the use of images and colour in Cardinal-Schubert's painting.

3. Influenced by the Mexican Revolution (1914–15) and the Russian Revolution (1917), Rivera believed that art should play a role in empowering working people by giving them an understanding of their own social and cultural history. By painting murals on the walls of public buildings, Rivera made his work accessible to the people. Comment on how looking at these paintings and knowing more about class history might empower a Mexican worker. How have contemporary Aboriginal artists accomplished a similar goal?

Two Poems

The following poems offer two further perspectives on the power of art to change our lives or to reveal truths about ourselves. The first selection is an excerpt from Wallace Stevens's long poem "The Man with the Blue Guitar" originally published in 1937. The second poem is by a contemporary poet, Rhona McAdam.

The Man with the Blue Guitar

❧ *Wallace Stevens*

I

The man bent over his guitar,
A shearsman of sorts. The day was green.

They said, "You have a blue guitar,
You do not play things as they are."

The man replied, "Things as they are
Are changed upon the blue guitar."

And they said then, "But play, you must,
A tune beyond us, yet ourselves,

A tune upon the blue guitar
Of things exactly as they are."

Coat of Many Poems

Rhona McAdam

She has hung him
round with lovely words,
made him
an admirable piece of work,

He doesn't need to say
anything. She is not even sure
if he is still there
beneath the weight
of decoration.

She listens
but hears nothing.
He has made tracks
beyond the reach of artifice.
He is doing fine
without rhyme and image and she
has his beautiful shell.

ᔓ In his poetry, Wallace Stevens tried to reconcile the products of imagination with reality. He wrote many poetry collections, and the well-known poem "The Man with the Blue Guitar" was the title piece for a collection published in 1937. Stevens's *Collected Poems* (1954) won him a Pulitzer Prize. (*Born Pennsylvania 1879; died 1955*) Rhona McAdam lived on Vancouver Island and in Edmonton, Alberta, before moving to London, England, in 1990. She has worked as an information technology trainer, as well as a technical author. She won the Alberta Poetry Award for her collection of poems *Hour of the Pearl* (1987). "Coat of Many Poems" appeared in *Creating the Country* (1989). (*Born Duncan, British Columbia 1957*)

Connecting

1. It has been said that, in his poem, Wallace Stevens puts words to Picasso's belief that "art is the lie to help us see the truth." Explain how the poem supports Picasso's belief. Justify your answer by referring to specific lines from the text.
2. a) Explain who you think the "he" is in McAdam's poem. Who is "she"?
    b) What is the significance of the lines "He has made tracks / beyond the reach of artifice"?
3. In your own words, explain what both writers are saying about art in these poems. Compare their message with that of another writer or painter in this Echo.

☐ REFLECTING ON THE ECHO

1. Select one of the following quotations and write an essay explaining how one of the selections in the Echo does or does not support the quote.

    "Art is coming face to face with yourself."
        Jackson Pollock

    "The task which the artist implicitly sets himself, is to overthrow existing values, to make of the chaos about him an order which is his own, to sow strife and ferment, so that by the emotional release those who are dead may be restored to life."
        Henry Miller

    "The subject matter of art is life, life as it actually is; but the function of art is to make life better."
        George Santayana

2. Identify a work of art that for you holds a personal connection or significance. Reflect in a letter to a friend or in a journal why you think this particular work is important to you.
3. Conduct a formal debate based on the resolution: An artist can never know the measure of his or her success.

ECHO

Snapshots

ᔪ Gordon Pengilly

A THIRTY-FIVE YEAR OLD MAN WEARING A DETROIT RED WINGS HOCKEY SWEATER, ADDRESSES THE AUDIENCE. THE SNAPSHOTS HE SHOWS TO US ARE ALL LIFE-SIZED AND ALL BLACK AND WHITE EXCEPT FOR THE VERY LAST ONE. BY THE END OF THE PERFORMANCE HE'LL BE SURROUNDED BY THEM.

MAN

A snapshot, in hockey, not to be confused with a slapshot or wristshot, is the quickest of releases in the shooter's repertoire. It is a shot in front of the body without pulling the puck back to the feet (as in a wristshot) and by flicking the blade of the stick at the puck using only the wrists. The release minimizes preparation and follow-through and is handy in tight situations around the net.

A snapshot is also another word for photograph, of course, a moment of joy or calamity or some other kind of incident or portrait frozen in time.

I haven't laced on a pair of skates for years.

This is a snapshot of my two sons in their green and white hockey uniforms. The Bisons. The taller one is Rob and the shorter one is Ray. Ray, though smaller, is actually older than Rob by a year and a half. He plays on defence. He's toughnosed, secure in himself. Has a good low shot from the point. As far as kids go he's pretty quiet. Still waters run deep, my mom used to say. When you talk to him he looks you square in the eye. Rob is a forward. Excellent skater, puck handler, goal scorer. To try and put a bodycheck on him is like trying to put a bodycheck on a string, as some sage defenceman once said of Wayne Gretzky. When you talk to him his eyes are all over the room. Scanning the room for a new distraction or escape. And he's a chatter box. Their both great kids—my sons—and I'd always be there for them.

This is a snapshot of my wife Melanie, in our backyard, standing in her flower garden. She works hard at her garden, she's very proud of it. She works hard at everything she does and she loves to succeed. She has high standards, high expectations. I can see her in both of our sons in different proportions. Different arrangements of both of us in both of them. Melanie is a very good mother. Very good hockey mom.

And I'm the hockey dad. Or I was. I'm currently under suspension. Family matter.

This is a snapshot of my office away from the house. There is my bookshelf, my desk, my computer. The snapshots of my kids in their hockey uniforms and my wife in her flower garden sit on my desk. In the background you can see my old blue sofa. It was the sofa Melanie and I bought at a second-hand store after we got married. I moved it here after we bought our new one. It's kind of ugly but it's still in good shape.

I'm sleeping on it.

Melanie asked me to leave five days ago. To sleep on it. She asked me not to come home until I've slept on it sufficiently. To dwell on my gambling problem. Those bloody VLTs. They're eating me alive.

We tell the boys that their dad needs to be alone for a while to take a good look at himself. How long is a while Ray asks. Melanie and I look at each other and Melanie says a few days. Then Rob asks if I'm still going to go to their games. Melanie says ask your dad and I say not for a while. We'd anticipated both questions and still answered them poorly. It was the hardest day of my life.

This is a snapshot of me and the boys playing hockey on the street in front of our house last summer.

These are my fingers clawing at my scalp while gazing at that snapshot. I'm on the outside looking in tonight and it's killing me inside.

I don't know how it all began. Or especially why. Melanie says I'll never really know until I get some help about it. See a counsellor. She's right. I know she's right. I just haven't come out and admitted it yet. I'm still sleeping on it. I'm waiting for something else to happen, for something reflexive or pure or wiser than me to jump over the boards and save me. With minimum preparation. And a quick release.

My little office away from home is just down the street from the Lord Nelson Tavern. They have big screen there. I used to meet with my buddies after work to have a few beers and watch a hockey game. That was before they got those bloody VLTs in there. Before I got hooked. This past year or so I've been sitting in there by myself. Watching the fruit jump. Without my buddies. They've tired of me, too.

It was my turn to take the boys to their game. Melanie had something on with one of her girlfriends and she had to be free to go by a certain time. I stopped off at the Nelson for a quick beer and a few quick coins in the fruit machine. The machine was hot. I went up two hundred. Time flew.

I drove like a demon to get home. Got stopped by a cop. Got a two hundred dollar speeding ticket. And when I finally got home Melanie's car was gone and so were the boys. I went to the rink and told Melanie about getting stopped by the cop but she saw fruit jumping in my eyes and said she didn't want to sit with me. So I left the building. Went out.

This is a snapshot of me when I'm shaking hands with Gordie Howe. It's 1963 and he's in the prime of his career. He's just won the Canadian Athlete of the Year Award and he was doing a promotional tour at Eaton's in the sports department. The Great Gordie. Old Elbows, signing autographs. And me looking out through my shiny brown eyes from the depths of my innocent soul.

My dad took the snapshot. He said you walk right up to that big guy there and ask him to sign that picture. I had a hockey magazine with his picture on the cover. Detroit Red Wings. Number 9. Red and white home uniforms. He was skating with the puck behind the net with Carl Brewer chasing him. Johnny Bower stood in the net looking over his shoulder. Toronto Maple Leafs. Blue and white road uniforms. In 1963 we didn't have colour TV. When my Dad gave me that magazine for my birthday it was the first time I'd seen the colours of the uniforms of any NHL hockey players. Newspapers weren't in colour, I'd never been to a league game and didn't collect hockey cards yet. Sure I *knew* all the colours of the Original Six teams without the aid of coloured pictures but to actually see those colours was awesome to me.

Gordie was recovering from a wrist surgery in the off-season that year of my ninth birthday and as he stood in the sports department of Eaton's that day he was squeezing a rubber ball in his hand for therapy. That big infallible man with those incredible sloping shoulders. Squeezing the juice out of a little rubber ball.

What is the team colour of the Tampa Bay Lightning? I don't know. The Nashville Predators? Haven't a clue. What's the insignia of the Florida Panthers? A panther I'll wager but I don't have a clear image of it. As far as professional hockey goes I've been on the outside for quite a while now.

The colour of fruit. I know the colour of fruit.

This is a snapshot of me sitting in my car outside my office. I could go to the corner and turn left and drive to the rink to watch my boys play hockey tonight or I could turn right and go watch the fruit jump at the Lord Nelson Tavern. Or I could do both. That's been my problem though. *Trying* to do both. Being a husband and a father and being a problem gambler. Bad mix. I blame expansion. Thirty teams in the NHL is too many. The talent's been watered down, the intensity is gone, player-team allegiances have all but vanished. If I'm not mistaken, Yzerman and Mario are the only active players with more than ten years' experience who have toiled on one single team their entire careers. I used to love watching a game down at the Nelson with my buddies. Don't anymore. Stopped caring. I blame the expansion. I blame expansion for my gambling problem.

And you know what else? My boys don't collect hockey cards anymore. It's passé. Instead they download pictures and stories and stats off the Internet and produce their own magazines. Whole magazines! Thirty, forty pages worth! If you put them on a rack downtown somewhere you wouldn't know they weren't the real thing.

Technology, sloth, escalating salaries, stupid uniforms...

How could you love a team called the Mighty Ducks? I blame them for my sadness.

When I got home that night five nights ago to find that my wife and boys had gone to the rink without me I knew I'd been existing on borrowed time and I knew the collector was on his way.

The first night on the sofa in my office I imagine killing myself. They hold the funeral on the frozen pond on the farm where I was raised. I'm wearing my old Red Wing's sweater.

I cry myself to sleep.

I'm sitting in my car. I could go to the rink or I could go to the Nelson. I decide to go to the rink. Watch the boys play. Surprise everybody. Tell Melanie I've decided to see a counsellor about my problem. Go home after. Sleep in our own bed with the woman I love. My boys asleep down the hall.

I drive to the corner. I break into that greasy sweat I know so well. That nauseous feeling. Dizziness. Hands start to shake. Can't be seen in public like this. I need a quick fix.

When I was a kid, when I played hockey, I wasn't that tough and I wasn't that pretty to watch—but I was sneaky quick.

The Nelson is nearly empty this evening. Lyle Lovett is singing on the jukebox:

> Last night you know I couldn't sleep
> I was tossing, turning and counting sheep
> To tell the truth
> The next thing I knew
> I woke up on the outside
> In the middle of the avenue.

The waitress wears a Flame's sweater. She calls me by name. She goes for my beer and the mere sight of those sparkling monsters across the room begins to ease my pain. The effect is immediate, organic. My body moves towards them. I feel like I'm gliding on ice holding on to my father's coat. Except my father isn't there, and neither is his coat.

. . . I'll only play one roll of quarters then I'll go to the rink catch the last two periods see Melanie go home with my family to go to sleep get control of my life my life . . .

I'm having a weird dream. I'm playing hockey on the same team as my two boys. It occurs to me that Gordie Howe was the only hockey player to play on a professional team with his sons, Mark and Marty, with the Houston Aeros in the old WHA. Melanie is in the stands taking snapshots of us and I'm feeling really good about myself until I realize that I don't have any pants on. My sweater is just long enough to cover up my genitals and I convince myself that nobody will notice and the game goes on. I score a goal on a really pretty three-way passing play from Rob and Ray and the crowd goes crazy. I look up at the scoreboard and see that it's turned into a huge VLT. The fruit start to jump and I'm suddenly nauseous. I can barely move my legs but I make my way to the bench where I find out that Gordie Howe is our coach. He's staring at me and he's squeezing the juice out of a little red rubber ball. The juice is red, too, like blood, and I suddenly lose my stomach.

I wake up on the sofa in my own vomit. It's morning. I remember leaving my car in the parking lot behind the Nelson, too drunk to drive, after losing five hundred dollars to the fruit monster.

I imagine killing myself. And this time it scares the hell out of me.

> *Last night you know I couldn't sleep*
> *I was tossing, turning and counting sheep*
> *To tell the truth*
> *The next thing I knew...*

This is a snapshot of Dave. Dave is my counsellor. He's a recovering gambling addict, he's been clean for ten years. When he looks at me he looks right through me.

This is a snapshot of what he sees inside of me.

I haven't seen my boys play hockey for a month. I don't understand the inner-psychology behind it but I've been keeping myself from going to their games, even since I've come home. I tell myself I'll start being hockey dad again when I've earned it, when I've earned some self-respect.

Dave plays hockey with a group of guys every Friday night. I've joined up.

We're playing outside tonight and it's damn cold. My feet hurt, my chest aches, my face is burning up—I haven't felt this good for a long, long time. The stars are above and the ice is below...

I crash into the boards. The stars are now in my head. I get up again. I glance over and see Melanie and my two boys leaning on the outside of the boards looking in at me. I had no idea they were going to be here. They cheer for me. Melanie has a camera.

This is a snapshot of me shooting a snapshot. *He hits the goal post!* I love the sound that makes. You know the sound I mean. The ring of truth.

LIGHTS FADE TO BLACK

꿍 Award-winning playwright Gordon Pengilly lives in Alberta. He has been playwright in residence for several companies including Theatre Calgary, Theatre New Brunswick, and the Banff Centre for the Arts. Pengilly also writes for radio and is poetry editor for *Dandelion* magazine. His plays include *Swipe* (1981) and *Drumheller* (2000).

RESPONDING

Meaning

1. Explain how Pengilly connects the two meanings of the word "snapshot." Illustrate the connection with specific reference to the text.
2. "This is a snapshot of what he sees inside of me." What is the picture that he shows the audience at this point? What does it reveal about the speaker?

Form and Style

3. Pengilly uses the snapshots to frame his monologue. Make a list of all the snapshots he describes. Explain how the sequence of pictures structures his narrative over time. Why is the final picture in colour while all the others are in black and white?
4. What techniques does Pengilly use to make the monologue conversational in tone?

Exploring Context

5. Pengilly titles his work, "a candid portrayal about addiction and hockey." How is this piece about both addiction and hockey?

Creative Extension

6. Using the Internet and other sources, research gambling addiction. Present your findings in an oral report.
7. Put yourself in the role of the production designer for this monologue. Create a sketchbook of abstract or representative designs that could be used in place of the traditional snapshots suggested in the text. Provide a brief written commentary on why you have designed each image as you have.

The Search for Signs of Intelligent Life in the Universe

ᔓ Written by Jane Wagner
Performed and co-produced by Lily Tomlin

TRUDY

Frankly, infinity doesn't affect me personally one way or the other.

You think too long about infinity, you could go stark raving mad.
But I don't ever want to sound negative about going crazy.
I don't want to overromanticize it either, but frankly,
goin' crazy was the *best* thing ever happened to me.
I don't say it's for everybody;
some people couldn't cope.

But for me it came at a time when nothing else seemed to be
working. I got the kind of madness Socrates talked about,
"A divine release of the soul from the yoke of
custom and convention." I refuse to be intimidated by
reality anymore.
After all, what is reality anyway? Nothin' but a
collective hunch. My space chums think reality was once a
primitive method of
crowd control that got out of hand.
In my view, it's absurdity dressed up
in a three-piece business suit.

I made some studies, and
reality is the leading cause of stress amongst those in
touch with it. I can take it in small doses, but as a lifestyle
I found it too confining.
It was just too needful;
it expected me to be there for it *all* the time, and with all
I have to do—
I had to let something go.

Now, since I put reality on a back burner, my days are
jam-packed and fun-filled. Like some days, I go hang out
around Seventh Avenue; I love to do this old joke:
I wait for some music-loving tourist from one of the hotels
on Central Park to go up and ask someone,
"How do I get to Carnegie Hall?"
Then I run up and yell,
"Practise!"
The expression on people's faces is priceless. I never
could've done stuff like that when I was in my *right* mind.
I'd be worried people would think I was *crazy.*
When I think of the fun I missed,
I try not to be bitter.

See, the human mind is kind of like . . .

a piñata. When it breaks open,
there's a lot of surprises inside. Once you get the piñata
perspective, you see that losing your mind
can be a peak experience.

I was not always a bag lady, you know.
I used to be a designer and creative consultant. For big
companies!
Who do you think thought up the colour scheme
for Howard Johnson's?
At the time, nobody was using
orange and aqua
in the same room together.
With fried clams.

Laugh tracks:
I gave TV sitcoms the idea for canned laughter.
I got the idea, one day I heard voices
and no one was there.

Who do you think had the idea to package panty hose
in a plastic goose egg?

One thing I personally don't like about panty hose:
When you roll 'em down to the ankles the way I like 'em, you
can't walk too good. People seem amused, so what's a little
loss of dignity? You got to admit:
It's a look!

The only idea I'm proud of—

my umbrella hat. Protects against sunstroke, rain and
muggers. For *some* reason, muggers steer clear of people
wearing umbrella hats.

So it should come as no shock . . . I am now creative consultant to
these aliens from outer space. They're a kinda cosmic
fact-finding committee. Amongst other projects, they've been
searching all over for Signs of Intelligent Life.

It's a lot trickier than it sounds.

ᔓ   Jane Wagner is a playwright, writer of screenplays and teleplays, designer, and producer.
The Search for Signs of Intelligent Life in the Universe (1986) won both a New York Drama
Desk Award for "Unique Theatrical Experience" and a New York Drama Critics' Circle
award. Her teleplay *J.T.* won a Peabody Award. She has collaborated on several projects
with Lily Tomlin. Lily Tomlin has created a multitude of memorable comic characters for
television, stage shows, films, and Broadway. She was a regular on the television series
Laugh-In between 1970 and 1973, as well as the series *Murphy Brown* with Candice Bergen
in 1996. She won an Oscar nomination as "Best Supporting Actress" for her role in the
movie *Nashville* (1975). (*Jane Wagner born Tennessee 1935; Lily Tomlin born Michigan 1939*)

RESPONDING

Meaning

1. What do you know about Trudy from what she says? What do you know about her from
    what is not said? Write a character sketch of her using both explicit and implicit infor-
    mation to support your view.
2. What is the nature of the social commentary made through this monologue? Support your
    answer with specific references to the text.

Form and Style

3. *Structural irony* involves the use of a naïve or deluded hero or unreliable narrator, whose view of the world differs widely from the true circumstances recognized by the author and readers. Explain whether or not you feel that Trudy's monologue is an example of structural irony.

4. Describe the *tone* of this monologue. How does the author create this tone?

Exploring Context

5. A reviewer of the play *The Search for Signs of Intelligent Life in the Universe* wrote: "What Oscar Wilde, at his best, did for witty epigram, Jane Wagner does for the ironic observation, the simple statement made out of context, and the scrambled truth which, suddenly and with great force, makes more sense than it ever did before."

    Find an example from the monologue of "an ironic observation," "a statement made out of context," or "a scrambled truth" that rings true for you. Explain why you find it particularly effective.

Creative Extension

6. *The Search for Signs of Intelligent Life in the Universe* was a one-woman show in which Lily Tomlin played several diverse characters. Research the play. Choose another character and compare that role with the role of Trudy. What social commentary does each offer?

7. Assume the role of a newspaper columnist who interviews Trudy for a series of articles on "The Urban Dispossessed." Write the article that would appear in your column following the interview.

Short Fiction

Isabel Allende on short fiction:

There is something magic in . . . storytelling. You tap into another world. The story becomes whole when you tap into the collective story, when other people's stories become part of the writing, and you know that it's not your story only. I have a feeling that I don't invent anything. That somehow I discover things that are in another dimension. That they are already there, and my job is to find them and bring them to the page.

The Allure of "the Other"

Why are we both fascinated and frightened by "otherness"?

What draws us to different places, to people who are not like us, to different cultures and worlds? Is it our fear of being "the isolate" that fosters a desire to belong? Is it a desire to experience that from which we feel excluded? Or, is it a need for human connection that drives us to want to feel one with the world? In this Echo section, a short story, two paintings, a poem, and an essay allow us to examine "otherness" and why it both frightens and fascinates us.

Learning Goals

- examine a theme from different perspectives
- analyze how difference in genres, forms, styles, and media contribute to meaning
- create original texts in response to a variety of works

Going to the Moon

ᕫ *Nino Ricci*

In this selection, Nino Ricci tells the story of a young boy who feels isolated and like an interloper in his world. He dreams of other worlds and other places, but the promise they hold is not always as he dreamed.

Windsor seemed a kind of purgatory to me, a temporary stop between whatever hell my parents had left behind in Italy and the vague promise of the skyline that opened up beyond the Detroit River. In winter that skyline's tall buildings stood unnaturally still and crisp in the cold air, on the verge, it seemed, of singing; in summer they shimmered and burned in the heat and smog. But always they had a strange, unreal quality, at once both toy-like and profound, as if my eyes could not believe their own power to hold so much in a glance.

My great-uncle Bert had come over before the war, smuggling himself into Canada after he'd been turned away at New York and then working his way on road crews up the St. Lawrence and along the Great Lakes till he'd arrived finally in Windsor. "I stopped here because it was so close to the border," he said. "In those days there were people who would take you across the river at night, in little boats. But by the time I had enough money to pay them, well, I got lazy."

Uncle Bert had shown me a picture once of the tiny room at the back of his old shoe-repair shop on Erie Street where he'd lived alone for twenty years, a room as grey and bare and gloomy as a prison cell. It seemed astonishing to me that he'd done that, that in all his years in Windsor he'd never so much as set foot in America, though its image had loomed over him daily, close enough to throw a stone at; and astonishing that we had all ended up in Windsor on account of him, family after family, aunts and uncles and cousins, stuck there in our narrow brown brick houses out of sheer inertia, like Dorothy falling asleep on the road to Emerald City. When my parents told stories about Italy they always talked about *miseria,* a word that meant "poverty" but that conjured up in my anglicized mind images of vague tortures and chastisements; though according to my mother we were poor in Canada as well, owed thousands of dollars to the bank for our house, which was why she and my father both worked their long odd hours, my father at the Chrysler plant or in his basement workshop, building cabinets and tables he sold for extra money, his face always puckered as he worked as if he had just swallowed something sour, and my mother at different places, sometimes at a butcher's shop and sometimes cleaning houses and sometimes picking beans or tobacco on the farms outside Windsor.

My father had built a second kitchen in our basement, our upstairs kitchen too small to eat in comfortably and our dining room, with its heavy polished wood table, reserved for when we had special company, a non-Italian or someone from out of town. Whenever my uncle Mike came in from Ohio my mother made it seem as if eating in the upstairs dining room was something we did every day, putting on a new, strange, friendly personality then, talking to Uncle Mike and his American wife in English and letting their kids call her Aunt Tony instead of Zia Antonia; but normally she guarded the dining room like an avenging angel, keeping the doors that led into it perpetually closed and forever warning my brother Joe and me never to set foot in it while she was away at work. A tall china cabinet stood in one corner, housing small arrangements of silverware and copper pots that emerged from behind their glass doors only for their monthly cleaning; and on the cabinet's top, underneath a clear glass dome, sat a golden pendulum clock which my mother wound every Sunday after church with a special key, bringing an old chair in from the kitchen to reach it and setting aside its dome with a tenderness that seemed oddly out of keeping with the work-swollen ruddiness of her hands, with the hard set of her shoulders and chin. Two copper mementos, of John Kennedy and Pope John XXIII, hung on the far wall, and velour curtains covered the window; but the room's gloomy elegance made it seem sad somehow, as if it knew that it didn't belong to the rest of the house, its only purpose to remind us of the things that were forbidden to us.

Joe and I attended school at Assumption Separate. Before I started there I had looked up to Joe, because he was six years older and had his own paper route; but at school he seemed diminished, some of the older English boys calling him Mustasho because of the dark hairs that had begun to sprout on his upper lip. When the boys began to pick on me as well, Joe muttered insults at them; but I saw from the dark look that crossed his face then, and from the unthinking grimace he made when he found me waiting for him at the school entranceway at the end of the day, that it humiliated him to have a younger brother, to be made more conspicuous by my presence beside him, and I had the sense that we were both of us merely interlopers at school, moving uncertainly through a world that refused to admit us, that we had to hide ourselves within like animals changing the colour of their fur to fit into a landscape.

But each morning when my class filed into the grade one classroom and I saw again the varnished desktops, the polished floors, the multicoloured alphabet that ran across the tops of the blackboards, I felt the small bright hope that my life could be different, that the things that marked me out could be erased, a hope made urgent, desperate, by the love that I felt for our teacher Miss Johnson. Miss Johnson was one of the few lay teachers at Assumption, and she stood out from the stiff formality of the priests and nuns like a burst of colour in a grey landscape, coming to school in lipstick and high heels, in dress suits with trim vests and jackets, in blouses of shimmering silk, and leaving behind a fragrance of herself when she passed our desks that lingered like a spirit; and we were all in love with her, proudly, self-importantly, all hoped to be chosen by her to wipe the blackboards or fetch chalk from the storeroom. I felt protected in that common love, in the importance I gained in sharing it, as if I'd been included in a game that could have no losers, no chance for ridicule or shame. Once near the beginning of the year Miss Johnson picked me out to stay in at recess to help her with a bulletin board, and while she stood shoeless on the seat of a desk, reaching down a braceleted arm for the pictures and pins I was to hand to her, she began to hum some song softly to herself as if she had forgotten that I was standing there beneath her; and it made me feel oddly relieved to be taken for granted like that, to have been drawn unthinkingly into the small private sphere of Miss Johnson's aloneness as if there were nothing strange or remarkable about me.

During first term Miss Johnson taught us about stars and planets. Every day she set some new vision before us like a brightly wrapped gift, brought in pictures and models of our solar system, read us stories about space travel and distant life. When we had learned to write she had us each compose in our careful inch-high letters a question to the astronauts at NASA, stuffing all of them afterwards into a large brown envelope; and a few weeks later, as if we had sent out like Noah a messenger who returned now with proof of a world that existed outside our own, a large packet arrived for us from NASA filled with brochures and posters and satellite photographs, so that while all the other classes in the school were doing up bulletin boards about Advent or All Saints' Day or the next year's Centennial, our own boards were filled with images of space, our prized centrepieces a foldout of an Apollo rocket and a poster-sized photo of the moon's Sea of Tranquillity.

One afternoon for art Miss Johnson had us push all our desks to the sides of the classroom and then covered the floor with two adjoining lengths of newsprint, shimmying along them in stockinged feet to join them together with long strips of masking tape. We spent the rest of that afternoon on hands and knees, paint trays and brushes and jars full of tinted water spread out on the floor around us as each of us, assigned to our own little squares of terrain on the newsprint, painted out our private versions of a lunar landscape. We ended up with a great hodgepodge of strange forms, green mountains vying with eerie yellow cities, four-armed monsters perched over ocean-filled craters, and in one corner Miss Johnson's own contribution, two bubble-headed astronauts looking out over the whole scene with expressions of alarm. When the paint had dried we folded our landscape at the seams, rolled it up, and deposited it at the back of our cloakroom; but thereafter, whenever rain kept us inside for recess or we had been especially well behaved, Miss Johnson would ask us again to move our desks into tight little rows at the sides of the classroom, and we would know that we were going to the moon.

To get to the moon we had to strap ourselves firmly into our seats and close our eyes. Miss Johnson would start the countdown, and on zero our spaceship would lift off and begin to climb; and as the earth receded and our ship veered off into space, Miss Johnson, to hide the crinkling of paper as she laid out our landscape, would lead us in our moon song:

Zoom, zoom, zoom,
We're going to the moon.
Zoom, zoom, zoom,
We're going very soon.
If you want to take a trip,
Step into my rocket ship.
Zoom, zoom, zoom,
We're going to the moon.

Now stray comets and satellites were flashing past our windshield as the moon balanced in the vastness of space, grew larger and larger, until with a bump and a lurch we touched down and opened our eyes to see its surface unfurled beside us; and when we had removed our safety straps and taken off our shoes and packed ourselves carefully into our spacesuits, we stepped out into space, our bodies moving weirdly because of the lack of gravity, and set off like tiny gods across the watercolour strangeness of the moon.

In the new year, Miss Johnson pinned to the centre of our largest bulletin board autographed photos of the three astronauts who would be flying *Apollo I* in February, the caption "Bon Voyage" stapled beneath them in black cut-out letters. She promised she'd bring a television into the classroom the day of the launch so that we could catch the liftoff together; and in a lower corner of the blackboard we kept a running countdown of the days remaining, all of us competing every day to change the number, anxious to show our excitement over an event that Miss Johnson had deemed worthy of our attention. But the liftoff never took place: with twenty-five days still left on our blackboard counter, the astronauts whose faces had become so familiar to our class were burnt to death when a fire broke out in their cockpit during a preflight test. I saw pictures of the fire at home on the television news, of the billowing smoke, of the burnt-out rocket, the charged solemnity of the reports stirring me in a vague memory of when John Kennedy had died; and it was strangely thrilling to see so much attention being paid to a thing that I had thought of as merely personal, as belonging only to Miss Johnson and our grade one class, as if suddenly something that had been a kind of fiction, a story that Miss Johnson had made up to indulge us, following its fixed course, had become pressingly, dangerously real, unpredictable, unknown.

At school the pictures came down, the blackboard counter was erased, Miss Johnson wheeling the school television into our classroom finally to watch not a liftoff but a long funeral procession; and for a few days we wore our sorrow for the astronauts as self-importantly as we had worn our love for Miss Johnson, wanting to be true to the grown-up sense of tragedy, of loss, which Miss Johnson tried to impart to us. But afterwards, when our bulletin boards were done up with Centennial themes like the boards in other classrooms, our lunar landscape forgotten now under the bench at the back of the cloakroom, and when the songs we sang were Centennial songs, as devoid of meaning as the hymns we sang in church, I felt cheated somehow, felt that I had touched for a moment some larger world that had receded again, that had remained as elusive finally as the promise of the tall buildings across the river or of the golden pendulum clock that sat in my mother's dining room.

All my life, it seemed suddenly, was merely waiting for the fulfilment of that promise, for a redemption from the narrowness and meanness of the world I came from; but it seemed possible finally that nothing would change, that I was stranded in my own small world as on some barren planet, with no way to bridge the gap between the promise and the hundred small humiliations that kept me from it, that refused simply to fall away from me like an old skin. When the chrome zipper on my winter coat split and my mother, instead of buying me a new coat as I hoped she would, as I thought other mothers would, merely sewed buttons down the coat's front and cut crude holes for them along the track of the broken zipper, I was certain that the kids at school, that Miss Johnson, would see in those makeshift repairs my mother's swollen hands, our poverty, our strangeness; and the next morning I left the house in only my sweater, my parents already at work and Joe merely shaking his head at my stubbornness as if he couldn't be bothered to fight with me, to pretend that he didn't understand. But at school one of the teachers saw me shivering outside the entranceway and sent me inside before the first bell had rung, and by then I had understood already how hopeless my situation was, how my humiliation was not something that other people did to me but something I carried inside me like a sin, that was there even if other people did not see it. I had begun to cry by the time I got to my classroom, and knowing that Miss Johnson would be there, making her silent mysterious preparations for the day, I slipped into the cloakroom and huddled onto the bench at the back, not wanting her to see me like that; but she must have heard the sound of my crying, for suddenly she was standing over me, with her silk blouse and her limpid eyes and her perfume smell, and she was so beautiful and soft and gently rounded, and her quick sad concern for me so misdirected, so much the promise of all the things I would not have, that I only cried harder, only thought, we'll never go to the moon again, we'll never go to the moon.

That summer Uncle Mike's son Benny was killed in the war in Vietnam. They had been to visit us at Easter, Benny in his uniform, seeming much older than I remembered him, and afterwards my mother and father had had an argument.

"He's an idiot," my father had said. "He thinks the war is a game."

"He has to go, he doesn't have a choice."

"He doesn't have to go, he volunteered, your brother told me himself."

But when the news came that Benny had been killed there were no arguments, only awkward, oppressive silence that seemed to carry some unexplained burden of guilt. My father could not get time off work for the funeral but my mother went down on the bus, dressed strangely in a dark dress and hat and in nylons and high heels. I thought that going to the States would change her in some way, or that she would return with some unexpected gift, something exciting and strange, that could not be found in the Woolco mall; but she came back a few days later empty-handed, changed only in that she was more short-tempered and curt than usual. I thought she was angry about the time she had missed from work; but one evening before bed I caught a glimpse of her through the kitchen doorway sitting at the table with her head in her hands as if she were crying, and I understood then that she had been carrying the shame of Benny's death inside her the whole time, that his death was not a special thing like the deaths of the Apollo astronauts but was merely private and grim, a blemish or failure that needed to be hidden away and forgotten like any other.

That was the summer, too, of the riots in Detroit, and for days the news was filled with images of fires and gunfights and broken windows. My mother forbade Joe and me to leave our neighbourhood while the riots were still going on, but when the two of us stole down to the riverfront one evening with two of our cousins we found that Windsor outside our own neighbourhood was still much what it had always been, people talking on the street corners as if nothing had happened, traffic flowing unabated on the main streets, the river wrapped in its usual twilight gloom. But across the river, the streets, cloaked in the shadows of dusk, seemed almost deserted; it was only when I stared hard that I began to make out some movement along the riverfront, the dim outlines of Jeeps and cars, a few shadowy figures. Higher up, though, where the afterglow of sunset still held the sky in unearthly blue, great clouds of dark smoke had formed and were leaning against the taller buildings as if to topple them into the river; and for a long time we sat at the water's edge staring silently at the skyline as if we were watching a movie, were waiting for it to draw to some inevitable conclusion. But then night settled in around us, leaving us stranded there at the river's edge as on an island; and finally we rose up together and began to make our way home.

Nino Ricci was born in Canada to Italian immigrants. Like many other contemporary Canadian writers, he writes about ethnicity, the search for cultural identity, and a sense of isolation in stories such as "Going to the Moon." *Lives of the Saints* (1990), the first novel in his popular trilogy, received international attention and a Governor General's Award. Ricci's novels have been translated into many languages. He is also an active member of the Canadian Centre of International PEN. (*Born Leamington, Ontario 1959*)

RESPONDING

Meaning

1. What is the significance to the story of Miss Johnson and the detailed description of her appearance and apparel? What does she represent to the narrator?

2. a) The author uses a series of parallel events to reinforce the story's theme. What is the theme and how do these events help to reinforce it?

    b) How does the moon act as a *metaphor* in developing the theme?

Form and Style

3. How does the author develop the tension between cultures often felt by those who immigrate to a new land? Refer to specific details and techniques (e.g., description of setting in the first paragraph, choice of words and images in the story, use of contrasts, etc.) in your answer.

4. An *allusion* is a reference to a well-known person, place, event, story, or work of art that is meant to extend the reader's understanding. In the third paragraph, Ricci uses an allusion to describe his family's situation in Windsor. What is the allusion and why is it particularly effective?

Exploring Context

5. According to Nino Ricci, "the artist is someone who stands outside the community and therefore sees it in starker, perhaps more realistic terms than those who are inside it and don't question its rules." How does this quotation inform your understanding of Ricci's story? In what ways is the narrator an "outsider"? What insights does this position allow him?

Creative Extension

6. Write a letter from the narrator's mother to her family in Italy in which she describes the funeral of her nephew and her thoughts and feelings about his death. Be sure to keep in mind the story's theme.

7. Write a poem or short story about a moment of disillusionment or disappointment. Structure your poem or story around an extended metaphor or symbol of your own devising, just as Ricci has used the abortive moon flight as a symbol of dashed hopes in his story.

The Virgins[1]

 ❦   *Derek Walcott*

In this poem, the speaker explores his sense of isolation in a world that has changed and lost its innocence to the "American dream."

> Down the dead streets of sun-stoned Frederiksted,[2]
> the first free port to die for tourism,
> strolling at funeral pace, I am reminded
> of life not lost to the American dream;
> but my small-islander's simplicities

can't better our new empire's civilized
exchange of cameras, watches, perfumes, brandies
for the good life, so cheaply underpriced
that only the crime rate is on the rise
in streets blighted with sun, stone arches
and plazas blown dry by the hysteria
of rumour. A condominium drowns
in vacancy; its bargains are dusted,
but only a jewelled housefly drones
over the bargains. The roulettes spin
rustily to the wind—the vigorous trade[3]
that every morning would begin afresh
by revving up green water round the pierhead
heading for where the banks of silver thresh.

---

1 The title refers to the Virgin Islands, a group of 100 small islands in the Caribbean.
2 Frederiksted is the largest seaport in St. Croix, the largest of the American Virgin Islands.
3 trade here also refers to the trade wind.

ଽ Poet Derek Walcott is also a playwright and theatre director. His poems are frequently
ironic journeys of self-discovery. He received widespread recognition with the collections
In a Green Night (1962), *The Castaway* (1965), and *The Gulf* (1970). "The Virgins" was
published in *The Star-Apple Kingdom* (1980). Walcott received a Nobel Prize for Literature
in 1992. (*Born Castries, St. Lucia 1930*)

Connecting

1. Describe the speaker in this poem. What emotions does he or she express? How might
    this poem be considered "an ironic journey of self-discovery" for the speaker?
2. Explain the significance of the reference to the American dream in line 4?
3. What parallels and contrasts can you draw between the themes and the speaker or
    protagonist in this poem and those in Nino Ricci's story "Going to the Moon"?

Two Paintings on a Theme

*The two paintings below present two perspectives on the theme of isolation and "otherness". Both
paintings depict solitary figures and convey the mixed emotions of sadness and joy.*

Melancholy: The Street

Giorgio de Chirico

Giorgio de Chirico, "Melancholy: The Street", 1924–25. ©Estate of Giorgio de Chirico / SODRAC (Montréal) 2002.

The Poetess

❦ *Tosa Mitsushize*

❦ The Italian painter Giorgio de Chirico was noted for the atmosphere of strangeness and uneasiness his paintings conveyed through his use of empty spaces, illogical shadows, and unexpected perspectives. He is considered an originator of Metaphysical painting, which was noted for setting people and objects in new and unusual relationships and settings. De Chirico is also considered a precursor of Surrealist painting. *(Born Volo, Greece 1888, died 1978.)* Tosa Mitsushize was an artist of the Tosa School during the Edo period in Japan (1615–1868). These artists often depicted literary and historical figures and subjects in a colourful if conservative style. This painting is of the poetess Ono no Kamachi, a solitary figure in her time.

Connecting

1. Describe the mood that emanates from de Chirico's painting. Support your answer with reference to specific elements in the art. Consider the use of perspective, colour, shadows and light, and the size and placement of figures and buildings.

2. What emotions are conveyed by Mitsushize's painting? What elements and techniques contribute to these emotions?

3. How does the atmosphere conveyed by these two works of art relate to the theme of isolation and "otherness"? What specific parallels can you draw between these paintings and Nino Ricci's story "Going to the Moon"?

Am I Blue?

❧ *Alice Walker*

In this essay, Alice Walker explores the theme of isolation and "otherness" through a number of analogies. Her insights are wide-ranging and thought-provoking.

"Ain't these tears in these eyes tellin' you?"

For about three years my companion and I rented a small house in the country that stood on the edge of a large meadow that appeared to run from the end of our deck straight into the mountains. The mountains, however, were quite far away, and between us and them there was, in fact, a town. It was one of the many pleasant aspects of the house that you never really were aware of this.

It was a house of many windows, low, wide, nearly floor to ceiling in the living room, which faced the meadow, and it was from one of these that I first saw our closest neighbour, a large white horse, cropping grass, flipping its mane, and ambling about—not over the entire meadow, which stretched well out of sight of the house, but over the five or so fenced-in acres that were next to the twenty-odd that we had rented. I soon learned that the horse, whose name was Blue, belonged to a man who lived in another town, but was boarded by our neighbours next door. Occasionally, one of the children, usually a stocky teenager, but sometimes a much younger girl or boy, could be seen riding Blue. They would appear in the meadow, climb up on his back, ride furiously for ten or fifteen minutes, then get off, slap Blue on the flanks, and not be seen again for a month or more.

There were many apple trees in our yard, and one by the fence that Blue could almost reach. We were soon in the habit of feeding him apples, which he relished, especially because by the middle of summer the meadow grasses—so green and succulent since January—had dried out from lack of rain, and Blue stumbled about munching the dried stalks half-heartedly. Sometimes he would stand very still just by the apple tree, and when one of us came out he would whinny, snort loudly, or stamp the ground. This meant, of course: I want an apple.

It was quite wonderful to pick a few apples, or collect those that had fallen to the ground overnight, and patiently hold them, one by one, up to his large, toothy mouth. I remained as thrilled as a child by his flexible dark lips, huge, cube-like teeth that crunched the apples, core and all, with such finality, and his high, broad-breasted *enormity*; beside which, I felt small indeed. When I was a child, I used to ride horses, and was especially friendly with one named Nan until the day I was riding and my brother deliberately spooked her and I was thrown, head first, against the trunk of a tree. When I came to, I was in bed and my mother was bending worriedly over me; we silently agreed that perhaps horseback riding was not the safest sport for me. Since then I have walked, and prefer walking to horse-back riding—but I had forgotten the depth of feeling one could see in horses' eyes.

I was therefore unprepared for the expression in Blue's. Blue was lonely. Blue was terribly lonely and bored. I was not shocked that this should be the case; five acres to tramp by yourself, endlessly, even in the most beautiful of meadows—and his was—cannot provide many interesting events, and once rainy season turned to dry that was about it. No, I was shocked that I had forgotten that human animals and non-human animals can communicate quite well; if we are brought up around animals as children we take this for granted. By the time we are adults we no longer remember. However, the animals have not changed. They are in fact *completed* creations (at least they seem to be, so much more than we) who are not likely to change; it is their nature to express themselves. What else are they going to express? And they do. And, generally speaking, they are ignored.

After giving Blue the apples, I would wander back to the house, aware that he was observing me. Were more apples not forthcoming then? Was that to be his sole entertainment for the day? My partner's small son had decided he wanted to learn how to piece a quilt; we worked in silence on our respective squares as I thought . . .

Well, about slavery: about white children who were raised by black people, who knew their first all-accepting love from black women, and then, when they were twelve or so, were told they must "forget" the deep levels of communication between themselves and "mammy" that they knew. Later, they would be able to relate quite calmly, "My old mammy was sold to another good family." "My old mammy was___ ____." Fill in the blank. Many more years later a white woman would say: "I can't understand these Negroes, these blacks. What do they want? They're so different from us."

And about the thousands of American men who marry Japanese, Korean, Filipina, and other non-English-speaking women and of how happy they report they are, "*blissfully*," until their brides learn how to speak English, at which point the marriages tend to fall apart. What then did the men see, when they looked into the eyes of the women they married, before they could speak English? Apparently only their own reflections.

I thought of society's impatience with the young. "Why are they playing the music so loud?" Perhaps the children have listened to much of the music oppressed people like their parents danced to before they were born, with its passionate but soft cries for acceptance and love, and they have wondered why their parents failed to hear.

I do not know how long Blue had inhabited his five beautiful, boring acres before we moved into our house; a year after we had arrived—and had also travelled to other valleys, other cities, other worlds—he was still there.

But then, in our second year at the house, something happened in Blue's life. One morning, looking out the window at the fog that lay like a ribbon over the meadow, I saw another horse, a brown one, at the other end of Blue's field. Blue appeared to be afraid of it, and for several days made no attempt to go near. We went away for a week. When we returned, Blue had decided to make friends and the two horses ambled or galloped along together, and Blue did not come nearly as often to the fence underneath the apple tree.

When he did, bringing his new friend with him, there was a different look in his eyes. A look of independence, of self-possession, of inalienable *horse*ness. His friend eventually became pregnant. For months and months there was, it seemed to me, a mutual feeling between me and the horses of justice, of peace. I fed apples to them both. The look in Blue's eyes was one of unabashed "this is *it*ness."

It did not, however, last forever. One day, after a visit to the city, I went out to give Blue some apples. He stood waiting, or so I thought, though not beneath the tree. When I shook the tree and jumped back from the shower of apples, he made no move. I carried some over to him. He managed to half-crunch one. The rest he let fall to the ground. I dreaded looking into his eyes—because I had of course noticed that Brown, his partner, had gone—but I did look. If I had been born into slavery, and my partner had been sold or killed, my eyes would have looked like that. The children next door explained that Blue's partner had been "put with him" (the same expression that old people used, I had noticed, when speaking of an ancestor during slavery who had been impregnated by her owner) so that they could mate and she conceive. Since that was accomplished, she had been taken back by her owner, who lived somewhere else.

Will she be back? I asked.

They didn't know.

Blue was like a crazed person. Blue *was*, to me, a crazed person. He galloped furiously, as if he were being ridden, around and around his five beautiful acres. He whinnied until he couldn't. He tore at the ground with his hooves. He butted himself against his single shade tree. He looked always and always toward the road down which his partner had gone. And then, occasionally, when he came up for apples, or I took apples to him, he looked at me. It was a look so piercing, so full of grief, a look so *human*, I almost laughed (I felt too sad to cry) to think there are people who do not know that animals suffer. People like me who have forgotten, and daily forget, all that animals try to tell us. "Everything you do to us will happen to you; we are your teachers, as you are ours. We are one lesson" is essentially it, I think. There are those who never once have even considered animals' rights: those who have been taught that animals actually want to be used and abused by us, as small children "love" to be frightened. But most disturbing of all, in Blue's large brown eyes was a new look, more painful than the look of despair: the look of disgust with human beings, with life; the look of hatred. And it was odd what the look of hatred did. It gave him, for the first time, the look of a beast. And what that meant was that he had put up a barrier within to protect himself from further violence; all the apples in the world wouldn't change that fact.

And so Blue remained, a beautiful part of our landscape, very peaceful to look at from the window, white against the grass. Once a friend came to visit and said, looking out on the soothing view: "And it *would* have to be a white horse; the very image of freedom." And I thought, yes, the animals are forced to become for us merely "images" of what they once so beautifully expressed. And we are used to drinking milk from containers showing "contented" cows, whose real lives we want to hear nothing about, eating eggs and drumsticks from "happy" hens, and munching hamburgers advertised by bulls of integrity who seem to command their fate.

As we talked of freedom and justice one day for all, we sat down to steaks. I am eating misery, I thought, as I took the first bite. And spit it out.

ᘓ   Alice Walker began writing while attending college. She worked as an editor of *Ms.* magazine and has taught at several colleges. Her work as a poet, novelist, and essayist is highly
acclaimed. The novel, *The Color Purple* (1982), won a Pulitzer Prize and was made into a
successful film. Another novel, *Possessing the Secret of Joy*, and her collected poems, *Her
Blue Body Everything We Know*, were published in 1992. "Am I Blue?" appeared in *Living
by the Word: Selected Writings 1973–1987*. (*Born Eatonton, Georgia 1944*)

Connecting

1. a) How, according to the narrator, was Blue similar to humans?
    b) Explain how Walker uses a number of *analogies* to establish this similarity. Choose
        one of these analogies and evaluate its effectiveness.
2. What is the thematic significance of the title, "Am I Blue"?
3. In addition to the sense of isolation, the theme of possible salvation runs through each
    of the selections in this Echo. Focusing on two of the selections, elaborate on this theme.
    Support your answer with direct quotations from the selections. [Consider how Blue's
    isolation is overcome, at least for a time. How does the protagonist in Ricci's story resolve
    his sense of isolation and longing for another world?]

☐ REFLECTING ON THE ECHO

1. The motif of isolation and "otherness" is a common one in art and literature. Select
    another work from your own reading or viewing that focuses on a character who is
    isolated and longs for another place or connection where he or she can feel a sense
    of belonging. Write an essay analyzing this theme and showing how it is developed.
2. Choose one of the selections in this Echo and transpose it into a different form. Trans-
    form it into a visual or musical representation, a short dramatic scene or dramatic mono-
    logue, a work of short fiction, or a work of non-fiction such as a letter, editorial, or journal.
    You may add details, but whatever you add should be consistent with the theme, tone,
    and characters in the original piece. Discuss how the process of changing form
    enhanced your understanding of the selection and the new form you used.
3. The "outsider" is a common character in many contemporary films. Select a film that
    centres around an "outsider" and write a critical review of it. Focus on how the charac-
    ter is portrayed and developed, how the central conflict is resolved, and how the film-
    makers used particular techniques to convey the main theme.

A Girl's Story

✑ David Arnason

You've wondered what it would be like to be a character in a story, to sort of slip out of your ordinary self and into some other character. Well, I'm offering you the opportunity. I've been trying to think of a heroine for this story, and frankly, it hasn't been going too well. A writer's life isn't easy, especially if, like me, he's got a tendency to sometimes drink a little bit too much. Yesterday, I went for a beer with Dennis and Ken (they're real-life friends of mine) and we stayed a little longer than we should have. Then I came home and quickly mixed a drink and started drinking it so my wife would think the liquor on my breath came from the drink I was drinking and not from the drinks I had had earlier. I wasn't going to tell her about those drinks. Anyway, Wayne dropped over in the evening and I had some more drinks, and this morning my head isn't working very well.

To be absolutely frank about it, I always have trouble getting characters, even when I'm stone cold sober. I can think of plots; plots are really easy. If you can't think of one, you just pick up a book, and sure enough, there's a plot. You just move a few things around and nobody knows you stole the idea. Characters are the problem. It doesn't matter how good the plot is if your characters are dull. You can steal characters too, and put them into different plots. I've done that. I stole Eustacia Vye from Hardy and gave her another name. The problem was that she turned out a lot sulkier than I remembered and the plot I put her in was a light comedy. Now nobody wants to publish the story. I'm still sending it out, though. If you send a story to enough publishers, no matter how bad it is, somebody will ultimately publish it.

For this story I need a beautiful girl. You probably don't think you're beautiful enough, but I can fix that. I can do all kinds of retouching once I've got the basic material, and if I miss anything, Karl (he's my editor) will find it. So I'm going to make you fairly tall, about five-foot eight and a quarter in your stocking feet. I'm going to give you long blond hair because long blond hair is sexy and virtuous. Black hair can be sexy too, but it doesn't go with virtue. I've got to deal with a whole literary tradition where black-haired women are basically evil. If I were feeling better I might be able to do it in an ironic way, then black hair would be okay, but I don't think I'm up to it this morning. If you're going to use irony, then you've got to be really careful about tone. I could make you a redhead, but redheads have a way of turning out pixie-ish, and that would wreck my plot.

So you've got long blond hair and you're this tall slender girl with amazingly blue eyes. Your face is narrow and your nose is straight and thin. I could have turned up the nose a little, but that would have made you cute, and I really need a beautiful girl. I'm going to put a tiny black mole on your cheek. It's traditional. If you want your character to be really beautiful there has to be some minor defect.

Now, I'm going to sit you on the bank of a river. I'm not much for setting. I've read so many things where you get great long descriptions of the setting, and mostly it's just boring. When my last book came out, one of the reviewers suggested that the reason I don't do settings is that I'm not very good at them. That's just silly. I'm writing a different kind of story, not that old realist stuff. If you think I can't do setting, just watch.

There's a curl in the river just below the old dam where the water seems to make a broad sweep. That flatness is deceptive, though. Under the innocent sheen of the mirroring surface, the current is treacherous. The water swirls, stabs, takes sharp angles and dangerous vectors. The trees that lean from the bank shimmer with the multi-hued greenness of elm, oak, maple, and aspen. The leaves turn in the gentle breeze, showing their paler green undersides. The undergrowth, too, is thick and green, hiding the poison ivy, the poison sumac and the thorns. On a patch of grass that slopes gently to the water, the only clear part of the bank on that side of the river, a girl sits, a girl with long blond hair. She has slipped a ring from her finger and seems to be holding it towards the light.

You see? I could do a lot more of that, but you wouldn't like it. I slipped a lot of details in there and provided all those hints about strange and dangerous things under the surface. That's called foreshadowing. I put in the ring at the end there so that you'd wonder what was going to happen. That's to create suspense. You're supposed to ask yourself what the ring means. Obviously it has something to do with love, rings always do, and since she's taken it off, obviously something has gone wrong in the love relationship. Now I just have to hold off answering that question for as long as I can, and I've got my story. I've got a friend who's also a writer who says never tell the buggers anything until they absolutely have to know.

I'm going to have trouble with the feminists about this story. I can see that already. I've got that river that's calm on the surface and boiling underneath, and I've got those trees that are gentle and beautiful with poisonous and dangerous undergrowth. Obviously, the girl is going to be like that, calm on the surface but passionate underneath. The feminists are going to say that I'm perpetuating stereotypes, that by giving the impression the girl is full of hidden passion I'm encouraging rapists. That's crazy. I'm just using a literary convention. Most of the world's great books are about the conflict between reason and passion. If you take that away, what's left to write about?

So I've got you sitting on the riverbank, twirling your ring. I forgot the birds. The trees are full of singing birds. There are meadowlarks and vireos and even Blackburnian warblers. I know a lot about birds but I'm not going to put in too many. You've got to be careful not to overdo things. In a minute I'm going to enter your mind and reveal what you're thinking. I'm going to do this in the third person. Using the first person is sometimes more effective, but I'm always afraid to do a female character in the first person. It seems wrong to me, like putting on a woman's dress.

Your name is Linda. I had to be careful not to give you a biblical name like Judith or Rachel. I don't want any symbolism in this story. Symbolism makes me sick, especially biblical symbolism. You always end up with some crazy moral argument that you don't believe and none of the readers believe. Then you lose control of your characters, because they've got to be like the biblical characters. You've got this terrific episode you'd like to use, but you can't because Rachel or Judith or whoever wouldn't do it. I think of stories with a lot of symbolism in them as sticky.

Here goes.

Linda held the ring up towards the light. The diamond flashed rainbow colours. It was a small diamond, and Linda reflected that it was probably a perfect symbol of her relationship with Gregg. Everything Gregg did was on a small scale. He was careful with his money and just as careful with his emotions. In one week they would have a small wedding and then move into a small apartment. She supposed that she ought to be happy. Gregg was very handsome, and she did love him. Why did it seem that she was walking into a trap?

That sounds kind of distant, but it's supposed to be distant. I'm using indirect quotation because the reader has just met Linda, and we don't want to get too intimate right away. Besides, I've got to get a lot of explaining done quickly, and if you can do it with the character's thoughts, then that's best.

Linda twirled the ring again, then with a suddenness that surprised her, she stood up and threw it into the river. She was immediately struck by a feeling of panic. For a moment she almost decided to dive into the river to try to recover it. Then, suddenly, she felt free. It was now impossible to marry Gregg. He would not forgive her for throwing the ring away. Gregg would say he's had enough of her theatrics for one lifetime. He always accused her of being a romantic. She'd never had the courage to admit that he was correct, and that she intended to continue being a romantic. She was sitting alone by the river in a long blue dress because it was a romantic pose. Anyway, she thought a little wryly, you're only likely to find romance if you look for it in romantic places and dress for the occasion.

Suddenly, she heard a rustling in the bush, the sound of someone coming down the narrow path from the road above.

I had to do that, you see. I'd used up all the potential in the relationship with Gregg, and the plot would have started to flag if I hadn't introduced a new character. The man who is coming down the path is tall and athletic with wavy brown hair. He has dark brown eyes that crinkle when he smiles, and he looks kind. His skin is tanned, as if he spends a lot of time outdoors, and he moves gracefully. He is smoking a pipe. I don't want to give too many details. I'm not absolutely sure what features women find attractive in men these days, but what I've described seems safe enough. I got all of it from stories written by women, and I assume they must know. I could give him a chiselled jaw, but that's about as far as I'll go.

The man stepped into the clearing. He carried an old-fashioned wicker fishing creel and a telescoped fishing rod. Linda remained sitting on the grass, her blue dress spread out around her. The man noticed her and apologized.

"I'm sorry, I always come here to fish on Saturday afternoons and I've never encountered anyone here before." His voice was low with something of an amused tone in it.

"Don't worry," Linda replied. "I'll only be here for a little while. Go ahead and fish. I won't make any noise." In some way she couldn't understand, the man looked familiar to her. She felt she knew him. She thought she might have seen him on television or in a movie, but of course she knew that movie and television stars do not spend every Saturday afternoon fishing on the banks of small, muddy rivers.

"You can make all the noise you want," he told her. "The fish in this river are almost entirely deaf. Besides, I don't care if I catch any. I only like the act of fishing. If I catch them, then I have to take them home and clean them. Then I've got to cook them and eat them. I don't even like fish that much, and the fish you catch here all taste of mud."

"Why do you bother fishing then?" Linda asked him. "Why don't you just come and sit on the riverbank?"

"It's not that easy," he told her. "A beautiful girl in a blue dress may go and sit on a riverbank any time she wants. But a man can only sit on a riverbank if he has a very good reason. Because I fish, I am a man with a hobby. After a hard week of work, I deserve some relaxation. But if I just came and sat on the riverbank, I would be a romantic fool. People would make fun of me. They would think I was irresponsible, and before long I would be a failure." As he spoke, he attached a lure to his line, untelescoped his fishing pole, and cast his line into the water.

You may object that this would not have happened in real life, that the conversation would have been awkward, that Linda would have been a bit frightened by the man. Well, why don't you just run out to the grocery store and buy a bottle of milk and a loaf of bread? The grocer will give you change without even looking at you. That's what happens in real life, and if that's what you're after, why are you reading a book?

I'm sorry. I shouldn't have got upset. But it's not easy you know. Dialogue is about the hardest stuff to write. You've got all those "he saids" and "she saids" and "he replieds." And you've got to remember the quotation marks and whether the comma is inside or outside the quotation marks. Sometimes you can leave out the "he saids" and the "she saids" but then the reader gets confused and can't figure out who's talking. Hemingway is bad for that. Sometimes you can read an entire chapter without figuring out who's on what side.

Anyway, something must have been in the air that afternoon. Linda felt free and open.

Did I mention that it was warm and the sun was shining?

She chattered away, telling the stranger all about her life, what she had done when she was a little girl, the time her dad had taken the whole family to Hawaii and she got such a bad sunburn that she was peeling in February, how she was a better water-skier than Gregg and how mad he got when she beat him at tennis. The man, whose name was Michael (you can use biblical names for men as long as you avoid Joshua or Isaac), told her he was a doctor, but had always wanted to be a cowboy. He told her about the time he skinned his knee when he fell off his bicycle and had to spend two weeks in the hospital because of infection. In short, they did what people who are falling in love always do. They unfolded their brightest and happiest memories and give them to each other as gifts.

Then Michael took a bottle of wine and a Klik sandwich out of his wicker creel and invited Linda to join him in a picnic. He had forgotten his corkscrew and he had to push the cork down into the bottle with his filletting knife. They drank wine and laughed and spat out little pieces of cork. Michael reeled in his line, and to his amazement discovered a diamond ring on his hook. Linda didn't dare tell him where the ring had come from. Then Michael took Linda's hand, and slipped the ring onto her finger. In a comic-solemn voice, he asked her to marry him. With the same kind of comic solemnity, she agreed. Then they kissed, a first gentle kiss with their lips barely brushing and without touching each other.

Now I've got to bring this to some kind of ending. You think that writers know how stories end before they write them, but that's not true. We're wracked with confusion and guilt about how things are going to end. And just as you're playing the role of Linda in this story, Michael is my alter ego. He even looks a little like me and he smokes the same kind of pipe. We all want this to end happily. If I were going to be realistic about this, I suppose I'd have to let them make love. Then, shaken with guilt and horror, Linda would go back and marry Gregg, and the doctor would go back to his practice. But I'm not going to do that. In the story from which I stole the plot, Michael turned out not to be a doctor at all, but a returned soldier who had always been in love with Linda. She recognized him as they kissed, because they had kissed as children, and even though they had grown up and changed, she recognized the flavour of wintergreen on his breath. That's no good. It brings in too many unexplained facts at the last minute.

I'm going to end it right here at the moment of the kiss. You can do what you want with the rest of it, except you can't make him a returned soldier, and you can't have them make love then separate forever. I've eliminated those options. In fact, I think I'll eliminate all options. This is where the story ends, at the moment of the kiss. It goes on and on forever while cities burn, nations rise and fall, galaxies are born and die, and the universe snuffs out the stars one by one. It goes on, the story, the brush of a kiss.

ᔥ Poet and short-story writer David Arnason founded the *Journal of Canadian Fiction*, which he edited for several years, and was one of the founders of Turnstone Press. Among his popular short-story collections are *Fifty Stories and a Piece of Advice* (1982), *The Circus Performers' Bar* (1984), *The Happiest Man in the World and Other Stories* (1989), and *The Pagan Wall* (1992). Arnason teaches creative writing and Canadian literature at the University of Manitoba. (*Born Gimli, Manitoba 1940*)

RESPONDING

Meaning

1. a) Explain the *irony* of the title, "A Girl's Story."
    b) This story includes elements of *satire*. What is being satirized? Support your answer with specific evidence from the story.

2. How does the incident of the fishing act as a *metaphor* in this story?

Form and Style

3. a) This story is self-reflexive; that is, the story incorporates in the narrative references to the actual act of writing the story. What effect does this have on the reader's attitude to the story? How does it affect the *tone* of the piece?

4. One technique for creating humour is to *juxtapose* a grand or romantic image with something more ordinary. Identify three examples of this kind of humour in the last three paragraphs of the story. Why do you think the author chose to use this technique?

Exploring Context

5. a) Self-reflexivity is part of a literary movement called Postmodernism. Using a good dictionary of literary terms, look up the term Postmodernism and write a brief summary of its major characteristics.
    b) Apply what you have learned about Postmodernism to "A Girl's Story." What characteristics of this literary movement are or are not present in the story? Support your answer with specific reference to the text.

Creative Extension

6. The narrator ends the story with the kiss and tells the reader "You can do what you want with the rest of it, except you can't make him a returned soldier, and you can't have them make love then separate forever." Take over the story and, using the self-reflexive style, create a new ending.

7. Assume the role of either Michael or Linda and write a monologue describing your views on the story, the narrator, and his method of writing. Stay true to the character developed in the story.

The Happy Man

✑ Naguib Mahfouz

He woke up in the morning and discovered that he was happy. "What's this?" he asked himself. He could not think of any word which described his state of mind more accurately and precisely than "happy." This was distinctly peculiar when compared with the state he was usually in when he woke up. He would be half-asleep from staying so late at the news-paper office. He would face life with a sense of strain and contemplation. Then he would get up, whetting his determination to face up to all inconveniences and withstand all difficulties.

Today he felt happy, full of happiness, as a matter of fact. There was no arguing about it. The symptoms were quite clear, and their vigour and obviousness were such as to impose themselves on his senses and mind all at once. Yes, indeed; he was happy. If this was not happiness, then what was? He felt that his limbs were well proportioned and functioning perfectly. They were working in superb harmony with each other and with the world around him. Inside him, he felt a boundless power, and imperish-able energy, an ability to achieve anything with confidence, precision, and obvious success. His heart was overflowing with love for people, animals, and things, and with an all-engulfing sense of optimism and joy. It was as if he were no longer troubled or bothered by fear, anxiety, sickness, death, argument, or the question of earning a living. Even more important than that, and something he could not analyze, it was a feeling which penetrated to every cell of his body and soul; it played a tune full of delight, pleasure, serenity, and peace, and hummed in its incredible melodies the whispering sound of the world, which is denied to the unhappy.

He felt drunk with ecstasy and savoured it slowly with a feeling of surprise. He asked himself where it had come from and how; the past provided no explanation, and the future could not justify it. Where did it come from, then, and how?! How long would it last? Would it stay with him till breakfast? Would it give him enough time to get to the newspaper office? Just a minute though, he thought . . . it won't last because it can't. If it did, man would be turned into an angel or something even higher.

So he told himself that he should devote his attention to savouring it, living with it, and storing up its nectar before it became a mere memory with no way of proving it or even being sure that it had ever existed.

He ate his breakfast with a relish, and this time nothing distracted his attention while he was eating. He gave "Uncle" Bashir, who was waiting on him, such a beaming smile that the poor man felt rather alarmed and taken aback. Usually he would only look in his direction to give orders or ask questions, although, on most occasions, he treated him fairly well.

"Tell me, 'Uncle' Bashir," he asked the servant, "am I a happy man?"

The poor man was startled. He realized why his servant was confused; for the first time ever he was talking to him as a colleague or friend. He encouraged his servant to forget about his worries and asked him with unusual insistence to answer his question.

"Through God's grace and favour, you are happy," the servant replied.

"You mean, I should be happy. Anyone with my job, living in my house, and enjoying my health should be happy. That's what you want to say. But do you think I'm really happy?"

The servant replied, "You work too hard, sir;" after yet more insistence, "It's more than any man can stand...."

He hesitated, but his master gestured to him to continue with what he had to say.

"You get angry a lot," he said, "and have fierce arguments with your neighbours...."

He interrupted him by laughing loudly. "What about you?" he asked. "Don't you have any worries?"

"Of course, no man can be free of worry."

"You mean that complete happiness is an impossible quest?"

"That applies to life in general...."

How could he have dreamed up this incredible happiness? He or any other human being? It was a strange, unique happiness, as though it were a private secret he had been given. In the meeting hall of the newspaper building, he spotted his main rival in this world sitting down thumbing through a magazine. The man heard his footsteps but did not look up from the magazine. He had undoubtedly noticed him in some way and was therefore pretending to ignore him so as to keep his own peace of mind. At some circulation meetings, they would argue so violently with each other that sparks began to fly and they would exchange bitter words. One stage more, and they would come to blows. A week ago, his rival had won in the union elections, and he had lost. He had felt pierced by a sharp, poisoned arrow, and the world had darkened before his eyes. Now here he was approaching his rival's seat; the sight of him sitting there did not make him excited, nor did the memories of their dispute spoil his composure. He approached him with a pure and carefree heart, feeling drunk with his incredible happiness; his face showed an expression full of tolerance and forgiveness. It was as though he were approaching some other man toward whom he had never had any feelings of enmity, or perhaps he might be renewing a friendship again. "Good morning!" he said without feeling any compunction.

The man looked up in amazement. He was silent for a few moments until he recovered, and then returned the greeting curtly. It was as though he did not believe his eyes and ears.

He sat down alongside the man. "Marvelous weather today. . . ." he said.

"Okay. . . ." the other replied guardedly.

"Weather to fill your heart with happiness."

His rival looked at him closely and cautiously. "I'm glad that you're so happy. . . ." he muttered.

"Inconceivably happy. . . ." he replied with a laugh.

"I hope," the man continued in a rather hesitant tone of voice, "that I shan't spoil your happiness at the meeting of the administrative council. . . ."

"Not at all. My views are well-known, but I don't mind if the members adopt your point of view. That won't spoil my happiness!"

"You've changed a great deal overnight," the man said with a smile.

"The fact is that I'm happy, inconceivably happy."

The man examined his face carefully. "I bet your dear son has changed his mind about staying in Canada?!" he asked.

"Never, never, my friend," he replied, laughing loudly. "He is still sticking to his decision. . . ."

"But that was the principle reason for being so sad. . . ."

"Quite true. I've often begged him to come back out of pity for me in my loneliness and to serve his country. But he told me that he's going to open an engineering office with a Canadian partner; in fact, he's invited me to join him in it. Let him live where he'll be happy. I'm quite happy here—as you can see, inconceivably happy. . . ."

The man still looked a little doubtful. "Quite extraordinarily brave!" he said.

"I don't know what it is, but I'm happy in the full meaning of the word."

Yes indeed, this was full happiness; full, firm, weighty, and vital. As deep as absolute power, widespread as the wind, fierce as fire, bewitching as scent, transcending nature. It could not possibly last.

The other man warmed to his display of affection. "The truth is," he said, "that I always picture you as someone with a fierce and violent temperament which causes him a good deal of trouble and leads him to trouble other people."

"Really?"

"You don't know how to make a truce; you've no concept of intermediate solutions. You work with your nerves, with the marrow in your bones. You fight bitterly, as though any problem is a matter of life and death!"

"Yes, that's true."

He accepted the criticism without any difficulty and with an open heart. His wave expanded into a boundless ocean of happiness. He struggled to control an innocent, happy laugh, which the other man interpreted in a way far removed from its pure motive.

"So then," he asked, "you think it's necessary to be able to take a balanced view of events, do you?"

"Of course. I remember, by way of example, the argument we had the day before yesterday about racism. We both had the same views on the subject; it's something worth being zealous about, even to the point of anger. But what kind of anger? An intellectual anger, abstract to a certain extent; not the type which shatters your nerves, ruins your digestion, and gives you palpitations. No so?"

"That's obvious; I quite understand. . . ." He struggled to control a second laugh and succeeded. His heart refused to renounce one drop of its joy. Racism, Vietnam, Palestine . . . no problem cold assail that fortress of happiness which was encircling his heart. When he remembered a problem, his heart guffawed. He was happy. It was a tyrannical happiness, despising all misery and laughing at any hardship; it wanted to laugh, dance, sing, and distribute its spirit of laughter, dancing, and singing among the various problems of the world.

He could not bear to stay in his office at the newspaper; he felt no desire to work at all. He hated the very idea of thinking about his daily business and completely failed to bring his mind down from its stronghold in the kingdom of happiness. How could he possibly write about a trolley bus falling into the Nile when he was so intoxicated by this frightening happiness? Yes, it really was frightening. How could it be anything else, when there was no reason for it at all, when it was so strong that it made him exhausted and paralyzed his will; apart from the fact that it had been with him for half a day without letting up in the slightest degree?!

He left the pages of paper blank and started walking backward and forward across the room, laughing and cracking his fingers. . . .

He felt slightly worried; it did not penetrate deep enough to spoil his happiness but paused on the surface of his mind like an abstract idea. It occurred to him that he might recall the tragedies of his life so that he could test their effect on his happiness. Perhaps they would be able to bring back some idea of balance or security, at least until his happiness began to flag a little. For example, he remembered his wife's death in all its various aspects and details. What had happened? The event appeared to him as a series of movements without any meaning or effect, as though it had happened to some other woman, the wife of another man, in some distant historical age. In fact, it had a contagious effect which prompted a smile and then even provoked laughter. He could not stop himself laughing, and there he was guffawing, ha . . . ha . . . ha!

The same thing happened when he remembered the first letter his son had sent him saying that he wanted to emigrate to Canada. The sound of his guffaws as he paraded the bloody tragedies of the world before him would have attracted the attention of the newspaper workers and passersby in the street, had it not been for the thickness of the walls. He could do nothing to dislodge his happiness. Memories of unhappy times hit him like waves being thrown onto a sandy beach under the golden rays of the sun.

He excused himself from attending the administrative council and left the newspaper office without writing a word. After lunch, he lay down on his bed as usual but could not sleep. In fact, sleep seemed an impossibility to him. Nothing gave him any indication that it was coming, even slowly. He was in a place alight and gleaming, resounding with sleeplessness and joy. He had to calm down and relax, to quiet his senses and limbs, but how could he do it? He gave up trying to sleep and got up. He began to hum as he was walking around his house. If this keeps up, he told himself, I won't be able to sleep, just as I can't work or feel sad. It was almost time for him to go to the club, but he did not feel like meeting any friends. What was the point of exchanging views on public affairs and private worries?! What would they think if they found him laughing at every major problem? What would they say? How would they picture things? How would they explain it? No, he did not need anyone, nor did he want to spend the evening talking. He should be by himself and go for a long walk to get rid of some of his excess vitality and think about his situation. What had happened to him? How was it that this incredible happiness had overwhelmed him? How long would he have to carry it on his shoulders? Would it keep depriving him of work, friends, sleep, and peace of mind?! Should he resign himself to it? Should he abandon himself to the flood to play with him as the whim took it? Or should he look for a way out for himself through thought, action, or advice?

When he was called into the examination room in the clinic of his friend, the specialist in internal medicine, he felt a little alarmed. The doctor looked at him with a smile. "You don't look like someone who's complaining about being ill," he said.

"I haven't come to see you because I'm ill," he told the doctor in a hesitant tone of voice, "but because I'm happy!"

The doctor looked piercingly at him with a questioning air.

"Yes," he repeated to underline what he had said, "because I'm happy!"

There was a period of silence. On one side, there was anxiety, and on the other, questioning and amazement.

"It's an incredible feeling which can't be defined in any other way, but it's very serious. . . ."

The doctor laughed. "I wish your illness were contagious," he said, prodding him jokingly.

"Don't treat it as a joke. It's very serious, as I told you. I'll describe it to you. . . ."

He told him all about his happiness from the time he had woken up in the morning till he had felt compelled to visit him.

"Haven't you been taking drugs, alcohol, or tanquilizers?"

"Absolutely nothing like that."

"Have you had some success in an important sphere of your life: work...love...money?"

"Nothing like that either. I've twice as much to worry about as I have to make me feel glad...."

"Perhaps if you were patient for a while...."

"I've been patient all day. I'm afraid I'll be spending the night wandering around...."

The doctor gave him a precise, careful, and comprehensive examination and then shrugged his shoulders in despair. "You're a picture of health," he said.

"And so?"

"I could advise you to take a sleeping pill, but it would be better if you consulted a nerve specialist...."

The examination was repeated in the nerve specialist's clinic with the self-same precision, care, and comprehensiveness. "Your nerves are sound," the doctor told him. "They're in enviable condition!"

"Haven't you got a plausible explanation for my condition?" He asked hopefully.

"Consult a gland specialist!" the doctor replied, shaking his head.

The examination was conducted for a third time in the gland specialist's clinic with the same precision, care, and comprehensiveness.

"I congratulate you!" the doctor told him. "Your glands are in good condition."

He laughed. He apologized for laughing, laughing as he did so. Laughter was his way of expressing his alarm and despair.

He left the clinic with the feeling that he was alone, alone in the hands of his tyrannical happiness, with no helper, no guide, and no friend. Suddenly, he remembered the doctor's sign he sometimes saw from the window of his office in the newspaper building. It was true that he had no confidence in psychiatrists even though he had read about the significance of psychoanalysis. Apart from that, he knew that their tentacles were very long and they kept their patients tied in a sort of long association. He laughed as he remembered the method of cure through free association and the problems which it eventually uncovers. He was laughing as his feet carried him toward the psychiatrist's clinic, and imagined the doctor listening to his incredible complaints about feeling happy, when he was used to hearing people complain about hysteria, schizophrenia, anxiety, and so on.

"The truth is, Doctor, that I've come to see you because I'm happy!"

He looked at the doctor to see what effect his statement had had on him but noticed that he was keeping his composure. He felt ridiculous. "I'm inconceivably happy. . . ." he said in a tone of confidence.

He began to tell the doctor his story, but the latter stopped him with a gesture of his hand. "An overwhelming, incredible, debilitating happiness?" he asked quietly.

He stared at him in amazement and was on the point of saying something, but the doctor spoke first. "A happiness which has made you stop working," he asked, "abandon your friends, and detest going to sleep? . . ."

"You're a miracle!" he shouted.

"Every time you get involved in some misfortune," the psychiatrist continued quietly, "you dissolved into laughter? . . ."

"Sir . . . are you familiar with the invisible?"

"No!" he said with a smile, "nothing like that. But I get a similar case in my clinic at least once a week!"

"Is it an epidemic?" he asked.

"I didn't say that, and I wouldn't claim that it's been possible to analyze one case into its primary elements as yet."

"But is it a disease?"

"All the cases are still under treatment."

"But are you satisfied without any doubt that they aren't natural cases? . . ."

"That's a necessary assumption for the job; there's only. . . ."

"Have you noticed any of them to be deranged in? . . ." he asked anxiously, pointing to his head.

"Absolutely not," the doctor replied convincingly. "I assure you that they're all intelligent in every sense of the word. . . ."

The doctor though for a moment. "We should have two sessions a week, I think?" he said.

"Very well. . . ." he replied in resignation.

"There's no sense in getting alarmed or feeling sad. . . ."

Alarmed, sad? He smiled, and his smile kept on getting broader. A laugh slipped out, and before long, he was dissolving into laughter. He was determined to control himself, but his resistance collapsed completely. He started guffawing loudly. . . .

ॐ Naguib Mahfouz began writing when he was seventeen and is now highly respected throughout the Arabic-speaking world. In novels such as *The Children of Gebelawi* (1959), *Small Talk on the Nile* (1966), and *Miramar* (1967), Mahfouz frequently uses allegory and symbolism to address political concerns. An English translation of his short story "The Happy Man" appeared in *God's World* (1973). Mahfouz won the Nobel Prize for Literature in 1988. *(Born Cairo, Egypt 1911)*

RESPONDING

Meaning

1. In your own words, explain what this story suggests about the human capacity for happiness.

2. a) A *caricature* is a comic exaggeration of a character's particular traits. Are there elements in the protagonist's characterization that are close to caricature? Explain.
    b) Which elements of his character and situation are realistic and believable?
    c) How do these various elements affect your response to his dilemma?

Form and Style

3. The author uses a series of *metaphors* to describe the protagonist's feelings of happiness. Identify two metaphors you found particularly effective and explain why.

4. What is the basic *irony* in the happy man's situation? How does the author play on the humour inherent in the situation?

Exploring Context

5. Existentialism is a philosophy of life that emphasizes personal choice and subjectivity; that is, the idea that our everyday choices, actions, and reactions determine who and what we are. Find out more about existentialism, using the Internet and other sources. Write a summary of what you have discovered, and explain how "The Happy Man" reflects elements of this philosophy.

Creative Extension

6. Write a poem or song lyric based on the theme of the quest for happiness. Consider how you will structure your piece (use of refrains, syntax, etc.) to convey your thoughts and emotions. Choose your diction and imagery carefully. Present a dramatic reading or performance of your piece.

7. With a partner, present a dramatic reading of one scene from the story. Use gestures, pauses, and facial expressions to emphasize the humour in the scene.

Your Mouth Is Lovely

ᗒ Nancy Richler

Learning Goals

- examine how specific text elements develop theme
- analyze setting and characterization
- assess the narrator's and writer's viewpoint
- write journal entries in character
- create a visual representation

Belarus, 1896.

Four years I stayed with Lipsa and four years I forgot I wasn't hers. I don't blame Lipsa. She was a busy woman. There were six children in her house —five of her own and me. Her husband was a peddlar and was gone for days, sometimes weeks at a time. Lipsa plucked chickens, sold eggs, took in other women's babies and washing. One winter she packed matches for the factory in Mozyr. Another she made cigarettes to sell in the market. She had no time to remind me of my misfortune.

We worked, all of us, packing matches, rolling cigarettes, pushing carts of laundry to and from the river, but we had our pleasures too. I took mine from the eggs I cleaned for market. Delicate and fragile they were, each one heavy with the secret of life. I removed dirt and feathers with three-year-old fingers without ever breaking a shell.

In my fifth year, my father remarried. It was unusual for a widower to have waited so long, unusual for a man to have lived alone—a young man, at that, and for so many years. There had been talk, of course. None of it good. My mother was thought to be behind his unnatural behaviour. She had walked into the Pripet river immediately after my birth and her body had never been recovered. There was no saying where her restless spirit hovered.

A woman in my father's position would have been forbidden to marry. *Agunah*, we would have called her, an abandoned wife. Our village had two. Sima, whose husband was surely dead—his blood-spattered coat had been found in the forest shortly after his disappearance—and Fruma, whose husband had left for America ten years earlier and forgotten to send for her. Unfortunates those women were. They remained bound to an absence for the rest of their lives. Abandoned men, however, could more easily obtain dispensation from their marriages. And in the fifth year of my life, my father obtained his.

Tsila was the name of his bride. Avram the Hero's eldest daughter. He was called The Hero because fifteen years earlier when his house had caught fire in the middle of the night he had run outside alone and sat on the snow, head in his hands, rocking and weeping, while his wife ushered their five children to safety.

Tsila was twenty already when my father married her. A tall girl, she was slender as a reed and had long, velvet hair the colour of honey. Hard working and practical, with clever hands and a strong back, all things being equal, she could have married much younger and found a far better match than a shoemaker whose first wife's spirit had never been properly put to rest. But all things are never equal: Tsila's face was marked by Divine anger. Across her left cheek and extending down to her chin was the unmistakable red handprint of the angel that had slapped her before birth.

In a sweet-natured girl, such a birthmark might have been talked away as a mistake, a momentary lapse in Divine judgment. "Look at her hair," a clever matchmaker might have pointed out. "Her eyes like emeralds. Her voice like a flute. And her disposition . . ." But Tsila wasn't sweet. Sour as spoiled milk, there were those who said that when the angel marked her face, he also placed a slice of lemon under her tongue, prohibiting her from sampling any of the more pleasant seasonings life might offer.

Their wedding took place two days after Purim, and my father sent for me soon after. Spring was early that year; the roads were rivers of mud. Lipsa walked with me along the planks of wood that had been laid across the mud to prevent us from drowning in it. "You'll be a good girl," Lipsa said as we walked. I stared at the dark sludge that oozed through the spaces between the planks. "You'll be helpful and you'll do as she says."

The day was mild, the air thick with the smells it had held frozen all winter. "She's your mother now," Lipsa said. I inhaled unfurling greens, thawing excrement, softening earth. "You had no mother, but now you do."

Past the butcher's we walked, the smells of fresh blood, chicken's feet. Past Reizel's stand of rotting fruit. It was Thursday. Lipsa's husband would be home tomorrow. Sometimes, if he'd been away a long time, he brought us small gifts. Once he had brought us candies. Hard yellow balls so sour they raised sweat from my forehead. "I was never your mother," Lipsa said.

We turned down the narrow passage where Malka the Apostate had lived. I wasn't usually allowed in that passage. Malka's mother had long since died of shame but her wails could still be heard on certain nights of the year. A fat drop of water fell on my face. I looked up at Lipsa. Her eyes were black stones. More drops fell. Lipsa clutched my hand tighter and hurried us along. We were close to the outskirts of town now—the planks of wood didn't extend this far. With each step we sank ankle deep into mud. A lark sang but I couldn't see it. The mud was alive, sucking hungrily at our feet.

I hadn't been to my father's house since my birth, hadn't seen him except in passing, had never heard his voice. We started up the hill. I knew that when we reached the top we would be there. The rain was falling more steadily now. Lipsa adjusted her kerchief, gave her chin a quick pat. She had a tuft of coarse black hair that grew out of her chin like the beard of a goat. Saturday evenings, when the men were at *shul* and we waited at home for the three stars that would end Shabbes and star the week, she would take me onto her lap. The hair on her chin tickled my cheek when she laughed.

We reached the top of the hill and stopped in front of a one-storey house. It looked like any other house. The walls were logs, the roof steep, the windows on either side of the door were squares of yellow light in the darkening afternoon. Chickens scratched in the mud of the yard. From somewhere in the shadows, a cow moaned. Smoke piled straight up out of the chimney as if it wasn't sure where to blow. Lipsa released my hand and thrust a small cloth bundle in my arms. "You're a lucky girl," she said. "I couldn't have kept you forever."

Tsila was tending her stove when I pushed open the door. Down on her knees, her back turned to me. I knew enough not to approach a creature that wasn't prepared to face me, not to enter a new life that greeted me with its back. I stood in her doorway waiting.

"Don't just stand there dripping rain," she said without turning around.

I had known she wouldn't want me. Lipsa's oldest had warned me. "Why would she want you?" Rohel had asked. "A new bride like her just starting out and you, a misfortune from her husband's first marriage?"

"In or out," Tsila said. "Don't you know it's bad luck to tarry on a threshold?"

Against my own judgment, I entered.

"Do you know how to tend a fire?" she asked, still bent over her stove.

I determined it was better to hold my tongue.

"Are you mute?" she asked and turned half around.

The side of her face that she presented to me was unmarked, and although I had not seen beauty in my life until then, I recognized it immediately in the profile I beheld.

"Well, sit down then," she said and gestured vaguely towards the window.

I followed her gesture and saw the small table by the window that she had indicated. Alongside the table were two chairs. I stood between them, uncertain which to choose.

"Sit," Tsila said, pointing to the one closer to the stove and settling herself on the other. "Here," she said, and pushed a plate of cookies my way.

It was Thursday and the cookies looked fresh. Who had fresh cookies at the end of a week, unless there was a special occasion, a special guest, something to celebrate? I reached over and took one. They were almond bars, dipped in sugar then baked until they formed a sweet crust. At Lipsa's we would have dipped them in tea.

Tsila watched me eat, then took one for herself. "I suppose your father will have to make another chair now," she allowed.

At Lipsa's there had never been a moment in the day or the night when the sounds of human life unfolding could not be heard. Her home was one of several grouped around a small courtyard, each one filled to bursting with its noisy generations. Reb Sender's nightly tantrums, his mother's snores, the whooping laughter of the Halpern old maid, the low moans of the fish monger's wife—all that and more had filled the two rooms of Lipsa's house and passed freely through the walls that barely separated us from our neighbours. "There's time enough for quiet in the world to come," Lipsa said once to a neighbour who complained. "We don't have to invite it before its time."

But in the house where Lipsa had just left me, the house where I had had the misfortune to be born, quiet had already descended. I strained my ears, but nowhere was there the hum of human conversation, the shrieks of children playing, voices raised in anger or lowered in fear or in love. Even Tsila's intake and output of breath was unaccompanied by sigh or cough. I knew I had not yet crossed into the world to come, but I couldn't feel certain. I listened for human sound but all I could hear was my own blood racing through my head.

We sat for a long while, Tsila mending, me clutching my bundle of belongings in case Lipsa should come back to return me to the noisy world of the living. I was still wearing my coat and was both too hot and shivering at the same time.

"It's good you don't look like her," Tsila finally uttered. It was late in the afternoon by then and already dark. I started at the sound of her voice but felt a relief so great that I immediately began to weep. "Don't be silly," she said harshly. A harshness sweet and reassuring in its earthly tones. I wept harder. She looked at me without expression then laid her cool hand on mine. "Don't be silly," she said again and again. "A man doesn't like to be reminded of past misfortune every time he looks at his daughter's face."

She didn't speak again. She continued her mending, I clutched my bundle of belongings, the rain fell on the roof and windows. I cleared my throat once to check if my voice had taken flight. For some time I had felt it flutter in my throat as if it longed to break free, return to Lipsa and abandon me to the silence, but it had not, as yet. Tsila looked at me. Eyes of a cat, one of Lipsa's daughters had said about her. "What are you staring at?" she asked, then turned back to her mending.

Eventually I heard footsteps approaching. My father, I knew, though I had never heard his footfall before. I looked up as the door opened and met his eyes for the first time. A man of the earth, people said about him, and I recognized immediately the clay of the riverbank in the hues of his face and beard. His eyes were the colour of mud.

He looked away and began to shake the rain off his clothes. He stamped his feet a few times, took off his cap to shake it, then shook his clothes yet again.

"Nu," Tsila said after a while. "Are you going to stand there all night shaking like a dog?"

My father took off his coat and hung it on the peg by the door.

"Maybe you can take your daughter's coat too . . . unless she prefers to sit wrapped up like an old woman as if I'm denying her heat."

I stood up, walked over to my father and handed him my coat. His hands were large, his nails darkly stained from the blacking of the threads he used for his work. I didn't dare raise my eyes to his face.

"A glass of tea?" Tsila offered getting up from her chair as I returned to mine.

My father said "please"—I had never heard a man say please to a woman before—and sat down in the chair Tsila had just vacated. I jumped up and joined Tsila at the stove.

"Sit," she said to me, then to my father, "She hops around like a wounded bird, but she doesn't talk too much."

My father nodded again and risked a look at my face.

My father, Aaron Lev, was still a young man at that time—no more than twenty-two or twenty-three—but already he had the bearing of one well advanced in years. His life had long become a wound from which he knew he would never recover and he bore it uneasily, in the stoop of his back— a slight hunch that swelled between the blades of his shoulders and pushed him inexorably downwards.

He was a strong man, but not well built. Out of balance, he was, as if the Creator had assembled him hastily at the end of too long a day, throwing in handfuls of this quality or that without considering necessary counters and complements. Intelligence he had been given, but not the tongue to express it; a large appetite, but the stomach of an invalid. His heart was too delicate for a man of his circumstances, his feet too small for a man of his size. Walking up the hill to his home, his large hulk stooped over his tiny feet, he gave the appearance, more obviously than most, of one perpetually teetering on the edge of his own destiny.

The Stutterer, he was called in our village, though he had long learned to hold his tongue. He had been born at the start of the typhus and was just learning to speak as the worst of the fever swept the village. Was it grief that strangled his tongue? Perhaps, though my mother also lost her parents to the fever and her tongue, by all accounts, was smooth and unfettered.

He was raised by his mother's cousin, a kind enough man, but one prone to bouts of melancholia so severe that only ceaseless recitation of the psalms enabled him to endure each new day that rose up against him. The cousin's wife was more able—she supported the family by selling the bread she baked—but her meagre stores of kindness had long been expended on her own children. Hungry, but not starving, literate but not educated, Aaron was apprenticed at nine and betrothed at fifteen to Henye, also fifteen—her dowry provided by the Society for Widows and Orphans. Henye resisted the arrangement at first. Her reasons were vague—premonitions, uneasy dreams. But she did at last acquiesce so that by sixteen, Aaron Lev was a bridegroom, and by seventeen, a widower and a father. A widower whose wife's body was never found and a father whose child brought him no joy.

My father drank his tea in small even gulps. The tea was hot—I could see steam rise off it—but he didn't pour it into his saucer or slurp it up with cooling sucks of air. He drank precisely, quietly, as if heat didn't burn his mouth.

Tsila placed a plate of potatoes and onions on the table and a pitcher of sour milk between us. I waited for my father to recite the blessing for fruits that have been pulled from the earth, but he thanked Tsila first. Before God. "Thank you, Tsila," he said, and I looked up in confusion.

I watched his eyes meet Tsila's. What passed between them was strange, certainly. There was a look on my father's face—a softness—that could have been part of a spell. But there was boldness as well, a boldness that didn't speak of bewitching. And wasn't it Tsila who looked away first? Her cheeks that filled with blood? I watched them look at each other and understood that the dangers in the household were many.

I tried to eat the meal she had laid before me, but her potatoes and onions seared the inside of my mouth. I took a sip of cooling milk, then turned the whole mess back into my plate.

"My food's not good enough for your daughter," she said.

I pushed my plate to the edge of the table. I didn't know why—the dangers in that room were many, but unnamed. My father watched me push my plate. Tsila watched me too. I pushed it over the edge and heard it land with a dull thud. Potatoes and onions splattered the floor and I waited for the blow to the back of my head that might have exploded what was building within me.

"No one's taught her anything," Tsila said, her voice dull with resentment. "She's been living like an animal, and now I'm to raise her."

I opened my mouth to protest but no words came and I couldn't fill my lungs. My father averted his eyes as if I was obscene.

"Well come on then," Tsila said to me. "Clean up your mess."

My father closed his eyes to recite the grace after meals, taking a long time, although only the short grace was required since we'd not eaten bread. When he finished, he remained with his eyes closed, his head nodding, as if reluctant to break off his communication with God and return to the scene before him.

There were those who said it was my mother herself who inhabited the air of that house. *He'd do well to find new quarters before bringing home a new bride*, they whispered, and maybe they were right. Was it my mother I was feeling tightening my chest, smothering conversation and laughter? I didn't know, but as I filled my lungs with the air of that place I felt my blood begin to starve.

My father pushed himself back from the table. I heard his chair scrape against the boards of the floor, then felt him standing over me. He was a giant of a man, very close now. I smelled the leather of his workday, saw the patterns of dried mud splattered up the legs of his pants. His hands hung at his sides. One hand—it was open and very large—began to swing towards me. A careful swing, deliberate and slow, a swing that might have turned into a slap or a caress. It stopped an inch from the skin of my cheek—I felt the heat of him, my own burning skin radiating out to meet his—then it swung back to hang again, clumsy and useless as an oversized paw. His step was heavy as he retreated to the door.

"Will you be late?" Tsila asked him.

The wind was up and from the north. I heard it against the rear wall of the house.

"Don't wait up," my father said.

I stared at them, uncomprehending. The wind was high—surely they must hear it—and coming from the swamps.

"The wind," I said, but Tsila was already on her feet approaching my father in the doorway. She stood close to him, her face turned up towards his. Something glinted in the mud of his eyes. He stroked her cheek once, easily, then stepped out into the night.

Our village sat on the edge of the Polyseh swamp. To our south were pine forests where the air was sweet and trees grew straight and thick, but to our north stretched an endless tract of roadless swamp. The Pripet river meandered through the Polyseh, flooding freely over most of its flat course and turning here and there to avoid any obstacle that might disturb its lazy flow. Our village occupied one such obstacle—a slight rise in the land that the river curved around rather than cutting a path through. We sat in the crook of the river's curve—a few streets, a crowd of wooden houses, some cultivated fields that flooded every spring, a market, several churches, two synagogues.

Why our town existed, no one knew; how it had started, no one remembered. The trees, probably. In the forest were thick pines that men could cut, then float down the river to the steppes of Little Russia where they had the grain that we lacked, but no lumber. From such endeavours others grew: a few mills, the match factories—so that by the time of my birth in 1892 there were almost fifty Jewish families eking out their lives in that clearing on the edge of the swamp.

The swamp was an unhealthy place—a wilderness where snakes lurked in the black waters, vapours and mists befouled the air, and the earth opened itself like water to swallow the foot that dared to walk upon it. There were lights in its vapours, lights anyone could see. They moved about in strange, weaving patterns and sometimes they moaned. Those lights were the souls that had departed our world but not yet entered the next, souls without peace that were detained between worlds for reasons only He could know. Lonely and comfortless, they waited for north winds so they could ride into town and look for solace among the living. It was on such a wind that my mother would come for me. Rohel had told me. You could smell them coming, damp and musty as they wafted from the swamp. We closed our windows against them.

"The wind," I said to Tsila when she shut the door behind my father. I had never known anyone to venture out when the wind from the north was blowing so strong, but Tsila seemed unconcerned. She looked at me for a long time, impatience growing all the while.

"Your head is filled with *bubbe meises*," she said. "What *wind*? The wind is wind. That's all it is."

I didn't answer, but her impatience grew. "I'm not interested in the foolishness Lipsa taught you."

It wasn't just Lipsa, and Tsila knew that. The streets of our town were all but deserted on nights such as this, for who could say with perfect confidence that the souls of their loved ones had found their final place of rest?

"Do you think your mother is waiting to snatch your father? Is that what you think? That she'll rush in to snatch him now when she never wanted him in life? Idiocy," she said, but she did rub her fingers on the amulet she wore around her neck, whether from habit or to ward off the evil her scornful words might have invited, I couldn't know for certain. "Your mother wasn't one to tarry," she said.

She led me then to a corner of the room—behind the stove, against the back wall of the house. There was a wooden bench there, small and narrow as I was, and upon it, a straw mattress, a quilt and a pillow. The quilt was the colour of young leaves and stitched with blue. The pillow was white and unstained. I had not seen such brightness in the objects of Lipsa's home.

"You'll sleep here," Tsila said, and I closed my eyes.

"Now what?" she asked, but how could I explain?

I had occupied until then the middle furrow of a tamped down mattress, wedged between Lipsa's two middle girls. Our blanket was rough but warm, leached of all colour and ripe with the smells of our accumulated nights. There I had drifted easily into sleep, the warmth of living flesh keeping me from drifting too far, the breath of other lungs leading my own breath into morning. What Tsila led me to was my bed, I knew, but how could it offer me rest when I was expected to enter it alone?

Tsila watched me undress then ran her hand across my naked back, my neck and through my loosened hair. Her touch, unburdened by affection, was lighter than Lispa's. She probed at my temples and between the partings of my hair but found neither louse nor flea.

"I'll bathe you tomorrow," she said.

I turned away from her to recite my *Shema*, the same prayer that I had recited every night from the first moment my lips could form the words. "Sleep is a perilous journey," Lipsa had instructed. If death should overtake us before morning we should enter its embrace with praise of His Name on our lips.

"Are you finished?" Tsila asked. I hadn't even shut my eyes yet, had not begun to summon the necessary concentration. Out of the corner of my eye I saw the brightness of the bed. I shut my eyes to clear my mind of distractions that were leading me away from Him.

"*Nu?*" Tsila said.

"*Hear O Israel,*" I began, but as I did so my mind exploded with colours. The pale green of the quilt, the blue of its stitching, the honey of her hair, the crimson of her birthmark—new life, eternity, sweetness, anger —each colour had a meaning, and more beyond. I fell silent before it.

"Even this she didn't teach you? *Hear O Israel,*" Tsila prodded.

"*The Lord is our God,*" I continued, then stopped. White now, as brilliant as the new pillow on which I was to rest my head, refracting to the emerald of her eyes, the unyielding copper that glinted in his. Longing—but for what?—swept through me like wind. Then fear—of what I didn't know. It was a sin, I knew to summon His presence only to defile it in this way.

I felt Tsila's hands on my shoulders. She turned me—a half-turn—to face her. My eyes were still closed, but upon them I soon felt a presence, a pressure, cool and calming. Tsila's hand. My eyelids fluttered against it.

"*Hear O Israel,*" she began and I listened, word by word, my mind ablaze. "*Blessed is the Holy Name,*" she continued, praise of His Name calming the colours, each in its turn until they rested, still vivid, but quiet beneath her hand.

She removed her hand and met my eyes with her own. She shook her head slightly as if dismayed by what stood before her. "We'll begin tomorrow," she said and extinguished the lamp by my bed.

When I awoke the next morning harm had befallen me. The storm had passed with the night, and sunlight flooded the room. My skin felt hot, as if the air of the room had scorched it, but my core had grown cold in the night and I shivered underneath the bright quilt. I felt a pain in my throat, but did not yet understand its meaning. Tsila was tending the oven. Her hair, unbound, fell golden across her back.

"*Nu?*" she asked when she saw my open eyes.

I pushed back the quilt and swung my legs over the side of the bed.

The floor was smooth and solid on the soles of my feet, but the room spun around me.

"*Modeh Ani*," Tsila prodded. The prayer upon waking. This too Lipsa had taught me, but when I attempted to utter the words, I could not. The prayer was there, lodged in my heart, but the instrument for its delivery had been taken from me.

"*I stand before Thee*," I rasped. The theft had been incomplete. A ragged shard of my voice still remained, but it hurt to use it, so raw and sore was the place from which the rest had been torn.

I waited in terror. Afraid of Tsila's anger, yes, but more of the damage that had been done to me.

"*King of the Universe*," Tsila went on. "*Who has mercifully returned my soul to me...*"

"My mother," I whispered to Tsila without thinking, understanding at once who had swept through me the night before as I stood by my bed trying to recite the evening prayer.

Tsila looked up from her oven. I saw her as from a great distance away. She was kneeling as she had knelt the day before, but her face was turned to me now. She put down the poker she had been using, arose and walked over to me. Her hand was rough on my forehead.

"You have a fever," she said. "Get back into bed."

I obeyed her, as Lipsa had told me I must, drinking the tea that she gave me and allowing her to wrap a warm towel around my neck, but she was misguided to think that tea and a towel might bring back what had been taken.

"Sleep now," she told me, and I did. Through that day, and the following.

I awoke at one point to the sound of whispers. It was night then, the lamps extinguished and darkness pressing against the windows. I lay in the darkness confused, a stream of whispers and I heard his laughter too now, a low rumble. And yet more whispers. My body shook under the quilt, but my cheeks burned.

I curled myself into a ball—only my hot forehead exposed. I lay like that, burning and shivering all at once until I felt a breath on my skin. Balm that breath was, soothing as a cool hand, and though I had not felt her touch until then, I knew at once whose it was.

I must have called out—but how? and with what?—because when I opened my eyes both Tsila and my father stood by my bed, Tsila's hand on my brow now.

"My mother," I whispered. Come for me, at last.

"It's the fever," Tsila said.

"Should we not call Lipsa?" I heard my father suggest as I fell back into sleep.

Lipsa's lips were pinched tight, her eyes unnaturally bright—two dark stars glittering out of a milky face.

"How long has this been?" she asked, then without awaiting an answer told Tsila to boil water with the lemons and honey she had brought.

"My mother," I whispered to her, but she placed her finger on my lips to silence me.

"*My mother, my mother,*" Tsila complained. She was suddenly by my bed, waving her wooden spoon around. "What kind of curse have you brought into my house?"

Lipsa rested her hand on Tsila's waving arm. "Go stir the lemon. It shouldn't boil too hard." She removed her hand from Tsila and lay her fingers on the point of violation. My throat fluttered beneath her touch. I waited for her to appeal to my mother. I had heard her make such appeals before. Just the week before my father's wedding I had accompanied her to the cemetery where she had begged Channa-Gitl to loosen her hold on her daughter's heart. Two years after Channa-Gitl's death, the daughter was still so stricken with grief that she was barren and unfit as a wife. *Have mercy on your poor daughter,* Lipsa cried out to Channa-Gitl. *Release her from her mourning. Free her for the life that is still hers to bring forth.* I closed my eyes now and waited for a similar appeal to my mother.

"Your mother wouldn't do this," Lipsa said quietly. She removed her fingers from my throat and I felt a damp warmth. A towel. She was laying a towel at my throat, no different from the towels Tsila had been laying throughout the week. "Your mother doesn't need your voice," Lipsa said to me. "What would she need with your voice?" But Lipsa's own voice trembled and there was fear in her face.

"It's your father who needs your voice," she said to me. "Your father who needs to hear your sweet voice."

"What, sweet?" Tsila muttered. "She has the voice of a crow."

"And Tsila, Tsila needs it too," Lipsa said.

"What do I need with her voice?" Tsila asked. "She wants to be mute all her life? Excellent." She handed the concoction she had boiled to Lipsa. "Let her be mute. Deaf too if she wants."

In Tsila's voice, too, though, there was the tremble of fear and it was from her that I understood just how close the angel of death hovered. *Leave her be now*, Tsila was imploring. *She is ugly, unloved, not worth your trouble. Go and find yourself a sweeter child.*

Lipsa brought a spoonful of syrup to my lips and I swallowed it. Hot, sour and sweet, it stung my throat as it passed through.

"Your father and Tsila need to hear your voice," Lipsa said as she continued spooning syrup down my throat. "What's a household without the voices of children?"

She pushed a lock of damp hair off my forehead.

"The next time I see Tsila, I want to hear you've been singing for her. Do you understand me?" I nodded miserably, hot tears sliding down my cheeks. "Tsila's your mother now," Lipsa said.

Mud filled my throat, a thick and sticky layer of it. It gurgled and thickened with each breath I tried to take. I strained for breath, gulping air in huge and useless swallows, but the mucus only spread across my throat, blocking the passage to my lungs.

Tsila forced steam through my nose and mouth with towels so hot they burned the skin of my face. But though the steam filled my nostrils and mouth, it couldn't penetrate the mud. I strained harder, clawing at the air, then at my throat that wouldn't admit it. With each failed breath my legs kicked up from the bed, then fell back. Tsila gripped my head against her lap, pressing harder with her hot, rough towels.

I heard Lipsa's voice again then felt her hands upon my head, and though her touch was gentle, the very hairs on my head ached beneath her fingers.

"Master of the universe," I heard her say.

"Save this child . . ." The prayer continued, but in Tsila's voice now.

I opened my eyes. It was daytime and nighttime at once. Candles burned in the room, yet light poured through the window. Moonlight or sunlight, I didn't know, but in that one beam of light I saw the suspended dust of the room begin to dance in a slow and swirling pattern. It circled my ankles once, twice, then again and again, gently tugging and lifting my now weightless legs from the bed. And though I did not see my mother among the particles of dust, I knew she was there, lifting and pulling me towards her. In the shadow behind me, though, Tsila clutched me against her hard and bony lap, holding me to the roughness of life.

Around the edges of my eyes a darkness began to gather. The dust still swirled, but it moved within a shrinking circle of light. Faster and wilder as the darkness pressed in around it—I watched, entranced, until the cool smoothness of Tsila's hand shut my burning eyelids. "Lord of my fathers, I beseech you," I heard from the shadow behind me. "Guide my hand in the act I am about to perform." My head was pulled back, my throat bared like that of a calf prepared for slaughter. "*Hear O Israel…*" Tsila whispered in my ear, preparing me to die. My mind followed the path of her words.

In peace will I both lay me down and sleep. For thou, Lord, makest me dwell alone in safety.

My father sat by my bed when he thought me asleep, softly reciting the psalms. Time had passed. I don't know how long. A cold wind still blew through the chinking of the walls, but Tsila had begun her Passover cleaning.

My fever had left me, and with it my strength. I awoke each morning and placed my feet on the floor, and each morning the air of that place pushed me backwards into my bed. The wound in my throat where Tsila had cut through the mud still hurt me, but air moved freely through my throat to my lungs. Every few hours Tsila boiled a new towel in water and laid it upon the wound.

The Lord is nigh unto them that are of a broken heart… None of them that take refuge in Him shall be desolate.

My father recited in the darkness. His work days were long; he was never in the house in daylight except on the Sabbath. I would hear him early in the morning, before the sun rose and at night again, after the first calling of the nightingale: *I am come into deep waters and the flood over-whelms me. I am weary with crying; my throat has dried.*

I had not spoken since my illness. It was not from stubbornness, though Tsila accused me of that. Where my voice had once been, there was now only pain. I showed Tsila without words the ache that I felt there.

"Pain is no excuse for your stubbornness," she scolded me as she brought me cup after cup of honeyed tea. Her face was pale and strained, her eyes rimmed with red as vivid as her birthmark. "Life is painful, but you don't see people lying down dead in the streets because of it."

"Should we not call Lipsa?" my father suggested.

"Has that woman not caused enough damage already?" Tsila asked.

My father's eyebrows arched with surprise but he didn't answer right away. He took a swallow of tea, then another as he considered the question put before him. "What damage?" he asked finally. "What damage?"

Tsila's eyes, flat with exhaustion from all the weeks of my illness and convalescence, lit now with anger. "What would you call cutting us off from a living? Doing us a good turn, perhaps?"

Tsila was a seamstress, but all the weeks of my illness no one had come to our house to be fitted for a dress or to pick up an order. No one had crossed our threshold at all, except Lipsa. My father still left for work before dawn each morning, but Tsila sat idle save for keeping house and nursing me.

"People were afraid, Tsila," my father said.

"Afraid of what? And by whose tale-bearing?"

My father closed his eyes as he often did when faced with an argument with Tsila. He pinched the bridge of his nose between his thumb and forefinger as if that might somehow give him the strength for the harsh words that loomed.

"It was safe for Lipsa to cross our threshold all those weeks but not my customers? What, Lipsa can't infect other children but my customers can?"

"Lipsa is a healer. She can't heal the sick without going to them."

"It wasn't Lipsa who healed your daughter, Aaron Lev. And I didn't see her calling for a quarantine when Freyde's Itche burned with fever last summer."

"It wasn't diphtheria."

"*Diphtheria.*" Tsila spat the word. "Don't give me diphtheria. Lipsa thinks I've stolen the child from her so now she tries to starve us."

"Tsila, Tsila," my father chided. "She's not trying to starve us. Why would Lipsa try to starve us? She's a good woman and besides, she knows the child is ours."

"Yours. She has always known the child is yours, but when five years passed and still you didn't call for her . . ."

"I always meant to."

"Still, you didn't until you were married to me."

"I don't think . . ."

"You never think," Tsila spat back. "Just what business do you think Lipsa still has here? In my home."

My father didn't answer.

"You don't answer because you don't know anything. I am the one who knows. I am the one who watches her scuttling up the hill, hunched and oily as a cockroach rushing to do her evil sorceries. I am the one who knows what she wants. She wants the child back in her clutches, Aaron Lev —on my own good health I swear this to you . . ."

"Don't," my father said, but too late.

"Her potions are nothing. Do you understand me, Aaron Lev? You think she has a potion that will return your daughter's voice, but I am the one who can return your daughter's voice. I am the one who saved your daughter from death."

"Only the Eternal One . . ."

"You know nothing," Tsila spat and my father fell silent.

"The child will speak again. Trust me, Arele. Have I not loosened your own tongue and freed it from its fetters?"

My father did not answer.

"Your daughter will speak, Aaron Lev. I will lead her to words."

"Water," I called out that night in my sleep. The first words I had uttered since falling ill. When I opened my eyes, Tsila was standing beside my bed. "Water," I said again, and she handed me a glass of the cool water I had called for. I drank it empty and handed it back to her.

"What do you say?" she whispered.

"Thank you," I said.

"Again?"

"Thank you," I repeated, and she dropped to her knees beside my bed.

"Your mouth is lovely," she whispered to me, the same words I had heard Lipsa say to her two youngest boys when they uttered their first words.

Help us guard his little mouth from obscenities, Lipsa had said. *May he never lie, but speak only words of Torah and wisdom, pleasing to God and men. Amen.*

Tsila said none of that. She stayed half-kneeling against my bed, her face close to mine, her long soft hair falling around my head. "Your lips are a crimson thread," she whispered, softly tracing the outline of my mouth with her finger.

We started then, the very next day, with Bes, the second letter of the alphabet.

"Aleph was chosen to be first, it's true, but what came of it?" Tsila asked.

She looked at me, awaiting my response, but I had no response. I didn't know about the letters.

"Bes came second. A disadvantage, no?" I nodded and that seemed to satisfy her.

"But look," she said, pulling an egg from the basket beside her. "Bavtzah," she pronounced as proudly as if she herself had created it. She placed the egg in my hand. It was warm, and heavy with promise. "Bavtzah," I said as I handed it back to her.

"Bayis," Tsila said next, sweeping her hand to indicate the house that encased us.

"Bimah," I repeated. The podium at the front of a shul. But now Tsila wasn't satisfied. "We've hardly even started and already you're daydreaming."

"I'm not daydreaming," I protested.

"You can't afford to daydream," she said. "Other girls, yes, they can daydream all they want, but you—you cannot afford to daydream when I am trying to teach you the Aleph-Bes. Do you understand me?"

I did not understand her, but nodded my head anyway.

"Do you want to end up like Simple Sorel?"

It was said that something had scared Sorel in her infancy and that was why she walked around with her hands covering her ears and eyes humming lullabies to herself all day.

"I'm not like Sorel," I said.

"Sorel wasn't like Sorel either until she started daydreaming and scaring herself half to death. Now you pay attention."

"I am paying attention."

"So then what else starts with the letter Bes?"

I thought about it, making the sound B over and over again. Tsila tapped her long fingers on the table.

"Bagel," I said.

"Bagel," Tsila repeated. "And what else?"

"Bracha," I said. "Binyamin, Booba . . ."

"Good," she said, with obvious surprise. "Bagel, Bracha, Binyamin, Baytzah—a lot of words, no?"

I nodded, but she wasn't looking at me.

"But most of all," she said, "most important of all the words Bes leads into the world . . . Can you think what it is?" She looked at me with hope. I wanted to satisfy her, but couldn't. She opened the Chumash on the table before us, opened it to the first page of the first book. Genesis. The beginning.

"Breshis," I said, before she could.

She looked at me. Her eyes were flashing emerald light. Her colour was high, obscuring the mark of anger in her cheek. "Breshis," she repeated. "The beginning. Do you see?" she asked, excitement swelling in her voice. "Second in line after the letter Aleph, yes, but chosen by God to begin the Torah, to begin all creation. Do you understand?"

I was only a child, and an ignorant one at that, but I sensed a blasphemy in the charged atmosphere of our lesson.

"And where's the Aleph?" she asked. "The great first letter?" Her eyes were lit as if by fever.

"Nu?" she prodded.

"I don't know," I said.

"Exactly." She took my finger, the second finger of my right hand and pointed to the third letter in the word "breshis."

"Aleph," she said. "First in line but silent now after Bes."

She sat back in satisfaction and I waited for her to bring out the sweets she would now lay before me, the drop of honey she would now place on my tongue. Lipsa's boys had been carried to *cheder* their first day, Lipsa herself had baked the sweets and provided the honey. A light golden honey, she had chosen. "Knowledge is sweetness," she whispered to her boys as the letters of the Aleph-Bes paraded before them for the first time.

"I'm not your mother," Tsila said, her face still flushed, her eyes flashing sparks of light. "I mean no cruelty, but I am not your mother. You and I have an understanding on that, no?"

I nodded my head, though uncertain as to the nature of the understanding I was entering.

"I will raise you and teach you to be a human being among human beings." She paused as if to digest the significance of such a promise. "But as for your mother... This is your mother now." She indicated the letters before us, a long line of unnamed letters, their mysteries still unrevealed.

"Your first mother was unfaithful to you."

I wouldn't nod my head to that. I knew the commandments even if I could not read them.

"But you mustn't blame her," Tsila went on. "All mothers are unfaithful to their daughters."

Another blasphemy. I felt it in the knotting of my stomach and the flutter in my throat.

Tsila looked at my face and laughed. "You mustn't close your ears when I tell you the truth." Her laugh was light, almost kind.

"I'm going to tell you many truths. And what I'm going to give you will be faithful. Far more faithful than your mother could be."

❧   Nancy Richler lives in Vancouver, B.C. Her first novel, *Throwaway Angels*, was shortlisted for the 1996 Arthur Ellis Award for Best First Crime Novel. "Your Mouth is Lovely" appeared in the *Journey Prize Anthology 2000*. The Journey Prize is awarded annually to a new and developing writer of distinction in Canada. Submissions from literary journals across the country are published in the *Journey Prize Anthology* each year. (*Born Montreal, Quebec 1957*)

RESPONDING

Meaning

1. References to various kinds of "voices" and silences occur throughout the story. Find several of these references, and explain how they relate to a key theme of the story.

2. In her portrait of Tsila, Richler negotiates a balance between perpetuating the stereotype of the "evil stepmother" and undermining it. Provide two examples of how she achieves this balance. What effect does this have on the reader?

Form and Style

3. The physical setting of the story is rich in symbolism and detail. What symbolic meaning might the following aspects of the setting have in the story:
    a) mud?
    b) the swamp?
    c) the wind?
    How do these aspects contribute to the overall mood of the story? How do they reflect the inner feelings of the narrator?

4. Describe the narrative viewpoint of the story. Why do you think Richler chose to tell the story from this point of view?

Exploring Context

5. Using at least three examples, show how Richler develops a critique of the lives of women within the setting of the story. Do you feel the author is, or is not, biased in this critique? Support your interpretation.

Creative Extension

6. Write a series of journal entries that Tsila, the stepmother, might have written from the time the girl arrives at her door, to the end of her illness. Include her impressions of the girl, her own thoughts and fears, and her feeling towards her husband and Lipsa. The voice you create should reflect the character of Tsila revealed in the story.

7. Create a visual representation of a character or scene from the story. Your visual representation could be a drawing, painting, storyboard, or stage setting in which you indicate where various props and characters would be if the scene were dramatized on stage or film. Include a short commentary explaining your choices and techniques.

The Night Face Up

✎ Julio Cortazar

Halfway down the long hotel vestibule, he thought that probably he was going to be late, and hurried on into the street to get out his motorcycle from the corner where the next-door superintendent let him keep it. On the jewelry store clock at the corner he saw that it was ten to nine; he had time to spare. The sun filtered through the tall downtown buildings, and he—because for himself, for just going along thinking, he did not have a name—he swung onto the machine, savouring the idea of the ride. The motor whirred between his legs, and a cool wind whipped his pantlegs.

He lets the ministries zip past (the pink, the white), and a series of stores on the main street, their windows flashing. Now he was beginning the most pleasant part of the run, the real ride: a long street bordered with trees, very little traffic, with spacious villas whose gardens rambled all the way down to the sidewalks, which were barely indicated by low hedges. A bit inattentive perhaps, but tooling along the right side of the street, he allowed himself to be carried away by the freshness, by the weightless contraction of this hardly begun day. This involuntary relaxation, possibly, kept him from preventing the accident. When he saw that the woman standing on the corner had rushed into the crosswalk while he still had the green light, it was already somewhat too late for a simple solution. He braked hard with foot and hand, wrenching himself to the left; he heard the woman scream, and at the collision his vision went. It was like falling asleep all at once.

He came to abruptly. Four or five young men were getting him out from under the cycle. He felt the taste of salt and blood, one knee hurt, and when they hoisted him up he yelped, he couldn't bear the pressure on his right arm. Voices which did not seem to belong to the faces hanging above him encouraged him cheerfully with jokes and assurances. His single solace was to hear someone else confirm that the lights indeed had been in his favour. He asked about the woman, trying to keep down the nausea which was edging up into his throat. While they carried him face up to a nearby pharmacy, he learned that the cause of the accident had gotten only a few scrapes on the legs. "Nah, you barely got her at all, but when ya hit, the impact made the machine jump and flop on its side...." Opinions, recollections of other smashups, take it easy, work him in shoulders first, there, that's fine, and someone in a dustcoat giving him a swallow of something soothing in the shadowy interior of the small local pharmacy.

Within five minutes the police ambulance arrived, and they lifted him onto a cushioned stretcher. It was a relief for him to be able to lie out flat. Completely lucid, but realizing that he was suffering the effects of a terrible shock, he gave his information to the officer riding in the ambulance with him. The arm almost didn't hurt; blood dripped down from a cut over the eyebrow all over his face. He licked his lips once or twice to drink it. He felt pretty good, it had been an accident, tough luck; stay quiet a few weeks, nothing worse. The guard said that the motorcycle didn't seem badly racked up. "Why should it," he replied. "It all landed on top of me." They both laughed, and when they got to the hospital, the guard shook his hand and wished him luck. Now the nausea was coming back little by little; meanwhile they were pushing him on a wheeled stretcher toward a pavilion farther back, rolling along under trees full of birds, he shut his eyes and wished he were asleep or chloroformed. But they kept him for a good while in a room with that hospital smell, filling out a form, getting his clothes off, and dressing him in a stiff, greyish smock. They moved his arm carefully, it didn't hurt him. The nurses were constantly making wisecracks, and if it hadn't been for the stomach contractions he would have felt fine, almost happy.

They got him over to X-ray, and twenty minutes later, with the still-damp negative lying on his chest like a black tombstone, they pushed him into surgery. Someone tall and thin in white came over and began to look at the X-rays. A woman's hands were arranging his head, he felt that they were moving him from one stretcher to another. The man in white came over to him again, smiling, something gleamed in his right hand. He patted his cheek and made a sign to someone stationed behind.

It was unusual as a dream because it was full of smells, and he never dreamt smells. First a marshy smell, there to the left of the trail the swamps began already, the quaking bogs from which no one ever returned. But the reek lifted, and instead there came a dark, fresh composite fragrance, like the night under which he moved, in flight from the Aztecs. And it was all so natural, he had to run from the Aztecs who had set out on their manhunt, and his sole chance was to find a place to hide in the deepest part of the forest, taking care not to lose the narrow trail which only they, the Motecas, knew.

What tormented him the most was the odour, as though, notwithstanding the absolute acceptance of the dream, there was something which resisted that which was not habitual, which until that point had not participated in the game. "It smells of war," he thought, his hand going instinctively to the stone knife which was tucked at an angle into his girdle of woven wool. An unexpected sound made him crouch suddenly stock-still and shaking. To be afraid was nothing strange, there was plenty of fear in his dreams. He waited, covered by the branches of a shrub and the starless night. Far off, probably on the other side of the big lake, they'd be lighting the bivouac fires; that part of the sky had a reddish glare. The sound was not repeated. It had been like a broken limb. Maybe an animal that, like himself, was escaping from the smell of war. He stood erect slowly, sniffing the air. Not a sound could be heard, but the fear was still following, as was the smell, that cloying incense of the war of the blossom.[1] He had to press forward, to stay out of the bogs and get to the heart of the forest. Groping uncertainly through the dark, stooping every other moment to touch the packed earth of the trail, he took a few steps. He would have liked to have broken into a run, but the gurgling fens lapped on either side of him. On the path and in the darkness, he took his bearings. Then he caught a horrible blast of that foul smell he was most afraid of, and leaped forward desperately.

"You're going to fall off the bed," said the patient next to him. "Stop bouncing around, old buddy."

He opened his eyes and it was afternoon, the sun already low in the oversized windows of the long ward. While trying to smile at his neighbour, he detached himself almost physically from the final scene of the nightmare. His arm, in plaster cast, hung suspended from an apparatus

---

1 The war of the blossom was the name the Aztecs gave to a ritual war in which they took prisoners for sacrifice. The Aztecs' gods saw humans as flowers to be uprooted.

with weights and pulleys. He felt thirsty, as though he'd been running for miles, but they didn't want to give him much water, barely enough to moisten his lips and make a mouthful. The fever was winning slowly and he would have been able to sleep again, but he was enjoying the pleasure of keeping awake, eyes half-closed, listening to the other patients' conversation, answering a question from time to time. He saw a little white push-cart come up beside the bed, a blond nurse rubbed the front of his thigh with alcohol and stuck him with a fat needle connected to a tube which ran up to a bottle filled with a milky, opalescent liquid. A young intern arrived with some metal and leather apparatus which he adjusted to fit onto the good arm to check something or other. Night fell, and the fever went along dragging him down softly to a state in which things seemed embossed as though opera glasses, they were real and soft and, at the same time, vaguely distasteful; like sitting in a boring movie and thinking that, well, still, it'd be worse out in the street, and staying.

A cup of a marvelous golden broth came, smelling of leeks, celery, and parsley. A small hunk of bread, more precious than the whole banquet, found itself crumbling little by little. His arm hardly hurt him at all, and only in the eyebrow where they'd taken stitches a quick, hot pain sizzled occasionally. When the big windows across the way turned to smudges of dark blue, he thought it would not be difficult for him to sleep. Still on his back so a little uncomfortable, running his tongue over his hot, too-dry lips, he tasted the broth still, and with a sigh of bliss he let himself drift off.

First there was a confusion, as of one drawing all his sensations, for that moment blunted or muddled, into himself. He realized that he was running in pitch darkness, although, above, the sky criss-crossed with treetops was less black than the rest. "The trail," he thought, "I've gotten off the trail." His feet sank into a bed of leaves and mud, and then he couldn't take a step that the branches of shrubs did not whiplash against his ribs and legs. Out of breath, knowing despite the darkness and silence that he was surrounded, he crouched down to listen. Maybe the trail was very near, with the first daylight he would be able to see it again. Nothing now could help him to find it. The hand that had unconsciously gripped the haft of the dagger climbed like a fen scorpion up to his neck where the protecting amulet hung. Barely moving his lips, he mumbled the supplication of the corn which brings about the beneficent moons, and the prayer to Her Very Highness, to the distributor of all Motecan possessions. At the same time he felt his ankles sinking deeper into the mud, and the waiting in the darkness of the obscure grove of live oak grew intolerable to him. The war of the blossom had started at the beginning of the moon and had been going on for three days and three nights now. If he managed to hide in the depths of the forest, getting off the trail farther up past the marsh country, perhaps the warriors wouldn't follow his track. He thought of the many prisoners they'd already taken. But the number didn't count, only the consecrated period. The hunt would continue until the priests gave the sign to return. Everything had its number and its limit, and it was within the sacred period, and he on the other side from the hunters.

He heard the cries and leaped up, knife in hand. As if the sky were aflame on the horizon, he saw torches moving among the branches, very near him. The smell of war was unbearable, and when the first enemy jumped him, leaped at his throat, he felt an almost-pleasure in sinking the stone blade flat to the haft into his chest. The lights were already around him, the happy cries. He managed to cut the air once or twice, then a rope snared him from behind.

"It's the fever," the man in the next bed said. "The same thing happened to me when they operated on my duodenum. Take some water, you'll see, you'll sleep all right."

Laid next to the night from which he came back, the tepid shadow of the ward seemed delicious to him. A violet lamp kept watch high on the far wall like a guardian eye. You could hear coughing, deep breathing, once in a while a conversation in whispers. Everything was pleasant and secure, without the chase, no . . . But he didn't want to go on thinking about the nightmare. There were lots of things to amuse himself with. He began to look at the cast on his arm, and the pulleys that held it so comfortably in the air. They'd left a bottle of mineral water on the night table beside him. He put the neck of the bottle to his mouth and drank it like a precious liqueur. He could now make out the different shapes in the ward, the thirty beds, the closets with glass doors. He guessed that his fever was down, his face felt cool. The cut over the eyebrow barely hurt at all, like a recollection. He saw himself leaving the hotel again, wheeling out the cycle. Who'd have thought that it would end like this? He tried to fix the moment of the accident exactly, and it got him very angry to notice that there was a void there, an emptiness he could not manage to fill. Between the impact and the moment that they picked him up off the pavement, the passing out or what went on, there was nothing he could see. And at the same time he had the feeling that this void, this nothingness, had lasted an eternity. No, not even time, more as if, in this void, he had passed across something, or had run back immense distances. The shock, the brutal dashing against the pavement. Anyway, he had felt an immense relief in coming out of the black pit while the people were lifting him off the ground. With pain in the broken arm, blood from the split eyebrow, contusion on the knee; with all that, a relief in returning to daylight, to the day, and to feel sustained and attended. That was weird. Someday he'd ask the doctor at the office about that. Now sleep began to take over again, to pull him slowly down. The pillow was so soft, and the coolness of the mineral water in his fevered throat. The violet light of the lamp up there was beginning to get dimmer and dimmer.

As he was sleeping on his back, the position in which he came to did not surprise him, but on the other hand the damp smell, the smell of oozing rock, blocked his throat and forced him to understand. Open the eyes and look in all directions, hopeless. He was surrounded by an absolute darkness. Tried to get up and felt ropes pinning his wrists and ankles. He was staked to the ground on a floor of dank, icy stone slabs. The cold bit into this naked back, his legs. Dully, he tried to touch the amulet with his chin and found they had stripped him of it. Now he was lost, no prayer could save him from the final . . . From afar off, as though filtering through the rock of the dungeon, he heard the great kettledrums of the feast. They had carried him to the temple, he was in the underground cells of Teocalli itself, awaiting his turn.

He heard a yell, a hoarse yell that rocked off the walls. Another yell, ending in a moan. It was he who was screaming in the darkness, he was screaming because he was alive, his whole body with that cry fended off what was coming, the inevitable end. He thought of his friends filling up other dungeons, and of those already walking up the stairs of the sacrifice. He uttered another choked cry, he could barely open his mouth, his jaws were twisted back as if with a rope and a stick, and once in awhile they would open slowly with an endless exertion, as if they were made of rubber. The creaking of the wooden latches jolted him like a whip. Rent, writhing, he fought to rid himself of the cords sinking into his flesh. His right arm, the strongest, strained until the pain became unbearable and he had to give up. He watched the double door open, and the smell of the torches reached him before the light did. Barely girdled by the ceremonial loin-cloths, the priests' acolytes moved in his direction, looking at him with contempt. Lights reflected off the sweaty torsos and off the black hair dressed with feathers. The cords went slack, and in their place the grap-pling of hot hands, hard as bronze; he felt himself lifted, still face up, and jerked along by the four acolytes who carried him down the passageway. The torchbearers went ahead, indistinctly lighting up the corridor with its dripping walls and a ceiling so low that the acolytes had to duck their heads. Now they were taking him out, taking him out, it was the end. Face up, under a mile of living rock which, for a succession of moments, was lit up by a glimmer of torchlight. When the stars came out up there instead of the roof and the great terraced steps rose before him, on fire with cries and dances, it would be the end. The passage was never going to end, but now it was beginning to end, he would see suddenly the open sky full of stars, but not yet, they trundled him along endlessly in the reddish shadow, hauling him roughly along and he did not want that, but how to stop it if they had torn off the amulet, his real heart, the life-center.

In a single jump he came out into the hospital night, to the high, gentle, bare ceiling, to the soft shadow wrapping him round. He thought he must have cried out, but his neighbours were peacefully snoring. The water in the bottle on the night stand was somewhat bubbly, a translucent shape against the dark azure shadow of the windows. He panted, looking for some relief for his lungs, oblivion for those images still glued to his eyelids. Each time he shut his eyes he saw them take shape instantly, and she sat up, completely wrung out, but savouring at the same time the surety that now he was awake, that the night nurse would answer if he rang, that soon it would be daybreak, with the good, deep sleep he usually had at that hour, no images, no nothing . . . It was difficult to keep his eyes open, the drowsiness was more powerful than he. He made one last effort, he sketched a gesture toward the bottle of water with his good hand and did not manage to reach it, his fingers closed again on a black emptiness, and the passageway went on endlessly, rock after rock, with momentary ruddy flares, and face up he choked out a dull moan because the roof was about to end, it rose, was opening like a mouth of shadow, and the acolytes straightened up, and from on high a waning moon fell on a face whose eyes wanted not to see it, were closing and opening desperately, trying to pass to the other side, to find again the bare, protecting ceiling of the ward. And every time they opened, it was night and the moon, while they climbed the great terraced steps, his head hanging down backward now, and up at the top were the bonfires, red columns of perfumed smoke, and suddenly he saw the red stone, shiny with the blood dripping off it, and the spinning arcs cut by the feet of the victim whom they pulled off to throw him rolling down the north steps. With a last hope he shut his lids tightly, moaning to wake up. For a second he thought he had gotten there, because once more he was immobile in the bed, except that his head was hanging down off it, swinging. But he smelled death, and when he opened his eyes he saw the blood-soaked figure of the executioner-priest coming toward him with the stone knife in his hand. He managed to close his eyelids again, although he knew now he was not going to wake up, that he was awake, that the marvelous dream had been the other, absurd as all dreams are—a dream in which he was going through the strange avenues of an astonishing city, with green and red lights that burned without fire or smoke, on an enormous metal insect that whirred away between his legs. In the infinite lie of the dream, they had also picked him up off the ground, someone had approached him also with a knife in his hand, approached him who was lying face up, face up with his eyes closed between the bonfires on the steps.

⌖ Julio Cortazar was raised in Argentina, but in 1951, he moved to France. His short stories and novels borrowed techniques from Surrealism, a movement in art, literature, and film. Surrealists tried to depict thoughts from the subconscious mind in unconventional ways. Cortazar achieved his first major success with a book of stories called *Bestiario* in 1951 (selections appear in *The End of the Game and Other Stories*, 1967). His novel *Rayuela* (*Hopscotch*), published in 1963, was widely praised and won Cortazar an enthusiastic international following. (*Born Brussels, Belgium 1914; died 1984*)

RESPONDING

Meaning

1. The two worlds depicted in the story stand in sharp contrast: the one, a world seemingly full of order and civilization; the other, a world of chaos, fear, and instinct. Yet the author seems to suggest that the two are not as separate as we would like to think. What aspects of the story indicate that chaos and order are really two sides of the same coin?

2. What is the significance of the story's title?

Form and Style

3. Examine the techniques Cortazar uses to heighten the suspense of the story. How does he manage to sustain the suspense even through the relatively calm periods when the protagonist escapes into the hospital room?

4. a) Read the first two paragraphs closely. How does the author use diction and imagery to emphasize the theme of order and civilization?

   b) Now read the two paragraphs that first describe the Aztec world (beginning "It was unusual as a dream . . . "). How does the author use diction and imagery to establish the contrast between the two worlds?

Exploring Context

5. The psychiatrist Carl Jung believed that dreams often express our most hidden desires and fears—parts of ourselves that we do not want to or are too afraid to acknowledge when awake. He claimed that these neglected, or repressed, aspects of our personality often manifest themselves in dreams in the form of a relentless pursuer. How does this theory apply to the protagonist in the story? From this perspective, what is the significance of the ending?

Creative Extension

6. Assume the role of a movie publicist and create an advertising poster for the movie version of "The Night Face Up." Use your own drawings or illustrations from newspapers, magazines, computer graphics programs, etc.

7. Use a variety of sources to prepare a report on one aspect of ancient Aztec or Motecan culture. Present your report to a group or the whole class.

The Fly

❧ Katherine Mansfield

"Y'are very snug in here," piped old Mr. Woodifield and he peered out of the great, green-leather armchair by his friend the boss's desk as a baby peers out of its pram. His talk was over; it was time for him to be off. But he did not want to go. Since he had retired, since his . . . stroke, the wife and the girls kept him boxed up in the house every day of the week except Tuesday. On Tuesday he was dressed and brushed and allowed to cut back to the City for the day. Though what he did there the wife and girls couldn't imagine. Made a nuisance of himself to his friends, they supposed. . . . Well, perhaps so. All the same, we cling to our last pleasures as the tree clings to its last leaves. So there sat old Woodifield, smoking a cigar and staring almost greedily at the boss, who rolled in his office chair, stout, rosy, five years older than he, and still going strong, still at the helm. It did one good to see him.

Wistfully, admiring, the old voice added, "It's snug in here, upon my word!"

"Yes, it's comfortable enough," agreed the boss, and flipped the *Financial Times* with a paper-knife. As a matter of fact he was proud of his room; he liked to have it admired, especially by old Woodifield. It gave him a feeling of deep, solid satisfaction to be planted there in the midst of it in full view of that frail old figure in the muffler.

"I've had it done up lately," he explained, as he explained for the past —how many?—weeks. "New carpet," and he pointed to the bright red carpet with a pattern of large white rings. "New furniture," and he nodded towards the massive bookcase and the table with legs like twisted treacle. "Electric heating!" He waved almost exultantly towards the five transparent, pearly sausages glowing so softly in the tilted copper pan.

But he did not draw old Woodifield's attention to the photograph over the table of a grave-looking boy in uniform standing in one of those spectral photographers' parks with photographers' storm clouds behind him. It was not new. It had been there for over six years.

"There was something I wanted to tell you," said old Woodifield, and his eyes grew dim remembering. "Now what was it? I had it in my mind when I started out this morning." His hands began to tremble, and patches of red started to show above his beard.

Poor old chap, he's on his last pins, thought the boss. And, feeling kindly he winked at the old man, and said jokingly, "I tell you what. I've got a drop of a little something here that'll do you good before you go out into the cold again. It's beautiful stuff. It wouldn't hurt a child." He took a key off his watch-chain, unlocked a cupboard below his desk, and drew forth a dark, squat bottle. "That's the medicine," said he. "And the man from whom I got it told me on the strict Q.T. it came from the cellars at Windsor Castle."

Old Woodifield's mouth fell open at the sight. He couldn't have looked more surprised if the boss had produced a rabbit.

"It's whisky, ain't it?" he piped feebly.

The boss turned the bottle and lovingly showed him the label. Whisky it was. "D'you know," said he, peering up at the boss wonderingly, "they won't let me touch it at home." And he looked as though he was going to cry.

"Ah, that's where we know a bit more than the ladies," cried the boss, swooping across for two tumblers that stood on the table with the water-bottle, and pouring a generous finger into each. "Drink it down. It'll do you good. And don't put any water with it. It's sacrilege to tamper with stuff like this. Ah!" He tossed off his, pulled out his handkerchief, hastily wiped his moustaches, and cocked an eye at old Woodifield, who was rolling his in his chaps.

The old man swallowed, was silent a moment, and then said faintly, "It's nutty!"

But it warmed him; it crept into his chill old brain—he remembered.

"That was it," he said, heaving himself out of his chair. "I thought you'd like to know. The girls were in Belgium last week having a look at poor Reggie's grave, and they happen to come across your boy's. They're quite near each other, it seems."

Old Woodifield paused, but the boss made no reply. Only a quiver in his eyelids showed that he heard.

"The girls were delighted with the way the place was kept," piped the old voice. "Beautifully looked after. Couldn't be better if they were at home. You've not been across, have yer?"

"No, no!" For various reasons the boss had not been across.

"There's miles of it," quavered old Woodifield, "and it's all as neat as a garden. Flowers growing on all the graves. Nice broad paths." It was plain from his voice how much he liked a nice broad path.

The pause came again. Then the old man brightened wonderfully.

"D'you know what the hotel made the girls pay for a pot of jam?" he piped. "Ten francs! Robbery, I call it. It was a little pot, so Gertrude says, no bigger than a half-crown. And she hadn't taken more than a spoonful when they charged her ten francs. Gertrude brought the pot away with her to teach 'em a lesson. Quite right, too; it's trading on our feelings. They think because we're over there having a look 'round we're ready to pay anything. That's what it is." And he turned towards the door.

"Quite right, quite right!" cried the boss, though what was quite right he hadn't the least idea. He came round by his desk, followed the shuffling footsteps to the door, and saw the old fellow out. Woodifield was gone.

For a long moment the boss stayed, staring at nothing, while the grey-haired office messenger, watching him, dodged in and out of his cubbyhole like a dog that expects to be taken for a run. Then: "I'll see nobody for half an hour, Macey," said the boss. "Understand? Nobody at all."

"Very good, sir."

The door shut, the firm heavy steps recrossed the bright carpet, the fat body plumped down in the spring chair, and leaning forward, the boss covered his face with his hands. He wanted, he intended, he arranged to weep. . . .

It had been a terrible shock to him when old Woodifield sprang that remark upon him about the boy's grave. It was exactly as though the earth had opened and he had seen the boy lying there with Woodifield's girls staring down at him. For it was strange. Although over six years had passed away, the boss never thought of the boy except as lying unchanged, unblemished in his uniform, asleep for ever. "My son!" groaned the boss. But no tears came yet. In the past, in the first months and even years after the boy's death, he had only to say those words to be overcome by such grief that nothing short of a violent fit of weeping could relieve him. Time, he had declared then, he had told everybody, could make no difference. Other men perhaps might recover, might live their loss down, but not he. How was it possible? His boy was an only son. Ever since his birth the boss had worked at building up this business for him; it had no other meaning if it was not for the boy. Life itself had come to have no other meaning. How on earth could he have slaved, denied himself, kept going all those years without the promise for ever before him of the boy's stepping into his shoes and carrying on where he left off?

And that promise had been so near being fulfilled. The boy had been in the office learning the ropes for a year before the war. Every morning they had started off together; they had come back by the same train. And what congratulations he had received as the boy's father! No wonder; he had taken to it marvellously. As to his popularity with the staff, every man jack of them down to old Macey couldn't make enough of the boy. And he wasn't in the least spoilt. No he was just his bright natural self, with the right word for everybody, with that boyish look and his habit of saying, "Simply splendid!"

But all that was over and done with as though it had never been. The day had come when Macey handed him the telegram that brought the whole place crashing about his head. "Deeply regret to inform you . . ." And he had left the office a broken man, with his life in ruins.

Six years ago, six years . . . How quickly time passed! It might have happened yesterday. The boss took his hands from his face; he was puzzled. Something seemed to be wrong with him. He wasn't feeling as he wanted to feel. He decided to get up and have a look at the boy's photograph. But it wasn't a favourite photograph of his; the expression was unnatural. It was cold, even stern-looking. The boy had never looked like that.

At that moment the boss noticed that a fly had fallen into his broad inkpot, and was trying feebly but desperately to clamber out again. Help! help! said those struggling legs. But the sides of the inkpot were wet and slippery; it fell back again and began to swim. The boss took up a pen, picked the fly out of the ink, and shook it on to a piece of bottling-paper. For a fraction of a second it lay still on the dark patch that oozed round it. Then the front legs waved, took hold, and, pulling its small, sodden body up, it began the immense task of cleaning the ink from its wings. Over and under, over and under, went a leg along a wing as the stones go over and under a scythe. Then there was a pause, while the fly, seeming to stand on the tips of its toes, tried to expand first one wing and then the other. It succeeded at last, and, sitting down, it began, like a minute cat, to clean its face. Now one could imagine that the little front legs rubbed against each other lightly, joyfully. The horrible danger was over; it had escaped; it was ready for life again.

But just then the boss had an idea. He plunged his pen back into the ink, leaned his thick wrist on the blotting-paper, and as the fly tried its wings down came a great heavy blot. What would it make of that? What indeed! The little beggar seemed cowed, stunned, and afraid to move because of what would happen next. But then, as if painfully, it dragged itself forward. The front legs waved, caught hold, and, more slowly this time, the task began from the beginning.

He's a plucky little devil, thought the boss, and he felt a real admiration for the fly's courage. That was the way to tackle things; that was the right spirit. Never say die; it was only a question of . . . But the fly had again finished its laborious task, and the boss had just time to refill his pen, to shake fair and square on the new-cleaned body yet another dark drop. What about it this time? A painful moment of suspense followed. But behold, the front legs were again waving; the boss felt a rush of relief. He leaned over the fly and said to it tenderly, "You artful little b . . ." And he actually had the brilliant notion of breathing on it to help the drying process. All the same, there was something timid and weak about its efforts now, and the boss decided that this time should be the last, as he dipped the pen deep into the inkpot.

It was. The last blot fell on the soaked blotting-paper, and the draggled fly lay in it and did not stir. The back legs were stuck to the body; the front legs could not be seen.

"Come on," said the boss. "Look sharp!" And he stirred it with his pen —in vain. Nothing happened or was likely to happen. The fly was dead.

The boss lifted the corpse on the end of the paper-knife and flung it into the waste-paper basket. But such a grinding feeling of wretchedness seized him that he felt positively frightened. He started forward and pressed the bell for Macey. "Bring me some fresh blotting-paper," he said sternly, "and look sharp about it." And while the old dog padded away he fell to wondering what it was he had been thinking about before. What was it? It was . . . He took out his handkerchief and passed it inside his collar. For the life of him he could not remember.

🔊 Katherine Mansfield spent her life moving between homes in England and her native New Zealand. She drew on her childhood in New Zealand in story collections such as *Bliss and Other Stories* (1920) and *The Garden Party and Other Stories* (1920). Her stories, influenced by Anton Chekhov, often display pathos, irony, and an intensity of feeling. *(Born Wellington, New Zealand 1888; died 1923)*

RESPONDING

Meaning

1. a) Why has Mansfield included the details and dialogue about the newly decorated office?
   b) What is the purpose of the anecdote about the pot of jam?
2. Explain the *symbolism* of the fly and the boss's actions towards it.

Form and Style

3. The protagonist in this story remains nameless. Why has Mansfield named Woodifield and Macey, and yet left the protagonist with the informal title, "the boss"?
4. At times, the narrator seems to be speaking the thoughts inside the boss's head; yet Mansfield has maintained a distance between narrator and protagonist that allows us more insight into the boss's situation than he has himself. Use examples from the text to show how she achieves this, and evaluate its effect on the story.

Exploring Context

5. Katherine Mansfield has been credited as a master of the short story in English. Using a variety of research resources, read and compare two or three stories by Mansfield. Some possibilities include "The Garden Party," "Miss Brill," and "A Doll's House." Use a chart to explore similar themes and stylistic devices. Write a paper describing Mansfield's distinctive style of writing.

Creative Extension

6. On your own or with a partner, script a monologue in which the boss explains his "various reasons" for not visiting his son's grave. Use words, gestures, and facial expressions to show or hint at the speaker's internal struggle to grapple with his true feelings regarding the tragedy. Perform your monologue for a group or record it on audio or videotape.
7. Reggie and the boss's son might have been killed at either Ypres or Passchendaele. Using print and electronic sources, research and write a vivid description of one of these battles from the point of view of a foot soldier on the front lines.

Juliet

ও Helen Fogwill Porter

Learning Goals

- investigate character revelation
- examine narrative flow
- evaluate effects of specific textual references
- script a dramatic scene
- create a media work based on the story's theme

"Your hair looks lovely," Sandra says, passing me the hand mirror.

"Smells nice, too,'" I say. "Remember how the old perms used to stink?"

Sandra nods, smiling, then asks me if I have a rake.

"A rake," I repeat. "You mean for raking up leaves and grass?"

Sandra laughs. "No, no, a comb. Like this one." She holds up a purple comb with a handle and wide spaces between the teeth.

"Oh, yes, I've got one of those somewhere. I didn't know they were called rakes."

As Sandra explains to me how to lift my hair instead of combing it in the usual way, I keep thinking about the word rake. It's an appropriate name for that kind of comb. And I must have heard it used in that way before.

I've never been able to do anything with hair, my own or anyone else's. When the girls were small I always kept their hair cut short, the way I'd worn mine as a child. "Unhandy," that was my mother's word for me. Whenever she said it she'd follow it up with praise for my high marks at school.

My father always took me to get my hair cut. We'd walk to Murphy's Barbershop at the crossroads, and he'd have his hair trimmed at the same time. I liked the feeling of the clippers on my neck, the swish of the brush and the smell of the green liquid floating in the air.

In their teens Janet and Abigail let their hair grow, curled and styled it themselves. They both inherited Doug's manual dexterity, thank God.

I pay Sandra, and she reminds me to come back in six weeks for a trim. When I'm halfway home I realize that I didn't give her a tip. I've never forgotten to tip Sandra before.

Rake. That word keeps repeating itself in my head. Rake. A simple four-letter word. As I continue walking home a shiver runs through my body. The weather is warm for May. What in the frig is wrong with me? I was fine when I got up this morning, fine when I left the house. Fine right up to the moment Sandra said that word. Rake.

Last night I heard an interview on the radio about recovered memory. I can't resist listening to programs like that. As I often do these days, I talked back to the radio. "God, she was thirteen when the abuse happened. How could anyone ever forget something like that?"

I'm home already. Remembering nothing I saw or heard on the way. Is this what it's like to be in a fugue state? It often happens to me when I'm lost in thought. It can be wonderful, when something good has just happened or is about to happen. Or when you're falling in love: "I know how it feels to have wings on my heels / And to fly down the street in a trance." I haven't felt that way for a long time.

After school I'd walk along LeMarchant Road with Nadine until we reached her house. Then I'd walk on alone. Sometimes I wouldn't know where I was until I got to the Parkers'. I'd always stop there, just to look at the long graceful cream-and-white house with windows that someone later told me were made of antique mouth-blown glass. In the fall there were piles of leaves outside the Parkers' gate, from the maple and chestnut trees that grew just inside the wrought-iron fence. I'd kick my way through the leaves till I got to the graveyard. Then I'd cross to the other side of the road.

Today my walk home was fraught with—fraught with what? Something I don't want to think about? Something I don't want to remember.

Sometimes when I'm with Lucy and Charlotte and Liz one of us will say, "Well, you know, one in four women has been sexually abused as a child. So which one of us is it?" We all laugh then, and change the subject. We were surprised when Charlotte told us about her cousin Susan. It was Susan's grandfather. Not the one she shared with Charlotte.

My father has been dead for ten years, my mother for fifteen. I was the first-born of five; Dad said he learned from me how to be a father. He was inconsolable when anything bad happened to one of us. "I can't stand it, Amy," he told my mother after I hadn't been chosen for a speaking part in the operetta at school. Eventually I gave up telling him things like that.

My father loved Shakespeare and had introduced my mother to the play when the Glossop-Harris Repertory Company came regularly to St. John's from England. "He'd always buy a big box of chocolates for us to take to the T.A. Hall. That's where the plays were put off," my mother told me. "I don't know where he got the money."

My father had already resolved to name their first daughter Juliet. Fortunately, my mother also liked the name. "Not Juliette," he told me many times, wrinkling his nose.

I'm sitting at my kitchen table now, a cup of strong tea in front of me. I'm not sure how it got there. I take a sip to warm myself. Why am I so cold? The sun is streaming through the window; the kitchen is the warmest room in the house.

Rake. Juliet. Juliette. The three words are circling around each other in my head. Damn that Sandra. What has she started? Poor Sandra, such a gentle person, painstaking in her work, kind to the children who come to get their hair cut.

It's not Sandra. It's me. Am I turning strange now that I've retired? When I worked at the library I had no time to dwell on myself.

I drink the tea, carry my cup to the sink. There's a slight sound from the hallway. The mail is late today.

Three letters and the phone bill. One letter is from my sister Jessica in Fort McMurray. Another from Nadine who lives in Little Rock, Arkansas. She married an American serviceman who was stationed at Pepperrell Air Force Base. Several of my schoolmates married Americans; they ended up all over the States. Doug and I were so young when we started going together that I never even dated an American. Once in a while I still feel sorry about that.

The third envelope is large and square, probably a card. It's not my birthday or anything. The postmark says Paris. But it's not the postmark that takes my attention. It's the "Juliette" scrawled in thick black ink. My back is cold, the way it feels at night when the duvet slips off me. "Cover over my left shoulder," Doug would repeat as he pulled the blankets snugly around me. "You'll be saying that when they throw the gravel on your grave." It's Doug who's in his grave, healthy, vigorous Doug who died suddenly of a massive heart attack.

Most people spell my name correctly. I make sure of that. Two or three times throughout my school years I had to correct teachers. In grade six Miss MacDonald patted my shoulder and said, "Don't worry, Juliet, I'll never spell your name that way again." Then she erased the offending "te" from the blackboard. Some of the girls laughed. I'd been reading Anne of

Green Gables and identified strongly with Anne when Mr. Phillips left the "e" off the end of her name.

I pick up the envelope and study it. Then I tear it open. Inside there's a card with a picture of the Champs Elysees on it. "Dear Juliette," says the short note. "I remember you told me you've always wanted to go to Paris. This is my first trip and it's everything I thought it would be. Hope you make it over here soon." It's signed "Laura."

Letter. Juliette. Rake. The louse rake . . .

I'm fifteen years old, in grade ten at Queen Victoria Academy. Nadine and I are laughing as we walk up the school steps together. The bell is ringing for the start of afternoon classes. We run up two flights of stairs to our classroom on the third floor. I'm breathless when I sit down at my desk. I lift the hinged top to take my history book out. There's a large folded sheet of paper in there, with "Juliette" on it in big loopy letters. I open it and begin to read, my head holding the desk top in place. "Dear Juliette"—the name is in block letters, underlined—"Your face might look okay if you washed it once in a while. And those long streely dresses you've been wearing, did you inherit them from your great-grandmother? As for your hair, why don't you comb it occacionally?" It registers with me that "occasionally" is also spelled wrong. "And don't forget the louse rake!"

There's more, much more, but I don't read it. I drop the letter back into the desk, take out my history book and sit back in my seat. My hands are trembling and my face is hot. I know it must be blood red.

Everyone in the classroom is unusually attentive to Miss Lambert's words about Alexander the Great. Nobody is looking at me. I hear a sound like a stifled giggle but I keep my eyes on the page in front of me.

After school, avoiding Nadine, I hurry to the girls' bathroom, lock myself into a cubicle and read the rest of the letter. It's more of the same. I look down at the blue-and-white polka-dot skirt I'm wearing, given to me by our neighbour, Mrs. Leary. Her daughter Pat bought a lot of new clothes before she left for nursing school in Halifax. Mrs. Leary also gave me several blouses, a slip, and three dresses.

"I'll hem them up for you when I get a chance," Mom said when I showed them to her. "It's great for you to have something nice to wear to school now that you're allowed to leave your uniforms off."

I tear the sheets of paper into tiny pieces and flush them down the toilet.

"Juliet, is that you in there?" It's Nadine. She rattles the cubicle door. "What's keeping you so long? Monthly, is it?"

In the distance I hear a shout of laughter.

"No," I say. "No, Nadine, I just feel a bit sick to my stomach." I flush the toilet again.

"Sure you're okay?" Nadine asks when I come out. I go to the nearest wash basin and splash cold water on my face.

Several girls are standing together over near the showers. They're whispering and giggling. Louise is there, and Dorothy and Thelma. And Betsy Stewart. Betsy is doing most of the talking.

"So long, Nadine. Toodle-oo, Juliet," Thelma calls as we pass. She emphasizes the last syllable of my name. "Don't do anything we wouldn't do." They all laugh.

"Think they're it, don't they?" Nadine mutters. "They are, if you put 'sh' in front of it."

Betsy had come to our school at the beginning of the year. Her father was an officer at Pepperrell. Without even trying she had been accepted into the Louise Mercer crowd. They're mostly girls whose fathers are well-off-doctors, lawyers, businessmen. Thelma's father is not one of them. He works at the post office with my father. It helps that Thelma is very pretty, gets all her clothes from her sister in the States, and can coax her blond hair into any style she finds in *Seventeen*.

"You haven't said a word since we left the school," Nadine says as we pass St. Clare's Hospital. "Still feeling sick?"

"No, I'm fine now." I try to smile. Nadine starts telling me about Cliff, the good-looking fellow from Bell Island she met at the roller rink.

"And he's getting his licence next month," she finishes as we approach her house.

As I walk on alone, I try to think of a place where I can run to cry. No matter where I go at home someone will hear me. I still share a room with Jessica; Rosalind and Cordelia are always in and out. And Mom will want me to take Duncan off her hands while she's cooking supper.

I don't tell anyone about the letter. I especially don't want my parents to know. Dad would cry and Mom would get mad. And what good would any of it do?

It's years since I've thought about that day in grade ten, consciously, anyhow. Nobody knows about the letter except me. And the girls who wrote it. I know it was the work of more than one girl, even though only one hand held the pen. For a few years after I finished school I'd sometimes run into girls from my class. We'd stop and chat and all the while I'd be asking myself, "Was she involved, was she, was she?"

Back when I found that letter the meanness didn't bother me as much as my belief that those girls were right to despise me. I was dirty, sloppy, streelish, untidy, unhandy. Even lousy. I couldn't pretend that I'd never found a louse or a nit in my thick, tangly hair. That's the real reason I never told anyone.

I pick up Laura's card and read it again. I don't know Laura very well; we met at the yoga class Abby talked me into joining. I don't even remember telling her I'd always wanted to go to Paris. It was nice of her to write.

It's time to start supper. Janet and Bob and the boys are coming and I promised them beef stroganoff. While I'm taking the meat out of the fridge I remember a story my mother told me more than once about a woman in her church group.

"They never ask Mrs. Norman to bring anything homemade," Mom would say as she squeezed her shortbread dough into long curly fingers or chopped up the vegetables for her beet salad. She would always wear a clean pair of underpants on her head when she was handling food. "She'd be asked to bring a quart of milk or a pound of butter, something like that. Poor soul, they said she wasn't very careful."

I wash my hands and begin to cut the round steak into small cubes.

Helen Fogwill Porter lives in Newfoundland and has published fiction, non-fiction, poetry, humour, drama, and criticism in Canada and overseas. Most of Porter's work is set in St. John's, and she pays close attention to regional speech patterns. *January, February, June or July* was shortlisted for the W. H. Smith/Books in Canada First Novel Award in 1989 and won the Young Adult Canadian Book Award. "Juliet" appeared in *Dropped Threads: What We Aren't Told* (2001), an anthology edited by Carol Shields and Marjorie Anderson. *(Born St. John's, Newfoundland 1939)*

RESPONDING

Meaning

1. What is revealed about the narrator's character through the details of her environment, both as a child and as an adult?

2. How does the word "rake" function on several levels in the story?

Form and Style

3. At times the narrator makes reference to instances of abuse. Do you feel that these references reinforce or weaken the story's narrative? Support your opinion.

4. How does the narrator manage to maintain a narrative flow, even while moving backward and forward in time? Give specific examples from the text.

Exploring Context

5. The narrator makes it clear that she and her siblings were named after characters in Shakespearean plays. Explore a variety of resources and, using a graphic chart, indicate how Juliet, Duncan, Jessica, and Rosalind are characters whose roles in Shakespearean dramas support the theme of this short story.

Creative Extension

6. In groups of four, script and present the scene in which Louise, Dorothy, Thelma, and Betsy Stewart write the letter to the narrator.

7. Create one aspect of a media campaign promoting respect for difference and diversity. Brainstorm a list of ideas, develop a simple, memorable core message for your campaign, and design a poster, pamphlet, radio spot ad, or storyboard for a short television commercial to convey your message. Display your campaign.

Araby

❦ James Joyce

North Richmond Street, being blind, was a quiet street except at the hour when the Christian Brothers' School set the boys free. An uninhabited house of two storeys stood at the blind end, detached from its neighbours in a square ground. The other houses of the street, conscious of decent lives within them, gazed at one another with brown, imperturbable faces.

The former tenant of our house, a priest, had died in the back drawing room. Air, musty from having been long enclosed, hung in all the rooms, and the waste room behind the kitchen was littered with old useless papers. Among these I found a few paper-covered books, the pages of which were curled and damp: *The Abbot*, by Walter Scott, *The Devout Communicant*, and *The Memoirs of Vidocq*. I liked the last best because its leaves were yellow. The wild garden behind the house contained a central apple-tree and a few straggling bushes under one of which I found the late tenant's rusty bicycle pump. He had been a very charitable priest; in his will he had left all his money to institutions and the furniture of his house to his sister.

When the short days of winter came dusk fell before we had eaten our dinners. When we met in the street the houses had grown sombre. The space of sky above us was the colour of ever-changing violet and towards it the lamps of the street lifted their feeble lanterns. The cold air stung us and we played till our bodies glowed. Our shouts echoed in the silent street. The career of our play brought us through the dark muddy lanes behind the houses where we ran the gauntlet of the rough tribes from the cottages, to the back doors of the dark dripping gardens where odours arose from the ashpits, to the dark odorous stables where a coachman smoothed and combed the horse or shook music from the buckled harness. When we returned to the street, light from the kitchen windows had filled the areas. If my uncle was seen turning the corner we hid in the shadow until we had seen him safely housed. Or if Mangan's sister came out on the doorstep to call her brother in to his tea, we watched her from our shadow peer up and down the street. We waited to see whether she should remain or go in and, if she remained, we left our shadow and walked up to Mangan's steps resignedly. She was waiting for us, her figure defined by the light from the half-opened door. Her brother always teased her before he obeyed and I stood by the railings looking at her. Her dress swung as she moved her body and the soft rope of her hair tossed from side to side.

Every morning I lay on the floor in the front parlour watching her door. The blind was pulled down to within an inch of the sash so that I could not be seen. When she came out on the doorstep my heart leaped. I ran to the hall, seized my books and followed her. I kept her brown figure always in my eye and, when we came near the point at which our ways diverged, I quickened my pace and passed her.

This happened morning after morning. I had never spoken to her, except for a few casual words, and yet her name was like a summons to all my foolish blood.

Her image accompanied me even in places the most hostile to romance. On Saturday evenings when my aunt went marketing I had to go to carry some of the parcels. We walked through the flaring streets, jostled by drunken men and bargaining women, amid the curses of labourers, the shrill litanies of shop-boys who stood on guard by the barrels of pigs' cheeks, the nasal chanting of street-singers, who sang a *come-all-you* about O'Donovan Rossa, or a ballad about the troubles in our native land. These noises converged in a single sensation of life for me: I imagined that I bore my chalice safely through a throng of foes. Her name sprang to my lips at moments in strange prayers and praises which I myself did not understand. My eyes were often full of tears (I could not tell why) and at times a flood from my heart seemed to pour itself out into my bosom. I thought little of the future. I did not know whether I would ever speak to her or not or, if I spoke to her, how I could tell her of my confused adoration. But my body was like a harp and her words and gestures were like fingers running upon the wires.

One evening I went into the back drawing-room in which the priest had died. It was a dark rainy evening and there was no sound in the house. Through one of the broken panes I heard the rain impinge upon the earth, the fine incessant needles of water playing in the sodden beds. Some distant lamp or lighted window gleamed below me. I was thankful that I could see so little. All my senses seemed to desire to veil themselves and, feeling that I was about to slip from them, I pressed the palms of my hands together until they trembled, murmuring: *O love! O love!* many times.

At last she spoke to me. When she addressed the first words to me I was so confused that I did not know what to answer. She asked me was I going to *Araby*. I forget whether I answered yes or no. It would be a splendid bazaar, she said; she would love to go.

"And why can't you?" I asked.

While she spoke she turned a silver bracelet round and round her wrist. She could not go, she said, because there would be a retreat that week in her convent. Her brother and two other boys were fighting for their caps and I was alone at the railings. She held one of the spikes, bowing her head towards me. The light from the lamp opposite our door caught the white curve of her neck, lit up her hair that rested there and, falling, lit up the hand upon the railing. It fell over one side of her dress and caught the white border of a petticoat, just visible as she stood at ease.

"It's well for you," she said.

"If I go," I said, "I will bring you something."

What innumerable follies laid waste my waking and sleeping thoughts after that evening! I wished to annihilate the tedious intervening days. I chafed against the work of school. At night in my bedroom and by day in the classroom her image came between me and the page I strove to read. The syllables of the word *Araby* were called to me through the silence in which my soul luxuriated and cast an Eastern enchantment over me. I asked for leave to go to the bazaar on Saturday night. My aunt was surprised and hoped it was not some Freemason affair. I answered few questions in class. I watched my master's face pass from amiability to sternness; he hoped I was not beginning to idle. I could not call my wandering thoughts together. I had hardly any patience with the serious work of life which, now that it stood between me and my desire, seemed to me child's play, ugly monotonous child's play.

On Saturday morning I reminded my uncle that I wished to go to the bazaar in the evening. He was fussing at the hallstand, looking for the hat-brush, and answered me curtly:

"Yes, boy, I know."

As he was in the hall I could not go into the front parlour and lie at the window. I left the house in bad humour and walked slowly towards the school. The air was pitilessly raw and already my heart misgave me.

When I came home to dinner my uncle had not yet been home. Still it was early. I sat staring at the clock for some time and, when its ticking began to irritate me, I left the room. I mounted the staircase and gained the upper part of the house. The high cold empty gloomy rooms liberated me and I went from room to room singing. From the front window I saw my companions playing below in the street. Their cries reached me weakened and indistinct and, leaning my forehead against the cool glass, I looked over at the dark house where she lived. I may have stood there for an hour, seeing nothing but the brown-clad figure cast by my imagination, touched discreetly by the lamplight at the curved neck, at the hand upon the railings and at the border below the dress.

When I came downstairs again I found Mrs. Mercer sitting at the fire. She was an old garrulous woman, a pawnbroker's widow, who collected used stamps for some pious purpose. I had to endure the gossip of the tea-table. The meal was prolonged beyond an hour and still my uncle did not come. Mrs. Mercer stood up to go: she was sorry she couldn't wait any longer, but it was after eight o'clock and she did not like to be out late, as the night air was bad for her. When she had gone I began to walk up and down the room, clenching my fists. My aunt said:

"I'm afraid you may put off your bazaar for this night of Our Lord."

At nine o'clock I heard my uncle's latchkey in the halldoor. I heard him talking to himself and heard the hallstand rocking when it had received the weight of his overcoat. I could interpret these signs. When he was midway through his dinner I asked him to give me the money to go to the bazaar. He had forgotten.

"The people are in bed and after their first sleep now," he said.

I did not smile. My aunt said to him energetically:

"Can't you give him the money and let him go? You've kept him late enough as it is."

My uncle said he was very sorry he had forgotten. He said he believed in the old saying: *All work and no play makes Jack a dull boy.* He asked me where I was going and, when I had told him a second time he asked me did I know *The Arab's Farewell to his Steed*. When I left the kitchen he was about to recite the opening lines of the piece to my aunt.

I held a florin tightly in my hand as I strode down Buckingham Street towards the station. The sight of the streets thronged with buyers and glaring with gas recalled to me the purpose of my journey. I took my seat in a third-class carriage of a deserted train. After an intolerable delay the train moved out of the station slowly. It crept onward among ruinous houses and over the twinkling river. At Westland Row Station a crowd of people pressed to the carriage doors; but the porters moved them back, saying that it was a special train for the bazaar. I remained alone in the bare carriage. In a few minutes the train drew up beside an improvised wooden platform. I passed out on to the road and saw by the lighted dial of a clock that it was ten minutes to ten. In front of me was a large building which displayed the magical name.

I could not find any sixpenny entrance and, fearing that the bazaar would be closed, I passed in quickly through a turnstile, handing a shilling to a weary-looking man. I found myself in a big hall girdled at half its height by a gallery. Nearly all the stalls were closed and the greater part of the hall was in darkness. I recognized a silence like that which pervades a church after a service. I walked into the centre of the bazaar timidly. A few people were gathered about the stalls which were still open. Before a curtain, over which the words *Café Chantant* were written in coloured lamps, two men were counting money on a salver. I listened to the fall of the coins.

Remembering with difficulty why I had come I went over to one of the stalls and examined porcelain vases and flowered tea sets. At the door of the stall a young lady was talking and laughing with two young gentlemen. I remarked their English accents and listened vaguely to their conversation.

"O, I never said such a thing!"

"O, but you did!"

"O, but I didn't!"

"Didn't she say that?"

"Yes. I heard her."

"O, there's a . . . fib!"

Observing me the young lady came over and asked me did I wish to buy anything. The tone of her voice was not encouraging; she seemed to have spoken to me out of a sense of duty. I looked humbly at the great jars that stood like eastern guards at either side of the dark entrance to the stall and murmured:

"No, thank you."

The young lady changed the position of one of the vases and went back to the two young men. They began to talk of the same subject. Once or twice the young lady glanced at me over her shoulder.

I lingered before her stall, though I knew my stay was useless, to make my interest in her wares seem more real. Then I turned away slowly and walked down the middle of the bazaar. I allowed the two pennies to fall against the sixpence in my pocket. I heard a voice call from one end of the gallery that the light was out. The upper part of the hall was now completely dark.

Gazing up into the darkness I saw myself as a creature driven and derided by vanity; and my eyes burned with anguish and anger.

છ James Joyce knew the Irish poet W. B. Yeats, and along with Yeats, he fostered the Irish cultural revival in the early part of the twentieth century. Although Joyce lived mostly in Europe after 1902, his work continued to focus on Ireland. His most significant short-story collection was *Dubliners* (1914), which Joyce claimed to have written in a style of "scrupulous meanness." "Araby" is from this collection. Joyce used a stream of consciousness technique in his famous novels *A Portrait of the Artist as a Young Man* (1916) and *Ulysses* (1921), which is a long novel describing the events of only one day in Dublin. *(Born Dublin, Northern Ireland 1882; died 1941)*

RESPONDING

Meaning

1. How would you describe the theme of the story? Identify details of setting and description that help to reinforce the theme.

2. At the end of the story, the boy experiences a moment of epiphany. In literature, an *epiphany* is a sudden revelation of the essential truth about a character, situation, or experience. What is the nature of the boy's epiphany? How does Joyce use *foreshadowing* to prepare the reader for this moment of revelation?

Form and Style

3. What imagery does Joyce use to describe Mangan's sister? What does this choice of imagery add to the story?

4. What is the narrator's attitude towards his younger self? How does this point of view affect the emotional impact of the ending?

Exploring Context

5. "Araby" comes from a collection of James Joyce's stories called *Dubliners*. In these stories, Joyce critiques the society of Ireland, his native land. What aspects of Irish society does Joyce critique in this story?

Creative Extension

6. Assume the role of the young boy in the story and write a series of at least four diary entries leading up to and including his reaction to the abortive trip to the bazaar.

7. Locate a copy of *Dubliners* by James Joyce. Choose another story from the collection, and write a comparative essay that examines one aspect (style, plot, characterization, theme) of the two pieces.

King of the Raft

⌇ Daniel David Moses

There was a raft in the river that year, put there, anchored with an anvil, just below a bend, by the one of the fathers who worked away in Buffalo, who could spend only every other weekend, if that, at home. The one of the mothers whose husband worked the land and came in from the fields for every meal muttered as she set the table that that raft was the only way the father who worked in the city was able to pretend he cared about his sons. Her husband, also one of the fathers, who had once when young gone across the border to work and then, unhappy there, returned, could not answer, soaking the dust of soil from his hands.

Most of the sons used the raft that was there just that one summer in the usually slow-moving water during the long evenings after supper, after the days of the fieldwork of haying and then combining were done. A few of them, the ones whose fathers and mothers practised Christianity, also used it in the afternoons on sunny Sundays after the sitting through church and family luncheons. And the one of the sons who had only a father who came and went following the work—that son appeared whenever his rare duties or lonely freedom became too much for him.

The sons would come to the raft along a footpath the half mile from the road and change their overalls or jeans for swimsuits among the gold-enrod and milkweed on the bank, quickly, to preserve modesty and their blood from mosquitoes, the only females around. Then one of the sons would run down the clay slope and stumble in with splashing and a cry of shock or joy for the water's current temperature. The other sons would follow, and, by the time they all climbed out onto the raft out in the stream, through laughter would become boys again.

The boys used that raft in the murky green water to catch the sun or their breaths on, or to dive from when they tried to touch the mud bottom. One of the younger ones also used to stand looking across the current to the other side, trying to see through that field of corn there, the last bit of land that belonged to the Reserve. Beyond it the highway ran, a border patrolled by a few cars flashing chrome in the sun or headlights through the evening blue like messages from the city. Every one of the boys used the raft several times that summer to get across the river and back, the accomplishment proof of their new masculinity. And once the younger one who spent time looking at that other land, crossed and climbed up the bank there and explored the shadows between the rows of corn, the leaves like dry tongues along his naked arms as he came to the field's far edge where the asphalt of that highway stood empty.

Towards the cool end of the evenings, any boy left out on the raft in the lapping black water would be too far from shore to hear the conversations. They went on against a background noise of the fire the boys always built against the river's grey mist and mosquito lust, that they sometimes built for roasting corn, hot dogs, marshmallows. The conversations went on along with or over games of chess. Years later, one of the older boys, watching his own son play the game with a friend in silence, wondered if perhaps that was why their conversations that year of the raft about cars, guitars, and girls—especially each other's sisters—about school and beer, always ended up in stalemate or check. Most of the boys ended up winning only their own solitariness from the conversations by the river. But the one who had only a father never even learned the rules of play.

One sunny Sunday after church in late summer, the one who had only a father already sat on the raft in the river as the rest of the boys undressed. He smiled at the boys who had gone across through the corn, who made it into the water first. Then he stood up and the raft made waves as gentle as those in his blue-black hair—I'm the king of the raft, he yelled, challenging the boy who had seen the highway to win that wet wooden square. And a battle was joined, and the day was wet and fair, until the king of the raft, to show his strength to the rest of the boys still on shore, took a hank of the highway boy's straight hair in hand and held the highway boy underwater till the highway boy saw blue fire and almost drowned. The story went around among the mothers and the fathers and soon that son who had only a father found himself unwelcome. Other stories came around, rumours about his getting into fights or failing grades or how his father's latest girlfriend had dyed her Indian hair blond. And the boy who almost had drowned found he both feared the king of the raft and missed the waves in his blue-black hair.

One muggy evening when pale thunderheads growled in from the west, the boy who had almost drowned, who had the farthest to go to get home, left the raft and the rest by the river early. On the dark road he met the king, who had something to say. They hid together with a case of beer in a cool culvert under the road. The king of the raft was going away with his father to live in Buffalo in the United States and thought the boy who had almost drowned could use what was left of this beer the king's father would never miss. The boy who had almost drowned sipped from his bottle of sour beer and heard the rain beginning to hiss at the end of the culvert. He crawled and looked out in time to see the blue fire of lightning hit a tree. In the flash he saw again the waves in the king's blue-black hair, the grin that offered another beer. The boy who had almost drowned felt he was going down again, and, muttering some excuse, ran out into the rain. The king yelled after him that old insult boys use about your mother wanting you home.

The boy who had almost drowned found he could cross through the rain, anchored by his old running shoes to the ground, though the water came down like another river, cold and clear and wide as the horizon. He made it home and stood on the porch, waiting for the other side of the storm, hearing hail hitting the roof and water through the eaves filling up the cistern. Later, out of the storm, he could still hear far off a gurgling in the gully and a quiet roar as the distant river tore between its banks. The storm still growled somewhere beyond the eastern horizon.

The raft was gone the next evening when the boys came to the bank and the current was still too cold and quick to swim in. No one crossed the river for the rest of the summer. The king of the raft never appeared again anywhere. In the fall, a rumour came around about his going to work in the city and in the winter another one claimed he had died. The boy who had crossed through the rain thought about going down even quicker in winter river water. Then a newspaper confirmed the death. In a traffic accident, the rain boy read. None of the boys had even met that impaired driver, that one of the fathers, surviving and charged without a license. One of the mothers muttered as she set another mother's hair about people not able to care even about their kids. The rain boy let the king of the raft sink into the river, washing him away in his mind, and decided he would someday cross over and follow the highway through that land and find the city.

ⓢ Daniel David Moses is a registered Delaware, who was born on the Six Nations Reserve in Ontario. In the poetry collections *Delicate Bodies* (1980) and *The White Line* (1991), Moses uses lyrical language to describe tribal traditions, as well as images of mainstream Canada. Moses has also published short stories and many plays, including *The Indian Medicine Shows* (1995), which were performed in Toronto. *(Born Ohsweken, Ontario 1952)*

RESPONDING

Meaning

1. a) Explain the *symbolism* of the raft in the story.
    b) Why did the raft suddenly disappear from the river? Support your interpretation.
2. Describe the relationship between the two boys. Why does the boy who almost drowned find that "he both feared the king of the raft and missed the waves in his blue-black hair"?

Form and Style

3. The two main incidents in the plot are the near-drowning of the boy by "the king of the raft," and the final meeting of the two boys in the culvert. What recurrent symbols and images does the writer use to link these two events?
4. a) The author has chosen to keep the characters in the story nameless. Why? How does he reinforce this namelessness?
    b) How does this stylistic choice affect your reading of the story?

Exploring Context

5. Daniel David Moses is an Aboriginal writer who grew up on the Six Nations reserve near Brantford, Ontario. This story is set on a reserve, and the characters are Aboriginal. Would you say, then, that the story would appeal primarily to Aboriginal readers? Why or why not?

Creative Extension

6. Assume the role of the "rain boy" and prepare a *eulogy* for "the king of the raft."
7. The city in the story is a symbol both of danger and of freedom. Create a poem, a visual interpretation, or a multimedia presentation that reflects your image of "the city."

The Flash

Italo Calvino

It happened one day, at a crossroads, in the middle of a crowd, people coming and going.

I stopped, blinked: I understood nothing. Nothing, nothing about anything: I didn't understand the reasons for things or for people, it was all senseless, absurd. And I started to laugh.

What I found strange at the time was that I'd never realized before. That up until then I had accepted everything: traffic lights, cars, posters, uniforms, monuments, things completely detached from any sense of the world, accepted them as if there were some necessity, some chain of cause and effect that bound them together.

Then the laugh died in my throat, I blushed, ashamed. I waved to get people's attention and "Stop a second!" I shouted, "there's something wrong! Everything's wrong! We're doing the absurdest things! This can't be the right way! Where will it end?"

People stopped around me, sized me up, curious. I stood there in the middle of them, waving my arms, desperate to explain myself, to have them share the flash of insight that had suddenly enlightened me: and I said nothing. I said nothing because the moment I'd raised my arms and opened my mouth, my great revelation had been as it were swallowed up again and the words had come out any old how, on impulse.

"So?" people asked, "what do you mean? Everything's in its place. All is as it should be. Everything is a result of something else. Everything fits in with everything else. We can't see anything absurd or wrong!"

And I stood there, lost, because as I saw it now everything had fallen into place again and everything seemed natural, traffic lights, monuments, uniforms, towerblocks, tramlines, beggars, processions; yet this didn't calm me down, it tormented me.

"I'm sorry," I answered. "Perhaps it was me that was wrong. It seemed that way. But everything's fine. I'm sorry," and I made off amid their angry glares.

Yet, even now, every time (often) that I find I don't understand something, then, instinctively, I'm filled with the hope that perhaps this will be my moment again, perhaps once again I shall understand nothing, I shall grasp that other knowledge, found and lost in an instant.

⸎ Italian novelist and short-fiction writer Italo Calvino delighted readers around the world with his deceptively simple, fable-like stories. His major works include *Cosmicomics* (1968), *Invisible Cities* (1972), and *If on a Winter's Night a Traveler* (1979). During his later years, Calvino became an avid film enthusiast and renowned lecturer. The English translation of "The Flash" appeared in *Numbers in the Dark and Other Stories* (1995). (*Born Cuba 1923; died 1985*)

RESPONDING

Meaning

1. Why do you think the narrator moves so quickly from finding the world "senseless" and "absurd" to finding that "everything had fallen into place again"?
2. What is the explanation for the "angry glares" from the people in the crowd?

Form and Style

3. A *paradox* is a statement or idea that seems to be contradictory or absurd, but in fact holds a truth. Find an example of paradox in "The Flash," and explain its use in this context.
4. Identify the moment of climax in the story. How does the author create mounting excitement leading up to this climax, and a sense of falling action after it?

Exploring Context

5. Calvino lived in Italy during World War II and was active in the Italian Resistance, fighting against the German occupation. "The Flash" was written around this time. What political significance can you see in the story? Explain.

Creative Extension

6. Script or improvise the dialogue between the narrator and a psychiatrist whom he or she consults to discuss his/her moment of "enlightenment." Present the scene to a group or record it on audio or videotape.
7. Compare the *epiphany* described in this short story with that experienced by the boy in "Araby." Write a short comparative essay explaining the similarities and differences between the two incidents.

The Passenger

ॐ Franz Kafka

I stand on the platform of the trolley car and am completely insecure about my footing in this world, in this city, in my family. Nor could I indicate even casually what demands I might rightfully make in any direction. In no way can I defend myself for standing on the platform, clutching this strap, letting this trolley carry me along, defend people for scurrying out of the way or walking quietly or window-shopping. Of course, no one is asking me for a defense, but that's beside the point.

The trolley approaches a stop, a girl comes over to the steps, ready to get out. She is as obvious to me as if I had run my fingers over her. She is wearing black, the pleats of her skirt barely stir, her blouse is snug and has a collar of white, fine-meshed lace, her left hand is propped flat against the side of the trolley, the umbrella in her right hand is poised on the second step from the top. Her face is brown, her nose, slightly pinched on the sides, has a broad, round tip. She has a lot of brown hair and small, stray hairs on her right temple. Her small ear lies close to her head, but by standing near her I can see the entire ridge of her right ear conch and the shadow at its root.

I wondered back then: How come she's not astonished at herself, how come she keeps her mouth shut and says nothing along those lines?

ॐ Czech novelist and short-story writer Franz Kafka wrote about nightmarish worlds, where lonely individuals became caught up in situations they could not control. Kafka's unfinished novels, such as *Der Schloss (The Castle)*, were published after his death in the 1920s. His famous short story, "Die Verwandlung" ("The Metamorphosis"), published in 1915, is about a man who turns into an insect. An English translation of "The Passenger" appeared in *The Metamorphosis and Other Stories* (1993). (*Born Prague, former Czechoslovakia 1883; died 1924*)

RESPONDING

Meaning

1. What is the importance in the story of the trolley car, the platform, and the title? Support your interpretations.

2. Why does the young woman "keep her mouth shut and [say] nothing along those lines"?

Form and Style

3. How does the author create a contrast between himself and the girl? What is the purpose of this contrast?

4. Assess the effectiveness of the author's choice of first-person narrative.

Exploring Context

5. Compare the experience of the narrator in this story with that of the narrator in "The Flash." What similarities and differences do you see in the two descriptions?

Creative Extension

6. Create a one-act play in which the narrator and the female passenger strike up a conversation. Add more characters if you wish. If there is time, perform the play for the class.

7. *Flash fiction* can be seen as somewhere between poetry and short stories in form. Rewrite the story in the form of a poem; use line endings, spacing, and other conventions of poetry to enhance the expression of the piece. You may choose to cut or add words, as well.

Murder in the Dark

ꕥ Margaret Atwood

Learning Goals

- examine irony and humour
- assess the author's use of analogy
- analyze narrative voice
- write an original piece of flash fiction

This is a game I've played only twice. The first time I was in Grade Five, I played it in a cellar, the cellar of a large house belonging to the parents of a girl called Louise. There was a pool table in the cellar but none of us knew anything about pool. There was also a player piano. After a while we got tired of running the punchcard rolls through the player piano and watching the keys go up and down by themselves, like something in a late movie just before you see the dead person. I was in love with a boy called Bill, who was in love with Louise. The other boy, whose name I can't remember, was in love with me. Nobody knew who Louise was in love with.

So we turned out the lights in the cellar and played *Murder in the Dark*, which gave the boys the pleasure of being able to put their hands around the girls' necks and gave the girls the pleasure of screaming. The excitement was almost more than we could bear, but luckily Louise's parents came home and asked us what we thought we were up to.

The second time I played it was with adults; it was not as much fun, though more intellectually complex.

I heard that this game was once played at a summer cottage by six normal people and a poet, and the poet really tried to kill someone. He was hindered only by the intervention of a dog, which could not tell fantasy from reality. The thing about this game is that you have to know when to stop.

Here is how you play:

You fold up some pieces of paper and put them into a hat, a bowl or the centre of the table. Everyone chooses a piece. The one who gets the x is the detective, the one who gets the black spot is the killer. The detective leaves the room, turning off the lights. Everyone gropes around in the dark until the murderer picks a victim. He can either whisper "You're dead," or he can slip his hands around a throat and give a playful but decisive squeeze. The victim screams and falls down. Everyone must now stop moving around except the murderer, who of course will not want to be found near the body. The detective counts to ten, turns on the lights, and enters the room. He may now question anyone but the victim, who is not allowed to answer, being dead. Everyone but the murderer must tell the truth. The murderer must lie.

If you like, you can play games with this game. You can say: the murderer is the writer, the detective is the reader, the victim is the book. Or perhaps, the murderer is the writer, the detective is the critic, and the victim is the reader. In that case the book would be the total *mise en scene*, including the lamp that was accidentally tipped over and broken. But really it's more fun just to play the game.

In any case, that's me in the dark. I have designs on you, I'm plotting my sinister crime, my hands are reaching for your neck or perhaps, by mistake, your thigh. You can hear my footsteps approaching, I wear boots and carry a knife, or maybe it's a pearl-handled revolver, in any case I wear boots with very soft soles, you can see the cinematic glow of my cigarette, waxing and waning in the fog of the room, the street, the room, even though I don't smoke. Just remember this, when the scream at last has ended and you've turned on the lights: by the rules of the game, I must always lie.

Now: do you believe me?

ಳ Margaret Atwood is one of Canada's most prominent contemporary writers. She is a poet, novelist, short-story writer, and writer of non-fiction and critical essays. Atwood's many novels include *The Handmaid's Tale* (1986) and *The Blind Assassin* (2000). Short-story collections include *Dancing Girls* (1977), *Bluebeard's Egg* (1983), and *Wilderness Tips* (1991). Atwood's work has been translated into over thirty languages, and she has been awarded several Canadian and international awards including the Giller Prize and the Booker Prize. The above selection is from *Murder in the Dark: Short Fiction and Prose Poems* (1983). (*Born Ottawa, Ontario 1939*)

RESPONDING

Meaning

1. Explain the *irony* in the anecdote about the poet and the dog.
2. Explain Atwood's *analogy* of the writer as murderer. Is the analogy an effective one in your view? Why or why not? Support your opinion.

Form and Style

3. Point out three or four examples of humour in the story. Identify the techniques Atwood uses to create this humour and comment on their effectiveness.

4. The narrator in the story speaks in the first person, and is a writer. Is this Margaret Atwood speaking to us directly? Discuss.

Exploring Context

5. a) Compare Atwood's narrative voice in this story with that in her poems and other writings in the Echo on pages 47–59. What would you say characterizes Atwood's writing style?

   b) Does this piece fit the theme of that Echo section? Provide reasons for your answer.

Creative Extension

6. In groups or with a partner, discuss whether it is fair to look for autobiographical details in works of fiction. Should a work of art stand on its own, independent of its author? Or, is it fair to consider aspects of the author's life and ideas when interpreting his or her creations?

7. Write an original piece of flash fiction. Focus your piece on a game, a specific incident, or a specific moment which may or may not involve an epiphany. Exchange your work with a partner or in a small group and elicit responses to your storyline and style.

Essays

Virginia Woolf on essays:

A novel has a story; a poem rhyme; but what art can the essayist use in these short lengths of prose to sting us wide awake?...He must know—that is the first essential—how to write. His learning may be profound...but in an essay it must be fused by the magic of writing.... There is no room for the impurities of literature in an essay. Somehow or other, by dint of labour or bounty of nature, or both combined, the essay must be pure—pure like water or pure like wine, but pure from dullness, deadness, and deposits of extraneous matter.... The merit [of essays] consists in the fact that they do not adumbrate, or initiate, or anticipate anything; they exist, perfect, complete, entire in themselves.

To Err is Human

✎ Lewis Thomas

Everyone must have had at least one personal experience with a computer error by this time. Bank balances are suddenly reported to have jumped from $379 into the millions, appeals for charitable contributions are mailed over and over to people with crazy-sounding names at your address, department stores send the wrong bills, utility companies write that they're turning everything off, that sort of thing. If you manage to get in touch with someone and complain, you then get instantaneously typed, guilty letters from the same computer, saying, "Our computer was in error, and an adjustment is being made in your account."

These are supposed to be the sheerest, blindest accidents. Mistakes are not believed to be part of the normal behaviour of a good machine. If things go wrong, it must be a personal, human error, the result of fingering, tampering, a button getting stuck, someone hitting the wrong key. The computer, at its normal best, is infallible.

I wonder whether this can be true. After all, the whole point of computers is that they represent an extension of the human brain, vastly improved upon but nonetheless human, superhuman maybe. A good computer can think clearly and quickly enough to beat you at chess, and some of them have even been programmed to write obscure verse. They can do anything we can do, and more besides.

It is not yet known whether a computer has its own consciousness, and it would be hard to find out about this. When you walk into one of those great halls now built for the huge machines, and stand listening, it is easy to imagine that the faint, distant noises are the sound of thinking, and the turning of the spools gives them the look of wild creatures rolling their eyes in the effort to concentrate, choking with information. But real thinking, and dreaming, are other matters.

On the other hand, the evidences of something like an *unconscious*, equivalent to ours, are all around, in every mail. As extensions of the human brain, they have been constructed with the same property of error, spontaneous, uncontrolled, and rich in possibilities.

Mistakes are at the very base of human thought, embedded there, feeding the structure like root nodules. If we were not provided with the knack of being wrong, we could never get anything useful done. We think our way along by choosing between right and wrong alternatives, and the wrong choices have to be made as frequently as the right ones. We get along in life this way. We are built to make mistakes, coded for error.

We learn, as we say, by "trial and error". Why do we always say that? Why not "trial and rightness" or "trial and triumph"? The old phrase puts it that way because that is, in real life, the way it is done.

A good laboratory, like a good bank or a corporation or government, has to run like a computer. Almost everything is done flawlessly, by the book, and all the numbers add up to he predicted sums. The days go by. And then, if it is a lucky day, and a lucky laboratory, somebody makes a mistake: the wrong buffer, something in one of the blanks, a decimal misplaced in reading counts, the warm room off by a degree and a half, a mouse out of his box, or just a misreading of the day's protocol. Whatever, when the results come in, something is obviously screwed up, and then the action can begin.

The misreading is not the important error; it opens the way. The next step is the crucial one. If the investigator can bring himself to say, "But even so, look at that!" then the new finding, whatever it is, is ready for snatching. What is needed, for progress to be made, is the move based on the error.

Whenever new kinds of thinking are about to be accomplished, or new varieties of music, there has to be an argument beforehand. With two sides debating the same mind, haranguing, there is an amiable understanding that one is right and the other wrong. Sooner or later the thing is settled, but there can be no action at all if there are not the two sides, and the argument. The hope is in the faculty of wrongness, the tendency toward error. The capacity to leap across mountains of information to land lightly on the wrong side represents the highest of human endowments.

It may be that this is a uniquely human gift, perhaps even stipulated in our genetic instructions. Other creatures do not seem to have DNA sequences for making mistakes as a routine part of daily living, certainly not for programmed error as a guide for action.

We are at our human finest, dancing with our minds, when there are more choices than two. Sometimes there are ten, even twenty different ways to go, all but one bound to be wrong, and the richness of selection in such situations can lift us onto totally new ground. This process is called exploration and is based on human fallibility. If we had only a single centre in our brains, capable of responding only when a correct decision was to be made, instead of the jumble of different, credulous, easily conned clusters of neurons that provide for being flung off into blind alleys, up trees, down dead ends, out into blue sky, along wrong turnings, around bends, we could only stay the way we are today, stuck fast.

The lower animals do not have this splendid freedom. They are limited, most of them, to absolute infallibility. Cats, for all their good side, never make mistakes. I have never seen a maladroit, clumsy, or blundering cat. Dogs are sometimes fallible, occasionally able to make charming minor mistakes, but they get this way by trying to mimic their masters. Fish are flawless in everything they do. Individual cells in a tissue are mindless machines, perfect in their performance, as absolutely inhuman as bees.

We should have this in mind as we become dependent on more complex computers for the arrangement of our affairs. Give the computers their heads, I say; let them go their way. If we can learn to do this, turning our heads to one side and wincing while the work proceeds, the possibilities for the future of mankind, and computerkind, are limitless. Your average good computer can make calculations in an instant which would take a lifetime of slide rules for any of us. Think of what we could gain from the near infinity of precise, machine-made miscomputation which is now so easily within our grasp. We would begin the solving of some of our hardest problems. How, for instance, should we go about organizing ourselves for social living on a planetary scale, now that we have become, as a plain fact of life, a single community? We can assume, as a working hypothesis, that all the right ways of doing this are unworkable. What we need, then, for moving ahead, is a set of wrong alternatives much longer and more interesting than the short list of mistaken courses that any of us can think up right now. We need, in fact, an infinite list, and when it is printed out we need the computer to turn on itself and select, at random, the next way to go. If it is a big enough mistake, we could find ourselves on a new level, stunned, out in the clear, ready to move again.

ර While having a distinguished career as a doctor, Lewis Thomas published a number of poems. In 1974, he published the essay collection *The Lives of a Cell: Notes of a Biology Watcher*, which found a sizeable audience and won the National Book Award. Later essay collections include *The Medusa and the Snail* (1976), which contains "To Err is Human." (*Born Flushing, New York 1913; died 1993*)

RESPONDING

Meaning

1. Thomas uses a very unusual idea to frame this persuasive essay. Which sentence best summarizes this idea? Justify your answer with evidence from the essay.

2. Explain the meaning of the following statements. How do they connect to the main idea of the essay? How do they contribute to Thomas's argument?
   a) As extensions of the human brain, [computers] have been constructed with the same property of error, spontaneous, uncontrolled, and rich in possibilities.
   b) Mistakes are at the very base of human thought, embedded there, feeding the structure like root nodules.
   c) Sometimes there are ten, even twenty different ways to go, all but one bound to be wrong, and the richness of selection in such situations can lift us onto totally new ground.
   d) If it is a big enough mistake, we could find ourselves on a new level, stunned, out in the clear, ready to move again.

Form and Style

3. Thomas begins his essay using an example with which he feels most readers will identify: personal experience with computer error. He goes on to state that computers, at their best, are infallible, then questions whether or not this can be true. How effective is this as a beginning to a persuasive essay? Justify your answer.

4. A *paradox* is a statement of striking contradiction that provokes the reader into seeing another sense in which the statement would be true. How are the following statements examples of paradox? How do they contribute to Thomas's thesis?
   a) ...if it is a lucky day, and a lucky laboratory, somebody makes a mistake...and then the action can begin.
   b) What is needed, for progress to be made, is the move based on the error.
   c) The capacity to leap across mountains of information to land lightly on the wrong side represents the highest of human endowments.
   d) The lower animals do not have this splendid freedom. They are limited, most of them, to absolute infallibility.
   e) What we need then, for moving ahead, is a set of wrong alternatives much longer and more interesting than the short list of mistaken courses that any of us can think up right now.

Exploring Context

5. History is full of attempts to persuade others to a certain point of view, or to argue a point in such a way that others will agree. Persuasion is most often characterized by emotionally charged language that appeals to feelings, while argument uses facts and logic to appeal to reason. Which approach does Thomas use? Support your views with evidence from the text.

Creative Extension

6. Thomas writes that computers "can do anything we can do and more besides." Is this true? Conduct a class debate on this statement.

7. Write a science fiction story or create a script for a short film that elaborates on the notion of computer error in a computer-dependent society. Will your theme agree or disagree with Thomas's idea that error is essentially positive?

Science and Beauty

☙ Isaac Asimov

One of Walt Whitman's best-known poems is this one:

When I heard the learn'd astronomer,
When the proofs, the figures, were ranged in columns before me,
When I was shown the charts and diagrams, to add, divide and
    measure them,
When I sitting heard the astronomer where he lectured with
    much applause in the lecture-room,
How soon unaccountable I became tired and sick,
In the mystical moist night-air, and from time to time,
Look'd up in perfect silence at the stars.

I imagine that many people reading those lines tell themselves, exultantly, "How true! Science just sucks all the beauty out of everything, reducing it all to numbers and tables and measurements! Why bother learning all that junk when I can just go out and look at the stars?"

That is a very convenient point of view since it makes it not only necessary, but downright aesthetically wrong, to try to follow all that hard stuff in science. Instead, you can just take a look at the night sky, get a quick fix, and go off to a nightclub.

The trouble is that Whitman is talking through his hat, but the poor soul didn't know any better.

I don't deny that the night sky is beautiful, and I have in my time spread out on a hillside for hours looking at the stars and being awed by their beauty (and receiving bug-bites whose marks took weeks to go away).

But what I see—those quiet, twinkling points of light—*is not all the beauty there is.* Should I stare at a single leaf and willingly remain ignorant of the forest? Should I be satisfied to watch the sun glinting off a single pebble and scorn any knowledge of a beach?

Those bright spots in the sky that we call planets are worlds. There are worlds with thick atmospheres of carbon dioxide and sulfuric acid; worlds of red-hot liquid with hurricanes that could gulp down the whole earth; dead worlds with quiet pock-marks of craters; worlds with volcanoes puffing plumes of dust into airlessness; worlds with pink and desolate deserts—each with a weird and unearthly beauty that boils down to a mere speck of light if we just gaze at the night sky.

Those other bright spots, which are stars rather than planets, are actually suns. Some of them are of incomparable grandeur, each glowing with the light of a thousand suns like ours; some of them are merely red-hot coals doling out their energy stingily. Some of them are compact bodies as massive as our sun, but with all that mass squeezed into a ball smaller than the earth. Some are more compact still, with the mass of the sun squeezed down into the volume of a small asteroid. And some are more compact still, with their mass shrinking down to a volume of zero, the site of which is marked by an intense gravitational field that swallows up everything and gives back nothing; with matter spiralling into that bottomless hole and giving out a wild death-scream of X-rays.

There are stars that pulsate endlessly in a great cosmic breathing; and others that, having consumed their fuel, expand and redden until they swallow up their planets, if they have any (and someday, billions of years from now, our sun will expand and the earth will crisp and sere and vaporize into a gas of iron and rock with no sign of the life it once bore). And some stars explode in a vast cataclysm whose ferocious blast of cosmic rays, hurrying outward at nearly the speed of light reaching across thousands of light-years to touch the earth and supply some of the driving force of evolution through mutations.

Those paltry few stars we see as we look up in perfect silence (some 2500, and no more, on even the darkest and clearest night) are joined by a vast horde we don't see, up to as many as three hundred billion— 300 000 000 000—to form an enormous pinwheel in space. This pinwheel, the Milky Way galaxy, stretches so widely that it takes light, moving at 186 282 miles each *second*, a hundred thousand *years* to cross it from end to end; and it rotates about its centre in a vast and stately turn that takes two hundred million years to complete—and the sun and the earth and we ourselves all make that turn.

Beyond our Milky Way galaxy are others, a score or so of them bound to our own in a cluster of galaxies, most of them small, with no more than a few billion stars in each; but with one at least, the Andromeda galaxy, twice as large as our own.

Beyond our own cluster, other galaxies and other clusters exist; some clusters made up of thousands of galaxies. They stretch outward and outward as far as our best telescopes can see, with no visible sign of an end—perhaps a hundred billion of them in all.

And in more and more of those galaxies we are becoming aware of violence at the centres—of great explosions and outpourings of radiation, marking the death of perhaps millions of stars. Even at the centre of our own galaxy there is incredible violence masked from our own solar system far in the outskirts by enormous clouds of dust and gas that lie between us and the heaving centre.

Some galactic centres are so bright that they can be seen from distances of billions of light-years, distances from which the galaxies themselves cannot be seen and only the bright star-like centres of ravening energy show up—as quasars. Some of these have been detected from more than ten billion light years away.

All these galaxies are hurrying outward from each other in a vast universal expansion that began fifteen billion years ago, when all the matter in the universe was in a tiny sphere that exploded in the hugest conceivable shatter to form the galaxies.

The universe may expand forever or the day may come when the expansion slows and turns back into a contraction to reform the tiny sphere and begin the game all over again so that the whole universe is exhaling and inhaling in breaths that are perhaps a trillion years long.

And all of this vision—far beyond the scale of human imaginings—was made possible by the works of hundreds of "learn'd" astronomers. All of it; *all* of it was discovered after the death of Whitman in 1892, and most of it in the past twenty-five years, so that the poor poet never knew what a stultified and limited beauty he observed when he "look'd up in perfect silence at the stars."

Nor can we know or imagine now the limitless beauty yet to be revealed in the future—by science.

ℰ Isaac Asimov was born in Russia but moved to the United States as a child. An associate professor of biochemistry in Boston, he wrote essays and books to explain scientific matters to the general public. "Science and Beauty" appeared in his essay collection *The Roving Mind* (1983). Some of his highly popular science-fiction stories appear in the collection *I, Robot* (1950). (*Born Petrovichi, Russia 1920; died 1992*)

RESPONDING

Meaning

1. What arguments does Asimov make to support his *thesis statement* "but what I see— those quiet, twinkling points of light—is not all the beauty there is"? Does Asimov succeed in making his case? Support your opinion.

2. What scientific information does Asimov provide about "those quiet, twinkling points of light" to make the connection between science and beauty? Provide your answer under the headings: planet, star, galaxy, universe. Use point-form notes, a web, or another organizer.

Form and Style

3. In the sixth paragraph, Asimov uses a device called the *rhetorical question*. Basically, he asks a question (two, in fact) to which the answer is so obvious, the reader must respond as Asimov desires and thus agree with him. How effective is this use of rhetorical question? How does it forward Asimov's argument about science and beauty?

4. Asimov's essay is an excellent example of *coherence* in writing—each part of the essay is seamlessly linked to the parts before and after it. Explain, using an outline of "Science and Beauty," how he accomplishes this coherence.

Exploring Context

5. Asimov's essay was written in 1983. Research some more recent discoveries in astronomy. What content additions to his essay could Asimov make, if he were still alive to do so?

Creative Extension

6. People have been fascinated with the night sky since the dawn of time. Research stories from different ancient cultures created to account for what they saw. Share the best of them with the class during a storytelling/reading session.

7. Using words and ideas from Asimov's essay, write a poem expressing the beauty in the science of the night sky. Alternatively, choose another aspect of science in which you find beauty and create a poem, short essay, photo essay, or personal prose piece expressing your ideas.

It's all real, but it's not all true

↩ Catherine Bush

I am continually amazed by the assumptions that people make about writers based upon their work. You're a vegetarian, so you won't like this restaurant, someone (another writer!) once said to me, when it's the central character in my first novel who doesn't eat meat. A former boyfriend was surprised that I wasn't a natural redhead. My mother had red hair, didn't she? No, only the astronaut mother I was writing about.

After a couple of books, the autobiographical fallacy—the temptation to read a writer's life into her fiction—will turn any author into a peculiar, portmanteau creature: I'd be the daughter of a scientist and a mother in space, an animal-rights activist who's had a duel fought over her, *and* who lives simultaneously in Toronto and London.

It shouldn't matter whether a work of fiction has obvious origins in the writer's life. What *should* count is whether we believe in the created world and characters—the strength of both the writer's and reader's conviction. Ideally, the author should perform what English writer Jeanette Winterson refers to as "the Indian rope trick," and disappear into the work.

Yet the impulse to search for autobiographical traces remains. Some novels court this by drawing quite explicitly on real life. Every review of Saul Bellow's novel *Ravelstein* comments on the fact that his eponymous protagonist bears a striking resemblance to Bellow's late friend, the philosopher Allan Bloom. This tension creates its own *frisson*, but the parallel (and whether the portrait's an accurate or distorted representation of Bloom) should be irrelevant to the consideration of the novel as fiction. (It might matter to Bloom, were he alive, or to those who knew him, but that's a separate issue.)

Like many writers, I sometimes feel shoehorned by stubbornly autobiographical readings, frustrated by a connect-the-dots approach to the work. It's a bit like watching someone try to stuff a forest through a keyhole. Fiction's authenticity, its access to "truth," doesn't depend on neat links between the writer's life and invention. Write what you know, beginning authors are often told, but there are many ways to know something.

The ability to imagine sympathetically and passionately, to bridge the gap between self and other, is perhaps a more potent route to knowledge than familiarity.

We live in a culture that favours the confessional gesture and fixates on the exposure of secrets. Acts of transformation risk being deemed mere disguise rather than a route to truth. Yet human behaviour is wonderfully paradoxical. Why should confession ultimately be more authentic than speaking in code, or lying? Each reveals something, depending on how you look at it.

Media obsession with personality means that these days the writer's own story is more readily hyped than the work. This may go partway toward explaining the temptation to read fiction as veiled autobiography. It may also mean that readers, steeped in the cult of personality, find it difficult to encounter the work without recasting this as an imaginative encounter with the author.

There's also something about the intimate, nearly unmediated way in which we experience stories (whether read or told to us) that elides writers and their fiction. (We're less swift, I think, to insist on autobiographical readings of filmmakers' work.) Mere words separate reader from writer. An author's voice is practically a presence in our heads. Because, at its best, the experience feels so seamless, we want desperately to see how it's achieved. Searching for biographical clues is a first, if simplistic, step toward examining the process of artistic creation.

Crucially, we often fail to distinguish how fiction can be profoundly personal without being autobiographical. Often readers look for superficial points of conjunction, while writers mine deeper psychic territory—obsessions, fears, private imagery—rather than the narrative content of their lives. As crucially, they manipulate material for reasons that have nothing to do with fidelity to the original experience. Writers live through their narratives instead of reflecting their lives in them.

Yet the dirty little secret of the autobiographical fallacy is that we all do it, even those of us who know better. We just search for clues more covertly. Why can't we help ourselves? Because, I sometimes think, story-telling has its origins not just in parable or entertainment, but in gossip. We want to know stuff about other people. And gossip, though much maligned, also serves a useful social function: It connects people.

Still, I'd like to make a plea for reading fiction as fiction. At root, fiction is metaphor—not one thing compared to another, but one thing transformed into something else. The art's in the leap. We need to allow ourselves, without looking back, to be transported.

ॐ Catherine Bush lives in Toronto, but she has taught creative writing at Concordia University and the University of Florida. She is the author of the novels *Minus Time* (1993) and *The Rules of Engagement* (2000), which were both nominated for City of Toronto Book Awards. *The Rules of Engagement* was also a *New York Times* Notable Book. Her non-fiction has appeared in numerous publications, including *New York Times Magazine* and Toronto's *Globe and Mail*. "It's all real, but it's not all true" appeared in the *Globe and Mail* on May 6, 2000. (*Born Toronto, Ontario 1961*)

RESPONDING

Meaning

1. Why is Bush bothered by the human tendency to assume works of fiction are, in fact, semi-autobiographical pieces about their author? What is this tendency called?

2. A *précis* is a summary in which the most important points in a longer piece of writing are presented in a concise, logical, and readable form. Write a précis of this persuasive essay.

Form and Style

3. a) This essay is written in the first-person point of view. How would it be different if written in third-person? Does Bush's choice of point of view contribute to the autobiographical fallacy she argues against or not? Support your opinion.

   b) If this piece of writing were fiction, would the first-person point of view contribute to the autobiographical fallacy? Explain.

4. Bush's first paragraph is concrete; her final paragraph is abstract. How does each support her thesis? How do they support each other? Are these choices effective or not in your opinion?

Exploring Context

5. Bush points to the differences between autobiography and fiction in this essay. Research and outline the major characteristics of these two forms. How well has Bush's essay contributed to your understanding of these forms? What else could she have said that would also have supported her thesis?

Creative Extension

6. Develop a pamphlet that gives tips on how to write fiction and how to read it in ways that avoid the autobiographical fallacy Bush writes about.

7. Choose any author of fiction in this book and read the selection. Read one or two more pieces by this author (this will require research), and then research facts about the author's life. Does this writer's life/writing support or refute Bush's thesis? Explain your views in an oral presentation or *seminar*.

The Enchanted Forest

ꙮ Bill Reid

...gradually I became aware of the old island here that flowered once for Dutch sailors' eyes—a fresh, green breast of the new world. It's vanished trees...had once pandered in whispers to the last and greatest of all human dreams; for a transitory enchanted moment man must have held his breath in the presence of this continent, compelled into an aesthetic contemplation he neither understood nor desired, face to face for the last time in history with something commensurate to his capacity for wonder.[1]

So wrote Scott Fitzgerald, concerning Long Island, New York, in *The Great Gatsby*, more than half a century ago.

Last month, on another island, almost as remote from Fitzgerald's as possible while still being part of North America, I had the great privilege of feeling something of the sense of wonder of those old Dutch sailors. With some friends, I went ashore at Windy Bay on Lyell Island, which lies off the east coast of Moresby in the southern Queen Charlottes. All my conscious life, because of my kinship with the Haida people and my involvement in their art and history, and because of the austere, remote beauty of the islands themselves, the Charlottes have been my spiritual and occasionally my actual home. But never have I felt the full impact of their magic as I did at Windy Bay.

There is grander scenery on the west coast, wider vistas to the north. But this could be the setting for the Peaceable Kingdom. A fine river empties into the bay through a grassy meadow, an old Haida village site lies at the edge of the forest, marked only by the lush grass that distinguishes the places where the people once lived.

Then there's the forest itself—great old spruces, hemlocks and cedars, some straight and tall, some twisted into incredible baroque shapes—not a gloomy place at all, so old that there are many open spaces to let in the

---

1 The quotation is taken from the last page of Fitzgerald's novel, published by Charles Scribner's Sons, New York, 1925.

light, which falls softly on the deep moss that carpets the ground. The game trails along the river are so well worn and the terrain so gentle that even I, who am neither very young nor very strong, could stroll easily for a mile or so along the river. A couple of yearling does didn't even look up as we passed within feet of them, and a black bear went on eating grass, waiting for the salmon that would soon fill the river.

Our time there should have been one of unqualified delight. But we all carried ashore with us the knowledge that the wave of technological assault that had begun on that other island and changed most of the continent, devastating much of it, was lapping at the shores of Windy Bay.

On the other side of the island we had seen the huge swath, miles long and nearly a hillside wide, that marked the rapid advance of the loggers. If present plans are followed, sometime within the next five years they will advance over the hilltop and move down the river valley to the sea. Nothing will remain of the grand old forest but stumps. The moss will be ripped away by the machines and skidded logs, a tangle of branches and other waste will cover the ground, the clear water of the river will be muddied by the unchecked runoff from the bare hills.

In the warm, moist, generous climate of the Charlottes, in fifty years or so the trees will be back, a dense, impenetrable thicket, and in five hundred years, if left alone, Windy Bay perhaps, just perhaps, may be something like it was when we saw it last month.

This is not intended as a diatribe aimed at the most important part of our economy. I'm not opposed to logging, loggers, or the lumber industry. I don't want to see my fellow residents of British Columbia starve in the forest, and as one who's spent many years using beautiful British Columbian wood in my work, I'd be a ridiculous hypocrite if I proposed the end of the tree harvest. But can't we, while we still have a little bit of a last chance, institute true multi-use of the forest, with due regard for its own regeneration, the wildlife it nurtures, and, most important and most neglected, its aesthetic values—that is, the nurture it affords to human life?

At this moment what is happening on the poor old Charlottes resembles a desperate attempt to loot a treasure house before the owners—you and I—realize what's going on and take measures to stop it. This on our famous Misty Isles, home of the fabled Haidas, one of the places in our country still imbued with romance, a world-renowned, unique ecological area.

To my way of thinking, sustained yield in tree farming, as in other farming, should mean bringing at least some of the crop to maturity. We should have fifty-year-old trees, hundred-year-old trees, five-hundred-year-old trees. After all, our great-great-grandchildren may enjoy seeing some big trees in mature forests, and may also find some use for beautiful, clear lumber. They may not feel overjoyed that their ancestors got a little richer by using it all up at once.

And what better place to set aside those five-hundred-year-old trees than the proposed South Moresby Park area, which includes Lyell Island and Windy Bay? Now that control of that particular tree farm licence is back in local hands, let us hope that enough people within the companies, the government, and the population at large will be found with their "capacity for wonder" sufficiently intact to preserve this tiny remnant for the enchantment of all, as a vital memorial to all that's been lost between those old Dutchmen's time and ours, and as a continuing promise for the future.

It may be argued that few will ever set eyes on such a remote spot, but those who still hold to what is left of the "last and greatest of human dreams" will find their way here, or find solace in the knowledge that it still exists unspoiled. Let's not waste *this* last time in history to save something commensurate to *our* capacity for wonder.

ço   Many people credit Haida sculptor Bill Reid with the revival of Northwest Coast Aboriginal arts, which he started studying in 1951. Among his internationally acclaimed works are the 4.5-ton sculpture, *Raven and the First Humans*, in the Museum of Anthropology at the University of British Columbia, and the *Spirit of the Haida Gwaii*, commissioned for the Canadian Embassy in Washington, DC. An outspoken proponent of Aboriginal rights in Canada, Reid first published "The Enchanted Forest" in the *Vancouver Sun*, October 1980. It also appears in *Solitary Raven: The Selected Writings of Bill Reid* (2000). In 1994, he received a Lifetime Achievement Award as a part of the National Aboriginal Achievement Awards. (*Born Vancouver, British Columbia 1920; died 1998*)

RESPONDING

Meaning

1. Like all persuasive essays, this one has a purpose. What is Reid's purpose? Quote his *thesis statement*.

2. What reasons does Reid offer to support his thesis and to get his reader to agree with him? How compelling are these reasons, in your opinion?

Form and Style

3. Reid does not actually state his thesis until well into his essay. This is unusual in persuasive writing, which usually offers the thesis statement much earlier. What does Reid spend time and space doing before getting to his point? Is this an effective approach? Support your view.

4. Reid opens with a quotation from Fitzgerald's *The Great Gatsby*. How does this quotation frame the content of his essay?

Exploring Context

5. This essay was written during times of environmental and political activism against clear cut logging on Lyell and Moresby Islands in the southern Queen Charlotte Islands of BC. Research this protest. What were the various issues? How were they resolved? Create a timeline of the events you discover. How does this knowledge enhance your understanding of Reid's position?

Creative Extension

6. View paintings by Emily Carr and other artists of Haida villages and the BC coastal wilderness. Evaluate how these paintings match Reid's descriptions of the same region. Explain your evaluation in a multimedia presentation.

7. Assume you are Bill Reid and write a journal entry about the trip to Windy Bay. How is this writing different from the writing he did on the same topic for his "Enchanted Forest" essay? Present your findings in a short informal talk or written commentary.

Forget Prince Charming

✑ June Callwood

I don't believe for a moment that a perfect mate exists and if such a freak of nature did occur that person would not be a heavenly match for me because I am imperfect and we would clash. But I have three granddaughters of marriageable age and I frequently advise them on such matters as how to run their lives and what they should require of a mate.

The primary consideration, I tell them, is that they cannot expect perfection. No human relationship is friction-free. Even siblings who are fond of one another have clashes, and they come from the same gene pool. There is no possibility that two adults from different backgrounds will agree on everything, and discord over trivia is not evidence of a mismatch.

The notion of a perfect mate exists because of the temporary insanity that accompanies courtship, when people experience what Freud called "the oceanic feeling." Self-protective edges disappear in a wash of uncritical attentiveness. The two in love become one sensate being, their emotions so attuned to one another that the existential loneliness of the human condition is masked. People in the first fiery intensity of romantic attachment bring out the sweetness in one another and are all the better for it.

Amazingly, the pounding heart is not always an idiot; some inner wisdom or instinct seems to guide many people to the right choice, and one they might never have made cognitively. Besides, passionate physical attraction is nature's plan for the species and without it relationships are cold gruel. The major flaw in ecstatic beginnings, however, is the expectation they arouse that, lifelong, the partnership will be effortless. No fundamental problems are ever resolved by two people moving in together; the best hope is that a stable relationship will enable each person to work on them.

All long-term couplings survive on a mutual ability to compromise, which is the same glue that holds our peculiar country together. Some matters are not negotiable, of course; violence and betrayal are definitely deal-breakers. But happily married people make concessions to one another's peculiarities all the time, and the exchange rarely is 50–50. The totality has to feel fair to both, but real life is far too complex for a balance scale to be relevant.

A wise Canadian child psychologist, the late Dr. William Blatz, was asked the secret of his serene marriage. He replied, "I make the dressing and she makes the salad." A dressing is a *lot* quicker to make than a salad, but people got the picture. The wedlock was a collaboration effort.

It may be significant that our granddaughters have scattered beyond the immediate reach of my wise counsel on the subject of choosing a mate. One is in India, either near the Ganges or Thailand doing something for *The New York Times*. No matter. We stay in contact through e-mail and I proffer endless help in what I take to be their pursuit of love and fulfillment, which may be synonymous states.

What I have been saying to them since they were so small I could hold them on my lap is that successful mating has little to do with finding Prince Charming, who in my experience frequently is a narcissistic dope. Romantic novelists have the ideal all wrong, I explain. The first quality they should seek in their partner is integrity. Someone who cheats on an expense account or can't admit fault will be dishonest in a myriad of other ways as well. For the long haul, they want a truth speaker.

Punctuality is an important clue to character, I continue. Chronic tardiness indicates to me a lack of respect for the waiting person that goes to the heart of consideration for others. I also insist on compassion, which rests on the fine bedrock of empathy. A helpful clue to this attribute can be found in the way the person behaves around small children. Anyone who stops to admire a baby probably had good parenting and will hang in with loyalty and kindness through the adversities that most certainly lie ahead.

I also stress humour, by which I don't mean joke telling, which can also be an indication of the need for attention and a paucity of anything interesting to say. However humour that springs from awareness of life's absurdities is the hallmark of a humane outlook. The ability to put matters in perspective and a knack for leavening bad times with a comical observation make life infinitely more bearable. My husband had something genuinely funny to say while we were burying our son, and it helped a great deal.

Come to think of it, my prescription for informed mate choosing seems to be a description of my own mate. We've been married almost fifty-seven years and so far it is working out all right, so what can I say. I'll keep you posted (little joke of my own there).

ॐ In the 1950s, June Callwood began publishing her essays in established Canadian magazines. Her books, including *Love, Fear, Hate and Anger* (1964) and *Portrait of Canada* (1981), explore a variety of subjects, frequently social activism. She was appointed an Officer of the Order of Canada in 1986. "Forget Prince Charming" appeared in the *National Post* in 2000 following an invitation to Canadian writers to describe their "perfect mate." *(Born Chatham, Ontario 1924)*

RESPONDING

Meaning

1. What reasons does Callwood offer for giving up on the notion of a perfect mate? What qualities does she suggest are important in a mate? List the reasons and qualities.

2. What is your opinion of Callwood's comments on the search for a perfect mate and qualities for which one should look? Do you agree or disagree with her advice? Beside each item in the list you created in question 1, provide a personal opinion.

Form and Style

3. Callwood's essay is essentially presented in two parts, although there is no obvious dividing line between them. What are these two parts? How do the two parts complement each other?

4. Although her essay is essentially about finding a suitable mate, Callwood manages to work in a variety of information about other topics: sibling rivalry, Freud, the Canadian tendency to compromise, the lives of her granddaughters, her personal life. Does this additional information help or hinder the development of her essay? Does it support or distract from her thesis? Support your answer.

Exploring Context

5. The topic of love is a perennial favourite for artists and songwriters. Review a sampling of love songs or poems, both traditional and modern. How do Callwood's ideas fit with the ideas on love presented in these works of art? Do you detect any difference in the attitude toward love over time?

Creative Extension

6. Create a readers' quiz like those found in magazines such as *Cosmopolitan* or *Seventeen*, titled "How Great Is Your Mate?" Present the quiz along with instructions for interpreting the results.

7. Evaluate a famous love story using Callwood's ideas for important qualities in a mate as criteria. Should the relationship have succeeded or failed, according to Callwood? Present your findings in a short oral or written report.

The Education Debate
What is education for, anyway?

What do you expect from your education? What is the purpose of an education, and how well does education fulfill its purpose? These questions have been debated for centuries, though it may seem that the debate has never been more heated than it is at the present moment. In this Echo, through essays, poems, a novel excerpt, and an editorial cartoon, you will explore several perspectives on this issue.

Learning Goals
- examine an issue from a variety of perspectives
- make personal connections with a variety of texts
- use a variety of strategies to better understand and interpret texts
- communicate ideas in a variety of forms

The Closing of the (North) American Mind

Robert Nielsen

In this provocative essay, Robert Nielsen reviews a book by American philosopher Allan Bloom. This book critiques the American education system, which Nielsen considers to be in the same state of disarray as the Canadian one. What do you think?

> *Instead of encouraging us to think and live well, "higher education," according to this scathing best-seller, is offering shifting values and irresponsible freedom.*

Now that higher education is within easier reach of Canadians than ever before, it's time to ask: What's so high about it? That's the question we are urged to consider by Allan Bloom's book, *The Closing of the American Mind*, which has surprised its author and publisher by becoming an international best-seller. In Canada as well as the United States, it has provoked keen debate over what the aims of education should be.

If we are content merely to have our universities train doctors, lawyers, engineers, scientists, and other professionals, they are probably serving us adequately. But if we share Bloom's fervent belief that universities should also offer students pathways to "the good life" of wisdom and virtue, then they are letting us down badly.

Subtitled "How higher education has failed democracy and impoverished the souls of today's students," the book scathingly indicts the universities for abandoning moral truth in favour of a shallow, shifting mix of "values." This moral relativism tends to justify whatever current opinions and behaviour students feel comfortable with; and they may pass through four years without ever encountering a professor—or book—that challenges them to do some serious thinking about their ideas.

Bloom, a classical scholar and philosopher, has taught at several North American universities, including the University of Toronto, and his criticisms are applicable to the Canadian as well as to the American scene. Bloom finds today's students "nice" in that they are tolerant and willing to concede everybody the rights they claim for themselves. They are not, he said, especially moral or noble. They don't fall in love, they have sexual "relationships" that are easy to start and easy to abandon. They have little idealism. "There is a whole arsenal of terms for talking about nothing—'caring,' 'self-fulfillment,' 'expanding consciousness,' and so on."

Students have no understanding of evil and even doubt its existence, thus lacking awareness of the depths as well as the heights of human nature. They read few books, and find neither pleasure nor insights for living in the great literature of the past; in history, no lessons for the present.

Futile Propaganda. The universities, of course, don't shape these "flat-souled" young people. They arrive on campus as products of homes, schools, and a commercially packaged youth culture far more influential than either parents or teachers in forming their tastes and attitudes. Here Bloom widens his target to our modern society itself.

Even in relatively happy homes, he says, "the dreariness of the family's spiritual landscape passes belief." Parents have quit their traditional role of instilling beliefs in religion, morals, and patriotism. Once "the Bible was the common culture, one that united the simple and the sophisticated, rich and poor, young and old." Now neither it nor other great books passed down to us are read and discussed in the home because "nobody believes that the old books do, or could, contain the truth." Claims Bloom: "Fathers and mothers have lost the idea that the highest aspiration they might have for their children is for them to be wise—as priests, prophets, and philosophers are wise. Specialized competence and success are all they can imagine."

In default of moral education at home, the schools give courses in "value clarification." These prompt children to talk about abortion, sexism, and the arms race, "issues the significance of which they cannot possibly understand." Such education is little more than propaganda, Bloom contends, and futile propaganda at that. The values at which the children arrive will change as public opinion changes—because they are not grounded in experience or passion, the bases of moral reasoning.

Meanwhile reading and writing are widely ill-taught in public schools, and television replaces reading in the home. This compels universities to set up remedial classes for the many high-school graduates who cannot read or write well enough to cope with first-year courses.

Delusive Openness. How do the universities respond to the masses of uncivilized young people? In general, Bloom maintains, by accommodating in every field except science and professional training the students' ignorance and paltry aims.

Literate or not, earnest or trifling, rich or poor, nearly every student, says Bloom, enters university with one fixed belief—that truth is relative. Students assume that ideas are valid only for their own time and place, or perhaps only for the individual holding them; that there are no universal and eternal verities for people to learn and live by. This leaves everyone free to think and do as they please, without worrying about right and wrong, so long as they don't infringe on others' freedom to do likewise. The only sin is intolerance.

Such "openness," Bloom says, actually leads to closed minds because it makes students incurious about real distinctions between good and bad, between right and wrong, between truth and error, instead of leading them to seek knowledge and certitude. In Bloom's view, "to deny the possibility of knowing good and bad is to suppress true openness."

Bloom says education should make students curious about man's highest aspirations, as opposed to his low and common needs. And they have to become aware that the answer is not obvious, but neither is it unavailable. It can't be found, however, without consulting the great thinkers and writers of the past.

The quest should be led by the humanities—literature, philosophy, and history. But the humanities faculties are in poor shape to carry out the task after caving in to the demands of a student "rabble" in the 1960s, Bloom alleges. Relaxed academic standards and easy grading made it hard for a student to flunk out. Junk courses were devised to cater to the demands for political "relevance."

The universities are quieter now, but Bloom warns against assuming that they have recovered their quality and integrity. Students can choose humanities courses in cafeteria style, picking out a list of soft ones that will get them an arts degree without giving them coherent knowledge.

At the same time, the faculties go their separate ways. At the University of Toronto, science students need take only three of their twenty courses in either arts or social science, and non-science students need take no science at all. The different faculties compete for students, but don't even try to collaborate in offering anyone a rounded education.

"These great universities," Bloom writes, "which can split the atom, find cures for the most terrible diseases, and produce massive dictionaries of lost languages, cannot generate a modest program of general education for undergraduate students." A good program of liberal education, he says, "feeds the student's love of truth and passion to live a good life." He adds that it is easy to devise courses of study that thrill those who take them; the difficulty is getting them accepted by the faculty.

Students come to US universities ignorant and cynical about their country's history, Bloom says. Their cynicism, at least, stands to be increased by "revisionist" historians who promote either or both of two poisonous distortions of history. They malign the character and ideas of the American founding fathers, and they pervert recent history to make the United States rather than the Soviet Union the villain in the contest between communism and democracy. (Some of these revisionists have moved north to places on Canadian university faculties, where they fuel anti-Americanism.) Thus young Americans are taught to be apologetic instead of proud of a political heritage that made their country the leading democracy and themselves perhaps the most privileged youth ever.

A milder form of this erosion is happening in Canada, where the British heritage used to be central to the teaching of literature and history. "Now," says Thomas Pangle, a former student of Bloom's who is today a professor of political philosophy at the University of Toronto, "a Canadian student is not expected to know any more about English literature than a student in Missouri. If a university teacher quotes Dickens or Shakespeare, he can't count on the students sensing any echoes." Canadian universities have generally gone along with the trend, although at the University of Toronto the eminent scholar Northrop Frye held the fort by insisting on the study of the Bible and Shakespeare.

"Ignorant Shepherds." Bloom's is a profound book, full of rewards to the attentive reader because of the richness of his thought and the clarity, energy, and wit of his writing. Near the end he offers a poignant metaphor of where we now stand in relation to the great tradition of human learning:

"We are like ignorant shepherds living on a site where great civilizations once flourished. The shepherds play with the fragments that pop up to the surface, having no notion of the beautiful structures of which they were once a part. All that is necessary is a careful excavation to provide them with life-enhancing models."

The restoration, if it comes, will be no easy task. The causes of the ills Bloom exposes in our education and our society are too deep for quick fixes—although a return to competent teaching of the three R's in school would be a useful beginning.

It is no surprise that the book has come under sharp attack. It defies almost every tenet of fashionable modern thought, and leaves no academic ox ungored. What is surprising, and heartening, is the phenomenal response to it. A year after its publication it was still on *The New York Times* best-seller list. This can only mean that many people sense a hollowness at the core of modern life which cannot be filled by more science and technology, more wealth and comforts, more sex and amusements.

A critic who credited the book's success to smart promotion was corrected by New York author Midge Decter, a close observer of today's youth. "The reason the book sold well," she says, "is that a lot of people, young people in particular, found themselves and their own feelings of emptiness reflected in it. The people who started the great publicity snowball were young people who read this and said, 'My God, that's us.'"

There are indeed young people who want more from university than a few years of irresponsible freedom. They feel cheated. Bloom's book offers a wealth of clues to what they are missing, and to what must be done to make higher education worthy of the name. From it young readers will emerge, it is hoped, champions of healthy change—change that restores the ancient goal of thinking and living well.

For many years, Robert Nielsen was a foreign correspondent for *The Toronto Star*. Currently retired, he lives in Perth-Andover, New Brunswick.

RESPONDING

Meaning

1. Summarize Nielsen's (Bloom's) opinion of "higher" education. Do you agree or disagree with this opinion? Why? (If you have no knowledge of colleges and universities, think about the public school system, which Nielsen also criticizes. What is your opinion of that? Why?)

2. At post-secondary institutions, "the sciences" include subjects such as Biology, Physics, Chemistry, Mathematics, and Geography while the arts, or Humanities, are subjects such as English, French, History, and Philosophy. Why would Nielsen (Bloom) argue that students should take both arts and sciences? Defend your answer with evidence from the essay.

Form and Style

3. Nielsen uses three sub-headings in his essay. What are they? How does each one contribute to his overall argument? Do you prefer essays with or without sub-headings? Explain.

4. This essay uses formal, academic *diction*. Explain the meaning of the following terms and phrases from the essay:
   a) scathingly indicts
   b) moral relativism
   c) it defies almost every tenet of fashionable modern thought, and leaves no academic ox ungored
   How does this diction affect the *tone* of the essay? Rewrite one paragraph in a more informal tone and discuss the effects.

Exploring Context

5.   Consider the subtitle of Bloom's book (see paragraph three of the essay). Given what the essay says about higher education, what do you think is the link between higher education and democracy? How has higher education failed democracy? Why are the "souls" of today's students "impoverished" according to these writers? Do you agree?

Creative Extension

6.   Write a critical response to Nielsen's essay. Your response may be in the form of an editorial or short persuasive essay. Be sure to carefully develop your argument.

7.   Create a newscast on the topic of "Education Today," or develop a short documentary. Interview teachers and students, administration and clerical/support staff, and parents to gather information and opinions. Internet research, including a visit to the Ministry of Education Web site to discover the province's "Aims or Goals of Education," and library research would also be appropriate.

Brave New World

ॐ   *Aldous Huxley*

In this excerpt from Aldous Huxley's famous futuristic novel, everything is geared to social stability. Life starts with the mechanical Bokanovsky process, which produces beings designed for specific tasks. Once born, the beings are psychologically trained and conditioned for their planned social destiny. Consider what point Huxley is making about higher education.

The room into which the three were ushered was the Controller's study.

"His fordship will be down in a moment." The Gamma butler left them to themselves.

Helmholtz laughed aloud.

"It's more like a caffeine-solution party than a trial," he said, and let himself fall into the most luxurious of the pneumatic armchairs. "Cheer up, Bernard," he added, catching sight of his friend's green unhappy face. But Bernard would not be cheered; without answering, without even looking at Helmholtz, he went and sat down on the most uncomfortable chair in the room, carefully chosen in the obscure hope of somehow deprecating the wrath of the higher powers.

The Savage meanwhile wandered restlessly round the room, peering with a vague superficial inquisitiveness at the books in the shelves, at the soundtrack rolls and the reading machine bobbins in their numbered pigeon-holes. On the table under the window lay a massive volume bound in limp black leather-surrogate, and stamped with large golden T's. He picked it up and opened it. MY LIFE AND WORK, BY OUR FORD. The book had been published in Detroit by the Society for the Propagation of Fordian Knowledge. Idly he turned the pages, read a sentence here, a paragraph there, and had just come to the conclusion that the book didn't interest him, when the door opened, and the Resident World Controller for Western Europe walked briskly into the room.

Mustapha Mond shook hands with all three of them; but it was to the Savage that he addressed himself. "So you don't much like civilization, Mr. Savage," he said.

The Savage looked at him. He had been prepared to lie, to bluster, to remain sullenly unresponsive; but reassured by the good-humoured intelligence of the Controller's face, he decided to tell the truth, straightforwardly. "No." He shook his head.

Bernard started and looked horrified. What would the Controller think? To be labelled as the friend of a man who said he didn't like civilization—said it openly and, of all people, to the Controller—it was terrible. "But, John," he began. A look from Mustapha Mond reduced him to abject silence.

"Of course," the Savage went on to admit, "there are some very nice things. All that music in the air, for instance . . ."

"Sometimes a thousand twangling instruments will hum about my ears and sometimes voices."

The Savage's face lit up with sudden pleasure. "Have you read it too?" he asked. "I thought nobody knew about that book here, in England."

"Almost nobody. I'm one of the very few. It's prohibited, you see. But as I make the laws here, I can also break them. With impunity, Mr. Marx," he added, turning to Bernard. "Which I'm afraid you *can't* do."

Bernard sank into a yet more hopeless misery.

"But why is it prohibited?" asked the Savage. In the excitement of meeting a man who had read Shakespeare he had momentarily forgotten everything else.

The Controller shrugged his shoulders. "Because it's old; that's the chief reason. We haven't any use for old things here."

"Even when they're beautiful?"

"Particularly when they're beautiful. Beauty's attractive, and we don't want people to be attracted by old things. We want them to like the new ones."

"But the new ones are so stupid and horrible. Those plays, where there's nothing but helicopters flying about and you *feel* the people kissing." He made a grimace. "Goats and monkeys!" Only in Othello's words could he find an adequate vehicle for his contempt and hatred.

"Nice tame animals, anyhow," the Controller murmured parenthetically.

"Why don't you let them see *Othello* instead?"

"I've told you, it's old. Besides, they couldn't understand it."

Yes, that was true. He remembered how Helmholtz had laughed at *Romeo and Juliet*. "Well then," he said, after a pause, "something new that's like *Othello*, and that they could understand."

"That's what we've all been wanting to write," said Helmholtz, breaking a long silence.

"And it's what you never will write," said the Controller.

"Because, if it were really like *Othello* nobody could understand it, however new it might be. And if it were new, it couldn't possibly be like *Othello*."

"Why not?"

"Yes, why not?" Helmholtz repeated. He too was forgetting the unpleasant realities of the situation. Green with anxiety, and apprehension, only Bernard remembered them; the others ignored him. "Why not?"

"Because our world is not the same as Othello's world. You can't make flivvers without steel—and you can't make the tragedies without social instability. The world's stable now. People are happy; they get what they want, and they never want what they can't get. They're well off; they're safe; they're never ill; they're not afraid of death; they're blissfully ignorant of passion and old age; they're plagued with no mothers or fathers; they've got no wives, or children, or lovers to feel strongly about; they're so conditioned that they practically can't help behaving as they ought to behave. And if anything should go wrong, there's *soma*.[1] Which you go and chuck out of the window in the name of liberty, Mr. Savage. *Liberty!*" He laughed. "Expecting Deltas to know what liberty is! And now expecting them to understand *Othello*! My good boy!"

The Savage was silent for a little. "All the same," he insisted obstinately, "*Othello's* good, *Othello's* better than those feelies."

"Of course it is," the Controller agreed. "But that's the price we have to pay for stability. You've got to choose between happiness and what people

---

used to call high art. We've sacrificed the high art. We have the feelies and the scent organ instead."

"But they don't mean anything."

"They mean themselves; they mean a lot of agreeable sensations to the audience."

"But they're . . . they're told by an idiot."

The Controller laughed. "You're not being very polite to your friend, Mr. Watson. One of our most distinguished Emotional Engineers . . ."

"But he's right," said Helmholtz gloomily. "Because it *is* idiotic. Writing when there's nothing to say . . ."

"Precisely. But that requires the most enormous ingenuity. You're making flivvers out of the absolute minimum of steel—works of art out of practically nothing but pure sensation."

The Savage shook his head. "It all seems to me quite horrible."

"Of course it does. Actual happiness always looks pretty squalid in comparison with the over-compensations for misery. And, of course, stability isn't nearly so spectacular as instability. And being contented has none of the glamour of a good fight against misfortune, none of the picturesqueness of a struggle with temptation, or a fatal overthrow by passion or doubt. Happiness is never grand."

෴ Aldous Huxley was a novelist, short-story writer, and journalist. His story collection *Limbo* (1920) was followed by *Crome Yellow* (1921), which launched his reputation as a witty and satirical commentator on contemporary events. With the popular novel *Brave New World* (1932), Huxley turned his attention to the threat of world domination by scientific totalitarianism. *(Born Surrey, England 1894; died 1963)*

Connecting

1. a)   The Controller argues that people would rather have stability than liberty, and that true happiness or contentment isn't really exciting. How does he support these arguments?
    b)   Do you agree or disagree with the Controller that this is a desirable way to live? How might this society be an extension of Nielsen's concerns for our society?

2.   Why does this futuristic society repress all old, classic literature such as Shakespeare? What is your opinion of this suppression? How does it connect to the education debate issues outlined by Robert Nielsen?

3. a)   The fourth paragraph refers to a trial. What or who do you think is on trial? Why?
    b)   What might be the outcome of the trial? Make a prediction and explain your ideas. How might an educated populace—educated in Bloom's sense—have prevented the trial?

ECHO

Legacy II

> *Leroy V. Quintana*

This poem presents a different view of education. What does it suggest about life and learning?

Grandfather never went to school
spoke only a few words of English,
a quiet man; when he talked
talked about simple things

planting corn or about the weather
sometimes about herding sheep as a child.
One day pointed to the four directions
taught me their names

<blockquote>

El Norte

Poniente   Oriente

El Sur[1]

</blockquote>

He spoke their names as if they were
one of only a handful of things
a man needed to know

Now I look back
only two generations removed
realize I am nothing but a poor fool
who went to college

trying to find my way back
to the centre of the world
where Grandfather stood
that day

---

1 El Norte and El Sur are Spanish for north and south; Poniente means west (where the sun sets) and Oriente means east (where the sun rises).

> Leroy V. Quintana was born in Albuquerque, New Mexico, and was raised by his Mexican grandparents. He served in Vietnam from 1967 to 1968, where he kept a notebook that became the source for many of his poems. He is the author of six books of poetry, including *The Great Whirl of Exile* (1991). He has won the American Book Award twice, and lives in San Diego, where he is Professor of English at Mesa College. (*Born New Mexico 1944*)

Connecting

1. Describe the character of the grandfather in this poem and his education. What is the significance of the four directions he points out to his grandson?

2. What view of education does this poem present? Why does the grandfather stand at the centre of the world, while the grandson is "a poor fool"?

3. How do the views of education in this poem fit in with those expressed in the writing by Nielsen? What would those writers say about who is at the centre of the world and who is "a poor fool"?

Cartoon

      ❧ *Carl Wiens*

Editorial cartoonists often use their art to comment on important social and political issues. They make their point through thoughtful use of images and through techniques such as exaggeration and caricature. This cartoon makes a strong point in the education debate.

ɕ Carl Wiens is an editorial cartoonist. His cartoons have appeared in newspapers such as the *Globe and Mail*. This cartoon appeared with a column by Robert Fulford in the *Globe and Mail* in 1991.

Connecting

1. What is the dominant image in this cartoon? Describe the other elements in the cartoon. How do they relate to the main image? Based on this analysis, summarize the cartoon's message.

2. What does this cartoon say about our ability to think as individuals? Explain.

3. How does this cartoon relate to the education debate? If blame is to be assigned for the "closing of the (North) American mind," where does this cartoon assign it? How does the society depicted by Huxley connect to this cartoon?

The Role of the Teacher

ɕ *Irving Layton*

This expository essay provides a very different perspective on the education debate. Layton argues that society itself is to blame for any downfall in the education system because people don't have a vision for what education could be. He also emphasizes the importance of the teacher.

In the past few years, educational institutions have been under severe attack. As the volume of criticism has mounted, a feeling has grown that schools and universities are not achieving that which they were intended to: namely, the enrichment of the individual's life by giving him the tools of self-improvement and the cultivated mind to use them. Naturally the bulk of this criticism has fallen upon the teacher, that poor cultural maid-of-all-work in our society, and the nearest, or at any rate, the most tangible object to seize upon in a fit of anger. Of course the fault does not lie there, or not mainly. Often it lies with unprogressive or penny-pinching school boards who engage teachers whose unsuitability is fully known to them in advance. And behind the incompetent teacher and the conservative school board stands a society which has no comprehensive vision of what education is or the aims that it ought to pursue. If we're going to start blaming, let's call the shots right.

No instructed observer denies that there are proportionately fewer general readers today than even twenty-five years ago. To increasingly larger numbers, books have become objects of curiosity; like an atomic pile, something heard about but hardly ever seen. In such a situation, the hardest hit have been the humanities. While every kind of narrow specialism is having a field day, the generous disciplines of the mind, philosophy, art, literature, are being discarded like old running-shoes. A constricted scientism, lacking both a sense of direction and a concern for values, has penetrated every nook and cranny of our society. The end of this process no one yet foresees, but already institutions of liberal learning are fast becoming anachronistic.

Little minds, dry, scholastic, pedantical, are not going to make the world over, or provide it with the intellectual light it requires to lead it out safely from our present-day moral and political dilemmas. Nor little hearts, untouched by concern for humanity. If education means anything, it should mean the creation of individuals with a strong sense of social responsibility, a regard for people, an attitude of helpfulness towards them that springs from an imaginative awareness of human need. In the long run, it means education for individual and collective freedom. A society where such persons abounded would place its mystics, seers, and artists in the front rank for they do the two things most vitally needed by an "open society": they interpret and help to shape the moral conscience of the human race, and they continuously enlarge the boundaries of human sensibility.

These reflections lead one to assay the role of the teacher. Without beating about the bush, let it be said at the outset that his function is paramount. Nowadays it's the usual thing to pay lip service in praise of the teacher's significance and utility—particularly on graduation day or when the cornerstone for a new school building is being laid; for the rest of the year he is grossly undervalued, underpaid, and almost all but forgotten. Yet his, nevertheless, is the power and the glory. His influence is incalculable, extending beyond the one or two years during which a teacher may have a particular class. It is usually from a gifted teacher that a child catches his first glimpse of harmony or wisdom and gets his first hint of the intellectual adventure which may engage him for the rest of his life.

But for a teacher to communicate the vision of the good life, he must first have that vision himself. If his own light does not burn steadily, he cannot hope to kindle it in anyone else. A teacher—what is he, if not an inspired seeker after the truth? In teaching as in the writing of poetry, techniques and formulae may support, but can never supplant inspiration.

Only by pursuing knowledge, that is, by constantly enlarging his own intellectual horizons, can the teacher retain his original freshness and enthusiasm. In the successfully creative teacher, knowledge spills over like water from a seemingly inexhaustible fountain. This kind of teacher is always an inspiration to his pupils. Furthermore the knowledge which he acquires in his free time and which he shares with others eventually trickles into the remotest corners of the community he lives in and helps to enlarge the area of good sense upon which the preservation of civilized values ultimately depends.

ॐ Irving Layton is a poet, short-story writer, and essayist. Born in Romania, he immigrated to Canada in 1913 with his family and settled in Montreal. He became known as a prolific and versatile writer who was not afraid to voice controversial issues. His poetry collection *A Red Carpet for the Sun* (1959) won a Governor General's Award and his work has been published internationally. *(Born Romania 1912)*

Connecting

1. Who is to blame for the problems in education according to Layton? Who does he say is being blamed unreasonably?
2. Do you agree that the purpose of schools and universities is to enrich the individual's life by giving him/her the tools of self-improvement and the cultivated mind to use them? Explain your thoughts on this issue.
3. What is the role of the teacher as far as Layton is concerned? Do you agree with this role?
4. How does Layton's perspective fit with the other perspectives you have read about in this Echo? Does it agree or disagree with the ideas held by the other writers? Or, does it provide a unique perspective in its own right?

□ REFLECTING ON THE ECHO

1. Stage a panel discussion in your class to further explore the issues in education. Have four people take on the following different perspectives:
   - we should be preparing students for the world of work and we are failing to do so
   - we should be preparing students to be critical thinkers with decent moral values and we are failing to do so
   - we should be preparing students for life—in and out of work—and we are succeeding
   - we should be concerned more with issues around quality of life, information-inundation, and globalization than the education system because the education system merely reflects the realities of society. If you want to fix the education system, assuming it needs fixing, you need to fix society first.

   Each panel member should prepare a statement with references to the reading selections that best support his or her perspective and be prepared to answer questions from the audience. One other student acts as moderator. Audience members are responsible for asking pertinent, intelligent questions of the panel.
2. Create a script for a thirty-second public information advertisement on education for television or radio. Consider short testimonials and interviews with students, teachers, etc., and focus on key images to get across your ideas. Point out some of the key current issues in education and some proposed reforms. If possible, record or videotape your ad.
3. Write an editorial expressing your view in the education debate. If one of the selections in this Echo was closest to your view, refer to it and refute the views of the other writers.

The Japanese Tea Ceremony

Julia V. Nakamura

A *Chanoyu* (Tea Ceremony) from invitation to the last thank-you call of the guests on the day following the ceremony is an artistic impression. The old masters wrote the score—as Beethoven wrote his—but each artist playing the same notes expresses his own self. The more a "player" brings to the score, or to the Tea Ceremony, the more intense, the more beautiful the result. The basic score does not change; the "melody" is always the same.

The entire score of a *Chanoyu* is a symphony in three movements, lasting about four hours, generally beginning at noon, although the hour is flexible. The first session is a meal and is called *Kaiseki*. This is followed by a short recess during which guests return to the "waiting bench" in the garden. To signal the beginning of the second part the host beats a gong near the tea room—five or seven times. This too is part of the artistic experience and guests listen critically. At best it should remind one of "wind through the forest." The second session is called *Koicha*, which means thick tea, and it is the finest quality. To prepare it the powdered tea is placed in the bowl, hot water poured over it, and vigorously stirred with a whisk till it is the consistency of spinach soup and the colour of liquid jade. Every guest drinks from the same bowl. Each guest wipes the rim where his lips touched the bowl and gives it a slight turn before handing it over to the next guest. Reminiscent, is it not, of some Protestant Communion services!

A host may choose to serve all three courses or any one of them. Modern demands on people's time, and today's tempo, make a four-hour service of this type impracticable. The most popular phase, therefore, is the afternoon tea—*Usacha* (weak tea)—which is thinner, of a grade inferior to that used for *Koicha*, far less ceremonious, and made afresh for each guest.

The etiquette begins with the invitation which may be extended by a man or woman, to men or women, or both, generally five in number. A host may decide to serve a ceremonial tea to celebrate a birth, a birthday, an engagement, a retirement, almost any occasion upon which Westerners might have a tea, cocktail party, or dinner party. The *Chanoyu* may be given to bring good friends together or may include persons between whom there is a strain in an effort to restore harmony to their relationship. Reply to the invitation is made in whatever manner is convenient, in addition to which it is considered polite to call on the host the day before the party to express one's thanks in advance.

Guests have clearly defined responsibilities. They are expected to assemble in the tea garden a quarter of an hour before the appointed time in order to admire the garden, to meditate in an effort to shed the cares of the "outside" world before entering the tea room. If a principal guest (guest of honour) has not been designated by the host, the guests at this time decide who is to be guest number one, guest number two, and so on. The guest of honour is the leader and spokesman, and he takes his place closest to the host in the tea room. The other guests follow his lead in the predetermined order. This is one occasion when age or rank need not be a determining factor. In the tea temple there is equality! Guests are expected to bring an extra pair of *tabi* (white socks with a pocket for the large toe) to wear into the tea room, and a *fukasa* (square of silk) used as a cushion in handling and admiring the tea utensils. They bring a small folding fan and a pad of *kaishi* (small-sized white paper) carried in a bag designated for this purpose.

Although the house, the tea room, and the garden are thoroughly cleaned as soon as the invitation is issued, just before the guests arrive the garden is swept again and sprinkled with water to give the feeling of freshness. And then, according to the season, the host with studied carelessness strews pine needles, or autumn leaves, to produce the effect of unpretentious rusticity, and archaic imperfection (*sabi*), of naturalness and beauty.

The garden signifies the first stage of meditation, the passage into self-illumination. The path is intended to break connection with the outside world, and to produce a fresh sensation conducive to the full enjoyment of aestheticism in the tea room. Tea Masters differed in the emphasis on the metamorphosis they wished to produce during the walk. Some sought to achieve serenity, others purity, others loneliness. The essence of the garden, as in the other parts, is restraint, creative beauty, self-expression. Okakuro Kakuzo explains it succinctly: "Art, to be fully appreciated, must be true to contemporaneous life . . . it is not that we should ignore the claims of posterity, or disregard the creations of the past, but we should try to assimilate them into our consciousness. Slavish conformity to traditions and formulas fetters the expression of individuality. . . ." This delicate balance of past, present and future which the Japanese have achieved is perhaps the secret of their dynamic position in the world despite the handicap of a late start, a devastating defeat on the battlefield, and a severe poverty of natural resources.

Since the garden is the first step in this aesthetic experience hosts take great pains to prepare the garden with artistry, to make of it a beautiful and tranquil introduction. The guests arrive early in order to appreciate the garden before it is time to appear in the tea room, which they approach, in order of precedence, by walking single file over special stepping stones which have been chosen with great care for their regular irregularity and beauty of line. Before entering the tea room each performs token gestures of purification at the special earthen wash basin, rinsing hands and mouth. When Samurai wore swords; these were left outside—the tea room being pre-eminently a place of peace—together with the *haori* (a short over-garment never worn in a tea room) and, of course, the sandals. Even the *tabi* are changed for clean ones as cleanliness is a prime consideration. No one wears rings or watches to a Tea Ceremony. The metal on these may mar or scratch the exquisite tea ware and the watch enslaves the mind. The door to the tea room is twenty-seven by thirty-six inches, forcing each guest to creep through, a symbolic act of humiliation.

The tea room is usually four and a half mats (*tatami*) in size. Each *tatami* is seventy-two by thirty-six inches, which is the smallest area in which an adult can sit, work, and sleep. The *tatami* is a standard architec-tural unit in Japan. The size of the tea room, four and a half mats, is deter-mined by a passage in the *Sutra* (Buddhist Writings), where there is the story of a saint welcoming eighty-four thousand disciples of Buddha in a room of this size. The allegory is based on the theory of the non-existence of space to the truly enlightened. The tea room may be an independent structure, or part of an existing room partitioned off by a screen (*sho-ji*). It is simple and devoid of luxury (*wabi*). When not in use it is kept empty and scrupulously clean.

ॐ The above excerpt is from *The Japanese Tea Ceremony* (1965) by Julia Nakamura.

RESPONDING

Meaning

1. A *Chanoyu* is a complicated ceremony. Take notes on its various components, either in the form of a chart or web. Include the following categories: process, purpose, guest roles, garden, tea room, host, etiquette.

2. At first glance, the fact that guests aren't permitted to wear watches because "they enslave the mind" might seem ironic, given the number of rules in a tea ceremony. How can a ritual that is so laden with rules also be considered "a real art—a most exquisite art"?

Form and Style

3. Nakamura uses an *extended metaphor* to describe the tea ceremony. What is her metaphor? How effective is it? Describe the component parts of the comparison.

4. This is an *expository essay*, which means its purpose is to explain (in this case, the Japanese tea ceremony). How does the organization of the content support this purpose?

Exploring Context

5. Nakamura states that "in a country so crowded as Japan, politeness is a means of self preservation" and that "the Tea Ceremony [teaches] propriety to those whose lives may touch all levels of society." How does the Tea Ceremony promote politeness and propriety? Research other Japanese ceremonies and customs that perform the same functions.

Creative Extension

6. Convert the steps and components of the tea ceremony into a flow chart that also does justice to the statement that the tea ceremony is "an artistic interpretation."

7. Write an expository essay that explains a Canadian or personal "ritual" for foreign readers. For example, you might explain the ritual of the graduation at your school; traditions followed in your family on birthdays or special occasions; or customs and procedures surrounding going to a play, concert, or other performance.

Of Revenge

ॐ Francis Bacon

Revenge is a kind of wild justice; which the more man's nature runs to, the more ought law to weed it out. For as for the first wrong, it does but offend the law; but the revenge of that wrong puts the law out of office. Certainly, in taking revenge, a man is but even with his enemy; but in passing it over, he is superior; for it is a prince's part to pardon. And Solomon, I am sure, said, *It is the glory of a man to pass by an offence.* That which is past is gone, and irrevocable; and wise men have enough to do with things present and to come: therefore they do but trifle with themselves, that labour in past matters. There is no man does a wrong for wrong's sake; but thereby to purchase himself profit, or pleasure, or honour, or the like. Therefore why should I be angry with a man for loving himself better than me? And if any man should do wrong merely out of ill nature, why, yet it is but like the thorn or briar, which prick and scratch, because they can do no other. The most tolerable sort of revenge is for those wrongs which there is no law to remedy; but then let a man take heed the revenge be such as there is no law to punish; else a man's enemy is still beforehand, and it is two for one. Some, when they take revenge, are desirous the party should know from where it come: this is the more generous. For the delight seems to be not so much in doing the hurt as in making the party repent: but base and crafty cowards are like the arrow that flies in the dark. Cosmus, duke of Florence, had a desperate saying against perfidious or neglecting friends, as if those wrongs were unpardonable: *You shall read* (said he) *that we are commanded to forgive our enemies; but you never read that we are commanded to forgive our friends.* But yet the spirit of Job was in a better tune: *Shall we* (said he) *take good at God's hands, and not be content to take evil also?* And so friends in a proportion. This is certain, that a man that studies revenge keeps his own wounds green, which otherwise would heal and do well. Public revenges are for the most part fortunate; as that for the death of Caesar; for the death of Pertinax; for the death of Henry the third of France; and many more. But in private revenges it is not so. Nay rather, vindictive persons live the life of witches; who as they are mischievous, so they end infortunate.

ᛋ Sir Francis Bacon was an essayist and philosopher. He published his first book of essays in 1597 and was one of the first people to write essays in English. He also wrote works in Latin, such as *De Sapientia Veterum* (1609), later translated as *The Wisdom of the Ancients* (1619). Writing in a beautiful, concise style, Bacon based his philosophy on knowledge gained from observation, rather than abstract theory. (*Born London, England 1561; died 1626*)

RESPONDING

Meaning

1. Bacon shares many different ideas on revenge in this essay. List them in your own words and in the order they appear.
2. What is your opinion of Bacon's ideas regarding revenge? Explain.

Form and Style

3. Unlike most modern essays, this essay is written as one long paragraph. Indicate where logical paragraph breaks might go and provide reasons for your decisions.
4. Francis Bacon is famous for writing *aphorisms*—short, pithy statements of a belief or truth as the writer sees it. One example is "revenge is a kind of wild justice; which the more man's nature runs to, the more ought law to weed it out."

    Identify four other aphorisms in the essay. "Translate" each one (including the one above) into today's English. Then decide whether or not you agree with the views expressed in these aphorisms.

Exploring Context

5. Bacon (1561–1626) was a great thinker in two distinct areas of endeavour in Elizabethan England: science and writing. He is credited with pointing the way to the modern scientific method, i.e., a generalized conclusion is arrived at through analysis of particular instances, otherwise known as inductive thinking. How is his essay scientific in approach? What qualities of his essay make it an ancestor of our modern essay?

Creative Extension

6. Bacon's essay is an *expository* one. Write your own expository essay using Bacon's style of *aphorism* on one of the following topics: marriage; homework and studying; or truth. Once you are done, locate a copy of Bacon's essay on these same topics and compare your efforts and ideas with his.
7. Bacon makes the following points about revenge:
   a) in taking revenge, a person is even with his or her enemy, but in passing it over, he or she is superior
   b) the past is gone and not worth troubling over
   c) people focused on revenge keep their hurt feelings and anger alive
   d) vindictive people end in misfortune.

   In groups of four, create a short dramatic scene to illustrate one of these statements.

The Black Widow

ꙮ Gordon Grice

Learning Goals

- identify specific evidence to support key statements
- analyze divisions in an essay and suggest subtitles
- assess use of two different points of view
- create songs or poems to reflect key ideas and emotions
- create a series of visual representations

I hunt black widow. When I find one, I capture it. I have found them in discarded wheels and tires and under railroad ties. I have found them in house foundations and cellars, in automotive shops and toolsheds, in water meters and rock gardens, against fences and in cinderblock walls. I have found them in a hospital and in the den of a rattlesnake, and once on the bottom of the chair I was sitting in.

Sometimes I raise a generation or two in captivity. The egg sacs produce a hundred or more pinpoint cannibals, each leaving a trail of gleaming light in the air, the group of them eventually producing a glimmering tangle in which most of them die, eaten by stronger sibs. Finally I separate the three or four survivors and feed them bigger game.

Once I let several egg sacs hatch out in a container about eighteen inches on a side, a tight wooden box with a sliding glass top. As I tried to move the box one day, the lid slid off and I fell, hands first, into the mass of young widows. Most were still translucent newborns, their bodies a swirl of brown and cream. A few of the females had eaten enough to molt; they had the beginnings of their blackness. Their tangle of broken web clung to my forearms. They felt like trickling water in my arm hairs.

I walked out into the open air and raised my arms into the stiff wind. The widows answered the wind with new strands of web and drifted away, their bodies gold in the late sun. In about ten minutes my arms carried nothing but old web and the husks of spiderlings eaten by their sibs.

I have never been bitten.

The black widow has the ugliest web of any spider. The orb weavers make those seemingly delicate nets that poets have traditionally used as symbols of imagination, order, and perfection. The sheet-web spiders weave crisp linens on the grass. But the widow makes messy-looking tangles in the corners and bends of things and under logs and debris. Often the web is littered with leaves. Beneath it lie the husks of insect prey, their antennae still as gargoyle horns, cut loose and dropped; on them and the surrounding ground are splashes of the spider's white urine, which looks like bird guano and smells of ammonia even at a distance of several feet. This fetid material draws scavengers—ants, sow bugs, crickets, roaches, and so on—which become tangled in vertical strands of silk reaching from the ground up into the web. The widow comes down and, with a bicycling of the hind pair of legs, throws gummy silk onto this new prey.

When the prey is seriously tangled but still struggling, the widow cautiously descends and bites the creature, usually on a leg joint. This is a killing bite; it pumps neurotoxin into the victim. The widow will deliver a series of bites as the creature dies, injecting substances that liquefy the organs. Finally it will settle down to suck the liquefied innards out of the prey, changing position two or three times to get it all.

Before the eating begins, and sometimes before the victim dies from the slow venom, the widow usually moves it higher into the web. It attaches some line to the prey with a leg-bicycling toss, moves up the vertical web strand that originally snagged the prey, crosses a diagonal strand upward to a higher point on a different vertical strand, and here secures the line. It has thus dragged the prey's body up off the ground. The whole operation is like that of a person moving a load with block and tackle. It occurs in three dimensions—as opposed to the essentially two-dimensional operations of orb weavers and sheet weavers.

You can't watch the widow in this activity very long without realizing that its web is not a mess at all but an efficient machine. It allows complicated uses of leverage and also, because of its complexity of connections, lets the spider feel a disturbance anywhere in the web—usually with enough accuracy to tell the difference at a distance between a raindrop or leaf and viable prey. The web is also constructed in a certain relationship to movements of air so that flying insects are drawn into it. This fact partly explains why widow webs are so often found in the face-down side of discarded car wheels—the wheel is essentially a vault of still air that protects the web, but the central hole at the top allows airborne insects to fall in. An insect that is clumsy and flies in random hops, such as a June beetle, is especially vulnerable to this trap. The widow often seems to choose her building sites according to indigenous smells rather than creating her own stinking waste pile from scratch. The webs turn up, for example, in piles of trash and rotting wood. A few decades ago, the widow was notorious for building its home inside the works of outdoor toilets. Scraping around with a stick before using the toilet was a common practice.

The architectural complexities of the widow web do not particularly impress the widows. They move around in these webs almost blind, yet they never misstep or get lost. In fact, a widow forcibly removed from its web and put back at a different point does not seem confused; it will quickly return to its habitual resting place. Furthermore, widows never snare themselves, even though every strand of the web is a potential trap. A widow will spend a few minutes every day coating the clawed tips of its legs with the oil that lets it walk the sticky strands. It secretes the oil from its mouth, coating its legs like a cat cleaning its paws.

The human mind cannot grasp the complex functions of the web but must infer them. The widow constructs it by instinct. A brain smaller than a pinhead contains the blueprints, precognitive memories the widow unfolds out of itself into actuality. I have never dissected with enough precision or delicacy to get a good specimen of the black widow brain, but I did glimpse one once. A widow was struggling to wrap a praying mantis when the insect's forelegs, like scalpels mounted on lightning, sliced away the spider's carapace and left exposed the clear droplet of bloody brain.

Widows reportedly eat mice, toads, tarantulas—anything that wanders into that remarkable web. I have never witnessed a widow performing a gustatory act of that magnitude, but I have seen them eat scarab beetles heavy as pecans; carabid beetles strong enough to prey on wolf spiders; cockroaches more than an inch long; and hundreds of other arthopods of various sizes. Widows begin life by eating their siblings. An adult female will fight any other female; the winner often eats the loser. A popular game among Mexican children is to stage such fights and bet on the outcome. The children put widows on a stick and pass it around so that everyone can see. Sometimes one female ties another up and leaves without killing her. I have come across such black pearls wrapped in silk and, upon peeling off the skin, seen the pearls unfold their legs and rush away.

Many widows will eat as much as opportunity gives. One aggressive female had an abdomen a little bigger than an English pea. She snared a huge cockroach and spent several hours subduing it, then three days

consuming it. Her abdomen swelled to the size of a largish marble, its
glossy black stretching to a tight red-brown. With a different widow,
I decided to see whether that appetite was really insatiable. I collected
dozens of large crickets and grasshoppers and began to drop them into
her web at a rate of one every three or four hours. After catching and consuming her tenth victim, this bloated widow fell from her web, landing
on her back. She remained in this position for hours, making only feeble
attempts to move. Then she died.

The first thing people ask when they hear about my fascination with the
widow is why I am not afraid. The truth is that my fascination is rooted
in fear.

   I have childhood memories that partly account for my fear. When
I was six my mother took my sister and me to the cellar of our farmhouse
and told us to watch as she killed a widow. With great ceremony she
produced a long stick (I am tempted to say a ten-foot pole) and, narrating
her technique in exactly the hushed voice she used for discussing religion
or sex, went to work. Her flashlight beam found a point halfway up the
cement wall where two marbles hung together—one crisp white, the
other a glossy black. My mother ran her stick through the dirty silver web
around them, and as it tore it sounded like the crackling of paper in fire.
This sound is unique to the widow's powerful web—anybody with a little
experience can tell a widow's work from another spider's by ear. The black
marble rose on thin legs to fight off the intruder. As the plump abdomen
wobbled across the wall, it seemed to be constantly throwing those legs
out of its path. The impression it gave was of speed and frantic anger, but
actually a widow's movements outside the web are slow and inefficient.
My mother smashed the widow onto the stick and carried it up into the
light. It was still kicking its remaining legs. Mom scraped it against the
sidewalk, grinding it into a paste. Then she returned for the white marble
—the widow's egg sac. This, too, came to an abrasive end.

   My mother's stated purpose was to teach us how to recognize and
deal with a dangerous creature we would probably encounter on the farm.
But of course we also took the understanding that widows were actively
malevolent, that they waited in dark places to ambush us, that they were
worthy of ritual disposition, like an enemy whose death is not sufficient

but must be followed with the murder of his children and the salting of his land and whose unclean remains must not touch our hands.

The odd thing is that so many people, some of whom presumably did not first encounter the widow in such an atmosphere of mystic reverence, hold the widow in awe. Various friends have told me that the widow always devours her mate, or that her bite is always fatal to humans—in fact, it almost never is. I have heard told for truth that goods imported from the Orient are likely infested with widows and that women with bouffant hairdos have died of widow infestation. Any contradiction of such tales is received as if it were a proclamation of atheism.

The most startling contribution to the widow's mythical status I have ever encountered was *Black Widow: America's Most Poisonous Spider,* a book that appeared in 1945. Between genuine scientific observations, the authors present the widow as a lurking menace with a taste for human flesh. . . .

We project our archetypal terrors onto the widow. It is black; it avoids the light; it is a voracious carnivore. Its red markings suggest blood.

The widow's venom is, of course, a soundly pragmatic reason for fear. The venom contains a neurotoxin that can produce sweats, vomiting, swelling, convulsions, and dozens of other symptoms. The variation in symptoms from one person to the next is remarkable. The constant is pain. A useful question for a doctor trying to diagnose an uncertain case: "Is this the worst pain you've ever felt?" A "yes" suggests a diagnosis of black widow bite. Occasionally people die from widow bites. The very young and the very old are especially vulnerable. Some people seem to die not from the venom but from the infection that may follow; because of its habitat, the widow carries dangerous microbes.

Some researchers hypothesized that the virulence of the venom was necessary for killing beetles of the scarab family. This family contains thousands of species, including the June beetle and the famous dung beetle the Egyptians thought immortal. All the scarabs have thick, strong bodies and unusually tough exoskeletons, and many of them are common prey for the widow. The tough hide was supposed to require a particularly nasty venom. As it turns out, the venom is thousands of times more virulent than necessary for this purpose. The whole idea is full of the widow's glamour: an emblem of eternal life killed by a creature whose most distinctive blood-coloured markings people invariably describe as an hourglass.

No one has ever offered a sufficient explanation for the dangerous venom. It provides no evolutionary advantages: all of the widow's prey victims would find lesser toxins fatal, and there is no particular benefit in killing or harming larger animals. A widow that bites a human being or other large animal is likely to be killed. Evolution does sometimes produce such flowers of natural evil-traits that are neither functional nor vestigial but utterly pointless. Natural selection favours the inheritance of useful characteristics that arise from random mutation and tends to extinguish disadvantageous traits. All other characteristics, the ones that neither help nor hinder survival, are preserved or extinguished at random as mutation links them with useful or harmful traits. Many people—even many scientists —assume that every animal is elegantly engineered for its ecological niche, that every bit of an animal's anatomy and behaviour has a functional explanation. This assumption is false. Nothing in evolutionary theory sanctions it; fact refutes it.

We want the world to be an ordered room, but in a corner of that room there hangs an untidy web. Here the analytical minds find an irreducible mystery, a motiveless evil in nature, and the scientist's vision of evil comes to match the vision of a God-fearing country woman with a ten-foot pole. No idea of the cosmos as elegant design accounts for the widow. No idea of a benevolent God is comfortable in a world with the widow. She hangs in her web, that marvel of design, and defies teleology.

᪇ Gordon Grice has worked as a teacher, newspaper reporter, and contributing editor for *Oklahoma Today* magazine. He writes poetry, as well as non-fiction. After his essay "The Black Widow" appeared in *High Plains Literary Review*, it was published in *The Best American Essays, 1996*. Grice's book *The Red Hourglass: Lives of the Predators* was published in 1998. (*Born Oklahoma 1965*)

RESPONDING

Meaning

1. Grice states that his fascination with black widow spiders is rooted in fear. What does he mean? Find evidence in the essay of his fascination. What evidence is there of his fear?

2. The last sentence of the essay points out that the black widow is a marvel of design and also defies teleology (its specific purpose in nature). Explain this statement. List the characteristics of the spider that demonstrate it is a design marvel. What are the characteristics that defy teleology?

Form and Style

3. a) This *expository essay* is in five sections, which the author indicates with extra spacing rather than headings or subtitles. What content is dealt with in each section?
   b) What might appropriate subtitles be for each of the sections? Why do you think the writer has chosen not to use them?

4. "The Black Widow" uses both first- and third-person *points of view*. How does this combination help Grice achieve his objective of conveying both his fear and fascination with his topic?

Exploring Context

5. Grice's essay is part of a growing genre of essays in which abstract science is made both interesting and accessible to the average reader. Stephen Jay Gould, David Suzuki, Steven Hawking, Jared Diamond, and Rachel Carson are all writers in this genre. Read one or two selections by one of these writers and compare them with Grice's essay. Comment on similarities and differences in topic, style, and form.

Creative Extension

6. Review what you wrote about Grice's fascination with, and fear of, the black widow spider. Using words and phrases from both your writing and the original essay, compose a pair of poems or songs to illustrate Grice's dual and conflicting feelings. Title one "Fascination" and the other, "Fear."

7. Grice's essay is written in five sections or "movements." Create a series of five visual representations—illustration, painting, collage, sculpture, found object assemblage—that reflect both the content of the section and the feelings about black widow spiders each section conveys.

Sojourners

ও Annie Dillard

earning Goals

examine appropri-
ateness of a title

describe poetic
techniques and their
effects

analyze an essay's
structure and its
purpose

create an illustrated
poster

write a descriptive
essay using an
extended metaphor

If survival is an art, then mangroves are artists of the beautiful: not only that they exist at all—smooth-barked, glossy-leaved, thickets of lapped mystery—but that they can and do exist as floating islands, as trees upright and loose, alive and homeless on the water.

I have seen mangroves, always on tropical ocean shores, in Florida and in the Galapagos. There is the red mangrove, the yellow, the button, and the black. They are all short, messy trees, waxy-leaved, laced all over with aerial roots, woody arching buttresses, and weird leathery berry pods. All this tangles from a black muck soil, a black muck matted like a mud-sopped rag, a muck without any other plants, shaded, cold to the touch, tracked at the water's edge by herons and nosed by sharks.

It is these shoreline trees which, by a fairly common accident, can become floating islands. A hurricane flood or a riptide can wrest a tree from the shore, or from the mouth of a tidal river, and hurl it into the ocean. It floats. It is a mangrove island, blown.

There are floating islands on the planet; it amazes me. Credulous Pliny described some islands thought to be mangrove islands floating on a river. The people called these river islands *the dancers,* "because in any consort of musicians singing, they stir and move at the stroke of the feet, keeping time and measure."

Trees floating on rivers are less amazing than trees floating on the poisonous sea. A tree cannot live in salt. Mangrove trees exude salt from their leaves; you can see it, even on shoreline black mangroves, as a thin white crust. Lick a leaf and your tongue curls and coils; your mouth's a heap of salt.

Nor can a tree live without soil. A hurricane-born mangrove island may bring its own soil to the sea. But other mangrove trees make their own soil—and their own islands—from scratch. These are the ones which interest me. The seeds germinate in the fruit on the tree. The germinated embryo can drop anywhere—say, onto a dab of floating muck. The heavy root end sinks; a leafy plumule unfurls. The tiny seedling, afloat, is on its way. Soon aerial roots shooting out in all directions trap debris. The sapling's networks twine, the interstices narrow, and water calms in the lee. Bacteria thrive on organic broth; amphipods swarm. These creatures grow and die at the trees' wet feet. The soil thickens, accumulating rainwater, leaf rot, seashells, and guano; the island spreads.

More seeds and more muck yield more trees on the new island. A society grows, interlocked in a tangle of dependencies. The island rocks less in the swells. Fish throng to the backwaters stilled in snarled roots. Soon, Asian mudskippers—little four-inch fish—clamber up the mangrove roots into the air and peer about from periscope eyes on stalks, like snails. Oysters clamp to the submerged roots, as do starfish, dog whelk, and the creatures that live among tangled kelp. Shrimp seek shelter there, limpets a holdfast, pelagic birds a rest.

And the mangrove island wanders on, afloat and adrift. It walks teetering and wanton before the wind. Its fate and direction are random. It may bob across an ocean and catch on another mainland's shores. It may starve or dry while it is still a sapling. It may topple in a storm, or pitchpole. By the rarest of chances, it may stave into another mangrove island in a crash of clacking roots, and mesh. What it is most likely to do is drift anywhere in the alien ocean, feeding on death and growing, netting a makeshift solid as it goes, shrimp in its toes and terns in its hair.

We could do worse.

I alternate between thinking of the planet as home—dear and familiar stone hearth and garden—and as a hard land of exile in which we are all sojourners. Today I favour the latter view. The word "sojourner" occurs often in the English Old Testament. It invokes a nomadic people's sense of vagrancy, a praying people's knowledge of estrangement, a thinking people's intuition of sharp loss: "For we are strangers before thee, and sojourners, as were all our fathers: our days on the earth are as shadow, and there is none abiding."

We don't know where we belong, but in times of sorrow it doesn't seem to be here, here with these silly pansies and witless mountains, here with sponges and hard-eyed birds. In times of sorrow the innocence of other creatures—from whom and with whom we evolved—seems a mockery. Their ways are not our ways. We seem set among them as among lifelike props for a tragedy—or a broad lampoon—on a thrust rock stage.

It doesn't seem to be here that we belong, here where space is curved, the earth is round, we're all going to die, and it seems as wise to stay in bed as budge. It is strange here, not quite warm enough, or too warm, too leafy, or incredible, or windy, or dead. It is not, frankly, the sort of home for people one would have thought of—although I lack the fancy to imagine another.

The planet itself is a sojourner in airless space, a wet ball flung across nowhere. The few objects in the universe scatter. The coherence of matter dwindles and crumbles toward stillness. I have read, and repeated, that our solar system as a whole is careering through space toward a point east of Hercules. Now I wonder: what could that possibly mean, east of Hercules? Isn't space curved? When we get "there" how will our course change and why? Will we slide down the universe's inside arc like mud slung at a wall? Or what sort of welcoming shore is this east of Hercules? Surely we don't anchor there, and disembark, and sweep into dinner with our host. Does someone cry, "Last stop, last stop"? At any rate, east of Hercules, like east of Eden, isn't a place to call home. It is a course without direction: it is "out." And we are east.

These are enervating thoughts, the thoughts of despair. They crowd back, unbidden, when human life as it unrolls goes ill, when we lose control of our lives or the illusion of control, and it seems that we are not moving toward any end but merely blown. Our life seems cursed to be a wiggle merely, and a wandering without end. Even nature is hostile and poisonous, as though it were impossible for our vulnerability to survive on these acrid stones.

Whether these thoughts are true or not I find less interesting than the possibilities for beauty they may hold. We are down here in time, where beauty grows. Even if things are as bad as they could possibly be, and as meaningless, then matters of truth are themselves indifferent: we may as well please our sensibilities and, with as much spirit as we can muster, go out with a buck and wing.

The planet is less like an enclosed spaceship—spaceship earth—than it is like an exposed mangrove island beautiful and loose. We the people started small and have since accumulated a great and solacing muck of soil, of human culture. We are rooted in it; we are bearing it with us across nowhere. The word "nowhere" is our cue: the consort of musicians strikes up, and we in the chorus stir and move and start twirling our hats. A mangrove island turns drift to dance. It creates its own soil as it goes, rocking over the salt sea at random, rocking day and night and round the sun, rocking round the sun and out toward east of Hercules.

ᶜ𝒮 Annie Dillard has been called a naturalist, theologian, and philosopher. She is known for her acute eye for detail, her curiosity about the natural and spiritual world, and her ability to make insightful connections. Her works include the novel *The Living* (1992), the collection of personal essays *Teaching a Stone to Talk* (1982) in which "Sojourners" appears, and another collection of essays called *Pilgrim at Tinker Creek*, which won a Pulitzer Prize for general non-fiction in 1975. Dillard's writing appears in many magazines, including *Harper's*, *The Christian Science Monitor*, and *Cosmopolitan*. (*Born Pennsylvania 1945*)

RESPONDING

Meaning

1. Look up a definition of "sojourners." Is this an appropriate title for this essay? Why or why not?
2. a) Floating mangrove trees amaze Dillard. Why? List her reasons.
    b) What else is she amazed by according to this essay? Provide a short list.

Form and Style

3. Before Annie Dillard was an essayist, she was a poet. Her essays use many of the techniques of poetry: figurative language, imagery, sensory appeal, rhythm, etc. Choose ten sentences or phrases that are most poetic in your opinion. Describe the poetic techniques Dillard uses and their effect on the reader.
4. a) "Sojourners" shifts gears twice, which divides the essay into three distinct, but related sections. What are these distinct sections? How are they connected?
    b) How does Dillard signal these shifts to the reader? What is the purpose of this essay structure?

Exploring Context

5. One of Dillard's essay collections, *Teaching a Stone to Talk*, demonstrates her interest in silence, mystery, the natural world, and spirituality. "Sojourners" is consistent with the general interests, or context, established by her work. Describe the elements of this essay that show these characteristics. Find another essay by Dillard and compare it to "Sojourners." ("Seeing" is one excellent possibility.)

Creative Extension

6. This essay makes the claim that mangroves are "artists of the beautiful." What other natural organisms—either flora or fauna—merit the same description, in your opinion? Provide three examples in an illustrated poster format and present your poster to the class.
7. Dillard compares us and our planet earth to the wandering mangrove islands in an *extended metaphor*. How do you think of the planet and its people? Write a descriptive essay using an extended metaphor of your own.

Confronting Conflict

Is war worth it?

People have been going to war for centuries. Why? The reasons are multiple. What are the costs? Human beings suffer under the conditions of war. How do we know if and when we have sacrificed too much? How do we pick up the pieces and continue life after war? This Echo section explores, through a number of short essays, poems, and art, the issues and ramifications of armed conflict.

Learning Goals

- examine an issue from multiple perspectives
- analyze how differences in form and style affect meaning
- communicate through print, visual representation, and oral speaking in response to a variety of texts

On the Road to Berlin

   ❀ *Ernie Pyle*

In this descriptive essay, journalist Ernie Pyle describes the American invasion of Normandy during World War II. The Americans are on the road to Berlin in their efforts to help liberate Europe from Nazi Germany, but there is always a cost to heroism.

I took a long walk along the historic coast of Normandy in the country of France. It was a lovely day for strolling along the seashore. Men were sleeping on the sand, some of them sleeping forever. Men were floating in the water, but they didn't know they were in the water, for they were dead.

The water was full of squishy little jellyfish about the size of a man's hand. Millions of them. In the centre of each of them was a green design exactly like a four-leafed clover. The good-luck emblem. Sure. Hell, yes.

I walked for a mile and a half along the water's edge of our many-miled invasion beach. I walked slowly, for the detail on that beach was infinite.

The wreckage was vast and startling. The awful waste and destruction of war, even aside from the loss of human life, has always been one of its outstanding features to those who are in it. Anything and everything is expendable. And we did expend on our beachhead in Normandy during those first few hours.

For a mile out from the beach there were scores of tanks and trucks and boats that were not visible, for they were at the bottom of the water—swamped by overloading, or hit by shells, or sunk by mines. Most of their crews were lost.

There were trucks tipped half over and swamped, partly sunken barges, and the angled-up corners of jeeps, and small landing craft half submerged. And at low tide you could still see those vicious six-pronged iron snares that helped snag and wreck them.

On the beach itself, high and dry, were all kinds of wrecked vehicles. There were tanks that had only just made the beach before being knocked out. There were jeeps that had burned to a dull grey. There were big derricks on caterpillar treads that didn't quite make it. There were half-tracks carrying office equipment that had been made into a shambles by a single shell hit, their interiors still holding the useless equipage of smashed typewriters, telephones, office files.

There were LCTs turned completely upside down, and lying on their backs, and how they got that way I don't know. There were boats stacked on top of each other, their sides caved in, their suspension doors knocked off.

In this shore-line museum of carnage there were abandoned rolls of barbed wire and smashed bulldozers and big stacks of thrown-away life belts and piles of shells still waiting to be moved. In the water floated empty life rafts and soldiers' packs and ration boxes and mysterious oranges. On the beach lay snarled rolls of telephone wire and big rolls of steel matting and stacks of broken, rusting rifles.

On the beach lay, expended, sufficient men and mechanism for a small war. They were gone forever now. And yet we could afford it.

We could afford it because we were on, we had our toehold, and behind us there were such enormous replacements for this wreckage on the beach that you could hardly conceive of the sum total. Men and equipment were flowing from England in such a gigantic stream that it made the waste on the beachhead seem like nothing at all, really nothing at all.

But there was another and more human litter. It extended in a thin little line, just like a high-water mark, for miles along the beach. This was the strewn personal gear, gear that would never be needed again by those who fought and died to give us our entrance into Europe.

There in a jumbled row for mile on mile were soldiers' packs. There were socks and shoe polish, sewing kits, diaries, Bibles, hand grenades. There were the latest letters from home, with the address on each one neatly razored out—one of the security precautions enforced before the boys embarked.

There were toothbrushes, and razors, and snapshots of families back home staring up at you from the sand. There were pocket books, metal mirrors, extra trousers, and bloody abandoned shoes. There were broken handled shovels, and portable radios smashed almost beyond recognition, and mine detectors twisted and ruined.

There were torn pistol belts and canvas water buckets, first-aid kits, and jumbled heaps of life belts. I picked up a pocket Bible with a soldier's name in it, and put it in my jacket. I carried it half a mile or so and then put it back down on the beach. I don't know why I picked it up, or why I put it down again.

Soldiers carry strange things ashore with them. In every invasion there is at least one soldier hitting the beach at H-hour with a banjo slung over his shoulder. The most ironic piece of equipment marking our beach—this beach first of despair, then of victory—was a tennis racket that some soldier had brought along. It lay lonesomely on the sand, clamped in its press, not a string broken.

Two of the most dominant items in the beach refuse were cigarettes and writing paper. Each soldier was issued a carton of cigarettes just before he started. That day those cartons by the thousand, water-soaked and spilled out, marked the first savage blow.

Writing paper came second. The boys had intended to do a lot of writing in France. The letters—now forever incapable of being written—that might have filled those blank abandoned pages!

Always there are dogs in every invasion. There was a dog still on the beach, still pitifully looking for his masters. He stayed at the water's edge, near a boat that lay twisted and half sunk at the waterline. He barked appealingly to every soldier who approached, trotted eagerly along with him for a few feet, and then, sensing himself unwanted in all the haste, he would run back to wait in vain for his own people at his own empty boat.

Over and around this long thin line of personal anguish, fresh men were rushing vast supplies to keep our armies pushing on into France. Other squads of men picked amidst the wreckage to salvage ammunition and equipment that was still usable.

I stepped over the form of one youngster whom I thought dead. But when I looked down I saw he was only sleeping. He was very young, and very tired. He lay on one elbow, his hand suspended in the air about six inches from the ground. And in the palm of his hand he held a large, smooth rock.

I stood and looked at him a long time. He seemed in his sleep to hold that rock lovingly, as though it were his last link with a vanishing world. I have no idea at all why he went to sleep with the rock in his hand, or what kept him from dropping it once he was asleep. It was just one of those little things without explanation that a person remembers for a long time.

The strong, swirling tides of the Normandy coast line shifted the contours of the sandy beach as they moved in and out. They carried soldiers' bodies out to sea, and later they returned them. They covered the corpses of heroes with sand, and then in their whims they uncovered them.

As I plowed out over the wet sand, I walked around what seemed to be a couple of pieces of driftwood sticking out of the sand. But they weren't driftwood. They were a soldier's two feet. He was completely covered except for his feet; the toes of his GI shoes pointed toward the land he had come so far to see, and which he saw so briefly.

Ernie Pyle was a popular American war correspondent during World War II. He wrote six columns a week for twenty-four newspapers around the world. Because of his sympathetic descriptions of soldiers and his willingness to share their discomforts, he was able to write moving accounts of the war and the soldiers in it. His war dispatches are collected in three books: *Here Is Your War* (1943), *Brave Men* (1944), in which "On the Road to Berlin" appears, and *Last Chapter* (1946). In 1945, he won a Pulitzer Prize for his reporting. (*Born Indiana 1900; died 1945*)

RESPONDING

Meaning

1. a) Descriptive essays often do not have a clear *thesis statement*, but this one has an obvious purpose nonetheless. What is the purpose of this essay?
   b) Is there a single sentence that performs the function of the thesis statement? Which one? Support your choice.

2. Why is this essay called "On the Road to Berlin"? What does the title have to do with the content and purpose of the essay?

Form and Style

3. This descriptive essay is essentially a catalogue of the casualties of war: human and equipment. Select three of the most effective descriptions for each category of casualty and list them. Why are these six so effective in your opinion?

4. Pyle uses *irony* twice in this essay. Identify these two instances. Are these effective uses of irony? Why or why not? How do they contribute to Pyle's overall description?

Exploring Context

5. There have been a number of famous war correspondents over the course of the twentieth century. Ernest Hemingway and Virginia Irwin covered World War II, Martha Gellhorn reported on the Spanish Civil War, Wallace Terry covered the Vietnam War, Arthur Kent reported on the Persian Gulf War, Ruth Fremson covered Bosnia and Kosovo, Peter Arnett covered Afghanistan during the Russian occupation, and Kate Adie reported on the conflicts in Northern Ireland, to list just a few. Review the work of some of these war correspondents. How does their writing and approach compare to Pyle's?

Creative Extension

6. Pyle was a news journalist who specialized in print. Many of today's war correspondents work in visual media. Create a three minute "live" news broadcast on the Normandy invasion based on Pyle's descriptive essay and your own research.

7. Using the library and Internet, research paintings of World War II, particularly those of the Normandy landing. In a short multimedia presentation, describe the paintings and how they relate to Pyle's essay.

These Fought in Any Case

꿍 *Ezra Pound*

This poem includes parts of the Latin phrase "Dulce et decorum est pro patria mori" which translates to "Sweet and fitting it is to die for one's country." The poet disagrees, however.

> These fought in any case,
>   And some believing,
>   Pro domo, in any case ...

Some quick to arm,
some for adventure,
some from fear of weakness,
some from fear of censure,
some for love of slaughter, in imagination,
learning later...
some in fear, learning love of slaughter;

Died some, pro patria,
    non 'dulce' non 'et décor'...
walked eye-deep in hell
believing in old men's lies, then unbelieving
came home, home to a lie,
home to many deceits,
home to old lies and new infamy;
usury age-old and age-thick
and liars in public places.

Daring as never before, wastage as never before.
Young blood and high blood,
fair cheeks, and fine bodies;
fortitude as never before

frankness as never before,
disillusions as never told in the old days,
hysterias, trench confessions,
laughter out of dead bellies.

ဆ Poet Ezra Pound was born in the United States, but moved to London in 1908. He
befriended other modernist writers, including Ernest Hemingway and Gertrude Stein, and
he edited many of T. S. Eliot's poems. Pound's largest work was the series of 117 *Cantos*
(1925–1969), in which he attempted to reappraise history. "These Fought in Any Case"
is taken from his long poem *Hugh Selwyn Mauberley* (1920). (*Born Hailey, Idaho 1885;
died 1972*)

ECHO

Connecting

1. Who are the "these" who fought in this poem? What reasons are offered for their decision to fight?
2. Pound incorporates into his poem parts of the Latin phrase "Dulce et decorum est pro patria mori." How does he succeed in demonstrating he doesn't agree with the phrase?
3. a) What lies are told, according to this poem? How do these lies connect to the statements and powerful images in the last stanza?
   b) Were the soldiers Pound writes of able to pick up the pieces of their lives after war? How do you know?
4. What side of war does this poem show? Do you agree or disagree with the sentiments expressed?

Crazed Man in Concentration Camp

ɕ *Agnes Gergely*

There is another side of war: that lived by the people who are forcibly ejected from their homes, separated from their loved ones and possessions, and marched off to concentration or refugee camps. In this poem, a man finally reaches the breaking point.

> All through the march, besides bag and blanket
> he carried in his hands two packages of empty boxes,
> and when the company halted for a couple of minutes
> he laid the two packages of empty boxes neatly at
>   each side,
> being careful not to damage or break either of them,
> the parcels were of
> ornamental boxes
> dovetailed by sizes each to each
> and tied together with packing-cord,
> the top box with a picture on it.
> When the truck was about to start, the sergeant
> Shouted something in sergeant's language,
> They sprang up suddenly,
> And one of the boxes rolled down to the wheel,
> The smallest one, the one with the picture:
> "It's fallen," he said and made to go after it,
> but the truck moved off
> and his companions held his hands
> while his hands held the two packages of boxes

and his tears trailed down his jacket.
"It's fallen," he said that evening in the queue—
and it meant nothing to him to be shot dead.

Translated by Edwin Morgan

෯ Agnes Gergely was born in Budapest. She has worked as a secondary school teacher, a
   producer for radio, and an editor. She publishes books of poetry and novels. (*Born
   Budapest 1933*)

Connecting

1. a) How do you know the dovetailed, decorative boxes are important to the man? Why
        don't his friends let him go after the box when he drops it?
    b) What does the box symbolize in the poem?
2. What two interpretations can be derived from his statement "it's fallen"? What was the
    queue for? Why did it mean nothing to him to be shot dead?
3. How successfully might this man's friends pick up the pieces of their lives after the war,
    assuming they survive the camp? What might become of the sergeants? What does this
    poem show of war and its effects on people?

A Story of War and Change

෯ *Reza Kiarash*

*In this personal narrative, a nineteen-year-old Iranian paramedic describes a New Year's Eve
during the Gulf War when he tries to save the life of a wounded soldier. His experiences are
shocking, but real.*

It's New Year's Eve, and everyone is waiting for the radio to announce the
moment. I am with a small group of soldiers. The table we prepared is very
odd. The New Year's table is supposed to have sweets, greens, and fruit, but
ours has bullets, guns, and grenades. Finally the radio says it: the New Year
has begun. Everybody is screaming and shooting into the air, but this doesn't
go on long because now a heavy bombardment begins. It is the enemy's New
Year's gift for us. Our side is silent now. There is no movement, and everyone is in his refuge and shelter. Some soldiers are on duty in trenches or at
posts made of wooden rails and sandbags. These men are in more danger
than the others. They are not ready for this kind of fire attack. Suddenly the
phone rings, and my heart starts pumping faster and faster. I know it's for
me. That's my job—it comes in fire attacks when someone gets wounded.
I pick up the phone. They need me at the third post, so I call the driver. We

take the ambulance and move to the front, where we reach the "Death Fur-row," so named because several men had been killed there. This part of the front is the worst I've seen so far. I leave the driver with the ambulance because the fire is too heavy. Now I run—no, not exactly run—sometimes run, and sometimes go flat on my belly to protect myself against fragments of bombs and shells. I am getting closer and closer. I can see the light, a huge light. It can't be fire. Yes, it is. Soldiers are calling for help, so I follow the voices. The first soldier tells me that the third post is on fire and three sol-diers are trapped inside. I ask for help to go there, but everyone refuses. They are afraid, because the two front lines of war are so close together that soldiers can talk to enemy soldiers. Again I ask them to come with me to the third post, which by now is like a theatre screen with everybody watching. Then I give up trying to get help, and go alone. I can see the three soldiers. Two of them seem dead. They must be dead, because they are burnt. Another one has fallen beside the post. I go over to him. I try to talk to him, but there is no response. I find out why: he is wounded badly in the head. I try to carry him but he's so heavy I can't, so I go back to the soldiers. First of all I ask the sergeant of the group for help. He refuses. He says that's my problem, not his. I insult him because the wounded man is his own soldier. I remember how the day I joined the platoon this sergeant talked to the new soldiers about the war, and especially his boldness at war. He seemed brave to me then, but now I leave him with his boldness. Two other soldiers finally come to help me, and we carry the wounded man through the trench to the ambu-lance. I put him inside, then try to stop his bleeding. I find his vein and inject him with a serum to replace his lost blood. He can't breathe anymore, because his nose and mouth are full of blood. There is no way for air to get in, so I use the oxygen tank and suction tube to open his windpipe. We are halfway to the hospital when suddenly the suction stops working. There is something wrong with it. I can't fix it now, and he is turning black. Time is going fast for him and for me. Now I make my decision. I put my mouth on his bloody mouth. I am exhaling air into his mouth. I can taste the salty blood. I am thinking about home, my mother, and my friends, though I don't know how I can think about these things at this time. I exhale the air. I put my mouth on his mouth, but before I give it to him, he throws up on me or, I should say, in my mouth. I don't stop. I clean my mouth, his mouth, and start all over again. The driver is watching me in the mirror and asks if I'm all right. I tell him "Yes, just drive fast. There is no time to be disgusted."

I get the man alive to the hospital. I know he is not going to live, but this is my job—to keep soldiers alive and help them. I am surprised that a person who was in high school six months ago can change that much in this short a time. I am proud of myself and glad that I've not changed like that sergeant.

ᔥ   Reza Kiarash was a paramedic in the Iranian army. Of the 100 men in his platoon during the war with Iraq, only ten were not killed or wounded. He was one of them. After the war, he moved to Spain and then Canada, where he entered university. This personal essay was originally published in *The Eyeopener*, a student newspaper. *(Born Shushtar, Iran 1965)*

Connecting

1. a)   Describe the style of this personal essay. Refer to specific lines and paragraphs in the text.
    b)   How does this style help Kiarash tell his story? What impact does it have on the reader?
2.   What side of war does this personal story reveal? Describe the effects of this particular war on the soldiers, the sergeant, and Kiarash.
3.   How does the beginning of this story use *irony* to depict war and its costs? Is this use of irony effective? Explain.
4.   Kiarash eventually leaves Iran and settles in Canada. How might this move help him, and others like him, deal with the aftermath of war?

Dressing Station in the Field

ᔥ   *Alfred Bastien*

❧ Alfred Bastien was a well-known Belgian artist before World War I broke out. In 1914 he joined the Belgian army and in 1917 was seconded to the Canadian army until 1918. He produced many works of art depicting the Canadian war experience, particularly the experiences of the famous French-Canadian 22nd Battalion (the Van Doos) to which he was attached. (*Born Brussels, Belgium 1873; died 1955*)

Connecting

1. During World War I, artists such as Alfred Bastien were sent to the front to record the action. Bastien was attached to the famous French-Canadian 22nd Battalion (the Van Doos). Patriotism and support for the war effort were a major focus of news reports and images from the war in many countries. Why do you think the artist chose to paint this scene? What message does it convey?

2. In small groups, discuss which aspects of the painting you find most striking and why. Refer to specific visual techniques in your discussions (e.g., foreground, texture, colour, etc.).

3. Write a short commentary on this painting from your perspective today. Consider why the artist created the painting, what impact it might have had at the time, what is most striking about it, the effects of techniques used, and what impact the painting has today.

The dead of September 11

 ❧ *Toni Morrison*

Sometimes there are no words for the costs of war. The events of September 11, 2001, when the World Trade Centre in New York was destroyed by terrorist planes, left many people shocked and grieving. In this emotional piece, American writer Toni Morrison attempts to find some solace.

Some have God's words; others have songs of comfort for the bereaved. If I can pluck courage here, I would like to speak directly to the dead—the September dead. Those children of ancestors born in every continent on the planet: Asia, Europe, Africa, the Americas . . . ; born of ancestors who wore kilts, obis, saris, geles, wide straw hats, yarmulkes, goatskin, wooden shoes, feathers, and cloths to cover their hair. But I would not say a word until I could set aside all I know or believe about nations, war, leaders, the governed and ungovernable; all I suspect about armour and entrails. First I would freshen my tongue, abandon sentences crafted to know evil— wanton or studied; explosive or quietly sinister; whether born of a sated appetite or hunger; of vengeance or the simple compulsion to stand up before falling down. I would purge my language of hyperbole; of its eagerness to analyze the levels of wickedness; ranking them; calculating their higher or lower status among others of its kind.

Speaking to the broken and the dead is too difficult for a mouth full of blood. Too holy an act for impure thoughts. Because the dead are free, absolute; they cannot be seduced by blitz. To speak to you, the dead of September, I must not claim false intimacy or summon an overheated heart glazed just in time for a camera. I must be steady and I must be clear, knowing all the time that I have nothing to say—no words stronger than the steel that pressed you into itself; no scripture older or more elegant than the ancient atoms you have become.

And I have nothing to give either—except this gesture, this thread thrown between your humanity and mine: I want to hold you in my arms and as your soul got shot of its box of flesh to understand, as you have done, the wit of eternity: its gift of unhinged release tearing through the darkness of its knell.

ᔕ   Toni Morrison is best known as a novelist whose works record the lives and experiences of African Americans. Before she began writing, she worked as a teacher of English and a senior editor at a publishing house. Her writing has a lyrical quality and reflects an oral storytelling culture. Her novels include *Tar Baby* (1981), *Beloved* (1987), which won the Pulitzer Prize, and *Jazz* (1992). The selection above appeared in *Vanity Fair* magazine in 2001. *(Born Ohio 1931)*

Connecting

1.   In this selection, Toni Morrison expresses the great difficulty in finding words for the dead. What does she feel she cannot say, and does not want to say?
2.   How does she find some solace for the dead in the final paragraph of her writing? How, through this piece of writing, does the writer offer solace to herself?
3.   Write a reader response for this piece. What thoughts does it leave you with about the events of September 11? What additional perspective does this piece provide in your look at the issues of conflict and war?

The Love That Feels Like Home

ᔕ   *Lorna Crozier*

In this essay, Crozier describes one way to recover from the effects of war and other disastrous events. Her suggestion is also a preventative one, if people would avail themselves of it.

Historians tell us that our century is the bloodiest on record. As a species we haven't progressed in the things that matter. We haven't learned how to control our hate or our feelings of superiority—religious or racial—over others of our kind. None of our so-called advances mean anything when measured against this.

W. H. Auden's most quoted and debated assertion comes from his eulogy for William Butler Yeats: "...poetry makes nothing happen." It's a pronouncement that's difficult to argue with. Try writing a poem that protests against Russia's treatment of the Chechens and see how quickly Moscow changes its policies. Yet people keep returning to poetry in times of grief and crisis as if it offers some kind of solace, as if it can change a life.

Almost four hundred years ago, Shakespeare linked the poet with the lover and the madman. His *menage à trois* makes sense: throughout the centuries, poets keep offering love as the antidote to the ills of humankind. Perhaps there is a madness in their faith in something so various and fickle.

In the nineteenth century Matthew Arnold summarized the character of his time with the following lines:

And we are here as on a darkling plain
Swept with confused alarms of struggle and flight,
Where ignorant armies clash by night.

What better description of our own violent decades? Arnold preceded these lines with what's become a famous plea:

Ah, love, let us be true
To one another!

In a similar vein, towards the end of his life Yeats, who wrote so movingly of the Irish troubles, cried out in a poem called *Politics*:

But O that I were young again
And held her in my arms!

We can read these lines as a cop-out, a way of turning our backs on social and political commitment, but we can also see them as something else. They voice a primary and necessary step toward learning how to live more adamantly, responsibly, and tenderly in the world: first, these poets tell us, you must love.

This imperative remains in the most famous revision of a single line of poetry in the English language. W. H. Auden's original line was:

We must love one another or die.

In the new version:

We must love one another and die.

An older Auden abandons the romantic idealism, the assertion that love defeats death, if only metaphorically.

Although the revision is closer to the hard facts of our existence and is more in keeping with Auden's clear-eyed observations of the human condition, he keeps the affirmation in the first half of his line. The cliché tells us there are two certainties that characterize our time on earth, death and taxes; a well-lived life must consist of a third—love.

The love these poets talk about is wilder than the love espoused by many theologians, particularly those of the fundamentalist variety. It is sexual, animal, gentle, and ferocious. It's a love that becomes spiritual because it's grounded in the sensual—the smells, tastes, and touch of another's skin.

In his recent collection of essays, the poet Tim Lilburn reminds us of what Plato said in the Phaedrus. Lilburn writes:

…when we love something or someone, we are reminded obscurely of another presence, absolute beauty, that feels most like home.

Poets have been speaking about the love that feels like home since the first words were chanted across a fire. They will continue to praise and desire it when we move into the years that stretch ahead.

In doing so, perhaps poems make everything happen. They speak of a love that begins in the private but reaches out into the world and shapes the way we live on our own darkling plain.

෬ Lorna Crozier is an award-winning Canadian poet. Both *The Garden Going on Without Us* (1985) and *Angels of Flesh, Angels of Silence* (1989) were nominated for Governor General's Awards. *Inventing the Hawk* (1992) received a Governor General's Award. Her essay "The Love That Feels Like Home" was written for a CBC series entitled "Canadian Authors on 2000." (*Born Swift Current, Saskatchewan 1941*)

Connecting

1. What is Crozier's *thesis statement?* What are the points offered to support it? Do you agree or disagree with her central idea? Explain.

2. Usually, when people speak of love, they refer to the emotional love between a man and a woman. What broader definition of love is Crozier working with? What is "the love that feels like home"?

3. Read the two poems in this Echo. Do you agree with Crozier that these poems help human beings deal with war and its aftermath? Research other poems that celebrate war, protest war, depict the reality of war, and deal with the aftermath of war. Does your answer to the question change when you have done this further reading?

☐ REFLECTING ON THE ECHO

1. Reread the first paragraph of Crozier's essay in this Echo. Now that you have finished the material in this Echo as a whole, do you agree with her statements about our species and advances? Explain your views in a short informal talk.

2. The focus question for this Echo was "Is war worth it?" Consider how each of the selections answered that question (think about it either from the author's or the speaker's perspective). Write the title of each piece along a continuum with "Yes" at one end and "No" at the other. Under each title, explain why you placed the selection where you did on the continuum.

3. Write a speech in which you describe your thoughts on the topic of war. Answer the question: "Is war worth it?" Present the speech to the class. Consider using visuals, quotations from key writers, audio recordings, testimonials, and any other material that serves to reinforce or support your ideas.

The Ironic Narrator of James Joyce's "Araby"

ℑ Janice E. Patten

Although James Joyce's story "Araby" is told from the first-person viewpoint of its young protagonist, we do not receive the impression that a boy tells the story. Instead, the narrator seems to be a man matured well beyond the experience of the story. The mature man reminisces about his youthful hopes, desires, and frustrations. More than if a boy's mind had reconstructed the events of the story for us, this particular way of telling the story enables us to perceive clearly the torment youth experiences when ideals, concerning both sacred and earthly love, are destroyed by a suddenly unclouded view of the actual world. Because the man, rather than the boy, recounts the experience, an ironic view can be presented of the institutions and persons surrounding the boy. This ironic view would be impossible for the immature, emotionally involved mind of the boy himself. Only an adult looking back at the high hoops of "foolish blood" and its resultant destruction could account for the ironic viewpoint. Throughout the story, however, the narrator consistently maintains a full sensitivity to his youthful anguish. From first to last we sense the reality to him of his earlier idealistic dream of beauty.

The opening paragraph, setting the scene, prepares us for the view we receive of the conflict between the loveliness of the ideal and the drabness of the actual. Descriptive words show the narrator's consciousness of the boy's response to beauty and the response of the neighbourhood people, who are blind to beauty: North Richmond Street is "blind"; its houses, inhabited by "decent" people, stare unseeingly at one another—and all this is under a sky of "ever-changing violet," in a setting of gardens marred by the "odours of ash-pits" and "dark odorous stables." The boy's own house, which had formerly been inhabited by a priest, is placed in a garden like that of Eden. It is a place of potential holiness, shown to us in the irony of the garden's barrenness and the priest's worldliness: the garden has now only a "central apple tree" and a "few straggling bushes"; the priest had

died and left behind him evidence of his preoccupation with secular literature and with collecting money and furniture.

Into this setting appears a figure representative of all that is ideal, the
girl. The narrator shows us in a subtly ironic manner that in his youthful
adoration of Mangan's sister she is, confusedly, the embodiment of all his
boyish dreams of the beauty of physical desire and, at the same time, the
embodiment of his adoration of all that is holy. In his dark environment
Mangan's sister stands out, a figure always shown outlined by light, with
the power to set aflame in him a zeal to conquer the uncaring and the
unholy. Her image, constantly with him, makes him feel as though he
bears a holy "chalice" through a "throng of foes"—the Saturday evening
throng of drunken men, bargaining women, cursing labourers, and all the
others who have no conception of the mystical beauty his young mind has
created in this world of material ugliness.

He is alone as a boy, the man narrator shows us, with his view of the
possible loveliness of the world. Even the aunt and uncle with whom he
lives are callous to his burning need to go to the bazaar, which looms in
his imagination as a place of mystical Eastern enchantment, to purchase a
gift worthy of his loved one. Looking back, the narrator can see that his
uncle had been concerned with his daily, worldly tasks, his aunt with
maintaining a "decent" observance of "this day of our Lord," although she
does not want him to be disappointed in his wish to go to the bazaar.
From the vantage point of maturity, the narrator can realize that the aunt
and the uncle perhaps once possessed an awareness of the romantic, an
awareness that has since been clouded by the drabness of North Richmond Street.

Like Stephen Dedalus of Joyce's *Portrait of the Artist as a Young Man*, the
boy, then, must seek for the high, the inviolate, by himself. And, also like
Stephen, he finds instead the world. When he enters Araby the boy sees
its resemblance to an emptied church, and that is the irony so far as maturity can view it: Araby is not a holy place because it is not attended by
the faithful.

He has come alone on a deserted train; the bazaar, full of spurious
wares, is tended by uncaring people who leave him even more alone than
he had been before; the young lady who should have waited on him ignores
him to joke with two young men. The young lady's inane remarks to the

young men have a ring in the memory of the mature narrator reminiscent of his adored one's remarks. Both are concerned with the material, the crass.

The narrator can, with his backward look, supply us with two apprehensions: one, the fully remembered, and thus fully felt, anguish of a too sudden realization of the disparity between a youthful dream of the mystic beauty of the world and his actual world; and two, the irony implicit in a view that can see the dream itself as a "vanity."

᧕ Janice E. Patten received her Ph.D. in English Literature at the University of California in 1992. She works as a lecturer with the Department of English at San Jose State University, publishing many articles on authors of the Romantic period. She also runs the literature Web site literarylink.com.

RESPONDING

Meaning

1. Patten's title tells us she believes the narrator of "Araby" is an ironic one. What evidence does she offer for this belief?
2. The last paragraph is a challenging one that treats the notion of irony on two different levels. What are these two levels? How is the narrator doubly ironic, according to Patten?

Form and Style

3. There are two forms of literary essay: one that analyzes a particular piece(s) of literature for meaning, structure, style, or content; and one that uses examples from literature to support an idea about the world. Which is this? How do you know?
4. Although her topic would allow Patten to skip to various parts of "Araby" to support her ideas, she chooses to move through the story chronologically as she analyzes it. What effect does this have on the reader? How does this choice help Patten make her point about the story's narrator?

Exploring Context

5. Find two more literary essays, preferably about "Araby." How do they compare to "The Ironic Narrator" in terms of content, style, and form? What statements can you make about literary essays in general based on these three examples?

Creative Extension

6. Reread "Araby" by James Joyce on pages 287–292 of this anthology. Do you agree with Janice Patten's interpretation of the story? Why or why not? Did her essay lead you to discover elements of the story you had not seen before? Discuss.
7. Write your own literary essay on "Araby" or on another selection of your choice. Decide on the interpretation you will present and outline evidence you will use to support your views.

Fathers and Sons (And What About Mothers and Daughters?)

✒ Jeanne Addison Roberts

earning Goals

summarize key ideas

assess the validity of those ideas

analyze an essay's structure and organization

develop a graphic organizer

present a dramatic reading

The two all-time favourite characters of Shakespeare's plays are Falstaff and Hamlet, and it is exciting to have the opportunity to read together the plays that these two superstars inhabit, *Henry IV, Part I,* and *Hamlet.* At first glance the characters and the plays may not seem to have much in common.... Falstaff is billed as a secondary character in a history play and distinguished for his "humorous conceits"; Hamlet is the central figure of a tragedy. Falstaff is old ("inclining to threescore," 2.4.438) and fat; Hamlet is young and glamorously athletic (we feel we know this even though the text identifies Hamlet's age as 30, 5.1.152–153 and 5.1.167, and his mother worries about the duel because her son is "fat and scant of breath," 5.2.313).

What is there, then, about the two of them that audiences have always found so intriguing and memorable? Perhaps the strongest quality they share is an insatiable addiction to language. Both are witty, quick, articulate, fascinated by turning words over to play with meanings; both are fluent in verse and prose. In sheer linguistic volume, both loom large. In addition, both characters occupy positions peripheral to the establishment and can comment on conventional society from wry outsider perspectives that everyone sometimes shares. Both have a flair for the dramatic and like to score in personal power struggles.

Even more important is the complexity and ambiguity of the characters. Both are appealing in their wit, their humanity, and their underdog positions, but each is also revealed as capable of cruelty, deception, childish irresponsibility, and even criminal behaviour. No two experiences of the plays ever evoke precisely the same responses to Falstaff and Hamlet, and no critic ever has the last word about either.

Unforgettable as the two characters are, however, they are only parts of the complex appeal of their plays. Probably written within three years of each other (*Henry IV, Part I,* in 1596–97; *Hamlet* in 1600–1601) when their author was in his early thirties, shortly after the death of his only son, both plays deal with aspects of one of the most important of human relationships—child to parent, youth to authority. In these two plays, of course, the focus is on sons and fathers—Prince Hal and Henry IV in one case, Hamlet and his father and uncle in the other. Both plays introduce secondary father-son relationships, but Hamlet might be thought of as a kind of archetypal "son" and Falstaff as a type of imagined benign "father." Both plays explore the young male's struggle to become "king" (both literally, over a kingdom, and metaphorically, over himself), to achieve an independent but relational identity, and to find justice in an unjust world.

Each play sets a young man in a troubled kingdom ruled by a guilty king who reached his position by violence and maintains it precariously. Each young man must attempt to achieve kingship over himself and his country by negotiating between his absolute ideals and the grey realities of the world. As Henry V, Hal succeeds gloriously, if briefly, as a military leader, while Hamlet's bloody revenge costs him his life. The paths of both winner and loser should be of immediate and engrossing concern to the adolescent male faced with comparable problems. . . .

Like Hal, Hamlet is haunted by his father—not by his faults but by his imagined perfection. The suggestion of Freud and Ernest Jones that Claudius and the elder Hamlet are two aspects of one father and that young Hamlet identifies with both seems to me a useful insight. Hamlet remembers the elder Hamlet as a mythical giant, the titan Hyperion, loving but not lustful. He discovers in Claudius the lecherous satyr of avid and repulsive sexual engagement. (Children rarely believe, in spite of the evidence, that their parents could be sexual beings.) Hamlet can neither become the perfect father nor kill the imperfect one, although he repeatedly chides himself for prolonging delay. When he does act, it is to cause the death of Polonius, an essentially harmless old man (and a father) and two relatively innocent bystanders, Rosencrantz and Guildenstern.

Like Hotspur, Fortinbras and Laertes offer complementary examples of sons who delight in action, but their actions are no guarantee of success. We know that after a period of calculated delay, Prince Hal as Henry V invades France with dubious legitimacy and having won a glorious victory, leaves a son who will lose all that his father has gained (Epilogue, *Henry VI*). Hotspur and Laertes die, and Fortinbras's success in battle does not seem to qualify him to bring order to the chaos of Denmark.

Father-son reconciliation often requires painful compromise, and the consequences may be far from satisfactory. Reconciliation may be impossible. But however they end, the problems of resolving generational conflict are as relentlessly recurring as generations. Drama does not solve such problems, but it opens them to empathy and exploration. The father-son struggles seem as immediate today as they must have seemed to Elizabethan audiences.

You will have noticed that I earlier used the word "humanity" in regard to Falstaff and Hamlet as if it were a universal term, but how valid is such a concept? Specifically, how does it relate to women and other minority groups in these two plays (women may not be a numerical minority, but like others minorities, they continue to be under-represented in power structures)? It is hard to think of a Shakespeare play in which women are as peripheral to the action as they are in *Henry IV, Part I*. Most of the men seem to have neither mothers, wives, nor daughters (Hotspur, Glendower, and Mortimer are technically exceptions). We have brief glimpses of Glendower's daughter, now Mortimer's wife, but she speaks and sings only in Welsh. Mistress Quickly puts in appearances primarily as an ignorant innkeeper who fractures the language and is exploited and mocked by Falstaff. Hotspur has a witty and assertive wife, but her assertiveness does her little good. Her longest speech is a description of her husband (2.3.39–67). Eleven of her sixteen speeches are one-liners, and she appears in only two scenes.

The women in *Hamlet* are peripheral in a different way. Ophelia seems to be a model of the role for women advocated by Elizabethan advice books—that they should be chaste, silent, and obedient. She is obedient at the expense of her own feelings. She has little to say; her best speech is a description of Hamlet in happier days (3.1.163–175). And she is probably chaste (unless possibly she is pregnant by Hamlet, as she is in one of the sources, and her mad songs are certainly suggestive). She is also passive, even in the face of death. Gertrude has more lines, but they do not establish a self. She seems to be rather a figment of her son's fevered imagination than a developed female character. Like Hamlet, we do not know for sure whether she has been adulterous, whether she was an accomplice in murder, whether she goes back to Claudius's bed after her son's injunction to stay away, or even whether she drinks the poisoned cup knowingly and deliberately or merely because she is thirsty. Actors are rarely able to bring the character to life.

In other Shakespeare plays, women are sometimes actively involved in politics, war, murder, and social upheavals. Particularly in the comedies, they may even be leaders in love. But in these two plays, audiences are forced to focus on men.

Fortunately for the survival of Shakespeare, in spite of outmoded gender roles, there seem to be elements in his work that engage audiences so powerfully that it is tempting to entertain the possibility of a few "universals." Some struggle between the young and their parents of the same sex is probably as unavoidable for women as for men. Experiencing the struggle dramatically in the present climate may actually have special meaning for a girl who wants to radically modify traditional expectations. If, like Hal, she does not want to replicate exactly the life of her parent, she may well learn to become a "king" as he does, by experimenting with a series of "parents." Or her inability to reconcile opposing models of adulthood may lead, like Hamlet's, to tragedy. Her reconciliation with her mother may be as uneasy as Hal's with King Henry or as impossible as Hamlet's with his two "fathers."

If there is a message about universality in these two plays, the hope clearly lies in the male characters. Falstaff and Hamlet and the issues of their plays seem to hold some clues. Dramatic characters are not "people," and drama is not life, though we inevitably imagine for the moment that both things are true. But the enduring popularity of Falstaff and Hamlet suggests that among all Shakespeare's "characters," these two possess a complexity and an immediacy that connect them with a broad spectrum of audiences. They may indeed approach the "universal." And as long as families survive, the issues dramatized in their plays can hardly avoid some relevance, even if only to give us the opportunity to rethink them.

৶ Jeanne Addison Roberts is a past president of the Shakespeare Association of America and is a professor of literature emeritus at the American University in Washington, DC. She has written many books and articles, including *The Shakespearean Wild* (1991).

RESPONDING

Meaning

1. Roberts offers two simple reasons for the audience appeal of *Hamlet* and *Henry IV*. What are they? If you have read or seen either of these plays, would you agree with her?

2. a) Summarize Roberts's explanation of the more complex reason(s) behind the appeal of the plays. Are these valid reasons, in your view? Support your opinion. (Even if you have not read either or both of these plays, you can answer this question based on your assessment of what appeals to audiences.)

   b) How is the title an appropriate one for the essay, given Roberts's beliefs and arguments?

Form and Style

3. Roberts states that the two plays—*Hamlet* and *Henry IV*—do not have much in common, but then goes on to show how much they do in fact have in common. What do you think of this technique—making a statement and then rebutting it?

4. a) Make a rough outline of this essay. Is it an example of the classic essay structure (introduction, body, conclusion), or is Roberts using another technique or organization?

   b) Is there an obvious *thesis statement*, which usually occurs in the introduction? If not, what might a good thesis statement be that encompasses everything you've noted in your outline?

Exploring Context

5. With your teacher's help, find one or two key speeches from either *Hamlet* or *Henry IV*. Discuss how the speech or speeches mesh with the ideas in Roberts's essay.

Creative Extension

6. Develop a graphic organizer that illustrates Roberts's points about *Hamlet*, *Henry IV*, and their similarities and differences. Post your organizer in the classroom, then tour the room with the other students to discuss their ideas and representations.

7. Present a dramatic reading of the speeches you identified in question 5 above. How does your reading enhance your understanding and appreciation of the characters and meaning in the texts?

April Fools on Polar Circus

ॐ Janet Roddan

Learning Goals

- discuss appropriateness of an essay's title
- assess effectiveness of stylistic techniques
- trace patterns of imagery
- create a personal narrative essay, feature article, or short story
- develop a storyboard and shooting script

Polar Circus is a long, alpine climb, 457 metres of vertical gain, involving both snow and ice pitches on Cirrus Mountain in the Athabascan Icefields of the Canadian Rockies. Janet Roddan's story relates a female ascent of this route on April Fool's Day, 1988.

The dance with fear fascinates me. Learning to accept fear, to take it in without letting it take over is one of the challenges of climbing ice. Climbing leads me into myself, through my hidden doors, into corners and attics. The doorway through fear always appears ominous, locked shut, insurmountable, impossible. Fear talks to me, whispers my weakness; it speaks of conditions, of my own mortality—it whispers "hubris." Fear sharpens my senses. It dances through my body. It tunes me. It wraps its fingers around my heart and squeezes gently. I learn to welcome fear and the edge it brings me, the whispered warnings, the adrenaline. The tango with fear makes me wise.

Two fireflies glimmer in the darkness. The tiny puffs of light float slowly upward and burn deeper into a maze of ice, snow, and rock. Snatches of our conversation drift up. We are on a quest, in search of ice. A note of opera breaks the white silence. We are singing as we approach the climb.

I learn the language; I articulate the right series of moves, body positions, ice axe and crampon placements to dance with a frozen tongue of ice. To talk with the mountain is strong medicine. Ice climbing allows me the privilege of witnessing the world. The couloir leads us into the mountain, up there to wild, silent places that wait, unconcerned with whether we view them or not.

An initial pitch of ice, steep enough to burn our calves, increases the intensity with which we communicate with this frozen world. This pitch is followed by a long, rambling walk, past the Pencil, a once free-standing pillar of ice that now lies broken and crushed in a heap. Then on up to the knoll, where we look out from the dark, claustrophobic couloir to see sun on the peaks. We continue to snake along a snowfield and arrive at last at the base of the route proper, six long pitches of undulating ice . . . varied, interesting, alpine.

Kafka said, "The words of literature are an ice axe to break the sea frozen inside us." We use our ice axes to shatter our frozen worlds into crystals of ice and fear. One of the strong pulls of ice climbing is the tremendous range of feelings one is forced to endure—tingling, shivering pain . . . bubbling, shining elation. We hold on, struggling to control the fear that pounds through our veins and capillaries. But just as fear begins to steal into the soul, a good axe placement thunks into the ice. This solid, physical connection to the world causes the fear to recede . . . first from the arms, then from the mind . . . then even more gradually fear's fingers release the heart, which eventually slows and quiets. The intensity is replaced with warm, smooth, flowing beats. The rhythm takes hold, and the dance begins again.

The last two pitches of the climb cascade out of the notch like an enormous wedding gown. Today's brides approach slowly, touched by the mystery and majesty of the place. We are filled with our fear and our audacity. We encourage each other; we push each other. Our vows are strong, but it is April, late in the season for ice climbing. The ice is rotten; the climb is falling down. Time melts and falls away along with great chunks of ice as I rail and pound against it. The dance becomes a struggle.

The entire world shrinks to a section of frozen water in front of my face. The ice is dripping wet and soggy. The rhythm has been broken. I force myself to breathe, to generate my own flow, to create my own beat. But nothing feels right. A chasm fifteen feet [4.5 m] wide opens up between Barb, my partner, and me. Impossible to return. I fight. I hit hard to get good placements. A big block of ice disengages itself; my tool is embedded in it. Time stops, and in slow motion I swing onto my other ice axe. I "barndoor" open and the block of ice topples over my shoulder. I look down to see the ice explode beside Barb, who suddenly looks tiny and hunched in her small belay stance.

"I don't know about this, Barb," I shout down, hoping she will offer an easy way out. I reason to come down. But she calls back, "It depends on how much you want it." Indeed. How much do I want it? Doubt slides in with spaghetti arms and little shivers that evaporate my courage.

But desire, commitment, and an incredible dislike for down climbing drive me. Up. One move at a time. Filled with solemn focus, I proceed. The final veil is gently torn away. The great Goddess reveals her face of frozen water. I witness her dark, foreboding pinnacles, her places of silent, quiet peace, her vistas too vast to contain in a single glance. Tingling, shivering, we arrive at the summit notch at 4 p.m., a happy marriage of fear, sweat, intelligent strength, and smiles.

The vast mystery that spreads out before us causes us to stop and look and take it in for heartbeats of silence. Endless jagged peaks. The silent contract, the ceremony is almost complete. We rappel down the climb. The ropes pull, snagging a few times just to remind us that it's not over yet. A climb is never over until you are back in the car. And even then, the journey that we are all on keeps going. As we descend, night overtakes us. We turn on our headlamps, tiny pins of light in a blanket of darkness.

The April fools, married with fear and laughter on Polar Circus, return to the car, smiling in the darkness, two tiny fireflies humming and buzzing softly.

Janet Roddan studied film at the Vancouver Film School and currently teaches video production in high school. An enthusiastic mountain climber, she makes short outdoor videos that attempt to capture the spirit of outdoor sports. Roddan has made several short videos that explore the connection between climbing and dance, such as *The Granite Ocean*. "April Fools on Polar Circus" appeared in *Leading Out: Mountaineering Stories of Adventurous Women*, edited by Rachel daSilva (1992).

RESPONDING

Meaning

1. Given the content of this essay, why is the title "April Fools on Polar Circus" appropriate?
2. Roddan writes that "the tango with fear makes me wise." Does it, in your opinion? Provide phrases that illustrate "the tango with fear." What evidence is there that it makes the climber "wise"?

Form and Style

3. Many writers believe that strong writing is characterized by using a combination of long, complex sentences and short simple ones. Find examples of passages using both in Roddan's essay. Comment on the effectiveness of her style. Is this strong writing in your opinion? Justify your views.

4. Roddan uses two sets of linked images to tell her story: dance imagery and wedding imagery. Trace the development of these images by listing the sentences and phrases that Roddan uses to extend each set.

Exploring Context

5. Although this selection tells a story, it is not an example of short fiction. It is, however, a personal narrative essay. What qualities are personal? What makes it narrative? What characteristics make it an essay?

Creative Extension

6. Write a personal narrative essay, feature article, or short story for a magazine about a time when you were faced with an intimidating, yet exhilarating challenge. Use imagery in your writing. Design your piece on computer, if possible.

7. "April Fools on Polar Circus" lends itself well to cinematography. Create a storyboard and shooting script for this essay as if you were a director/writer responsible for bringing Roddan's story to the screen.

Snapshot: Lost Lives of Women

∽ Amy Tan

When I first saw this photo as a child, I thought it was exotic and remote, of a faraway time and place, with people who had no connection to my American life. Look at their bound feet! Look at that funny lady with the plucked forehead!

The solemn little girl is, in fact, my mother. And leaning against the rock is my grandmother, Jingmei. "She called me Baobei," my mother told me. "It means Treasure."

The picture was taken in Hangzhou, and my mother believes the year was 1922, possibly spring or fall, judging by the clothes. At first glance, it appears the women are on a pleasure outing.

But see the white bands on their skirts? The white shoes? They are in mourning. My mother's grandmother, known to the others as Divong, "The Replacement Wife," has recently died. The women have come to this place, a Buddhist retreat, to perform yet another ceremony for Divong. Monks hired for the occasion have chanted the proper words.

And the women and little girl have walked in circles clutching smokey sticks of incense. They knelt and prayed, then burned a huge pile of spirit money so the Divong might ascend to a higher position in her new world.

This is also a picture of secrets and tragedies, the reasons that warnings have been passed along in our family like heirlooms. Each of these women suffered a terrible fate, my mother said. And they were not peasant women but big city people, very modern. They went to dance halls and wore stylish clothes. They were supposed to be the lucky ones.

Look at the pretty woman with her finger on her cheek. She is my mother's second cousin, Nunu Aiyi, "Precious Auntie." You cannot see this, but Nunu Aiyi's entire face was scarred from smallpox. Lucky for her, a year or so after this picture was taken, she received marriage proposals from two families. She turned down a lawyer and married another man. Later she divorced her husband, a daring thing for a woman to do. But then, finding no means to support herself or her young daughter, Nunu eventually accepted the lawyer's second proposal—to become his number two concubine.[1] "Where else could she go?" my mother asked. "Some people said she was lucky the lawyer still wanted her."

Now look at the small woman with a sour face (*third from left*). There's a reason that Jyou Ma, "Uncle's Wife," looks this way. Her husband, my great-uncle, often complained that his family had chosen an ugly woman for his wife. To show his displeasure, he often insulted Jyou Ma's cooking. One time Great-Uncle tipped over a pot of boiling soup, which fell all over his niece's four-year-old neck and nearly killed her. My mother was the little niece, and she still has that soup scar on her neck. Great-Uncle's family eventually chose a pretty woman for his second wife. But the complaints about Jyou Ma's cooking did not stop.

Doomma, "Big Mother," is the regal-looking woman seated on a rock. (The woman with the plucked forehead, far left, is a servant, remembered only as someone who cleaned but did not cook.) Doomma was the daughter of my great-grandfather and Nu-pei, "The Original Wife." She was shunned by Divong, "The Replacement Wife," for being "too strong," and loved by Divong's daughter, my grandmother. Doomma's first daughter was born with a hunchback—a sign, some said, of Doomma's own crooked nature.

---

1 a concubine was a secondary wife who had a low status in Chinese society of the time

Why else did she remarry, disobeying her family's orders to remain a widow forever? And why did Doomma later kill herself, using some mysterious means that caused her to die slowly over three days? "Doomma died the same way she lived," my mother said, "strong and suffering lots."

Jingmei, my own grandmother, lived only a few more years after this picture was taken. She was the widow of a poor scholar, a man who had the misfortune of dying from influenza when he was about to be appointed a vice-magistrate. In 1924 or so, a rich man ... forced my grandmother into becoming one of his concubines. My grandmother, now an outcast, took her young daughter to live with her on an island outside of Shanghai. She left her son behind, to save his face. After she gave birth to another son she killed herself by swallowing raw opium buried in the New Year's rice cakes. The young daughter who wept at her deathbed was my mother.

My mother could never talk about any of this, even with her closest friends. "Don't tell anyone," she once said to me. "People don't understand. My mother was a good woman, high-class. She had no choice."

I told her I understood.

"How can you understand?" she said, suddenly angry. "You did not live in China then. You do not know what it's like to have no position in life. I was her daughter. We had no face! We belonged to nobody! This is a shame I can never push off my back." By the end of the outburst, she was crying.

On a recent trip with my mother to Beijing, I learned that my uncle found a way to push the shame off his back. He was the son my grandmother left behind. In 1936 he joined the Communist party—in large part, he told me, to overthrow the society that forced his mother into concubinage. He published a story about his mother. I told him I had written about my grandmother in a book of fiction. We agreed that my grandmother is the source of strength running through our family. My mother cried to hear this.

My mother believes my grandmother is also my muse, that she helps me write. "Does she still visit you often?" she asked while I was writing my second book. And then she added shyly, "Does she say anything about me?"

"Yes," I told her. "She has lots to say. I am writing it down."

This is the picture I see when I write. These are the secrets I was supposed to keep. These are the women who never let me forget why stories need to be told.

↪ Amy Tan's parents left China in 1949 to settle in the United States. Their daughter grew up in San Francisco. Before she began writing novels, she worked as a reporter, editor, and consultant to programs for children with disabilities. Her first novel, *The Joy Luck Club* (1989), was a finalist for the prestigious National Book Critics Circle Award and was made into a major motion picture, for which Amy Tan wrote the screenplay. "Snapshot: Lost Lives of Women" appeared in *Life* magazine in April 1991. (*Born California 1952*)

RESPONDING

Meaning

1. a) In commenting on the women in the photograph, Tan says, "...they were not peasant women but big city people, very modern.... They were supposed to be the lucky ones." This comment contrasts with the actual circumstances in which the women found themselves. Find two or three key phrases that indicate the status of women in China in 1922.
   b) Discuss what you know about the status of women in other countries, including Canada, at this time. What similarities and differences do you find?

2. Amy Tan says that she first thought of this photo as "exotic and remote...with people who had no connection to my American life." By the end, she has discovered a very strong connection. What is this connection and how did she come to it?

Form and Style

3. This personal essay makes extensive use of illustrations to support the statement: "Each of these women suffered a terrible fate...." In a chart, list the women by name and summarize their "terrible fates."

4. Amy Tan uses a number of stylistic techniques to make this essay particularly vivid. Select an example of each of the following and comment on its effectiveness.
   a) quotations
   b) questions
   c) exclamations
   d) first and last paragraphs and the connection between them

Exploring Context

5. This autobiographical piece appeared in *Life* magazine. Locate copies of the most recent issues of this magazine. Based on the contents and features in the issues you examine, determine the magazine's main audience. Discuss how Amy Tan's piece fits the purpose and audience of the magazine.

Creative Extension

6. Select a photograph that has a special significance for you. In writing or in an audiotaped talk, describe the photo in detail and comment on what it means to you.

7. Write a letter to one of the women in "Lost Lives of Women." Feel free to ask questions, present challenges, and indicate your feelings about the circumstances in which the woman lives. Be sure to use a respectful tone.

Non-fiction

Writers on non-fiction:

I hate all things fiction … there should always be some foundation of fact for the most airy fabric—and pure invention is but the talent of the liar.

(Lord Byron, 1817)

There is no longer any such thing as fiction or non-fiction; there's only narrative.

(E. L. Doctorow, 1988)

To separate [non-fiction] and poetry—therefore history and poetry—to set them up at opposite ends of the world of discourse, is to separate seeing from the feel of seeing, emotion from the acting of emotion, knowledge from the realization of knowledge.

(Archibald MacLeish, 1959)

Describing Circles

ଔ Rohinton Mistry

Learning Goals

- consider alternative titles for a piece
- assess the purpose of particular incidents and references
- evaluate transitions and narrative flow
- develop a multimedia presentation

It was still raining when we stopped outside Hotel Bhagsu. I took my socks off the taxi's corroded chrome door handles, where they had hung to dry for almost four hours, and pulled them over my clammy feet. The socks were still soggy. Little rivulets ran out of my shoulder bag as I squelched into the lobby. The desk clerk watched with interest while I fastidiously avoided a trail of water that ran from the leaky umbrella stand to the door. Why, with the shoes already sopping wet? he must have wondered. I was not sure myself—perhaps to emphasize that I did not generally go about dripping water.

As I signed the register, shaking raindrops from my hands, the desk clerk said that the candles would be sent to my room before dark. "Candles", I asked?

He had assumed I would know: "There is a small problem. Electricity workers are on strike." Worse, the strikers were sabotaging the power lines. No electricity anywhere, he emphasized, in case I was considering another hotel: not in Upper Dharmsala, not in lower Dharmsala, nowhere in Kangra District.

I nodded, putting out my hand for the room key. But he held on to it.

With that circular motion of the head which can mean almost anything, he said, "There is one more problem." He continued after a suitable pause: "There is no water. Because of heavy rains. Rocks fell from the mountains and broke all of the water pipes."

He seemed surprised by the lack of emotion with which I greeted his news. But I had already glimpsed the handiwork of the pipe-breaking avalanches during my four-hour taxi ride. The car had laboured hard to reach McLeod Gunj, up the winding, rock-strewn mountain roads, grinding gears painfully, screeching and wheezing, negotiating segments that had become all but impassable.

Perhaps a bit disappointed by my stolidity, once again the desk clerk assured me it was the same in Upper and Lower Dharmsala, and in all of Kangra District; but management would supply two buckets of water a day.

So there was no choice, the hotel would have to do. I requested the day's quota hot, as soon as possible, for a bath. He relinquished my room key at last. It's brass tag had Hotel Bhagsu engraved on one side. "What is Bhagsu?" I asked him, picking up my bag.

"In local language, means Running Water," he said.

The room had an enormous picture window. The curtains, when thrown open, revealed a spectacular view of Kangra Valley. But I could not linger long over it, urgent matters were at hand. I unzipped the bag and wrung out my clothes, spreading them everywhere: over the bed, the chair, the desk, the doorknob. Wet and wretched, I sat shivering on the edge of the bed, waiting for the hot water and remembering the warnings to stay away from Dharmsala while it was in the clutches of the dreaded monsoon.

When the Dalai Lama fled Tibet in 1959, just hours before the Chinese conducted a murderous raid on his palace in Lhasa and occupied the country, he found refuge in India. For months afterwards, other Tibetans followed him, anxious to be with their beloved spiritual leader. The pathetic bands of refugees arrived, starving and frostbitten—the ones lucky enough to survive the gauntlet of teacherous mountain passes, the killing cold, and, of course, Chou En-lai's soldiers.

The Dalai Lama (whose many wonderfully lyrical, euphonious names include Precious Protector, Gentle Glory, and Ocean of Wisdom) spent his first months of exile in anguish and uncertainty. Faced with unabating news of the endless atrocities upon

the body and soul of Tibet, he eventually decided that Dharmsala was where he would establish a government-in-exile. Perhaps this quiet mountain hamlet in the Himalayas reminded him of his own land of ice and snow. Soon, a Tibetan colony evolved in Dharmsala, a virtual country-within-a-country. Visitors began arriving from all over the world to see Namgyal Monastery, Tibetan Children's Village, the Dalai Lama's new temple, or to study at the Library of Tibetan Works and Archives.

As a child, it always struck me with wonderment and incredulity that I should have an uncle who lived in Dharmsala. In this remote mountain hamlet he ran the business which has been in the Nowrojee family for five generations. To me, a thousand miles away in Bombay, this land of mountains and snow had seemed miraculously foreign. Photographs would arrive from time to time, of uncle and aunt and cousins wrapped in heavy woollens, standing beside three-foot-deep snow drifts outside their home, the snow on the roof like thick icing on a cake, and the tree branches delicately lined with more of the glorious white substance. And in my hot and sticky coastal city, gazing with longing and fascination at the photographs, I would find it difficult to believe that such a magical place could exist in this torrid country. Now there, somewhere in the mountains, was a place of escape from heat and dust and grime. So, to visit Dharmsala became the dream.

But for one reason or another, the trip was never taken. Those old photographs: snow-covered mountains and mountain trails; my cousins playing with their huge black Labrador; uncle and aunt posing in the *gaddi* dress of native hill people, a large hookah between them: those old black and white photographs curled and faded to brown and yellow. Years passed, the dog died, my cousins got married and settled elsewhere, and my uncle and aunt grew old. Somehow, the thousand miles between Bombay and Dharmsala were never covered. There was always some logistical or financial problem, and travelling third class on Indian trains was only for the foolish or the desperate.

Then, by a quirk of fate I undertook a different journey, a journey ten thousand miles long, to Canada, and I often thought about the irony of it. So this time, back in Bombay to visit family and friends, not monsoon rain nor ticket queues nor diarrhoea nor avalanches could keep me away from Dharmsala.

Thus twenty-eight hours by train first class brought me to Chakki Bank, in Punjab. It was pouring relentlessly as the first leg of the long journey ended. "Rickshaw, *seth*, rickshaw?" said a voice as I stepped off the train. I quickly calculated: there could be a big demand for transportation in this weather, it might be prudent to say yes. "Yes," I said, and settled the price to Pathankot bus station.

Outside, auto rickshaws—three wheelers—were parked along the station building in a long line. Enough for everyone, I thought. They had black vinyl tops, and plastic flaps at the side which could be fastened shut, I noted approvingly. I followed my man.

And we came to the end of the line. There, he placed my bag in a pitiful cycle rickshaw, the only one amidst that reassuringly formidable squadron of auto rickshaws. The cycle rickshaw had open sides; and old gunny sacks tied to the top of the frame formed a feeble canopy. I watched in disbelief, appalled by my bad luck. No, stupidity, I corrected myself, for it was clear now why he had come inside the station to solicit a fare. That should have made me suspicious. Once upon a time it would have.

The cycle rickshawalla saw my reaction. He pointed pleadingly at the seat, and I looked him in the face, something I never should have done. I am trusting you, his eyes said, not to break our contract. The auto rickshaws taunted me with their waterproof interiors as I stared longingly after them. Their owners were watching, amused, certain I would cave in. And that settled it for me.

Within seconds of setting off, I was ruing my pride. The gunny sacks were as effective as a broken sieve in keeping out the rain, and despite my raincoat I was soon drenched. The downpour saturated my bag and its contents— I could almost feel its weight increasing, minute by minute. The cycle rickshawalla struggled to pedal as fast as he could through streets ankle-deep in water. His calf muscles contracted and rippled, knotting with the strain, and a mixture of pity and anger confused my feelings. I wished the ride would end quickly.

In Pathankot, he convinced me a taxi was better than a bus in this weather. Afterwards, I was glad I took his advice: on the mountains, buses had pulled over because the avalanches, the pipe-breaking avalanches, had made the roads far too narrow. Meanwhile, I waited as the rickshawalla and the taxi driver haggled over the former's commission.

And four hours later I was draping my underwear, socks, shirts, and pants over the doorknob, armchair, lampshade, and window. There was a knock. The houseboy (who doubled as waiter, I discovered later in the restaurant) staggered in with two steaming plastic buckets, one red and the other blue. He looked around disbelievingly at my impromptu haberdashery. "All wet," I explained. He smiled and nodded to humour the eccentric occupant.

I wondered briefly where the water in the buckets came from if the pipes were broken. My guess was a well. In the bathroom, I splashed the hot water over me with a mug.

Dharmsala is a collection of settlements perched across the lower ridges of the Dhauladur range. The Dhauladur range itself is a southern spur of the Himalayas and surrounds the Kangra Valley like a snow-capped fence. McLeod Gunj, at seven thousand feet, is one of the highest settlements. I had passed others on my way up by taxi: Lower Dharmsala and Kotwali Bazaar, the main commercial centre crowded with hotels, shops, and restaurants; Forsyth Gunj, a one-street village; and, of course, the huge military cantonment, which was the beginning of everything, back in the British days.

Early in this century, the British were considering making Dharmsala their summer capital; they found the plains unbearable in the hot season. But an earthquake badly damaged the place in 1905, and they chose another hill station, Simla, a bit farther south. (Later, my uncle would describe it differently: the official in charge of selecting the capital was travelling from Dalhousie to Dharmsala when he caught dysentery on the way, reached Dharmsala, and died. The idea of Dharmsala as summer capital was promptly abandoned.)

I wanted to see more of McLeod Gunj and Upper Dharmsala. But first

I was anxious to meet my aunt and uncle. Next morning, I telephoned them at their general store, and they were delighted to hear my voice. The line was so bad, they thought I was calling from Bombay. No, I said, Hotel Bhagsu, and they insisted I come immediately, their place was only a five-minute walk away.

It was still drizzling. Along the side of the hotel, under every rain spout, was a plastic bucket. My red and blue were there as well. The houseboy was standing guard over them, watching them fill with the run-off from the roof. He looked away guiltily at first when he saw me. Then he must have decided to put the best face on things, for he acknowledged me by smiling and waving. He seemed like a child caught red-handed at mischief.

My uncle and aunt were sorry for the way my visit had begun. "But didn't anyone tell you? This is not a good season for Dharmsala," they said. I had been warned, I admitted, but had decided to come anyway. They found this touching, and also confusing. Never mind, Uncle said, perhaps half our troubles would soon be over: the military cantonment had dispatched its men to find and repair the sabotaged power lines. The only snag was, as soon as they mended one, the strikers snipped through some more.

As for water, said my aunt, not to worry, their supply had not been affected, I could shower there.

Not affected? How? Just then, customers arrived, asking for candles. My aunt went to serve them and my uncle told the story.

During the devastation of the 1905 earthquake, the Nowrojee store was practically the only structure that survived. Uncle's grandfather had handed out food and clothing and blankets from store supplies till proper relief was organized by the British District Commissioner. When McLeod Gunj was back on its feet, the District Commissioner wanted to show his gratitude to the family. He gifted a mountain spring to their house. That private pipeline was still operating after eighty-odd years and had survived the present avalanches.

I promised I would use their shower in the evening. Then more customers entered, and he had to assist my aunt. Local people were inquiring if the newspaper delivery was expected to get through to Dharmsala. Foreign tourists in designer raincoats were seeking out the sturdy black umbrella which, locally, was the staple defence against the rains. The tourists were also laying in a stock of Bisleri mineral water.

There was a lull in business after this surge. My aunt suggested that Uncle take me around Dharmsala for a bit, she could hold the fort alone. So we set out for a walk.

At first the going was slow. Almost every person we passed stopped to exchange a few words, mainly about the weather, and which roads were closed and which were still passable. But it was heartening to see the Tibetan monks, in their crimson robes, always smiling joyfully. For a people who had suffered such hardships and upheavals, struggling to start life over again in a strange land, they were remarkably cheerful and happy. Perhaps this, and their Buddhist faith, is what sustained them. They had the most wonderful beaming, smiling faces. Just like their spiritual leader, whom I had watched some time ago on *60 Minutes*, whose countenance seems to radiate an inner well-being.

Exchanging *namaskaars* with everyone we met (the folded-hands greeting, which translates into: I greet the God in you, common to Hindus and Buddhists), we arrived at a tall gold-crowned structure at the centre of a group of buildings. It was a *chorten*, a religious monument, dedicated to the memory of all those suffering under Chinese occupation in Tibet. The faithful were circling round it, spinning rows of prayer wheels and reciting mantras.

We left the little square and the buildings which housed Tibetan handicraft shops, restaurants, and hotels. Farther down were the Tibetan homes: shacks and shanties of tin and stone, and every window was adorned with flowers in rusty tin cans. Faded prayer flags fluttered in the trees overhead.

The road climbed steeply. Before I knew it, the buildings and the *chorten* were below us. My uncle turned and pointed. There used to be a beautiful park there, he said, at the centre of McLeod Gunj, but it had to go when the refugees came.

During our walk I gathered he loved the Tibetan people, and had done much to aid them. I could hear the respect and admiration in his voice when he talked about the Dalai Lama, whom he had helped back in 1959 to acquire suitable houses and properties where the Tibetans could start rebuilding their lives. But now as my uncle told the story of Dharmsala and the arrival of refugees, I could not help feeling that there was also some resentment toward these people who had so radically changed and remade in their own image the place where he was born, the place he loved so dearly. My aunt, who likes the hustle and bustle of big cities and gets her share of it by visiting relatives periodically, said he would pine away if she ever insisted they leave Dharmsala.

We continue to climb, and on the mountain spur that dominates the valley rose the golden pinnacles of Thekchen Choeling, the Island of Mahayana Teaching, the complex which was the new residence of the Dalai Lama. His cottage had a green corrugated roof, and the temple was a three-story lemon-yellow hall topped by gold spires. On a low verandah surrounding the temple, a woman was performing repeated prostrations. She was making a circuit of the temple, measuring her progress with her height.

We removed our shoes and went inside. The main hall had a high throne at one end: the Dalai Lama's throne, on which he sat when he gave audiences and preached. There would be no audiences for the next few days, though, because he was away in Ladakh to deliver the Kalachakra—Wheel of Time—Initiation. Behind the throne was a larger-than-life statue of the Buddha in the lotus position. The Buddha was locked in a huge glass case. Myriads of precious and semi-precious stones formed a halo around the Buddha's solid gold head, and hence the locked glass: things had changed in Dharmsala; the increase in population and the tourist traffic forced the monks to take precautions.

The changes were having other effects, too. The mountain slopes were being rapidly deforested by the poverty-stricken population's hunger for firewood. And, as elsewhere in the world, the disappearance of trees was followed by soil erosion. My uncle had pointed out the gashed and scarred hills on our climb up. He said that so many mudslides and rockfalls were unheard of in the old days;

and there was less and less snow each year.

I thought of those photographs from my childhood. Their memory suddenly seemed more precious than ever. The pristine place they had once captured was disappearing.

Inside the temple, at the throne's right, more statues were displayed. One of them had multiple heads and arms: Chenrezi, the awareness-being who symbolizes compassion in the Tibetan pantheon. The legend went that Chenrezi was contemplating how best to work for the happiness of all living things, when his head burst into a thousand pieces as he realized the awesome nature of the task. The Buddha of Limitless Light restored him to life, giving him a thousand heads to represent the all-seeing nature of his compassion, and a thousand arms to symbolize the omnipresence of his help. But now Chenrezi, along with other statues bedecked with gold and jewels, was locked behind a floor-to-ceiling collapsible steel gate.

The rain finally ceased. My uncle wished the mist would clear so he could show me Pong Lake in the distance. When the moon shone upon the water, he said, it took one's breath away. But the mist sat over the valley, unmoving.

Descending the temple road, we saw several monks, prayer beads in hand, walking a circular path around the complex. They were simulating the Lingkhor, the Holy Walk circumscribing the Potala, the Dalai Lama's place in Tibet. Round and round they walked, praying, perhaps, for a time when he would be back in his palace, and they treading the original Lingkhor.

Inside: the woman, making a mandala of her prostrations around the temple. Outside: the monks, creating circles of prayer around their beloved leader's residence. Circles within circles. The Wheel of Time.

Back at the general store, bad news awaited: the taps were dry. The Tibetan refugees (everyone, Tibetans included, used that word, despite their having lived here thirty years; perhaps clinging to this word kept alive the hope of returning to their Land of Snows) had discovered that the Nowrojee pipeline still held water. They had cut it open to fill their buckets. Strangely, my uncle and aunt were not too upset. It had happened before. They just wished the people would come to the house and fill their buckets from the taps instead of cutting the pipe.

Later that night, I found my way back to Hotel Bhagsu with a borrowed flashlight. My uncle accompanied me part of the way. Near the incline that led to the hotel, where the road forked, there was a little lamp in an earthen pot, sitting at the very point of divergence. How quaint, I thought. A friendly light to guide the traveller through the pitch-black night. But my uncle grabbed my arm and pulled me away. He said to tread carefully to the right of the lamp, by no means to step over it.

What was it? Something to do with Tibetan exorcism rites, he answered. Did he believe in such things? He had lived here too long, he said, and seen too much, to be able to disbelieve it completely. Despite my skepticism, he succeeded in sending a shiver down my spine. It was only the setting, I explained to myself: a pitch-dark mountain road, the rustling of leaves, the swirling of mists.

Back at the hotel, the desk clerk apologetically handed me the stubs of two candles. Dharmsala was out of candles, what remained had to be strictly rationed. I asked for water.

One more day, I decided, then I would leave. There was not much to do. The avalanches had closed the roads farther north, and the side trips I had planned to Dalhousie, Kulu, and Manali were not feasible. The houseboy knocked.

He was carrying the red bucket. "Where is the blue?" He shook his head: "Sorry, not enough rain. Today only one bucket."

The electricity was back next morning, I discovered thankfully. Around nine, I went to the empty restaurant and ordered tea and toast. Afflicted with a bad stomach, I had been virtually living on toast for the past three days. The houseboy in the persona of waiter took my order cheerfully and left.

Thirty minutes later I was still waiting. The door marked EMPLOYEES ONLY was ajar, and I peered into the kitchen. It was empty. The backyard beyond the kitchen window was deserted too. I went to the front desk. No one. Finally, I ran into the night watchman, who had just woken. "What is going on?" I asked him with manufactured testiness, remembering long-forgotten roles and poses. "Waiter has disappeared, no one in the kitchen, no one on duty. What has happened? Is this a hotel or a joke?"

He studied his watch and thought for a moment: "Sunday today? Oh yes. Everyone is watching *Ramayan*. But they will come back. Only five minutes left."

The *Ramayana* is one of the two great Sanskrit epics of ancient India. The other is the *Mahabharata*, which recently found its way in translation onto Western stages in Peter Brook's production. But when the *Ramayana*, the story of the god Rama, was made into a Hindi TV serial, sixty million homes began tuning in every Sunday morning, and those who did not own TVs went to friends who did. In the countryside, entire villages gathered around the community set. Before the program started, people would garland the TV with fresh flowers and burn incense beside it. Classified ads

in newspapers would read: Car For Sale—But Call After *Ramayan*. Interstate buses would make unscheduled stops when the auspicious time neared, and woe betide the bus driver who refused. Ministerial swearing-in ceremonies were also known to be postponed.

The series ended after seventy-eight episodes, which, however, were not sufficient to cover the entire epic. In protest, street sweepers went on strike and there were demonstrations in several cities. The Ministry of Information and Broadcasting then sanctioned a further twenty-six episodes in order to bring *Ramayan* and the strike to their proper conclusions.

But the story does not end there. Not satisfied with burning incense and garlanding their television sets on Sunday mornings, people began mobbing the actor who played the role of Rama, genuflecting wherever he appeared in public, touching his feet, asking for his blessing. To capitalize on the phenomenon, Rajiv Gandhi's Congress Party enlisted the actor-god to campaign for their candidate in an upcoming election. The actor-god went around telling people that Rama would give them blessings if they voted for the Congress Party, and how it was the one sure way to usher in the golden age of Rama's mythical kingdom of Ayodhya.

At this point, the intellectuals and political pundits sadly shook their sage heads, lamenting the ill-prepared state of the masses for democracy. Suspension of disbelief was all very well when watching television. But to extend it to real life? It showed, they said, the need for education as a pre-requisite if democracy was to work successfully.

When it was time to vote, however, the masses, despite the actor-god and the shaking heads of the intellectuals, knew exactly what to do. The Congress candidate went down in a resounding defeat, and the actor-god became sadly human again.

My waiter returned, promising immediate delivery of my tea and toast. I threw my hands in the air and pretended to be upset: How long was a person supposed to wait? Was this a hotel or a joke? In response to my spurious annoyance, he affected a contrite look. But like me, his heart was not in it. Like the voters and the actor-god, we played out our roles, and we both knew what was what.

In Bombay, at the beginning of the trip, I had listened amusedly when told about the power of the serial. Intriguing me was the fact that what was, by all accounts, a barely passable production lacking any kind of depth, with embarrassingly wooden acting, could, for seventy-eight weeks, hold a captive audience made up not only of Hindus but also Muslims, Sikhs, Parsis, Christians—cutting right across the religious spectrum.

Could it be that under the pernicious currents of communalism and prejudice, there were traces of something more significant, a yearning, perhaps, which transcended these nasty things, so that the great Sanskrit epic of ancient India, a national heritage, could belong to all Indians?

I had not expected to receive a personal demonstration of the Sunday morning power that *Ramayan* wielded. Least of all in this faraway mountain hamlet. In a way, though, it was fitting. Everywhere, *Ramayan* brought diverse communities together for a short while, to share an experience. But in Dharmsala, the native population and the refugees have been sharing and living together for many years. Even the electricity saboteurs cooperated with the show. Of course, shortly after *Ramayan* the region was once again powerless.

Halfway between McLeod Gunj and Forsyth Gunj was an old English church my uncle had told me about. The pure scent of pine was in the air as I walked to it. The rock face of the mountain appeared to have burst into fresh green overnight. The rains had given birth to countless little streams and rivulets that gurgled their descent. Sometimes, at a bend in the road, the noise of water was so loud, it seemed that a huge waterfall was waiting round the corner. But it was only the wind and the mountains playing tricks, orchestrating, weaving, and blending the music of the new-born runnels and brooks into one mighty symphony of a cataract.

The church of the beautiful name came into view: the Church of Saint John in the Wilderness, a lonely reminder of the British Raj. It looked very much like any English parish church. The grounds were in grave neglect. A tall pine had fallen across the walkway, brought down by the rains, no doubt. Sunday-morning service was in progress. Tourists and local residents made up the scanty congregation.

I walked around to the back and found myself in the churchyard. A ten- or twelve-foot monument dominated the cemetery. Intrigued, I went closer. James Bruce, 8th Earl of Elgin and 12th Earl of Kincardine (1811-1863) read the inscription, barely legible. And then, the positions he had held in the far-flung corners of the Empire: Governor of Jamaica; Governor-General of Canada; Viceroy and Governor-General of India.

I examined other gravestones. But weather and time had successfully effaced most of the words. A date here, a first name there: Dear Wife . . . , or, Faithful Husband . . . , and then, Final Rest . . . , and, Heavenly Peace—these fragments were all I could read.

I went back to Lord Elgin's grave and sat before it on a stone ledge. The churchyard was deserted. I read again the words carved in stone, thinking about this Viceroy who had died in Dharmsala, so far from his own country. I imagined the long journeys he had undertaken for Queen and Country: what had he thought about this ancient country? Had he enjoyed his stay here? How might he have felt at having to live out his life in distant lands, none of them his home? Sitting on the moss-grown ledge, I thought about this man buried here, who, a hundred and twenty-five years ago and more, had governed them both, my old country and my new; I thought about the final things.

The weather-beaten gravestones, the vanished epitaphs, the disappearing inscriptions, somehow brought back to me the fading, indistinct photographs of uncle and aunt, cousins and dog, snow on the rooftops and trees. How far away was it—that Dharmsala of my imagination and of my uncle's youth—how far from what I had seen? As far away, perhaps, as the world of empire in whose cause Lord Elgin had undertaken his travels.

I thought about my own journey: from Dharmsala of childhood fantasies to the peaceful churchyard of Saint John in the Wilderness; and then, amidst the gentle ruins of weather-worn, crumbling gravestones, back to the fading, curling photographs. To have made this journey, I felt, was to have described a circle of my own. And this understanding increased the serenity of the moment.

It started to drizzle. I put on my raincoat and opened the umbrella. As it gathered strength, the rain streamed down the sides of Lord Elgin's monument and blurred the words I had been reading. Thoughts of departure, of descending from the tranquillity of the mountains into the dusty, frenetic plains, began gnawing at the edges of the moment. But I pushed them away. I sat there a little longer, listening to the soothing patter as the rain fell upon the leaves and upon the gravestones all around.

୯ Rohinton Mistry is a short-story writer and novelist who emigrated to Canada from Bombay in 1975. He has become known for the vivid details in his writing and for his captivating narratives. His first novel *Such a Long Journey* (1991) examined the political events that led to the creation of Bangladesh. The novel won the Governor General's Award, the Commonwealth Writers Prize for Best Book, and was shortlisted for the Booker Prize. *A Fine Balance* (1995) won the Giller Prize and the Commonwealth Writers Prize for Best Book. Some of Mistry's stories have been collected in *Tales from Firozsha Baag* (1987). "Describing Circles" appeared in *The Third Macmillan Anthology* (1990) edited by John Metcalf and Kent Thompson. (*Born Bombay, India 1952*)

RESPONDING

Meaning

1. This travel piece tells the story of Mistry's long-delayed visit to his aunt and uncle in northern India. In a small group, decide which of the following would best suit the meaning and intention of the author if you were to re-title the text. Consider each suggestion and why it would be appropriate or not.
   a) It all Started With a Photo
   b) Circles within Circles
   c) Dharmsala Dilemma
   d) Exchanging *Namaskaars*
   e) If I hear "There is a small problem" one more time...

2. Without rereading the travelogue, write a short journal entry on the one section or episode that you remember best. In the journal entry, consider why that particular part of the narrative attracted you. Share your journal entry with two other students. Discuss what cues prompt you to think and remember.

Form and Style

3. Skim the entire selection and list the episodes when the idea of "water" is the focus. Label the incident's purpose to the narrative in each case (e.g., humour, reflection, information, or plot progression).

4. This personal narrative is told in six different sections. How does Mistry signal his shifts from section to section to his reader? How effective is this non-chronological approach to personal narrative writing, in your opinion?

Exploring Context

5. This selection fits into a very popular genre of writing: travel writing. Travel writing has always been well-received by the public, but surged in popularity during Georgian and Victorian times (late 1700s and 1800s). What is appealing about travel writing? Create a list of criteria for successful travel writing. How well does Mistry's "Describing Circles" fit your list?

Creative Extension

6. Travel writers often go on tour and give oral presentations, accompanied by slides or other visual representations of their adventures. Create a travel presentation based on Mistry's experiences, or develop a presentation based on a trip of your own. Alternatively, choose an area of the world you would like to visit and present a virtual trip.

7. Arrange with your teacher to have a guest speaker come to your class and inform fellow students on India or Tibet. This cultural exploration activity can be arranged by contacting the local MAGMA association in your area. Be prepared with questions you would ask the guest speaker to address.

Cellphones

ᕬ Rex Murphy

Learning Goals

- examine the purpose of satire
- analyze and experiment with tone
- discuss the connotations and effects of words and phrases
- create a song parody
- compose a satirical commentary

There may be more obnoxious agencies of human misery and torment than the cellphone. But they are few: Being mistaken for a wheat field by a cloud of locusts. Being buried alive with a loop of the soundtrack from the *Titanic*. Attending a constitutional conference. Being mistaken for a pundit. Interviews from film festivals.

In Toronto (the vanguard of so much of what we recognize as true human enlightenment on this planet), there is a movement to have the use of cellphones in cars banned by law.

I'm not so sure that this is altogether such a healthy idea.

The wonderful dexterity and nimbleness of Toronto pedestrians is one of the glories of the globe. They owe their superb conditioning, that urban agility, to the terrors of the in-car cellphone.

Watching a group of them at any crosswalk in this city is like being in your own *National Geographic* special. Cheetahs are sluggish, gazelles are clumsy, in comparison with the Toronto pedestrian staring down (in limb-threatening combo) a Porsche, a yuppie, and her portable hand-held, ear-welded cell.

Every person who crosses a street in this city knows that the BMW bearing down on them is really a mobile telephone booth with a licence to kill. Everyone knows that if it's a choice between keeping one eye on the road and one out for pedestrians, or hitting the speed dial to negotiate the finer points of the divorce settlement at 80 miles an hour, the cellphone is going to win every time.

It's helpful to think of the great highways leading into this city, the 401 and the Don Valley, as essentially a giant switchboard on radial tires, travelling at 140 km per hour. And of the people behind the wheel on these highways—not as drivers, that would be too plain—but as communicators.

So busy are they, absorbing information from their stockbrokers, their mistresses, or their nannies, they have no time at all to acknowledge more mundane, vehicular data: that they've just cut off an eighteen-wheeler transport truck, and are about to vacuum up some poor Ford Taurus under the bonnet of their chattering SUV. Reach out and touch someone is such a vivid little slogan.

The windshield in any car with a cellphone could just as well be made of lead as glass, for its only purpose is to maintain the privacy of the call, not to clarify the direction of the car. And now that cellphones also have Internet capacity, to the wonderful ability of talking and driving at the same time, we may add the exquisite pleasures of mobile authorship; composing witty e-mails while whizzing through the red light and nailing the bike courier, is such an exemplary function of the human brain—which, as all will acknowledge, is simply wasted merely keeping track of the traffic and people in front of you.

Some people say cellphones are as bad as alcohol. I think this is a slander on booze. Alcohol is something, which when added to the human mind makes it lazy, and careless, and stupid. Cellphones in cars gravitate to those minds that are that way already.

Should we ban them? I think Mothers Against Drunk Driving should open a subsidiary. I may give them a call.

꿍 Rex Murphy is known throughout Canada as a quick-witted and accomplished writer and broadcaster. Host of CBC radio's *Cross Country Checkup*, Murphy also delivers opinion pieces on diverse topics on CBC television's *The National*, where "Cellphones" was heard on January 19, 2001. His book reviews and commentaries appear in the *Globe and Mail* and the *Ottawa Citizen*. He has won several national and provincial broadcasting awards. *(Born Carbonear, Newfoundland)*

RESPONDING

Meaning

1. With a partner, decide on an appropriate subtitle or header for this piece. Your choice should clearly reflect the *tone* and purpose of the commentary. Justify your answer.
2. Writers of *satire* may choose to mock trivial things with the purpose of attacking larger issues. Ultimately, their goal is to bring about social change. What is the true purpose of this satire? Support your opinion.

Form and Style

3.   a) The *tone* of a text is created through a number of elements including rhetorical devices, *diction* (word choice or vocabulary), and type of evidence. Identify the author's tone in this piece. List devices and diction to support your answer.
   b) Summarize any one of the paragraphs of "Cellphones" in a different tone. Comment on the effects.

4. Discuss the specific *connotations* (additional or implied meanings) Murphy wishes to convey through his use of the following phrases and expressions:
   a) a cloud of locusts
   b) being buried alive with a loop of the soundtrack from the *Titanic*
   c) attending a constitutional conference
   d) interviews from film festivals

Exploring Context

5. What other modern-day conveniences or recent technological advances could be the focus of such a commentary? What characteristics of that item would be main targets of the *satire?*

Creative Extension

6. Model the *tone* of this essay by writing and delivering a similar commentary on the first "horseless carriage" (automobile), the first ballpoint pen, promoting computers in the school, allowing student representatives on School Boards, or another topic of your choice. Alternatively, scan the letters to the editor in a newspaper and create a satirical commentary based on one of the pieces. Present your commentary orally or record it on audio tape.

7. Choose a paragraph from this commentary and create a song parody. *Parody* is a type of satire that humorously copies and exaggerates elements of an original piece. The purpose is to make fun of the human condition in society.

How Wise is it to Separate Our Emotions From the Rest of Our Being?

୬ Bronwen Wallace

A few years ago, I did a stint on a Canada Council Arts jury that had the task of deciding which projects, among hundreds, would receive support funding. One of the applications described a video project dealing with sexual abuse. As usual, the pros and cons of the project were discussed at length by the six jury members. I had a great deal to contribute, since I was also working at Kingston Interval House at the time, and my fellow jurists valued my opinion on the usefulness of the project. One person, however, was vigorously opposed to the application and, as the discussion became more intense, I found myself crying.

"Found myself crying" is exactly the right phrase. I didn't intend to cry; I didn't even want to cry. But cry I did. No great, heaving sobs, mind you, but tears sufficient to be noticeable and to bring on one of those tense silences that displays of emotion of this sort often elicit.

I was mortified. Here I was trying to engage in a rational discussion about the merits of a project in which I had no direct investment, organized by people I didn't even know, and here I was weeping because someone else disagreed with me. It didn't help, either, when the project was eventually approved later in the session. Then, of course, I worried that the other jury members had felt pressured by my outburst, that I would be perceived as one of those manipulative women who gets her way by crying.

This incident came back to me recently when I read an article about how crying at the workplace can damage a woman's credibility and her career. Although there was some disagreement about isolated displays of emotion, all executives quoted in this article seem to agree that repeated expressions are detrimental. One interviewee, Pittsburgh author Paula Bern, was quoted as saying, "You've got to be calloused and tough if you're a woman in power. If you can't keep your emotions under control, you shouldn't run for public office or expect to be in high-level management."

Keeping "your emotions under control." I wonder about that. What does it do to us, for example?

A few years ago, the *Whig-Standard* ran an article by Jodi Vernon about tears and some of the research connected to them. Some of the findings are very interesting. It would appear, for instance, that crying easily—or not crying at all—is learned, rather than genetic. Women *do* cry more than men, not because they are "naturally" more emotional, but because there are strong enough sanctions against men expressing emotion through tears.

Yet the research indicates that tears are very healthy. Non-criers are most likely to have high blood pressure, peptic ulcers, cardiac problems, headaches, and skin eruptions than people who cry more easily. In addition, researchers in one experiment studied the tears of subjects who cried when viewing a sad movie and found that they contained higher levels of protein and albumin, which are considered toxic "stress" chemicals, than the tears produced when the subjects were exposed to fresh-cut onions.

It would appear, then, that crying may be more than a psychological release. One of the reasons you feel better after a good cry could be that your tears have actually cleansed your body of toxins produced by stress. The article quotes Hans Selye, the late author of *The Stress of Life*, as saying: "We are just beginning to see that many common diseases are due largely to errors in our adaptive response to stress, rather than by direct damage by germs, poisons, and other external agents."

All of this brings up important questions about how wisely—and indeed, how easily—we can really separate our emotions from the rest of our being. For me, it also means taking a hard look at what we mean when we talk about keeping our emotions "under control." Recognizing how we feel and deciding how we are going to express it appropriately is one thing. Disregarding or denying how we feel in order to appear in control is another. Too often, we confuse the two. Studies of violent, abusive men, for example, show that they are often incapable of recognizing and expressing such feelings as fear, sadness, or vulnerability. But that does not mean these feelings are "under control"; rather, it means that they often get expressed as anger. Or in my own case, if I had realized that, given my work situation, the discussion of the video project was likely to be stressful, I might have been able to express that in words and not suddenly "found myself" crying.

And how much can we really separate what we "feel" from what we "think"? To what extent is our culture's emphasis on rationality the result of a truly *irrational* fear of emotion and its place in any decision-making process? What's wrong with emotions being part of decisions anyway?

I think it's important to look critically at where this attempt to separate rationality from emotion has got us. At present, we in Kingston, Ontario live in one of the most highly polluted areas in North America, the Windsor-Montreal corridor. We live in a province whose government, according to a recent new report, does not have any idea how much of its remaining timber the forest industry can safely cut without doing even more damage to the ecology. We live on a planet where $900-billion is spent annually on arms, while 40 000 children die every day, most of them of starvation.

I would argue that this state of affairs has grown out of emotions such as fear, greed, and anger. I would also argue that it is largely the result of decisions made by people who consider themselves rational human beings whose ability to make such decisions is unclouded by "dangerous" emotions.

If that's the case, I'd say we need a lot more tears in the workplace.

꿍 Bronwen Wallace was a prominent Canadian poet and essayist. Her concerns for workers and women led her to work with autoworkers, co-found a women's bookstore, and work in a battered women's shelter. She was also a creative writing teacher and filmmaker. Her book of essays *Arguments with the World: Essays by Bronwen Wallace* was published in 1992. *(Born Kingston, Ontario 1945; died 1989)*

RESPONDING

Meaning

1. In groups of four, preferably consisting of two males and two females, discuss the significance of the following statements in the context of the editorial and in the context of your own experience, where possible:
    a) I was mortified.
    b) You've got to be calloused and tough if you're a woman in power.
    c) women *do* cry more than men
    d) crying is a psychological release
    e) Studies of violent, abusive men, for example, show that they are often incapable of recognizing and expressing such feelings as fear, sadness, and vulnerability.
2. For what audience is this editorial intended? Support your reasoning.

Form and Style

3. a) Although Wallace seems to focus on explaining a specific incident in her career, the incident opens the door to the discussion of other issues as well. Write an outline of this editorial's organization.

    b) Look carefully at the proof and specifics Wallace uses to support her deductions and conclusion. Identify three examples and comment on their effectiveness.

4. a) What stereotypes does Wallace allude to in this editorial? What is her attitude toward them?

    b) Explain the *irony* in the *Whig-Standard*'s article about tears and the research connected to them.

Exploring Context

5. Outline carefully the social context of the incident that begins the editorial: "If tears are not accepted in public or work situations, does that mean women will never be fully accepted in the workplace?" Address this statement informally in the same group you worked with in question 1.

Creative Extension

6. Discuss the appropriateness of the last paragraph as a conclusion. Create two different endings to this editorial. Explain your reasoning.

7. Use the Internet and search cartoon sites. Find gender-related work cartoons. Choose one that would be appropriate to add to this text, and one that would be inappropriate based on Wallace's message.

The Power of Imagination

What draws us to imaginary worlds?

Why do we read fictional stories, fairy tales, and myths? What draws us to television dramas, fantasy movies, video games based on a daring quest, or even soap operas? Is it pure escape—or, do we see things in these imaginary worlds that tell us something essential about ourselves and our world? Do we see certain characters, plots, and patterns recurring again and again in these stories? This Echo, through exploring the universal appeal of one of the greatest fantasy writers of the twentieth century— J. R. R. Tolkien—addresses these questions. The Echo includes a critical review, profile, modern song, art, and essay.

Learning Goals

- analyze theme in a variety of genres
- recognize archetypal patterns in literature
- examine how aspects of form and style affect expressions of themes and ideas
- create original texts in response to specific texts

Lord of the Geeks

✑ *Julian Dibbell*

J. R. R. Tolkien Still Feeds the Nerd Nation's Imagination

In this critical review, Julian Dibbell explores the extraordinary reactions to J. R. R. Tolkien's epic fantasy The Lord of the Rings. *The work has been both praised and defiled, but ultimately it has endured and has inspired both an incredibly loyal following and new incarnations, including a motion picture. Why such appeal?*

In 1961, five years after publication of the final volume in John Ronald Reuel Tolkien's three-part fantasy epic, *The Lord of the Rings*, the formidable English literary critic Philip Toynbee announced with great relief that popular enthusiasm for Tolkien was now thoroughly tapped out and his works were finally on their way to "merciful oblivion." Nice call, Phil: Four years later, the first American paperback edition of *The Lord of the Rings* appeared, and the modestly best-selling book—the tale of brave little hobbit Frodo Baggins's quest to destroy the Ring of Power and save Middle Earth from the Dark Lord Sauron—blew up to a youth-cultural legend. Three million copies were sold between 1965 and 1968; the curly-haired Frodo and his white-bearded wizardly protector Gandalf became hippie icons; and merry pranksters decked the walls of college campuses with such grafitti as "J. R. R. Tolkien is hobbit forming" and "Frodo Lives."

He still does, in case you hadn't noticed. Even as you read this, the living face of Frodo Baggins is probably shining, ten feet tall, on a movie screen near you, embodied by teen actor Elijah Wood in New Line Cinema's *Fellowship of the Ring*, the first installment in a slavishly faithful three-film rendering of the *Ring* trilogy. The movie will land like a mothership in the midst of a global fandom that has by now swelled the sales figure for Tolkien's masterwork to over 50 million copies (not counting the 40 million sales of its 1938 predecessor, *The Hobbit*). The Tolkienite hordes have been flooding Web sites for months with gossip and debate about the film. Add in every on-line discussion about the genealogy of the kings of Gondor, every argument over the syntax of the Elven Quenya dialect, and the monthly textual output of the world's Tolkien-flavoured chat rooms and message boards probably exceeds, kilobyte for kilobyte, the 1400 pages of *The Lord of the Rings* itself. In short, the year 2001 finds Tolkien's following bigger and busier than at any other period in the four decades since Philip Toynbee wrote its obituary.

What that amounts to in the greater pop cultural scheme of things, of course, is harder to say than it used to be. Back in the days when Tolkien was still alive and in the habit of referring to his shaggy, puff-sleeved fans as "my deplorable cultus" (he was a straitlaced, arch-conservative Catholic himself), they were easily mistaken for flower children, or at least fellow travellers on the road to a global transformation of consciousness through drugs, electrified music, and other forms of postindustrial enchantment. But now that the world-historical context has simmered down and a somewhat tamer generation has filled out the hobbit-loving ranks, everyone can see they're just geeks.

Or something even geekier, arguably: ur-geeks. Keepers of the geek flame. For if *The Lord of the Rings* is not the *sine qua non* of geek culture, it's hard to think what is. After all, the vast genre of fantasy fiction is, along with sci-fi, one of the two great narrative flows feeding the Nerd Nation's imaginative life, and nobody doubts that Tolkien single-handedly invented it. And that's not even counting the immense subcultural contingent that is *Dungeons & Dragons* and every role-playing game descended from it—from the complex, on-line time-stuck *EverQuest* to the Japanimated children's saga *DragonBallZ*—all of which testify to the formative influence of the Tolkien mythos. Throw in *Star Wars* (as Tolkienesque a space opera as ever there was) and the argument is pretty much a lock: Without the lucidly imagined geography of Middle Earth and the archetypal characters Tolkien stocked it with—the grave wizards, stout dwarves, evil orcs, and above all, plucky, permanently adolescent hobbits—geekdom as we know it would simply not exist.

If you feel that's no particularly meaningful achievement, I understand. But maybe you could indulge me and imagine, just for a moment, that the fact that we live in a world increasingly made by geeks actually makes their collective imagination worth understanding. Think about computers, their evolution shaped by a hacker culture that insisted some of the earliest dot-matrix printers be programmed to produce the elvish F'anorian script. Think about the Internet, whose founding architects included the *D&D* fanatic who created *The Adventure*, the very first, very Tolkienized on-line role-playing game. Think, for a moment, about these profoundly transformative technologies. And then consider the possibility that the structures of feeling we inherit from them might just have some intimate connection to the dream life of the people who designed them. Consider, in other words, the possibility that *The Lord of the Rings*, geek culture's defining literary creation, might just be one of the defining literary creations of our age.

That *The Lord of the Rings* belongs among the most important works of modern Western literature is not an unheard-of notion, but it's not exactly a blue-ribbon one either. True, in some of the first reviews of the trilogy, Tolkien's best friend, C. S. Lewis, did call it a groundbreaking successor to the *Odyssey*, and W. H. Auden reckoned it was right up there with Milton's *Paradise Lost*. But when Übercritic Edmund Wilson published a bruising smackdown in *The Nation* ("Oo, Those Awful Orcs," April 14, 1956) dismissing the book as "balderdash" and "juvenile trash," he sent Tolkien's critical stock into a long, steady tailspin from which it has yet to recover. By late 1996, when a survey of British readers crowned *The Lord of the Rings* "the greatest book of the 20th century," the dismay that set in among Britain's credentialed literati was as predictable as it was over-the-top. Germaine Greer, who arrived at Cambridge as a student in 1964, wrote "it has been my nightmare that Tolkien would turn out to be the most influential writer of the twentieth century. The bad dream has materialized." Nor does the official stance seem to have softened any since. Just a few weeks ago critic Judith Shulevitz went to the trouble of reminding us all, in the pages of *The New York Times Book Review*, that no modern work of fiction in which people say things like "There lie the woods of L—thlrien . . . Let us hasten!" can be anything less than "death to literature itself."

Shulevitz made these remarks in response to claims very much to the contrary, advanced in T. Shippey's new critical assessment, *J. R. R. Tolkien: Author of the Century*, published by Houghton Mifflin last month. Shippey is a professor of Old English, just as Tolkien was—Shippey even shared teaching duties with Tolkien at Oxford for a brief time—and he seems to take just a tad personally the general critical disdain heaped upon his former colleague. But while his indignation gets a little out of hand, his argument is a sober one, aimed at setting Tolkien alongside such epic poets of the twentieth-century condition as Orwell, Joyce, and Pynchon. *The Lord of the Rings*, he insists, constitutes "a deeply serious response to what will be seen in the end as the major issues of this century: the origin and nature of evil . . .; human existence . . . without the support of divine revelation; cultural relativity; and the corruptions and continuities of language." But in fact, deeply serious or not, Tolkien's actual responses to these issues are so deeply unengaged with the twentieth-century cultural mainstream as to seem willfully out of it.

A lovely list of issues indeed. The problem, though, is that, deeply serious or not, Tolkien's responses to them were those of a man whose head resided in the twentieth century but whose heart just wasn't in it. He was a medievalist in more ways than one, and to read his work as Shippey proposes, with the concerns of modernist literature in mind, is to invite the sort of exasperation you might feel if you were in the mood for *Madame Bovary* and got handed *Beowulf* instead. Tolkien's theory of evil? Well, orcs are, our heroes aren't, and that about sums it up. Tolkien's take on "human existence"? A hard gig, certainly, full of danger and tough decisions, but fortunately not enough to threaten the wise Gandalf, the noble Aragorn, the sly Saruman, or any of Tolkien's other characters with more than the occasional moment of psychological complexity. And as for "cultural relativity," hoo boy.

But ultimately, the real problem with Shippey's approach is the same one that dogs almost all attempts to wring serious literary meaning out of *The Lord of the Rings*: It fails to take Tolkien's literary project as seriously as he took it himself. "I cordially dislike allegory in all its manifestations," he famously wrote in one foreword to the trilogy, warning readers against the temptation of finding in it "any inner meaning or 'message.'" Nearly every thoughtful piece of Tolkien criticism makes some kind of nod to the letter of that admonition, but very few can resist violating its spirit. For some, the "inner meaning" of *The Lord of the Rings* has been a bluntly topical allegory of, say, World War II or eco-activism (Sauron is Hitler and the Ring is the atomic bomb; Sauron is the enemy of Gaia and the Ring is industrial technology). For more high-minded exegetes, like Auden and Shippey, the meanings are more abstract (Frodo's quest is the Quest of Everyman to come to know himself; Frodo's struggle with the Ring's corrupting influence is society's struggle with the burden of power). But either way, these critics' sense of the worthiness of the trilogy compels them to sniff out its significance, often as not at the expense of any true grasp of what Tolkien's point and power really are.

So what is his point then? What is his power? Strip away his meaning and what is left? Well, Middle Earth itself. Or rather his invention of it—a powerful, lifelong act that produced at least 12 volumes of background notes on the history and languages of that imaginary world. Some might call this make-believe, others might call it simulation, still others would call it hallucination. There is in America—and anywhere else the engines of postmodernity run at full tilt—growing cultural fascination with the elasticity of reality, and with it a growing urge to tinker at reality's stretchiest edges. Literature, as the critics now understand it, doesn't satisfy this urge. But child's play has always done the trick. Psychedelics too. And now, more and more, our technologies are at it as well. Already, deep, complex computer games like the Sims and Black and White anticipate an era when critics locate culture's centre of gravity not in books but in elaborate digital simulations. And when they do, a few may recall that it was Tolkien, lord of the geeks, who announced the shift.

❧ Julian Dibbell has published articles and reviews in magazines such as *Rolling Stone, Wired, Details,* and *The New York Times*. He writes on a variety of subjects, including pop music stars, movies, computer subcultures, science-fiction writers, and the politics of technology. His monthly column in the *Village Voice* is called "Strange Loops," and in it Dibbell analyzes the social and cultural implications of new digital technologies. "Lord of the Geeks" appeared in the *Village Voice* in 2001. Dibbell has also written a book, *My Tiny Life* (1998), a memoir of his experiences in an on-line, text-based virtual reality. *(Born California 1963)*

RESPONDING

Meaning

1. In groups of three, discuss what Dibbell means by the following phrases and references:

   a) lord of the geeks
   b) hippie icons
   c) like a mothership
   d) Tolkienite hordes
   e) "my deplorable cultus"
   f) Keepers of the geek flame
   g) a Tolkienesque space opera
   h) a growing urge to tinker at reality's stretchiest edges
   i) culture's centre of gravity

2. a) The critics and Tolkien himself have very different ideas about the purpose and creation of *The Lord of the Rings*. Summarize those two ideas.
   b) Scan Dibbell's article and find his allusion to Tolkien as a creator of an *archetype*, an original pattern, for this modern age. Cite examples of others following his pattern of fantasy.

Form and Style

3. List the stylistic techniques Dibbell uses that contribute to the freshness of his style of criticism. Which two devices particularly appealed to you? Why?

4. Analyze the effectiveness of the shifts in *tone* Dibbell makes throughout the piece. Cite the actual words and/or phrases that are the transitions or segues signalling the changes.

Exploring Context

5. Often, the age of the reader determines the attitude toward a certain text. Sometimes, the political and social climate influences the popularity of a text. How would you account for the popularity of *The Lord of the Rings* to so many age groups and generations? Name other texts that bridge the same gap. What elements do they have in common with *The Lord of the Rings*?

Creative Extension

6. From Dibbell's review, create a glossary of words that would not be understood and would have no point of reference at the time that Tolkien wrote the *Ring* series. Comment on how your glossary underlines the point Dibbell is making about the relevance of the *Ring* series.

7. Assume that Philip Toynbee is still alive. Write a letter or e-mail to him and explain why *The Lord of the Rings* and other such texts will never fall into "merciful oblivion." Alternatively, write a short editorial or review of one of the recent films of the series addressing the same topic.

ECHO

Tolkien's World

ᔆ *Paintings of Middle Earth*

Tolkien's books have captured the imaginations of many artists and inspired them to recreate scenes, characters, and worlds. The following visuals are just some examples of these imaginative recreations.

The Glow of Smaug

ᔆ *Carol Emery Phenix*

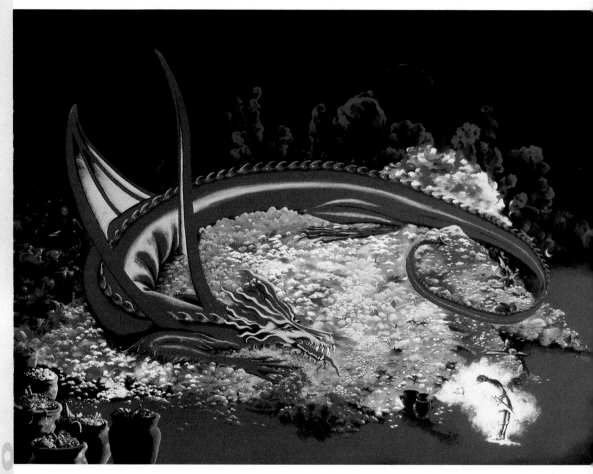

There he lay, a vast red-golden dragon, fast asleep; a thrumming came from his jaws and nostrils, and wisps of smoke, but his fires were low in slumber. Beneath him, under all his limbs and his huge coiled tail, and about him on all sides stretching away across the unseen floors, lay countless piles of precious things, gold wrought and unwrought, gems and jewels, and silver red-stained in the ruddy light.

The Hobbit

The Stone Trolls

Alan Lee

The sun was now high, and it shone down through the half-stripped branches of the trees, and lit the clearing with bright patches of light. They halted suddenly on the edge, and peered through the tree-trunks, holding their breath. There stood the trolls: three large trolls. One was stooping, and the other two stood staring at him.

Strider walked forward unconcernedly. 'Get up, old stone!' he said, and broke his stick upon the stooping troll.

Nothing happened. There was a gasp of astonishment from the hobbits, and then even Frodo laughed. 'Well!' he said. 'We are forgetting our family history! These must be the very three that were caught by Gandalf, quarrelling over the right way to cook thirteen dwarves and one hobbit.'

The Fellowship of the Ring

Riders at the Ford

ᘓ   *Ted Nasmith*

'By Elbereth and Luthien the Fair,' said Frodo with a last effort, lifting up his sword, 'you shall have neither the Ring nor me!'

Then the leader, who was now half across the Ford, stood up menacing in his stirrups, and raised up his hand. Frodo was stricken dumb. He felt his tongue cleave to his mouth, and his heart labouring. The sword broke and fell out of his shaking hand. The elf-horse reared and snorted. The foremost of the black horses had almost set foot upon the shore.

At that moment there came a roaring and a rushing: a noise of loud waters rolling many stones. Dimly Frodo saw the river below him rise, and down along its course there came a plumed cavalry of waves. White flames seemed to Frodo to flicker on their crests and he half fancied that he saw amid the water white riders upon white horses with frothing manes.

The Fellowship of the Ring

 5 Carol Emery Phenix lives in New Hampshire, USA, and has been enthralled by Tolkien's
    writings since age sixteen. She continues to illustrate his works. Ted Nasmith lives and
    works in Toronto. His work includes architectural renderings, singing, and songwriting, in
    addition to illustrations of Tolkien's writings created over a decade. His illustrations have
    appeared in many Tolkien calendars. Alan Lee worked on a special illustrated edition
    of *The Lord of the Rings*. All of the illustrations pictured here appeared in a book entitled
    Tolkien's World: Paintings of Middle Earth published by HarperCollins in 1992.

Connecting

1. In small groups, discuss the significance of the following characters and images. Use the
    context of the review, your own knowledge, or search for definitions to discover the
    connotations. In what other contexts or works (literary, visual, aural, virtual, or digital)
    have you encountered these or similar characters and images?

    a) trolls   e) a red sword
    b) wizards   f) a bridge
    c) dragons   g) a "ring"
    d) a secret fire/flame   h) hobbits

2. a) Which visual most appeals to you? Explain your choice with specific reference to the
        focus of the visual, the mood it evokes, the choice of colours and dominant images,
        and the theme.

    b) Which visual best captures the theme and mood of the written text that accompa-
        nies it? Justify your choice.

    c) Which artist do you believe captures Dibbell's vision of the Tolkien fantasy? Explain
        by direct references to the subject of the visual, the artist's style, and the artist's
        interpretation of the accompanying written text.

3. Read the following quotations by the artists. Discuss what each quotation means and
    what appealed to each artist about Tolkien's work. How do these quotations reveal what
    draws people to imaginary worlds? Try to match the quotation with the artist and the
    artwork.

    a) ...I discovered much of my identity, ironically, by becoming a sort of conduit for
        visual expression of Tolkien's masterpiece. It chose me as much as I came to own
        it. The sadness, bittersweetness, darkness, light, glory, mystery, and grandeur
        appeal to me.

    b) Tolkien succeeded in creating a world which exists beyond the scope of his own
        narrative. By establishing such a powerful imagined landscape, and firm founda-
        tions of history and myth, he has made Middle Earth available to all of us for our own
        imaginative wanderings.

    c) My first 'illustrative experience' came at the age of seven while listening to story
        readings every afternoon at school.... Since that time I have always found my most
        artistic satisfaction is in the giving of life and breath to that which lies in the imagi-
        nation, rather than just in the interpretation of reality.... particularly to Tolkien's
        weaving of his moral thinking into the fabric of his tale...

ECHO

The Battle of Evermore

Led Zeppelin

Tolkien's works have not only captured the imaginations of illustrators, but also of song writers and musicians. What common, archetypal figures do you recognize in this song by the British group Led Zeppelin?

Queen of Light took her bow
And then she turned to go,
The Prince of Peace embraced the gloom
And walked the night alone.

Oh, dance in the dark of night,
Sing to the morning light.
The dark Lord rides in force tonight
And time will tell us all.

Oh, throw down your plow and hoe,
Rest not to lock your homes.
Side by side we wait the might
Of the darkest of them all.

I hear the horses' thunder
Down in the valley below,
I'm waiting for the angels of Avalon,
Waiting for the eastern glow.

The apples of the valley hold
The seeds of happiness,
The ground is rich from tender care,
Repay, do not forget, no, no.
Oh, dance in the dark of night,
Sing to the morning light.

The apples turn to brown and black,
The tyrant's face is red.

Oh the war is common cry,
Pick up your swords and fly.
The sky is filled with good and bad
That mortals never know.

Oh, well, the night is long
The beads of time pass slow,
Tired eyes on the sunrise,
Waiting for the eastern glow.

The pain of war cannot exceed
The woe of aftermath,
The drums will shake the castle wall,
The ringwraiths ride in black,
Ride on.

Sing as you raise your bow,
Shoot straighter than before.
No comfort has the fire at night
That lights the face so cold.

Oh dance in the dark of night,
Sing to the mornin' light.
The magic runes are writ in gold
To bring the balance back.
Bring it back.

At last the sun is shining,
The clouds of blue roll by,
With flames from the dragon of darkness
The sunlight blinds his eyes.

♪ Led Zeppelin was a British rock group that produced albums between 1969 and 1980. Its music is still popular today. Many fans claim that the band, led by Robert Plant and heavily influenced by rhythm and blues songs, founded heavy-metal music. Classic songs, such as "Stairway to Heaven" and "The Battle of Evermore," are from the album *Untitled* (1971).

ECHO

Connecting

1. The lyrics of this song are based on a particular section of *The Lord of the Rings*, but the general theme can also be considered *archetypal*. List the elements of this song that reflect universal themes and symbols found in literature.

2. Reread the lyrics and, if possible, listen to the music on the Led Zeppelin CD *Untitled*. What is the *mood* and *tone* of the piece? Identify words and images that best capture the overall feeling of the song.

3. Review paragraph 7 of "The Lord of the Geeks" focusing on what Shippey wrote concerning *The Lord of the Rings*. Choose a stanza from Led Zeppelin's lyrics that reaffirms Shippey's statements.

The Purposes of Fantasy

♫ Natalie Babbitt

So what is it that really attracts us to imaginative worlds? In this essay, Natalie Babbitt offers some possible answers to that question. See if you agree.

When you say fantasy fiction to a group of average adults, you are apt to get reactions voiced in one of two ways: sniffily, as "that sort of thing is for children," or in a cooing tone, as "Oh, you mean nursery tales!" I'm not surprised by this phenomenon anymore, but it will always intrigue me that, considering the fundamental role fantasy plays in all of our lives, I find so little understanding of it.

True fantasy is not so much invented as it is distilled and interpreted— from impressions that go far back into prehistory, impressions that, so far as we can tell from the study of folktales, are common to us all whatever our age and nationality. By no means does true fantasy always amuse, and it does not aim to improve an audience so much as it aims to define the universe.

Our fantasies are sometimes kinder than reality, sometimes more horrifying, and nearly always more interesting. It's hard to accept the idea, then, that they spring and have always sprung from ignorance, fear, and superstition; but that seems to be the case.

Of course, we don't believe a person's soul can escape through his nose, but we do say "God bless you" when someone sneezes, don't we? And we do make sure a dead person's eyes are closed. I have not been able to verify this recently, but I seem to remember reading that the practice of putting coins on the dead one's closed eyelids came from a belief that evil spirits would be satisfied to take the money and leave the soul alone.

We are a very advanced civilization. We understand earth, and we understand the heavens. Some of us even understand molecular biology. But there is much inside our heads that, like the cockroach, has survived countless centuries of attack from common sense and the cold eye of science—vague stuff that breeds in dark corners and cannot be pinned down under microscope or through telescope—stuff that in spite of ourselves continues to influence much that we do. Nearly all of it has to do with the dismaying fact that we still don't know, after all this time, exactly where we came from or exactly where we're going. We are arguing still, and again, and always, about creation. We are baffled, outraged, challenged, and humbled by death. For all our indoor plumbing and instant coffee and flu shots and permanent press, we are still, as we were at the beginning, creatures of ignorance, superstition, and fear.

I find it interesting that of the two forces, good and evil, that we long ago took to personifying, the evil ones are surviving in the best condition. When things go wrong for us, as individuals or as a nation, we are quick to suspect there is a dark, malignant force at work. That force has been given many names down through the years, but even at its most general, when we call it simply Bad Luck, we tend to believe it is always present, waiting offstage, ready to strike at us just when things are going our way at last. We delight in horror in our movies, books, plays, and on television. A new retelling of Bram Stoker's *Dracula* brings us out in droves. At movie houses across the land, we wait in line to see skyscrapers burn, ships sink, and airplanes crash.

There is, however, something more in our attraction to these dramas than a simple taste for blood and violence, more in a desire to see someone else get swallowed by the evil so that it won't be ready to swallow us for a little while longer. We are attracted by the hero, who faces the evil, who may even dance on its teeth and still survive. For the hero, of course, is us. These stories, however they are presented, act out encounters with disaster. Many characters will be mauled, burned, drowned, or drawn and quartered, but not the hero—not us—because the hero knows how to placate the evil, how to shame the devil, when to pour the libation, when to ring the bell. The hero knows the rules. He will not die.

The hero, because he is us, is not a fantasy. True fantasy figures representing good have not survived so well as the evil ones, at least not among adults. They have been left mostly to the youngest children. Fairy god-mothers, brownies, the Easter bunny, and Santa Claus all have roots as old as Beelzebub's, but they seem to require too great a suspension of disbelief for adults. They do not battle evil directly but only stand behind the hero and cheer him on. They represent earthly rewards for good behaviour: In ancient terms, courtesy to the hag on the road and soft answers to the cruel stepmother; in modern terms, the straight-A report card, the tidy room, the little sister left unmolested. In short, the kind heart and the stainless life, which will surely be rewarded. We like to think children are the only ones who need a system of learning and reward, and so, as we grow older, we abandon Santa Claus and the rest as pure make-believe. They are not useful and no longer stir our imaginations. As Alan Watts has said, "Heaven is rather static and glistening as compared with the riots of imagination that have gone into the depiction of the Inferno . . . In general it seems that, in artistic representation, hell is exuberant and heaven is not." However this may be, our heads are certainly full of the noise of wings and voices, but almost never the wings and voices of the angels. On the whole, we seem more prepared for punishment than for reward, more inclined to believe we totter always on the brink of disaster rather than on the doorsill of paradise.

In literature the battle against evil began at the beginning and has never stopped, and since one of the definitions of literature is that it is a system for interpreting the real world in symbolic terms, we can tell a good deal about concepts of evil down through the years by reading novels. The adversary changes his face continually, masquerading as everything from a white whale to a corporate executive. Evil, in fact, floats comfortably into any category, any scapegoat, that a new generation or a new dilemma can suggest. The modern novel for adults has moved far afield from the magic of old tales.

Even so, both in and out of literature, it is interesting to observe how, for people of any age, the realm of fantasy can move itself about and shift its accessibility. It can exist across a prairie where it can only be reached via cyclone. It can lie on the other side of a wardrobe or down a rabbit hole. It can be found somewhere between here and madness in a place called the Twilight Zone. It can be all around us in nature, daring us to trace its foot-prints in the snow of the Himalayas or to dive for it in the waters of Loch Ness, or it can come right into our kitchens and dress us for a ball or claim to be butter when what we thought we had was margarine.

For the most part, in literature, at least, fantasy exists elsewhere than in the real world, and we must make a great journey to get to it. Sometimes the journey takes the wink of an eye; sometimes much, much longer. We will need a guide, a little protective magic, and a lot of courage to get there. Sometimes a writer can successfully suggest, as Richard Adams did in *Watership Down*, that it is all around us but is simply not available to humans. On the other hand, Shakespeare brings the two worlds together on the same plane again and again and manages to maintain the credibility of both even while they are interacting as a single unit.

Erich Fromm has suggested that the acceptance and understanding of this other world is contained in the subconscious mind, which he calls the storehouse of a "forgotten language . . . the common origin of dreams, fairy tales, and myth." But whether inside our own heads, as he says, or "outside over there," as Maurice Sendak would say, the other world will always be somewhere, as it always has been, because no matter how we may try to deny it, our need for it is very great, and I think there are two reasons for that need.

The first and most obvious is that it suggests answers to questions for which there are no observable answers in our physical, observable world. . . . I think the other great reason for our need for fantasy is that it makes things more diverting. . . .

We live every day with hopes large and small, for few if any of us believe that our lives as we are living them are perfect—that we are as happy as we would be if things, at least in some fashion, were different. Perhaps the things we wish were different are large, important things; perhaps they aren't. Mostly, they are a combination. . . . Some hopes are pinned on trivialities, some on life-changing possibilities but hope is a happy gas that expands to fit the space available. Without it there is nothing to keep us afloat.

Fantasy literature lets us share the hero's hopes and eventual triumph. In this century things haven't been very pleasant on this planet, but few of us are so deflated that we go out of our way to remind ourselves of that fact all the time, in spite of the thrust of much modern adult fiction. Most of us would rather read a book that ends on a note of hope—one of the special qualities of fantasy literature. It is not a sop for the terminally optimistic but an affirmation of one of the things that makes us, as a species, unique: the always present hope that something will happen to change everything for the better, once and for all.

↶ Author and illustrator Natalie Babbitt has published many novels and picture books for young readers. Like Tolkien, Babbitt creates fantastical worlds where forces of good and evil battle one another. She collaborated on a children's book with her husband in 1966 called *The Forty-Ninth Magician*. She also wrote and illustrated a book called *The Devil's Storybook* (1974). (*Born Ohio 1932*)

Connecting

1.   Before Babbitt began her lecture "The Purposes of Fantasy," she made this opening statement "...the <u>hero is universal</u> and <u>the path he follows is universal</u>—in myth, in fairy tale, in folktale...and so, at bottom, all fantasists are telling <u>the same story</u>." Explain what you understand by the underlined phrases. Refer to movies, TV shows/series, fantasy novels, etc., that you have read or viewed.

2.   Babbitt alludes to the role of fantasy in life. State one of the roles she says it plays. Which of the visuals from this Echo reflects or at least hints at that idea?

3.   Reread the last paragraph of this text. If what motivational writers say is correct, "that attitude is all," what conclusion can you make concerning fantasy readers?

Creator of a World

J. R. R. Tolkien died in 1973 at the age of eighty-one. The following obituary, which appeared in The New York Times, *provides an insightful look at his life, his work, and his universal appeal.*

John Ronald Reuel Tolkien cast a spell over tens of thousands of Americans in the nineteen-sixties with his 500 000-word trilogy, *The Lord of the Rings*, in essence a fantasy of the war between ultimate good and ultimate evil.

Creating the complex but consistent world of Middle Earth, complete with elaborate maps, Tolkien peopled it with hobbits, elves, dwarves, men, wizards, Ents and Orcs (goblins), and other servants of the Dark Lord, Sauron. In particular, he described the adventures of one hobbit, Frodo, son of Drogo, who became the Ring Bearer and the key figure in the destruction of the Dark Tower. As Gandalf, the wizard remarked, there was more to him than met the eye.

The story can be read on many levels. But the author, a scholar and linguist, for thirty-nine years a teacher, denied emphatically that it was allegory. The Ring, discovered by Frodo's uncle, Bilbo Baggins, in an earlier book, *The Hobbit*, has the power to make its wearer invisible, but is infinitely evil.

Tolkien admirers compared him favourably with Milton, Spencer, and Tolstoy. His English publisher, Sir Stanley Unwin, speculated that *The Lord of the Rings* would be more likely to live beyond his and his son's time than any other work he had printed.

Escapist Literature

But detractors, among them the critic Edmund Wilson, put down *The Lord of the Rings*, Tolkien's most famous and most serious fantasy, as a "children's book which somehow got out of hand." A *London Observer* critic condemned it in 1961 as "sheer escapist literature . . . dull, ill-written and . . . whimsical" and expressed the wish that Tolkien's work would soon pass "into merciful oblivion."

It did anything but. It was just four years later, printed in paperback in the United States by Ballantine and Ace Books, that a quarter of a million copies of the trilogy were sold in ten months. In the late sixties all over America fan clubs sprouted, such as The Tolkien Society of America, and members of the cult—many of them students—decorated their walls with the maps of Middle Earth. The trilogy was also published in hardcover by Houghton Mifflin and was a Book-of-the-Month Club selection.

The creator of this monumental, controversial work (or sub-creator as he preferred to call writers of fantasy) was an authority on Anglo-Saxon, Middle English, and Chaucer. He was a gentle, blue-eyed, donnish-appearing man who favoured tweeds, smoked a pipe, and liked to take walks and ride an old bicycle (though he converted to a stylish car with the success of his books).

From 1925 to 1959 he was a professor at Oxford, ultimately Merton Professor of English Language and Literature and a fellow of Merton College. He was somewhat bemused by the acclaim his extracurricular fantasy received—at endless interpretations that variously called it a great Christian allegory, the last literary masterpiece of the Middle Ages, and a philological game.

Tolkien maintained, however, that it wasn't intended as allegory. "I don't like allegories. I never liked Hans Christian Andersen because I knew he was always getting at me," he said.

The trilogy was written, he recalled, to illustrate a 1938 lecture of his at the University of Glasgow on fairy stories. He admitted that fairy stories were something of an escape from the world of factories, machine guns, and bombs. It was a joy, he said, that was the mark of the true fairy story: ". . . However wild its events, however fantastic or terrible the adventures, it can give to child or man that hears it, when the 'turn' comes, a catch of the breath, a beat and lifting of the heart, near to (or indeed, accompanied by) tears, as keen as that given by any form of literary art, and having a peculiar quality."

His own fantasy, it was said, had begun when he was correcting examination papers one day and happened to scratch at the top of one of the dullest, "in a hole in the ground there lived a hobbit." The hobbits began to take form.

They were, he decided, "little people, smaller than the bearded dwarves. Hobbits have no beards. There is little or no magic about them, except the ordinary everyday sort which helps them to disappear quietly and quickly when large stupid folk like you and me come blundering along, making a noise like elephants which they can hear a mile off. They are inclined to be fat in the stomach; they dress in bright colours (chiefly green and yellow); wear no shoes, because their feet grow natural leathery soles and thick warm brown hair like the stuff on their heads (which is curly); have long clever brown fingers, good-natured faces, and laugh deep fruity laughs (especially after dinner which they have twice a day when they can get it)."

Discovering England

He settled these protected innocents in a land called Shire, patterned after the English countryside he had discovered as a child of four arriving from his birthplace in South Africa, and he sent some of them off on perilous adventures. Most of them, however, he conceived as friendly and industrious but slightly dull, which occasioned his scribble on that fortuitous exam paper.

"If you really want to know what Middle Earth is based on, it's my wonder and delight in the earth as it is, particularly the natural earth," Tolkien once said. His trilogy was filled with his knowledge of geology and botany.

The author was born in Bloemfontein on Jan. 3, 1892, a son of Arthur Reuel Tolkien, a bank manager, and Mabel Suffield Tolkien, who had served as a missionary in Zanzibar. Both parents had come from Birmingham and when the boy's father died, his mother took him and his brother home to the English Midlands.

England seemed to him "a Christmas tree" after the barrenness of Africa, where he had been stung by a tarantula and bitten by a snake, where he was "kidnapped" temporarily by a black servant who wanted to show him off to his kraal. It was good, after that, to be in a comfortable place where people lived "tucked away from all the centres of disturbance."

At the same time, he once noted in an essay on fairy stories, "I desired dragons with a profound desire. Of course, I in my timid body did not wish them to be in the neighbourhood, intruding into my relatively safe world..."

His mother was his first teacher and his love of philology, as well as his longing for adventure, was attributed to her influence. But in 1904 she died.

The Tolkiens were converted to Catholicism, and he and his brother became the wards of a priest in Birmingham. (Some critics maintained that the bleakness of industrial Birmingham was the inspiration for his trilogy's evil land of the Enemy, Mordor.)

Served In World War I

Young Tolkien attended King Edward's Grammar School and went on to Exeter College, Oxford, on scholarship. He received his B.A. in 1915. But World War I had begun, and, at twenty-three, he began service in the Lancaster Fusiliers. A year later he married Miss Edith Bratt.

The war was said by his friends to have profoundly affected him. The writer C. S. Lewis insisted that it was reflected in some of the more sinister aspects of his writing and in his hero's joy in comradeship. Tolkien's regiment suffered heavy casualties and when the war ended, only one of his close friends was still alive.

Invalided out of the Fusiliers, Tolkien decided in the hospital that the study of language was to be his metier. He returned to Oxford to receive his M.A. in 1919, and to work as an assistant on the Oxford Dictionary. Two years later he began his teaching career at the University of Leeds.

Within four years, he was a professor, and had also published a Middle English Vocabulary and an edition (with E. V. Gordon) of *Sir Gawayne*

and the Green Knight. He received a call to Oxford, where his lectures on philology soon gave him an extraordinary reputation.

His students remember him as taking endless pains to interest them. One recalled that there was something of the hobbit about him. He walked, she said, "as if on furry feet," and had an appealing jollity.

Meanwhile, once he had scratched that word "hobbit" on the examination paper, his curiosity about hobbits was piqued, and the book of that name—the precursor of the more serious *The Lord of the Rings*—began to grow.

It was nurtured by weekly meetings with his friends and colleagues, including the philosopher and novelist, C. S. Lewis and his brother W. H. Lewis, and the mystical novelist, Charles Williams. The Inklings, as they called themselves, gathered at Magdalen College or a pub to drink beer and share one another's manuscripts.

C. S. Lewis thought well enough of *The Hobbit*, which Tolkien began to write in 1937 (and told to his children), to suggest that he submit it for publication to George Allen and Unwin, Ltd. It was accepted, and the American edition won a Herald Tribune prize as best children's book.

The author always insisted, however, that neither *The Hobbit* nor *The Lord of the Rings* was intended for children.

ECHO

"It's not even very good for children," he said of *The Hobbit*, which he illustrated himself. "I wrote some of it in a style for children, but that's what they loathe. If I hadn't done that, though, people would have thought I was loony."

"If you're a youngish man," he told a London reporter, "and you don't want to be made fun of, you say you're writing for children."

"*The Lord of the Rings*," he admitted, began as an exercise in "linguistic esthetics" as well as an illustration of his theory of fairy tales. Then the story itself captured him.

Took Fourteen Years to Write

In 1954, *The Fellowship of the Ring*, the first volume of the trilogy, appeared. *The Two Towers* and *The Return of the King* were the second and third parts. The work, which has a 104-page appendix and which took fourteen years to write, is filled with verbal jokes, strange alphabets, and names from the Norse, Anglo-Saxon, and Welsh. For its story, it calls, among others, on the legend of *The Ring of the Nibelung* and the early Scandinavian classic, the *Elder Edda*.

Meanwhile, Tolkien was also busy with scholarly writings, which included *Chaucer as a Philologist*; *Beowulf, The Monster and the Critics*; and *The Ancrene Wisse*, a guide for medieval anchoresses.

After retirement, he lived on in the Oxford suburb of Headington, "working like hell," he said, goaded to resume his writing on a myth of the Creation and Fall called *The Silmarillion*, which he had begun even before his trilogy. As he said in an interview, "A pen is to me as a beak is to a hen."

❧ John Ronald Reuel Tolkien was a scholar and writer of fantasy. He was born in South Africa and moved to England at the age of three. As a scholar at the University of Leeds, he studied the Anglo-Saxon literature, particularly epic and folklore, that would inform his books. His novel *The Hobbit* (1937) developed from bedtime stories that he told his children about a kind of gnome named Bilbo Baggins, who was sent on a quest to destroy evil. A similar theme and some of the same characters resurfaced in Tolkien's three-volume series, *The Lord of the Rings* (1954–1955). His novels quickly achieved cult status. *Fellowship of the Ring* was made into a feature film that opened in theatres in 2001, the first in the series. (*Born 1892 South Africa; died 1973*)

Connecting

1. Evaluate the author's introduction based on all you have experienced in this Echo.
2. List key ideas from this obituary that help clarify or explain sections from any of the preceding texts in this Echo.
3. Assume the persona of <u>one</u> of the following and write a letter to *The New York Times* editor reacting to this obituary: a member of the Tolkien family, Julian Dibbell, Natalie

Babbitt, Philip Toynbee (the critic Dibbell refers to in the first paragraph of his work), or one of the artists who created a visual shown in the preceding pages. (To make the response manageable, focus on two or three specifics from the obituary.)

4. Many teachers of the writing process repeat frequently, "write about what you know." Using the information found in Tolkien's obituary, write a persuasive paragraph arguing that this advice still holds true, even for writers of fantasy.

☐ REFLECTING ON THE ECHO

1. a) Create a fantasy story for a class of students your own age. Your work must retain what the critic Joseph Campbell says is the pattern for all fantasy "separation, adventure, and return". It must also include what Babbitt says is a prime ingredient: "the hero crosses some kind of threshold in order to be tested in the otherworld and then returns to the real world ... Fantasy, which covers things larger than life, must follow the complete round. The hero must return."

   b) In groups of three, create a CD or cassette tape of one of your fantasy stories complete with sound track and a series of visuals to complement the project.

2. Assume Tolkien's persona and write a letter to one of the artists whose work is in this Echo discussing their concept of your work. To ensure your persona is realistic, reread Dibbell's review and the obituary. You could also research and read at least three of Tolkien's personal letters to his publisher from *Letters of J. J. R. Tolkien* compiled by Humphrey Carpenter and Christopher Tolkien.

3. Conduct a *forum* based on the question: "Is it appropriate to introduce fantasy literature in the provincial English Language Arts program?" See the section on Xenotransplantation on pages 449–453 of this anthology for details on a forum.

ECHO

Rejection Shock

ᘓ Richard Nelson Bolles

The job hunt.

Ah, the job hunt.

What a ludicrous episode in our lives!

All of our lives if there's one thing we hate it's rejection. Most of us, most of the time, want to avoid rejection, like the plague. We want to be accepted, sometimes at any price.

We'll often reshape ourselves, be who our family or peers want us to be, just in order to avoid rejection.

We die to avoid rejection when we are very small, in our family.

We don't want to be rejected in school, by our class or friends, or the gang we run with.

We don't want to be rejected by the girl or boy that we are sweet on, in high school.

We don't want to be rejected by our college teachers, if we go there.

We don't want to be rejected by the person we fall in love with, and hope to marry.

Avoiding rejection is the story of our life.

And throughout that life, we'll do anything to avoid being rejected, and I mean *anything*. We'll even play the game of rejecting others before they have a chance to reject us. The history of human dating is littered with such games.

Thus we spend our life practising how to avoid being rejected. And then we have to go job-hunting.

Whoops!

It all goes out the window.

What we have spent our life trying to avoid, we here embrace. Job-hunting is *nothing but* a process of rejection, until the very end.

As we go *out there*, as we send resumes, write, call, and visit one prospective employer after another, this is what we run into:

NO NO NO NO NO NO NO NO NO NO NO NO NO NO NO
NO NO NO NO NO NO NO NO NO NO NO NO NO NO NO
NO NO NO NO NO NO NO NO NO NO NO NO NO NO NO
NO NO NO NO NO NO NO NO NO NO NO NO NO YES.

And we submit ourselves to this rejection process not once, but eight times in our lifetime, on average.

The thing which would astound a visitor from Mars, given how much we hate rejection, is not the frequency of our job hunts, but that we often *choose* to go job-hunting, rather than waiting until we are compelled to.

How many of us choose to do it? Well, in a survey conducted recently in the U.S. it was found that 39 million, or 33% of all workers, had thought seriously about chucking their jobs in a given year, and 16 million of them, or 14% of all workers, actually did, during the following two years.

REASONS FOR CHANGING CAREERS

We may be sick and tired of our job. We get bored, fed up, and hungry for something challenging, exciting, and risky, that demands more of us.

Our job may have gone through profound changes we do not like, so that it is no longer our dream job, if ever it once was. Jobs can alter profoundly in a day and a night. Our much-beloved supervisor moves on, leaving us working for a jerk. Or we are given additional responsibilities, without any raise in salary. Or we are promoted into an administrative position which uses none of the skills we like to use. Or, our workplace comes under stringent budget cuts. Or our funding is lost. Whatever. The job which was a perfect match for us just a couple of years ago, is now *"the job from hell."* And we want out.

We may find ourselves asking the question: "Is this *really* what I want to do for the rest of my life?" And if the answer is "No," then eventually we may screw up the courage to take the leap.

We may be stressed, burnt out, exhausted, and hungry
for something peaceful, calm, and secure, that demands
less of us.

We may want to change careers for deeper reasons.
Most of us are engaged in a life-long search for, and
journey toward, *meaning*—through all the varying jobs
or careers that we may hold in our life. We may want a
career that has more meaning.

Many of us believe ourselves to be both body and
spirit. When we are very young, the body preoccupies
us. Work is largely a matter of how we can find bread
to eat, and clothes to wear, and how we can put a roof
over our head. But as we move through the various
stages of our life, and get older, concern for our spirit
moves to the forefront of our consciousness. And we
begin to hunger for work which will honour our spirit's
values. For example, if we have been working too hard
(which 97% of the workforce has), we want to figure
out how we can have more time "to smell the flowers."

We may increasingly want to find the work we feel we
were *born* to do, what we speak of as *our vocation*, or
calling. We may hunger for work which is the deepest
fulfillment of our being, reflecting who we most truly are.

It may look as though we're going to be laid off or
fired, and we decide to leap before we're pushed.

If a career change looks appetizing, it does not matter what the state of the job market is. If your internal time clock has struck midnight, then *that is that.*

If we volunteer to go through this process of rejection, called the job hunt, it is because the goal, at the end, seems worth all the rejection we will have to go through, in order to reach it.

NOBODY'S JOB IS SAFE ANYMORE

Many times, of course, we don't volunteer to go through the job hunt. It is thrust upon us, sometimes when we least expect it—and least want to go through it. And this is happening to us increasingly, in the world's workplace.

The reason for this increase is that throughout the world, the workplace is being reshaped—as a profound kind of *workquake* is taking place beneath its surface. We are seeing throughout the world, in these days, a major and profound restructuring of the whole way in which business is done.

We all know this.

We have seen this restructuring attended by waves of unannounced and unexpected layoffs, as companies, organizations, corporations, the armed forces, defence work, and government programs *downsize.*

We have seen the increasing disappearance of well-paying jobs.

We have seen an increase in the number of hours that present full-time employees have to work, as employers prefer to use employees who already are being paid benefits, rather than hire new workers to whom such benefits would have to be given.

We have seen more and more of the unemployed forced to take part-time jobs, or work as "temporaries," through Temporary Employment Agencies.

We have seen the unemployed find new jobs where their paycheque is smaller, sometimes *much* smaller, than they were formerly accustomed to —forcing an attendant drop in their standard of living.

We have seen more and more workers anxious about their jobs. And with good reason.

What this all adds up to, is that nobody's job is safe anymore. Your job can disappear in a moment, in the twinkling of an eye. One day you'll have the job; the next day you won't. There may be some warning; or there may be none. You may get a decent, even handsome severance pay; or you may get nothing. Your boss may continue to be friendly toward you; or may treat you as though he or she never knew you.

You may understand why this happened to you; or you may not understand at all. If you are let go because your employer went out of business, you may be philosophical about it. But if you are caught in a "downsizing" or "restructuring," you will likely find it much more difficult to be so understanding—particularly if you have worked there *for years.* "Monday-morning quarterbacking" will be epidemic among the employees being let go.

Welcome to *The World of Work.*

Most of us don't understand the nature of that world until we bump our head or stub our toe on that nature. High school or college doesn't prepare us for it. Only out there in the hard school of life do we begin to slowly and painstakingly piece this information together, usually completing the task by the time we're sixty-five.

Earlier than that, all of this may come as a complete shock. Rejection shock. If you've been fired, laid-off, or "made redundant," you will probably be hurt, dejected, angry, and aghast.

And especially so, if you had worked at that place for quite a number of years, given them your loyalty and your best, expected to get their loyalty in return—but they let you go, anyway.

You are suffering from "Rejection Shock." And you are suffering from it because (*among other things*) you didn't expect to be treated this way. In fact, you didn't think *The World of Work* even functioned in this manner.

But it does.

If you study the world of work long enough—not as you would like it to be, but as it is—you will eventually realize there are twelve "rules" in *The World of Work* about Hiring and Firing—some of them a kind of *Bill of Rights* for the employer, some of them a kind of *Bill of Rights* for you. Here they are.

THE TWELVE RULES ABOUT HIRING AND FIRING

1 Nobody owes you a job.

4 Your employers may lay you off, or fire you, anytime they want to. They may do this because they have run out of money, and can't afford you anymore. They may do this because they have to decrease the size of their business, or are going out of business. They may do this because they find your skills do not match the work that they need to have done. Or they may do this because they have a personality conflict with you.

6 Your employers may fire you, or lay you off, without any warning or much notice at all to you, dumping you unceremoniously out on the street.

8 If you are fired, your former employer may do everything in the world to help you find other employment, or may do nothing.

10 As you look back, you may feel that your employers treated you very well, in accordance with their stated values—or you may feel that your employers treated you very badly, in total contradiction of their stated values.

11 If you were the only one who was fired or let go, the other employees may promise they will fight to save your job, but you need to be prepared for the fact that when the chips are down, they may actually do nothing to help you. You will feel very alone.

2 You have to fight to get a job.
   ("Fight" means "persevere," "use ingenuity," "compete.")

3 You have to fight to keep a job. Loyalty, years of service, or personal friendship with the boss, do not in any way guarantee you a job at that place for the rest of your life.

5 You may quit anytime you want to.

7 You may quit without any warning or much notice at all to your employer, leaving them high and dry.

9 If you quit, you may do everything you can to help your employer find a suitable replacement, or you may do nothing.

12 Nonetheless, you remain a rare and unique individual, no matter how the world of work treats you. Your worth is not defined simply by your work, but by your spirit, your heart, and your compassion toward others.

HOW TO PREPARE TO DEAL WITH REJECTION

Given that we spend all of our life trying to avoid rejection, how can we stand this kind of rejection that we meet when we lose our job, or have to go job hunting?

The key is preparation. Preparation begins above all else with your *philosophy of life*. It is immensely useful when you're going through a time where you feel rejected, to sit down and listen to a recording of some famous symphony—say Tchaikovsky's Fifth. The second movement is particularly instructive. As you listen to it, and think about what it is that makes it so interesting, you will be struck by the fact that there are two major themes or melodies in that movement, not just one. The horn melody, with which the movement opens, is sombre; the second melody, picked up by the strings, and the clarinet, is soaring and joyous. Throughout the remainder of the movement these two themes keep alternating. They keep reappearing and interacting with one another, with ever brightening intensity. Two themes; not just one.

What makes the music so interesting, of course, is that it mirrors our *life*. Our life, too, has not one theme but two major themes alternating throughout. We may describe these two themes in various ways. We may say:

Life is sometimes sombre; life is sometimes joyous.
Life is sometimes difficult; life is sometimes easy.
Life is sometimes tawdry; life is sometimes beautiful.
Life is sometimes worse; life is sometimes better.

Life finds us sometimes struggling; life finds us
    sometimes well off.
Life is sometimes sickness; life is sometimes health.
Life is sometimes depressing; life is sometimes elating.
Life is sometimes sorrow; life is sometimes happiness.
Life is sometimes death; life is sometimes resurrection.
Life sometimes casts us down; life sometimes exalts us.
Life is sometimes a battle; life is sometimes glorious.

To have a *philosophy of life* is to know this about life. And to know not to expect to find life always easy, or always happy. Nor, on the other hand, to expect to find it always difficult, and always a struggle. For most of us, the two themes alternate, in music and in life, both on this earth and beyond.

Thus, you need not feel your life has suddenly taken on a permanent turn for the worse when you lose your job, or are fired, when you are out pounding the pavements, and not finding anyone who wants you. Such a difficult time in life is *one* of the themes of life, and therefore in that sense *natural* and *inevitable*.

You've been laid off? The horns are sounding the sombre theme, in the movement of life. You're going through a difficult job hunt with lots of NOs? The horns, again.

But the most helpful thing to know about all of this is that it is not the permanent theme for the rest of your life. Your life has two themes, not one. This difficult sombre time will yield eventually to the lilting voice of strings, to the contrasting theme of joy and happiness, all in due time. You need to know this, and thus put this period of your life in some perspective.

This is how you begin, in dealing with rejection shock.

෴ "Rejection Shock" is the second chapter in Richard Nelson Bolles' best-selling *The 1995 What Color Is Your Parachute? A Practical Manual for Job-Hunters & Career-Changers*. Bolles has been interviewed on many news programs in the United States, such as CNN and ABC's *Nightline*. He lives in San Francisco. *(Born Wisconsin 1927)*

RESPONDING

Meaning

1. Summarize the first two pages of this text in *standard* English, the language used in academic, business, and professional fields. In other words, as you rewrite, rephrase the following colloquialisms:
   a) job-hunting
   b) ...gang we run with
   c) whoops
   d) chucking
   e) jerk
   f) screw up courage

2. *Jargon*, specialized language, is used frequently in this business-oriented excerpt. Explain the following in standard English:
   a) workquake
   b) downsize
   c) benefits
   d) temporaries
   e) restructuring
   f) made redundant

Form and Style

3. In a paragraph, explain the appropriateness of one of the visuals to its accompanying text. Comment also on the purpose and appropriateness of the visual in the *context* of the entire excerpt.

4. a) Identify the writing techniques (stylistic devices) the author uses to make this text interesting and accessible. Beside each technique, cite an example from the text.
   b) Write a journal entry reflecting on the author's style. Is it appropriate to the intended audience? the subject matter? Is it effective?

Exploring Context

5. There are more recent editions of this book. Speculate on how this chapter would be presented in the most recent edition. Comment on page design and layout, use of visuals, writing style, etc. Give reasons for your suggestions. Then go to the library or your local bookstore and look through the most up-to-date edition of *What Color Is Your Parachute?* Does it include a similar chapter? Why or why not? Were your speculations about changes in design, layout, and style correct?

Creative Extension

6. Argue that this text would be better presented as a Web page or government information pamphlet. Choose one of these forms and create it for your graduating class based on what you consider to be the most important concepts presented in the book chapter. Debrief your work by writing a short commentary on how your choice of form affected the presentation of the information.

7. Prepare a multimedia presentation for a Careers or Co-operative Education class, or a business organization. Use Bolles's chapter as your basis, but add to his text. Carefully select or create visuals, graphics, etc. Remember to keep your audience in mind as you draft your work (choose your language, *tone,* etc. appropriately). Apply the techniques of effective oral presentations including careful attention to pace, volume, intonation, juncture (pauses), and eye contact with your audience.

The Perils of Indifference

ᘓ Elie Wiesel

Mr. President, Mrs. Clinton, members of Congress, Ambassador Holbrooke, Excellencies, friends: Fifty-four years ago to the day, a young Jewish boy from a small town in the Carpathian Mountains woke up, not far from Goethe's beloved Weimar, in a place of eternal infamy called Buchenwald. He was finally free, but there was no joy in his heart. He thought there never would be again.

Liberated a day earlier by American soldiers, he remembers their rage at what they saw. And even if he lives to be a very old man, he will always be grateful to them for that rage, and also for their compassion. Though he did not understand their language, their eyes told him what he needed to know—that they, too, would remember, and bear witness.

And now, I stand before you, Mr. President—Commander-in-Chief of the army that freed me, and tens of thousands of others—and I am filled with a profound and abiding gratitude to the American people.

Gratitude is a word that I cherish. Gratitude is what defines the humanity of the human being. And I am grateful to you, Hillary—or Mrs. Clinton—for what you said, and for what you are doing for children in the world, for the homeless, for the victims of injustice, the victims of destiny and society. And I thank all of you for being here.

We are on the threshold of a new century, a new millennium. What will the legacy of this vanishing century be? How will it be remembered in the new millennium? Surely it will be judged, and judged severely, in both moral and metaphysical terms. These failures have cast a dark shadow over humanity: two World Wars, countless civil wars, the senseless chain of assassinations—Gandhi, the Kennedys, Martin Luther King, Sadat, Rabin—bloodbaths in Cambodia and Nigeria, India and Pakistan, Ireland and Rwanda, Eritrea and Ethiopia, Sarajevo and Kosovo; the inhumanity in the gulag and the tragedy of Hiroshima. And, on a different level, of course, Auschwitz and Treblinka. So much violence, so much indifference.

What is indifference? Etymologically, the word means "no difference" —a strange and unnatural state in which the lines blur between light and darkness, dusk and dawn, crime and punishment, cruelty and compassion, good and evil.

What are its courses and inescapable consequences? Is it a philosophy? Is there a philosophy of indifference conceivable? Can one possibly view indifference as a virtue? Is it necessary at times to practise it simply to keep one's sanity, live normally, enjoy a fine meal and a glass of wine, as the world around us experiences harrowing upheavals?

Of course, indifference can be tempting—more than that, seductive. It is so much easier to look away from victims. It is so much easier to avoid such rude interruptions to our work, our dreams, our hopes. It is, after all, awkward, troublesome, to be involved in another person's pain and despair. Yet, for the person who is indifferent, his or her neighbours are of no consequence. And, therefore, their lives are meaningless. Their hidden or even visible anguish is of no interest. Indifference reduces the other to an abstraction.

Over there, behind the black gates of Auschwitz, the most tragic of all prisoners were the "Muselmanner," as they were called. Wrapped in their torn blankets, they would sit or lie on the ground, staring vacantly into space, unaware of who or where they were, strangers to their surroundings. They no longer felt pain, hunger, thirst. They feared nothing. They felt nothing. They were dead and did not know it.

Rooted in our tradition, some of us felt that to be abandoned by humanity then was not the ultimate. We felt that to be abandoned by God was worse than to be punished by Him. Better an unjust God than an indifferent one. For us to be ignored by God was a harsher punishment than to be a victim of His anger.

Man can live far from God—not outside God. God is wherever we are. Even in suffering? Even in suffering.

In a way, to be indifferent to that suffering is what makes the human being inhuman. Indifference, after all, is more dangerous than anger and hatred. Anger can at times be creative. One writes a great poem, a great symphony, one does something special for the sake of humanity because one is angry at the injustice that one witnesses. But indifference is never creative. Even hatred at times may elicit a response. You fight it. You denounce it. You disarm it. Indifference elicits no response. Indifference is not a response.

Indifference is not a beginning, it is an end. And, therefore, indifference is always the friend of the enemy, for it benefits the aggressor—never his victim, whose pain is magnified when he or she feels forgotten. The political prisoner in his cell, the hungry children, the homeless refugees—not to respond to their plight, not to relieve their solitude by offering them a spark of hope is to exile them from human memory. And in denying their humanity, we betray our own.

Indifference, then, is not only a sin, it is a punishment. And this is one of the most important lessons of this outgoing century's wide-ranging experiments in good and evil.

In the place that I come from, society was composed of three simple categories: the killers, the victims, and the bystanders. During the darkest of times, inside the ghettoes and death camps—and I'm glad that Mrs. Clinton mentioned that we are now commemorating that event, that period, that we are now in the Days of Remembrance—but then, we felt abandoned, forgotten. All of us did.

And our only miserable consolation was that we believed that Auschwitz and Treblinka were closely guarded secrets; that the leaders of the free world did not know what was going on behind those black gates and barbed wire; that they had no knowledge of the war against the Jews that Hitler's armies and their accomplices waged as part of the war against the Allies.

If they knew, we thought, surely those leaders would have moved heaven and earth to intervene. They would have spoken out with great outrage and conviction. They would have bombed the railways leading to Birkenau, just the railways, just once.

And now we knew, we learned, we discovered that the Pentagon knew, the State Department knew. And the illustrious occupant of the White House then, who was a great leader—and I say it with some anguish and pain, because, today is exactly fifty-four years marking his death—Franklin Delano Roosevelt died on April the 12th, 1945, so he is very much present to me and to us.

No doubt, he was a great leader. He mobilized the American people and the world, going into battle, bringing hundreds and thousands of valiant and brave soldiers in America to fight fascism, to fight dictatorship, to fight Hitler. And so many of the young people fell in battle. And, nevertheless, his image in Jewish history—I must say it—his image in Jewish history is flawed.

The depressing tale of the *St. Louis* is a case in point. Sixty years ago, its human cargo—maybe 1000 Jews—was turned back to Nazi Germany. And that happened after the Kristallnacht, after the first state sponsored pogrom, with hundreds of Jewish shops destroyed, synagogues burned, thousands of people put in concentration camps. And that ship, which was already on the shores of the United States, was sent back.

I don't understand. Roosevelt was a good man, with a heart. He understood those who needed help. Why didn't he allow these refugees to disembark? A thousand people—in America, a great country, the greatest democracy, the most generous of all new nations in modern history. What happened? I don't understand. Why the indifference, on the highest level, to the suffering of the victims?

But then, there were human beings who were sensitive to our tragedy. Those non-Jews, those Christians, that we called the "Righteous Gentiles," whose selfless acts of heroism saved the honour of their faith. Why were they so few?

Why was there a greater effort to save SS murderers after the war than to save their victims during the war?

Why did some of America's largest corporations continue to do business with Hitler's Germany until 1942? It has been suggested, and it was documented, that the Wehrmacht could not have conducted its invasion of France without oil obtained from American sources. How is one to explain their indifference?

And yet, my friends, good things have also happened in this traumatic century: the defeat of Nazism, the collapse of communism, the rebirth of Israel on its ancestral soil, the demise of apartheid, Israel's peace treaty with Egypt, the peace accord in Ireland. And let us remember the meeting, filled with drama and emotion, between Rabin and Arafat that you, Mr. President, convened in this very place. I was here and I will never forget it.

And then, of course, the joint decision of the United States and NATO to intervene in Kosovo and save those victims, those refugees, those who were uprooted by a man whom I believe that because of his crimes, should be charged with crimes against humanity. But this time, the world was not silent.

This time, we do respond. This time, we intervene.

Does it mean that we have learned from the past? Does it mean that society has changed? Has the human being become less indifferent and more human?

Have we really learned from our experiences? Are we less insensitive to the plight of victims of ethnic cleansing and other forms of injustices in places near and far? Is today's justified intervention in Kosovo a lasting warning that never again will the deportation, the terrorization of children and their parents be allowed anywhere in the world? Will it discourage other dictators in other lands to do the same?

What about the children? Oh, we see them on television, we read about them in the papers, and we do so with a broken heart. Their fate is always the most tragic, inevitably. When adults wage war, children perish. We see their faces, their eyes. Do we hear their pleas? Do we feel their pain, their agony? Every minute one of them dies of disease, violence, famine. Some of them—so many of them—could be saved.

And so, once again, I think of the young Jewish boy from the Carpathian Mountains. He has accompanied the old man I have become throughout these years of quest and struggle. And together we walk towards the new millennium, carried by profound fear and extraordinary hope.

෴   During World War II, the Nazis deported the teenaged Elie Wiesel and his family from their home in Hungary to a concentration camp in occupied Poland. Wiesel's family died in the camp. He was liberated in April 1945, after which he moved to Paris and then settled in New York. He has documented wartime atrocities against the Jewish people in over forty books, including *Night* (1960), a chronicle of his Holocaust experiences. Wiesel was awarded the Nobel Prize for Peace in 1986. He delivered the speech "The Perils of Indifference" at the White House on April 12, 1999, as part of the Millennium Lecture series, hosted by President Bill Clinton and his wife, Hillary Rodham Clinton. *(Born Romania 1928)*

RESPONDING

Meaning

1. Identify or explain the meaning of the underlined words in the phrases below and discuss their significance in the context of Wiesel's speech.
    a) <u>he</u> will always be grateful to them for their rage
    b) <u>gratitude</u> is a word that I cherish
    c) the <u>legacy</u> of this...century...will be judged severely in both moral and meta-physical terms
    d) the *St. Louis*...[and its] human cargo was turned back to Nazi Germany...after the <u>Kristallnacht</u>

2.   Wiesel's focus is "indifference." List at least five of the descriptors he gives this term. Explain three of them.

Form and Style

3.   Scan the text again. Estimate the number of questions the speaker poses. What is the effect of this use of questions in a speech? Does the number add to or detract from the purpose of this text? Justify your response.

4.   List, with examples, four of the persuasive techniques Wiesel uses in this speech (e.g., use of powerful metaphors, repetition, parallelism, direct appeals to the audience, etc.). Share your list with a partner or small group. Together come up with a complete list of the techniques used in this speech and discuss their effectiveness.

Exploring Context

5.   This oral text was part of the Millennium Lecture series sponsored by the White House. Cite the paragraph that indicates that fact and explain the need for this type of lecture— to this occasion and to history.

Creative Extension

6.   In small groups, practise reading paragraph twelve of the speech (beginning "In a way, to be indifferent..."). Focus on key aspects of oral presentation, including *pitch* (the degree of highness or lowness of vocal tones), *stress* (the amount of emphasis given to syllables and words), and *juncture* (pauses or breaks between words and word groups). Read the paragraph in various ways and discuss the results. Decide on the most effective presentation. Then listen to short clips of other speeches and analyze the speaker's use of these techniques.

7.   Research articles written on the efforts of humanitarian aid workers and Red Cross workers to help the victims of Kosovo or another recent conflict. Concentrate your research and your interpretation of the articles on those humanitarian efforts. Prepare a speech of two to four minutes using techniques Wiesel employed to convince your audience that human nature is admirable after all. Record your speech on audio tape.

The Ethics of Xenotransplantation

✺ A Televised Forum

earning Goals

summarize and
explain key
arguments

examine others'
ideas to clarify and
expand on personal
understanding

understand the pur-
pose of a forum and
assess its success

transpose a forum
into a television or
Internet newscast

create a feature
article

Arlene Bynon with guests Dr. Margaret Somerville, *McGill Centre for
Medicine, Ethics & Law, Montreal, Quebec* and Alastair Gordon, *The Islet
Foundation*.

ARLENE BYNON: Xenotransplantation. The use of animal organs in human
transplants could help with Canada's low rate of organ donation. Now the
Commons health committee is holding public hearings to examine ways
to improve the rate of donation. They've heard from a host of medical and
ethical people with reservations on organ transplants. Today the case for
and against the use of animal organs. We're joined by Alastair Gordon
of the Islet Foundation, and from Ottawa, Dr. Margaret Somerville from
McGill University Centre for Medicine, Ethics, and Law. Welcome
Dr. Somerville.

DR. MARGARET SOMERVILLE: Thank you.

BYNON: I know there has been bad weather so you're stuck there in
Ottawa. Let me ask you first of all, what reservations . . . , what should
we be asking ourselves before we move more forward with this kind of
transplant?

SOMERVILLE: Well there's all of the usual reservations that we have about
medical research which you know, are good reservations. They're to make
sure when we do medical research we do it ethically. All of those apply to
xenotransplantation. But there's two other reservations. One of them I find
serious but not insurmountable. That is what we do to animals in order to
make them suitable as donors of these organs. 'Cause these animals have a
pretty terrible life. I think—pigs are intelligent animals. It seems as though
that's what we'll use. And so I think we have to be very sensitive to the
issues surrounding that. Some people think we shouldn't use those animals
at all in that way. The other set of issues relates to us. You see, most medical
research really only creates serious risks to the people who are the research
subjects. But there is a possibility, and we don't know whether this will

occur or not, that you could transfer an infective agent from the pig into the person who gets the organ and that person could then spread it . . . maybe to their family and ultimately, possibly, to everybody in the population. That's what we're worried about.

BYNON: Okay. Let's just stop on that point because is there new information that humans and animals transfer more diseases than we know because, you know, as many people say we have been using some aspects of animals' bodies like insulin or whatever for years? So what's different about it?

SOMERVILLE: Well, because I mean, we don't know. That's the point. Look, I'm not an expert. I'm an expert to the extent that I'm an expert on anything—that once I'm given the scientific facts, I can manage to do an ethical and legal analysis of those. What we know here is a lot of very reputable scientists, eminent scientists, say that we've got no idea what we might transfer when we, let's say, take a heart out of a pig and put it into a human. There could be all sorts of unknown things. We know about some of the things that we could transfer and we could watch out for those. But the other thing that people were talking about this morning in the committee of the House of Commons was that it could even be that, for instance, a virus that's in the pig which might not hurt us could combine with a virus that's in us which possibly doesn't hurt us at the moment and then you could have something new and very dangerous. And so there's all sorts of unknowns that we're dealing with here.

BYNON: Now, isn't that the case—I mean, that's how people believe HIV —I mean it was prevalent in a monkey. It didn't affect the monkey. Somehow it got into a human—

SOMERVILLE: Yes. Well, we've only been able to establish that authoritatively in the last few weeks. And also the other one that we're concerned about is mad cow disease. Now, that's a kind of an unusual transfer between a sheep and cow. But that's two different species where—I mean they've lived together for as long as humans have lived with animals. There was never that transfer until we did something unusual—feed the cows food that was made from sheep. And so we're doing something here—we're doing what we call crossing the species and an immunological barrier. And that's very different from simply living with another animal.

BYNON: Okay. Okay. I'd like to turn over to Alastair Gordon with the Islet Foundation. You've just heard some of this. I mean, you believe that this is a good thing, as Martha Stewart would say. Do you not have any reservations about xenotransplantation?

ALASTAIR GORDON: Any reservations I would have about xenotransplantation would have to be driven by actual scientifically compelling information. In other words, I think it's fairly immoral to allow death and suffering to continue in the face of a completely unarticulated fear, a fear that has never once been demonstrated, never proven.

BYNON: But it happened with HIV in monkeys. Isn't that . . . I mean it has happened.

GORDON: Well, if we take a look at the examples of HIV in monkeys, there was a transfer of disease from an animal to a human. It did not occur as a result of xenotransplantation.

BYNON: I know, but I think the example is clear that if, you know, if it happened by accident, couldn't it happen when we do things on purpose?

SOMERVILLE: Could I just also interrupt here and just sort of say what we're looking at here in terms of ethics? You see, I disagree with you that we've got to know about the risk. You see, what we're saying is we should take what's called a precautionary ethic. We should be reticent to do this until we know it's reasonably safe and ethical to do it. Whereas what you're saying is let's do it until we find out it's unsafe. We've had so many bad experiences in the past when we've done that. I mean, even if you look at our whole—

BYNON: Can you hang on, Dr. Somerville? Let Alastair Gordon answer.

GORDON: I think, Dr. Somerville, what I'm saying is we have a massive body of evidence that shows that there is no diseased transfer between pigs and human beings despite about a seventy-five year history in which we provided innumerable pathways for that to occur.

BYNON: Do you mean the insulin?

GORDON: For example, people with diabetes have injected insulin from pigs for the past seventy-seven years. For about the first two decades, that was a non-sterile product. People with burns have been treated with living pigskin. People working in slaughterhouses have certainly been exposed to pig tissue getting into open wounds and those were people that have in many cases had severely compromised immune systems at the turn of the century, including tuberculosis.

SOMERVILLE: Look, I accept that. I'm not the expert in the transfer of these organisms or these infected agents. But, if that's—and I accept what you say is true—but all of the people I listen to when I'm at these scientific meetings are world experts on immunology. And they know all of that and they're raising these concerns. And, in fact, the concerns are so great in Europe that it's very likely that Europe's going to put a moratorium on this.

BYNON: Okay. I just want to ask Alastair, do you think there should be control over it? Anything that would make—you know, put your mind at rest about transferring these kinds of diseases? Are there any kind of controls that we are doing?

GORDON: We're drafting xenotransplantation guidelines which will make sure that we are using purpose-bred pigs whose sole raison d'être is to be a tissue donor. And—

BYNON: What are these pigs like?

GORDON: They are are kept under very sterile, very humane conditions. Just touching on Dr. Somerville's point of the ethics of using animals in this way, human beings have a long history of using pigs for suede, paint brushes, and bacon. To use a pig to save a child from the horrors of diabetes or somebody from dying from liver disease is certainly to me a lot more ethically palatable than eating them and wearing them.

BYNON: Dr. Somerville, not a bad point there.

SOMERVILLE: No, no it's a different argument. You see, what you're mixing up is the kind of life that the pig has with what you do with the pig after you've killed it. I mean, I agree with you that if we use pigs for other purposes, then that helps to justify using them for this purpose. But those pigs could be, for instance, pigs that live anywhere and have a good life. You kill them and you use them for what you want to. These pigs are going to have a totally artificial, confined, terrible life. We know that, but we still may be justified in doing it as I believe—but not everybody agrees with that.

૭   The debate on the "Ethics of Xenotransplantation" appeared on the television show *Bynon*,
hosted by Arlene Bynon, on the Global Television network in March of 1999. Dr. Margaret
Somerville is a professor of law at McGill University in Montreal. Alastair Gordon is
the president of the Islet Foundation, an organization that funds research seeking a cure
for diabetes.

RESPONDING

Meaning

1.   What are the two reservations Dr. Somerville states concerning the transplanting of
animal organs in humans? Do you agree with the order in which she states them? Explain.

2.   Summarize, in a short paragraph and without using examples, the stand of each member
of the forum. Explain their stance from their perspective.

Form and Style

3.   Debates or *forums* usually balance logic with emotion (rhetoric). With a partner, list the
arguments made by each speaker. Then analyze each argument by placing the letter "L"
beside those based on logic, and the letter "E" beside those you consider to be emotional.
Is this debate balanced?

4.   A *forum*, according to the authors of the text *Mastering Effective English*, is "a group of
people assembled to discuss a question or questions of public interest . . . representing
two major points of view; [it] has as its main purpose to present fairly both sides of the
question, not to arrive at a plan of action or the adoption of a resolution."

   Has this forum been successful? Are you more informed? If so, what information do
you have now that you did not have before?

Exploring Context

5. This forum was presented on television. What advantages does television have over radio,
for example, as a medium for forums, debates, and talk shows? Recreate and videotape
a segment of this forum. Carefully consider camera shots and non-verbal cues in your
recreation. Discuss the results. Present your videotape to the class and outline your
findings.

Creative Extension

6. Transpose this forum into a television or Internet newscast. Reformat the information to
suit the new form and medium. Then write a short commentary noting the strategies you
used to reformat the information and the reasons for your decisions.

7. *Time* magazine has a section entitled "Society" wherein a writer studies a current issue
and investigates the impact it has had or could have on society. The articles often include
visuals, surveys, quotes, research, and information from interviews. Assume you are such
a writer. Create an article based on this forum. Use the information in the forum and build
on it through your own research and investigations.

The Iron Road

ᘓ Al Purdy

Learning Goals

- analyze theme or purpose
- examine structure
- identify poetic techniques and their effects
- present a readers' theatre inter- pretation
- write an original "coming-of-age" piece

Riding the boxcars out of Winnipeg in a
morning after rain so close to
the violent sway of fields it's
like running and running
naked with summer in your mouth
being a boy scarcely a moment and you
hear the rumbling iron roadbed singing
under the wheels at night and a door jerking open
mile after dusty mile riding into Regina with
the dust storm crowding behind you
night and morning over the clicking rails

The year was 1937, and I was seventeen. I rode the freight trains to Vancouver, along with thousands of other Canadians during the Great Depression. In the Hungry Thirties it seemed that half the population was on the move. The unemployed workmen of Toronto and Montreal and all the other big cities swarmed over the boxcars, moving west to the Prairies, west to Vancouver, wherever there might be hope of finding work.

There were also the professional hoboes, who always went in the opposite direction from where there was any rumour of employment. They lived in hobo jungles beside rivers and near the towns, never far from the railway yards. There they lit campfires, cooked food, washed clothing—if it was absolutely necessary—and told tales of the steel high-ways while standing over the fires at night. Of towns where housewives always invited you inside for dinner when you asked for a handout, and never handed you an axe while pointing sternly at the woodpile. Of towns where you never had to work, there was always plenty of beer. . . . But after a day or two in the jungle they got restless again, and boarded the train to Anywhere.

It was a dark night in early June when I caught my first train at the railway yards in Trenton, Ontario. It had chuffed in from the east an hour earlier, and was about to pull out for Toronto. The yards were full of shunting switch engines bustling back and forth in the night, red and green signal lights gleaming like the eyes of stationary cats, and every now and then you heard a hoarse, impatient scream from the whistles of the westbound train.

I'll never know how I had the nerve to board that train, for I was scared to death of it. I'd quit school a couple of years before and there was no work at all in Trenton. But that wasn't the reason why I was heading west. The reason was boredom. I wanted adventure. That was why I crouched in some bushes beside the tracks, almost too nervous to breathe, wondering how I'd ever manage to climb onto that boxcar. Was it something like getting on a bicycle or a horse? And where were the railway police hiding?

Suddenly the westbound train made a peculiar "toot-toot" that signalled departure—a sound I've heard many times since. Hoboes call it "the high-ball." Then a great metallic crash came from the couplings, and the train grunted away into the night. I broke cover and ran alongside, grabbing at the steel ladder of a passing boxcar, and climbed up onto the roof—collapsing on the swaying catwalk while all the vertebrae of the wriggling wooden serpent beneath me thundered west.

A few days later and miles from home, I received my first instructions from a professional bum about the proper method of boarding a moving train. A lean little man with a dark stubble of beard, he'd seen me swing onto a train by the rear ladder of a boxcar.

"That's the way guys get killed," he said. "Ya gotta do it the right way." He spat tobacco on the boxcar floor and gestured. "I seen guys lose a leg or arm falling under them wheels. Ya always go for the ladder at the front end of the car, never the one at the back end. If ya miss yer hold on the rear ladder ya fall between the cars and yer a gone goose. Always the front ladder. An remember that, kid."

There were other famous bums who wrote their names and deeds on boxcar walls or on the supports of watertanks with knife and pencil—Regina Sam Jones, Montana Slim, Midnight Frank. I've often wondered: why should a man call himself "Midnight Frank"? There was also the immortal Kilroy, who wrote "Kilroy was here" the length and breadth of the continent.

Farther west, at Broadview, Saskatchewan, the Mounties had a reputation for being very tough on bums. The stories about their toughness alarmed me so much that I crawled down the trap door of a threshing machine mounted on a flatcar before going through town. I crouched in the darkness of that monster, nervously waiting to be discovered and hauled off to jail. I heard the police tramping around outside, making a tremendous racket, but they didn't find me. When the train pulled out on its way west, I was the only illicit passenger left of the three score or so who had ridden with me into Broadview.

When I first started out for Vancouver I had some money in my pockets. But it was soon spent. I had to forsake the aristocratic habit of eating in restaurants and join the other bums knocking on doors to ask for handouts. It was embarrassing, but I got used to it. You nerved yourself, knocked on a door, and waited, wondering what might happen. The dignity of man was, of course, a lesser consideration than being hungry.

You might get a sandwich from a housewife, perhaps even a full meal, a "sitdown" we used to call it; but you might also be given an axe and directed to the woodpile; or a man in shirtsleeves might come to the door and tell you to "Beat it, bum!" It was all part of the game, and you didn't really hold any grudges for a harsh reception, you just kept on trying.

Sometimes you went to the bakery of whatever small town you happened to be passing through, asking the baker if he had any stale bread or buns. Most of the time you got something to eat, but occasionally there were long stretches on the train where it wasn't possible to ask for a handout. At such times you stayed hungry.

On my first trip west I hitchhiked north from Sault Ste. Marie, and was disheartened to find that the road ended at a little village called Searchmont (at that time the Trans-Canada Highway was not yet completed through Northern Ontario). Near midnight I boarded a freight travelling north and west, riding in an open-air gondola used to transport coal. After an hour it began to rain, and the coaldust made things worse. My face and hands were streaked with it. We stopped around 5 a.m. and it was still dark. I had no idea where I was, but the rain and coaldust were too miserable to be borne. I ripped the seal off a boxcar with my hunting knife and tried to get inside. But the door was too big and heavy for me to move, so I went back to my gondola and huddled under the rain in silent misery.

A railway cop materialized out of the greyness not long after I got
settled. He'd seen the broken seal, and knew I was responsible. He told
me that the settlement was named Hawk Junction, then locked me up in
a caboose with barred windows and a padlocked door. And I thought:
how would my mother feel now about her darling boy? At noon the railway cop took me to his house for dinner with his wife and children, gave
me some *Ladies Home Journals* to read, and casually mentioned that I could
get two years for breaking the boxcar seal.

When returned to my prison-on-wheels I felt panicstricken. I was only
seventeen, and this was the first time I'd ventured far away from home.
I examined the caboose-prison closely, thinking: two years! Why, I'd be
nineteen when I got out, an old man! And of course it was hopeless to
think of escape. Other prisoners had tried without success, and windows
were broken where they'd tried to wrench out the bars. And the door: it
was wood, locked on the outside with a padlock, opening inward. It was a
very springy door though: I could squeeze my fingertips between sill and
door, one hand at the top and the other a foot below. That gave me hope,
blessed hope, for the first time. My six-foot-three body was suspended in
air by my hands, doubled up like a coiled spring, and I pulled. Lord, how
I pulled! The door bent inward until I could see a couple of daylight
inches between door and sill. Then, Snap! and screws pulled out of the
steel hasp outside. I fell flat on my back.

Peering cautiously, right and left, I jumped to the ground, walking as
slowly and sedately as I could make myself—toward freedom. The urge to
run was hard to resist, especially when crossing a bridge over a wide river
along the tracks, and continuing steadily in the direction of Sault Ste.
Marie, 165 miles south of the railway divisional point. But that cop would
be looking for me, and so would other blue uniforms! Two years! Walking
the tracks would make me far too obvious, much too easy to find. So how
about making the journey twenty or thirty feet into the heavy forest lining
both sides of the right of way? That way I could see if anyone came after
me, and duck back among the trees. Brilliant, positively brilliant.

But the trees went uphill and down, turned leftways and rightways,
without any landmarks or anything to orient me with the tracks. I began
to feel uneasy: better stay close to the railway. Too late. I was deep into the
woods, not knowing in which direction to turn. I was lost—and didn't feel

stupid, just terrified. My heart began to pump hard, and I ran, with branches and leaves slapping my face, blundering into trees, splashing through little streams.

Finally I stopped, knowing panic was useless but feeling it anyway. The possibility of dangerous animals occurred to me: what about bears?—bears must live in these woods. I had no defense against them; the railway cop had confiscated my hunting knife. Besides, what good would such a feeble weapon be against an angry black bear? And the brown shape that flitted between the trees, not so much seen as realized, what was that?

I slept on the side of a hill, huddled around a mother-tree, and it was cold, cold. Morning was grey with a light rain falling, more mist than rain. By this time I'd thought of the sun as some kind of directional reference, but there was no sun. And just a couple of miles away I could hear engines shunting and butting back and forth in the railway yard, the sound seeming to come from all directions among the trees. Old logging trails meandered through the forest, but they were so old that when I tried to follow them they vanished in the vague greyness. Once I stumbled on an old hunting camp, so ancient that the lean-to logs were rotten. Later in the day, during my stumbling, lurching progress, I came on that hunting camp twice more, each time increasingly terrified about walking in circles.

At age seventeen I didn't believe in God, at least I told myself I didn't. But this was no time to take chances one way or the other. I prayed. Fervently, passionately, and with no reservations, I prayed to get out of that forest. And remembered the forty-some Sundays I'd attended church two years before, without listening to the preacher's sermon but in order to receive a prize for attendance. Since then I'd become a non-believer in that fire-and-brimstone God, but now for reasons of expediency I pretended to myself and to a possible Him that my backsliding was over—at least for as long as I was lost in this northern forest.

And maybe it worked: I still don't know. That railway bridge I'd crossed when leaving Hawk Junction popped into my head. Adolescent high school logic took over. The river and railway tracks would make two sides of a very large isosceles triangle. And carry it a step farther: if I could finally walk in something close to a straight line, which hadn't happened thus far, then I must finally locate either river or tracks. And the sun, now becoming a pale spot in the overhead grey, gave me some small direction. I walked and walked, and two hours later nearly fell head-first down an embankment into that blessed blessed river.

That same evening I boarded a passenger train just behind the engine, and rode south to the Soo in style, careless of legal consequences. But no cops appeared on the smokey, cindered horizon of fear. At the steel town I dived into a Scandinavian steambath to stop the shivering chill that I'd picked up from two days in the woods. And sleeping that night in a cheap flophouse, I was still shuddering a little, in slow motion.

I think my first sight of the mountains was worth all the hardships—waking early in the morning inside an empty boxcar and gazing down into a lake surrounded by forest stretching for miles and miles—cupped and cradled by the white peaks. And myself crawling round the side of a mountain like a fly on a sugar bowl. For the first time I realized how big this country was. And, naively, because I was only seventeen years old, I felt a tremendous exaltation at the sight. How marvellous to be alive and to ride a bare-backed train through such a country. And, naively, forty years later, I've not changed my mind.

Vancouver was a sprawling, dingy, beautiful giant of a waterfront city even in 1937. I walked down Water Street, over the puddles and wet grey concrete in the early morning. An old woman on an iron balcony called down for me to come up and see her daughter, mentioning explicitly certain delights that could be expected. Rather prudishly, I declined. I spent the afternoon at a movie, paying fifteen cents for the privilege of watching Dorothy Lamour disport herself in a sarong. But I'm not sure if the girl wouldn't have been a better bargain.

After the movie I was seized with a realization of the immense distance I had come from home. Originally I had meant to get a job fishing on a purse seiner at Vancouver, but the smelly old harbour depressed me. The Lions Gate Bridge, stretching spider-like across First Narrows, seemed alien; the streets themselves were unfriendly and peopled by strangers. I was homesick.

On the same day that I had arrived I slipped under the barrier at a level crossing and boarded a freight train moving east. And all the immense width of a continent was before me again, all the lakes and rivers and mountains—and the green country of childhood lay behind.

Riding into the Crowsnest mountains with
your first beard itching and a
hundred hungry guys fanning out thru
the shabby whistlestops for handouts and
not even a sandwich for two hundred miles
only the high mountains and knowing
what it's like to be not quite a child
any more and listening to the tough men
talk of women and talk of the way things are
in 1937—

❧ Canadian poet Al Purdy won a broad readership and a Governor General's Award with his collection *The Cariboo Horses* in 1965. The long lines and colloquial style that he used in many of his collections influenced the generation of Canadian poets that came after him. Some of his strongest poems emerged from his travels across Canada, such as those in *North of Summer: Poems from Baffin Island* (1967). "The Iron Road" is from *No Other Country*, a memoir published in 1977. Purdy's introduction to his memoir ends with the sentence "This is the map of my country, the cartography of myself." (*Born Wooler, Ontario 1918; died 2000*)

RESPONDING

Meaning

1. This memoir includes vivid details about the Great Depression era, but it is also very much about a personal journey. Quote lines that reveal Purdy's personal thoughts, feelings, and preoccupations.

2. Reread the closing paragraphs starting with "I was homesick" and ending with "...lay behind." What does Purdy mean when he says, "...the green country of childhood lay behind."

Form and Style

3. a) This memoir begins and ends with lines of poetry. Why do you think Purdy chose to frame his story in this way?
   b) Discuss why Purdy breaks the poetic narrative exactly where he does to embed his own story.

4. Purdy's style is very poetic. Identify examples of *personification*, *simile*, *alliteration*, and *onomatopoeia*. Comment on the effectiveness of these poetic devices in helping the reader empathize with the speaker.

Exploring Context

5. In small groups, research images of the Great Depression that occurred during the 1930s across North America. Mount a collection entitled "Visions of the Depression." How do these images help you understand the experiences Purdy describes in his memoir? Where possible, match photos to experiences in the memoir.

Creative Extension

6. Choose a segment of this memoir and present a readers' theatre interpretation. Alternatively, create a multimedia production incorporating visuals and audio recordings of other voices from the Depression. Comment on how the techniques you chose convey the mood and tone of Purdy's memoir.

7. Write about your own "initiatory" or "coming of age" journey. Consider the time frame, mode of transportation, challenges that might arise, and how the central character (yourself or a fictional character) changes. Use Purdy's memoir as a model or choose a different genre. You could write your piece as a short documentary (or fictional) film script, for example.

Deaf Music

❧ Margaret Hollingsworth

Every Saturday morning my mother strapped me into the canvas harness that housed my hearing aid. I was eight and didn't need her help, but she wanted to make sure it was secure; after all, sound was a priority in a music lesson. On weekdays I managed the buckles myself. My mother knew I hated the hearing aid, and she tried to bring me around by giving it a name—we called it Muriel. At home I was allowed to abandon it, but when it came to music there were different expectations.

My deafness was diagnosed when I was seven. Prior to this, in my Infants School, they were aware that I had speech problems (I was born with a cleft in my soft palate), but they dismissed them as something I'd eventually grow out of. Teachers paid special attention to me, and I learned to read and write along with the rest. I was loved and protected. The other children accepted me and never questioned my preference for non-verbal communication. Maybe the teachers told the kids to be kind to me; if they did I'm glad I didn't know.

When I moved up to Junior School at seven everything changed. I was supplied with the hearing aid, a rather crude model that was issued free on the British National Health Service. Everyone thought I would be delighted, but the reverse was true. Sound was a novelty, but nothing I needed. Suddenly I was different. Not special. Different. In the first week that Muriel arrived in my life, I shook uncontrollably; my palms were so sweaty my pencil seemed to be paddling and my writing slipped all over the page. I hated the crude noises that blasted into my ears. The whistling kettle, our neighbour's motorbike, even the wind, became enemies; people's voices were intrusive, unexpected, the sounds I heard often carried no meaning. When more than one person spoke at once, I ducked. The only way I could remain in control was by keeping my finger on the off switch. But there was no way of hiding the clumsy box that was strapped to my chest. It measured about three inches by four and it was almost an inch thick. The twin pink wires leading from the protruding pink receivers in my ears screamed "look at me." If I wore the amplifier under my gym slip, the fabric rubbed against the microphone, giving a raw, scratchy fore-ground to the jumble of sounds I was supposed to decipher. If I wore the harness over my clothes I was an immediate target of derision, the butt of the class wits, or of other kids who would run up as if to embrace me, then veer away at the last minute and scream into the microphone so that my head leapt with pain. The world of sound was jagged and spiky. Cruel.

I suffered the contraption for a week, and after that I dodged into the local park on my way to school, tore it off, and flung it into my school bag. The relief was immediate: my world flattened out and I was at its centre again. I sat at the back of the class, copied from the board and from the exercise book of the girl sitting next to me and kept my eyes firmly fixed on the teacher's face. Muriel's absence went unremarked since I worked at making myself invisible to the class of forty children. I maintained average marks and I cultivated a dreamy, abstracted air to account for my failure to answer questions.

The fact that I had no friends also went unnoticed. It didn't bother me—I was happy in my safe, predictable world, free of taunts. At home I killed Muriel off, which meant that I had to forgo the sound on our rented TV, but this was a small sacrifice. I devoured books, made models, and I had a sympathetic relationship with my ginger cat, Bill, who under-stood everything I said. My mother never drew attention to my deafness or my cleft palate. We sat together at night in the big armchair in front of the TV, and she encouraged me to put my ear against her breastbone so I could hear the vibrations of her voice; secure in the O of her arms, I joked and gossiped and teased, chattering non-stop. I hear her voice as soft and mellifluous, not hesitant and accented with northern vowel sounds like the voice that Muriel transmitted. This was all the proof I needed that Muriel was a distorter of the truth.

I was an only child (my father was never in the picture), and though she never put it into words, I knew my mother wanted to believe she had a normal child, and I usually did my best to back her up. When we went shopping, Muriel remained at home. We held hands and communicated by squeezes so no one ever had to hear me speak; we giggled a lot and I acted as if I were following the conversation when she stopped to chat with neighbours. It was a game. When we got home we always cooked a pan of french fries together. On the rare occasions when I went on an errand alone, she gave me a note which I handed to the shopkeeper, head bowed, pretending to be shy.

The music lesson was something new. My grandmother in Sheffield had died and left me her piano. All my parents' relatives lived "up north," and I had never met any of them. We wrote to them regularly, and they sent me gifts at Christmas and birthdays. I don't know if they were aware of my speech and hearing problems. One Christmas my Auntie Mary sent me a music box. I could feel the sound with my fingertips as I watched the ballerina whirl in front of her mirror and I longed to know the tune she danced to. When I set the box down and put my temple to the surface of the table I could almost make out the melody, though the top notes were missing. I wound it up so often it broke. I think this convinced my mother I was musical. The piano had been sitting unused in the front room for a year when she announced that I would be going to Miss Beamish's for a weekly half-hour lesson and I'd better be good at it, because we'd be going without the Sunday roast in order to pay for it.

Miss Beamish lived in a street of Victorian mansions. I refused to let my mother accompany me to my first lesson, and I stood outside the house for ages, wondering whether to go in. Between the sidewalk and the road was a wide flower bed, thick with rhododendron bushes. These provided the ideal cover for unhitching Muriel. She slid into my music case and I trotted up the wide staircase and planted my thumb on the doorbell, hoping it was working.

I don't think I had any expectations except that this would be a one-shot deal. I could certainly never have dreamed up Violet Beamish. She was a garage mechanic by day and a music teacher by night and at weekends. She had thick, pebbled glasses, grey wispy hair cut like a man's and her knuckles were ingrained with black oil. Her voice boomed and she spoke slowly so I felt immediately secure. She lived with her mother in one of the largest houses on the street. The old lady was always lost somewhere on the upper floors, I imagined her like Mrs. Rochester in the novel I was reading.

I followed Miss Beamish into an enormous room which she described as the music room. It was perfectly preserved from the mid-Victorian period, a crowded jungle of heavy furniture and marble tables with huge mirrors and gilt legs. There were mahogany shelves thick with a tantalizing collection of Victorian bric-a-brac. There were glass domes sheltering dried flowers and stuffed birds, Chinese vases full of peacock feathers, statues of Greek gods, an ivory chess set, and a gramophone with a huge bell big enough to house my head.

Reluctantly, I turned my back on this treasure house, and seated myself next to Miss Beamish on a bench at one of the two upright pianos which nestled between stacks of music. She placed my hands on the keys and indicated that I should watch and imitate. Then she hid her hands and I repeated the exercise. After several tries I managed a single octave scale. She seemed pleased. Jamming my knees under the keyboard augmented the sound; it passed through my thighs and up into my tummy. I was excited. This was something I could actually do.

Miss Beamish never asked me to repeat what I said, and never mentioned my deafness (I convinced myself she hadn't noticed). I was treated exactly the same as all her pupils. At the end of each lesson there was always a reward, a slice of toast, browned in front of the two-bar electric heater and slathered with butter. Sometimes she was late for the lesson and I worked my way round the magic room, studying the paintings of women in plumed hats and the foxed photographs of ancient clerics until she arrived straight from work, puffing like a bellows, still clad in her grimy overalls.

I practised on the piano for hours, working at being so proficient that I wouldn't need verbal correction. By the end of the year I had leapt ahead to Intermediate Level. At the start of each lesson Miss Beamish played the piece I was learning twice. I concentrated, watching, listening, and physically absorbing the rhythm of the music through the frame of the piano. I put all my senses into top gear, learning to trust them absolutely, and experienced my first taste of complete understanding, complete communion with someone who was not my mother. When I played particularly well, she hugged me and I buried my nose in her skin which smelt of Lily of the Valley perfume and motor oil. I felt I was betraying the intimacy I had with my mother, but I couldn't help it. I looked forward to my lessons with a passion that made me pray for the week to dissolve and for it to be forever Saturday.

I took my music exams and passed Grade Four and Five with distinction. I was not doing so well at school. My marks had fallen, and even though my lip-reading had improved, I was finding it harder to keep up. Sometimes I stayed away altogether, wandering the streets until home time. Once, the boy in the seat across the aisle flicked a folded note onto my desk. I opened it and read the word MORON printed in bold capitals. That night I locked myself in with the piano and pounded the keys till the pads on my fingertips hurt. I couldn't confide in my mother; I was terrified she would be ashamed of me, love me less, or worse still, leave me. I dared her to talk to my schoolteachers when she fussed over my school reports. The reports repeated the same refrain: Margaret could do better; Margaret must learn to pay attention.

At the beginning of the third year of music lessons, Miss Beamish came across Muriel as she rifled through my music bag for a lost sheet of manuscript paper. I had grown, but the hearing aid still looked mountainous. The two pink receivers dangled on their twin pink wires like fallen climbers as Miss Beamish held up the harness. I refused to look at her face but she grabbed my chin and waited till I had plugged Muriel in and turned up the volume to squealing point. "Do you wear this thing when you're practising?" I shook my head. "Do you realize how much time you have wasted? How far we could have progressed?" I shook my head again.

She put the lid of the piano down. "What is your mother thinking of?" I wanted to explain that my mother didn't know that I never wore my hearing aid, that Muriel distorted the sound, made it tinny, took away the purity I heard inside my head, the true sound, the sound that Beethoven must have heard (I had just discovered that he was deaf). Far from making me love him, I began to resent him bitterly. He was a handicapped cretin, all the world knew it was true, no matter how brilliant his music was. I opened my mouth to explain, but Miss Beamish clamped her hand over my lips. "It's time we stopped playing games, Margaret. Let's face it, you're deaf as that doorpost and I've heard parrots speak more clearly. Teaching you demands so much energy and you refuse to help yourself. You're draining me. It's all effort! You need to be shaken up. Do you want to spend the rest of your life on the sidelines?"

I was mortified—hadn't I proved to her that I wasn't on the sidelines? I was her star pupil. How could she think I was a parrot? I tore the receivers out of my ears, threw Muriel into my case, abandoned my music books, and rushed out of her house.

The next week I didn't go to my lesson, and I didn't touch the piano. The following Saturday I told my mother I was needed to help with a nature study project at school. We had no phone, so Miss Beamish didn't contact us. The Sunday roast was reinstated, but by the third week the need for my lesson was so great that it overtook my humiliation. I had no particular plan but I didn't bother to strap on the harness. My mother made no comment as she handed me my music case.

It was snowing, and I liked the feel of my silent footsteps as I made my way to Miss Beamish's house. The silence of snow is different from other silences; there are so many kinds and qualities of silence, the deaf know them intimately.

I rang the front doorbell as usual, but no one came. There was no note to say the bell was out of order, so I pushed on the door and went inside. The wide black-and-white-tiled entry hall was empty. I could see the music room through the double glass doors with their pink bevelled borders. The pictures and the ornaments were still in place, the electric heater was on. A light smell of motor oil hung on the air. I concentrated my attention on the soles of my feet, trying to detect whether Miss Beamish had taken another pupil in my place but there were no vibrations. I went in. The room was empty. Should I call her? I hesitated to shout her name, "Miss Beamish . . ." I couldn't get my tongue around a *sh* or an *s* sound, so I often substituted words that didn't contain those letters. If this was too hard I kept quiet.

I sat at the piano nearest the heater. My music was piled at one end, neatly separated from the rest of the scores. I picked up the top book. It was a volume of Chopin; I opened it randomly and started to play. The instrument responded immediately; my fingers were sure and confident, and I could feel the music spraying through my hands into my forearms, my elbows, my neck, my whole body, unreeling, unwinding, carrying me into a place I had missed so badly it made me dizzy. I was playing for Miss Beamish, the music was not forgiveness, not a gift, but an ecstatic "up yours."

Suddenly I sensed that someone was in the room. I looked up, expecting to see her standing in the doorway, her face all wrinkly and smiling, but the person I saw was a diminutive old woman, her thin grey hair plaited on top of her head, her body lost in a large flowered apron. This must be Miss Beamish's mother, Mrs. Rochester from upstairs. I saw her mouth moving, but couldn't make out any sound and her lips were tight as wires and impossible to read.

"I don't get you." A rare admission.

She came in and seemed to be repeating what she had just said, enlarging on it, shunting words at me. I watched her mouth and her filmy eyes, trying to concentrate, trying not to panic. No vestige of meaning filtered through.

"Weren't you told? I'm deaf like that door." It was the first time I'd ever admitted it aloud. Deaf was a word that was too close to death.

Her body was taut and erect, her hands clamped to her sides; her expression a blank, there were no clues.

She moved to the piano and picked up the red pen Miss Beamish used for correcting theory. She scrawled across my Chopin étude: Violet is gone.

I stared at her. She made a motion with her hands, bringing them together to make an implosion of air. What did it mean? Still, her face gave nothing away. Pushing her aside, I darted out of the house into the snow which seemed to be falling more erratically. It was suddenly chill. I realized I'd left my music behind, together with my coat and my bag containing Muriel. I couldn't go back. I was responsible for Miss Beamish's disappearance.

My mother showed me the death notice in the local paper. Violet Beamish had been trapped under a van when a jack collapsed. It was an accident.

The following day I wrote a note to my form mistress excusing myself from further classes on account of my deafness. I signed it with my mother's name. She hauled me into the staff room and rained questions on me, telling me (I think), that she had been ready to refer me to the local asylum for assessment. (I later found out that a good many deaf children have grown up in mental institutions.) Why, she demanded, had the staff not been informed of my handicap—I could have been put in a special class. I shook my head, and feigned ignorance though I wanted to bash her face in. There was no way to explain how my skin contracted at the words handicap and impediment or any substitute word that sweetened the pill, or how I cringed at unrequested kindness. My mother was the only one who understood.

Soon after, I failed the Eleven Plus exam which was a watershed in every child's life in Britain at that time (a pass opened up the possibility of higher education). I changed schools, and my mother found the money for a commercial hearing aid, much daintier than Muriel. It was easily concealed in my new training bra and I wore it more often, and gradually came to rely on it. Life began to change. The new school arranged for me to see another speech therapist. After weeks of no progress my enunciation improved, and, to my chagrin, my school reports called me plucky.

The next year I played centre in the netball team, and joined the stamp club. I even sheltered a secret ambition to be an actress. I made no protest when my mother sold the piano.

I left school at sixteen and found a job as a filing clerk in a large multinational corporation. I handed most of my weekly pay packet over to my mother, but I still managed to fund the course of intensive speech therapy that was required to exorcise my glottal *S*'s and *Sh*'s. The following year I had an operation: the hearing in one ear was restored, and I threw away my hearing aid for good.

I finally diffused the problem of my residual speech impediment by immigrating to Canada where it went unnoticed since voices are more nasal. I have travelled a long way since Miss Beamish died. My life has opened up immeasurably, but I still find it difficult to listen to Beethoven. In my most intimate moments I have yet to obtain the oneness I felt in those music lessons, and I have never been able to find the quality of inner stillness I knew when I wasn't wearing Muriel. Occasionally, when I come close, I catch a whiff of lily of the valley and motor oil.

Born in England, playwright Margaret Hollingsworth has lived in Canada since the 1960s. The book *Willful Acts* (1985) is an updated collection of her best-known plays, including *War Babies*, which was nominated for a Governor General's Award. "Deaf Music" appeared in the anthology *Going Some Place: Creative Non-fiction across the Prairies* (2000), edited by Lynne Van Luven. *(Born Sheffield, England 1940)*

RESPONDING

Meaning

1. Select at least two sections in this memoir where Hollingsworth reflects on the contrast between sound and "silence." Comment on the significance of these sections in the memoir. How do they enhance our insight into the world of people with hearing disabilities?

2. When Hollingsworth says, "I felt I was betraying the intimacy I had with my mother, but I couldn't help it," she suggests that the central issue is not "deafness" but acceptance and fulfilled human relationships. Find at least two other quotations from "Deaf Music" to support this interpretation and relate them to your own experience.

Form and Style

3. This selection represents a journey that begins with the statement, "Sound was a novelty, but nothing I needed" and ends with, "I threw away my hearing aid for good." Outline the key events in this journey and note how Margaret changes at each point.

4. a) The Canadian writer George Woodcock wrote: "[There are] four elements of auto-biography, the elements that distinguish it within the broader field of narrative unity, and mark it off, though never very decisively, from fiction. These elements are memory, documentation, reflection, and confession." Would you agree with this statement? Discuss to what extent Hollingsworth's memoir fits these criteria.

   b) "Deaf Music" appeared in a collection of "creative non-fiction." In small groups, discuss what you think the major characteristics of creative non-fiction are. How is "Deaf Music" a piece of creative non-fiction?

Exploring Context

5. Although we would not think to do so today, there was a time when it was thought best to "institutionalize" all people with "special needs." Margaret Hollingsworth used a number of coping strategies that kept her from institutionalization. Identify these strategies and comment on whether you or someone you know has used them, even though you do not have a hearing disability.

Creative Extension

6. Using your response to question 3 above, set this memoir to music. Select music that reflects each stage in Margaret's journey and record it on audiotape or CD. Consider including quotations from the memoir at particular points or use your own words to introduce sections.

7. Reflect on an activity that you participated in as a child or continue to participate in today. Write an autobiographical essay describing what the activity means to you. Use specific details and *diction* to develop a lively narrative.

Media

Marshall McLuhan on media:

When you talk back to ads, they become your servants. Since you cannot survive the effects of media if you huddle or hide, you must rush out and kick them in the guts—give them what for—right in the midriff.... The road to understanding media effects begins with arrogant superiority.

These are the hapless victims of all advertising, these people who think that merely by subjecting themselves to it without taking an interest in it they can be immune. The idea of immunity from environments and environments created by media... is a cherished illusion....

Advertising and Marketing: It's Not Always a Product

When we think of advertising and marketing, we often assume that they are used to sell us products. Advertisers and marketers have a much larger role in our society, being often called upon to promote abstract concepts, ideas, information, places, corporate and public images, and even social norms. The following pieces feature media texts designed to serve purposes beyond the sale of a tangible product.

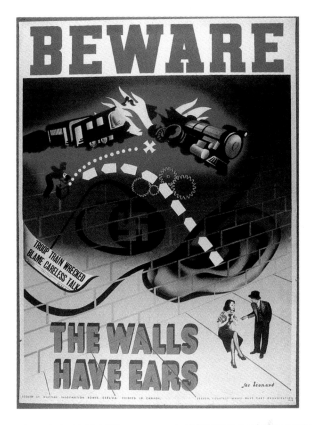

When fires in Mexico destroyed 490,000 acres of forest and 870,000 acres of grassland, Ford Motor Company, our dealers, and the government of Mexico joined together to plant more than 3 million trees in an effort to bring the ecosystem back into balance.

Land Lover Karen Arguello is part of our public affairs team. She put Ford and the Mexican government in the woods together.

Ford Motor Company

The most easterly point in North America, Cape Spear N

For your free travel guide or to make reservations,

storic Site.

Of all the sunrises in North America, this is the first. The yawn and stretch of a new day.

At the edge of the western world, there's a place where the day dawns first.

Here, you can see the oldest lighthouse in Newfoundland and Labrador live life on the edge, as it has for 160 years. In the far east of the western world.

NEWFOUNDLAND & LABRADOR
CANADA

www.gov.nf.ca/tourism/

...leen at **1-800-563-NFLD**

Government of Canada   Gouvernement du Canada

ILLEGAL and OFFENSIVE CONTENT on the INTERNET

THE CANADIAN STRATEGY TO PROMOTE SAFE, WISE AND RESPONSIBLE INTERNET USE: A SUMMARY

www.connect.gc.ca/cyberwise

Canada

More than one in two Canadians use the Internet

The Internet is a powerful tool. Used wisely it can turn a home, sc or library into a place of unlimited information, communication — family fun.

The Government of Canada aims to make Canada the most connected country in the world — and it is succeeding. On March 30, 1999, Canada became the first country in the world to connect all of its schools and public libraries to the Internet. By early 2001, more than one in two Canadians over the age of 12 were using the Internet.

Children and teens are drawn to this exciting medium, and pare appreciate the benefits that their children can receive from it. M families, however, are concerned about the risks children face or

Tackling illegal and offensive content on the Internet

Content on the Internet can violate Canada's laws. For example, child pornography and hate propaganda that are **illegal** on the are also illegal on the Internet — and Canada's law enforcemen community works hard to uphold our laws in cyberspace.

Some Internet content, however, is legal — but **offensive** to so people. Like many box office movies, Web sites can contain sexua explicit material and graphic violence. Other sites can offend a fa values, religion or culture.

Balancing freedom of expression with protecting our childre

Canadian families want to protect their children from offensive content, but opinions and values can and do vary. Canada must balance protection with freedom of expression — a right which Canadians hold dear.

There is no single solution. That's why the Government of Canad developed a five-point plan to give Canadians the comprehensive support they need.

For the complete Government of Canada strategy, go to:
www.connect.gc.ca/cyberwise

WHAT DO CANADIAN PARENTS SAY?

- Two in three parents say education is the biggest benefit of children's Internet use.
- Half say inappropriate content is their biggest concern.
- More than one in five say their children have come across se explicit material, that they are aware of.

What else do they say?
View the study *Canada's Children in a Wired World* at:
www.connect.gc.ca/cyberwise

CANADA'S FIVE-POINT PLAN

Using the Internet safely...wisely...responsibly...

1. GIVE CANADIANS THE TOOLS THEY NEED

In Canada today, knowledge is power. One of the Government of Canada's top priorities is to **educate** Canadians about illegal and offensive content on the Internet, and to **empower** Canadians to take action in their homes.

Canadian parents need a variety of options — everything from house rules for Internet use, to Web site labelling, to filters that limit access to undesirable sites. No one tool will suit all families, so the Government of Canada encourages, supports and funds many initiatives.

Looking for help?

Parents, community leaders, and educators can consult the following sources:

- Contact the Media Awareness Network (MNet) for how-to information on finding great children's sites, doing effective on-line searches, tracking where children go while on-line and protecting children from on-line predators (**www.media-awareness.ca**).

- Check out MNet's Web Awareness: Knowing the Issues (**www.webawareness.org**) for practical information and hands-on activities to give children "cyber smarts."

> ### RULES THAT WORK
>
> MNet's Online Rules can be posted beside your computer:
>
> √ When using the Internet, I will always use a pretend name or nickname that doesn't reveal anything about me.
>
> √ I will not open e-mail, files, links, pictures or games from people that I don't know or trust.
>
> √ I will not arrange to meet a friend I have made on the Internet unless one of my parents has been informed and will be present...
>
> Visit their site to get them all!
> **www.media-awareness.ca**

- The Internet safety portal, established by the Canadian Association of Internet Providers, provides information about hate propaganda, the use of the Internet to lure children, and consumer issues (**www.caip.ca**).

- Industry Canada's SchoolNet National Advisory Board has several brochures available to help teachers out in the classroom (**www.schoolnet.ca/snab/brochure**).

- Librarians can get information on special programs through MNet (see the address above), or the Canadian Library Association (**www.cla.ca**).

- Missing is a computer game, video and guide that teaches children how to surf safely and warns about child predators. It is available in 10 000 schools and libraries (**www.livewwwires.com**).

Looking for information on filters or Internet content labelling?

Industry Canada's *Strategis* Web site has a wealth of information on Internet-related topics: **strategis.gc.ca/internet**

2. WORK WITH SAFETY-MINDED SERVICE PROVIDERS

Since Internet service providers (ISPs) connect users to the Internet, they can perform an important service in dealing with illegal and offensive content on the Internet.

Today, the government works closely with the Canadian Association of Internet Providers (CAIP) and individual ISPs to encourage good business practices throughout the ISP industry. CAIP's Code of Conduct states that members will cooperate with law enforcement officials and adhere to Canada's laws.

For CAIP's Code of Conduct, go to: **www.caip.ca/issueset.htm**

IS YOUR ISP SAFETY-MINDED?

Your ISP can be your best safety guide. Ask safety questions!

- Does the company adhere to a code of conduct?
- Does it offer family-friendly services such as a "kid zone" or child-friendly search engine?
- Does it make Internet filters, or information about them, available to customers?
- What does the provider do if you make a complaint about something you find on the Internet?

What more can you ask? Go to: **www.connect.gc.ca/cyberwise**

3. ENFORCE THE LAW IN CYBERSPACE

In Canada, anything illegal off-line is illegal on-line. Canada's laws apply in cyberspace — but the law must keep pace with illegal uses of new technology. Canada plans to amend the *Criminal Code* to better deal with those who use the Internet to lure children.

Eliminating child pornography is a key concern for Canadians. RCMP computer crime investigators are located in all major centres in Canada and the police force works closely with Internet service providers. New Internet training for police officers focusses on the sexual exploitation of children, and includes investigative techniques for search and seizure of illegal computer data.

The fight against child pornography and hate propaganda cuts across the law enforcement community. The Criminal Intelligence Service of Canada coordinates national and international forces to combat child pornography and the victimization of children on and off the Internet.

4. INVESTIGATE HOTLINES

Today, Canadian parents tend not to complain about offensive ma even when they want to. Why? They don't know who to call.

In many countries, hotline investigators act as crime stoppers, handling complaints and contacting service providers and police when necessary. In Canada, government and the pr sector are examining the costs and benefits of establishing hotline to report illegal content on the Internet. More than of Canadian parents think setting up such a hotline would very effective.

5. WORK TOWARD GLOBAL ANSWERS

Canada cannot tackle illegal and offensive content on the Internet working alone. Governments, law enforcemen officers and industry must find solutions that transcend national boundaries.

Sharing expertise

- CAIP is sharing information with European service providers, and working with other countries to devise international solutions.

- Canada hosts global summits, conducts international studies and is helping draft the Council of Europe's convention on cybercrime.

Law enforcement across borders

- Canadian investigators work with experts from 30 countries in the Interpol Specialist Group on Crimes Against Children.

- To enhance cooperation among G-8 countries working togeth to share information on Internet-based investigations, 24-hour law enforcement points of contact have been established.

By working together, Canadians are creating a healthy environment to promote safe, wise and responsible Internet use.

Cat. No. C2-548/2001
ISBN 0-662-65442-0
53325B

For a copy
complete s
call (613) 947

20% recycled material

RESPONDING

Meaning

1. For each of the five previous media texts, identify what you perceive to be the intended audience and purpose (e.g., to sell, to persuade, to inform, etc.). Compare your answers with a partner and discuss any differences in opinion.

2. Each of the five selections focuses on an image or concept as a controlling idea. What is the central idea in each text? In what way(s) are these ideas different from what we find in the majority of advertisements and marketing texts we encounter?

Form and Style

3. *Propaganda* is defined as texts aimed at "persuading people to support a particular cause (usually political, social, or religious)." All of the previous texts include some elements of propaganda. What specific features of the writing and visual texts persuade the viewer of a particular point of view? Support your answers.

4. a) Visual elements are often designed to set a mood or tone for the written text. For each selection, determine what mood the creators were trying to evoke in the viewer? What visual elements did they use to set this mood?

   b) How does the form of the text (e.g. poster, print advertisement, brochure) change the way in which visual elements are used?

Exploring Context

5. Increasingly, corporations, non-profit organizations, and governments are using advertising and marketing to promote images and ideas. This "advocacy advertising" is usually less direct than product-selling advertising. Using a variety of media as sources, create a short presentation in which you provide examples of some of the ways organizations are using advertising and marketing to promote ideas. Comment on the effectiveness of the media texts you present.

Creative Extension

6. Choose a cause or social goal you feel strongly about, such as promoting recycling, preventing drinking and driving, promoting awareness of the hazards of smoking or drug use, good health, help for homeless people, child labour, etc. Focus on a central idea and image, choose a form (e.g., poster, pamphlet, print ad, television commercial story-board, etc.), and design a media text to powerfully present your vision and ideas. Develop your piece on computer if possible. Pay attention to particular techniques such as the size of visuals, headings and other type, perspective, etc.

7. Organize a panel discussion or debate in which you discuss the ethics of using persuasive techniques and media texts to promote images and particular points of view. Should corporations, non-profit groups, and governments be required to state explicitly the purpose of their advertisements and marketing tools?

Great Newspaper Ads

ଓ Carey Toane

Should newspapers be treated differently from any other medium? Is there a distinct creative process involved? We asked four 2000 gold Extra winners to share their secrets on award-winning newspaper creative.

TREVOR MCCONNELL
President, Christopher Finn
Productions, Calgary

Years working with newspaper creative: 22
Gold Extra for: "Fingers" (a PJ DDB ad that also won the Best of Show Award)
Marketer: Vancouver Aquarium

Concept: The campaign was pretty straightforward as a marketing exercise. The approach that the guys took was pretty typical, certainly of PJ, but I think of all good creative teams—to look for the most curious, the most interesting, the most startling ways of representing the subject. In the case of the crocodiles, these things are scary! They could eat you! So that was pretty hard to resist.
Pros of newspaper as a medium: It's a classic medium. If you can make it there, you can make it anywhere, so to do a great newspaper ad is a worthy

goal for any creative. I always really appreciate a great newspaper ad and I think most veteran creative people do. It's a great challenge.
Cons of newspaper as a medium: Your images have to be clear and sim-ple, especially if you're working in black and white, and with very read-able body copy. A newspaper will destroy 50% of whatever you put in. Also, it is so ephemeral. It's here in today's paper and then it's gone again. It often gets used for packing around people's dishes.
Cardinal rules of newspaper creative: Keep it simple, keep it stripped down, really look at the visual impact and always think of the newspaper ad in context. It's a good idea to take a newspaper ad, even in the comp [composition] stage, and just lay it in the paper and pay attention to the worst-case scenario. Always think of it as part of the page, part of the medium.

JACK NEARY
President and Chief Creative Officer, BBDO Canada, Toronto

Years working with newspaper creative: 21
Gold Extra for: "Stop Sign"
Marketer: DaimlerChrysler Canada for Jeep

Concept: It was a parking meter sticking out of the side of a mountain cliff, the implication being that Jeeps can go there and that's where they would park. That ad nicely captured, in one visual, without any words at all, the essence of the Jeep brand.
Pros of newspaper as a medium: Readers read, which is a more intellectually engaged activity than, say, watching television, which kind of washes over you. So you generally get a slightly more intelligent audience, and that allows you to be more sophisticated, conceptually. Also, because the production turnaround is a lot shorter than broadcast, you can be very topical. But ultimately, what I like about newspapers is the intimacy, the size of the page, the involvement of the reader. Those are all wonderful characteristics that your ad can take advantage of.
Cons of newspaper as a medium: I have to be careful here because one of my clients is the *Globe and Mail*.
Cardinal rules of newspaper creative: Respect the readers' intelligence. Don't

talk down to them. Too much advertising, historically, has taken this paternalistic view that we're the company and we know what's right for you. Buy this thing now. People don't like to be talked to that way in their personal lives, why would they want advertisers to talk to them like that? They're pretty bright; they can usually fill things in. You don't have to hammer them over the head. You can be subtle.

LISA FRANCILIA
Co-creative Director, Bryant Fulton & Shee Advertising, Vancouver

Years working with newspaper creative: 7
Gold Extra for: "Minivan"
Marketer: Rocky Mountaineer Railtours

Concept: The title is, "no one ever wrote a folk song about a minivan." We had never seen the Rockies the way we had when we went on the train ride. We wanted colour wherever we could, because that also helps, but we didn't want to do four-colour because that seems to blend in to the Travel section. We were trying to do something that captured what the train ride was really all about, what we had experienced, and the nostalgia with the sepia tones.

Pros of newspaper as a medium:
Everybody looks at a newspaper. Also, whereas outdoor ads should be simple, newspaper allows for a little bit more (detail). It's flexible. Sometimes you can do something really creative by putting something you wouldn't expect in the Food section, for example.

Cons of newspaper as a medium:
The reproduction quality is pretty bad in most newspapers, and we fight that all the time. It doesn't matter how amazing your photograph can be, it's kind of a gamble.

Cardinal rules of newspaper creative:
Media is really key for newspaper. I like to work closely with our media department to make sure that they're putting it in the right section, they're putting it on the right side of the page. All those little things really help. Looking at your competitors, sometimes what can really kill you is if you end up sandwiched next to something. Of course, you can't always control that, but it helps if you know what's going to be in your area, what section you're going to be in.

IAN GRAIS
Partner and Co-creative Director,
Rethink Communications,
Vancouver

Years working on newspaper creative: 10
Gold Extra for: "Proctologist"
Marketer: Stockhouse Media

Concept: Very early on we started looking at these stock certificates and realized that they were this lost art. They're beautiful pieces of artwork that are made not to be reproduced, like currency, so there are very detailed drawings on them. It was something that, symbolically, was easily recognizable by people, and they were completely relevant to the client, which is a stock information provider. Basically, they were a great form for turning into ads. They were a nice way to include a lot of information and have it all delivered in one punch.

Pros of newspaper as a medium:
A larger percentage of the population reads the newspaper than does specifically Canadian magazines, so it's a better way to reach people. There are also a lot of opportunities with newspapers because they have set sections, set formats. A lot of advertisers use that to their advantage. For example, we can run in the middle of the stock pages, or in the Lifestyle section, so that's an option that you have with newspapers, to play with positioning.

Cons of newspaper as a medium:
Whatever you do, it has to print well. With Stockhouse, we had a huge challenge in getting those certificates to print. When we got the artwork back, we collected papers from across the country to see the comparisons, and it

was shocking. A green ad in Vancouver was purple in Winnipeg and brown in Toronto.

Cardinal rules of newspaper creative: Good communication is good communication no matter what medium it's in. Having said that, too many advertisers try and cram too much information into the ads so that the impact, the visual nature of it, is lost. You still have to present something that's going to stop people. That's got to be the first priority of any advertisement, and newspaper is no exception.

ꝋ Carey Toane is a freelance writer based in Toronto. This report, "Great Newspaper Ads," appeared in 2001 in *Marketing* magazine. The Extra Awards are presented each year to the best Canadian newspaper ads in a variety of different categories by the Canadian Newspaper Association.

RESPONDING

Meaning

1. Each of the CDs (Creative Directors) interviewed in this article gives an opinion on the pros and cons of newspaper advertising. Prepare a chart that summarizes all the positive and negative aspects of newspaper advertising.

2. The introduction to the interview asks, "Should newspapers be treated differently from any other medium?" and "Is there a distinct creative process involved?" After reading the responses from the interviewees, what is your response to these questions?

Form and Style

3. This article was originally written for a trade journal for advertising professionals. What stylistic features has the writer used to make the article quick and easy to read? Why would the writer have structured the article this way?

4. Each of the Creative Directors interviewed outlines what he or she feels are the cardinal rules of being creative in newspaper advertising. What are the "rules" for creative newspaper advertising? Reflecting on newspaper advertisements that you have found interesting or appealing, what "rules" would you add to the list, as a consumer?

Exploring Context

5. Newspapers have changed considerably in the past thirty years, specifically in response to other media, such as television and the Internet. Using a recent copy of a newspaper as a resource, compare and contrast the advertising and visual techniques of the newspaper with those in other media forms such as magazines and the Internet. In what ways have other media forms influenced newspaper advertising? In what ways have newspaper advertisements remained unique?

Creative Extension

6. Using the "Cardinal rules of newspaper creative" as outlined in the article as a guide, create a newspaper advertisement promoting your school. Before you create your advertisement, look at several examples of ads in your local newspaper. Ensure that your advertisement meets the design requirements in terms of size and shape. Create your ad on computer if possible.

7. Research the most recent winners of the Extra awards, which are given each year by the Canadian Newspaper Association. Choose one of the winners and prepare a critical analysis of the ad either in writing or as a short presentation. What made this ad particularly effective? Keep the rules of effective newspaper advertising in mind as you prepare your analysis.

Atanarjuat: The Fast Runner

ℭ Paul Apak, Norman Cohn, Zacharias Kunuk,
Hervé Paniaq, Pauloosie Qulitalik

Film Synopsis: Evil in the form of an unknown shaman divides a small community of nomadic Inuit, upsetting its balance and spirit.

Twenty years pass. Two brothers emerge to challenge the evil order: Amajuat, the Strong One, and Atanarjuat, the Fast Runner. Atanarjuat wins the hand of the lovely Atuat away from the boastful son of the camp leader, Oki, who vows to get even. Oki ambushes the brothers in their sleep, killing Amajuat, as Atanarjuat miraculously escapes over the spring sea ice.

Director's Statement: "*Atanarjuat* is a universal story with emotions people all over the world can understand. It is also totally Inuit: a story we all heard as children, told and acted by Inuit. We show how Inuit lived hundreds of years ago and what their problems were, starting with their marriage problems. What happens when a woman is promised to one man but breaks a taboo and marries another? We show how our ancestors dressed, how they handled their dog teams, how they argued and laughed and went through hard times—how they confronted evil and fought back. They had to get along, to work things out no matter what. This is the story we are passing on to others, just like it was passed on to us."

CHARACTERS

Atanarjuat, 18—Lead male. A lean, fine-featured young man with intelligent dreamy eyes. He has the carefree, athletic gracefulness of someone for whom everything comes almost too easily. He is a confident hunter, well-dressed, and well-fed.

Amajuat, 20—Lead male. A powerful, physical young man—a force of nature. He is neither mean-spirited nor kind. Like his brother Atanarjuat, he is a confident hunter, well-dressed, and well-fed.

Atuat, 18—Lead female. A beautiful young woman, gentle, intelligent, and loving. She falls in love with Atanarjuat and defies Sauri's bidding to marry Oki.

Puja, 17—Friend of Atuat, sister of Oki. A lively, flirtatious young woman, always aware of male eyes on her. She's always ready to play one man against the other.

Panikpak, 40–60—She is an elegant, intelligent woman with a young girl's lively face. She exudes energy and at the same time gives an immediate sense of calmness and strength. She possesses spirit powers.

Qulitalik, 35—Panikpak's brother and a strong, handsome-featured man with piercing eyes. A shaman.

Sauri, 20–40—When young, he has a submissive manner concealing a bitter resentment of his powerful father, the murdered camp leader. When he becomes camp leader himself, he shows himself to be cunning, manipulative, and intimidating.

Oki, 21—Son of Sauri, he is an overbearing man who exudes a brutal arrogance concealing perpetually wounded feelings. He is a jealous and quick-tempered bully.

Tungajuak, 40–50—An evil shaman. An odd, yet mild-looking man who can transform his features into pure evil.

Kumaglak, 55—A camp leader radiating power. He is straight-backed, soft-spoken, totally confident. He is a man who is used to people doing whatever he says.

EXT.   QULITALIK'S MAINLAND TENT   EVENING

CLOSE-UP as Qulitalik's hands tie an arrowhead to its shaft. He and Atanarjuat work side by side, fully concentrated, in front of their tent facing a beautiful bay surrounded by jagged hills.

ATANARJUAT: *(casual)* Caribou bulls must be facing north now…

Qulitalik keeps working as if he hasn't heard.

ATANARJUAT: It would be good to have fresh meat . . .

Qulitalik keeps ignoring him. Atanarjuat takes a deep breath, then continues as if he's been thinking about this and preparing it.

ATANARJUAT: Look, I know I have to do something. I just don't know what it is. Maybe if I go hunting . . .

Qulitalik finally looks up. Quietly . . .

QULITALIK: You know what's out there when you're all alone. Are you ready to face that?

Much less scattered and confused, Atanarjuat recognizes the danger he's in but he needs to get moving. Qulitalik listens carefully evaluating his awareness and resolve.

ATANARJUAT: Do I have any other choice? I know what you're thinking. The spirit will follow me. Well . . . sooner or later I *have* to face it. It's the only way . . . (*looks Qulitalik in the eye*) So help me if you can.

Atanarjuat's determination seems to convince Qulitalik. He takes from his parka the walrus-skin pouch Panikpak gave his wife when they left Igloolik many years ago. Gravely, Qulitalik puts it on the ground between them.

QULITALIK: Your dung-picker. Fill it up with droppings from every animal. Caribou, lemming, fox . . . The more the better. It will help you when you need it.
ATANARJUAT: (*impressed*) How?
QULITALIK: When you see how much dung you can carry you'll *have* to let it out!

Qulitalik LAUGHS, then stands up. He shows his finished arrow to Atanarjuat.

QULITALIK: Still . . . not bad for an old man. I have lost so many of these in my lifetime. Come on . . . If you're going out there alone, at least protect yourself.

He walks off down the hill.

EXT.   TENT   DAY

Atanarjuat tightens a strap on his dog pack. As he heaves his tent bundle over his shoulders he seems a different man from the one we saw leave with Puja a year ago: heavier in spirit, with lines of pain and loss etched in his face. The small pouch hangs around his neck. The women watch nervously as Qulitalik checks his straps, then picks up a small stone and weighs it in his hand.

Atanarjuat heals body, soul, and spirit at Qulitalik's camp.

QULITALIK: Listen, Atanarjuat. You need to exercise your mind. Here . . . hold this rock in your left hand all day. When you know what to do with it, you can put it down.

Atanarjuat stares silently at the rock.

QULITALIK: Pay attention when you see and hear things. If you're strong enough you won't lose your concentration. And remember . . . (*'peeps' like a snow bunting*) when your pouch goes like that it's time to come back. Give thanks to the four winds from the highest peak and shout 'It's done!'

Qulitalik carefully removes the rabbit's foot from around his neck and hands it to Atanarjuat.

QULITALIK: Bring the rabbit's foot and your dung picker back to me. Wear them on you all the time. Never let them go.

DISSOLVE TO . . .

EXT.   INLAND   DAY/NIGHT

SLOW DISSOLVING MONTAGE reminiscent but different from the summer hunt with Puja. This trip has a darker edge, lonely and foreboding. Travelling alone in a vast landscape of minimalist beauty is mostly a SILENT affair, with odd whispers of subtle SOUNDS. Wind, water and his own footsteps take on strange echoes as Atanarjuat seems to be hunting something other than caribou . . .

Atanarjuat on the land caribou hunting.

THROUGH DISSOLVES Atanarjuat walks down a long valley framed by ridges of black stone . . . He sets up his tiny tent in dimming twilight . . . Kneeling to examine caribou tracks, he picks up droppings for the pouch, then looks around listening carefully . . . In light blowing snow a group of caribou lift their heads as he walks past . . .

DISSOLVE TO:

EXT. OUTSIDE CAMP EVENING

EXTREME WIDE VIEW Atanarjuat climbs over a ridge of large stones.

His POV: coming down he sees what looks like a dead polar bear carcass. As he approaches, it suddenly moves. With a hideous SOUND it stands revealing a bear's head on a human torso. The creature GROWLS like an angry bear, while it MOANS like a tortured person. It stands on bear's legs and moves toward Atanarjuat, reaching out with eerie, clawed human hands.

Atanarjuat is paralyzed by his terror. The creature grabs him and they struggle. With an agonizing GROAN the creature throws him to the ground. Atanarjuat suddenly remembers Qulitalik's rock in his hand and desperately throws it at the beast as hard as he can.

The rock hits the beast in the face. Startled, it MOANS, then . . . disappears. Just as startled, Atanarjuat looks down at his empty hand, then slowly closes it into a fist.

DISSOLVE TO:

EXT. INLAND NIGHT

Seen from a distant hilltop the lonely glow of a campfire seems like a golden spot in an endless night. BLEED IN CRACKLING SOUND of campfire burning and DISSOLVE TO . . .

EXT. INLAND NIGHT

EXTREME CLOSE UP into flames burning.

EXTREME CLOSE UP of Atanarjuat staring into firelight. HOLD as flickering shadows project strange fluid shapes on the screen of his face . . .

Slowly, he leans over and lies down on his side, making a pillow of his arms under his head. CLOSE ON his face again, still staring, waiting . . . He shuts his eyes. HOLD as the fire burns down, dimmer and dimmer, and he too seems to disappear . . .

EXT. INLAND NIGHT

Atanarjuat's Dream . . . Hallucination . . . Flashback . . . ?

POV: Rough-housing as young boys with Amajuat and Oki laughing . . .

JUMP TO:

*POV: Puja, leaning over him . . . She opens her eyes and looks down
possessively. She leans down further, further, a darkening shadow
closing down . . .*

DISSOLVE TO:

*POV: EXTREME CLOSE-UP terror! Smothering claustrophobic folds of
translucent tent skin press down. Distorted sunlight shines through. Amplified
crackling SOUND. POV twists around desperately. With an explosive SLAM!
a spearhead appears right in our face. POV turns fast only to be hit with a
spurt of blood.*

DISTORTED VOICE: Run, little brother . . !!! . . . . Run! Save yourself!

EXT.   INLAND   NIGHT

*Atanarjuat sits up with a fearful shout. His hands fly to his face, as if touching
blood; then to his neck, feeling for his charms. Covered with sweat, he looks
around hoping he is really awake. The fire still burns brightly. BLEED IN
SOUND of children playing . . .*

EXT.   SAURI'S CAMP   DAY

*Establishing. Three tents beside a powerful river. A busy camp with children
running around noisily.*

EXT.   SAURI'S TENT DAY

*A skin ball lands near some men chatting. Atuat's son Kumaglak runs up, but
Sauri gets hold of it first. The boy waits.*

KUMAGLAK: Give me the ball.

*Sauri throws it behind him to the other children. Kumaglak stares at him, then
walks away toward the river.*

EXT.   RIVER   DAY

A skin bucket scoops through rushing water. Atuat hands it back to Panikpak who sets it down. They watch little Kumaglak drift aimlessly along the river. Atuat fills a second bucket. Panikpak looks at her curiously. Atuat glances back with a shy smile.

ATUAT: What?

PANIKPAK: You look different today... What is it?

Atuat blushes shyly. Reluctant.

ATUAT: I have a strong feeling my husband is alive.

PANIKPAK: Why? What makes you think that today?

A hopeful Atuat leans toward Panikpak confidentially.

ATUAT: Before all this happened, whenever Atanarjuat made love to Puja I would feel uneasy inside. Even when I wasn't around, I always felt tension in my heart. Last night... I had that same feeling again.

PANIKPAK: Excellent! You're the one that holds the truth. I myself always believed in my heart he is alive. I knew him well even as a baby.

ATUAT: Why did you never say anything?

PANIKPAK: Who ever knows?

EXT.   INLAND   DAY

The weather has changed. Grey, damp, cooler. Fog coming in. Atanarjuat seems to sit in the same place we last saw him. The fire is out. He shivers uncontrollably and unsteadily stands up.

He looks around at the weather, shivers again. The wind PICKS UP suddenly. Loud and raw, it blows through his tangled hair, stings his eyes. He blinks hard to clear them.

ATUAT SPIRIT (OS): Husband! It's you!

So startled by the voice he literally jumps, Atanarjuat whirls around.

His POV: Atuat and Kumaglak walk out from behind his tent. They are almost real but not quite: holding hands, his wife and son seem joyful, beautiful, happy to see him. As they approach, Atuat's face changes to anguish and accusing anger...

ATUAT SPIRIT: How could you leave me behind? I love Oki now. Don't
bother to come back!

She turns to leave. Pulling her son's hand, Kumaglak resists.

KUMAGLAK SPIRIT: Father! Father!

The boy suddenly spits in Atanarjuat's face.

CUT TO:

*Atanarjuat's face and hair are wet in the drifting fog . . . His haunted eyes close
tight. They reopen, searching for something no longer there. Instead, an arm
snakes around his neck from behind, a hand on his shoulder. Horrified,
Atanarjuat glances at the hand, slowly turns his head . . .*

*His POV: Puja leans in so close we can feel her breath. She speaks in a
whisper, with an eerie smile.*

PUJA SPIRIT: I never loved you for one minute!

*With an ugly LAUGH she slaps his face. Atanarjuat squeezes his eyes shut,
squeezes them hard, afraid to open them.*

AMAJUAT SPIRIT (OS): Little Brother! Quick! Help me!

*Atanarjuat's POV: A smiling Amajuat stands facing him holding a dead young
caribou in his arms.*

AMAJUAT SPIRIT: You didn't even fight for me! You were so angry you
just ran away for yourself!

*Amajuat drops the caribou to reveal his parka covered with blood. He looks
down at his chest, surprised, then points accusingly.*

AMAJUAT SPIRIT: *You killed me!*

For the first time Atanarjuat suddenly answers back.

ATANARJUAT: No! . . . No!

*Atanarjuat's torment floods over him. A dam seems to break inside.
CRYING. . . .*

ATANARJUAT: NO!...I didn't kill you...*Angayu! [Older brother]* It's not true! You were supposed to protect me!

CLOSE ON Atanarjuat crying uncontrollably...uncontrollably...

ATANARJUAT: *You...were supposed to protect...me!*

CONTINUE CLOSING and DISSOLVE TO...

EXT. INLAND DAY

Bright sunshine. Atanarjuat stares around wildly, as if he just woke up. Everything seems normal, the weather completely clear. Back in ordinary reality, he looks like a fugitive from his worst nightmare. He exhales with relief.

QULITALIK (OS): Relax. It's all over now.

Qulitalik walks up calmly behind him, smiling and reassuring.

QULITALIK: You've been through a lot, I know. But you passed your test.

Atanarjuat's astonishment collapses into tears of relieved joy.

ATANARJUAT: I'm so glad to see you! I can't believe it! How did you find me?

QULITALIK: I've been with you the whole time, helping you understand what you've been through. It was all planned and you did very well! Where's your little rock?

Atanarjuat looks down sheepishly at his empty hand.

ATANARJUAT: An...un-being...attacked me. I must have thrown it at the beast. I wasn't thinking...

Qulitalik holds out his hand.

Atanarjuat reaches up to remove the charms from around his neck.

Qulitalik's hand reaches eagerly to take them. Too eagerly.

Surprised...then suspicious...Atanarjuat hesitates. With the charms just a few inches from Qulitalik's overeager hand, he slowly pulls them back...

POV: With a sudden terrifying THUNDERCLAP Qulitalik SCREAMS like a horrendous animal. Enraged, his body transforms slowly to the man-bear beast, the evil shaman Tungajuak, holding a harpoon. SCREAM segues to the beast's mocking LAUGH. HOWLING wind rushes back. The beast raises his harpoon to strike.

In resigned horror Atanarjuat's hand desperately hold the charms as the wind tried to blow them free. Calmly, the beast thrusts his harpoon with all his strength into Atanarjuat's chest. He shudders and falls as the harpoon hits with a violent, sickening THUD!

BEAST TUNGAJUAK: *(calmly)* Death come upon you!

In EXTREME CLOSE-UP Atanarjuat's hand slowly uncurls . . . the two charms still held . . . CUT TO BLACK. FADE TO SILENCE.

Later in the film, Atanarjuat is reunited with his wife Atuat.

ᕿ *Atanarjuat* premiered at the Cannes International Film Festival in 2001, where Director Zacharias Kunuk won the Camera d'or Prize for first feature film. The movie is the first in Canada to be written, produced, directed, and acted by Inuit. The writers—Paul Apak, Norman Cohn, Zacharias Kunuk, Hervé Paniaq, and Pauloosie Qulitalik—are associated with the movie's production company, Igloolik Isuma Productions, Canada's first Inuit independent production company. The film is based on an ancient Inuit oral legend which the filmmakers have adapted in order to preserve the story for future generations. They noted, "*Atanarjuat* demystifies the exotic, otherworldly aboriginal stereotype by telling a powerful, universal story—a drama set in motion by conflicts and emotions that have surfaced in virtually every [human] culture...."

RESPONDING

Meaning

1. *Atanarjuat* is a modern film retelling of an ancient Inuit legend, set in the Arctic at the dawn of the first millennium. Explain the bond between Atanarjuat and Qulitalik, using details from the script to support your answer. What universal human archetypes do the two characters represent? What characters from other mythic traditions, literature or films do they parallel?

2. In the confrontation between Atanarjuat and the "unbeing", there is both a physical encounter and a mystical one, with the creature attacking Atanarjuat through his own memories. Write a paragraph in which you describe the memories that the creature uses to attack Atanarjuat, and what these memories represent. In your paragraph, provide specific evidence that supports your analysis.

Form and Style

3. a) *Atanarjuat* is adapted from Inuit oral tradition and transposed into the visual medium of film. What stylistic features and visual images have the writers used to make the story visually appealing?

   b) What challenges do you think the filmmakers faced in transposing this oral story to film?

4. Just as a novelist or poet would use word symbols, the writers of this screenplay have used visual symbols to illuminate abstract ideas. What visual symbols are in the excerpt and what are they meant to represent? Comment on their effectiveness.

Exploring Context

5. The past twenty years have seen a rapid increase in film and video production by cultural groups who have historically not had access to these forms of communication. How might access to film and video change the presentation and interpretation of a culture's values and traditions?

Creative Extension

6. Choose a story, fable, or legend from your cultural heritage. Write a screenplay adaptation of the story, using correct screenplay technique. Consider the visual aspects of the screenplay (various camera angles, visual symbols, etc.), as well as effective audio techniques, music, and dialogue or voice-overs, to convey the theme of the story.

7. In small groups, assume you have been asked to create a media campaign advertising *Atanarjuat*'s release in theatres across the country. Together, decide how you will promote the film—in which media (television, newspapers, magazines, etc.) and using what forms (posters, print ads, movie trailer, radio spots, etc.). Justify your choices. Then create at least two promotional pieces and present them to the class or another group.

Monty Python's King Arthur Skit

ᘐ Graham Chapman, Terry Jones, Terry Gilliam,
Michael Palin, Eric Idle, John Cleese

Mist

Silence. Possibly atmospheric music.

After a few moments we hear horse's hooves getting closer and closer.

Out of the mist walks King Arthur followed by a servant who is banging two coconuts together.

Arthur raises his hand.

ART: Whoa there!

Servant makes noises of horse halting with a flourish.

Arthur peers through the mist.

Cut to shot from over his shoulder: A castle (e.g., Bodium) rising out of the mist.

On the castle battlements, a soldier is dimly seen.

SOLDIER: Halt! Who goes there?

ART: It is I, Arthur, son of Uther Pendragon, from the Castle of Camelot, King of all Britons, defeater of the Saxons, Sovereign of all England.

Pause.

SOLDIER: Get-away!

ART: It bloody well is. And this is my trusty servant, Patsy. We have ridden from the further corner of this land, in quest of the Holy Grail, the sacred chalice from which our Lord himself drank at the Last Supper. I must speak with your master.

SOLDIER: What! Ridden on a horse?

ART: Yea.

SOLDIER: You're using coconuts.

ART: What?

SOLDIER: You're using two empty halves of coconuts and banging them together.

ART: (*Scornful*) So? We have ridden since the snows of Winter covered this land. Our horses grew weary, unable to carry us further. We were forced to leave them by the Mountains, and continue with coconuts.

SOLDIER: Where did you get the coconuts?

ART: We found them.

SOLDIER: *Found* them? The coconut is a tropical fruit. It's not indigenous to these temperate areas.

ART: The swallow may fly south with the sun, or the house martin or the plover seek hot lands in winter, yet these are not strangers to our land.

A moment's pause.

SOLDIER: Are you suggesting coconuts migrate?

ART: Not at all. They could be carried.

SOLDIER: What? A *swallow* carrying a *coconut?*

ART: Why not?

SOLDIER: I'll tell you why not . . . because a swallow is about 8 inches long and weighs 5 ounces, and you'd be lucky to find a coconut under a pound.

ART: The swallow grips it by the husk.

SOLDIER: It's not a question of where he grips it, it's a simple question of dynamics—a 5½ ounce bird could not hold a one pound coconut.

ART: Cannot the tiny ant, building his home from the hard earth, move sixty times his own weight?

SOLDIER: (*Irritated*) What kind of ant are you talking about? There are 5000 different species.

ART: You speak with the tongue of snakes, I will no more of this.

SOLDIER: Not at all. It's just that ants are my special subject. Ants, bees, wasps, all the hymenoptera, and you often get people who just *bandy* the word "ant" around as if it meant something. It's like saying: "I am human." It's so unspecific.

Another soldier [S2] looms on the battlements.

S2: Is he talking about ants again?

Cut to Arthur looking bewildered.

SOLDIER: It just annoys me, the way people hear some sensational story about an ant moving 60 times its own weight, and . . .

S2: He's probably thinking of termites.

SOLDIER: There you go! *You're* just as bad! There's 2000 species of termite.

S2: Alright! Alright! Let me finish!

SOLDIER: They're a totally different order. They're isoptera. They're not remotely comparable.

S2: No. I'm saying that termites *generically* are able to move . . .

Arthur raises his eyes heavenwards, beckons to Patsy and they turn and go off into the mists.

We stay on the castle for a moment and hear:

SOLDIER: What do you mean "generically"? There's the "plodding termite," the "yellow Angolian termite," I mean you just can't say . . .

They leave the battlements, (Arthur and Patsy).

As they walk away into the beautiful medieval countryside, a roller caption starts.

ROLLER: According to ancient legend, the chalice used by
               Jesus Christ at the Last Supper was brought by
               Joseph of Arimathaea to England in the middle
               of the first century A.D. and deposited at Glastonbury.
               Subsequently it mysteriously disappeared. Many
               believers searched for it before King Arthur and his
               Knights of the Round Table dedicated their lives to its
               recovery. This then, was the Quest for the Holy Grail . . .

Bring up music, and take it down.

Possibly credits over Arthur progressing through wooded countryside. Credits end. They are still travelling through suitably Arthurian countryside with trees.

Monty Python and the Holy Grail was released in 1975. It starred the writers and performers of the British television comedy series *Monty Python's Flying Circus*, which ran from 1969 until 1975. The group included Graham Chapman, Terry Jones, Terry Gilliam, Michael Palin, Eric Idle, and John Cleese. The screenplay from the *Holy Grail* appeared in the book *Monty Python and The Holy Grail (Book)* in 1977. Other Monty Python movies include *The Life of Brian* (1979) and *The Meaning of Life* (1983).

The Life of King Arthur

ꞩ Translated by Judith Weiss and Rosamund Allen

9703. When Arthur had conquered Ireland, he travelled as far as Iceland, taking and conquering the whole land, and subduing it entirely to him; he wanted to rule everywhere. Gonvais, king of Orkney, Doldani, king of Gotland, and Rummaret of Wenelande all heard the news, each from their spies, that Arthur would come their way and destroy all the islands. There was not his equal in the whole world for military might, or anyone who could lead such an army. Afraid he would attack them and ravage their lands, they freely and without constraint went to him in Iceland. They brought him so many of their possessions, promised and gave so much, that peace was made and they became his men, holding their heritage from him. They promised and appointed a truce, and each gave hostages. In this way everybody stayed in peace, and Arthur returned to his ships; he came back to England and was welcomed with great joy.

9731. For twelve years after his return, Arthur reigned in peace. No one dared to make war on him; nor did he go to war himself. On his own, with no other instruction, he acquired such knightly skill and behaved so nobly, so finely and courteously, that there was no court so talked about, not even that of the Roman emperor. He never heard of a knight who was in any way considered to be praiseworthy who would not belong to his household, provided that he could get him, and if such a one wanted reward for his service, he would never leave deprived of it. On account of his noble barons—each felt he was superior, each considered himself the best, and no one could say who was the worst—Arthur had the Round Table made, about which the British tell many a tale. There sat the vassals, all equal, all leaders; they were placed equally round the table, and equally served. None of them could boast he sat higher than his peer; all were seated near the place of honour, none far away. No one—whether Scot, Briton, Frenchman, Norman, Angevin, Fleming, Burgundian, or Lorrainer

—whoever he held his fief from, from the West as far as Montgieu, was accounted courtly if he did not go to Arthur's court and stay with him and wear the livery, device, and armour in the fashion of those who served at that court. They came from many lands, those who sought honour and renown, partly to hear of his courtly deeds, partly to see his rich possessions, partly to know his barons, partly to receive his splendid gifts. He was loved by the poor and greatly honoured by the rich. Foreign kings envied him, doubting and fearing he would conquer the whole world and take their territories away.

9785. In this time of great peace I speak of—I don't know if you have heard of it—the wondrous events appeared and the adventures were sought out which, whether for love of his generosity, or for fear of his bravery, are so often told about Arthur that they have become the stuff of fiction: not all lies, not all truth, neither total folly nor total wisdom. The raconteurs have told so many yarns, the storytellers so many stories, to embellish their tales, that they have made it all appear fiction.

9799. Prompted by his own noble disposition, the advice of his barons, and the large body of knights he had equipped and nurtured, Arthur said he would cross the sea and conquer all France. But first he would go to Norway and make his brother-in-law Loth King there. Sichelin, the king, had died, without son or daughter; on his death-bed he had asked, as he had asked when in health, that Loth should be king of Norway and hold his domain and his kingdom. He was his nephew, he had no other heir, so Loth by right should have everything. If Sichelin had ordained this, and thought it would be so, the Norwegians considered both his command and his decree folly. When they saw that the king was dead, they utterly refused Loth the kingdom. They had no desire to call upon a foreigner or make a foreigner their lord; they would have to be all old greybeards before recognizing him. He would give to others abroad what he should give to them. They would make one of Sichelin's retainers king, who would cherish them and their sons. For this reason they thus made Riculf, one of their barons, king.

9831. When Loth saw he would lose his rights if he did not conquer them by force, he appealed to Arthur, his lord, and Arthur promised him that he would give him all the kingdom, and Riculf had been wrong to accept it. He summoned a large fleet and large army and entered Norway by force. He inflicted great damage on the land, burning towns and plundering houses. Riculf would not flee or leave the country; he thought he could defend himself against Arthur, and gathered together the men of Norway, but he had few men and few friends. He was conquered and slain. So many of the others were killed that very few were left. When Norway surrendered, Arthur gave it all to Loth, on condition that Loth held it from him and acknowledged him as overlord. Walwein had recently returned, a renowned and valiant knight, from St. Soplice, the Pope, may his soul rest in glory. He had given him armour, which was well bestowed. Walwein possessed bravery and great moderation; he had no time for pride or arrogance. He would do more than he said, and give more than he promised.

    ᕙ   The Monk Wace wrote *The Life of King Arthur* in the late Middle Ages, specifically the twelfth century. He was the first to mention the Round Table, which allowed the knights to be seated in such a way that none had precedence. This excerpt is taken from The Everyman Library edition of *The Life of King Arthur*, introduced and translated by Judith Weiss and Rosamund Allen.

RESPONDING

Meaning

1. The Monk Wace wrote the excerpt from *The Life of King Arthur* in the late Middle Ages. What characteristics are attributed to Arthur and how does Wace convey them? How do these differ from the presentation of Arthur's character in the modern film script?

2. The excerpt from *The Life of King Arthur* provides the first literary explanation of the origins of the Round Table. What, according to Wace, was its origin? Why did Wace choose to write of the Round Table in a section of the book where he was discussing various conquests by Arthur?

Form and Style

3. *Parody* is a mocking imitation of the style of a literary work. What aspects of the King Arthur legend are being parodied in the film screenplay excerpt?

4. Although some aspects of medieval life are portrayed in the screenplay excerpt, much of the humour is a result of deliberate *anachronism*—the misplacing of any person, thing, custom, or event outside its proper historical time. Identify the anachronisms in the screenplay and comment on their effects.

Exploring Context

5.   *Monty Python* was a British comedy troupe whose work originated on a British television show in the 1960s. The work of the group encompassed television shows, films, books, and recordings. Some critics have claimed that the longevity and popularity of the group was due to the absurdist nature of its humour. Examine other Monty Python work and write a critique of the humour techniques used by the group.

Creative Extension

6.   Write an essay comparing and contrasting the serious screenplay treatment of a legend in *Atanarjuat* with the satirical parodying in the screenplay of *Monty Python's King Arthur Skit.*

7.   Using the Monty Python screenplay as a template, create a humorous dialogue in which one party is trying to accomplish a serious end, while the other is distracted by inconsequential details. Make your argument as absurd as possible. Perform your dialogue for a group, or record it on audio or videotape.

Virtual Sleuthing

ᔍ Stevie Cameron

**The Internet can connect us to a universe of fascinating people—
even those who topple corrupt presidents**

They say our world shrinks as we get older; for me, as a journalist, the world is expanding and getting more interesting every day. The reason? The Internet and e-mail. This is how I've come to know an extraordinary woman, Sheila Coronel, the executive director of the Philippine Center for Investigative Journalism (PCIJ). We were introduced via e-mail by my friend Rod Macdonell, an investigative journalist on leave from the Montreal *Gazette* who now works for the World Bank in Washington.

Macdonell runs international training programs in investigative reporting. When he told me what Coronel was doing in Manila, I felt envy and awe—I have long wanted to do the same thing in Canada. "It's the best investigative journalism organization I have seen in the world," says Macdonell. "They publish books, a quarterly magazine, and stories—they go out and investigate and then they sell the story. They just helped bring down the president of the Philippines."

President Joseph Estrada, a former actor with no personal fortune, resigned in late January after PCIJ stories appeared about the tens of millions of dollars he'd spent on lavish homes for his wives and mistresses—money that came from the illegal gambling protection racket, kickbacks, and tobacco taxes—and about the front companies he controlled. The stories, picked up around the world, led to Estrada's impeachment, corruption charges, and final flight from the presidential palace while military helicopter gunships hovered overhead.

This was easily the biggest story of her career, Coronel says, and much of the original information came from a banking source who sent her text messages on her cellphone because he was too afraid to contact her any other way.

Coronel started in 1982 as a magazine writer, eventually moving to the *Manila Chronicle* to cover politics. In 1989, three years after the fall of the country's corrupt dictator, Ferdinand Marcos, she and a small group of colleagues set up the PCIJ to do investigative journalism. "We realized that the kind of reporting that we wanted to do we could never do in the newsroom," she explains. "We had high hopes when press freedom was restored back in 1986. We thought we would be able to write what we wanted then. Instead, we were stuck in the daily grind of journalism. We also found our freedoms being frittered away by the media's obsession with the superficial and sensational. We thought this was such a waste."

At first, Coronel was the only one working for the PCIJ full-time, out of a borrowed office with second-hand equipment. Eventually organizations such as the Ford and Asia Foundations and UNESCO began giving them money; today, the PCIJ has sixteen employees and runs on an annual budget of about $200 000 (US) a year. Only five of the staff are journalists, but the PCIJ gives grants to many freelancers so they can work on investigative reports. The PCIJ does both print and broadcast reporting and sells stories to fourteen mainstream newspapers and the public networks. No one has ever turned down a story.

"We often work in collaboration with TV public affairs programs," says Coronel. "Sometimes we work with their reporter and we provide the research. Or they come to us with an idea and we work together. Or else we do the entire thing—research, on-camera reporting, as well as video production—and sell the package to a program."

In Canada, we like to think an organization like the PCIJ isn't needed. But investigative journalism is just as unpopular among our most powerful citizens as it is in the Philippines, and many of our news organizations won't do it. Visit Coronel's site at www.pcij.org and see for yourself what this woman and her team have accomplished (you can also buy their books.)

For me, Sheila Coronel is an inspiration, but I never would have understood her work and its impact without the Internet and e-mail. With these resources, I was able to read PCIJ stories, study their site and staff, pull up newspaper stories from many countries about their work, and even interview her—all in just a few days. While nothing can replace the colour and texture of chasing a story in its own country, virtual journalism, if this is what we can call it, means a bigger and infinitely more fascinating world for all of us.

෧ Canadian journalist Stevie Cameron has worked as a freelance magazine writer, magazine editor, and columnist and reporter with the *Globe and Mail*. She created a national stir with her book *On the Take: Crime, Corruption and Greed in the Mulroney Years* (1994) about former Canadian prime minister Brian Mulroney. She was also the founding editor of the Toronto magazine *Elm Street*. "Virtual Sleuthing" appeared in its summer 2001 issue. (*Born Belleville, Ontario 1943*)

RESPONDING

Meaning

1. a) Based on the information in the article and your own experience, define investigative journalism. How and why is it considered different from mainstream journalism? Why would it be, as Stevie Cameron notes, "just as unpopular among our most powerful citizens" as it is in the Philippines?

    b) What does Stevie Cameron mean by "virtual journalism"? How has it affected her work and career?

2. The Philippine Center for Investigative Journalism (PCIJ) began as a one-person organization and has grown to become a formidable media operation. In your own words, trace the growth of PCIJ. What challenges has the organization faced? What have been its accomplishments? How do you explain the success of PCIJ?

Form and Style

3. This column is written in an informal, yet compact and precise style that often characterizes newsmagazine writing. Reread the article and note those features that reflect subjective personal writing and those that reflect the objective journalism of newspaper articles. Why would a magazine writer choose this blend of subjective and objective styles instead of one or the other?

4. In the article, Coronel provides an overview of how PCIJ operates as a media organization. In which media forms does PCIJ provide news? How might this ability to produce stories in various media forms be an advantage to an investigative journalism organization?

Exploring Context

5. When the Philippines restored freedom of the press in 1986, Coronel expected that journalists would be free to write what they wanted. Instead she found "our freedoms being frittered away by the media's obsession with the superficial and sensational." In Canada, does our media preserve our freedoms or concentrate on trivial and sensational matters? Write an editorial in which you support your position.

Creative Extension

6. Many media outlets feature investigative journalism. Examples include Canada's television show *W5*, the American show *60 Minutes,* newsmagazines such as *Maclean's,* and many Web sites. In groups, closely examine as many examples of investigative journalism as you can. Create a presentation in which you outline the unique features of investigative journalism, its goals, and why it is important to our society. Support your presentation with specific examples.

7. This article explored how e-mail and the Internet are expanding the world of journalists. Choose another career and investigate how these technologies are changing the work done in that career. If possible, interview someone in the career you have chosen. Share your findings with the class.

An Interview with Derrick de Kerckhove

ལྦ Blake Harris

In the late 1950s and 60s, Marshall McLuhan captured worldwide attention
with his unique analysis of the role that media technologies play in struc-
turing human cultures. Since then, McLuhan's phrases such as "the global
village" and "the medium is the message" have become standard terms in
our contemporary vocabulary. And in recent years, the wired generation
has virtually co-opted him as their "patron saint."

Following McLuhan's death in 1980, there was much speculation about
his true heir. However, by tracing an unbroken lineage, the most probable
inheritor of the McLuhan mantle is McLuhan's own colleague, Derrick de
Kerckhove (pronounced "kirk-hove").

De Kerckhove's close association with Marshall McLuhan during
the 1970s, as translator, assistant, and co-author, gave him privileged
access to the working mind of one of this century's pre-eminent media
philosophers.

Subsequently, as McLuhan's successor at the head of the McLuhan
Program in Culture and Technology in Toronto, de Kerckhove has been at
the centre of an international network of scholars, artists, and communication analysts dedicated to the study of McLuhan's vision of electronic media.
At the same time, de Kerckhove has been a sought-after consultant to
telecommunication firms, governments, international businesses, and
television networks.

In his own writing, de Kerckhove has extended and deepened some
of McLuhan's insights, as well as developed his own original and provocative theories. His book, *The Skin of Culture,* for instance, presents an
overview of research and speculation spanning more than a decade. Here,
he warns that our planet is at a precarious turning point that can lead
either to fragmentation or further globalization. Only by designing our
technologies—instead of letting them design us—will we be able to avert
social catastrophe.

As McLuhan did before him, de Kerckhove contends that what appear to be marginal qualities of the media often have the most powerful effects. For example, the fall of the Berlin Wall and the end of the Cold War were, he believes, inevitable events brought about by electronic telecommunications and information processing systems, as well as by television. Understanding and controlling these marginal qualities, he says, may turn out to be one of our most crucial undertakings, for new technologies "wage war" upon the cultures into which they emerge.

Now, in one of his rare media interviews, de Kerckhove goes beyond his published work to discuss the coming impact of new electronic network technologies upon government.

GT: You've emphasized that the electronic environment amplifies emotion rather than rational response.

DE KERCKHOVE: I'm glad you brought this up because that is true for radio and TV. That is true for broadcast media. It is absolutely provable for broadcast media, particularly for radio. It is absolutely not true in the interactive environment of networks. The network sensibility is by nature critical. It doesn't just buy or accept stuff. People on the Net ask questions. One of the most frequently asked questions is the frequently asked question! This is one of the exciting things about the Net that essentially enhances freedom for the individual.

GT: So, in a sense, the Internet is actually countering the emotional mediums of television and radio.

DE KERCKHOVE: Yes, and for two reasons. One, because it is interactive. And two, because it is text-based. Text is critical. All text is. What Marshall and I feared with radio and television was the fact that they didn't give you a hold on information. So that sensory-wise, you were just flooded with the stuff. Whether it was advertising to turn you into a consumer society or whether it was militarization to turn you into a war machine—as happened in the 30s and 40s, right on into the early 50s. What happens with the electronic networks is that they give you text and they give you interactivity. Those two things—text and interactivity—guarantee a certain freedom of mind.

One related problem would be if the mind itself connected in such a way as to warp you very strongly. For example, our relationship to computers—our personal relationship to computers—is program and therefore programmable. How far can it be programmed? That's another aspect of the question. But it's not an emotional aspect. You are not being programmed based on an emotional response, you are going to be programmed because of a rational response, which could be worse.

There is a lot more to think about when you think about text plus interactivity and freedom. Civil liberties. Electronic liberties, really. Information rights. At the McLuhan Program, we are working on that right now. We are very interested in developing a Bill of Information Rights, for example.

GT: In your writing, you have expanded upon McLuhan's idea that "When information moves at electric speed, the worlds of trends and rumours becomes the real world." This would tie in.

DE KERCKHOVE: Opinion and rumour are very close. A rumour is information that hasn't been verified. Opinion is a slightly different thing from a rumour, but they are in the same family. The opinion is what carries some emotional, persuasive weight in an oral society.

It's very interesting. Fighting opinion was a major battle of Plato and fighting opinion was also a major battle of Voltaire—fighting superstition, the world of opinions, rumours, all these fuzzy functions of human language which work well in oral situations, but do not work in text.

Elected government literally lives by rumour and opinion. That's obvious. They live by opinion polls. At the very beginning, a new government will sometimes make big decisions. But by and large, governments are governed by rumour, by spin-doctoring, by opinion-making.

GT: So it is also the pace of electronic network communications which changes, not just the way news is generated and relayed, but also response to that news?

DE KERCKHOVE: Yes. And the question is really there: what effect will the Net have on elected politics and on opinion-making? In scientific journals, for example, it takes six or more months for the news to come out. Basically some guy makes a wonderful discovery, then has it shot down by a couple of reviewers and the thing does not come out until there is enough correction to water it down to nothing. And then it gets published.

But for all its faults, the speed at which publishing went was the proper speed for verifying truth—the kind of truth we are all perfectly willing to live by. Just as the speed of the legal process is also a book, a text-based speed. But the speed of electronic information, also text-based, but instant —that speed creates a completely different relationship to rumour. There should be a kind of grammar of rumours that goes beyond simple definitions. Even the speed of television and radio was nothing like the speed of network data. The jury is still out on what this will mean.

GT: You've said electronic communications do away with local boundaries. What should local governments be doing to counter this tendency? How do they ensure that the network environment doesn't have an eroding effect?

DE KERCKHOVE: Well, for one thing, the generalized impact of electronic communication is decentralization—so the regionalization of government, the devolution of centralized government to the periphery, of central institutions to their outsourcing—this is to be expected generally.

And there is the whole question of standardization, which is necessarily central—standards of road maintenance, of education, of bandwidth access, of linguistic services. It's like being a company. A company has an identity of some kind and that identity is reflected in its design, its architecture, its corporate culture. And if a government wants to stay around, if a country wants to stay around, it pretty much has to project this kind of unity.

Boundaries can be very flexible. The whole world of real estate is being virtualized. Government buildings can go. They will eventually be replaced by networks. You can see that this is happening. But at the same time what you need is the other side, a sense of belonging, a sense of unity. If everything is peripheral and there is no more centre—if the centre cannot hold as the poetry goes—things do fall apart. A country falls apart. There has to be a balance. Government at all levels should approach network communication with interest but also with care. There has to be a balance between what you yield in controls, how much direct participation you allow, and how much body you want to keep.

I think governments today ought to pay increased attention to the social and cultural impact of networks and keep in mind this dual mandate, which is to yield more and more participatory response to the periphery, to the people, the electorate, keeping a good watch on those interest groups that could unbalance power. But at same time they have to make sure what they have got in place maintains that sense of unity and identity which keeps the country—or an area—together.

ᔓ Blake Harris has been a professional writer and researcher for more than twenty years. He writes about business, politics, government, education, entertainment, marketing, and new technologies. He has also written many short videos and films. This interview with Derrick de Kerckhove "Marshall McLuhan's Successor" appeared in the December 1996 issue of *Government Technology*, the leading American publication dealing with the impact of new technologies on state and local governments.

RESPONDING

Meaning

1. In this interview, de Kerckhove draws a distinction between the "emotional" mediums such as radio and TV and interactive networks such as the Internet. What arguments does he make to prove the Internet is not the same as radio and TV? Do you agree or disagree with his analysis? Explain.

2. Throughout the interview, de Kerckhove makes a number of predictions about how networks such as the Internet will change society and how both people and governments will act. Make a list of de Kerckhove's predictions and for each, provide your analysis of whether or not it is likely to come true.

Form and Style

3. The interviewer's questions are printed verbatim in this interview. In many newspaper and newsmagazine articles, the interviewer's questions are never printed, only the responses. Collect examples of interviews of both types. After examining the two styles, write an analysis of the advantages and disadvantages of each. In your analysis, consider aspects such as audience, article length, and requirements of the print medium.

4. This interview was originally published in a journal called *Government Technology*. How would this interview change if it were rewritten for
   a) a local newspaper
   b) a national newsmagazine
   c) an Internet Web site
   d) a television news program, or
   e) your class?
   Choose one of the above forms and develop a list of questions that might be asked of a media expert such as de Kerckhove to address the concerns of the specific audience.

Exploring Context

5. As quoted in the interview, Marshall McLuhan said, "When information moves at electric speed, the world of trends and rumours becomes the real world." Do you agree or disagree with this statement? Provide specific examples from modern media to support your position.

Creative Extension

6. Using de Kerckhove's ideas on media, government, and electronic communication, write a futuristic short story in which you present your vision of life twenty years from now.

7. What do you think should be included in a Bill of Information Rights or a Bill of Rights for Internet Use? In groups, draft ten to twelve key points for such a Bill of Rights. Develop your Bill for your school or local community. Justify your decisions. Review the government brochure on Internet safety, noting the layout and style of language used. Then create a pamphlet clearly presenting and elaborating on your points, or develop a Web page to post your ideas.

News in Different Media

Mars has long been the planet that has captured the imagination of both literary writers and the media. In the following news reports, we compare media texts about Mars from the Scientists at NASA, the mainstream Discovery Channel, and the tabloid newspaper Weekly World News. *Is it the same planet viewed from these three points of view?*

MARTIANS ARE BLOWING UP OUR SPACECRAFT!

Weekly World News

WASHINGTON—The latest bizarre mishap involving a space probe visiting Mars has revived controversial claims that hostile inhabitants of the Red Planet are shooting our vessels out of the sky!

"This pattern of our spacecraft disappearing mysteriously or being destroyed—either en route to Mars or on the surface—is so clear that to attribute it to 'coincidence' is unscientific," declared astronomer Dr. Jason Wismar, an outspoken critic of the space-exploration establishment.

"It's fairly obvious now that something or someone doesn't want us to go there." The latest disaster occurred September 23 when the $125 million Mars Orbiter suddenly burst into flames and plunged to its doom as it attempted to enter an orbit around the planet.

But that was far from the first catastrophe to strike NASA's star-crossed missions to Mars.

On August 21, 1993, Earth scientists suddenly lost contact with an earlier probe, the Mars Observer.

The spacecraft had cruised flawlessly across millions of miles of space, but vanished without a trace just as it reached Mars. To this day, the vessel's fate remains unknown.

And on September 27, 1997, the Mars Pathfinder mysteriously went dead, ceasing to radio messages back to Earth just 83 days after landing. The exact whereabouts of Sojourner, a six-wheeled robotic rover that rolled out of the lander to explore the Martian surface, remains a mystery.

The official explanation issued by NASA for the latest calamity is that engineers working on the Mars Orbiter had simply gotten mixed up. One team supposedly used English units such as feet and pounds while the other used the metric system, resulting in a fatal navigation error.

But Seattle-based Dr. Wismar and many others outside the space agency don't buy it. "Well, obviously that's a cover story," he said. "I know many of these aerospace engineers personally —and to suggest they could ever make such a stupid mistake is ludicrous. NASA just doesn't want to panic the public with talk of hostile space aliens blowing up our probes."

Respected British astrophysicist Dr. Jeremy Lackersby pooh-poohs the notion that live aliens are blowing up our spacecraft. He says it's much more likely that the Martians have been extinct for eons, but left behind an automated missile-defense system.

"It could well be something akin to the Star Wars program provoked by President Ronald Reagan," he said. Both he and Dr. Wismar are highly critical of US politicians—especially presidential candidates—who have been making noises about sending a manned mission to Mars.

"Sure, it would be great for American pride," said Dr. Wismar. "But to send American astronauts to Mars before we understand the danger would be worse than folly—it would be murder."

GIANT FLOOD CHANNELS UNCOVERED ON MARS
Richard Stenger

(CNN)—The largest valley system in the solar system, discovered underneath layers of hardened lava, ash, and dust on Mars, could have delivered enough water to fill an ocean within a matter of weeks, according to scientists.

Dwarfing anything on Earth, the flood channels were spotted by a satellite in Mars orbit that can peer with a laser instrument under the planet's surface.

The network of gorges, situated in the Western Hemisphere between a giant volcano and the possible remnants of an ocean, is ten times larger than its nearest rival on the red planet, according to the researchers.

Cataclysmic floods that at times unleashed 50 000 times the flow of the Amazon River most likely formed the outflow system, which boasts individual channels as wide as 125 miles (200 km), the scientists said.

"After picking the complex geologic picture apart like a jigsaw puzzle, we think there must have been several episodes of (volcanic) heating creating catastrophic floods," said James Dohm of the University of Arizona in Tucson this week.

Such discharges could have filled an ocean three times the size of the Mediterranean in less than two months, calculated the scientists from the University of Arizona and NASA.

Geological Survey. A smaller sea nearby could have filled within eight days. Scientists have speculated for some time that the desert planet teamed with water and periodic oceans billions of years ago. But the latest research lends weight to the theory that the planet experiences episodic changes that transform the surface in an instant, geologically speaking.

The presence of the northwestern valley slopes provides further evidence that Mars possesses vast underground stores of frozen water.

Occasional blasts of internal heat can melt the aquifers and release torrents of water, producing temporary oceans and seas, which sink back underground and return the planet to desert conditions, according to Dohm and colleagues.

Such volcanism could happen again and form an ocean or lake over the northern plains, the Arizona scientists theorize.

The team, which published their most recent findings in the June issue of the *Journal of Geophysical Research,* combined observations from the Mars Global Surveyor, currently in Mars orbit, and the Viking spacecraft, which circled the red planet in the 1970s.

NASA FACTS: MARS EXPLORATION ROVER

In 2003, two powerful new Mars rovers will be on their way to the red planet. With far greater mobility than the 1997 Mars Pathfinder rover, these robotic explorers will be able to trek up to 100 metres (about 110 yards) across the surface each Martian day. Each Mars 2003 rover will carry a sophisticated set of instruments that will allow it to search for evidence of liquid water that may have been present in the planet's past. The rovers will be identical to each other, but will land at different regions of Mars.

Mission Overview
Both rovers are planned for launch from Cape Canaveral, Florida, one on June 3, 2003, and the second on June 27. The first should reach Mars January 4, 2004, the other on February 25.

The landing for each will resemble that of the Pathfinder spacecraft. A parachute will deploy to slow the spacecraft and airbags will inflate to cushion the landing. Upon reaching the surface, the spacecraft will bounce about a dozen times, and could roll as far as one kilometre (0.6 mile). When it stops, the airbags will deflate and retract and the petals will open up, bringing the lander to an upright position and revealing the rover.

The landed portion of the Mars Exploration Rover mission features a design dramatically different from Mars Pathfinder's. Where Pathfinder had scientific instruments on both the lander and the small Sojourner rover, these larger rovers will carry all their instruments with them. Immediately after landing, the rover will begin reconnaissance of the landing site by taking a 360-degree visible colour and infrared image panorama. It will then leave the petal structure behind, driving off to begin its exploration. Using images and spectra taken daily from the rovers, scientists will command the vehicle to go to rock and soil targets of interest and evaluate their composition and their texture at microscopic scales. Initial targets may be close to the landing sites, but later targets can be far afield: These exploration rovers will be able to travel almost as far in one Martian day as the Sojourner rover did over its entire lifetime.

Rocks and soils will be analyzed with a set of five instruments on each rover, and a special tool called the rock abrasion tool, or irRAT ln will be used to expose fresh rock surfaces for study. Each rover has a mass of nearly 150 kilograms (about 300 pounds) and has a range of up to 100 metres (about 110 yards) per sol, or Martian day. Surface operations will last for at least 90 sols, extending to late April 2004, but could continue longer, depending on the health of the vehicles.

Science Goals

The mission seeks to determine history of climate and water at two sites on Mars where conditions may once have been favourable to life. The sites will be chosen by about a year before launch, on the basis of intensive study of orbital data collected by the Mars Global Surveyor spacecraft and other missions. Selection criteria will include clear evidence of ancient water, as indicated either by minerals that form under wet conditions or landscapes apparently shaped by water. Possibilities include former lakebeds or hydrothermal deposits. The rovers' instruments will be used to read the geologic record at the sites, and to evaluate how suitable the past conditions would have been for life.

RESPONDING

Meaning

1. For each news report, list those details that are objective facts and those that are opinions, including opinions attributed to an expert. Which article appears to have the most objectivity? Which has the least? Does your analysis match your expectations? Discuss.

2. Each of these news articles deals with different aspects of Mars, yet each highlights curiosity about the possibility of life on the planet. In what way is this curiosity approached in each article? Why is life on Mars such a prevalent topic in the media? Support your answer with examples from other media and literature you have studied.

Form and Style

3. Although one of these news items is a fact sheet from a government agency, one a news report from the Internet, and one from a tabloid newspaper, they all share stylistic similarities. In what ways is the writing style similar? Why would this be so? What differences do you note?

4. If you were the art director responsible for illustrating each of these articles, what visuals would you choose? In what ways would the visual elements chosen for each be different? Consider the intended audience, content, and style of writing in making your choices. Provide a rationale for your decisions.

Exploring Context

5. Tabloid newspapers have been around for several decades, but their form and content has changed considerably. Stories of aliens and the supernatural have decreased in popularity, whereas scandals about celebrities have increased. Do an informal survey of the cover stories featured in news tabloids. Provide an oral report of your findings. What characteristics of modern society account for your results?

Creative Extension

6. Based on the information in these articles and some further research, create a shooting script for a movie trailer. The trailer will be for a film about Mars—either a documentary or a science fiction film. Consider your audience and purpose, and choose appropriate music, narration, visual images, and graphics. Your trailer should capture some of the curiosity and wonder surrounding the planet. If you have access to video or film equipment, produce your trailer. Share your ideas with other groups. How are the trailers different when aimed at different audiences and produced for different purposes?

7. Choose a current issue or news event. Find examples of how the event or issue is covered in at least three different media (e.g., a TV news item, a newspaper story, and a magazine article). Analyze the differences in format, depth of coverage, style of language used, and enhancement with graphics, sound, or other elements. Share your findings with the class.

Selections from The One and the Many

❧ Poetry by Rabindranath Tagore
❧ Photographs by John M. Berridge

Fireflies

The fireflies, twinkling among leaves,
make the stars wonder.

Fireflies

I leave no trace of wings in the air,
      but I am glad I have had my flight.

Fireflies

These paper boats of mine are meant to dance
         on the ripples of hours,
                  and not to reach any destination.

Stray Birds 116

The earth hums to me today in the sun, like a
woman at her spinning, some ballad of the ancient
time in a forgotten tongue.

Stray Birds 110

Man goes into the noisy crowd to drown his
Own clamour of silence.

Stray Birds 77

Every child comes with the message that God
is not yet discouraged of man.

ɕ   Mystic, poet, and novelist Rabindranath Tagore helped inspire the Bengali literary revival.
He began publishing poems, short stories, and popular songs in India at the age of twenty.
He gained an international reputation after he translated his own work into English,
including the play *Chitra* in 1896 and the poetry collection *Gitanjali* ("Song offerings") in
1912. He won the Nobel Prize for Literature in 1913. (*Born Bengal, India 1861; died 1941*)
The above excerpt is from *The One and the Many*, a book compiled by John Berridge which
includes poems and other readings from Tagore's work along with photographs by Dr.
Berridge. For thirty-one years, John Berridge taught in the department of Religious Studies
at St. Francis Xavier University in Antigonish, Nova Scotia. In 2000, he took early retirement to pursue his interest in photography. *The One and the Many* (1997) contains fifty-
five of Dr. Berridge's photographs of India and Bangladesh. (*Born 1938*)

RESPONDING

Meaning

1. The photographer John Berridge states in the preface to the book, "It is my sincere hope that the photographs may also reflect something of Tagore's vision of the harmonious relationship between the One and the Many." Who are the "one" and who are the "many," as presented in the selections? Defend your answer with evidence from both the pictures and the poetic text.

2. a) According to Berridge, the poet Tagore believed that the common place "was always a source of wonder." How is this reflected in the photographs?

   b) Berridge also noted that in placing his photographs with particular poems, he followed "an intuitive rather than a literal approach." For each of the selections, detail what you feel connects the photograph and the poem. How does each reinforce or inform the meaning of the other?

Form and Style

3. Many of the selections written by Tagore are described as *aphorisms*, succinct statements of a general principle or truth, expressed memorably by condensing much wisdom into few words. Which of the selections are aphorisms? Provide evidence to support your answer.

4. Interpreting a written text visually, particularly one being translated from a different language and culture, is difficult. What specific photographic techniques, such as point of view, camera angle, lighting, focus, and foregrounding does Berridge use to interpret the written text?

Exploring Context

5. Rabindranath Tagore (1861–1941) was a Bengali monk, poet, and Nobel Prize winner who consciously tried to identify links between the cultural traditions of Western Europe and East India. The Nobel Prize in Literature is arguably the world's most famous award for writing. It is usually awarded to individuals from a variety of cultures, based on a whole body of work rather than a single piece of literature. Choose one winner of the Nobel Prize in Literature and write a biographical sketch. You may choose to augment your piece with samples of the winner's writings and/or photographs of the writer.

Creative Extension

6. Write or find three or four short poems (two to three lines) or *aphorisms* that have significance to you. Alternatively, choose a single word that describes an abstract idea (e.g., security, love, friendship). If you have access to a digital or film camera, create a photo series that illustrates your aphorisms or concept. If a camera is not available, find photographs or artworks from a magazine, newspaper, or other source. Mount the texts (visual and written) on a suitable background. Comment on your choices in a short informal talk.

7. If you are competent in another language, choose a piece of poetry in a language other than English and translate it into English. Reflect on the process of translation. Is it difficult to translate poetry? Why or why not? Share both your translation and your analysis of the process with the class. What difficulties did you have?

The Medium is the Message

Do we control the media, or do the media control us?

We may feel that we are very aware of the effects various media, such as television and the Internet, have on us. After all, we control how we use them. Or do we? Are we really aware of the full power of various media and how they influence our activities, relationships, and understandings? The Canadian media theorist Marshall McLuhan coined the phrase "the medium is the message." Through an illustrated book, essay, poem, storyboard for a television commercial, and piece of art, this Echo explores what that phrase means.

Learning Goals

- explore a major question through various texts
- examine various perspectives on a central issue
- analyze how differences in form and style affect the presentation of a theme
- create original texts to communicate ideas

McLuhan for Beginners

ᔐ   *W. Terrence Gordon*

The ideas of media philosopher Marshall McLuhan can be difficult to grasp. The following excerpt from an illustrated book attempts to distill McLuhan's ideas and make them accessible to a wide audience.

ᔐ   Writer W. Terrence Gordon published *McLuhan for Beginners* in 1997 to explain the theories of Marshall McLuhan, a Canadian communication theorist. McLuhan, who lived from 1911 until 1980, became internationally known in the 1960s for his theories about the effects of mass media on thought and behaviour. Many of his ideas appear in the book *Understanding Media* (1964). W. Terrence Gordon wrote a biography about McLuhan entitled *Marshall McLuhan: Escape into Understanding* (1997). *(Born 1942)*

(Re)Defining "Media"

When McLuhan first came to the attention of the general public in the 1960s, many assumed that he was promoting the end of book culture and embracing the age of television. In fact, he was cautioning that the then-new medium of television had enormous power. Publicly, he called it "the timid giant" and urged awareness of that power.

PRIVATELY, HIS AVERSION TO THE TUBE WAS SO STRONG THAT HE PLEADED WITH HIS SON ERIC NOT TO LET THE GRANDCHILDREN WATCH TV!!

Lewis Lapham says that McLuhan's thinking about media begins with two premises: on the one hand, he notes, McLuhan argued that "we become what we behold;" on the other, he stated that "we shape our tools, and thereafter our tools shape us." McLuhan saw media as make-happen rather than make-aware agents, as systems more similar in nature to roads and canals than to objects of art or models of behavior.

Most of us think of media (one "medium;" two or more "media") as sources that bring us news or information—namely the press, radio, and television. But McLuhan had his own ingeniously original definition of media. To him, a medium—while it may often be a new technology—is <u>any</u> extension of our bodies, minds, or beings...

-*clothing is an extension of skin*-

-*housing is an extension of the body's heat-control mechanism*-

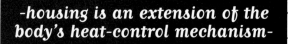

-*the stirrup, the bicycle, and the car extend the human foot*-

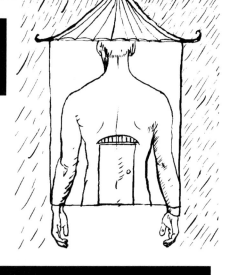

-*the computer extends our central nervous system*-

(Re)Defining "Message"

HOW, THEN, CAN THE MEDIUM
BE THE MESSAGE?

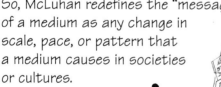

By saying "the medium is the message" McLuhan forces us to re-examine what we understand by both "medium" and "message." We have just seen how he stretched the meaning of "medium" beyond our usual understanding of the word. He does this for "message" too. If we define "message" simply as the idea of "content" or "information," McLuhan believes, we miss one of the most important features of media: their power to change the course and functioning of human relations and activities. So, McLuhan redefines the "message" of a medium as any change in scale, pace, or pattern that a medium causes in societies or cultures.

This yields the equation:

MEDIUM ● MESSAGE

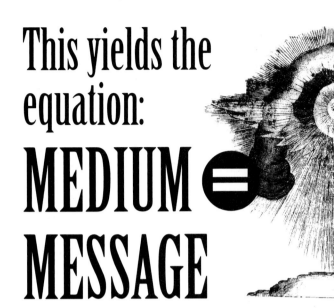

Media mates

Another reason for this new definition is that "content" turns out
to be an illusion, or at least a mask
for how media interact. They work in
pairs; one medium "contains"
another (and that one can contain
another, and so on). The tele-
graph, for example, contains the
printed word, which contains
writing, which contains speech.
So, the contained medium becomes the
message of the containing one!

Now because we don't usually notice this kind of interaction of
media, and because the effects of it are so powerful on us,
any message, in the ORDINARY sense of "content" or "information" is far less important than the medium itself.

ECHO

Classifying Media: Hot and Cool

McLuhan's basic classification of media as either "hot" or "cool" hinges on special senses of the words "definition" and "information"—and on our physical senses more than word-senses. McLuhan borrows from the technical language of television to make his point about definition. It's a two-part tale.

Part One:

TYPOGRAPHY IS ARCHITECTURE, AND T TYPOGRAPHER IS THE ARCHITECT. THE BUILD	TYPOGRAPHY IS ARCHITECTURE AND T TYPOGRAPHER IS THE ARCHITECT THE BUILD
TYPOGRAPHY IS ARCHITECTURE, AN THE TYPOGRAPHER IS THE ARCHITECT. TH	TYPOGRAPHY IS ARCHITECTURE AN THE TYPOGRAPHER IS THE ARCHITECT. TH
TYPOGRAPHY IS ARCHITECTURE, AND THE TYPOGRAPHER IS THE ARCHIT	TYPOGRAPHY IS ARCHITECTURE AND THE TYPOGRAPHER IS THE ARCHIT
TYPOGRAPHY IS ARCHITECTURE, A	TYPOGRAPHY IS ARCHITECTURE, A
TYPOGRAPHY IS ARCHITECTURE	TYPOGRAPHY IS ARCHITECTURE

In the TV world, "high-definition" means well-defined, sharp, solid, detailed, etc., in reference to anything visual. So, to McLuhan, letters of the alphabet, numbers, photographs, and maps, for example, are high-definition objects.

Forms and shapes and images that are not so distinct (like sketches and cartoons) are "low-definition." For these, our eyes must scan what is visible and fill in what is missing to "get the full picture." This "fill-in-the-blanks" principle applies to sounds (our sense of hearing) as well. So

A HIGH-DEFINITION MEDIUM

gives a lot of information and gives LITTLE to do

and →

A LOW-DEFINITION MEDIUM

gives A LITTLE information and makes the user WORK to fill in what is missing

Part Two:

When McLuhan speaks of the "information" that a medium transmits, he is not referring to facts or knowledge; rather, he is referring to how our physical senses respond to, or participate in, media.

HIGH-DEFINITION IS HOT

LOW-DEFINITION IS COOL

51

Here's how McLuhan classifies various media:

HOT

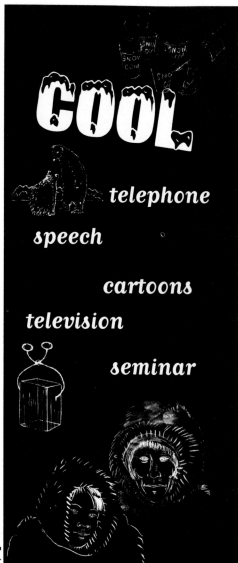

COOL

radio

print

photographs

movies

lectures

telephone

speech

cartoons

television

seminar

gain, McLuhan emphasizes the role of our physical senses and our perceptions and how we relate to media. "Hot" media are low in participation; "cool" media are high in participation. Participation does not refer primarily to intellectual involvement, but, like "definition" and "information," to how a medium engages our physical senses.

RESPONDING

Meaning

1. Marshall McLuhan is considered to be one of the most important thinkers about media of the twentieth century. In point form, summarize the major points McLuhan makes about media as outlined in this selection.

2. "The medium is the message" is probably the most famous quotation from McLuhan and in many ways represents the basis of his theories. In your own words, explain what this quotation means. Do you agree or disagree with McLuhan's premise? Why or why not?

Form and Style

3. a) Marshall McLuhan's ideas are often considered difficult or abstract for the average person to understand. What specific literary and visual techniques has Gordon used to communicate these ideas more easily to the reader? Support your answer with examples.
   b) What advantages does this text provide over reading the original works by McLuhan? What disadvantages?

4. Gordon uses visuals in a variety of ways. Create a chart in which you list each graphic and note whether it is a literal, metaphoric, or symbolic representation of the written text. For each example, explain how the visual reinforces or enhances the reader's understanding of the written text.

Exploring Context

5. Marshall McLuhan (1911–1980) set forward the bulk of his theories in the "television age" 1960s and 1970s, long before the Internet and modern communications technologies such as cellular phones, satellite television, and fax machines. Choose one of these more recent media forms and write a short essay in which you analyze how McLuhan's theories (as outlined in this selection) apply to this medium.

Creative Extension

6. Using "the medium is the message" as your theme, write a narrative piece in which you explore the ways that media affect your everyday life.

7. Analyze a comic book or a feature movie trailer using McLuhan's ideas. According to McLuhan's criteria, is it a hot or cool medium? In your analysis, focus on the effects of the medium rather than on the content. How do the visual images impact on thoughts and emotions? What does the medium motivate you to do? What biases and values seem implicit in the medium? How much control do you have over the influence of this medium?

The Warner Bros./Shakespeare Hour

ॐ *Bert Almon*

The following poem raises some interesting questions about the effects of modern media and how audiences react to media works. How are media works different from more traditional forms of art?

"Will you walk out of the air, my lord?"

The fine tuning won't prevent
channel 4 from drifting into 3
as a faint background
so that *Hamlet* is haunted
by ghostly figures
of the Coyote and the Roadrunner

As Hamlet says *"To be or not to be"*
I can make out the Coyote climbing
a ladder suspended in mid-air
Convention says he won't fall
until he tops the ladder and looks down
He'll smash on the desert floor
and come back renewed in another frame

Hamlet finishes his soliloquy
and greets the fair Ophelia
The Coyote has built a bomb
and lights the fuse
He has no trouble taking arms
while Hamlet is the man who looks down
and knows that resurrection
is not a convention of his play
We share his terror
rung by rung

Bert Almon was born in Texas, but he has lived in Canada since 1968, where he teaches modern poetry and creative writing at the University of Alberta. He has published several books of poetry, along with many academic articles. The collection *Earth Prime* won the Writers' Guild of Alberta poetry award in 1995, and Almon went on to publish *Mind the Gap* in 1996. (Born Texas 1943)

Connecting

1. This poem examines aspects of audience in the modern media-saturated world. What does the poem imply about the way a modern audience perceives a work of art?

2. a) Almon draws parallels between the predicaments of the cartoon character Wile E. Coyote and Hamlet. In what ways are the two characters alike?

b)   What contrast in conventions between the cartoon and the Shakespearean play does Almon highlight? What does this imply about the nature of traditional literary text as opposed to the nature of modern media text?

3.   "Marshall McLuhan saw media as <u>make-happen</u> rather than <u>make-aware</u> agents." In what ways does this poem explain and expand upon this idea? How does Almon demonstrate the way in which ideas are presented on television? What does the television in this poem "make-happen"? What does it not "make-aware"?

History? Education? Zap! Pow! Cut!

ᔕ   Pico Iyer

In this essay, journalist Pico Iyer takes an insightful look at both the perils and opportunities that modern media offer the current generation.

In his novel, *Vineland*, Thomas Pynchon, that disembodied know-it-all hiding out somewhere inside our nervous system, performs an eerie kind of magic realism on the McLuhanite world around us. His is an America, in 1984, in which reflexes, values, even feelings, have been programmed by that All-Seeing Deity known as the tube. Remaking us in its own image (every seven days), TV consumes us much more than we do it. Lovers woo one another on screens, interface with friends, cite TV sets as corespondents in divorce trials. And the children who have grown up goggle-eyed around the electric altar cannot believe that anything is real unless it comes with a laugh track: they organize their emotions around commercial breaks and hope to heal their sorrows with a Pause button. Watching their parents fight, they sit back and wait in silence for the credits. History for them means syndication; ancient history, the original version of *The Brady Bunch*.

All this would sound crazy to anyone who didn't know that it was largely true. As the world has accelerated to the fax and satellite speed of light, attention spans have shortened, and dimension has given way to speed. A whole new aesthetic—the catchy, rapid-fire flash of images—is being born. Advertising, the language of the quick cut and the zap, has literally set the pace, but Presidents, preachers, even teachers, have not been slow to get the message. Thus ideas become slogans, and issues sound bites. Op-ed turns into photo op. Politics becomes telegenics. And all of us find that we are creatures of the screen. The average American, by age forty, has seen more than a million television commercials; small wonder that the very rhythm and texture of his mind are radically different from his grandfather's.

Increasingly, in fact, televisionaries are telling us to read the writing on the screen and accept that ours is a post-literate world. A new generation of children is growing up, they say, with a new, highly visual kind of imagination, and it is our obligation to speak to them in terms they understand. MTV, *USA Today*, the PC, and the VCR—why, the acronym itself!—are making the slow motion of words as obsolete as pictographs. Writing in *The New York Times* not long ago, Robert W. Pittman, the developer of MTV, pointed out just how much the media have already adjusted to the music-video aesthetic he helped create. In newspapers, "graphs, charts, and larger-than-ever pictures tell the big story at a glance. Today's movie scripts are some twenty-five per cent shorter than those of the 1940s for the same length movies." Even TV is cutting back, providing more news stories on every broadcast and less material in each one.

There is, of course, some value to this. New ages need new forms, and addressing today's young in sentences of Jamesian complexity would be about as helpful as talking to them in Middle English. Rhetoric, in any case, is no less manipulative than technology, and no less formulaic. Though TV is a drug, it can be stimulant as well as sedative. And the culture that seems to be taking over the future is a culture so advanced in image making that it advertises its new sports cars with two-page photographs of rocks (though the Japanese, perhaps, enjoy an advantage over us insofar as their partly ideogrammatic language encourages them to think in terms of images: haiku are the music videos of the printed word). Nor would this be the first time that technology has changed the very way we speak: the invention of typography alone, as Neil Postman wrote in *Amusing Ourselves to Death*, "created prose but made poetry into an exotic and elitist form of expression." No less a media figure than Karl Marx once pointed out that the *Iliad* would not have been composed the way it was after the invention of the printing press.

Yet none of this is enough to suggest that we should simply burn our books and flood the classroom with TV monitors. Just because an infant cannot speak, we do not talk to him entirely in "goo"s and "gaah"s; rather, we coax him, gradually, into speech, and then into higher and more complex speech. That, in fact, is the definition of "educate": to "draw out," to teach children not what they know but what they do not know; to rescue them, as Cicero had it, from the tyranny of the present. The problem with visuals is not just that they bombard us with images and informations only of a user-friendly kind, but also that they give us no help in telling image from illusion, information from real wisdom. Reducing everything to one dimension, they prepare us for everything except our daily lives. Nintendo, unlike stickball, leaves one unschooled in surprise; TV, unlike books, tells us when to stop and think. "The flow of messages from the instant everywhere," as Daniel Boorstin points out, "fills every niche in our consciousness, crowding out knowledge and understanding. For while knowledge is steady and cumulative, information is random and miscellaneous." A consciousness born primarily of visuals can come terrifyingly close to that of the tape-recorder novels of the vid kid's most successful voice, Bret Easton Ellis, in which everyone's a speed freak and relationships last about as long as videos. Life, you might say, by remote control.

If today's computer-literate young truly do have the capacity to process images faster than their parents, they enjoy an unparalleled opportunity—so long as they learn to process words as well. They could become the first generation in history to be bilingual in this sense, fluent onscreen as well as off. We need not, when we learn to talk, forget to communicate in other ways. But only words can teach the use of words, and ideas beget ideas. So just as certain tribes must be taught how to read a TV set, we must be taught how to read the world outside the TV set. Much better, then, to speak up than down, especially when speech itself is threatened. Nobody ever said that thinking need be binary. Nobody, that is, except, perhaps, a computer.

꙳ Born in England to Indian parents, Pico Iyer immigrated to California at the age of seven. He became a staff writer at *Time* magazine in 1982. "History? Education? Zap! Pow! Cut!" was first published in *Time* on May 14, 1990. In 1995, the *Utne Reader* named Iyer one of the world's top 100 visionaries. His collected essays appear in *Tropical Classical: Essays from Several Directions* (1997). (Born Oxford, England 1957)

Connecting

1. In the introduction to this essay, Pico Iyer refers to "the McLuhanite" world around us. What ideas of Marshall McLuhan's presented in "McLuhan for Beginners" are represented in this introduction?

2. Discuss the meaning of each of the following quotations from the essay. Do you agree or disagree with Pico Iyer's point? Support your arguments
   a) ...reflexes, values, even feelings have been programmed by that All-Seeing Deity known as the tube.

b)   TV consumes us much more than we do it.
c)   . . . children who have grown up goggle-eyed around the electric altar cannot believe anything is real unless it comes with a laugh track.
d)   Watching their parents fight, they sit back and wait in silence for the credits.
e)   Thus ideas become slogans, and issues sound bites.
f)   Though TV is a drug, it can be stimulant as well as sedative.
g)   . . . we must be taught how to read the world outside the TV set.

3. What is Iyer's central thesis? Is he opposed to technological change? Is he opposed to modern media? Provide evidence to support your answer.

Storyboard: The House Hippo

ভ *Publicis Advertising Agency*

The following storyboard for a television commercial aimed at promoting media literacy in children confronts the question of just how much we believe of what we see on the screen.

ANNCR (MALE, 50ish, IN DOCUMENTARY STYLE): It's nighttime. In a kitchen just like yours. All is quiet. Or is it?

The North American House Hippo is found throughout Canada and the eastern United States.

House hippos are very timid creatures and are rarely seen, but they will defend their territory if provoked.

They come out at night to search for food, water, and materials for their nests.

House hippos will eat almost anything, but their favourite foods are chips, raisins, and the crumbs from peanut butter on toast.

House hippos usually build their nests in bedroom closets or kitchen cupboards using lost mittens, dryer lint, and bits of string. The nests have to be very soft and warm; house hippos sleep about 16 hours a day!

ECHO

ANNCR (FEMALE):
That looked really...real, but you knew it couldn't be true, didn't you? That's why it's good to think about what you're watching on TV and ask questions. Kind of like you just did.

A message from Concerned Children's Advertisers.

    Concerned Children's Advertisers (CCA) is a non-profit organization founded in 1990 by a group of Canadian companies that market and advertise products and services for children. The organization states that its goal is to combine marketing for children with the social responsibility of caring for children. CCA has produced a series of commercial messages on issues such as substance abuse prevention, issues of self-esteem, active living, and media literacy. "House Hippo" was produced in 1999 by Publicis Advertising Agency and won the Golden Marble award for best public service advertisement that year.

Connecting

1. The humour in this advertisement is based in large part on *hyperbole* (exaggeration for the purpose of emphasis) and *parody* (a mocking imitation). What elements of the ad are hyperbole and what is being parodied?
2. The cliché "Seeing is believing" is deliberately challenged in this advertisement. To what purpose did the advertiser go to such lengths to distort reality? Why would this be an effective way to promote advertising awareness?
3. According to McLuhan, television is a "cool" medium because it provides a little information and makes the user fill in what's missing. How does the House Hippo advertisement make the user fill in information?
4. In your opinion, do television viewers accept what they see on television as being reality? Provide specific examples to support your opinion.

Transmission Difficulties: The Operation

    Claude Breeze

Modern artists have also created works expressing their ideas and vision of contemporary media and its effects. This piece is by Canadian artist Claude Breeze.

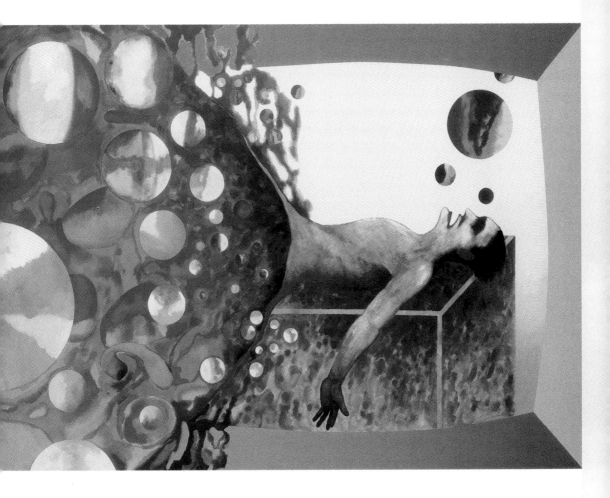

ᕒ The art of Claude Breeze is often political, with many abstract elements. Breeze works
in oil, acrylic, graphic arts, and mixed media. He is one of the featured artists in Ann
Newlands's *Canadian Art from its Beginnings to 2000* and Ian Thom's *Art BC: Masterworks
from British Columbia* (both published in 2000). His work has been exhibited in major
galleries and museums in Canada, the United States, and Europe. *(Born Nelson, British
Columbia 1938)*

Connecting

1. In small groups, discuss the message being communicated by the painter. Come to a
    consensus about
    a) the central focus of the painting
    b) what is happening in the painting
    c) what the figure's facial features, position, and expression convey
    d) what point the artist is making about television

2.   What is the significance of the painting's title, *Transmission Difficulties: The Operation*? How does it affect your interpretation of the painting?

3.   According to what you know of McLuhan's classification of media into hot/cool, high definition/low definition, which category would this painting fall into? Why?

☐ REFLECTING ON THE ECHO

1.   Write an essay in which you discuss the relationship between media and society. Was McLuhan right when he claimed that "we shape our tools and thereafter our tools shape us"? Refer to specific media texts as examples in your essay.

2.   Using a media form of your choice, create a piece in which you explore your own personal relationship to media. Do you see media as a friend, a tool, an annoyance, an enemy, or in some other way?

3.   For each point you summarized from *McLuhan For Beginners*, find an example in media that illustrates the point. Collect all of your examples into a scrapbook and present them to the class.

ECHO

Credits

༄

2-3 Lawrence Ferlinghetti, 'Constantly Risking Absurdity (#15)' from *A Coney Island of the Mind*, copyright © 1958 by Lawrence Ferlinghetti. Reprinted by permission of New Directions Publishing Corp.; **4-5** 'betting on the muse' by Charles Bukowski. Copyright © 1996 by Linda Lee Bukowski. Reprinted from *Betting on the Muse: Poems & Stories* with permission of Black Sparrow Press; **6-7** Karen Connelly, 'The Story' from *The Border Surrounds Us* by Karen Connelly. Used by permission, McClelland & Stewart Ltd. *The Canadian Publishers*; **8** Barbara Kingsolver, 'Naming Myself' from *Another America/Otra America* (Seattle, WA: Seal Press, 1992); **9** Richard Harrison, 'All-Star Action' from *Hero of the Play* (Toronto: Wolsak and Wynn, 1994). Reprinted by permission; **10** Leona Gom, 'Guilt' from *Private Properties* (Victoria: Sono Nis Press, 1986). Reprinted by permission of Sono Nis Press; **11** Bert Almon, 'This Day in History' from *Blue Sunrise* (Thistledown Press, 1980). Reprinted by permission; **16-17** Maxine Tynes, 'The Woman I Am in My Dreams' from *Poetic Voice of the Maritimes* (Hantsport, NS: Lancelot Press, 1996). Reprinted by permission of the author; **18** 'Today's Learning Child' from *Song of Eskatoni: More Poems of Rita Joe* (Charlottetown, PE: Ragweed Press, 1988). Reprinted by permission of the author; **19** Seamus Heaney, 'Field of Vision' from *Seeing Things* (London: Faber and Faber, 1991). Reprinted by permission of Faber and Faber Limited; **20** Joy Kogawa, 'Where There's A Wall' from *Woman in the Woods* (Oakville, ON: Mosaic Press, 1985). Reprinted by permission of Mosaic Press; **21** Marilyn Dumont, 'gravity' from *green girl dreams Mountains* (Lantzville, BC: Oolichan Books, 2000); **22-23** Tom Dawe, 'Ghosts' from *Island Spell: Poems* (St. John's, NF: Harry Cuff Publications, 1981); **24-25** Tom Wayman, 'Students' from *The Face of Jack Monroe* (Madeira Park, BC: Harbour Publishing, 1986). Reprinted by permission of Harbour Publishing; **31** Federico Garcia Lorca, 'The Six Strings,' translated by Donald Hall from *The Rattle Bag*, Seamus Heaney and Ted Hughes, eds. (London: Faber and Faber, 1982); **31-32** Wayne Keon, 'eagle's work' from *Border Lines: Contemporary Poems in English*, Andy Wainwright et al. eds. (Toronto: Copp Clark, 1995); **32** Kojo Laing, 'Dog' from *Godhorse* (Oxford: Heinemann International, 1989); **33** Dorothy Livesay, 'The Uninvited' from *Collected Poems: The Two Seasons of Dorothy Livesay*. Reprinted by permission of the Estate of Dorothy Livesay; **34-35** Anne Simpson, 'Myth' from *Light Falls Through You* by Anne Simpson. Used by permission, McClelland & Stewart Ltd. *The Canadian Publishers*; **36-37** Alice Major, 'puce fairy book' from *Time Travels Light* (Edmonton, AB: Rowan Books, 1992). Reprinted by permission of Rowan Books; **38-39** Michael Ondaatje, 'The Diverse Causes' from *The Cinnamon Peeler* (Toronto: McClelland & Stewart, 1992). Reprinted by permission of the author; **40** Ben Okri 'And If You Should Leave Me' (22 lines) from *An African Elegy* by Ben Okri published by Jonathan Cape. Used by permission of The Random House Group Limited; **41** Chinua Achebe, 'Refugee Mother and Child' © Chinua Achebe. Reprinted by permission of the author; **47-48** Margaret Atwood 'This is a photograph of me' from *The Circle Game* copyright © 1998 by Margaret Atwood. Reprinted by permission of Stoddart Publishing Co. Limited; **48-50** Margaret Atwood 'Morning in the Burned House' from *Morning in the Burned House* by Margaret Atwood. Used by permission, McClelland & Stewart Ltd. *The Canadian Publishers*; **51-55** Interview with Margaret Atwood extracted from *Writers & Company* by Eleanor Wachtel. Copyright © 1993 by Eleanor Wachtel. Reprinted by permission of Alfred A. Knopf Canada, a division of Random House of Canada Limited; **57-59** Margaret Atwood, 'There Was Once' from *Good Bones and Simple Murders* by Margaret Atwood. Used by permission, McClelland & Stewart Ltd. *The Canadian Publishers*; **67** Gabriela Mistral, 'The Goblet' from *Selected Poems of Gabriela Mistral* ed. and trans. by Doris Dana (Baltimore, MD: The Johns Hopkins University Press, 1971); **70** Dylan Thomas, 'Do Not Go Gentle Into That Good Night' from *The Poems* (London: J.M. Dent). Reprinted by permission of David Higham Associates Ltd.; **71** E.J. Pratt, 'From Stone to Steel' from *E.J. Pratt: Complete Poems*, Sandra Djwa and R.G. Moyles, eds. (Toronto: University of Toronto Press, 1989). Reprinted with permission of University of Toronto Press; **72** Anne Hébert, 'Night' from *Selected Poems* copyright © Anne Hébert, translation copyright © A. Poulin. Reprinted by permission of Stoddart Publishing Co. Limited; **91** Phyllis McGinley, 'Lancelot on Bicycle'; **92-94** Elton John and Bernie Taupin, 'Candle in the Wind', Warner Bros. Publications US Inc.; **94-98** Ernest Buckler, excerpts from *The Mountain and the Valley*, (Toronto: McClelland & Stewart, 1968); **100-101** 'The River

Merchant's Wife: A Letter', by Ezra Pound, from *Personae*, copyright © 1926 by Ezra Pound. Reprinted by permission of New Directions Publishing Corp.; **109-113** T.S. Eliot, 'The Love Song of J. Alfred Prufrock' from *Collected Poems 1909–1962* (London: Faber and Faber, 1974). Reprinted by permission of Faber and Faber Limited; **115-116** Yevgeny Yevtushenko, 'The City of Yes and the City of No' from *The Collected Poems, 1952–1990* (New York: Henry Holt, 1991). Reprinted by permission of the author; **122-131** Anton Chekhov, 'A Marriage Proposal', Barrett H. Clark, trans., 1914) © Samuel French, Inc.; **133-148** William Inge, *Glory in the Flower* copyright © 1958, by William Inge. Reprinted by permission; **150-151** *The Black and White* by Harold Pinter (1959). Reprinted by permission of the publishers, Faber and Faber Ltd.; **153-188** Michael Healey, 'The Drawer Boy' (Toronto: Playwrights Canada Press, 1999). Reprinted by permission; **190-192** excerpts from *The Farm Show*, A Theatre Passe Muraille Production; **195-196** Excerpt from 'The Man with the Blue Guitar' from *The Collected Poems of Wallace Stevens* by Wallace Stevens, copyright 1954 by Wallace Stevens and renewed 1982 by Holly Stevens. Used by permission of Alfred A. Knopf, a division of Random House, Inc.; **196** 'Coat of Many Poems' by Rhona McAdam from *Creating the Country* (Thistledown Press, 1989). Reprinted by permission of Thistledown Press; **198-203** Gordon Pengilly, 'Snapshots' is reprinted by permission of the author; **205-207** Pages 17-20 from *The Search for Signs of Intelligent Life in the Universe* by Jane Wagner. Copyright © 1986 by Jane Wagner Inc. Reprinted by permission of HarperCollins Publishers Inc.; **210-217** 'Going to the Moon' by Nino Ricci; **218-219** Derek Walcott, 'The Virgins' from *Sea Grapes* (New York: Farrar, Straus & Giroux, 1976); **222** Alice Walker, 'Am I Blue?' from *Living by the Word: Selected Writings 1973–1987* (San Diego: Harcourt Brace Jovanovich, 1988); **227-233** David Arnason, 'A Girl's Story' reprinted by permission of Talon Books Ltd.; **235-243** Naguib Mafhouz, 'The Happy Man' from *God's World*, Akef Abadir and Roger Allen, trans. (Minneapolis, MN: Bibliotheca Islamica, 1973). Reprinted by permission of Bibliotheca Islamica, Inc., Box 14474, Minneapolis, MN 55414, USA; **244-263** Nancy Richler, 'Your Mouth is Lovely' originally published in *The Journey Prize Anthology* (Toronto: McClelland & Stewart, 2000) © Nancy Richler. Reprinted by permission of HarperCollins Publishers; **265-272** Julio Cortázar, 'The Night Face Up' from *End of the Game and Other Stories* by Julio Cortázar, translated by Paul Blackburn, copyright © 1963, 1967 by Random House, Inc. Used by permission of Pantheon Books, a division of Random House, Inc.; **280-285** Helen Fogwill Porter: 'Juliet' from *Dropped Threads: What We Aren't Told* (2001) eds. Carol Shields and Marjorie Anderson; **294-296** Daniel David Moses, 'The King of the Raft' is used with permission of the author; **298-299** 'The Flash' extracted from *Numbers in the Dark and Other Stories by Italo Calvino*. English translation copyright © 1995 by Tim Parks. Reprinted by permission of Alfred A. Knopf Canada, a division of Random House of Canada Limited; **300** Franz Kafka, 'The Passenger', reprinted with the permission of Scribner, a Division of Simon & Schuster, Inc., from *The Metamorphosis and Other Stories*, translated by Joachim Neugroschel. Translation and introduction copyright © 1993, 1995, 2000 by Joachim Neugroschel; **302-303** Margaret Atwood, 'Murder in the Dark' from *Murder in the Dark* by Margaret Atwood. Used by permission, McClelland & Stewart Ltd. *The Canadian Publishers*; **306-309** 'To Err is Human', copyright © 1976 by Lewis Thomas, from *The Medusa and the Snail* by Lewis Thomas. Used by permission of Viking Penguin, a division of Penguin Putnam Inc.; **311-313** 'Science and Beauty' by Isaac Asimov appeared in the *Washington Post*, August 12, 1979, under the title 'Science and the Sense of Wonder'. © 1979 by The Washington Post, Inc. Published by permission of the Estate of Isaac Asimov c/o Ralph M. Vicinanza, Ltd.; **315-317** Catherine Bush, 'It's all real but it's not all true' from *The Globe and Mail*, 6 May 2000. Reprinted by permission of the author; **318-320** Bill Reid, 'The Enchanted Forest' from *Solitary Raven: The Selected Writings of Bill Reid*. Copyright © 2000 by Bill Reid. Published in Canada by Douglas & McIntyre Ltd. Reprinted by permission of the publisher; **322-323** June Callwood, 'Forget Prince Charming' from *National Post*, February 2001, is reprinted by permission of the author. June Callwood, C.C., O. Ont., is a journalist; **325-330** Robert Nielsen, 'The Closing of the (North) American Mind' from *The Closing of the American Mind* by Allan Bloom (New York: Simon & Schuster, 1987). Reprinted with permission from the November 1988 Reader's Digest; **331-334** Extract from *Brave New World* by Aldous Huxley published by Chatto & Windus. Reprinted by permission of The Random House Group Limited. © the Estate of Mrs. Laura Huxley; **335** Leroy V. Quintana, 'Legacy II' from *Grandparents' Houses* edited by Connie Streich

(New York: Greenwillow Books, 1984). Reprinted by permission of the author; **337-339** Irving Layton, 'The Role of the Teacher' from *Taking Sides: The Collected Social and Political Writings* published by Mosaic Press © 1977, Oakville, ON L6L 5N9. Reprinted by permission; **340-342** Excerpt from *The Japanese Tea Ceremony* copyright © 1965 Peter Pauper Press. Reprinted by permission; **346-351** 'Black Widow' from *The Red Hourglass* by Gordon Grice, copyright © 1998 by Gordon Grice. Used by permission of Dell Publishing, a division of Random House, Inc.; **353-356** 'Sojourners' from *Teaching a Stone to Talk: Expeditions and Encounters* by Annie Dillard. Copyright © 1982 by Annie Dillard. Reprinted by permission of HarperCollins Publishers Inc.; **361-362** 'Hugh Selwyn Mauberley IV' by Ezra Pound, from *Personae*, copyright © 1926 by Ezra Pound. Reprinted by permission of New Directions Publishing Corp.; **363-364** Agnes Gergely 'Crazed Man in Concentration Camp', translated by Edwin Morgan, from *New Hungarian Quarterly*; **364-366** Reza Kiarash, "A Story of War and Change' (originally titled 'New Year's Eve') from *The Eyeopener*, 16 January 1991. Reprinted by permission of the author; **367-368** Toni Morrison, 'The dead of September 11' from *Vanity Fair*, One Week in September issue, November 2001; **368-370** Lorna Crozier, 'The Love That Feels Like Home' from CBC Web site 'Canadian Authors on 2000'. Reprinted by permission of the author; **372-374** Janice Patten, 'The Ironic Narrator in James Joyce's "Araby"' from http://www.theliterarylink.com/araby_essays.html; **375-380** Jeanne Addison Roberts, 'Fathers and Sons (And What About Mothers and Daughters?)' from *Shakespeare Set Free*; **380-382** Janet Roddan, 'April Fools on Polar Circus' from *Leading Out: Mountaineering Stories of Adventurous Women* edited by Rachel da Silva, ed., (Seattle, WA: Seal Press, 1992); **384-387** Amy Tan, 'Lost Lives of Women' copyright © 1991 by Amy Tan. First appeared in *Life* Magazine. Reprinted by permission of the author and the Sandra Dijkstra Literary Agency; **390-401** Rohinton Mistry, 'Describing Circles' from *The Third Macmillan Anthology*, edited by John Metcalf and Kent Thompson (Toronto: Macmillan of Canada). Copyright © Rohinton Mistry 1990. Reprinted by permission of the author; **403-404** Rex Murphy, 'Cellphones' from *The National*, 19 January, 2001. Used by permission; **406-408** Bronwen Wallace, 'How wise is it to separate our emotions from the rest of our being?' from *Arguments with the World* edited by Joan Page (Kingston, ON: Quarry Press, 1992). Reprinted by permission of the Estate of Bronwen Wallace; **410-414** Julian Dibbell, 'Lord of the Geeks' from *The Village Voice*, 21 June 2001. Reprinted by permission of the author; **416** Quote from *The Hobbit* by J.R.R. Tolkien (London: George Allen & Unwin Publishers, 1937) reprinted by permission of HarperCollins Publishers; **417/418** Quotes from *The Fellowship of the Ring* by J.R.R. Tolkien (London: George Allen & Unwin Publishers, 1954) reprinted by permission of HarperCollins Publishers; **420-421** Jimmy Page and Robert Plant: 'Battle of Evermore', Atlantic Records, 1972; Superhype Publishing Inc.; Warner Bros. Music Corp.; **422-425** Excerpts from 'The Purposes of Fantasy' by Natalie Babbitt from *Innocence and Experience: Essays and Conversations on Children's Literature*, Barbara Harrison and Gregory Maguire, eds. (New York: Lothrop, Lee & Shepard, 1987). Reprinted by permission of the author; **426-430** 'J.R.R. Tolkien: Creator of a World' Copyright © 1973 by the New York Times Co. Reprinted by permission; **432-441** 'Rejection Shock' reprinted with permission from *What Color Is Your Parachute?* 1995 Edition by Richard Nelson Bolles. Copyright © 1995 by Richard Nelson Bolles, Ten Speed Press, Berkeley, CA; **449-452** Dr Margaret Somerville and Alastair Gordon, 'The Ethics of Xenotransplantation' is reprinted from http://www.islet.org/45.htm by permission; **454-460** Al Purdy, 'Iron Road' from *Starting from Ameliasburgh: The Collected Prose of Al Purdy*, Sam Solecki, ed. (Madeira Park, BC: Harbour Publishing, 1995). Reprinted by permission of Harbour Publishing; **462-469** Margaret Hollingsworth, 'Deaf Music' from *Going Some Place*, edited by Lynne Van Luven (Regina, SK, Coteau Books, 2000). Reprinted by permission of the author; **482-485** 'Great Newspaper Ads' by Carey Toane from *Marketing* magazine February 5, 2001, reprinted with permission; **487-497** Excerpt from *Atanarjuat: The Fast Runner* by Paul Apak, Norman Cohn, Zacharias Kunik, Herve Paniaq, Paulossie Qulitalik/Igloolik Isuma Productions Inc. This text contains extracts from the ATANARJUAT: THE FAST RUNNER original script that were not included in the final edit of the film; **499-501** King Arthur Skit from *Monty Python's Second Film: A First Draft* by Graham Chapman, Terry Jones, Terry Gilliam, Michael Palin, Eric Idle, and John Cleese (London: Methuen, 1977). Reprinted by permission of Methuen Publishing; **506-507** Stevie Cameron, 'Virtual Sleuthing' reprinted from *Elm Street*, Summer 2001, by permission of the author; **509-513** Blake Harris, interview with

Derek de Kerckhove from *Government Technology*, 1996; **520-525** Rabindranath Tagore, excerpts from *The One and the Many*, William Radice and Ketaki Kushari Dyson, trans. (Calgary, AB: Bayeux Arts, 1997). Reprinted by permission; **528-534** Excerpts from *McLuhan for Beginners* by W. Terrence Gordon, Illustrations by Susan Willmarth (New York: Writers & Readers Publishing, 1997); **535-536** 'The Warner Bros./Shakespeare Hour' by Bert Almon from *Deep North* (Thistledown Press, 1984). Reprinted by permission of Thistledown Press; **537-539** Pico Iyer, 'History? Education? Zap! Pow! Cut!' from *Time*, 14 May 1990. © Time Inc. 1990.

Visuals Credits

56 *All Things Fall* by Jack Chambers/1963/Private Collection/© The Estate of Jack Chambers; **69** BEN83452.Empress Theodora with her court of two ministers and seven women, c. 547 AD (mosaic) by Byzantine School (6th century). San Vitale, Ravenna, Italy/Bridgeman Art Library; **82** ONT90443. '"I am Half Sick of Shadows" Said the Lady of Shalott' 1915 (oil on canvas) by John William Waterhouse (1849–1917). Art Gallery of Ontario, Toronto, Canada/Gift of Mrs Phillip B. Jackson, 1971/Bridgeman Art Library; **84** Sidney Harold Meteyard, *"I am Half-Sick of Shadows" Said the Lady of Shalott* (1913), Julian Hartnoll, The Pre-Raphaelite Trust, London, England; **86** MAN62953. The Lady of Shalott by William Holman Hunt (1827–1910). Manchester City Art Galleries, UK/Bridgeman Art Library; **88** ART44562: Copyright Tate Gallery, London/Art Resource, NY; **90 (tl)** ONT90443. '"I am Half Sick of Shadows" Said the Lady of Shalott' 1915 (oil on canvas) by John William Waterhouse (1849–1917). Art Gallery of Ontario, Toronto, Canada/Gift of Mrs Phillip B. Jackson, 1971/Bridgeman Art Library, **(tm)** Sidney Harold Meteyard, *"I am Half-Sick of Shadows" Said the Lady of Shalott* (1913), Julian Hartnoll, The Pre-Raphaelite Trust, London, England, **(tr)** MAN62953. The Lady of Shalott by William Holman Hunt (1827–1910). Manchester City Art Galleries, UK/Bridgeman Art Library, **(bm)** ART44562: Copyright Tate Gallery, London/Art Resource, NY; **154** Theatre New Brunswick; **173** Photograph by Bruce Monk. Reproduced by permission of Tom Barnett and David Fox; **193** ART27012: Copyright Schalkwijk/Art Resource, NY; **194** ART26993: Copyright: Schalkwijk/Art Resource, NY; **220** HKH141618. Melancholy: The Street, c. 1924–25 (oil on canvas) by Giorgio de Chirico (1888–1978). Hamburg Kunsthalle, Hamburg, Germany/Bridgeman Art Library; **221** ART67251: Copyright Scala/Art Resource, NY; **366** *Dressing Station in the Field – Arras*, 1915. Painted in 1918 by Alfred Bastien (1873–1955). Canadian War Museum, CWM 8091; **384-385** Amy Tan; **416** Carol Emery Phenix, *The Glow of Smaug*. J.R.R. Tolkien, *Tolkien's World – Paintings of Middle Earth* (HarperCollins Publishers, 1992). Reproduced with the permission of the artist; **417** Alan Lee, *The Stone Trolls*. J.R.R. Tolkien, *Tolkien's World – Paintings of Middle Earth* (HarperCollins Publishers, 1992). Reproduced with the permission of the artist; **418** Ted Nasmith, *Riders at the Ford*. J.R.R. Tolkien, *Tolkien's World – Paintings of Middle Earth* (HarperCollins Publishers, 1992). Reproduced with the permission of the artist; **472** St. John Ambulance. Photographed by Keven Zacher; **473 (t)** Baldwin/Toronto Reference Library, **(bl)** Baldwin/Toronto Reference Library, **(br)** National Archives of Canada/C-090883; **474-475** Ford Motor Company; **476-477** Tourism Newfoundland & Labrador, St. John's Nfld.; **478-480** Reproduced with the permission of the Minister of Public Works and Government Services Canada, 2001; **490** Norman Cohn/Igloolik Isuma Productions; **491** MH Cousineau/Igloolik Isuma Productions; **497** Norman Cohn/Igloolik Isuma Productions; **520-525** © John Berridge; **540 (tl)** Concerned Children's Advertisers, **(bl)** Sekani/Second Line Search; **541** Sekani/Second Line Search; **542** Sekani/Second Line Search; **543** Breeze, Claude "Transmission Difficulties: the Operation", 1968, acrylic on canvas, 172.4 x 239 cm. National Gallery of Canada, Ottawa. Purchased 1969. Reproduced by permission of the artist.

Every reasonable effort has been made to trace the original source of text material and visuals contained in this book. Where the attempt has been unsuccessful, the publisher would be pleased to hear from copyright holders to rectify any omissions.